The Library Reference Series

LIBRARIANSHIP AND LIBRARY RESOURCES

The Library Reference Series
Lee Ash
General Editor

AMERICAN LIBRARY RESOURCES

A Bibliographical Guide

By
ROBERT B. DOWNS

GREGG PRESS
Boston 1972

This is a complete photographic reprint of a work
first published in Chicago by the American Library Association in 1951.

First Gregg Press edition published 1972.

Copyright 1951 by the American Library Association
Reprinted with permission.

Printed on permanent/durable acid-free paper in
The United States of America.

Library of Congress Cataloging in Publication Data

Downs, Robert Bingham, 1903-
  American library resources.

  Sponsored by the American Library Association Board
on Resources of American Libraries.
  1. Bibliography--Bibliography. 2. Libraries-United
States. I. American Library Association. Board on
Resources of American Libraries. II. Title.
[Z1002.D6 1972]   016.016   72-7111
ISBN 0-8398-0377-X

AMERICAN LIBRARY RESOURCES

American Library Resources

A BIBLIOGRAPHICAL GUIDE

Robert B. Downs, Director

University of Illinois Library and Library School

Sponsored by the American Library Association

Board on Resources of American Libraries

AMERICAN LIBRARY ASSOCIATION

Chicago, 1951

Copyright 1951 by the American Library Association
Manufactured in the United States of America
Library of Congress catalog card number: 51-11156

Preface

This bibliographical guide to American Library resources may be said to have had its inception some fifteen years ago when the compiler was assembling published references to facilities for study and research available in southern libraries. A few years later, in connection with a similar project for New York City libraries, a more extensive bibliography was prepared. Convinced of the value of such a record, the idea of a list national in scope was conceived, and is now brought to realization in the present work.

Financial support for the laborious task of compiling and checking entries, for correspondence and travel, and for incidental expenses was generously provided by the Rockefeller Foundation through the interest of Dr. David H. Stevens, then Director of the Division for the Humanities. Grateful acknowledgment is made of this assistance, which greatly expedited the project.

A deep obligation is felt also for the cooperation of the individual libraries in checking, revising and expanding lists of references relating to their holdings. Because of the size and importance of their contributions, special appreciation is due Verner W. Clapp, Robert C. Gooch, and their colleagues at the Library of Congress; G. W. Cottrell, Jr., of Harvard University Library; Karl Brown of the New York Public Library; Lyle H. Wright of the Henry E. Huntington Library; Warner G. Rice and Randolph G. Adams of the University of Michigan; Stanley Pargellis of the Newberry Library; Alexander D. Wainwright of the Princeton University Library; Ralph R. Shaw of the U. S. Department of Agriculture Library; and David H. Clift of Yale University Library. Comparable aid was received from dozens of other university, college, public, reference, state, and special libraries throughout the country, to all of which sincere gratitude is hereby expressed.

Much of the editorial responsibility for the guide was carried by Lucile W. Allen, who verified data and form, annotated many titles, and checked a variety of sources for additional references. Her efficient and intelligent help was invaluable. Preparation of the manuscript, always a tedious undertaking in a work of this nature, was done by Charlene M. Woodson, who actually likes to type bibliographies and indexes! She is entitled to a large meed of thanks.

It should be noted, finally, that the guide is under the sponsorship of the American Library Association's Board on Resources of American Libraries, whose members advised in its planning and development.

Robert B. Downs

March 1, 1951

Contents

Introduction	page 1

GENERAL

	item numbers
General Bibliography and Reference Books	1-22
Government Publications	23-53
Library Science	54-67
General Surveys of Libraries	68-115
Surveys of Individual Libraries	116-176
General Library Catalogs	177-280
Periodicals, Newspapers, and Journalism	281-482
Manuscripts	483-548
Rare Books	549-579
Printing History	580-948

PHILOSOPHY AND PSYCHOLOGY

General	949-958
Psychology	959-961
Occult Sciences	962-968
Ethics	969-971
Peace and War Ethics	972-979
Marriage and Divorce	980-982

RELIGION

General	983-1013
Bible	1014-1046
Hymnology	1047-1050
Missions	1051-1055
Christian Churches and Sects	1056-1213
Non-Christian Religions	1214-1253

SOCIAL SCIENCES

Sociology	1254-1268
Statistics	1269-1343
Political Science	1344-1451
Economics	1452-1570
Labor	1571-1668
Law	1669-1855
Public Administration	1856-1916
Welfare and Social Activities	1917-1948
Education	1949-2029
Commerce and Communication	2030-2137
Customs and Folklore	2138-2156

SCIENCE

General	2157-2183
History	2184-2194
Periodicals	2195-2208
Mathematics	2209-2228
Astronomy	2229-2244
Physics	2245-2250
Chemistry	2251-2276
Geology	2277-2295
Paleontology	2296
Biology and Anthropology	2297-2314

Botany	2315-2328
Zoology	2329-2342

MEDICINE
General	2343-2360
Catalogs and Surveys of Collections	2361-2384
Periodicals	2385-2401
History	2402-2416
Incunabula and Early Printing	2417-2434

TECHNOLOGY
General	2435-2453
Engineering	2454-2544
Aeronautics	2545-2581
Home Economics	2582-2590
Agriculture	2591-2673
Business	2674-2780
Chemical Technology	2781-2806
Manufactures	2807-2828
Building	2829

FINE ARTS
General	2830-2855
Landscape Architecture and City Planning	2856-2873
Architecture	2874-2902
Numismatics	2903-2908
Drawing	2909-2922
Decoration and Design	2923-2945
Painting	2946-2953
Engraving	2954-2993
Photography	2994-2999
Music	3000-3085
Amusements	3086-3145

LINGUISTICS
General	3146-3156
Germanic Languages	3157-3161
Romance Languages	3162-3167
Slavic Languages	3168-3169
Semitic Languages	3170-3171
Malay-Polynesian, etc.	3172-3174
American Indian	3175-3186
Other Languages	3187-3188

LITERATURE
General Literature	3189-3218
American Literature	3219-3347
Canadian Literature	3348
English Literature	3349-3579
German Literature	3580-3605
Scandinavian Literature	3606-3632
French Literature	3633-3659
Italian Literature	3660-3686
Spanish, Portuguese and Latin American Literature	3687-3721
Greek and Latin Literature	3722-3741
Celtic Literature	3742-3744
Slavic Literature	3745-3766
Oriental Languages and Literature	3767-3800
Juvenile Literature	3801-3821

GEOGRAPHY AND MAPS
General	3822-3868
America (General)	3869-3878
North America	3879-3895
United States (Individual States and Cities)	3896-3925
Latin America	3926-3934

BIOGRAPHY AND GENEALOGY
General	3935-3941
Individual Biography	3942-4134
Genealogy	4135-4177

Directories	4178-4183	United States State and Local History	4708-5280
HISTORY		Latin American History	5281-5370
General	4184-4197	Oceanian and Polar Regions History	5371-5386
Ancient History	4198-4227		
European History	4228-4327	Military and Naval History and Science	5387-5495
Asiatic History	4328-4365		
African History	4366-4387	World War I	5496-5539
Canadian History	4388-4394	World War II	5540-5578
United States History	4395-4707	Index	page 375

Introduction

Multiplication, especially within the past twenty-five years, of handbooks, check lists, bibliographies, calendars, surveys, union lists, union catalogs, and similar guides to American library resources has increased immeasurably our knowledge and consequently the availability of existing research facilities. Valuable resources previously hidden in obscure institutions, as well as important collections in libraries with national reputations, were brought to light for the first time. The saving of time for scholars, students, research workers, and librarians which has resulted from the provision of these bibliographical tools is immense, and of course materials have been revealed that would otherwise have remained undiscovered. To cite only two well-known examples, we can hardly realize now the difficulties confronting anyone attempting to locate a file of a scarce periodical before the appearance in 1927 of the Union List of Serials in Libraries of the United States and Canada, or a rare newspaper before the publication of American Newspapers, 1821-1936, and Brigham's American Newspapers.

As bibliographical finding aids have increased by leaps and bounds, now running into thousands of titles, the need for some type of control or central record has become evident. Many of the published guides are highly specialized, often confined to a minute field. Frequently they are issued in small editions, sometimes buried in journals of limited circulation, and therefore almost as likely to be overlooked as the collections they describe. Furthermore, works cutting across subject lines and containing data pertinent to various fields are easily missed by specialists unfamiliar with such general compilations.

These considerations led to development of the present comprehensive bibliographical guide to American library resources, under the sponsorship of the American Library Association's Board on Resources of American Libraries. Nothing of the kind has been projected previously except on a limited scale.*

In scope, the guide now presented is national in coverage and is inclusive of every field for which bibliographical information is available. Hence there are listed printed library catalogs, union lists of books and serials, descriptions of special collections, surveys of library holdings, calendars of archives and manuscripts, selected library reports, and similar works of potential usefulness to research workers. Occasional unpublished bibliographies and indexes, of which there are many in the country, have also been recorded. Sources of information concerning references included in the guide were numerous. A substantial percentage was contributed through correspondence with individual libraries; the bibliographical file of the Library of Congress Union Catalog added hundreds of valuable items; a check of library, bibliographical, historical and literary periodicals of the past twenty-five years turned up more titles; and personal visits to several major libraries proved profitable. The hundreds of check lists and other compilations issued by the Historical Records Survey and the American Imprints Inventory were incorporated almost in toto.

---

* E.g., The "Bibliography" in Winchell's Locating Books for Interlibrary Loan; Haskell and Brown's "Bibliography of Union Lists of Serials," appended to the Union List of Serials; and the bibliographical sections of Downs's Resources of New York City Libraries and Resources of Southern Libraries.

INTRODUCTION

From the outset, it was decided that no specific date limitations on the guide would be desirable. Few entries precede 1900, and these are principally library catalogs, check lists of special collections, and works of historical significance. The terminal date is roughly 1950, though no systematic search was undertaken for post-1949 publications. As one reviews older references in this field, it becomes clear that the study of library resources has long been of interest to American librarians. We find, for example, union lists of serials going back to the 1870's, and Longhead described California's library resources as early as 1878.* As stated previously, however, the most striking proliferation of such material has occurred chiefly in the last generation.

An obvious weakness in a guide to library resources restricted to published information is the uneven character of the publishing which has taken place. Certain libraries are extensively documented, bibliographically speaking, while others of perhaps equal or greater importance, at least in certain areas, may have done little to publicize their rich facilities. Most thoroughly covered of the general institutions are the Library of Congress and the New York Public Library. Among more specialized agencies, the Henry E. Huntington Library, Hispanic Society of America, William L. Clements Library, Hoover Library, National Archives, John Crerar Library, Newberry Library, and Pierpont Morgan Library are outstanding for their success in making their resources known to the scholarly world.

The importance of journal publications for publicity purposes should be noted. The New York Public Library Bulletin is the oldest of the type still current and has been the instrument for hundreds of bibliographies, check lists, calendars, and descriptive articles relating to that great library's holdings. More recently established and performing like services for the libraries they represent are the Harvard Library Bulletin, Yale University Library Gazette, Library of Congress Quarterly Journal of Current Acquisitions, University of Pennsylvania Library Chronicle, Newberry Library Bulletin, Princeton University Library Chronicle, Library Chronicle of the University of Texas, Journal of the Rutgers University Library, Boston Public Library Quarterly, Colby Library Quarterly, and Duke University's Library Notes. As a rule, these periodicals not only report systematically on current acquisitions, but are also retrospective, going back to describe older items and collections. They constitute, therefore, valuable storehouses of information concerning these several libraries.

In contrast to the libraries which have been so well covered bibliographically, we find a group of strong institutions that has been inactive in publishing, and which perforce does not show up to full advantage in the present compilation. Instances among universities are California, Chicago, Columbia, Illinois, Michigan (except Clements Library), Minnesota, Stanford (except Hoover Library), Northwestern, Indiana, Wisconsin, Ohio, and New York. A number of explanations may be offered for this situation: (1) a majority of the institutions named, it will be observed, are state universities, which in general are less free than privately endowed libraries with funds for bibliographical publishing; (2) with some exceptions, the libraries listed, and others of similar character, place less stress on special collections which lend themselves readily to descriptive accounts, and are more concerned with the development of their general resources; and (3) again with certain exceptions, these libraries are more recently founded, have achieved their status as major libraries later, and have concentrated attention on collecting materials rather than on publicizing their acquisition. The need is quite apparent for additional bibliographies, handbooks, check lists, and surveys to guide research workers to the extensive holdings of such libraries.

Approximately 6,000 titles (including subreferences) are included in the main body of this guide. In many cases, bibliographies listed do not fully represent collections with which they deal, because collections have continued to grow after publication of the bibliographies. Even when the references are incomplete or somewhat inconsequential in themselves, however, they have been recorded because they reveal the presence of important collections. It has also been the policy to be more generous in the inclusion of bibliographical works pertaining to library resources in regions not well provided with research materials. These titles may relate to holdings of slight value from a national viewpoint, but of considerable worth to the regions in which they are located.

Some types of material and subject fields have proved more attractive to bibliographers and no doubt adapt themselves better to bibliographical treatment than do others. Among general categories, a cursory examination of this compilation will show a heavy emphasis on such areas as serial publications, printing history, archives and manuscripts. It is not difficult to understand the popularity of union lists

---

* Longhead, Flora Haines Apponyi. The Libraries of California; Containing Descriptions of the Principal Private and Public Libraries Throughout the State. San Francisco: A. L. Bancroft and Co., 1878. 304p.

INTRODUCTION

of serials, because of their immediate utility, relative ease of preparation, and aid in programs of library cooperation. Hundreds, ranging from local to national and international levels, general and special, have appeared in the past two or three decades, and continue to come out in a steady flow. In printing history, the prodigious labors of the late Douglas C. McMurtrie and the American Imprints Inventory added immensely to our knowledge of the existence and location of imprints of the early periods of United States history. For European printing, primary emphasis bibliographically is on incunabula, though increasing attention is being paid to the two following centuries. In the field of archives and manuscripts, we are indebted especially to two agencies, the American Historical Association, for its pioneer surveys at the beginning of the present century, and to the Historical Records Survey, under Luther H. Evans' able direction in the 1930's and early 1940's. Currently, the most active single organization in this area is the National Archives.

Another general category, library catalogs in book form, was considered outmoded, except for special collections, until appearance of A Catalog of Books Represented by Library of Congress Printed Cards and its successors. Possibly a reversal in the universal trend to card catalogs may be impending. For the purposes of this guide, however, only selected examples of older catalogs have been included, as, for the most part, these are now obsolete.

In subject fields, the social sciences show tremendous vitality, bibliographically speaking, in large part due to the prolific publishing in this area by the Library of Congress and the New York Public Library. Literature and history also account for large blocks of references. Considerably less numerous are citations to fine arts collections. Science and technology are well represented, but with some emphasis on the historical side, since these are rapidly changing subjects, and bibliographies soon become out of date, thereby discouraging publication of bibliographical works intended for use over a long period of time.

Classification of references in the bibliography which follows is broadly by the Dewey Decimal System, with occasional exceptions, e.g., for linguistics. The decision to use this arrangement was made for two principal reasons: its simplicity and the general familiarity of library users with it. While recognizing its frequently illogical and unscientific features, it is believed the advantages mentioned counterbalance the drawbacks. Further, the detailed index appended should reveal any gold buried by the classification scheme.

Every item included in the bibliography has been given an individual number, and index citations are to entry numbers rather than to pages. Each title is listed only once, under what is considered the most appropriate heading, though, if unlimited space were available, additional listings under related headings might have been useful. Again, the index is intended to make up for any deficiencies in this respect.

In conclusion, it ought to be emphasized that a primary purpose of this work is to aid in programs of national and international library cooperation. Further development of the Library of Congress Union Catalog and regional union catalogs, new union lists and bibliographies, agreements for specialization of fields among institutions, photographic reproduction projects, interlibrary loans, and other types of cooperative action depend substantially on locating specific materials and collections. From an even wider point of view, e.g., bibliographical proposals on an international scale growing out of UNESCO, it is essential that existing information concerning library resources in various countries be brought together.

A fitting postscript to this, or any other, bibliographical compilation is the following quotation from Elliott Coues:

> Bibliography is never finished and always more or less defective, even on ground long gone over.... The writer would be accurate; yet he feels the weight of Stevens' satire: "If you are troubled with a pride of accuracy, and would have it completely taken out of you, print a catalogue."

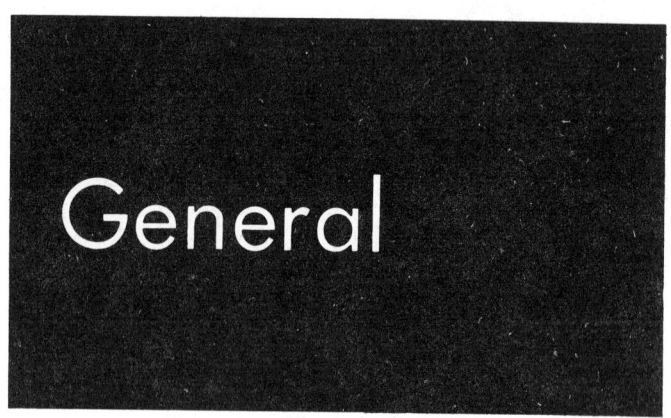

General

GENERAL BIBLIOGRAPHY AND REFERENCE BOOKS

1. ALA Junior Members Round Table. Local indexes in American libraries; a union list of unpublished indexes, ed. by Norma Olin Ireland and others. Boston: F. W. Faxon Co., 1947. 221p.
   Lists about 8,000 indexes for 950 libraries on 2,500 subjects.

2. American book-prices current. N. Y.: R. R. Bowker, 1895 to date.
   "In case of rare books location of the copies sold can sometimes be traced by applying to the auctioneer." (Mudge). A record of books, manuscripts and autographs sold in the principal auction rooms of the United States.

3. Carnegie Institution of Washington. Catalogue of publications and depositories of the Institution. Wash.: The Institution, 1948. 388p.
   P. 339 - 66 list libraries in the United States which receive all or selected publications of the Carnegie Institution.

4. "Current national bibliographies,"I-III. Library of Congress quarterly journal of current acquisitions, 6 (Aug. 1949), 28-33; 7 (Nov. 1949), 14-22; (Feb. 1950), 11-13.
   "It is expected to conclude the series in two future issues of the Quarterly Journal." Based upon Library of Congress collection.

5. Historical Records Survey. Bibliography of research projects reports; check-list of Historical Records Survey publications, prep. by Sargent B. Child and Dorothy P. Holmes. Wash.: Federal Works Agency, 1943. 110p. (WPA technical series, research and records bibliography, no.7)

6. John Crerar Library. A list of bibliographies of special subjects, July 1902. Chicago: The Library, 1902. 504p.
   Classified arrangement. Covers social, physical and natural sciences and their applications. Limited to material in John Crerar Library.

7. John Crerar Library. A list of cyclopedias and dictionaries with a list of directories, August 1904. Chicago: The Library, 1904. 272p.
   Contains 1,610 titles, covering general works and special subjects. Classified.

8. John Crerar Library. A list of reference indexes, special bibliographies and abstract serials in the John Crerar Library, comp. by H. Einar Mose. Chicago, 1930-32. 3v. (Reference list 4, 9, 20)

9. McKay, George Leslie, comp. American book auction catalogues, 1713-1934; a union list. N. Y.: New York Public Library, 1937. 540p.
   A list of 10,000 catalogs, with locations in 10 libraries.
   "Additions." New York Public Library Bulletin, 50 (1946), 177-84; 52 (1948), 401-12. Reprinted. 8p. Supplement 2. 2p.

10. New York Library Association, Junior Members Round Table, Local Indexes Committee. Local indexes in New York State libraries. N. Y., 1942? 42 numb. 1.
    A subject list of indexes, locating special collections in 62 libraries.

11. New York Public Library. "A bibliography of Slavonic bibliography in English," comp. by the Slavonic Division of the New York Public Library. New York Public Library bulletin, 51 (1947), 200-08. Reprinted. 11p.

"In most cases the items listed are available in the New York Public Library." 132 titles.

12. Philadelphia Bibliographical Center, and Union Library Catalogue. Union list of microfilms; a basic list of holdings in the United States and Canada. Philadelphia: Philadelphia Bibliographical Center, 1942. 379p. Supplements 1-5 (1942-46). Philadelphia, 1943-47.
    Lists 5,221 items in 127 institutions.

13. Ricci, Seymour de. The book collector's guide; a practical handbook of British and American bibliography. Philadelphia: Rosenbach Co., 1921. 649p.
    Locates copies of rare books in libraries and many private collections.

14. Spargo, John Webster. "Some reference books of the sixteenth and seventeenth centuries: a finding list." Bibliographical Society of America papers, 31 (1937), 133-75.
    150 titles located in 8 American and 3 foreign libraries.

15. Taylor, Archer and Mosher, Frederic J. Bibliographical history of anonyms and pseudonyms. Chicago: published for the Newberry Library by the University of Chicago Press, 1950. In press.

16. Texas, University, Library. An index of indexes and minor collections not fully displayed in the card catalog of the library of the University of Texas. Austin: Univ. of Texas Library, 1945. 29 numb. 1.

17. Union catalog of hand-copied books in Braille - grade one, grade two, and grade one and a half. Comp. October 1934. Wash.: Govt. Print. Off., 1936. 233p.
    A subject list locating books in 76 libraries.

18. A Union catalogue of photo facsimiles in North American libraries. Material so far received by the Library of Congress. Yardley, Pa.: F. S. Cook and Son, 1929. 64 numb. 1.
    Lists holdings of 16 libraries.

19. U. S. Library of Congress, Copyright Office. Catalog of copyright entries. July 1891-to date. Wash.: Govt. Print. Office, 1891-to date.

20. U. S. Library of Congress, Acquisitions Department. European imprints for the war years received in the Library of Congress and other federal libraries. Wash., 1946. 3 pts.
    Pt. 1, Italian imprints, 1940-45; pt. 2, German imprints, 1940-45; pt. 3, French imprints, 1940-45.

21. U. S. Library of Congress, General Reference and Bibliography Division. A guide to Soviet bibliographies, comp. by John T. Dorosh. Wash., Apr. 1950. 158p.

22. U. S. Library of Congress, Hispanic Foundation. A bibliography of Latin American bibliographies, by C. K. Jones, 2d ed. Wash.: Govt. Print. Off., 1942. 311p.

GOVERNMENT PUBLICATIONS

United States

23. Arkansas, University, Library. Checklist of Arkansas state publications received by the University of Arkansas Library. No. 1 - . 1943- to date. Fayetteville, 1944- to date.

24. California Library Association, Southern District. A union list of local documents in libraries of Southern California. [Los Angeles]: The Association, 1935. 166p.
    Attempts "to record all Southern California county, city and district documents." Locates copies in 49 libraries.

25. California State Library. "Catalog of state publications of California, 1850 to July, 1894." California State Library biennial report, (1892-94), 32-72.
    Publications listed are in California State Library.

26. Colorado State Board of Library Commissioners. Check list of Colorado public documents. Denver: Smith-Brooks Printing Co., 1910. 203p.
    "Prepared in Document department, Public Library, Denver." An entry for every document from earliest territorial days to Sept. 1, 1910.

27. Florida, University, Library. Short-title check list of official Florida publications received by the...Library. July/Aug. 1942- to

28 GENERAL

date. Gainesville, 1942- to date.
Bi-monthly.

28. Greely, Adolphus Washington. Public documents of the first fourteen congresses, 1789-1817. Wash.: Govt. Print. Off., 1900. 903p. (56th Congress, 1st sess. Senate document, no. 428). Supplement. American Historical Association annual report, (1903), 343-406.

"Unless otherwise stated, all originals herein mentioned are in the following libraries: Boston, Athenaeum Library; New York, Public Library; Washington, War Department Library." Supplement locates copies in 6 libraries.

29. Greely, Adolphus Washington. "Public documents of the early Congresses." American Historical Association annual report, I (1896), 1109-1248.

Locates good collections of documents and some individual titles listed in the bibliography.

30. Hodgson, James Goodwin. The official publications of American counties; a union list. Fort Collins, Colo., 1937. 594p.

Over 5,000 entries located in 194 libraries of all types.

31. Kuhlman, A. F. "The need for a comprehensive checklist bibliography of American state publications." Library quarterly, 5 (1935), 31-58.

"Bibliographies, catalogs, check lists, etc., of American state publications," many of which locate copies in specific libraries, p. 38-51.

32. Minnesota Historical Society. A bibliography of Minnesota Territorial documents, comp. by Esther Jerabek. St. Paul: The Society, 1936. 157p. (Minn. Hist. Soc. special bulletins, v. 3)

A check list of the Society's holdings. "All items listed in the bibliography are in the possession of the Minnesota Historical Society, unless otherwise indicated."

33. Minnesota Historical Society. Check list of Minnesota public documents. July 1923- Feb. 1941, no. 1-86. St. Paul: The Society, 1923-41.

Most of documents listed are in Minnesota Historical Society.

34. National Association of State Libraries. Collected public documents of the states; a check list, comp. by William S. Jenkins. Boston, 1947. 87p.

Locates copies of "unique or exceptionally rare items" in 27 libraries.

35. New Hampshire State Library. Check list of New Hampshire state documents received at the State Library, July 1, 1942 - June 30, 1944. [Concord, 1944] 12p.

36. New York Public Library. "Check list of United States state documents in the New York Public Library relating to finance." New York Public Library bulletin, 6 (1902), 293-314.

37. New York State Library. Check list of official publications of the State of New York. Albany, 1947-to date.

Monthly, with annual cumulations. Based on New York State Library holdings.

38. Rhode Island State Library. Checklist of legislative documents in the Rhode Island state archives, by Grace E. MacDonald. Providence: Oxford Press, 1928. 24p.

39. U. S. Library of Congress, General Reference and Bibliography Division. Post-war problems, a current list of printed U. S. government publications. Wash., 1944-46. 8v.

40. U. S. Library of Congress, Processing Department. Monthly check list of state publications. Wash.: Govt. Print. Off., 1910-to date.

Publications received by Library of Congress.

41. Virginia State Library. "Check list of Virginia state publications," 1926-to date. Virginia State Library bulletin, 16 (1927) - to date.

An annual list of all Virginia documents acquired by Virginia State Library and Virginia State Law Library.

42. Washington State Library. A reference list of public documents, 1854-1918, found in the files of the State Library. Olympia: F. M. Lamborn, Public Printer, 1920. 51p.

Latin America

43. Childs, James Bennett. Bibliography of

official publications and the administrative systems in Latin American countries. Wash., 1938. 44p. (Reprinted from Inter-American Bibliographical and Library Association first convention proceedings, 1938)

Based upon Library of Congress collection.

44. Childs, James Bennett. Colombian government publications. Wash., 1941. 41p. (Reprinted for the Library of Congress by the H. W. Wilson Co. from the Proceedings of the Third Convention of the Inter-American Bibliographical and Library Association.)

Based upon Library of Congress collection.

45. Childs, James Bennett. "Hispanic American government documents in the Library of Congress." Hispanic American historical review, 6 (1926), 134-42. Reprinted.

46. Childs, James Bennett. The Memorias of the Republics of Central America and of the Antilles. Wash.: Govt. Print. Off., 1932. 170p.

Copies located in Library of Congress, six other federal libraries, University of California, New York Public Library, and Pennsylvania Commercial Museum.

47. U. S. Library of Congress. A guide to the official publications of the other American Republics. James B. Childs, general ed. Wash. 1945-48. 18 pts. (Its Latin American series, no. 9-11, 15, 17, 19, 22-25, 27, 29-31, 33-37)

48. U. S. Library of Congress. Mexican government publications; a guide to the more important publications of the national government of Mexico, 1821-1936, by Annita M. Ker. Wash.: Govt. Print. Off., 1940. 333p.

Locates copies in 8 libraries in United States and various departments and libraries in Mexico City.

General

49. American Library Association. Committee on Foreign Documents. Partial list of French government serials in American libraries. Albany: Univ. of the State of N. Y., 1902. p.97-164. (New York State Library bulletin, no. 70, Bibliography, no. 33, p. 97-164)

Lists holdings of 16 libraries.

50. Childs, James Bennett. "Notes on some recent documentary materials." American political science review, 40 (1946), 1251-54; 4 (1947), 410-12, 634-37, 1078-85; 42 (1948), 641-46, 1076-80; 43 (1949), 431-38, 882-86.

Reviews documentary materials pertaining to countries outside United States. Based on Library of Congress collection.

51. Childs, James Bennett. "Official gazettes of foreign countries." In: American Library Association. Committee on Public Documents. Public documents, ed. by Jerome K. Wilcox... with Archives and libraries...Papers presented by the 1938 conference of the American Library Association. Chicago, 1938. p. 129-174.

An "endeavor to appraise the current informational content of foreign offical gazettes." Based on Library of Congress holdings.

52. List of the serial publications of foreign governments, 1815-1931, ed. by Winifred Gregory, for the American Council of Learned Societies, American Library Association, National Research Council. N. Y.: H. W. Wilson, 1932. 720p.

Lists foreign serials holdings of 85 American libraries.

53. U. S. Library of Congress, Division of Documents. Official publications of present-day Germany; government, corporate organizations and National Socialist Party, with an outline of the governmental structure of Germany, by Otto Neuburger. Wash.: Govt. Print. Off., 1942. 130p.

LIBRARY SCIENCE

54. Evans, Clara T. and Baer, Carlyle S. Census of book plate collections in public, college and university libraries in the United States. Wash.: Bruin Press, 1938. 48p.

Describes how collections were acquired, availability to public, arrangement, and method of increasing collections in 58 United States libraries.

55. Fearing, Daniel B. A list of angling bookplates. Newport, R. I., 1916. 40p.

Most of plates in compiler's collection presented to Harvard College Library.

56. Georgetown University. The Georgetown

University Library; miniatures commemorating the tercentenary of its founding (1640-1940). [Wash.: Georgetown University, 1940] 60p.

"Contents: Wagner, B. M., The manuscripts in the Riggs Memorial Library; Wilkinson, W. W. J., Incunabula; Parsons, W., Early Americana; Temple, P., The Library and its work today."

57. Harvard University Library. "Angling and watercraft bookplates in the Harvard College Library." Harvard alumni bulletin, 21 (1918), 131-33.

58. Illinois, University, Library. List of library reports and bulletins in the collection of the University of Illinois Library School, comp. by Florence Rising Curtis. Urbana: University of Illinois, 1912. 22p. (University of Illinois bulletin, v. 9, no. 12)

Includes foreign and domestic libraries. Gives holdings.

59. Jahr, Torstein Knutson Torstensen and Strohm, Adam Julius. Bibliography of cooperative cataloguing and the printing of catalogue cards, with incidental references to international bibliography and the Universal catalogue. (1850-1902) Reprinted from the Report of the librarian of Congress. Wash.: Govt. Print. Off., 1903. 116p.

Based upon Library of Congress collection.

60. Long Island Historical Society. "Emma Toedteberg and her book plates," by W. G. Bowdoin. Long Island Historical Society quarterly, 2 (1940), 35-46.

Description of collection of 6,000 bookplates owned by Society.

61. New York Public Library. "Causes and prevention of deterioration in book materials," comp. by Robert P. Walton. New York Public Library bulletin, 33 (1929), 235-66. Reprinted. 39p.

62. New York Public Library. "Check list of works relating to libraries of New York City in the New York Public Library." New York Public Library bulletin, 5 (1901), 227-32.

63. New York Public Library. "Insect pests of books; an annotated bibliography to 1935," comp. by Ralph H. Carruthers and Harry B. Weiss. New York Public Library bulletin, 40 (1936), 829-41, 985-94, 1049-64. Reprinted, 1937. 63p.

64. Newark Free Public Library, Business Branch. Business service in public libraries of 109 large cities; a survey conducted by Marian C. Manley. Newark: The Library, 1930. 48p.

Pt. 1, General policies; pt. 2, Collections.

65. Pan American Union, Columbus Memorial Library. Latin American booktrade and library journals in the Columbus Memorial Library of the Pan American Union. Wash.: Pan American Union, 1941. n. p. (Bibliographic series, no. 2, pt. 2, rev.)

66. Pan American Union, Columbus Memorial Library. Obras existentes en la Biblioteca Colón de la Unión Panamericana sobre organización de bibliotecas y sistemas de clasificacion. Wash., 1937. 16 numb. l. (Serie bibliográfica, no. 8. 2d. ed. rev.)

67. Walton, Clarence E. The three-hundredth anniversary of the Harvard College Library. Cambridge: Harvard College Library, 1939. 46p.

Describes the history and development of the Harvard College Library, and it collections.

GENERAL SURVEYS OF LIBRARIES

68. American Council on Education. American universities and colleges, ed. by A. J. Brumbaugh. 5th ed. Wash.: American Council on Education, 1948. 1,054p.

Gives general statement of number of volumes and special collections in libraries of about 1,000 educational institutions.

69. American library directory, 1948. N. Y.: Bowker, 1948. 731p.

"Index to special collections, special subjects and special libraries," p. 705-19.

70. Berthold, Arthur Benedict. "Directory of union catalogs in the United States." In: Downs, R. B., ed. Union Catalogs in the United States. Chicago: American Library Association, 1942, p. 349-91.

Describes scope, subject emphases, and special services of each catalog, with a list of libraries included.

GENERAL

71. Bibliographical Planning Committee of Philadelphia. Philadelphia libraries, a survey of facilities, needs and opportunities. Philadelphia: Univ. of Pennsylvania Press, 1942. 95p.

A survey of 157 libraries. Supplement (46p. bound in) gives chronology, classified lists and a guide to research materials of Philadelphia libraries.

72. Joint Committee on Library Research Facilities for National Emergency. Guide to library facilities for national defense. Rev. ed. Ed. by Carl L. Cannon. Chicago: American Library Association, 1941. 448p.

Selected information on resources of about 750 American libraries with collections of material pertinent to national defense.

73. Carlson, William H. "Library resources in the land of little water." ALA bulletin, 39 (1940), 617-22.

Describes library resources of Montana, Idaho, Wyoming, Colorado, New Mexico, Arizona, Utah and Nevada.

74. Chicago Library Club. Directory of libraries of the Chicago area. 2d. ed. Chicago: The Club, 1945. 135p.

Lists 833 libraries, with bibliographical, statistical and other data. Lists special collections. First issued 1933.

75. Clemons, Harry. A survey of research materials in Virginia libraries, 1936-37. Charlottesville, Va.: Alderman Library, 1941. 100p. (University of Virginia Bibliographical series, no. 1)

Describes material available in about 25 Virginia libraries.

76. "Collections in university libraries." In: World Almanac. N. Y., 1950, p. 537-43.

Lists special collections and other data for 41 large American university libraries.

77. Dean, Helen E. "A survey of special collections in Missouri libraries." The M. L. A. Quarterly, 3 (Dec. 1942), 67-71, 74; 4 (March 1943), 4-5, 17-18; 4 (June 1943), 24-28, 39.

Brief descriptions of special collections in a variety of fields.

78. Downs, Robert B. "Leading American library collections." Library quarterly, 12 (1942), 457-73.

250 libraries are represented as having leading collections in one or more of 75 subjects.

79. Downs, Robert B. "Notable materials added to American libraries, 1938-39." Library quarterly, 10 (1940), 157-91.

Locates and describes materials added to many libraries.

80. Downs, Robert B. "Notable materials added to American libraries, 1939-40." Library quarterly, 11 (1941), 257-301.

Locates and describes materials added to many libraries.

81. Downs, Robert B. "Notable materials added to American libraries, 1940-41." Library quarterly, 12 (1942), 175-220.

Locates and describes materials added to many libraries.

82. Downs, Robert B. Resources of New York City libraries; a survey of facilities for advanced study and research. Chicago: American Library Association, 1942. 442p.

A survey describing or mentioning the resources of nearly 400 libraries in New York City.

83. Downs, Robert B., ed. Resources of Southern libraries; a survey of facilities for research. Chicago: American Library Association, 1938. 370p.

Studies all classes of library research materials in 13 Southern states.

84. Hill, David Spence. The libraries of Washington; a study of the governmental and non-governmental libraries in the District of Columbia. Chicago: American Library Association, 1936. 296p.

Describes 269 libraries in Washington, D. C., giving size, scope, purpose, control, and relation to establishments they serve.

85. Hintz, Carl W. "Notable materials added to North American libraries, 1943-47." Library quarterly, 19 (1949), 105-18; 186-200.

Locates and describes materials added to many libraries.

86. Iben, Icko. "Resources of Illinois college and research libraries." I. L. A. record, 1 (March 1948), 1-10.

Tabulation, covering 64 institutions, notes special collections and strong subject fields.

87. Iben, Icko. A survey of research materials in Oklahoma libraries. Stillwater: A. & M. College, 1937. 44p.

88. Inland Empire Council of Teachers of English. Committee on Books. Northwest books. 2d. ed. Portland, Ore.: Binfords and Mort, 1942. 356p.
Includes brief notes on resources of libraries in Northwest region, p. 351-56.

89. Johnston, William D. "Library resources of New York City and their increase." Columbia University quarterly, 13 (1911), 163-72.
Locates some special collections in libraries of New York City.

90. Johnston, William D., and Mudge, Isadore G. Special collections in libraries in the United States. Wash., 1912. 140p. (U. S. Bureau of Education bulletin, no. 23, 1912.) "A supplementary list." Library journal, 38 (1913), 331-33.
A subject list of special collections and unique copies in more than 2,000 United States libraries.

91. Literary history of the United States, ed. by Robert E. Spiller and others. N. Y., Macmillan, 1948. 3v.
Volume 3, p. 3-26, lists bibliographical centers, catalogs, directories, union lists, special collections, guides to special fields, etc.

92. Longhead, Flora Haines Apponyi. The libraries of California; containing descriptions of the principal private and public libraries throughout the state. San Francisco: A. L. Bancroft and Co., 1878. 304p.
A pioneer survey now of historical interest.

93. New Jersey Library Association, Junior Members' Round Table, Union Catalog Comm. Survey of special collections in New Jersey libraries. N. Y.: H. W. Wilson, 1940. 113p.
A subject list describing collections in New Jersey libraries.

94. New Orleans Library Club. The libraries of New Orleans. New Orleans: The Club, 1945. 44p.
Describes collections of 64 libraries, including public and private school collections.

95. Pacific Northwest Library Association. Special collections in libraries of the Pacific Northwest, comp. by Charles W. Smith. Seattle: Univ. of Washington Press, 1927. 20p.
A subject list, giving approximate number of volumes in special collections in 37 American and 5 British Columbian libraries.

96. Paylore, Patricia P. "A survey of Arizona library resources with particular reference to special collections." Arizona librarian, 5 (1948), 9-15.
Surveys resources of 41 Arizona libraries, excluding school libraries.

97. Power, Ralph Lester, ed. Libraries of Los Angeles and vicinity. Los Angeles: Univ. of Southern California Press, 1921. 63p.
Describes about 50 libraries.

98. Prince, Huberta, comp. The Washington book mart. N. Y.: Oceana Publications, 1949. 260p.
Descriptive guide to libraries and other book agencies in Washington, D. C., including a brief account of resources.

99. Richardson, Ernest C. An index directory to special collections in North American libraries. Provisional ed. unedited. Yardley, Pa.: F. S. Cook & Son, 1927. 168p.
A list of special collections by localities and by subjects; gives name of collection, location, and number of volumes only.

100. Smith, Charles W., comp. Special collections in libraries of the Pacific Northwest. Seattle: Univ. of Wash. Press, 1927. 20p.
Arranged by subject fields.

101. Special Libraries Association. Special libraries directory of the United States and Canada. 3d ed. N. Y.: The Association, 1935. 263p.
Lists 1,475 libraries with their "important subjects" noted.

102. Special Libraries Association. Special library resources, ed. by Rose Vormelker. N. Y.: The Association, 1941-47. 4v.
"A source book for the holdings of American libraries in special subject fields."

103. Special Libraries Association, Boston Chapter. Directory of special libraries in Boston and vicinity. 4th ed. Boston, Mass., 1928. 24p.

Lists 133 libraries and gives "a survey of informational resources of Greater Boston."

104. Special Libraries Association, New York Chapter. Special libraries directory of greater New York. 5th ed. N. Y.: The Association, 1950. 110p.

Contains 641 entries, with data on subject interests of libraries.

105. Special Libraries Council of Philadelphia and vicinity. Directory of libraries and informational sources in Philadelphia and vicinity. 7th ed., ed. by Mrs. Catharine C. Grady. Philadelphia, 1947. 130p.

Lists 286 libraries, describing their general resources.

106. Special libraries directory of Indiana. South Bend, Ind.: Studebaker Corp., 1940. 24p.

Gives size and lists special collections for 110 Indiana libraries.

107. Swanton, Walter Irving. Libraries in the District of Columbia. Wash.: Nat. Res. Council, 1921. 19p. (Reprint and circular series of the Nat. Res. Council, no. 20)

A list of 170 libraries, giving characterization of contents, number of volumes in each, and subject classification of libraries.

108. Texas Library Association. Handbook of Texas libraries, no. 4. Houston: The Association, 1935. 151p.

Brief descriptions of collections.

109. U. S. Library of Congress, Legislative Reference Service. Library and reference facilities in the area of the District of Columbia. 3d ed. Wash.: Library of Congress, 1948. 132p.

Describes resources of 217 libraries.

110. Van Male, John. "Notable materials added to American libraries, 1941-42." Library quarterly, 14 (1944), 132-58.

Locates and describes materials added to many libraries.

111. Van Male, John. Resources of Pacific Northwest libraries; a survey of facilities for study and research. Seattle: Pacific Northwest Library Association, 1943. 404p.

Surveys resources of 108 libraries in British Columbia, Idaho, Montana, Oregon, and Washington.

112. Virginia Library Association. Handbook of Virginia libraries. Charlottesville: Univ. of Virginia, 1936. 92p.

Lists 847 libraries, notes size of collections, etc.

113. Wagner, Henry R[aup]. Willard Samuel Morse, a great collector. [Los Angeles] Printed for Dawson's Book Shop by the Ward Ritchie Press, 1939. 12p.

Briefly describes Joaquin Miller collection now in Claremont College Library, Mark Twain collection now in Yale University Library, and 23 other collections.

114. Williams, Edwin E. "Research library acquisitions from eight countries." Library quarterly, 15 (1945), 313-23.

Report on percentages of books procured in a typical year by leading American research libraries from Belgium, Canada, France, Italy, Mexico, Peru, Spain, and Sweden.

115. Winchell, Constance M. Locating books for interlibrary loan; with a bibliography of printed aids which show location of books in American libraries. N. Y.: H. W. Wilson, 1930. 170p.

A subject list of bibliographies which locate copies.

SURVEYS OF INDIVIDUAL LIBRARIES

116. Bauer, Harry C. "Books at the University of Washington." Pacific spectator, 3 (Winter 1949), 63-72.

Discusses facilities and resources.

117. Bibliographical Planning Committee of Philadelphia. A faculty survey of the University of Pennsylvania libraries. Philadelphia: Univ. of Penn. Press, 1940. 202p.

Lists resources in the general library and the departmental libraries of the University of Pennsylvania.

118. Bruner, Helen M. "Possibilities for research in the Sutro collection." Library journal, 60 (1935), 787-89.

Description of a collection now housed in

the San Francisco Public Library and administered as a branch of the California State Library.

119. California, University, Library, William Andrews Clark Memorial Library. William Andrews Clark Memorial Library. Report of the first decade, 1934-1944, ed. by Lawrence Clark Powell. Berkeley and Los Angeles: Univ. of California Press, 1946. 78p.

120. Chicago, University, Library. The university libraries, by M. Llewellyn Raney. Chicago: Univ. of Chicago Press, 1933. 250p. (The Univ. of Chicago survey, v. 7)

A comprehensive survey of the University of Chicago Library's holdings in various fields.

121. Columbia University Library. Bibliotheca Columbiana, published from time to time by the Friends of the Library of Columbia University. N. Y., no. 1-4 (April 1933 - August 1937).

Contains descriptions of important collections in the Library.

122. Connecticut State Library. A brief summary of its activities. Tercentenary edition. Hartford, 1935. 12p.

123. Currie, Florence B. "The Flack collection of the University of Missouri." Bibliographical Society of America papers, 17 (1923), 57-62.

Description of a collection of 6,000 books and pamphlets on European law and early French literature and history.

124. Duke University Library. The library of Duke University. Durham, N. C.: Friends of Duke University Library, 1949 [24]p. (Duke University Library notes, special no., Oct. 1949)

"The library collection," p. 12-21, describes research holdings in various fields.

125. Emory University Library. The Emory Library: where it stands. Atlanta: Emory University, 1948. 16p. (Emory University bulletin, v. 34, no. 17, Nov. 1, 1948)

General survey of Library's resources, with brief descriptions of special collections.

126. Emory University Library. A preliminary account of the special collections, chiefly manuscripts, in the Emory University libraries. [Atlanta, 1941] [4]p.

127. Harvard University Library. "The name of Gay." Harvard Library notes, 2 (1927), 143-47.

Survey of collections, in Harvard College Library, made by Frederick L. Gay, Ernest L. Gay, and George H. Gay. See also Harvard Library notes, 2 (1931), 242.

128. Henry E. Huntington Library. Aids to research in the Huntington Library, comp. by Lyle H. Wright. San Marino: The Library, 1940. 10p.

A list of bibliographical aids and subject indexes to Library's collections.

129. Henry E. Huntington Library. "Huntington Library collections." Huntington Library bulletin, 1 (1931), 33-106.

Brief descriptions of most important manuscripts and printed materials in Library.

130. Henry E. Huntington Library. "Research facilities of the Huntington Library." Huntington Library quarterly, 3 (1939), 131-45.

Three talks on scope and use of collections.

131. Indiana University Library. "The University as a collector." Indiana quarterly for bookmen, 2 (Jan. 1946), 7-18.

Discusses collections in Indiana University Library.

132. John Crerar Library. The John Crerar Library, 1895-1944; an historical account, [by Jens Christian Bay] Chicago, 1945. 206p.

Chapter VII describes collections.

133. Law, Robert A. "Two Texas libraries." Texas review, 5 (1920), 349-57.

Description of Rosenberg Library, Galveston, and Wrenn Library, University of Texas.

134. Lewis, Wilmarth S. The Yale collections. New Haven: Yale Univ. Press, 1946. 54p.

Summarizes outstanding collections in Sterling Memorial Library, Peabody Museum of Natural History, Yale University Art Gallery, and Yale Anthropological Collection.

135. Los Angeles Public Library. Handbook of central library collections. Los Angeles, 1940. 60 numb. 1.

136. Michigan, University, Library, Reference Dept. University of Michigan libraries: special collections, comp. by Margaret I. Inglis. 1946. 10p.

137. Missouri, University, Library. Survey of the resources of the University of Missouri Library for research work, by H. O. Severance. Columbia: Univ. of Missouri, 1937. 30p. (Univ. of Missouri bulletin, v. 38, no. 16, Library ser., no. 19)

138. Mood, Fulmer. A survey of the library resources of the University of California. Berkeley: Univ. of California Library, 1950. 837p. Microfilm.
   General survey of library resources in all branches of University of California.

139. New York Public Library. A guide to the reference collections of the New York Public Library, comp. by Karl Brown. N. Y.: The Library, 1941. 416p. Reprinted from the New York Public Library bulletin, May 1935 - Feb. 1941.

140. New York Public Library. History of the New York Public Library, by Harry Miller Lydenberg. N. Y.: The Library, 1923. 643p.
   Traces history of many important collections contained in Library.

141. New York Society Library. History of the New York Society Library, with an introductory chapter on libraries in colonial New York, 1698-1776, by Austin Baxter Keep. N. Y.: DeVinne Press, 1908. 60p.
   Describes growth of New York Society Library's collections of Americana, genealogy, newspapers, etc.

142. New York Society Library. The New York Society Library, founded in 1754; being a brief résumé of its history, together with its officers and benefactors. N. Y., 1949. 13p.
   Includes general description of Library's resources.

143. Newberry Library. Handbook. Chicago: The Library, 1938. 78p.
   A description of resources of Library, particularly in special fields of research.

144. North Carolina, University, Library. Library resources of the University of North Carolina, ed. by Charles E. Rush. Chapel Hill: Univ. of North Carolina Press, 1945. 264p.
   A comprehensive survey.

145. Oklahoma Library Commission. Oklahoma libraries, 1900 - 1937; a history and handbook. Oklahoma City: The Commission, 1937. 276p.
   History and description of libraries in Oklahoma, with mention of their special collections.

146. Oklahoma, University, Library. Oklahoma's crown jewel; the new library. Norman: Univ. of Oklahoma Press, 1930. 47p.
   Pages 25-47 are facsimiles or photographs of incunabula and other rarities in University of Oklahoma Library.

147. Pierpont Morgan Library. The Pierpont Morgan Library; a review of the growth, development and activities of the library during the period between its establishment as an educational institution in February 1924 and the close of the year 1929. N. Y.: [Plandome Press], 1930. 148p., 18 plates.

148. Pierpont Morgan Library. The Pierpont Morgan Library; review of the activities and acquisitions of the library from 1930 through 1935; a summary of the annual reports of the Director to the Board of Trustees. N.Y.: [Plantin Press, c1937]. 151p., 16 plates.

149. Pierpont Morgan Library. The Pierpont Morgan Library; review of its activities and acquisitions of the library from 1936 through 1940; a summary of the annual reports of the Director to the Board of Trustees. N. Y.: [Plantin Press], 1941. 127p., 19 plates.

150. Pierpont Morgan Library. The Pierpont Morgan Library; review of the activities and major acquisitions of the Library, 1941-1948. With a memoir of John Pierpont Morgan and the Pierpont Morgan Library, 1913 - 1943. N. Y.: [Gallery Press], 1949. 108p., 12 plates.

151. [Potter, Alfred C.] The library of Harvard University; descriptive and historical notes. 4th ed. Cambridge: Harvard Univ. Press, 1934. 186p. Earlier editions 1903, 1911, 1915.

152. Rochester, University, Library. "Our special collections." University of Rochester

153 GENERAL

Library bulletin, 4 (1949), 45-68.
Brief descriptions of 42 collections in various fields held by University of Rochester Library.

153. Rosenberg Library. Henry Rosenberg, 1824-1893. Galveston, Texas. [N.Y.: DeVinne Press] 1918. 226p.
Part 3, p. 139-226, describes Rosenberg Library, and its special collections.

154. Sondley Reference Library. A survey of research material. Asheville, N. C., 1940. 30p.
Description of Library's resources on Southeast history, American Indians, English and American literature, science, etc.

155. Thompson, C. Seymour. "The University Library." University of Pennsylvania Library chronicle, 1 (1933), 47-60.
Survey of Library's history and collections.

156. U. S. Library of Congress. The Library of Congress. Some notable items that it has; some examples of many others that it needs. Wash.: [Govt. Print. Off.] 1926 113p.

157. U. S. Library of Congress. The Library of Congress in relation to research, by Martin A. Roberts. Wash.: Govt. Print. Off., 1939. 55p.
P. 1-26, description of Library's collections in principal divisions.

158. U. S. Library of Congress. The Library of Congress, its collections and services. [Wash.: Govt. Print. Off., 1945] 24p.

159. U. S. Library of Congress. Some notes on the Library of Congress as a center of research, together with a summary account of gifts received from the public in the past forty years, by William Adams Slade. Wash.: Govt. Print. Off., 1939. 29p. (Reprinted from Annual report of the librarian of Congress for the fiscal year ended June 30, 1938.)
Describes some of the resources available to research workers in Library of Congress. Mentions the famous collections and projects.

160. U. S. Library of Congress. Special facilities for research. [Wash.: Govt. Print. Off., 1942] 8p.

161. U. S. Library of Congress, Reference Dept. A guide to special book collections in the Library of Congress, by Shirley Pearlove. Wash.: The Library, 1949. 66p.
Notes names of collections, location, description, and bibliographical references.

162. U. S. Library of Congress, Reference Dept. A report on certain collections in the Library of Congress. [Wash., 1942] 26 numb. l.

163. Vosper, Robert. "Books at U. C. L. A." Pacific spectator, 2 (Winter, 1948), 113-22.

164. Watkinson Library of Reference. Special collections in the Watkinson Library of Reference, by Ruth A. Kerr. Connecticut Library Association bulletin, 10 (1943), no. 3, 5, 7.
A brief description of collections.

165. Wesleyan University Library. Library handbook, 1942-43, Olin Memorial Library, Wesleyan University, comp. by Fremont Rider. 4th ed. Middletown, Conn., 1942. 79p.

Periodicals

The following current journals issued by individual libraries contain descriptions of collections, bibliographies, and other data on resources.

166. Boston Public Library quarterly, 1 (1949) to date.
Supersedes More books.

167. Colby Library quarterly, 1 (1943), to date.

168. Harvard Library bulletin, 1 (1947), to date.

169. New York Public Library bulletin, 1 (1897), to date.

170. Newberry Library bulletin, 1 (1944), to date.

171. Pennsylvania, University, Library. University of Pennsylvania Library chronicle, 1 (1933), to date.

172. Princeton University Library chronicle, 1 (1939), to date.

173. Rutgers University Library. The journal of the Rutgers University Library, 1 (1937), to date.

174. Texas, University, Library. Library chronicle of the University of Texas, 1 (1944), to date.

175. U. S. Library of Congress quarterly journal of current acquisitions, I (1943), to date.

176. Yale University Library gazette, 1 (1926), to date.

GENERAL LIBRARY CATALOGS

177. U. S. Bureau of Education. "List of printed catalogues of public libraries in the United States, arranged by the date of publication." U. S. Bureau of Education, Public libraries in the United States. Wash.: Govt. Print. Off., 1876. p. 568-622.

List of 1,010 catalogs, issued by college, university, public and other libraries from 1723 to 1876. Indicates number of volumes cataloged in each work.

178. Alabama Polytechnic Institute Library. Catalogue... complete to Nov. 20, 1894. Auburn, 1894. 90p.

179. Alabama, University, Library. Catalogue of the library of the University of Alabama, with an index of subjects, by Wilson G. Richardson. Tuscaloosa: M. D. J. Slade, 1848. 257p.

180. Allegheny College Library. Catalogus bibliothecae collegii Alleghaniensis. Meadville, Penn.: T. Atkinson, 1823. 139p.

Includes books received from James Winthrop, Isaiah Thomas, William Bentley, etc.

181. American Antiquarian Society Library. A catalogue of books in the library of the American Antiquarian Society. Worcester: The Society, 1836-37. ca. 350p.

Now only of historical value. An author list of the printed books only.

182. American Philosophical Society Library. Catalogue of the American Philosophical Society Library. Philadelphia, 1863-84. 1,390p. (4pts. in 2v.)

183. Arizona Territorial Library. Catalogue of the Territorial Library of Arizona. Phoenix: H. H. McNeil Co., 1905. 117p.

Law Department: p. 9-59; General library: p. 63-117. Now Arizona State Library.

184. Augustana College. Denkmann Memorial Library. Bibliography of the catalogued books of the Augustana College Library, comp. by Marcus Skarstedt. [Rock Island, Ill., 1917] 272p. (Augustana bulletin, ser. 13, no. 1, March 1, 1917)

Strong in material relating to the Lutheran Church.

185. Boston Athenaeum. Catalogue of the library of the Boston Athenaeum. 1807-71. Boston, 1874-82. 5v.

186. Boston Public Library. Catalogue of the Public Library of the City of Boston. Boston: J. Wilson & Son, 1854. 180p.

The Library's first general catalog.

187. Boston Public Library. Index to the catalogue of books in the Bates Hall of the Public Library of the City of Boston. First supplement. Boston: J. E. Farwell & Co., 1866. 718, 21p.

Supplement to 1861 index, including, in an appendix, index to Boston city documents, 1834-65.

188. Bowdoin College Library. A catalogue of the library of Bowdoin college; to which is added, an index of subjects. Brunswick [Me.]: Printed for the College, 1863. 832p.

189. Brooklyn Library. Analytical and classed catalogue of the Brooklyn Library. Authors, titles, subjects, and classes. Brooklyn, 1877-80. 1,110p.

Lists 60,000 volumes. Now part of Brooklyn Public Library.

190. Brown University Library. A catalogue of the library of Brown University, in Providence, Rhode Island. With an index of subjects. Providence, 1843. 560p.

191. Burnam, John Miller, ed. Summary catalogue of a part of the library of John M. Burnam. Cincinnati, O.: Univ. of Cincinnati Press [1906]. 84p. (University studies, pub. by the University of Cincinnati.

192 GENERAL

Ser. II, vol. 2, no. 3)

Now in University of Cincinnati Library. Strong in historical source material, Roman religion, patristics, palaeography and lexical apparatus.

192. California State Library. Catalogue of the California State Library, prep. by W. C. Stratton. Sacramento: O. M. Clayes, State Printer, 1866. 2v.

193. California State Library. Catalogue. General Department. Authors. Sacramento: J. D. Young, Supt. of State Printing, 1889. 1,172p.

-----. Supplementary catalogue. General Department. Authors. San Francisco: Caxton Printing Co., 1898. 980p.

194. California, University, Library. Library of the University of California. Contents index. v. 1. Berkeley, 1889-90. 519p.

Subject catalog of books in Library, plus analytics to serial publications of learned societies and periodicals.

195. Century Association Library. A catalogue of the James Lorimer Graham Library, [comp. by P. L. Ford] N. Y., 1896. 391p.

Graham books were given to Century Association about 1893.

196. Chicago Public Library. Philosophy, religion, medicine: finding list. Chicago: The Library, 1916. 454p.

"Includes all the books on the first two of these subjects now in the library, together with a revised list of those on medicine."

197. Cincinnati Public Library. Books for adult beginners, grades I to VII, comp. by the staff of the Readers' Bureau. Rev. ed. Chicago: American Library Association, 1946. 56p.

A special collection of books gathered by Readers' advisers of Cincinnati Public Library.

198. Cincinnati Young Men's Mercantile Library Association. Catalogue. Cincinnati: Truman & Spofford, 1855. 308p.

199. Clemson Agricultural College Library. Catalogue. Clemson College, S. C.: Clemson College Printery, 1913. 181p.

200. College of the City of New York Library. Catalogue of the Library of the College of the City of New York. New York, 1877-78. 2 vols.

Supersedes 1860 catalog.

201. Colorado State Library. Catalog of State Library of Colorado. Denver: Times Printing Co., 1884. 82p.

Arranged by types of material and subjects.

202. Columbia University Library. Catalogue of the books and pamphlets in the library of Columbia College, New York. N. Y.: J. W. Amerman, 1874. 412p.

Does not include law and mining collections.

203. Columbia University Libraries. Catalog of the Isadore Witmark collection of autographed books and musical scores in the Columbia University Libraries. N. Y.: The Library, 1942. 76p.

204. Dayton Public Library. Catalogue... authors, subjects, and titles. Dayton, Ohio: United Brethern Publishing House, 1884. 438p. Supplement, 1885. 50p. Supplement 2, 1888. 131p. Supplement 3, 1891. 154p.

205. Delaware State Library. Catalogue. Dover: The Index, 1900. 249p.

Limited chiefly to law collection.

206. Detroit Public Library. Catalogue of the Public Library of the City of Detroit. Detroit, 1868. 149p.

207. Folk, Edgar Estes, ed. A catalogue of the library of Charles Lee Smith. Wake Forest, N. C.: Wake Forest College Press, 1950. 654p.

A comprehensive general library now owned by Wake Forest College.

208. Georgia, University, Library. Catalogue of books in the library of the University of Georgia. Athens, Ga., 1858. 192p.

Arranged by subjects.

209. [Harvard University Library] A catalogue of the books and manuscripts of Harry Elkins Widener, by A. S. W. Rosenbach. Philadelphia: Privately Printed, 1918. 2v.

Collection now owned by Harvard University.

210. Harvard University Library. A catalogue of the library of Harvard University in Cambridge, Massachusetts. Cambridge: E. W. Metcalf & Co., 1830-31. 3v. in 4. First supplement. Cambridge: C. Folsom, 1834. 260p.

Volume 3 contains a catalog of maps and charts. Latest printed catalog of Harvard College Library.

211. Harvard University Library. The Farnsworth Room in the Harvard Library; a catalogue of books for readers. Cambridge: Harvard College Library, 1931. 141p.

A collection of about 5,000 volumes of cultural and recreational value.

212. Hispanic Society of America Library. List of printed books in the library of the Hispanic Society of America. N. Y., 1910. 20v.

213. Illinois State Library. Dictionary catalogue of the Illinois State Library (public documents excepted). Danville, Ill.: Illinois Print. Co., 1912. 814p. Earlier edition issued 1903. 712p.

214. Indiana State Library. Catalog, 1903. Indianapolis: W. B. Burford, 1905. 523p. Supplement. Indianapolis: W. B. Burford, 1905. 178p.; supplement, 1906. 439p.

215. Iowa State Library. Catalogue of the State Library of Iowa, comp. by Mary H. Miller. Des Moines: G. E. Roberts, State Printer, 1889. 275, 466p. (2 parts)

Supplements to catalog are to be found in biennial reports of State Librarian.

216. John Crerar Library. A list of books in the reading room, 1909. Chicago, 1909. 488p.

Revised edition of list first issued in 1900. Lists about 4,000 volumes.

217. Kansas State Library. Catalogue of the Kansas State Library, 1871, by D. Dickinson. Topeka, Kansas: S. S. Prouty, State Printer, 1871. 50p.

218. Kentucky State Library. Catalogue. Frankfort, 1928. 474p.

219. Louisiana State Library. Catalogue of the State Library of the State of Louisiana up to March 31, 1886. New Orleans: E. A. Brandao & Co., 1886. 228p.

Arranged by subjects and types of material.

220. Maryland State Library. Catalogue of the Maryland State Library... 1895, by L. H. Gadd. Annapolis: Maryland Republican Steam Print, 1895. 2 pt. in 1 v.

Pt. I, law; Pt. II, general literature.

221. Massachusetts Historical Society Library. Catalogue of the private library of Thomas Dowse, of Cambridge, Mass., presented to the Massachusetts Historical Society, July 30, 1856. Boston: Printed by J. Wilson & Son, 1870. 214p.

222. Massachusetts State Library. Catalogue of the State Library of Massachusetts. Boston: Rand, Avery and Co., 1880. 1,048p.

223. Michigan State Library. Catalogue of the Michigan State Library. United States documents, state documents, foreign exchanges. Lansing: Robert Smith Printing Co., 1898. 276p.

224. Mississippi State Library. Catalogue of the Mississippi State Library, by Mattie Plunkett. Nashville: Brandon Printing Co., 1902. 451p.

225. Nebraska State Library. Catalogue of the State Library, comp. by Guy A. Brown. Lincoln: Journal Co., 1884. 196p.

A catalog of the 25,000 volume collection.

226. Nevada State Library. Catalogue of books in the miscellaneous department February 1934. Carson City, 1934. 258p.

227. Nevada State Library. Catalogue of the Nevada State Library, by Jennie D. Fisher. Carson City: State Printing Office, 1890. 320p.

228. New Bedford Free Public Library. Catalogue of the Free Public Library, New Bedford, Mass. New Bedford: B. Lindsey, 1858. 354p.

Supplement. New Bedford: E. Anthony & Sons, 1869. 313p.

Second Supplement. New Bedford: E. Anthony & Sons, 1876. 476p.

229. New Hampshire State Library. Author list of the New Hampshire State Library, June 1, 1902. Manchester: John B. Clarke Co., 1904. 2v. Supplements issued 1904, 1906, 1908. 3v.

230. N. Y. Mercantile Library Association. Catalogue of books in the Mercantile Library of the City of New York. N. Y.: F. T. Taylor, 1866. 699p.

Supplement. N.Y.: J. Medole, 1869. 250, 15p.; Second supplement. N.Y.: J. Sutton & Co., 1872. 296p.

231. [New York Public Library.] Astor Library. Catalogue or alphabetical index of the Astor Library, comp. by Joseph Green Cogswell. N.Y.; C. Craighead, 1857-1866. 5v.
  Now in New York Public Library.

232. [New York Public Library.] Astor Library. Catalogue of the Astor Library (continuation). Cambridge, Mass.: Riverside Press, 1886-88. 4v.
  Now in New York Public Library.

233. [New York Public Library.] Lenox Library. Contributions to a catalogue of the Lenox Library. N. Y.: 1877-93. 7 numbers.
  Contents: 1. Voyages of Hulsius, etc.; 2. Jesuit relations, etc.; 3. Voyages of Thévenot; 4. Bunyan's Pilgrim's Progress, etc.; 5. Works of Shakespeare, etc.; 6. Works of Milton, etc.; 7. Waltonian collection.
  Material recorded is now in New York Public Library.

234. New York Public Library, Lenox Library. Short-title list. [N.Y., 1887-99]. 12 parts.
  Pt. I-II. Bibles; III. Americana; IV. Miscellaneous; V. Shakespeare, angling, Milton, Bunyan; VI. Aldines, etc.; VII. Astoin collections; VIII. Duyckinck collection; IX. Paintings, etc.; X. Miscellaneous collections; XI-XII. Drexel [Musical] collection.

235. New York Society Library. Alphabetical and analytical catalogue of the New York Society Library. With the charter, by-laws, etc., of the institution. N.Y.: R. Craighead, 1850. 621p.
  Includes a catalog of Winthrop library (originally owned by John Winthrop, founder of Connecticut).

236. New York Society Library. Catalogue of books from the circulating library of the late James Hammond of Newport, R. I., presented to the...library...by Robert Lenox Kennedy. N. Y.: John W. Amerman, 1868. 31p.

237. [New York University Library]. Katalog der von... Paul de Lagarde gesammelten und von ihm der Königlichen gesellschaft der wissenschaften zu Göttingen vermachten bibliothek. Göettingen: Kaestner, 1892. 85p.
  Catalog of a collection of theology, Greek and Latin literature, orientalia, and general linguistics now in New York University, University Heights Library.

238. North Carolina State Library. Catalogue of the North Carolina State Library, 1891. Raleigh: Josephus Daniels, 1891. 146p.
  Pt. 1, books; pt. 2, newspapers.

239. Ohio State Library. Catalogue of the Ohio State Library, 1875, comp. by William Holden. General Library. Columbus: Nevins & Myers, 1875. 727p. Supplement, no.1, 1875-82, 1882. 296 p.

240. Oregon State Library.' "Catalogue of the State Library to the twenty-first legislative assembly, 1901." In: Oregon State Library biennial report, 1901, p. 5-133.

241. Peabody Institute Library (Baltimore). Books counted by classes and divisions in the library up to May 31st, 1937; with a selected list of publications following each class. [Baltimore] 1937. [95]1.

242. Peabody Institute Library (Baltimore). Catalogue of the library of the Peabody Institute of the City of Baltimore. Baltimore; 1883-92. 5v.

243. Peabody Institute Library (Baltimore). Second catalogue of the library of the Peabody Institute of the City of Baltimore, including the additions made since 1882. Baltimore, 1896-1905. 8v.

244. Peabody Institute Library (Peabody, Mass.) Catalogue of the library of the Peabody Institute. Peabody, Mass.: Charles D. Howard, 1872. 483p. Supplement, 1787. 221p.

245. Pennsylvania, University, Library.

Catalogue of books belonging to the Library. Philadelphia: J. Dobson, 1829. 103p.

246. Philadelphia Library Company. A catalogue of the books belonging to the Library Company of Philadelphia. Philadelphia: C. Sherman & Co., 1835. 2v. V.3, A supplementary volume, issued 1856, lists titles added 1835-56, with index to whole.

247. Philadelphia Library Company, Loganian Library. Catalogue of the books belonging to the Loganian Library: to which is prefixed a short account of the institution, with the law for annexing the said library to that belonging to "The Library Company of Philadelphia." Philadelphia: C. Sherman & Co., 1837. 450p. Supplement, 1867. 32p.

248. Philadelphia Mercantile Library Company. Catalogue of the Mercantile Library of Philadelphia. Philadelphia: Mercantile Library Company, 1870. 707p.

249. Pittsburgh, Carnegie Library. Classified catalogue of the Carnegie Library of Pittsburgh. Series [1] - 4; Vol. 1-9, 1895-1916. Pittsburgh: Carnegie Library, 1907-1926. 11v.

250. Potter, Alfred C. "Catalogue of John Harvard's library." Colonial Society of Massachusetts publications, 21 (1919), 190-230.

251. Princeton University Library. Alphabetical finding list. Princeton: The Library, 1921. 5v.

"The list represents approximately those books that were in the University Library on July 1, 1920, though a few later additions are included."

252. Princeton University Library. Classed list. Princeton: The Library, 1920. 6v.

253. Providence Athenaeum. Catalogue of the library of the Providence Athenaeum. Providence: Knowles, Anthony & Co., 1853. 557p. Supplementary catalog issued 1861. 374p.

254. Riant, Paul Édouard Didier. Catalogue de la bibliothèque de feu M. le comte Riant... rédigé par L. de Germon et L. Polain. Paris: A. Picard et fils, 1896-99. 3v. in 2.

Scandinavian collection (1st part) is now in Yale University Library; Part 2, Crusades and Latin Orient, is in Harvard University Library.

255. Salem Athenaeum. A catalogue of the library of the Salem Athenaeum, in Salem, Massachusetts. Boston: J. Wilson & Son, 1858. 179p.

256. San Francisco Public Library. Catalogue. San Francisco: The Library, 1880-82. 3v. Supplementary catalogue. San Francisco, 1889. 391p.

257. Silas Bronson Library. Finding list of the Silas Bronson Library of Waterbury, Connecticut. New Haven: Price, Lee and Co., 1889. 139p. Catalogue of the Library issued 1870. 340p.

258. Streeter, Mary Eleanor, comp. "Books given by Henry Adams to Western Reserve University; a list of the books given by Henry Adams from his library to the Library of Adelbert College of Western Reserve University." Cleveland, 1948. 18 l. Typed.

259. Sumner, Charles. The collection of books and autographs, bequeathed to Harvard College Library, by the Honorable Charles Sumner. Cambridge: University Press, 1879. 28p. (Harvard University Library, Bibliographical contributions, no. 6)

260. Tennessee State Library. Catalogue of the general and law library. Nashville: [Jones, Purvis and Co.] 1871. 432p.

261. Union League Club of New York Library. Catalogue of the library...comp. by Ellsworth Totten. [N.Y.: G. P. Putnam's Sons], 1886. 451p.

262. U. S. Dept. of the Interior Library. Catalogue of the library of the Department of the Interior, including the additions made from May 31, 1877 to February 1, 1881. Wash.: Govt. Print. Off., 1881. 292p. Supplemental catalogue of books added...from February 1, 1881, to June 30, 1883. [Wash.: Govt. Print. Off., 1883] 15p. Supplemental catalogue... June 30, 1883 to December 31, 1884. Wash.: Govt. Print. Off. 1885. 13p.

263. U. S. Dept. of the Interior Library. List

264 GENERAL

of books added to the library of the Department of the Interior from December 1884 to June 1, 1892. Wash.: Govt. Print. Off., 1892. 26p.

264. U. S. Library of Congress. Alphabetical catalogue of the Library of Congress. Authors. Wash.: Govt. Print. Off., 1864. 1236p.

    About 80,000 volumes. The first and only general author catalog in one alphabet published by the Library of Congress. A subject catalog appeared in 1869, and an author catalog, A-Cragin only, 1878-80.

265. U. S. Library of Congress. A catalog of books represented by Library of Congress printed cards, issued to July 31, 1942. Ann Arbor, Mich.: Edwards Bros., 1942-46. 167v.

-----. Supplement. Cards issued August 1, 1942 - December 31, 1947. Ann Arbor, Mich.: Edwards Bros., 1948. 42v.

266. U. S. Library of Congress. Catalogue of the Library of the United States. Wash.: Printed by Jonathan Eliot, 1815. 170p.

    "The Jefferson collection, 6,500 volumes, purchased by Congress in 1815 to replace the library destroyed in 1814." "Classification based on that of Jefferson."

267. U. S. Library of Congress. Cumulative catalog of Library of Congress printed cards. Wash.: The Library, 1948 - to date.

    Shows locations in other libraries if catalog copy is supplied.

268. U. S. Library of Congress. Library of Congress subject catalog, a cumulative list of works represented by the Library of Congress printed cards. Wash., Jan. 1950 - to date.

269. Utah State Library. Catalogue of the Utah State Library, by H. W. Griffith. Salt Lake City: [Kelly and Co., 1910]. 115p.

270. Vanderbilt University Library. Catalogue. Nashville: Brandon Printing Co., 1886. 300p.

271. Vermont, University, Library. Alaphabetical and analytical catalogue of the University of Vermont, Burlington. Burlington: Free Press Office, 1854. 164p.

272. Virginia, University, Library. Catalogue of the library of the University of Virginia... Also, a notice of such donations of books as have been made to the University. Charlottesville: Gilmer, Davis & Co., 1828. 114p.

273. Washington State Library. Catalogue of the Washington State Library. Olympia: O. C. White, 1891. 329p.

    Law Department, p. 3-262; General Department, p. 265-321.

274. Widener, Harry Elkins. A catalogue of some of the more important books, manuscripts, and drawings in the library of Harry Elkins Widener. Philadelphia, 1910. 233p.

    Collection now in Harvard University Library.

275. Williams College Library. Catalogue of the Library of Williams College, Williamstown, Mass., 1875. North Adams, Mass.: James T. Robinson & Son, 1875. 233p.

276. Wilmington Institute Free Library. Finding list of the circulating department. Wilmington, Del., 1894-95. 2v.

277. Yale University, Brothers in Unity Library. Catalogue of the library of the Society of Brothers in Unity, Yale College, July 1851. New Haven: T. J. Stafford, 1851. 294p.

278. Yale University, Calliopean Society Library. Catalogue of the library of the Calliopean Society, Yale College, February 1846. New Haven: Printed by B. L. Hamlen, 1846. 94p.

279. Yale University Library. Catalogue of books in the library of Yale College. New Haven: Printed at the Journal office, 1823. 100p.

280. Yale University Library, Linonian and Brothers' Library. Catalogue of the Linonian and Brothers' Library, Yale College. New Haven: Tuttle, Morehouse & Taylor, 1873. 344p. First supplement. New Haven: Tuttle, Morehouse & Taylor, 1880. 220p.

PERIODICALS, NEWSPAPERS, AND JOURNALISM

General

281. Haskell, Daniel C. and Brown, Karl, comps. "Bibliography of union lists of serials." In: Union list of serials in libraries of the United States and Canada. N. Y.: H. W. Wilson, 1943. p. 3053-65.

A geographical list of bibliographies which may be found in the New York Public Library or other library specified.

282. Josephson, Aksel Gustav Salomon. A bibliography of union lists of serials. 2d. ed. Chicago: John Crerar Library, 1906. 28p.

283. Alabama Department of Archives and History. Check list of newspapers and periodical files in the Department of Archives and History. Montgomery: Brown Printing Co., 1904. 65p. (Bulletin, no. 3)

284. Arizona, University, Library. Union list of serials in the University of Arizona Library and associated libraries. Tucson: University of Arizona, 1933. 145p.

Lists holdings of 13 public and private collections.

285. Baker, Mary E. Tennessee serials, together with the holdings of Tennessee libraries. Knoxville, 1937. 57p.

Gives holdings of 25 public collections and one private collection in Tennessee.

286. Beer, William. "Check list of American periodicals, 1741-1800." American Antiquarian Society proceedings, n. s. 32 (1922), 330-45. Reprinted, 1923. 18p.

Covers period 1741 to 1800, inclusive, alphabetical by title, with locations of 98 titles in 17 libraries.

287. Bibliographical Center for Research, Rocky Mountain Region, Denver. Union list of periodicals currently received in the college and university libraries of Colorado and Wyoming (Denver Public Library is included). Boulder: University of Colorado Libraries, 1942. 136 numb. 1.

Lists holdings of 16 libraries.

288. Boston Public Library. A guide to serial publications founded prior to 1918 and now or recently current in Boston, Cambridge, and vicinity, comp. by Thomas Johnston Homer. Boston: The Library, 1922-36. 613p. (A-Ret)

Locates publications in 83 libraries or collections but does not give exact holdings.

289. Brody, Fannie M. "The Hebrew periodical press in America, 1871-1931: a bibliographical survey." American Jewish Historical Society publication, no. 33 (1934), 127-70.

List compiled from material in New York Public Library or from bibliographies.

290. Bucks County Historical Society Library. A check list of American and foreign periodicals in the library of the Bucks County Historical Society. Doylestown, Pa.: The Society, 1940. 118 [15]p.

291. California Library Association. List of California periodicals issued previously to the completion of the transcontinental telegraph (August 15, 1846 - October 24, 1861), by Katherine Chandler. San Francisco: The Association, 1905. 20p. (Publication, no. 7)

Locates copies in 25 California libraries and private collections.

292. California Library Association, Southern District. Union list of serials in libraries of southern California. Los Angeles: Los Angeles Public Library, 1939. 504p.

Records holdings of 75 libraries. Omits periodicals, local documents and newspapers.

293. California, University, Library. List of serials in the University of California Library. Berkeley: Univ. of California Press, 1913. 266p. (Its Library bulletin, no. 18)

294. Carberry, Hilda (Maurer), comp. Selected list of periodicals in Cincinnati libraries with special reference to scientific and technical publications. [Cincinnati] 1936. 129 numb. 1.

A union list.

295. Catholic University of America Library. Periodicals and serials in the library of the Catholic University of America, 1910. Wash.: The University, 1910. 113p.

296. Chicago Library Club. A list of serials in public libraries of Chicago and Evanston. Chicago, 1901. 185p. Supplement issued by

John Crerar Library, 1903; and revised supplement in 1906.
    Lists holdings of 15 libraries.

297. Chicago Public Library Omnibus Project. Bibliography of foreign language newspapers and periodicals published in Chicago. Chicago, 1942. 150 numb. l.
    Lists holdings of 97 libraries in United States.

298. Clark University Library. A union list of serials in twelve libraries in Worcester County, Massachusetts. Worcester: Clark University Library, 1949. 346p.
    Lists holdings of university, college, public and special libraries in area.

299. Colorado State College of Agriculture Library. Serial holdings of the Colorado State College library. Fort Collins, 1942- (Colorado State College library, Library bulletin, 10, pt. 1-6, A-M)
    Supersedes List of Serials, 1930.

300. Colorado, University, Library. List of serials in University of Colorado Library. Boulder, 1913. 82p. (Univ. of Colorado bulletin, v. 13, no. 1)
    Indicates holdings of 2,800 titles in University of Colorado Library.

301. [Conference of Eastern College Librarians] A list of periodicals bound complete with advertising pages in New England and New York City libraries. Hanover, N. H., 1935. 15p.
    Locations shown in 34 cooperating libraries.

302. Denver, University, Library. A union list of serials in certain Denver libraries, by Marguerite J. Schwab. [Denver:] University of Denver, 1942. 496 numb. l.
    Gives holdings of 9 libraries (not including the Denver Public Library).

303. DuPont de Nemours & Co. Technical Library. A list of periodicals currently received in the libraries of the Wilmington (Delaware) district. Wilmington: The Library, 1934. 29 numb. l.
    Locates titles but not holdings in 81 special and institutional libraries.

304. Flanders, Bertram Holland. Early Georgia magazines; literary periodicals to 1865. Athens: Univ. of Georgia Press, 1944. 289p.
    Locates files in 55 public and private collections.

305. Flanders, Ralph B. "Newspapers and periodicals in the Washington Memorial Library, Macon, Georgia." North Carolina historical review, 7 (1930), 220-23.
    Description of a collection of early Georgia newspapers and literary periodicals in Macon, Ga., Public Library.

306. Geiser, Samuel Wood. A check list of the bound serial publications in the fields of science and technology, philosophy and medicine in the public libraries of Dallas, Texas. [Dallas] 1928. 8p.
    Lists holdings of Dallas Public Library, Southern Methodist University and Baylor University College of Medicine.

307. Gilmer, Gertrude C. "A critique of certain Georgia ante-bellum literary magazines arranged chronologically, and a check list." Georgia historical quarterly, 18 (1934), 293-334.
    Locates files in American libraries.

308. Gilmer, Gertrude C., comp. "Maryland magazines - ante bellum, 1793 to 1861." Maryland historical magazine, 29 (1934), 120-31.
    Locates holdings of those titles which are in Maryland Historical Society.

309. Goan, Fava Eloise, ed. Union list of serials in Indiana libraries, recording the holdings of forty-six public, college, university, institutional and special libraries of the state. Lafayette: Indiana Union List Committee, 1940. 680p.
    Especially strong in serial publications dealing with Indianians or originating in Indiana.

310. Graham, Mary Elizabeth and Graham, Walter James. "Census of American newspapers and periodicals, 1690-1800, in American libraries." [Urbana, Ill.] 1934. 136 numb. l. Typed.
    808 titles located in 71 libraries.

311. Gregory, Winifred, ed. International congresses and conferences, 1840-1937;

a union list of their publications available in libraries of the United States and Canada. N. Y.: H. W. Wilson, 1938. 229p.
Lists holdings of over 100 libraries.

312. Griffin, Max L. "A bibliography of New Orleans magazines." Louisiana historical quarterly, 18 (1935), 491-556.
Covers period from 1834 to 1930. Locates files in 4 New Orleans libraries.

313. Historical Records Survey, Utah. Check list of newspapers and magazines published in Ogden. Ogden: Hist. Rec. Survey, 1938. 5 numb. l.

314. Hoole, Wm. S. A check list and finding list of Charleston periodicals, 1732-1864. Durham, N. C.: Duke Univ. Press, 1936. 84p.
Holdings of 67 libraries reported, not repeating those included in Union list of serials in the United States and Canada.

315. Hoole, W. Stanley. North Texas regional union list of serials, comprising the libraries of North Texas State Teachers College, Southern Methodist University, Southwestern Baptist Theological Seminary, Texas Christian University, Texas State College for Women, and the Public Libraries of Dallas and Fort Worth. Denton: North Texas State Teachers College, 1943. 532 l. Supplements issued 1945, 1946.

316. Illinois, University, Library. List of serials in the University of Illinois Library, together with those in other libraries in Urbana and Champaign, comp. by Francis K. W. Drury. Urbana: University of Illinois, 1911. 233p. (University of Illinois bulletin, v. 9, no. 2)
Represents holdings in 6 libraries.

317. John Crerar Library. A list of current periodicals. 4th ed., March, 1938. Chicago: The Library, 1938. 91p.

318. John Crerar Library. Supplement to the List of serials in public libraries of Chicago and Evanston. 2d ed., cor. to Nov. 1905, ed. by Clement W. Andrews. Chicago, 1906. 220, 28p.

319. Lamberton, John P. A list of serials in the principal libraries of Philadelphia and its vicinity. Philadelphia: Library Company, 1908. 309p. (Philadelphia Free Library bulletin, no. 8)
Locates 12,000 serials in 25 libraries in and around Philadelphia.

-----. Supplement. Philadelphia: Library Company, 1910. 88p. (Bulletin, no. 9)
Adds holdings of 2 more libraries and further information about others.

320. Litchfield, Dorothy Hale, ed. Classified list of 4,800 serials currently received in the libraries of the University of Pennsylvania and of Bryn Mawr, Haverford, and Swarthmore colleges. Philadelphia: Univ. of Penn. Press, 1936. 411p.
Includes holdings of Wistar Institute and the Cancer Research Laboratories. List includes only serials received since Jan. 1, 1933.

321. Lutrell, Estelle. Newspapers and periodicals of Arizona, 1859-1911. Tucson: Univ. of Arizona, 1950. 123p. (Univ. of Arizona general bulletin, no. 15, July 1949)
Bibliographical account giving locations of files of Arizona territorial newspapers.

322. McMillen, James A. The works of James D. B. DeBow, a bibliography of DeBow's review with a checklist of his miscellaneous writings. Hattiesburg, Miss.: Book Farm, 1940. 36p. (Heartman's hist. ser., no. 52)
Mentions files in Louisiana State University and Library of Congress.

323. McMurtrie, Douglas C. The French press of Louisiana; notes in supplement to Edward Larocque Tinker's "Bibliography of French newspapers and periodicals of Louisiana." [New Orleans, 1935] 19p. (Reprinted from the Louisiana historical quarterly, 18, (Oct., 1935), 947-65.
Locates issues where known.

324. Matthews, Albert. "New England magazines of the eighteenth century." Colonial Society of Massachusetts publications, 13 (1912), 69-74.
List is based on collections owned by 15 named libraries; no individual title is located.

325. Milwaukee Municipal Reference Library. Union list of periodicals in Milwaukee, by the Works Progress Administration and Municipal Reference Library. Milwaukee, 1939. 240 numb. l.
Lists holdings of 32 Milwaukee libraries.

326. Minnesota, University, Library. A list of periodicals received on subscription by the University of Minnesota Library from Axis and Axis-dominated countries during the years 1939-1944. Minneapolis: The Library, 1944. 164p.

327. Missouri Library Association, Committee on Cooperative Acquisitions. Union list of serials in the libraries of Missouri. Columbia, 1935. 228 numb. l.

Lists holdings of 31 libraries for 13,000 titles.

328. New Mexico, University, Library. List of serials in the University of New Mexico Library, together with those in other libraries in Albuquerque, May 1938. [Albuquerque: The Library, 1938] 153 numb. l.

329. New York Public Library. A check list of cumulative indexes to individual periodicals in the New York Public Library, comp. by Daniel C. Haskell. N. Y.: The Library, 1942. 370p.

Records about 25,000 indexes to 5,000 periodicals.

330. New York Public Library. "List of Jewish periodicals in the New York Public Library." New York Public Library bulletin, 6 (1902), 258-64.

331. New York Public Library. "Little magazines, a list," comp. by Carolyn F. Ulrich and Eugenia Patterson. New York Public Library bulletin, 51 (1947), 3-25.

Lists collection of little magazines in New York Public Library.

332. Ohio Library Association, College & University Section. Regional list of serials in the college and university libraries of Ohio. Ann Arbor, Mich.: Edwards Brothers, Inc., 1936. 205p.

"Union subject list of special collections in Ohio college, university and seminary libraries, 1935," p. 199-205. Lists holdings of 26 libraries, excluding 4 largest institutions.

333. Ohio State Library. Newspapers and periodicals in Ohio State Library, other libraries of the state, and lists of Ohio newspapers in the Library of Congress and the Library of the Historical Society of Wisconsin, comp. by C. B. Galbreath. Columbus: F. J. Heer, 1902. 268p.

Represents holdings of 22 Ohio libraries.

334. Oregon State College Library. List of serials in the Oregon Agricultural College Library, November 1, 1925. Corvallis: The College, 1925. 89p.

335. Pan American Union, Columbus Memorial Library. Catalogue of newspapers and magazines in the Columbus Memorial Library of the Pan American Union. Wash., 1931. 112 numb. l. (Bibliographic series, no. 6)

Arranged by countries of publication.

336. Pan American Union, Columbus Memorial Library. A list of literary and cultural magazines received in the Columbus Memorial Library of the Pan American Union. Wash.: The Union, 1940. 27 numb. l. (Bibliographic series, no. 22)

337. Philadelphia Free Library. Subject list of 3200 current periodicals received by the Free Library of Philadelphia. [Philadelphia] 1943. 122p.

338. Robbins, Roy Marvin. A bibliography of American periodicals found in the libraries of Cleveland and Oberlin, Ohio, to the year 1900. Cleveland: Western Reserve University, 1935. 58 numb. l.

Lists holdings of 12 libraries.

339. Rochester Public Library. Union list of serials in the libraries of Rochester, including periodicals, newspapers, annuals, publications of societies and other books, published at intervals. Rochester, N. Y.: The Library, 1917. 147p.

Lists holdings of 26 libraries.

340. Sampley, Arthur M. and Evans, Louise, eds. North Texas regional union list of serials. Rev. ed. Denton: North Texas State Teachers College, 1948. 769p.

Revision of 1943 list.

341. Scott, Franklin William. Newspapers and periodicals of Illinois, 1814-1879. Rev. and enl. ed. Springfield: Illinois State Historical Library, 1910. 610p. (Illinois State Historical Library collections, v. 6)

Locates copies in Illinois libraries and 6 libraries outside state.

342. Severance, Frank H. "Contributions towards a bibliography of the Niagara region; the periodical press of Buffalo, 1811-1915." Buffalo Historical Society publications, 19 (1915), 177-280.

Notes files in Buffalo Public Library and Buffalo Historical Society Library.

343. Skaggs, Alma Stone, ed. Serials currently received in Southern libraries; a union list. Chapel Hill, N. C., 1936. 194 numb. l.

Lists about 7,000 titles in 78 libraries.

344. Smith, Dorothy, ed. Union list of serials in Maine libraries, comp. by Dorothy Smith. Orono, Me.: University Press, 1937. 257p. (University of Maine studies, second series, no. 40)

Gives holdings of 11 libraries.

345. Smithsonian Institution. Catalogue of publications of societies and of periodical works; belonging to the Smithsonian Institution, January 1, 1866; deposited in the Library of Congress. Wash.: Smithsonian Institution, 1866. 591p. (Smithsonian Institution publication 179)

A list, by country, of society and periodical publications owned by Smithsonian Institution, and now on deposit in Library of Congress.

346. Special Libraries Association, Boston Chapter. Union list of periodicals and annuals taken by eleven special libraries in Boston. [Boston, 1921] 16p.

Lists titles only.

347. Special Libraries Association, Cincinnati Chapter. Union list of periodicals currently received by libraries in Cincinnati, 1934, comp. by Louise G. Prichard and Katherine B. Strong. Cincinnati: The Chapter, 1934. 95p.

Represents 45 libraries.

348. Special Libraries Association, Illinois Chapter. "A list of periodicals in the special libraries in the Chicago area." Illinois libraries, 26 (Oct. 1944), 343-433. Reprinted.

Supplements Union list of serials, covering holdings of 65 member libraries.

349. Special Libraries Association, Illinois Chapter. "A list of periodicals in the special libraries in the Chicago area." Illinois libraries, 32 (1950), 172-213, 258-312, 360-410, 474-504.

Lists holdings of 84 libraries.

350. Special Libraries Association, Michigan Chapter and the Detroit Public Library. Union list of serials in the libraries of metropolitan Detroit. Detroit: Wayne Univ. Press, 1946. 670p.

Records serial holdings of 39 libraries in Detroit as of January 1943.

351. Special Libraries Association, New York Chapter. Union list of periodicals in special libraries of the New York Metropolitan District, ed. by Ruth Savord and Pearl M. Keefer. N. Y.: H. W. Wilson, 1931. 238p.

Records holdings of about 7,500 serials in 72 libraries.

352. Special Libraries Association, Pittsburgh Chapter. Union list of periodicals in some of the special libraries of Pittsburgh, comp. by Henrietta Kornhauser and Mary M. Lynch, 2d ed. Pittsburgh: The Chapter, 1934. 139 numb. l.

353. Special Libraries Association, San Francisco Bay Region Chapter. Union list of serials of the San Francisco Bay region. Stanford University: Stanford Univ. Press, 1939. 283p.

Represents 40 libraries not in Union list of serials in the United States and Canada. Holdings as of January 1937. Supplement, 1937-41. San Francisco, 1942. 187p., represents holdings of 39 libraries.

354. Special Libraries Association, Southern California Chapter. Union list of periodicals in libraries of Southern California. 3d ed. Rev. & enl. [Los Angeles] 1941. 582p.

First edition, 1925, listed holdings of 24 libraries; second edition, 1931, gave holdings of 33 libraries; third edition, 1941, lists holdings of 61 libraries for 13,883 entries.

355. Stanford University Library. List of serials in the Leland Stanford Junior University Library. Stanford University, 1916. 169p.

Includes magazines, yearbooks, newspapers, and society and institutional publications.

356. Storkan, Charles Joseph. "Cleveland newspapers, magazines, and periodicals from their beginning to 1900." Cleveland: Western Reserve University, 1950. 259 l. Unpublished M. A. thesis.

A union list of Cleveland newspapers and periodicals wherever found.

357. Streeter, Mary Eleanor, comp. Periodicals and other serial publications currently received by all libraries of Western Reserve University, Case Institute of Technology, Western Reserve Historical Society, Cleveland Museum of Art, Cleveland Museum of Natural History, Cleveland Institute of Art, Garden Center of Greater Cleveland, Cleveland Hearing and Speech Center, and by the Cleveland Medical Library. Cleveland, O., 1950. 78 l.

358. Tashjian, Nouvart. "New York University index to early American periodical literature, 1728-1870." College and research libraries, 7 (1946), 135-37.

Description of Index, consisting of more than 1,000,000 cards, for 339 periodical titles published from 1728 to 1870, in Washington Square Library, New York University.

359. Tinker, Edward Larocque. Bibliography of the French newspapers and periodicals of Louisiana. Worcester: American Antiquarian Society, 1933. 126p.

Locates copies and gives holdings. Reprinted from American Antiquarian Society proceedings, n. s. 42 (1933), 247-370. Supplemented by D. C. McMurtrie's "French press of Louisiana," Louisiana historical quarterly, 18 (1935), 947-65.

360. Trinity College Library. A list of current periodicals in the libraries of Hartford. 2d ed. Hartford, Conn., 1926. 45p. (Trinity College bulletin, n. s. v. 23, no. 2)

First edition, 1916, represented 12 libraries.

361. Union list of serials for the Atlanta district; with supplemental titles and holdings from some other Georgia libraries. Atlanta: [Emory University] 1938. 146 numb. l.

Lists 3,700 titles and holdings of 21 libraries.

362. Union list of serials in libraries of the United States and Canada. 2d ed. edited by Winifred Gregory. N. Y.: H. W. Wilson, 1943. 3,065p.

Lists about 120,000 titles in more than 600 libraries. First edition issued in 1927. Supplement, January 1941 - December 1943, ed. by G. E. Malikoff. N. Y.: H. W. Wilson, 1945. 1,123p.

363. Washington University Library (St. Louis). Washington University serial list. Inventory of serial publications in the collections of the Library of Washington University (including department libraries) and libraries of Washington University Medical School and Missouri Botanical Garden, ed. by Winthrop Holt Chenery. St. Louis: The University, 1915. 86p.

Lists holdings of libraries.

364. Washington, University, Library (Seattle). Union list of periodicals in the University of Washington libraries and the Seattle Public Library. Seattle, Wash., 1914. 47p.

Lists holdings.

365. Watkinson Library of Reference. List of serials in the Watkinson Library. Hartford: Hartford Printing Co., 1929. 84p. (Bulletin 2)

Newspapers

366. American newspapers, 1821-1936. A union list of files available in the United States and Canada, ed. by Winifred Gregory under the auspices of the Bibliographical Society of America. N. Y.: H. W. Wilson, 1937. 791p.

Locations given in about 5,700 depositories, including libraries, county courthouses, newspaper offices, and private collections.

367. Ander, Oscar Fritiof. Swedish-American political newspapers; a guide to the collections in the Royal library, Stockholm, and the Augustana College Library, Rock Island. Stockholm and Uppsala, 1936. 28p.

368. Association of Research Libraries. Newspapers on microfilm, a union check list, ed. by George A. Schwegmann, Jr. Philadelphia: Office of the Executive Secretary; 1948. 176p.

"Includes all entries of newspapers on microfilm... reported to the National Union Catalog," from about 130 libraries.

369. Ayer, Mary Farwell. Check-list of Boston newspapers, 1704-1780. Boston: Colonial Society of Massachusetts, 1907. 399p. (Colonial Society of Massachusetts publications, v. 9.)

Lists holdings of 14 libraries.

370. Barthold, Allen J. "French journalists

in the United States, 1780-1800." Franco-American review, 1 (1937), 215-30.

Lists French-American newspapers, 1780-1800, with holdings in American and European libraries.

371. Bigelow, Frank B. "Early files of newspapers in the New York Society Library." Literary collector, 5 (1902), 38-42.

372. Brayer, Herbert O. "Preliminary guide to indexed newspapers in the United States, 1850-1900." Mississippi Valley historical review, 33 (1946), 237-58.

Arranged by states; gives locations and holdings of each title.

373. Brantley, Rabun Lee. Georgia journalism of the Civil War period. Nashville, Tenn.: George Peabody College for Teachers. 1929. 134p. (George Peabody College contributions to education, no. 58)

"Exhibit of all Georgia newspapers of the period 1860-65," p. 15-54, lists 111 titles and gives exact holdings in American libraries.

374. Brigham, Clarence Saunders, comp. "Bibliography of Winchester newspapers printed prior to 1820." Winchester (Va.) Historical Society annual papers, 1 (1931), 233-39.

Lists 9 titles, with holdings in various libraries.

375. Brigham, Clarence Saunders. History and bibliography of American newspapers, 1690-1820. Worcester: American Antiquarian Society, 1947. 2v. 1,508p.

Locates specific holdings in about 500 libraries and many private collections. A revision of his "Bibliography of American newspapers, 1690-1820," which appeared in American Antiquarian Society proceedings, 23-37 (1913-27).

376. Brown, Warren. Check list of Negro newspapers in the United States (1827-1946). Jefferson City, Mo.: Lincoln Univ., 1946. 37p. (Lincoln Univ. Journalism series, no. 2, July 1946)

Lists 467 newspapers with library holdings.

377. California Library Association, Southern District. A union list of newspapers in offices of publishers and in libraries of Southern California. [Los Angeles] California Library Assoc., 1936. 200 numb. l.

Lists holdings of 89 libraries.

378. Cappon, Lester J. Virginia newspapers, 1821-1935; a bibliography with historical introduction and notes. N. Y.: D. Appleton-Century Co., 1936. 299p. (Guide to Virginia historical materials, pt. 1)

Arranged alphabetically by names of towns, listing holdings in about 80 collections.

379. Chaplin, W. E. "Some of the early newspapers of Wyoming." Wyoming Historical Society miscellanies, (1919), 7-24.

Newspapers mentioned are in archives of Wyoming Historical Society.

380. Chicago, University, Libraries. Newspapers in libraries of Chicago; a joint check list. Chicago, 1936. 257 numb. l.

Lists holdings of 7 libraries. Preliminary edition, 1932. 89p.

381. Cook, Elizabeth Christine. "Newspapers in the American colonies, 1704-1750." In her: Literary influences in colonial newspapers, 1704-1750. N. Y., 1912. p. 268-72.

Locates files of 14 newspapers.

382. Crittenden, Charles C. North Carolina newspapers before 1790. Chapel Hill: Univ. of North Carolina Press, 1928. 83p. (James Sprunt historical studies, v.20, no. 1)

P. 60-62: "A list of North Carolina newspapers published before 1790 which are... in the Library of the University of North Carolina or in the collections of the North Carolina Historical Commission."

383. Duke University Library. A check list of the United States newspapers (and weeklies before 1900) in the general library, comp. by Mary Wescott and Allene Ramage. Durham: Duke Univ., 1932-37. 6 parts. (Bibliographical contributions of the Duke Univ. Libraries)

A detailed record of the Library's holdings.

384. "Early New York newspapers," In: Stokes, I. N. P., Iconography of Manhattan Island. N. Y., 1915-1928. v. 2, p. 413-52.

A check list of papers published from 1725 to 1811, giving holdings of Long Island Historical Society, New York Public Library, New York Historical Society, New York Society Library, and 9 other libraries.

385. Emig, Wilmer J. "A check-list of extant Florida newspapers, 1845-1876." Florida historical quarterly, 11 (1932), 77-87.

Locates copies in American collections and British Museum.

386. Fassett, Frederick Gardiner. A history of newspapers in the district of Maine, 1785-1820. Orono: Maine Univ. Press, 1932. 242p. (Univ. of Maine studies, 2d ser., no. 25)

Locates files in 6 libraries.

387. Ford, Worthington C. "Franklin's New England courant." Massachusetts Historical Society proceedings, 57 (1924), 336-53.

History and description of file of New England courant now in Massachusetts Historical Society.

388. Fox, Louis Hewitt. "New York City newspapers, 1820-1850, a bibliography." Bibliographical Society of America papers, 21 (1927), pts. 1-2.

Lists holdings of New York Public Library, New York Historical Society, American Antiquarian Society, Library of Congress, and occasional files elsewhere.

389. Gaeddert, G. Raymond. "First newspapers in Kansas counties, 1854-1886." Kansas historical quarterly, 10 (1941), 3-33, 124-49, 299-323, 380-411.

Locates files in Kansas State Historical Society.

390. Henry E. Huntington Library. Rare newspapers and their precursors, 1515-1918; an exhibition. 3d ed. San Marino, 1935. 14p.

391. Historical Records Survey, Wisconsin. A guide to Wisconsin newspapers: Iowa County, 1837-1940. Madison: Wisconsin Historical Records Survey, 1942. 142 numb. l.

Locates copies in 10 libraries and newspaper offices.

392. Historical Records Survey, Mississippi. Mississippi newspapers, 1805-1940; a preliminary union list of Mississippi newspaper files available in county archives, offices of publishers, libraries, and private collections in Mississippi. Jackson: Miss. Hist. Records Survey, 1942. 323p.

Holdings of 17 college and public libraries listed, plus newspaper and private collections.

393. Historical Records Survey, Texas. Texas newspapers, 1813-1939; a union list of newspaper files available in offices of publishers, libraries, and a number of private collections. Houston: San Jacinto Museum of History Assoc., 1941. 293p.

394. Historical Records Survey, Arkansas. Union list of Arkansas newspapers, 1819-1942; a partial inventory of Arkansas newspaper files available in offices of publishers, libraries, and private collections in Arkansas. Little Rock, 1942. 240p.

Locates holdings in 18 college and public libraries.

395. Historical Records Survey, Philadelphia. American Imprints Inventory. Check list of Philadelphia newspapers available in Philadelphia. 2d ed. Philadelphia: Historical Records Survey, 1937. 160 numb. l. First edition, 1936. 115 numb. l.

396. Historical Records Survey, American Imprints Inventory. A check list of the Kellogg collection of "patent inside" newspapers of 1876, preserved in Chicago Historical Society Library. Chicago: W. P. A. Hist. Rec. Survey, 1939. 99 numb. l. (American Imprints Inventory, no. 11)

397. Historical Records Survey, Louisiana. American Imprints Inventory. Louisiana newspapers, 1794-1940; a union list of Louisiana newspaper files available in offices of publishers, libraries, and private collections in Louisiana. Baton Rouge: Louisiana State University, 1941. 295p.

Lists holdings of 31 libraries and institutions, in addition to publishers.

398. Historical Society of Western Pennsylvania. Inventory of files of American newspapers in Pittsburgh and Allegheny County, Pennsylvania. Pittsburgh, 1933. 34p.

Lists holdings of 12 libraries and of some newspaper publishers.

399. "Index to newspapers on file in Michigan." Michigan library bulletin, 18 (Feb. 1927), 50-67.

Michigan newspaper files in libraries, newspaper offices, etc.

400. Indiana State Library. "A list of Indiana newspapers available in the Indiana State

Library, the Indianapolis Public Library, the library of Indiana University, and the Library of Congress, Washington, D. C." Indiana State Library bulletin, 11 (1916), no. 4. 31p.

401. James, Edmund Janes and Loveless, Milo J. A bibliography of newspapers published in Illinois prior to 1860. Springfield, Ill.: Hillips Bros., 1899. 94p. (Illinois State Historical Library publications, no. 1)

Locates some files, including a list of Missouri and Illinois newspapers, 1808-1897, in the St. Louis Mercantile Library.

402. Kansas State Historical Society, History of Kansas newspapers; a history of the newspapers and magazines published in Kansas from the organization of Kansas Territory, 1854, to January 1, 1916. Topeka: Kansas State Printing Plant, 1916. 373p.

Holdings of Kansas State Historical Society noted.

403. Kansas State Historical Society. A list of Kansas newspapers and periodicals received by the Kansas State Historical Society. Topeka: State Printer, 1948. 55p.

Annual publication. Lists 680 titles arranged by county and city of publication. Holdings not indicated.

404. Keidel, George C. "Early Maryland newspapers, a list of titles." Maryland historical magazine, 28 (1933), 119-37, 244-57, 328-44; 29 (1934), 25-34, 132-44, 223-36, 310-22; 30 (1935), 149-56.

Covers period from 1727 to 1860, and indicates titles held by Maryland Historical Society.

405. Kentucky Library Association. Check list of Kentucky newspapers contained in Kentucky libraries, comp. by Ludie Kinkead and T. D. Clark. Lexington, 1935. 44p., 10 numb. l.

Lists holdings of 22 libraries.

406. Knauss, James Owen. " A chronological list of Florida newspapers published before July, 1845, with a check list of all copies located." In his: Territorial Florida journalism, Deland, 1926, p. 86-128.

Locates copies in American Antiquarian Society, Library of Congress, New York Historical Society, and Yonge Library (University of Florida).

407. Knauss, James Owen. "Table of German American newspapers of the eighteenth century." In his: Social conditions among the Pennsylvania Germans in the eighteenth century. Lancaster, Pa., 1922, p. 169-202. (First printed in Proceedings of the Pennsylvania-German Society, v. 29)

Lists all copies located and gives holdings of each library.

408. Louisiana State University Library. Newspaper files in Louisiana State University Library. Baton Rouge, La., 1947. 119p.

409. Mabbott, Thomas Ollive and Jordan, Philip D. Catalogue of Illinois newspapers in the New York Historical Society. [Springfield, Ill., 1931]. 58p. (Reprint from Illinois State Historical Society journal, 24 (1931), no. 2)

410. McMurtrie, Douglas C. "A bibliography of Nevada newspapers, 1858 to 1875, inclusive." Gutenberg-Jahrbuch, 10 (1935), 292-312. Reprinted.

Locates copies of 87 titles with holdings in several American libraries.

411. McMurtrie, Douglas C. Washington newspapers, 1852-1890 inclusive; a supplement to Professor Meany's list. Seattle: Washington Univ. Press, 1935. 48p. (Reprinted and revised from Washington historical quarterly, January - April 1935.)

Gives locations and holdings in 9 libraries outside state of Washington.

412. Meany, Edmund Stephen. "Newspapers of Washington Territory." Washington historical quarterly, 13 (1922), 181-95, 251-68; 14 (1923), 21-29, 100-07, 186-200, 269-90; 26 (1935), 34-64, 129-43.

Locates some files, but does not indicate exact holdings. Pages in v. 26 are supplemental material, by Douglas C. McMurtrie.

413. Miller, Daniel. "Early German American newspapers." Pennsylvania-German Society proceedings and addresses, 19 (1908), pt. 22, p. 1-107.

Locates holdings throughout text.

414. Miller, Daniel. "The German newspapers of Berks County." Berks County Historical Society transactions, 3 (1912), 4-23.

Locates copies or single issues in libraries or private collections.

415. Millington, Yale O. "A list of newspapers published in the District of Columbia, 1820-1850." Bibliographical Society of America papers, 19 (1925), 43-65.
A specimen of each newspaper mentioned is in Library of Congress.

416. Minnesota, University, Division of Library Instruction. American newspapers in the University of Minnesota Library, 1719-1934. [Minneapolis] 1935. 12p. (Bibliographical projects, no. 2)

417. Minnesota, University, Library. American newspapers in the University of Minnesota Library [1719-1938] [Minneapolis, 1939] 26p.

418. Missouri State Historical Society. "List of old newspapers in the library of the Missouri State Historical Society." Missouri historical review, 5 (1910), 34-43.

419. Monmouth County Historical Association. "A check list of Monmouth County [N. J.] newspapers in the Monmouth County Historical Association." Monmouth County Historical Association bulletin, 1 (1935), 12-34.
A list of 19th and 20th century newspapers, arranged by localities and showing exact holdings.

420. Mott, David C. "Early Iowa newspapers; a contribution toward a bibliography of the newspapers established in Iowa before the Civil War." Annals of Iowa, 3d ser., 16 (1928), 161-233.
Gives holdings only when in Historical, Memorial and Art Department of Iowa.

421. Nelson, William. Notes toward a history of the American newspaper. N. Y.: C. F. Heartman, 1918. 644p. v. 1. (Heartman's historical series no. 31)
Published 1894-97 under title: Some account of American newspapers, particularly of the 18th century, and libraries in which they may be found. Gives holdings of 30 libraries. Covers states alphabetically from Alabama through New Hampshire.

422. New Mexico, University, Library. A check list of New Mexico newspapers. Albuquerque: Univ. of New Mexico Press, 1935. 31p. (Univ. of New Mex. bulletin, Sociological series, v. 2, no. 2).
Locates files in New Mexican libraries.

423. New York Public Library. "American newspaper reprints," comp. by Joseph Gavit. New York Public Library bulletin, 35 (1931), 212-23. Reprinted. 16p.
Alphabetically arranged by cities. Locates copies in various libraries.

424. New York Public Library. "A check list of newspapers and official gazettes in the New York Public Library," comp. by Daniel Carl Haskell. New York Public Library bulletin, 18 (1914), 683-722, 793-826, 905-38, 1079-1110, 1261-94, 1467-80; Supplement. 19 (1915), 553-69. Reprinted with alphabetical and chronological indexes, 1915. 579p.

425. New York times index. N. Y.: N. Y. Times, 1913 to date.
List of libraries holding files of New York times in each volume of Index.

426. North Carolina State Library. "Bibliography of bound newspapers in the North Carolina State Library." In: North Carolina State Library biennial report, 1924-26, p. 8-131.
List of holdings of about 5,000 volumes, principally North Carolina papers.

427. Ohio State Archaeological and Historical Society. Union list of Ohio newspapers available in Ohio, comp. by Arthur D. Mink. Columbus: The Society, 1946. 124p.
Lists holdings of 162 Ohio libraries.

428. Pennsylvania Historical Survey. A checklist of Pennsylvania newspapers. V. 1, Philadelphia County. Harrisburg: Pennsylvania Historical Commission, 1944. 323p.
Lists 700 newspapers published since 1719, with locations in Pennsylvania. Volume 2 (Western Pennsylvania) in preparation.

429. Purcell, George W. "Survey of early newspapers in the middle western states." Indiana magazine of history, 20 (1924), 347-63.
Locates an occasional issue.

430. Qualls, LeRoy L. Newspapers in the University of Illinois Library. Illinois libraries, 24 (1942), 71-77.
Describes newspaper collection of over 20,000 volumes in University of Illinois Library.

431. Ray, Grace Ernestine. Early Oklahoma

newspapers; history and description of publications from earliest beginnings to 1889. Norman: Univ. of Oklahoma [1928] 119p. (Univ. of Oklahoma bulletin, n. s. no. 407, Studies, no. 28)

Locates some of files in Oklahoma Historical Society.

432. Rex, Wallace Hayden. Colorado newspapers bibliography, 1859-1933. Denver: Bibliographical Center for Research, 1939. 69p., 394, 72, 184 numb. l.

Locates files, chiefly in Colorado libraries.

433. Stevens, Harry R. "United States newspapers in the Duke University Library." Library notes, a bulletin issued for the Friends of Duke University Library, no. 22 (July 1949), 1-4.

A general survey, analyzing collection by region, and listing major titles.

434. Stump, Vernon Caradine. "Early newspapers of Cincinnati." Ohio archaeological and historical quarterly, 34 (1925), 169-83.

Locates one title in Historical and Philosophical Society of Ohio, and two other titles in Mercantile Library [of Cincinnati?]

435. Thwaites, Reuben Gold. "The Ohio Valley press before the war of 1812-15." American Antiquarian Society proceedings, n. s. 19 (1909), 309-68. Reprinted 1909. 62p.

Appendix, p. 354-68, is a union list of newspapers of the region: Western Pennsylvania, Kentucky, Ohio, Indiana, and Missouri, from the beginning of the press in each state to 1812.

436. U. S. Library of Congress, Periodical Division. Check list of American eighteenth century newspapers in the Library of Congress. New ed. Wash.: Govt. Print. Off., 1936. 401p. 1st ed. published 1912.

437. U. S. Library of Congress, Periodical Division. Check list of American newspapers in the Library of Congress, comp. by A. B. Slauson. Wash.: Govt. Print. Off., 1901. 292p.

438. U. S. Library of Congress, Serials Division. Newspapers currently received, September 1949. Wash., 1949. 40 numb. l. Frequently revised.

439. Virginia Historical Society. "Virginia newspapers in public libraries; annotated list of Virginia newspapers in the Library of Congress, [Virginia Historical Society, and Virginia State Library]." Virginia magazine of history and biography, 8 (1901), 337-46; 9 (1902), 1-11, 130-38, 289-97, 411-13; 10 (1903), 225-29, 421-23.

440. Virginia State Library. "List of newspapers in the Virginia State Library, Confederate Museum, and Valentine Museum." Virginia State Library bulletin, 5 (1912), [285]-425.

441. Virginia, University, Library. "A check list of newspapers to 1821 in the Alderman Memorial Library, University of Virginia," comp. by Glenn Curtis Smith. University of Virginia Library annual report on historical collections, no. 9 (1938-39), 26-30.

Arranged by states, and exact holdings indicated.

442. Wall, Alexander J. "Early newspapers, with a list of the New-York Historical Society's collections of papers published in California, Oregon, Washington, Montana, and Utah." New-York Historical Society bulletin, 15 (1931), 39-66.

Lists principally California papers, 1847-73.

443. Western Pennsylvania Historical Survey. Inventory of files of American newspapers in Pittsburgh and Allegheny County, Pennsylvania. Pittsburgh: The Survey, 1933. 34p. (Bibliographical contributions, no. 2)

Locates copies in 12 libraries and in publishers' offices.

444. Western Reserve Historical Society. Ohio newspapers in Western Reserve Historical Library. Cleveland, 1944. 101p.

445. Wickersham, James. Alaskan newspapers and periodicals; preliminary check list prepared for the use of Hon. James Wickersham, delegate from Alaska, by Hugh Morrison. Wash., 1915. 28 (i.e. 27) numb. l.

Based on Library of Congress holdings.

446. Wilmington Institute Free Library. Union list of Delaware newspapers in H. Historical Society Library, I. Wilmington Institute Free Library, E. Every Evening

office, U. University of Delaware Library. Wilmington, Del.: The Library, 1933. 22 numb. 1.

447. Winship, George P. "Newport newspapers in the eighteenth century." Newport Historical Society bulletin, 14 (Oct. 1914), 1-19.
   Locates copies.

448. Wisconsin State Historical Society Library. Annotated catalogue of newspaper files in the library of the... Society. 2d ed., comp. by Ada Tyng Griswold. Madison: The Society, 1911. 591p.

449. Wisconsin State Historical Society. Supplementary catalogue of newspaper files... listing the papers acquired... 1911-1917. Madison: [The Society] 1918. 91p. (Bulletin of information, no. 93).

450. Yale University Library. A list of newspapers in the Yale University Library. New Haven: Yale Univ. Press, 1916. 216p.

Foreign periodicals and newspapers

451. American Antiquarian Society Library. "List of newspapers of the West Indies and Bermuda in the library of the American Antiquarian Society," by Waldo Lincoln. American Antiquarian Society proceedings, n. s. 36 (1926), 130-55. Reprinted.

452. American Library Association, Committee on Library Cooperation with Latin America. List of Latin American serials; a survey of exchanges available in U. S. libraries, prep. by Abel Plenn. Chicago: American Library Association, 1941. 70p.
   Locates files in 17 libraries in the United States.

453. Benedictis, Jack de, comp. A comparative and selected list of Soviet Russian newspapers and periodicals available at the library of the University of California and at the Hoover Library on War, Revolution, and Peace. Stanford University, University of California, 1948. 70p.

454. Bond, Richmond P. "Some early English newspapers and periodicals at Yale." Yale University Library gazette, 13 (1939), 69-75.

455. Butler, Ruth Lapham. "Files of periodicals published in South American countries which now form a part of the Edward E. Ayer collection of the Newberry Library of Chicago." Hispanic American historical review, 19 (Feb. 1939), 106-08.
   Listed alphabetically by titles under each country.

456. Cabon, Adolphe. "Un siècle et demi de journalisme en Haiti." American Antiquarian Society proceedings, 49 (1940), 121-205.
   Footnotes locate copies in American libraries.

457. Craig, Mary Elizabeth. The Scottish periodical press, 1750-1789. Edinburgh: Oliver and Boyd, 1931. 113p.
   A bibliographical list, p. 95-104, locates copies in 13 British and 19 American libraries.

458. Crane, Ronald Salmon and Kaye, F. B. "A census of British newspapers and periodicals, 1620-1800." Studies in philology, 24 (1927), 1-205.
   Lists 970 titles in 62 American libraries, showing holdings. Also lists 1,445 items not to be found in America.

459. Harvard University Library. "French newspapers, etc." Harvard Library notes, 2 (1925), 11-13.
   In Harvard Library.

460. Henry E. Huntington Library. "Check list of English newspapers and periodicals before 1801 in the Huntington Library"; comp. by Anthony J. Gabler. Huntington Library bulletin, no. 2 (1931), 1-66. Reprinted, Cambridge, Mass., 1931. 66p.
   Newspapers and periodicals published in England, Scotland and Ireland in the 17th and 18th centuries.

461. Limouze, A. S. "Early English periodicals in the [Duke] University Library." Library notes, a bulletin issued for the Friends of Duke University Library, no. 21 (Jan. 1949), 6-8.
   Survey of holdings, listing important titles.

462. Morize, André, ed. Survey of bulletins, memoirs, etc., published by learned societies in France, existing in American libraries.

Princeton: Princeton Univ. Library [192-?], unpaged.

Lists 68 libraries, surveying holdings of French periodicals of literary interest.

463. New York Public Library. "Latin-American periodicals current in the Reference Department." New York Public Library bulletin, 24 (1920), 503-07. Reprinted. 7p.

Arranged by countries.

464. New York Public Library. "Russian, other Slavonic and Baltic periodicals in the New York Public Library," comp. by Herman Rosenthal. New York Public Library bulletin, 20 (1916), 339-72. Reprinted. 36p. The Library also published "List of Russian and other Slavonic periodicals in the New York Public Library," in its Bulletin, 6 (1902), 231-34.

465. Pan American Union, Columbus Memorial Library. Latin American newspapers (other than official) received in the library of the Pan American Union. [Wash., 1942] 11 numb. l.

466. Pan American Union, Columbus Memorial Library. Latin American university journals and serial publications; a tentative directory, by Katherine Lenore Morgan. Wash.: Pan American Union, Division of Intellectual Cooperation, 1944. 74 numb. l.

Based on holdings of Pan American Union library.

467. U. S. Library of Congress. Latin American periodicals currently received in the Library of Congress and in the Library of the Department of Agriculture, ed. by Charmion Shelby. Wash.: The Library, 1944. 249p.

Alphabetical list of 1,578 titles. Does not show holdings. Index by countries and publishing agencies.

468. U. S. Library of Congress. "A list of current German serial publications including periodicals, monographs in series and books in parts received by the Library of Congress in 1935 or later years." [Wash., 1940] 120, 17 numb. l. Typed.

"A list of incomplete German books, published in parts": 17 numb. l. at end.

469. U. S. Library of Congress, European Affairs Division. The European press today. Wash.; 1949. 152p.

-----. The press in Turkey. Supplement to the report, The European press today. Wash., 1949. 6 l.

An annotated bibliography of periodical publications in Europe, based on Library of Congress holdings.

470. U. S. Library of Congress, Hispanic Foundation. Latin American periodicals current in the Library of Congress, prep. by Murray M. Wise. Wash.: Hispanic Foundation, Library of Congress, 1941. 137 l.

471. [U. S. Library of Congress, National Union Catalog] "Check list of certain periodicals." [Wash., 1942.] 4 v. Typed. Loose-leaf.

"In 1942 the Library of Congress enlisted the cooperation of some 300 libraries in reporting their holdings of some 3000 scientific and technical series published in Continental Europe and the warring countries of Asia, 1939 to date."

472. U. S. Library of Congress, Periodical Division. A check list of foreign newspapers in the Library of Congress. 2d ed. Wash.: Govt. Print. Off., 1929. 209p.

473. U. S. Library of Congress, Periodicals Division. "Learned society and institution serials received from Europe (except Great Britain), Africa, Asia and Australia, from 1938 to date." Wash., Dec. 7, 1942. 153p. Typed.

474. U. S. Library of Congress, Periodicals Division. List of German periodicals received in the Library of Congress in 1941. Wash., Nov. 1941. 34p.

475. U. S. Library of Congress, Periodicals Division. "Newspapers and periodicals from enemy-occupied countries of Europe." Wash., 1943. 48p. Typed.

476. U. S. Library of Congress, Periodicals Division. "Newspapers and periodicals from the Axis countries of Europe." Wash., 1943. 19p. Typed.

477. U. S. Library of Congress, Periodicals Division. "Periodicals received from Europe

478 GENERAL

(except Great Britain), Africa, Asia and Australia, from 1938 to date." Wash., Oct. 3, 1942. 102p. Typed.

478. Virginia State Library. "French newspapers of 1848-50 in the Virginia State Library," comp. by Earl G. Swem. Virginia State Library bulletin, 9 (1916), 285-347.

479. Winship, George Parker. "Early South American newspapers." American Antiquarian Society proceedings, n. s. 19 (1908), 239-49.
    Locates some titles in Lenox Library (New York Public Library), or John Carter Brown Library.

Journalism

480. Mott, Frank Luther, comp. A list of unpublished theses in the field of journalism on file in the libraries of American universities. Minneapolis: Amer. Assoc. of Schools & Depts. of Journalism & Amer. Assoc. of Teachers of Journalism, 1936. p. 330-355.
    Issued as a second section of v. 13, no. 3, of Journalism quarterly. A subject list, giving name of the institution where thesis is on file.

481. New York Public Library. "Journalism; a list of references in English," comp. by Carl Leslie Cannon. New York Public Library bulletin, 27 (1923), 147-57, 219-36, 263-308, 440-45, 466-539, 565-627, 645-710. Reprinted with additions, 1924. 360p.
    Classified arrangement.

482. Salmon, Lucy M. The Justice collection of material relating to the periodical press in Vassar College Library. [Poughkeepsie, N. Y.] 1925. 20p.
    Description of the collection.

MANUSCRIPTS

General

483. Boston Public Library. A brief description of the Chamberlain collection of autographs. Boston: The Trustees, 1897. 65p.

484. Boston Public Library. Medieval manuscripts in the Boston Public Library, by Zoltan Haraszti. Boston, 1928. 29p. (Reprinted from More Books, March 1928.)

485. Butler, Ruth Lapham. A check list of manuscripts in the Edward E. Ayer collection. Chicago: Newberry Library, 1937. 295p.
    Arranged geographically in four divisions: North America, Spanish America, Phillipine Islands, and Hawaiian Islands. A fifth division is on Indian, Philippine and Hawaiian languages.

486. Chicago, University, Library. A descriptive catalogue of manuscripts in the libraries of the University of Chicago, prep. by Edgar J. Goodspeed. Chicago: Univ. of Chicago Press [1912] 128p.

487. Garrett, Robert. "Recollections of a collector." Princeton University Library chronicle, 10 (1949), 103-16.
    Account of Garrett collection of manuscripts in Princeton University Library.

488. Harvard University Library. "Autographs." Harvard Library notes, 2 (1929), 224-30.
    Survey of collections in Harvard College Library.

489. Harvard University Library. "Manuscript collections." Harvard Library notes, 2 (1929), 220-24.
    General survey of manuscript collections in Harvard College Library.

490. Haselden, R. B. "Manuscripts in the Huntington Library." Archives and libraries, (1939), 71-79.
    Describes only outstanding manuscript collections in fields of English and American history in Henry E. Huntington Library.

491. Henry E. Huntington Library. "Some explorations in San Marino," by Sir William Beveridge. Huntington Library bulletin, 2 (1931), 67-85.
    Survey of Battle Abbey, Stowe, Huntingdon, and Ellesmere manuscript collections in Huntington Library.

492. Hispanic Society of America. Fourteen Spanish manuscript documents in the collection of the Hispanic Society of America. N. Y., 1926. 9p. (Hispanic notes and monographs)

493. Hispanic Society of America Library. Manuscripts in the library, ed. by A. D.

Savage. N. Y., 1927-31. 13 nos. B1-B8, B10-13, B130.

Fourteenth and 15th century manuscripts; B130 belongs to the 17th century. Transliterations with introductions, notes, and references.

494. Historical Records Survey - Calif. List of the letters and documents of rulers and statesmen in the William Andrews Clark Memorial Library (University of California at Los Angeles). Los Angeles: Southern California Historical Records Survey, 1941. 161 numb. 1.

495. Illinois, University, Library. "Descriptions of manuscripts at the University of Illinois." Urbana, 1934. 3 pt. in 1 v. Typed.

Pt. 1, literary manuscripts; pt. 2, mathematical manuscripts; pt. 3, other manuscripts.

496. Ives, S. A. "Corrigenda and addenda to the descriptions of the Plimpton manuscripts as recorded in the DeRicci census." Speculum, 17 (1942), 33-49.

Corrects data relating to manuscripts now in the Plimpton Collection of Columbia University Library. Medieval and Renaissance mss.

497. Lincoln, Charles Henry. "The manuscript collections of the American Antiquarian Society." Bibliographical Society of America papers, 4 (1909), 59-72.

Description of collections.

498. Miner, Dorothy E. "Collection of manuscripts and rare books in the Walters Art Gallery." Bibliographical Society of America papers, 30 (1936), 104-19.

Describes collections in library of Walters Art Gallery in Baltimore. Over 750 illuminated manuscripts from the 9th to the 18th century.

499. Modern Language Association of America. Reproductions of manuscripts and rare printed books. N. Y.: Modern Language Assoc. of Amer. [1942]. 36p.

Record of materials now on deposit in Library of Congress.

500. Modern Language Association of America. "Rotographs of manuscripts and rare printed books." PMLA, Publications of the Modern Language Association of America, 45 (June 1930), [6p.] (unnumb. prelim. paging).

Deposited in Library of Congress.

501. New York Public Library. "Manuscript collections in the New York Public Library." New York Public Library bulletin, 5 (1901), 306-36; Supplement, 19 (1915), 149-65. Original list reprinted. 31p. Supplement is part of an article, "The Manuscript Division of the New York Public Library," 135-65; the whole was reprinted, 33p.

Supplemented by annual lists of accessions in February issues of Bulletin, since 1935.

502. New York Public Library. "Medieval manuscripts in the New York Public Library," by Seymour de Ricci. New York Public Library bulletin, 34 (1930), 297-322. Reprinted. 28p.

Lists and describes 137 items.

503. Pierpont Morgan Library. The letter; an exhibition illustrating the practice of letterwriting through 3500 years. [N. Y.: The Library, 1950] [6]p.

Brief notes on clay tablets, papyri, illuminated manuscripts, autograph letters and printed books, shown February-April 1950.

504. Pierpont Morgan Library. The written word; inscriptions, texts and illuminated manuscripts from 3200 B. C. to the invention of printing in the XVth century. Handlist of an exhibition held December 14, 1944 to April 14, 1945. [N. Y.: The Library, 1945] 64p.

505. "Recent acquisitions." Mississippi Valley historical review, 35 (Dec. 1948), 546-55; 36 (Dec. 1949), 569-75.

Beginning 1948, the December issue of each year, annual "list of the more important manuscript acquisitions of university, state and city libraries," omitting Library of Congress and National Archives.

506. Ricci, Seymour de and Wilson, Jerome. Census of medieval and renaissance manuscripts in the United States and Canada. N. Y.: H. W. Wilson, 1935-40. 3v.

Records locations in 486 collections in the United States and 12 in Canada.

507. Richardson, Ernest Cushing, ed. A union world catalog of manuscript books, preliminary studies in method. I. The world's collections of manuscript books; a preliminary survey. N. Y.: H. W. Wilson, 1933. 40p.

Pages 1-4 list manuscript collections in

the United States, alphabetically by states and cities.

508. Richardson, Ernest Cushing, ed. A union world catalog of manuscript books; preliminary studies in method. III. A list of printed catalogs of manuscript books. N. Y.: H. W. Wilson, 1935. 386p.

Locates copies in Library of Congress, Harvard, New York Public Library, etc.

509. Rochester, University, Library. Catalogue of the autograph collection of the University of Rochester, comp. by Robert F. Metzdorf. Rochester, N. Y.: Univ. of Rochester Library, 1940. 176p.

Lists 1,031 items, including wide variety of names well known in literature and history.

510. U. S. Library of Congress. "Annual reports on acquisitions: manuscripts." Library of Congress quarterly journal of acquisitions, 3 (May 1946), 36-49; 4 (May 1947), 80-94; 6 (May 1949), 80-94.

511. U. S. Library of Congress. "Autographs in the John Davis Batchelder deposit," comp. by Jean Campbell. Wash., 1933. 86p. Typed.

512. U. S. Library of Congress, Division of Manuscripts. Accessions of manuscripts, broadsides and British transcripts, July 1920-21 - 1925. Wash.: Govt. Print. Off., 1922-26. 5v.

513. U. S. Library of Congress, Division of Manuscripts. Handbook of manuscripts in the Library of Congress. Wash.: Govt. Print. Off., 1918. 750p.

514. U. S. Library of Congress, Division of Manuscripts. "List of manuscript collections in the Library of Congress to July, 1931, by Curtis Wiswell Garrison." Wash.: Govt. Print. Off., 1932. p. 123-249. ("Reprinted from the Annual report of the American Historical Association for 1930.")

515. U. S. Library of Congress, Division of Manuscripts. List of manuscript collections received in the Library of Congress, July 1931 to July 1938; comp. by C. Percy Powell. Wash.: Govt. Print. Off., 1939. 33p. (Reprinted from the Annual report of the American Historical Association for 1937.")

516. U. S. Library of Congress, Division of Manuscripts. The manuscript collections in the Library of Congress. Wash.: Govt. Print. Off., 1916. 9p.

517. U. S. Library of Congress, Division of Manuscripts. Manuscripts in public and private collections in the United States. Wash.: Govt. Print. Off., 1924. 98p.

Enlarged edition of Check list of collections of personal papers in historical societies, university and public libraries, and other learned institutions in the United States, 1918.

Illuminated manuscripts

518. Brooklyn Museum. "Illuminated manuscripts," by Susan A. Hutchinson. Brooklyn Museum quarterly, 13 (1926), 72-80; 14 (1927), 126-35.

Description of manuscripts in the Museum's collection.

519. Brooklyn Museum. "The Mary Benson bequest of illuminated manuscripts and autograph letters," by Susan A. Hutchinson. Brooklyn Museum quarterly, 6 (1919), 222-27.

A brief description of 8 volumes of Horae Beatae Mariae Virginis (Books of Hours), one missal, and some autographs in the Brooklyn Museum.

520. New York Public Library. "An exhibition of illuminated manuscripts in the Spencer Collection," by Philip Hofer. New York Public Library bulletin, 37 (1933), 939-46.

521. New York Public Library. "The Landevennec Gospels; a Breton illuminated manuscript of the ninth century," by Charles Rufus Morey. New York Public Library bulletin, 33 (1929), 643-53. Reprinted. 64p.

522. New York Public Library. "The Tickhill Psalter; an English illuminated manuscript of the early fourteenth century," by Donald Drew Egbert. New York Public Library bulletin, 36 (1932), 663-78. Reprinted. 20p.

The Library also published in 1940 The Tickhill Psalter and related manuscripts, 112 facsimiles in 56 leaves.

523. Philadelphia Free Library. A descriptive catalogue of the John Frederick Lewis collection of European manuscripts in the

Free Library of Philadelphia, comp. by Edwin Wolf II. Philadelphia, 1937. 219p.

524. Pierpont Morgan Library. The animal kingdom; illustrated catalogue of an exhibition of manuscript illuminations, book illustrations, drawings, cylinder seals, and bindings. New York, November 19, 1940 - February 28, 1941. [N. Y.: The Library, 1940] 70p., 12 plates.

525. Pierpont Morgan Library. Catalogue of manuscripts... from the libraries of William Morris, Richard Bennett, Bertram, Fourth Earl of Ashburnham, and other sources, now forming part of the Library of J. Pierpont Morgan. London: Chiswick Press, 1906. 210p.

Full descriptions of 120 items and color reproductions.

526. Pierpont Morgan Library. The Christmas festival illustrated through illuminated manuscripts and drawings in the Pierpont Morgan Library. New York, December 16, 1935 to January 31, 1936. [N. Y.: The Library, 1935] [42]p., facsims.

Catalog of 125 illuminated manuscripts and 22 drawings, from the 9th to the 16th century.

527. Pierpont Morgan Library. Exhibition of illuminated manuscripts held at the New York Public Library from November 1933 to April 1934. N. Y.: Pierpont Morgan Library, 1934. 85p. 100 plates.

Lists and describes 134 manuscripts, 20 illuminated leaves, and leather and metal bookbindings from the 9th to the 16th century. From collection in Pierpont Morgan Library.

528. Pierpont Morgan Library. The first Christmas. Sixteen reproductions from illuminated manuscripts in an exhibition held at the Pierpont Morgan Library, November 1946 to February 1947. [N. Y.: The Library, 1946] [36]p.

529. Pierpont Morgan Library. Illuminated manuscripts from the Pierpont Morgan library; catalogue of an exhibition held at the New York Public Library. N. Y.: New York Public Library, 1934. 32p.

530. Pierpont Morgan Library. Sixteen illustrations from an exhibition of religious symbolism in illuminated manuscripts, at the Pierpont Morgan Library. New York, March 20 - May 20, 1944. [N. Y.: The Library, 1944] [16]p.

Oriental manuscripts

531. Faris, Nabih Amin. A demonstration experiment with Oriental manuscripts (Princeton University Arabic manuscripts. Garrett Manuscripts 1-383). N. Y.: H. W. Wilson, 1934. 73p. (A union world catalog of manuscript books, preliminary studies in method, no. 4)

532. Faris, Nabih Amin. "Special Collections at Princeton; III. Garrett collection of Arabic manuscripts." Princeton University Library chronicle, 1 (1940), 19-25.

533. Haverford College Library. "A catalogue of manuscripts (chiefly Oriental) in the library of Haverford College," by Robert W. Rogers. Haverford College studies, 4 (1890), [28]-50.

534. Martin, F. R. The Nizami manuscript from the library of the Shah of Persia, now in the Metropolitan Museum at New York. Vienna, 1927. 18p.

535. Martinovitch, Nicholas N. "Arabic, Persian and Turkish manuscripts in the Columbia University Library." American Oriental Society journal, 49 (1929), 219-33. Reprinted.

Check list of 47 manuscripts.

536. Matthews, Charles D. "Manuscripts and a Mamlūk inscription in the Lansing collection in the Denver Public Library." American Oriental Society journal, 60 (Sept. 1940), 370-82.

Descriptions of several early Arabic items. Collection described further in author's article "Reliques of the Rev. Dr. John G. Lansing," Moslem World, 30 (July 1940), 269-79.

537. Metropolitan Museum of Art. A catalogue of the collection of Persian manuscripts, including also some Turkish and Arabic, presented to the Metropolitan Museum of Art, New York, by Alexander Smith Cochran; prep. and ed., by A. V. Williams Jackson and Abraham Yohannan. N. Y.: Columbia Univ. Press, 1914. 187p. (Columbia Univ. Indo-Iranian series, v. 1)

538. Nemoy, Leon. "Notes on some Arabic manuscripts on curious subjects in the Yale University Library." In: Papers in honor of Andrew Keogh. [New Haven, 1938] p. 45-66.

539. New York Public Library. "An exhibition of Oriental and European manuscripts." New York Public Library bulletin, 18 (1914), 3-10.

Illustrates history of writing and bookmaking in various nations from ancient times to 16th century.

540. Newberry Library. The Arabic and Turkish manuscripts in the Newberry Library; described by Duncan Black Macdonald. Chicago: The Library [1912] 18p. (Newberry Library publications, no. 2)

541. Philadelphia Free Library. Oriental manuscripts of the John Frederick Lewis collection in the Free Library of Philadelphia; a descriptive catalogue with forty-eight illustrations, by Muhammed Ahmed Simsar. Philadelphia, 1937. 248p.

542. Poleman, Horace I. A census of Indic manuscripts in the United States and Canada. New Haven: American Oriental Society, 1938. 542p. (American oriental series, v. 12)

Nearly 8,000 items located in 69 public and 38 private libraries.

543. Poleman, Horace I. "Three Indic manuscripts". Library of Congress quarterly journal of current acquisitions, 1 (Apr.-June, 1944), 24-29.

In Library of Congress.

544. Princeton University Library. A catalogue of Turkish and Persian manuscripts belonging to Robert Garrett, and deposited in the Princeton University Library; by Nicholas N. Martinovich. Princeton: Princeton Univ. Press, 1926. 46p.

Superseded by 1939 catalog.

545. Princeton University Library. Descriptive catalog of the Garrett collection of Persian, Turkish, and Indic manuscripts, including some miniatures, in the Princeton University Library, by Mohamad E. Moghadam and Yahya Armajani. Princeton: Princeton Univ. Press, 1939. 94p.

546. Princeton University Library. "The Garrett collection of manuscripts." Princeton University Library chronicle, 3 (1942), 113-48.

Consists of separate articles on Arabic and Islamic, Western European, Greek, Persian and Indo-Persian, Indic manuscripts and the papyri included in the Garrett collection at Princeton.

547. Princeton University Library. A list of Arabic manuscripts in Princeton Library, by Enno Littmann. Princeton: The Library, 1904. 84p.

548. U. S. Library of Congress. Indic manuscripts and paintings, the Library of Congress. Wash.: Govt. Print. Off., 1939. 16p.

Catalog of an exhibition of 97 items from Library of Congress, University of Pennsylvania and other collections in the United States. Locations given, arranged by languages.

RARE BOOKS

549. Alden, J. E. "Some recent additions to the rare book collection." [University of Pennsylvania] Library chronicle, 15 (1949), 59-70.

Classical authors in French translation; Italian literature; English literature; horological collection; musical library of Francis Hopkinson; American literature; Theodore Dreiser collection.

550. Campbell, Jean. "The reference works in the Rosenwald collection." Library of Congress quarterly journal of current acquisitions, 3 (Oct. 1945), 67-68.

Early dictionaries, catalogs, recipe books, and similar works in collection received by Library of Congress.

551. Century Association Library. Rare books in the library of the Century Association exhibited in the art gallery, February and March, 1934. [New Rochelle: Walpole Prtg. Off.] 1934. 36p.

552. Clark, Ethel B. "The Founders Room Library at Dumbarton Oaks." Harvard Library bulletin, 4 (1950), 141-71.

Description of several thousand rare books, autograph letters, literary and music manuscripts.

553. Clark University Library. List of books and pictures in the Clark Memorial Collection. Worcester: Clark University Press, 1906. [80]p. (Clark University Library publications, v. 2, no. 1, July 1906.)

A list of manuscripts, printed books and pictures given to University by Jonas Gilman Clark.

554. Columbia University Library. "University Library collections: monumenta and rariora," by V. G. Simkhovitch. Columbia University quarterly, 13 (1911), 173-82.

Describes some monumenta and rariora in several collections in Columbia University Library.

555. Columbia University, Teachers College Library. Catalogue of the Ellen Walters Avery collection of books. N. Y., 1897. 63p.

Lists 609 titles, illustrated and fine editions in literature, natural sciences, etc.

556. English, Thomas Hopkins. "The Treasure room of Emory University." Southwest review, 29 (1943), 30-36.

General description of special collections relating to Methodism, Joel Chandler Harris, etc.

557. Goff, Frederick R., comp. "Catalog of fine books and manuscripts selected for exhibition at the Library of Congress from the Lessing J. Rosenwald collection, October 1945." Library of Congress quarterly journal of current acquisitions, 3 (Oct. 1945), 5-51.

Detailed descriptions of 80 titles, chronologically arranged, 1460-1890.

558. Goff, Frederick R. "A catalog of important recent additions to the Lessing J. Rosenwald collection selected for exhibition at the Library of Congress, June 1948." Library of Congress quarterly journal of current acquisitions, 5 (May 1948), 3-51.

Detailed descriptions of 82 titles, chronologically arranged 1474-1947.

559. Grosvenor Library. "Rare books in the Grosvenor Library." Grosvenor Library bulletin, 27 (1945), no. 2.

Stresses first editions of American authors, drama, Masonic literature, and printing history.

560. [Jackson, William A.] The Houghton Library; report of accessions for the year 1941/42 - date. Cambridge, Mass.: Harvard Univ. Printing Office, 1942 - date.

Annual report of accessions of Rare Book division of Harvard College Library.

561. Jackson, William A. "The new rare book library." Harvard University Library notes, 4 (1941), 23-24.

Description of Houghton Library at Harvard.

562. New York Public Library. "One hundred treasures; an exhibition to mark the one-hundredth anniversary of the New York Public Library." New York Public Library bulletin, 53 (1949), 277-89.

Annotated list of 100 greatest rarities in the Library's collections.

563. [Newberry Library] Catalogue of the collection of books, manuscripts, and works of art, belonging to Mr. Henry Probasco. [Cambridge: Welch, Bigelow & Co.] 1873. 407p.

Collection of rare books and manuscripts acquired by Newberry Library in 1890.

564. Parma, V. Valta. The rare book collection of the Library of Congress, New Rochelle, N. Y.: Walpole Printing Office, 1931. [18]p.

565. Pierpont Morgan Library. The first quarter century of the Pierpont Morgan Library; a retrospective exhibition in honor of Belle DaCosta Greene. [N. Y.: The Library, 1949] 67p., 50 plates.

Catalog of 256 items representative of Library's collections.

566. Pierpont Morgan Library. Flowers of ten centuries; catalogue of an exhibition, April 28 to July 26, September 15 to November 15. N. Y.: [The Library], 1947. 70p., 12 plates.

Catalog of 187 items, including illuminated manuscripts, printed books, engravings and drawings.

567. Pierpont Morgan Library. Guide to an exhibition held on the occasion of the New York World's Fair, 1939. [N. Y.: The Library, 1939] 27p.

Hand list of items shown. Representative of Library's collections.

568. Pierpont Morgan Library. Illustrated catalogue of an exhibition held on the occasion of the New York World's Fair 1939. New

York: The Pierpont Morgan Library, May through October, 1939. N. Y.: The Library, 1939. 78p., 21 plates.

335 items selected from each of important types of collections in Library: papyri, illuminated manuscripts, printed books, bookbindings, etc.

569. Pierpont Morgan Library. Illustrated catalogue of an exhibition held on the occasion of the New York World's Fair 1940. New York, May through October, 1940. [N. Y.: The Library, 1940] 41p., 9 plates.

152 items: illuminated manuscripts, metal book covers and other bindings, autograph manuscripts, letters and documents, drawings and Gutenberg Bible.

570. Plimpton, George A. "Greek manuscripts and early printed books in the Plimpton Library." American Philological Association transactions, 65 (1934), 260-70.

Describes a collection now in Columbia University.

571. Rosenwald, Lessing J. "The formation of the Rosenwald collection." Library of Congress quarterly journal of current acquisitions, 3 (Oct. 1945), 53-62.

Description of collection and mention of rare titles.

572. St. John's Seminary Library, Camarillo, Calif. Catalogue of books and manuscripts in the Estelle Doheny collection. Los Angeles, 1940. 297p.

Part two, Los Angeles, 1946. 77p. Records about 500 additional titles of illuminated manuscripts, incunabula, Bibles, English literature, Californiana, and Kate Greenaway. Original catalog lists illuminated manuscripts, incunabula, Bibles, 16th century books, French books, first editions of American and English literature, William Morris and Kelmscott Press and other private presses, and fine bindings.

573. Texas, University, Library. The rare book collections of the University of Texas Library. Austin, Tex. [1943?] 8p.

574. Thompson, C. S. "The gift of Louis XVI." University of Pennsylvania Library chronicle, 2 (1934), 37-48; 60-67.

Discussion and list of 36 titles in 100 volumes received by University of Pennsylvania in 1784.

575. Transylvania Library; a list of old periodicals, transactions, reports, general and medical. Lexington, Ky. 1922. 40p. (Transylvania College bulletin, v. 13, no. 3, March 1922)

Material listed is in Transylvania College Library.

576. U. S. Library of Congress. "Annual report on acquisitions: rare books." Library of Congress quarterly journal of acquisitions, 3 (May 1946), 49-59; 4 (May 1947), 95-102; 5 (May 1948), 53-67; 6 (May 1949), 95-106.

577. U. S. Library of Congress. A catalog of important recent additions to the Lessing J. Rosenwald collection selected for exhibition at the Library of Congress, June 1947, comp. by Frederick R. Goff. Wash., 1947. 52p.

Lists 80 titles, chronologically arranged from 1459 to 1664. Detailed descriptions. Reprinted from Library of Congress quarterly journal of current acquisitions, 4 (1947), 3-56.

578. U. S. Library of Congress, John Boyd Thacher Collection. The collection of John Boyd Thacher in the Library of Congress. Wash.: Govt. Print. Off., 1931. 3v.

Volume 1 is a reissue of Catalogue of the John Boyd Thacher collection of incunabula, 1915; v. 2 lists books relating to French Revolution, early Americana, etc.; v. 3 lists autographs relating to French Revolution and European notables.

579. Winship, George P. "The Harvard Treasure Room." Harvard Library notes, 3 (1939), 210-16.

Survey of Harvard College Library's rare book collection.

PRINTING HISTORY

General

580. Bennett, Richard. A catalogue of the early printed books and illuminated manuscripts collected by Richard Bennett. [Guildford, England], 1900. 55p.

Collection now in Pierpont Morgan Library.

581. Boston Public Library. Five hundred years of printing; an exhibit of the work of famous presses from Gutenberg to the present

day, in the Treasure room of the Boston Public Library, June - October, 1940. Boston: The Library, [1940] 27p.

582. Boston Public Library. A list of books on the history and art of printing and some related subjects in the Public Library of the city of Boston and the libraries of Harvard College and the Boston Athenaeum. Boston: The Library, 1906. 38p.

583. Clements, William L. A check list of books published before 1700 belonging to the library of William L. Clements. Bay City, 1920. 15p.

Now in William L. Clements Library, University of Michigan.

584. Colby College Library. Catalogue of a mid-century centennial exhibition of books published in 1850. Waterville, Me.: The Library, 1950. 16p.

From Colby College Library collection.

585. Colby College Library. "Eighteen-fifty - 'annus mirabilis.'" Colby Library quarterly, 2 (1950), 225-37.

Exhibition of works of 20 English and American authors published in 1850. Material from Colby College Library.

586. Columbia University Library. An exhibition commemorating the five hundredth anniversary of the invention of printing, Low Memorial Library, January 15 - April 15, 1940. [N. Y., 1940] 11p.

587. Connecticut State Library. 500 years of printing, 1440-1940; an exhibition at the Connecticut State Library. [Hartford, 1940] 65p.

Locates copies of 225 titles, all but three loaned by libraries in Hartford or elsewhere in Connecticut.

588. Dobell, Bertram. Catalogue of books printed for private circulation. Collected by Bertram Dobell, and now described and annotated by him. London: Pub. by the author [1891]-1906. 4 pt. in 1v.

Part of collection, 1,611 volumes, acquired by Library of Congress.

589. Goff, Frederick. "Almost books." New colophon, 1 (Apr. 1948), 125-33.

Copyright records. Describes collection in Library of Congress of about 36,000 pieces of title pages dating from 1790 to 1870.

590. Grolier Club. "Microscopic books in the library of the Grolier Club." (Its: Officers, Committees... 1911, p. 119-51.) Reprinted under title: A short list of microscopic books in the Library of the Grolier Club. N. Y., 1911. 121-51p.

591. Henry E. Huntington Library. The Alice and George Millard collection, illustrating the evolution of the book, acquired for the Huntington Library by a group of their friends. [Los Angeles, 1939] 15p.

592. Henry E. Huntington Library. Fine books; an exhibition of written and printed books selected for excellence of design, craftsmanship and materials. San Marino, 1936. 16p., 15 facsims.

A selection of 30 volumes from several centuries and various parts of Europe and United States.

593. Henry E. Huntington Library. Great books in great editions; an exhibition commemorating the 500th anniversary of the invention of printing, prep. by Roland Baughman and Robert Schad. San Marino: The Library, 1940. 47p.

Describes 25 titles in Library. Important texts, typographically excellent, and in fine condition.

594. Hispanic Society of America Library. List of books printed before 1601 in the library of the Hispanic Society of America, comp. by Clara Louisa Penney. N. Y.: The Society, 1929. 274p.

Lists over 250 incunabula and about 2,364 16th century works, consisting of first and rare editions of books of Hispanic interest, printed in Portugal, Mexico, Peru, Italy, Netherlands, etc.

595. Hispanic Society of America Library. List of books printed 1601-1700, in library of the Hispanic Society of America, by Clara Louisa Penney. N. Y.: The Society, 1938. 972p.

About 5,800 entries. Appendices: 1. 15th-16th century books not included in List of books printed before 1601; 2. check list of printing sites and printers of Hispanic books, 1468?-1700. Cervantes section (over 400 entries) "is carried beyond the year 1700 and is inclusive of accessions through the year 1937."

596. Hollins College Library. The Lucy Winton McVitty memorial collection of manuscripts, incunabula, and books relating to the history of printing and the study of incunabula. Hollins College, Va. [1943] 15p.

    Collection given to Hollins College in 1943.

597. Long Island Historical Society. Manuscripts and early printed books bequeathed to the Long Island Historical Society by Samuel Bowne Duryea. Brooklyn, 1895. 40p.

    Description of 32 manuscripts and 16 printed books.

598. Mills College Library. Thirty books and manuscripts from the Albert M. Bender collection of Mills College. Mills College, Calif.: Bibliophile Society, 1937. 46p.

    Describes 30 of 3,800 items in Bender collection.

599. New York Public Library. "A gazetteer of Hebrew printing," by Aron Freimann. New York Public Library bulletin, 49 (1945), 355-74, 456-68, 530-40, 913-39. Reprinted with revisions and additions, 1946. 86p.

    A large portion of material is in New York Public Library. Locations given in 8 other libraries.

600. New York Public Library. "One hundred books and manuscripts; an exhibition. List of the books and manuscripts shown." New York Public Library bulletin, 41 (1937), 455-62. Reprinted. 8p.

    Chiefly of interest for book history.

601. New York Public Library. "Printing from the 16th to the 20th century; introduction to the catalogue of an exhibition," comp. by Charles Flowers McCombs. New York Public Library bulletin, 44 (1940), 71-92. Reprinted. 8p.

    Lists 137 titles, 1454-1930.

602. Newark Free Public Library. The Richard C. Jenkinson collection of books chosen to show the work of the best printers. Newark, N. J.: The Library, 1925-29. 2v.

    Lists 1,268 examples of printing of various periods and countries, now in Newark Free Public Library.

603. Newberry Library. 500 years of printing; an exhibition in commemoration of the five-hundredth anniversary of the European invention of printing from movable type. Chicago: The Library [1940] 29p.

604. Pierpont Morgan Library. Catalogue of a collection of books formed by James Toovey principally from the Library of the Earl of Gosford, the property of J. Pierpont Morgan. N. Y., 1901. 192p.

    Includes Aldine Press books and fine bindings.

605. Pierpont Morgan Library. Catalogue of... early printed books from the libraries of William Morris, Richard Bennett, Bertram, Fourth Earl of Ashburnham, and other sources, now forming part of the Library of J. Pierpont Morgan. London: Chiswick Press, 1907. 3v., facsims.

    V. 1: Xylographica, Germany and Switzerland. V. 2: Italy and part of France. V. 3: France (end), Netherlands, Spain, England.

606. Stanford University, Library. Finely printed books presented to the Library. A catalogue. Stanford University, 1927. 33p.

    Arranged alphabetically under presses, with author index.

607. Syracuse Public Library. Catalogue of the J. William Smith collection, comp. by Caroline M. Daggett. Syracuse, N. Y., 1910. 43p.

    Includes manuscripts, incunabula, examples of fine printing, etc., in Syracuse Public Library, J. William Smith collection.

608. Taylor, Archer. Renaissance guides to books: an inventory and some conclusions. Berkeley, Calif.: Univ. of California Press, 1945. 130p.

    List of renaissance bibliographies published prior to 1700, with location of copies in American libraries.

609. Transylvania College Library. Transylvania Library; a list of rare and curious old works on medicine, law and the humanities printed before 1700. Lexington, Ky., 1919. 51p. (Transylvania College bulletin, v. 11, no. 3, Nov. 1919.)

    Lists 171 titles of works in Library, and gives a general description of whole collection of 28,000 items.

610. U. S. Library of Congress. "Books in the John Davis Batchelder deposit," comp. by Jean Campbell. Wash., 1935. 74p. Typed.

611. U. S. Library of Congress. Exhibit of books, manuscripts, bindings, illustrations, and broadsides selected from the collection of John Davis Batchelder, Esquire [presented to the Library of Congress, 1936]. Wash.: Govt. Print. Off., 1938. 62p.

612. Vassar College Library. A list of rare books, manuscripts and autographs in Vassar College Library, with notes by Mary M. Shaver. Poughkeepsie, N. Y., 1917. 38p.
Arranged by types and presses.

613. Williams College, Chapin Library. Short-title list, comp. by Lucy Eugenia Osborne. Portland, Me.: Southworth-Anthoensen Press, 1939. 595p.
Lists incunabula, Americana, manuscripts, etc., in Chapin Library.

614. Yale University Library. Catalogue of the William Loring Andrews collection of early books in the Library of Yale University, ed. by Addison VanName. New Haven: Yale Univ. Press, 1913. 56p.

Incunabula

615. Annmary Brown Memorial. The Annmary Brown Memorial; a booklover's shrine, by Margaret Bingham Stillwell. Providence, 1940. 27p.
Relates to the Memorial's incunabula collection.

616. Annmary Brown Memorial Library. Catalogue of books mostly from the presses of the first printers showing the progress of printing... through the second half of the fifteenth century; collected by Rush C. Hawkins, catalogued by Alfred W. Pollard, and deposited in the Annmary Brown Memorial at Providence, Rhode Island. Oxford: University Press, 1910. 339p.

617. Boston Public Library. A check list of the incunabula in the Boston Public Library, by Zoltan Haraszti. Boston: The Library, 1935. 12p.

618. Brown University, John Carter Brown Library. A list of books printed in the fifteenth century in the John Carter Brown Library and the General Library of Brown University, Providence, Rhode Island. Oxford: University Press, 1910. 19p.

619. Bühler, Curt F. "English incunabula in America." Library quarterly, 11 (1941), 497-501.
Statistical comparison of holdings of leading English and American libraries.

620. Bühler, Curt F. "The incunabula of the Grenville Kane collection." Princeton University Library chronicle, 11 (Autumn 1949), 26-36.
Purchased by Princeton University Library.

621. Chicago, University, Library. "Fifteenth-century books in the University of Chicago," by J. C. M. Hanson. University record, 9 (1923), 156-63. Reprinted.

622. Daley, Charles Marie. Dominican incunabula in the Library of Congress. N. Y.: U. S. Catholic Historical Society, 1932. 88p. ("Reprinted from Historical records and studies, v. 22, Oct. 1932.")

623. Daley, Charles Marie. "Incunabula of Albertus Magnus in the Library of Congress." Catholic historical review, 17 (1932), 444-63.

624. Duff, Edward Gordon. Fifteenth century English books: a bibliography of books and documents printed in England and of books for the English market printed abroad. [Oxford]: Oxford Univ. Press, 1917. 136p. (Bibliographical Society, Illustrated monographs, no. 18.)
Locates copies in some American libraries.

625. Faye, C. U. Fifteenth century printed books at the University of Illinois. Urbana: Univ. of Illinois Press, 1949. 160p. (Illinois contributions to librarianship, no. 4)
Lists 431 typographica and 3 xylographica in the University of Illinois Library, with an index of printers, presses, publishers and places.

626. Gesamtkatalog der wiegendrucke, hrsg. von der Kommission für den Gesamtkatalog der wiegendrucke... Leipzig: K. W. Hiersemann, 1925-40. v. 1-8[1]
Locates copies in American and European libraries.

627. Goff, Frederick R. "Incunabula in the Library of Congress." Library of Congress quarterly journal of current acquisitions, 1 (Jan.-March, 1944), 3-14.

　　Summary of Library of Congress holdings of 15th century books, with description of outstanding items in the Rosenwald collection.

628. Grolier Club. Catalogue of early printed books presented to the Grolier Club by David Wolfe Bruce. N. Y., 1894. 33p.

　　Lists 85 titles of incunabula and early imprints on literary history of typography.

629. Grolier Club. A description of the early printed books owned by the Grolier Club with a brief account of their printers and the history of typography in the fifteenth century. N. Y.: The Club, 1895. 77p.

630. Haraszti, Zoltán. "Fifteenth-century books in the library." More books, 4 (1929), 353-80; 5 (1930), 5-23, 61-85, 353-78, 421-40; 6 (1931), 174-92, 231-40, 425-35; 7 (1932), 11-20, 263-84; 8 (1933), 381-96; 9 (1934), 5-19, 253-63, 297-306; 10 (1935), 1-8, 81-95; 11 (1936), 157-80, 210-29, 329-44, 381-97; 15 (1940), 355-79, 409-28; 16 (1941), 43-70, 235-60, 403-32; 17 (1942), 183-212, 247-60, 413-30; 18 (1943), 96-121, 163-78, 275-92.

　　Descriptive catalog of 15th century printed books and single leaves of incunabula in Boston Public Library.

631. Harvard University Library. "Fifteenth century books." Harvard Library notes, 1 (1921), 85-86, 89-116.

　　In Harvard Library.

632. "Hebrew incunabula in America (a census)." Journal of Jewish bibliography, 2 (April-July 1940), 67-77.

　　Locates copies in 38 public and private collections.

633. Henry E. Huntington Library. Incunabula in the Huntington Library, comp. by Herman Ralph Mead. San Marino, Calif., 1937. 386p. (Huntington Library lists, no. 3)

　　Lists about 5,200 items.

634. Hispanic Society of America Library. Incunabula in the library. N. Y.: The Society, 1928. 5 pts. (Hispanic notes and monographs.)

　　Each number devoted to bibliographical descriptions of one or two incunabula.

635. John Crerar Library. A list of books exhibited... including incunabula and other early printed books in the Senn collection. Chicago, 1907. 32p.

636. Josephson, A. G. S. "The incunabula in the Senn collection at the John Crerar Library." American Medical Association journal, 52 (1909), 1749-51. Reprinted. 6p.

637. Keogh, Andrew. "The Gutenberg Bible as a typographical monument." Yale University Library gazette, 1 (1926), 1-6.

　　Locates all copies of the Gutenberg Bible in this country in 1926. See also Antiquarian bookman, 6 (Nov. 15, 1950), pt. 2, 7-12.

638. McMurtrie, Douglas C. Miniature incunabula; some preliminary notes on small books printed during the fifteenth century. Chicago: Privately printed. 1929. 11p.

　　Locates 2 titles in Newberry Library and 1 title in Pierpont Morgan Library.

639. Marston, Thomas E. "A fifteenth century library." Yale University Library gazette, 21 (1947), 31-35.

　　A general description of 196 incunabula and 8 sixteenth-century books added to Yale University Library.

640. Marx, Alexander. "Hebrew incunabula." Jewish quarterly review, 11 (1920), 98-119.

　　Locates copies of Hebrew incunabula mentioned in two books reviewed: Cassuto, U. Incunaboli Ebraici a Firenze, and Katalog 151 von Ludwig Rosenthal's Antiquariat. Hebräische Inkunabeln 1475-1490.

641. Michigan, University, Library. Early printed books in the Stephen Spaulding collection at the University of Michigan. [Wash., 1940] 8p.

　　Lists 122 items.

642. Michigan, University, Library. A list of incunabula in Ann Arbor, June 1940. Ann Arbor: Univ. of Mich. Press, 1940. 32p.

　　Short-title list of 310 books held by the University of Michigan and 12 in private libraries in Ann Arbor.

643. Newberry Library. A check list of fifteenth-century books in the Newberry Library and in other libraries of Chicago, comp. by Pierce Butler. Chicago: The

Library, 1933. 362p.

Lists 1,613 incunabula in Newberry and 182 in 10 other Chicago libraries.

644. Newberry Library. The first fifty years of the printed book, 1450-1500. Notes descriptive of an exhibition. Chicago: The Library, 1925. 17p.

645. North Carolina, University, Library. Incunabula in the Hanes collection, comp. by Olan V. Cook. Chapel Hill, 1940. 125p. (Hanes Foundation publications, no. 1)

Records 536 titles in University of North Carolina Library.

646. Pierpont Morgan Library. Check list of fifteenth-century printing in the Pierpont Morgan Library, comp. by Ada Thurston and Curt F. Bühler. N. Y.: Pierpont Morgan Library, 1939. 348p.

Records 1,850 15th century type-printed books and 24 block books and woodcut single sheets owned by Library.

647. Pierpont Morgan Library. The fifteenth-century book, an exhibition arranged for the 500th anniversary of the invention of printing; list of books exhibited with an introduction by Lawrence C. Wroth. [N. Y.]: Pierpont Morgan Library, 1940. 28p.

About 100 titles drawn from Library's collection.

648. Princeton University Library. Early printing in Italy, with special reference to the classics, 1469-1517. [Princeton, 1940] 32p.

Guide to an exhibition.

649. Radin, Max. "The Sulzberger collection of Soncino books in the library of the Jewish Theological Seminary." Bibliographical Society of America papers, 7 (1912/13), 79-89.

650. Ricci, Seymour de. A census of Caxtons. Oxford: University Press, 1909. 196p. (Bibliographical Society, Illustrated monographs, no. 15).

Locates copies in 5 American libraries.

651. Rider, Fremont. "Holdings of incunabula in American University libraries." Library quarterly, 9 (1939), 273-84.

Statistics of number of incunabula held by 94 American university libraries.

652. Rider, Fremont. Incunabula in American libraries; a supplementary list. Library quarterly, 10 (1940), 361-65.

A record of number of volumes of incunabula held by 102 libraries not covered by original list published in 1939.

653. Shaffer, Ellen Kate. Nuremberg chronicle. Los Angeles: Dawson's Book Shop, 1950. 61p.

"Census of copies of the five editions of the Nuremberg Chronicle in North America," p. 55-[58]. Includes public and private owners.

654. Smith, George D., booksellers, N. Y. Monuments of early printing in Germany, the Low countries, Italy, France and England, 1460-1500. N. Y.: G. D. Smith, 1916. 96p.

Now a part of Huntington Library.

655. Sotheby, Wilkinson & Hodge. Chatsworth Library; the famous Devonshire collection of works printed by or from the types of William Caxton. London [1914]. 16p.

Acquired en bloc by Huntington Library.

656. Stillwell, Margaret Bingham. Incunabula in American libraries; a second census of fifteenth-century books owned in the United States, Mexico, and Canada. N. Y.: Bibliographical Society of America, 1940. 619p.

Records 35,232 copies, 11,132 titles, in 332 public and 390 private collections.

657. Tucker, Ethelyn M. "Incunabula in the library of the Arnold Arboretum." Arnold Arboretum journal, 4 (1923), 56-60.

In Harvard University.

658. U. S. Library of Congress. Exhibit of books printed during the XVth century and known as incunabula; selected from the Vollbehr collection purchased by act of Congress 1930; list of books. Wash.: Govt. Print. Off., 1930. 78p.

List of about 1,700 of 3,000 items in collection. Arranged by types, subjects, and presses.

659. U. S. Library of Congress. Loan exhibition of incunabula from the Vollbehr collection; books printed before 1501. Wash.: Govt. Print. Off., 1928. 8p.

Collection now in Library of Congress.

660. U. S. Library of Congress. The Vollbehr

collection of incunabula. [Wash.: Govt. Print. Off., 1929] 4p.

661. U. S. Library of Congress. The Vollbehr collection of incunabula and the Gutenberg Bible. [Wash.: Govt. Print. Off., 1939][4]p.

662. Walters, Henry. Incunabula typographica; a descriptive catalogue of the books printed in the fifteenth century (1460-1500) in the library of Henry Walters. Baltimore, 1906. 522p.

Collection now in Walters Art Gallery, Baltimore, Maryland.

663. Winship, George Parker. Vollbehr incunabula. [N. Y., Pynson printers, 1926.] 18p.

Now in Library of Congress.

Great Britain

664. Allen, Don C. "A short title catalogue of English books prior to 1700 in the library of the State College of Washington." Research studies of the State College of Washington, 5 (1937), supp., 109-26.

665. Bishop, William Warner. A checklist of American copies of "Short-title catalogue" books. Ann Arbor: Univ. of Michigan Press, 1944. 250p. (University of Michigan General library publications, no. 6). 2d ed. Ann Arbor: Univ. of Michigan Press, 1950. 203p.

Records holdings of about 100 American libraries.

666. California State Library, Sutro Branch. Catalogue of English pamphlets in the Sutro Library. San Francisco: The Library, 1941. 2 parts.

Pt. 1, 1562-1642; pt. 2, 17th century periodicals.

667. Clark, William Andrews. The library of William Andrews Clark, Jr. The Kelmscott and Doves Presses. San Francisco: J. H. Nash, 1921. 123p.

Now in University of California, Los Angeles.

668. Colby College Library. "Kelmscott complete." Colby Library quarterly, 2 (1950), 238-40.

Report on complete collection, 53 titles, of Kelmscott Press books in Colby College Library.

669. Henry E. Huntington Library. "Huntington library supplement to the record of its books in the Short title catalogue of English books, 1475-1640," comp. by Cecil Kay Edmonds. Huntington Library bulletin, no. 4 (1933), 152p.

Additions and corrections to the Bibliographical Society's Short Title Catalogue of English Books, 1475-1640.

670. [Henry E. Huntington Library] An illustrated catalogue of English pamphlets, etc. from 1640-1830. Tunbridge Wells, England: P. M. Barnard, bookseller [1923] 83p.

Acquired en bloc by Huntington Library.

671. McManaway, James G. "Survey of the Harmsworth collection." Amherst graduates' quarterly, 27 (August 1938), 329-36.

In Folger Shakespeare Library, Washington, D. C. About 10,000 English books for period 1475-1640.

672. Madan, Falconer. Summary description of a library of Oxford books, collected during fifty years. [London: Dryden Press, 1928?] [8]p.

Collection purchased by Yale University Library in 1930.

673. Morrogh, Charles A. Catalogue of illustrated works and first editions in the library of Charles Morrogh. N. Y., 1902. 115p.

Collection purchased by Henry E. Huntington. Contained 54 Kelmscott Press books and 57 volumes illustrated by Cruikshank.

674. Nash, Ray. "Rastell fragments at Dartmouth." The Library, 4th ser., 24 (1943), 66-73.

Describes a collection of 16 early 16th century English black-letter fragments from Rastell press.

675. New York Public Library. "Check list of early English printing, 1475-1640, in the New York Public Library," comp. by Daniel Carl Haskell. New York Public Library bulletin, 29 (1925), 484-512, 545-78. Reprinted. 66p.

676. Newberry Library. Books printed by William Morris at the Kelmscott press. An exhibition at the Newberry Library, Chicago, 1927. [Chicago], 1927. 14p.

677. Newberry Library. Check list of books printed in English before 1641, comp. by Mae I. Stearns. Chicago, 1923. 198p. (Special publications, no. 20)

All items are in Newberry Library.

678. Newberry Library. English books and books printed in England before 1641 in the Newberry Library; a supplement to the record in the Short title catalogue, comp. by Gertrude L. Woodward. Chicago, 1939. 118p.

679. Pollard, Alfred William and Redgrave, G. R. A short-title catalogue of books printed in England, Scotland and Ireland, and of English books printed abroad, 1475-1640. London: Bibliographical Society, 1926. 609p.

Locates copies in over 150 libraries, of which 15 are American.

680. Virginia, University, Library. Early English books at the University of Virginia; a short-title catalogue, comp. by C. William Miller. Charlottesville: Alderman Library, 1941. 29p. (Univ. of Virginia bibliographical series, no. 3)

Lists 237 items, 1534-1640.

681. Wing, Donald Godard. Short-title catalogue of books printed in England, Scotland, Ireland, Wales, and British America and of English books printed in other countries, 1641-1700. N. Y.: Index Society, 1945-48. 2v. V. 1, A-England; v. 2, England-Oz.

Lists about 24,500 items with locations in 210 libraries.

682. Yale University Library. "Check list of the John Baskerville collection of Perry Williams Harvey, including some specimens of work of contemporary continental printers." Yale University Library gazette, 11 (1936), 63-80.

Collection now in Yale University Library.

683. Yale University Library. "A selection of Baskerville imprints in the Yale University Library," described by Rebecca Dutton Townsend and Margaret Currier. In: Papers in honor of Andrew Keogh. [New Haven, 1938] p. 285-97.

United States

GENERAL

684. Adams, Randolph G. The passports printed by Benjamin Franklin at his Passy press. Ann Arbor: Univ. of Michigan, 1925. 10p.

Describes examples in William L. Clements Library, University of Michigan, and in a private collection.

685. American Antiquarian Society Library. "Early American broadsides, 1680-1800," prep. by Nathaniel Paine. American Antiquarian Society proceedings, n. s. 11 (1897), 455-516. Reprinted, 1897. 64p.

Chronological list of about 200 titles, with detailed descriptions, in American Antiquarian Society Library. Supplementary list in Society's Proceedings, n. s. 12 (1898), 315-17.

686. American Antiquarian Society Library. "A list of early American imprints in the Library of the American Antiquarian Society, 1640-1700," prep. by Nathaniel Paine. American Antiquarian Society proceedings, n. s. 10 (1895), 281-350. Reprinted, 1896. 80p.

Chronological arrangement, with detailed bibliographical descriptions.

687. Boston Public Library. Catalogue of a collection of early New England books made by the late John Allen Lewis (1819-1885). Boston, 1892. 31p.

Rich in material relating to the history of printing in Boston, particularly issues of press of John Foster.

688. Chapin, Howard Millar. Calendrier français pour l'année 1781 and the printing press of the French fleet in American waters during the Revolutionary War. Providence, 1914. [9]p. (Contributions to Rhode Island bibliography, no. 2)

Locates copies.

689. Chicago Public Library Omnibus Project. Check list of books printed in America before 1800 in the libraries of Chicago. Chicago: The Project, 1941. 401p.

3,459 titles located in 7 Chicago libraries.

690. Eames, Wilberforce. "The Antigua Press and Benjamin Mecom, 1748-1765."

American Antiquarian Society proceedings, n. s. 38 (1928), 303-48.

Chronological list of works printed on island of Antigua (British West Indies), Boston, New York and Burlington (N. J.) by Benjamin Mecom, Benjamin Franklin's nephew. Lists 67 titles and locates all known copies.

691. Evans, Charles. American bibliography. A chronological dictionary of all books, pamphlets and periodical publications printed in the United States of America from the genesis of printing in 1639 down to and including the year 1820. Chicago: Blakely Press, 1903-34. 12v.

Completed only through 1799. Locates copies.

692. Flanders, Louis W. Simeon Ide, yeoman, freeman, pioneer printer... Bibliography of the imprints of Simeon Ide, by R. W. G. Vail. Rutland, Vt.: Tuttle Co., 1931. 347p.

Printer in Ipswich, N. H. (1815-16), Vermont (1817-35), Claremont, N. H. (1836-79). Bibliography, p. 141-72, locates copies in American Antiquarian Society.

693. Ford, Paul L. The New England primer: a history of its origin and development; with a reprint of the unique copy of the earliest known edition. N. Y.: Dodd Mead & Co., 1897. 354p.

Bibliography appended often locates copies.

694. Gaskill, Nelson B. Imprints from the press of Stephen C. Ustick, with its several locations... 1794-1836. Wash., 1940. 93p.

Lists imprints of Philadelphia, Mount Holly and Burlington (N. J.), Washington, and Alexandria (Va.). Locates copies in 53 libraries.

695. Green, Samuel Abbott. A supplementary list of early American imprints belonging to the library of the Massachusetts Historical Society. With dates of two early commencements at Cambridge. Cambridge: J. Wilson & Son, 1898. 15p. (Reprinted from Massachusetts Historical Society proceedings, 2d. ser. 12 (1898), 273-86)

Second supplement, Massachusetts Historical Society proceedings, 2d ser., 12 (1899), 380-423; third supplement, Massachusetts Historical Society proceedings, 2d ser. 17 (1903), 13-75. Locations in other collections frequently indicated.

696. Heartman, Charles F. American primers, Indian primers, Royal primers, and thirty-seven other types of non-New England primers issued prior to 1830; a bibliographical check list. Highland Park, N. J.: Printed for Harry B. Weiss, 1935. 159p.

Copies located in 36 institutional and private libraries.

697. Heartman, Charles F. The New England primer issued prior to 1830; a bibliographical check list. N. Y.: R. R. Bowker, 1934. 148p. Earlier editions, N. Y., 1915. 117p.; N. Y., 1922. 190p.

Copies located in 30 public and private collections.

698. Henry E. Huntington Library. "American imprints, 1648-1797, in the Huntington Library, supplementing Evans' American bibliography," comp. by Willard O. Waters. Huntington Library bulletin, no. 3 (Feb. 1933), 1-95. Reprinted, Cambridge, Mass., 1933. 95p.

699. Henry E. Huntington Library. Confederate imprints in the Henry E. Huntington Library, by Willard O. Waters. Chicago, 1930. 18-109p. (Reprinted from Bibliographical Society of America papers, 23 (1929), pt. 1)

Lists imprints unrecorded in previously published bibliographies of such material.

700. Merritt, Percival. "The Royal primer." In: Bibliographical essays; a tribute to Wilberforce Eames. [Cambridge: Harvard Univ. Press], 1924, p. 35-60.

Locates copies of editions from 1750 to 1818 in New York Public Library, American Antiquarian Society, Boston Public Library, Huntington Library, British Museum, and several private collections.

701. Michigan, University, William L. Clements Library. Early American printing, an exhibition. Ann Arbor, 1927. 21p. (Bulletin, no. 15)

702. Michigan, University, William L. Clements Library. Historic examples of American printing and typography; a guide to an exhibition. Ann Arbor: William L. Clements Library, [1940] 66p. (Bulletin, no. 32)

Bibliographical descriptions and reproductions of title pages of examples of American printing from 1544 to 1837.

703. Roberts, Martin A. "Records in the Copyright Office of the Library of Congress deposited by the United States district courts, 1790-1870." Bibliographical Society of America papers, 31 (1937), 81-101. Reprinted, 1939. 19p.

704. Sondley, Reference Library. "American imprints: 1752-1820." Asheville, N. C. Leaves from the Sondley, 1 (Apr., 1946), [6]p.

705. Thomas, Isaiah. The history of printing in America, with a biography of printers, and an account of newspapers... 2d ed. With the author's corrections and additions, and a catalogue of American publications previous to the revolution of 1776. Pub. under the supervision of a special committee of the American Antiquarian Society... Albany, N. Y.: J. Munsell, printer, 1874. 2v. (Archaeologia Americana. American Antiquarian Society. Transactions and collections, v. 5 and 6) ---Appendixes. Catalogue of publications in what is now the United States, prior to the revolution of 1775-6 [comp. by Samuel F. Haven, Jr. (also issued separately.)]
Sometimes locates copies.

ALABAMA

706. Duke University Library. Check list of Alabama pamphlets in the Duke University Library, 1823-1941. [Durham, 1942] 53 l.
Lists 316 titles chronologically.

707. Ellison, Rhoda Coleman. A check list of Alabama imprints, 1807-1870. University, Ala.: Univ. of Alabama Press, 1946. 151p.
Lists 1,658 items, with locations in 30 collections.

708. Historical Records Survey - Alabama, American Imprints Inventory. Check list of Alabama imprints, 1807-1840. Birmingham, Alabama: Hist. Rec. Survey, 1939. 159p. (American Imprints Inventory, no. 8)
Lists 345 titles in 107 public and private collections.

ARKANSAS

709. Allen, Albert H., Arkansas Imprints, 1821-1876. N. Y.: Pub. for the Bibliographical Society of America, by R. R. Bowker Co., 1947. 236p.
Locates 766 titles in 270 libraries.

710. Historical Records Survey - Arkansas, American Imprints Inventory. A check list of Arkansas imprints, 1821-1876. Little Rock: Ark. Historical Records Survey, 1942. 139 numb. l. (American Imprints Inventory, no. 39)
Lists 596 titles with locations in about 350 libraries.

ARIZONA

711. Historical Records Survey - Arizona, American Imprints Inventory. A check list of Arizona imprints, 1860-1890. Chicago: Hist. Rec. Survey, 1938. 81p. (American Imprints Inventory, no. 3)
Locates copies of 161 items in 29 libraries.

712. McMurtrie, Douglas C. The beginnings of printing in Arizona, with an account of the early newspapers and a bibliography of books, pamphlets and broadsides printed in Arizona, 1860-1875. Chicago: Black Cat Press, 1937. 44p.
Locates 35 imprints in 16 libraries.

CALIFORNIA

713. California, University, Library, William Andrews Clark Memorial Library. The private press of Thomas Perry Stricker. [Los Angeles, 1947] 12p.
Includes biographical notes and a check list.

714. Cowan, Robert Ernest. A bibliography of the Spanish press of California, 1833-1845. San Francisco, 1919. 31p.
Locates copies of some 66 items in 10 public and private collections.

715. Harding, George L. "A census of California Spanish imprints, 1833-1845." California Historical Society quarterly, 12 (1933), 125-36. Reprinted.
Locates copies of 74 imprints.

716. Henry E. Huntington Library. The work of the Grabhorn Press; notes on an exhibition, prep. by Roland Baughman. [San Marino, 1945] 8p.

717. Historical Records Survey - California, American Imprints Inventory. A check list of California non-documentary imprints, 1833-1855. San Francisco, 1942. 109 numb. l.

(American Imprints Inventory, no. 31)
Locates 489 titles in about 150 libraries.

718. Wagner, Henry Raup. California imprints, August 1846-June 1851. Berkeley, Cal., 1922. 97p.
Locates copies in public and private collections.

719. Waters, Willard O. "Los Angeles imprints, 1851-1876: a check list." Historical Society of Southern California quarterly, 19 (1937), 63-94.
Locates copies in 10 libraries, all except Library of Congress in California.

COLORADO

720. McMurtrie, Douglas C. and Allen, Albert H. Colorado imprints not listed in the bibliography on "Early printing in Colorado". Evanston: Priv. Print., 1943. 4 numb. 1.
Locates 20 imprints.

721. McMurtrie, Douglas C. and Allen, Albert H. Early printing in Colorado, with a bibliography of the issues of the press, 1859 to 1876 inclusive, and a record and bibliography of Colorado territorial newspapers. Denver: A. B. Hirschfeld Press, 1935. 305p.
Locates copies, with holdings, in 17 public and 2 private collections.

722. McMurtrie, Douglas C. A preliminary check list of Colorado imprints, 1859-1876. Chicago, 1932. 63p.
Locates copies in Library of Congress, Colorado Historical Society, and occasionally in other collections.

CONNECTICUT

723. Bates, Albert Carlos. "The work of Hartford's first printer." In: Bibliographical essays, a tribute to Wilberforce Eames. [Cambridge: Harvard University Press] 1924, p. 345-61.
Lists 51 of Thomas Green's Hartford imprints, 1764-68, locating copies in Connecticut Historical Society, Library of Congress, New York Historical Society, Vermont State Library, Watkinson Library (Hartford), and Yale University.

724. Connecticut Historical Society. Examples of Connecticut imprints of the eighteenth century, exhibited by the Connecticut Historical Society and the Watkinson Library. Hartford, 1935. 32p.

725. Sills, R. Malcolm. "W. J. Linton at Yale - the Appledore private press, Hamden, Connecticut, 1875-1897." Yale University Library gazette, 12 (1938), 43-52.
All but 4 items are in Yale University Library.

DELAWARE

726. Hawkins, Dorothy Lawson. "A checklist of Delaware imprints up to and including 1800; a contribution to the history of printing in Delaware." Columbia University, Master's essay, 1928, 74p. Unpublished typescript.
Locates copies in 16 libraries.

727. Hawkins, Dorothy Lawson. "James Adams; the first printer of Delaware." Bibliographical Society of America papers, 28 (1934), 28-63.
Locates copies of titles mentioned, when known, in several libraries.

DISTRICT OF COLUMBIA

728. McMurtrie, Douglas C. "The beginnings of printing in the District of Columbia." Americana, 27 (1933), 265-89.
Locates a few rare items.

GEORGIA

729. McMurtrie, Douglas C. Located Georgia imprints of the eighteenth century not in the DeRenne Catalogue. Savannah, Ga.: Privately printed. 1934. 44p. (Reprinted from Georgia historical quarterly, March 1934).
Describes and locates 71 imprints in 16 American libraries.

IDAHO

730. Historical Records Survey - Idaho, American Imprints Inventory. A check list of Idaho imprints, 1839-1890. Chicago: WPA Historical Records Survey, 1940. 74 numb. 1. (American Imprints Inventory, no. 13)
Lists 180 titles with locations in 93 libraries.

731. McMurtrie, Douglas C. A short-title check list of books, pamphlets, and broadsides

printed in Idaho, 1839-1890. Chicago: The Historical Records Survey, 1938. 45p. (American Imprints Inventory, Imprints memoranda, no. 2)

Gives holdings of 20 libraries.

ILLINOIS

732. Historical Records Survey. American Imprints Inventory. Check list of Chicago ante-fire imprints, 1851-1871. Chicago: Hist. Rec. Survey, 1938. 727p. (American Imprints Inventory, no. 4)

Lists 1,880 titles distributed among 142 libraries and private collections.

733. McMurtrie, Douglas C. A bibliography of Chicago imprints, 1835-1850. Chicago: Wright Howes, 1944. 112p.

Locates 227 titles in over 100 libraries.

734. McMurtrie, Douglas C. A bibliography of Peoria imprints, 1835-1860. Springfield, Illinois: Privately printed, 1934. 30p. (Reprinted from Illinois State Historical Society journal, July, 1934.)

Locates 71 titles in 22 libraries.

735. McMurtrie, Douglas C. Early Illinois copyright entries, 1821-1850. Evanston, 1943. 20p. ("Reproduced from the Bulletin of the Chicago Historical Society, Vol. 2, p. 50-61, 92-101.")

Locates known copies in 37 libraries.

736. McMurtrie, Douglas C. The first printers of Chicago, with a bibliography of the Chicago press, 1836-1850. Chicago: Cuneo Press, 1927. 42p.

-----. Notes in supplement to "The first printers of Chicago." Chicago: Priv. print., 1931. 14p.

Locates copies of imprints.

737. McMurtrie, Douglas C. The first printing in Peoria, Illinois. Chicago: Ludlow Typograph Co., 1929. 30p.

Locates copies of 20 items, 1835-60, in New York Public Library, Peoria Public Library, Chicago Historical Society, and Huntington Library.

738. Wirick, Harriet P. "A check list and study of Illinois imprints through 1850." Urbana: Univ. of Illinois, 1932. 127 numb. l.

M. A. thesis. Typescript, unpublished.

Excludes newspapers, periodicals and documents. Copies located in 15 libraries.

INDIANA

739. Hepburn, William M. Notes on Bruce Rogers of Indiana. 1945. 11p. (Reprinted from Indiana quarterly for bookmen, July, 1945)

Describes Rogers collection in Purdue University Library.

740. McMurtrie, Douglas C. "Indiana imprints, 1804-1849; a supplement to Mary Alden Walker's 'Beginnings of printing in the state of Indiana,' published in 1934." Indiana Historical Society publications, 11 (1937), 307-93.

Locates items in 41 libraries; includes 25 broadsides.

741. Walker, Mary Alden. The beginnings of printing in the state of Indiana. Comprising a brief analysis of the literary production, and a list of items printed to 1850. Crawfordsville, Ind.: R. E. Banta, 1934. 124p.

Locates items in 46 libraries.

IOWA

742. Historical Records Survey - Iowa. American Imprints Inventory. A check list of Iowa imprints, 1838-1860, in supplement to those recorded by Alexander Moffit in the Iowa Journal of History and Politics for January 1938. Chicago: WPA Historical Records Survey, 1940. 84 numb. l. (American Imprints Inventory, no. 15)

Locates 195 titles in 77 libraries.

743. Moffit, Alexander. "Check list of Iowa imprints, 1837-1860." Iowa journal of history and politics, 36 (1938), 1-95.

Locates imprints in 47 libraries.

KANSAS

744. Historical Records Survey - Kan. American Imprints Inventory. Check list of Kansas imprints, 1854-1876. Topeka: WPA Historical Records Survey, 1939. 773p. (American Imprints Inventory, no. 10)

Contains 1,594 titles and locates holdings of 187 libraries.

745. McMurtrie, Douglas C. and Allen, Albert H. A forgotten pioneer press of Kansas. Chicago: John Calhoun Club, 1930. 30p.

Describes and locates copies printed by Ioway and Sac Mission press.

746. McMurtrie, Douglas C. and Allen, Albert H. Jotham Meeker, pioneer printer of Kansas, with a bibliography of the known issues of the Baptist Mission Press at Shawanoe, Stockbridge, and Ottawa, 1834-1854. Chicago: Eyncourt Press, 1930. 169p.

Locates known copies of 89 items.

747. McMurtrie, Douglas C. Pioneer printing of Kansas. Topeka, 1935. 16p. (Extract from Kansas historical quarterly, Nov. 1931.)

Locates copies of titles when known.

KENTUCKY

748. Historical Records Survey - Kentucky, American Imprints Inventory. Supplemental check list of Kentucky imprints, 1788-1820, ed. by John Wilson Townsend. Louisville: Historical Records Survey, 1942. 241p. (American Imprints Inventory, no. 38)

Locates over 1,300 titles in 30 libraries. Supplementary to check lists for years 1787-1810 and 1811-1820, comp. by D. C. McMurtrie and A. H. Allen.

749. Jillson, Willard Rouse. The first printing in Kentucky; some account of Thomas Parvin and John Bradford and the establishment of the Kentucky Gazette in Lexington in the year 1787, with a bibliography of seventy titles. Louisville: C. T. Dearing Print. Co., 1936. 57p.

Locates some items.

750. Jillson, Willard Rouse. Rare Kentucky books, 1776-1926; a check and finding list of scarce, fugitive, curious and interesting books and pamphlets with annotations and prices current appended. Louisville, 1939. 199p.

Locations given in 9 Kentucky libraries and in the Library of Congress.

751. McMurtrie, Douglas C. and Allen, Albert H. Check list of Kentucky imprints, 1787-1810. Louisville: Historical Records Survey, 1939. 205p. (American Imprints Inventory, no. 5)

323 titles located in 103 collections.

752. McMurtrie, Douglas C. and Allen, Albert H. Check list of Kentucky imprints, 1811-1820, with notes in supplement to the Check list of 1787-1810 imprints. Louisville: Historical Records Survey, 1939. 235p. (American Imprints Inventory, no. 6)

429 titles located in 158 libraries and 24 private collections.

753. McMurtrie, Douglas C. and Allen, Albert H. "A supplementary list of Kentucky imprints, 1794-1820, additional to those recorded in American Imprints Inventory check lists nos. 5 and 6." Kentucky State Historical Society register, 42 (1944), 99-119.

Locates copies in 21 libraries.

754. McMurtrie, Douglas C. Proof sheets of a bibliography of Kentucky imprints, 1787-1822. Chicago, 1932 [1934]. 113 l.

Locates most of 681 titles in 58 libraries.

LOUISIANA

755. Foote, Lucy Brown. Bibliography of the official publications of Louisiana, 1803-1934. Baton Rouge, La.: Hill Memorial Library, Louisiana State University, 1942. 579p. (Historical Records Survey, American Imprints Inventory, no. 19)

Lists holdings in Louisiana State University Library, Howard Memorial Library (New Orleans), University of Illinois Library, and 30 other libraries if not in the above three.

756. McMurtrie, Douglas C. Denis Brand, imprimeur du roi à la Nouvelle Orléans. Paris, 1929. 14p.

Locates 20 imprints of Denis Brand, from 1764 to 1770.

757. McMurtrie, Douglas C. Early printing in New Orleans, 1764-1810, with a bibliography of the issues of the Louisiana press. New Orleans: Searcy & Pfaff, 1929. 151p.

Bibliography, p. 87-144, locates all known copies of 161 imprints.

758. McMurtrie, Douglas C. Louisiana imprints, 1768-1810; in supplement to the bibliography in "Early printing in New Orleans." Hattiesburg, Miss.: The Book Farm, 1942. 65p. (Heartman's historical series, no. 62)

Locates 70 titles in 13 libraries.

MAINE

759. Boardman, Samuel Lane. Peter Edes, pioneer printer in Maine, a biography. Bangor: Printed for the De Burians, 1901. 159p.

Edes imprints described and located, chiefly in Maine libraries.

760. McMurtrie, Douglas C. Maine imprints, 1792-1820; an open letter to R. Webb Noyes, Esq. Chicago: Privately printed, 1935. 12 numb. 1.

Lists 28 Maine imprints, 1792-1820, not recorded by Noyes, with locations in 15 libraries.

761. Noyes, Reginald Webb. A bibliography of Maine imprints to 1820. Stonington, Me.: The Author, 1930. 22,[132]p. Supplement, 1934. 11 1.

Lists 965 numbered items. Locations shown in 19 libraries. Supplement gives additional information.

MARYLAND

762. Baer, Elizabeth, comp. Seventeenth century Maryland, a bibliography. Baltimore: John Work Garrett Library, 1949. 219p.

Locates copies in 112 American institutional libraries, also foreign and private libraries. Contains 209 entries, arranged chronologically.

763. Wheeler, Joseph Towne. The Maryland press, 1777-1790. Baltimore: Maryland Historical Society, 1938. 226p.

Lists 550 items, located in 34 libraries or collections.

764. Wroth, Lawrence C. A history of printing in colonial Maryland: 1686-1776. [Baltimore] Typothetae of Maryland, 1922. 275p.

P. 157-256: "Maryland imprints; an annotated bibliography of books, broadsides and newspapers printed in Maryland from 1689 to 1776." Locates copies in 19 American libraries and elsewhere.

MASSACHUSETTS

765. American Antiquarian Society Library. "Remarks on the early American engravings and the Cambridge Press imprints (1640-1692) in the Library of the American Antiquarian Society," by Nathaniel Paine. American Antiquarian Society proceedings, n. s. 17 (1906), 280-98. Reprinted, 1906. 21p.

Includes chronological list of imprints, with detailed descriptions.

766. Dartmouth College Library. The Isaiah Thomas donation. Hanover, N. H.: The Library, 1949. 36p.

Catalog of 248 titles presented to Dartmouth College by Thomas; chiefly books printed between 1790 and 1816 and printed or published by Thomas.

767. [Eames, Wilberforce] Bibliographic notes on Eliot's Indian Bible and his other translations and works in the Indian language of Massachusetts. Wash.: Govt. Print. Off., 1890. 58p. (Reprinted in Pilling's Bibliography of the Algonquian languages, 1891. p. 127-84.)

Often locates copies seen.

768. Eames, Wilberforce. A list of editions of the Bay psalm book. N. Y., 1885. 14p.

Reprinted from Sabin, v. 16. Locates copies.

769. [Ford, Worthington Chauncey] Broadsides, ballads, etc., printed in Massachusetts, 1639-1800. [Boston]: Massachusetts Historical Society, 1922. 483p.

Lists locations in 25 libraries for 3,423 items, arranged chronologically.

770. Gilmore, Barbara. A Puritan town and its imprints; Northampton, 1786-1845. Northampton, Mass.: Hampshire Bookshop, 1942. 104p.

Locations shown in 7 libraries. Includes newspapers.

771. Green, Samuel Abbott. John Foster, the earliest American engraver and the first Boston printer. Boston: Massachusetts Historical Society, 1909. 149p.

Locates copies of Foster imprints in many libraries.

772. Green, Samuel A. A list of early American imprints belonging to the library of the Massachusetts Historical Society. Cambridge: J. Wilson & Son, 1895. 137p. (Reprinted from Massachusetts Historical Society proceedings. 2d ser. 9 (1895), 410-540)

Covers period from 1643 to 1700.

773. Henry E. Huntington Library. The work of the Merrymount Press and its founder Daniel Berkeley Updike (1860-1941); an exhibition, prep. by Gregg Anderson. San Marino: The Library, 1942. 35p.

Huntington Library acquired Merrymount Press library in 1949.

774. Historical Records Survey - Mass., American Imprints Inventory. A check list of Massachusetts imprints, 1801-1802. Boston, 1942. 2v. (American Imprints Inventory, nos. 40, 45)

Volume 1 lists 394 titles, and v. 2 lists 377, each in about 500 libraries.

775. Jones, Matt B. "The early Massachusetts-Bay Colony seals; with bibliographical notes based upon their use in printing." American Antiquarian Society proceedings, n. s. 44 (1934), 13-44. Reprinted, 1935. 34p.

Appendix has chronological list, 1672-91, of Massachusetts Bay session laws, proclamations, etc., carrying impressions of seals with locations of copies in 15 public and private collections.

776. Litchfield Historical Society. The publications of Thomas Collier, printer, 1784-1808, comp. by Samuel H. Fisher. Litchfield: The Society, 1933. 98p.

Lists 126 items chronologically, locating copies in 20 libraries.

777. Littlefield, George Emery. The early Massachusetts press, 1638-1711. Boston: Club of Odd Volumes, 1907. 2v.

Locates occasional copies throughout the text.

778. McKeon, Newton Felch and Cowles, Katharine Conover, eds. Amherst, Massachusetts imprints, 1825-1876. Amherst, Mass.: Amherst College Library, 1946. 191p.

Locates 710 imprints in more than 300 libraries.

779. Michigan, University, William L. Clements Library. "Catalogue of an exhibition for the bicentenary of Isaiah Thomas," prep. by F. L. D. Goodrich. The quarto, no. 20 (Jan. 1950). 4p.

Items dated 1759 to 1808.

780. Nichols, Charles L. Isaiah Thomas, printer, writer & collector... With a bibliography of the books printed by Isaiah Thomas. Boston: [Merrymount Press]: Printed for the Club of Odd Volumes, 1912. 144p.

Locations frequently indicated.

781. Roden. Robert F. The Cambridge press, 1638-1692: a history of the first printing press established in English America, together with a bibliographical list of the issues of the press. N. Y.: Dodd, Mead & Co., 1905. 193p.

Bibliography, p. 145-85, often locates copies.

782. Spargo, John. Anthony Haswell, printer-patriot-ballader; a biographical study with a selection of his ballads and an annotated bibliographical list of his imprints. Rutland, Vt.: Tuttle Co., 1925. 293p.

A printer of Worcester and Springfield, Mass. (1780-82), and Bennington, Vt. (1783-1815). Copies of imprints located in 19 libraries.

783. Swan, Bradford F. "Some thoughts on the Bay Psalm book of 1640, with a census of copies." Yale University Library gazette, 22 (1948), 49-76.

Locates and describes in detail 11 copies known to be in existence in 1948.

784. Tapley, Harriet Silvester. Salem imprints, 1768-1825; a history of the first fifty years of printing in Salem, Massachusetts. Salem: Essex Institute, 1927. 512p.

Locations indicated in 18 institutional and private collections.

MICHIGAN

785. Historical Records Survey - Mich., American Imprints Inventory. Preliminary check list of Michigan imprints, 1796-1850. Detroit: Michigan Historical Records Survey, 1942. 224p. (American Imprints Inventory, no. 52)

Locates 943 titles in about 360 libraries.

786. McMurtrie, Douglas C. Early printing in Michigan, with a bibliography of the issues of the Michigan Press, 1796-1850. Chicago: John Calhoun Club, 1931. 351p.

Exact holdings shown in 33 public and private collections.

MINNESOTA

787. Historical Records Survey - Minn., American Imprints Inventory. Check list of Minnesota imprints, 1849-1865, by Mamie R. Martin. Chicago: Hist. Rec. Survey, 1938. 219p. (American Imprints Inventory, no. 2)

Lists locations of 656 titles in 33 libraries.

MISSISSIPPI

788. McMurtrie, Douglas C. A bibliography of Mississippi imprints, 1798-1830. Beauvoir Community, Miss.: The Book Farm, 1945. 168p.

Lists 290 items with locations. Supersedes author's Preliminary check list of Mississippi imprints, 1798-1830 and his Short title list of books, pamphlets and broadsides printed in Mississippi, 1811-1830.

789. McMurtrie, Douglas C. Preliminary check list of Mississippi imprints, 1798-1810. Chicago, 1934. 53p.

Locates 44 titles in 13 libraries.

790. McMurtrie, Douglas Crawford. A Short-title list of books, pamphlets and broadsides printed in Mississippi, 1811 to 1830. Chicago, 1936. 47p.

Locates titles in 36 libraries.

791. Sydnor, Charles S. "The beginning of printing in Mississippi." Journal of southern history, 1 (1935), 49-55.

Locates 5 early Mississippi imprints.

MISSOURI

792. Breckenridge, James M. William Clark Breckenridge, historical research writer and bibliographer of Missouriana. St. Louis: The Author, 1932. 380p.

P. 249-99: "Bibliography of early Missouri imprints, 1808-1850," locates titles in Library of State Historical Society of Missouri.

793. Historical Records Survey - Mo. American Imprints Inventory. A preliminary check list of Missouri imprints, 1808-1850. Wash.: Hist. Rec. Survey, 1937. 225p. (American Imprints Inventory, no. 1)

Records 694 imprints with locations in 87 libraries.

794. McMurtrie, Douglas C. Early Missouri book and pamphlet imprints, 1808-1830. Chicago, 1937. 17 numb. 1. (Originally appeared in American book collector, 1 (1932), 96-103, 159-62, 231-34.)

Describes and locates imprints in 15 libraries.

MONTANA

795. McMurtrie, Douglas C. Montana imprints, 1864-1880; bibliography of books, pamphlets and broadsides printed within the area now constituting the state of Montana. Chicago: Black Cat Press, 1937. 82p.

Locates 164 titles in 37 libraries or collections.

NEBRASKA

796. Historical Records Survey - Neb., American Imprints Inventory. A check list of Nebraska non-documentary imprints, 1847-1876. Lincoln, 1942. 132p. (American Imprints Inventory, no. 26).

Lists 503 titles with locations in about 150 libraries.

NEVADA

797. Historical Records Survey - Nev. American Imprints Inventory. A check list of Nevada imprints, 1859-1890. Chicago: Historical Records Survey, 1939. 127 numb. 1. (American Imprints Inventory, no. 7)

Locates copies of 520 titles in 73 public and private collections.

NEW HAMPSHIRE

798. Dartmouth College Library. "Private press; brief description of the Printer's Devil Press, the Arts Press, Baker Library Press, and the Windward Press." Dartmouth College Library bulletin, 2 (May 1935), 46-49.

Bibliography of items printed on press in Dartmouth College Library.

799. McMurtrie, Douglas C. The beginnings of printing in New Hampshire. London: Bibliographical Society, 1934. p. 340-63. "Reprinted... from the Transactions of the Bibliographical Society, the Library, Dec. 1934."

Locates copies of titles when known.

800. Nash, Ray. Pioneer printing at Dartmouth; with a check list of Dresden imprints,

by Harold Goddard Rugg. Hanover: George T. Bailey, 1941. 40p.

Locates Dresden imprints in 26 libraries. Text quotes from some manuscripts in Dartmouth College Library.

801. Whittemore, Caroline. "A check list of New Hampshire imprints, 1756-1790." M. S. Thesis, Columbia University, 1929. 137 l. Typescript, unpublished.

Locates copies in 30 libraries.

NEW JERSEY

802. Hill, Frank Pierce and Collins, Varnum L. Books, pamphlets and newspapers printed at Newark, New Jersey, 1776-1900. Newark, 1902. 296p.

Locates copies in Newark Public Library and New Jersey Historical Society Library.

803. Historical Records Survey - New Jersey. American Imprints Inventory. Check list of New Jersey imprints, 1784-1800, by Lucile M. Morsch. Baltimore: WPA Hist. Rec. Survey, 1939. 189p. (American Imprints Inventory, no. 9)

Locates copies of 501 titles in 33 libraries.

804. Humphrey, Constance H. "Check-list of New Jersey imprints to the end of the Revolution." Bibliographical Society of America papers, 24 (1930), 43-149.

Copies located in 25 libraries.

805. McMurtrie, Douglas Crawford. A bibliography of Morristown imprints, 1798-1820. Newark, N. J., 1936. 31p. Reprinted from New Jersey Historical Society proceedings, 54 (1936), 129-55.

Locates 73 titles in 24 libraries.

806. Miller, George J. "David A. Borrenstein, a printer and publisher at Princeton, N. J., 1824-1828." Bibliographical Society of America papers, 30 (1936), 1-56.

"A bibliography of the printing of David A. Borrenstein" locates copies in 9 American and several British libraries.

807. Morsch, Lucile M. Check list of New Jersey imprints, 1784-1800. Baltimore, 1939. 189p. (American Imprints Inventory, no. 9)

Copies located in 33 libraries.

808. Rose, Grace D. "Early Morristown imprints." New Jersey Historical Society proceedings, 53 (1935), 156-63.

Lists 34 titles, all of which are in Morristown Library.

NEW MEXICO

809. Historical Records Survey - Illinois. American Imprints Inventory. Check list of New Mexico imprints and publications, 1784-1876. Detroit: Mich. Hist. Rec. Survey, 1942. 115p. (American Imprints Inventory, no. 25)

Locates 300 imprints in 103 libraries.

810. McMurtrie, Douglas C. "The history of early printing in New Mexico, with a bibliography of the known issues of the New Mexico press, 1834-1860." New Mexico historical review, 4 (1929), 372-410. Reprinted.

Locates 80 titles.

811. McMurtrie, Douglas C. "Some supplementary New Mexico imprints, 1850-1860." New Mexico historical review, 7 (1932), 165-75.

Supplementary material to his "The history of early printing in New Mexico." Locates 41 additional titles.

812. Wagner, Henry R. "New Mexico Spanish press." New Mexico historical review, 12 (1937), 1-40.

Lists and locates 30 New Mexico imprints, 1834-45.

NEW YORK

813. Benton, Joel. "Some early Hudson River imprints." Literary collector, 3 (1901-02), 119-22.

Lists early imprints of Poughkeepsie, Hudson, Newburgh, and Stanford, most of which are now in the Adriance Library, Poughkeepsie.

814. Ford, Paul L., ed. The journals of Hugh Gaine, printer. N. Y.: Dodd, Mead, 1902. 2v.

V. 1, p. 85-174: "Bibliography of the issues of Hugh Gaine's press, 1752-1800." Locates copies in 14 libraries.

815. Foreman, Edward R. "Proposed bibliography of Rochester publications, together with check list of Rochester publications, 1816-1860." Rochester Historical Society publication fund series, 5 (1926), 171-250.

Location given for titles in Rochester Historical Society Library.

816. Hill, William H. A brief history of the printing press in Washington, Saratoga and Warren counties, state of New York. Together with a check list of their publications prior to 1825. Fort Edward, N. Y.: Priv. print., 1930. 117p.

Most of imprints were taken from New York Public Library, New York State Library or the author's collection.

817. Historical Records Survey - Illinois. American Imprints Inventory. A check list of Utica imprints, 1799-1830. Chicago, 1942. 179p. (American Imprints Inventory, no. 36)

Lists 572 titles with locations in about 400 libraries.

818. Historical Records Survey - N. Y. American Imprints Inventory. "Preliminary check list of Batavia imprints, 1819-1876." New York history, 24 (1943-44), 423-32, 565-69; 25 (1944), 69-79, 228-33, 381-87.

Locates 117 Batavia imprints in 104 libraries.

819. McMurtrie, Douglas C. "Additional Buffalo imprints, 1812-1849." Grosvenor Library bulletin, 18 (1936), 69-91. Reprinted 1936.

Additional to list published in the Grosvenor Library bulletin, v. 16. 1934. Descriptions and locations of 64 additional Buffalo imprints.

820. McMurtrie, Douglas C. "Additional Geneva imprints, 1815-1849." Grosvenor Library bulletin, 18 (1936), 93-99. Reprinted 1936.

Additional to list published in the Grosvenor Library bulletin, v. 17. 1935. Locates 15 additional imprints in Geneva.

821. McMurtrie, Douglas C. "A bibliography of books, pamphlets and broadsides printed at Auburn, N. Y., 1810-1850." Grosvenor Library bulletin, 20 (1938), 69-152.

Locates 403 titles in 120 libraries.

822. McMurtrie, Douglas C. "A bibliography of books and pamphlets printed at Geneva, N. Y., 1800-1850." Grosvenor Library bulletin, 17 (1935), 81-112. Reprinted 1935.

Locates 158 titles in 37 libraries.

823. McMurtrie, Douglas C. "A bibliography of books and pamphlets printed at Ithaca, N. Y., 1820-1850." Grosvenor Library bulletin, 19 (1937), 45-105. Reprinted 1937.

Locates 257 titles in 64 libraries.

824. McMurtrie, Douglas C. "A bibliography of books, pamphlets and broadsides printed at Canandaigua, N. Y., 1799-1850." Grosvenor Library bulletin, 21 (1939), 61-107. Reprinted 1939.

Locates 190 titles in 84 libraries.

825. McMurtrie, Douglas C. A check list of books, pamphlets, and broadsides printed at Schenectady, N. Y., 1795-1830. Chicago, 1938. 35p.

Locates 94 imprints in 39 libraries.

826. McMurtrie, Douglas C. A check list of eighteenth century Albany imprints. Albany: University of the State of New York, 1939. 83p. [Univ. of the State of N. Y. bulletin, no. 1155, Jan. 2, 1939] N. Y. State Library, Bibliography bulletin, no. 80)

Locates 255 titles in 76 libraries.

827. McMurtrie, Douglas Crawford. A check list of the imprints of Sag Harbor, L. I., 1791-1820. Chicago: Historical Records Survey, 1939. 61p. (American Imprints Inventory, no. 12)

Locates 46 titles in 36 libraries.

828. McMurtrie, Douglas C. Issues of the Brooklyn press; a list of books and pamphlets printed in Brooklyn, New York, from 1790 through 1820, in supplement to Wegelin's Bibliography. Brooklyn: Brooklyn Public Library, 1936. 22p.

Locates 58 supplementary items and gives additional locations of titles listed by Wegelin.

829. McMurtrie, Douglas C. "Pamphlets and books printed in Buffalo prior to 1850; being a supplement to the list compiled by Dr. F. H. Severance and published in the Buffalo Historical Society publications, v. 6, appendix A., 1903." Grosvenor Library bulletin, 16 (1934), 58-107.

Locates copies in 36 libraries.

830. McMurtrie, Douglas C. A preliminary check list of books and pamphlets printed in Geneva, N. Y., 1800-1850. Buffalo: Grosvenor Library, 1935. 25 numb. l.

Locates copies in 16 libraries.

831. McMurtrie, Douglas C. Rochester imprints, 1819-1850, in libraries outside of Rochester; an informal check list. Chicago: Privately printed, 1935. 93p.

Locates 286 titles in 40 libraries outside of Rochester.

832. McMurtrie, Douglas C. A short-title of books, pamphlets and broadsides printed in Auburn, N. Y., 1810 to 1850. Chicago: Chicago Historical Society, 1936. 79 numb. l.

Locates copies in 24 libraries.

833. McMurtrie, Douglas C. A short-title list of books, pamphlets and broadsides printed in Ithaca, N. Y., 1811 to 1850. Buffalo: Grosvenor Library, 1936. 55 numb. l.

Locates copies in 54 libraries.

834. New York Public Library. "The first year of printing in New York, May, 1693 - April, 1694," by Wilberforce Eames. New York Public Library bulletin, 32 (1928), 3-24. Reprinted. 25p.

Locates copies, in New York Public Library and elsewhere, of all known imprints.

835. New York Public Library. "New York broadsides, 1762-1779." New York Public Library bulletin, 3 (1899), 23-33.

Lists and describes 86 broadsides in New York Public Library.

836. New York Public Library. "Solomon King, early New York bookseller and publisher of children's books and chapbooks," by Harry B. Weiss. New York Public Library bulletin, 51 (1947), 531-44. Reprinted, 16p.

Locates copies in 6 libraries.

837. Roach, George W. "Preliminary check list of Batavia imprints, 1819-1876." New York history, 24 (1943), 423-32, 565-69; 25 (1944), 69-79, 228-33, 381-87.

Locates 117 imprints.

838. Rutherfurd, Livingston. John Peter Zenger, his press, his trial and a bibliography of Zenger imprints, also a reprint of the first edition of the trial. N. Y.: Dodd, Mead & Co., 1904. 275p. Reprinted in 1941 by Peter Smith. 275p.

Locates copies of Zenger imprints in 10 libraries.

839. Wegelin, Oscar. "The Brooklyn, New York, press, 1799-1820." Bibliographical Society of America bulletin, 4 (1912), 37-47.

Check list of publications, locating copies in 7 libraries.

840. Williams, John Camp. An Oneida County printer, William Williams, printer, publisher, editor; with a bibliography of the press at Utica, Oneida County, New York, from 1803-1838. N. Y.: Scribner, 1906. [214]p.

No locations, but notes 5 libraries on which bibliography is based.

NORTH CAROLINA

841. McMurtrie, Douglas C. "A bibliography of North Carolina imprints, 1761-1800." North Carolina historical review, 10 (1933), 214-34; 13 (1936), 47-86, 143-66, 219-54.

A continuation of his The first twelve years of printing in North Carolina, 1749-1760. Locates copies of each imprint.

842. McMurtrie, Douglas C. Eighteenth century North Carolina imprints, 1749-1800. Chapel Hill: Univ. of N. C. Press, 1938. 198p.

Locations of 237 titles given in 57 libraries.

843. McMurtrie, Douglas Crawford. The first twelve years of printing in North Carolina, 1749-1760; with a bibliography of the issues of the North Carolina press, 1749-1760. Raleigh, 1933. 23p. (Reprinted from North Carolina historical review, 10 (1933), 214-34.)

Locates 30 of the 32 imprints described.

844. Weeks, Stephen B. The press of North Carolina in the eighteenth century; with... a bibliography of the issues. Brooklyn, N. Y.: Historical Printing Club, 1891. 80p.

Locates copies if in University of North Carolina or State Library at Raleigh.

NORTH AND SOUTH DAKOTA

845. Allen, Albert H., ed. Dakota Imprints, 1858-1889. N. Y.: Pub. for the Bibliographical Society of America, by R. R. Bowker Co., 1947. 221p.

Locates 774 titles in over 100 libraries, including all Dakota libraries.

846. McMurtrie, Douglas C. Preliminary check list of North Dakota imprints, 1874-1890. Evanston, Ill., 1943. 32 numb. l.

Locates 177 imprints in 38 public and private collections.

OHIO

847. Historical Records Survey - Ohio. American Imprints Inventory. A check-list of Ohio imprints, 1796-1820. Columbus: Ohio Hist. Rec. Survey, 1941. 202 numb. l. (American Imprints Inventory, no. 17)

Locates 590 titles in about 275 libraries.

848. Kyle, Eleanor R. "Early Ohio imprints." Urbana, 1932. 170 numb. l. M. A. thesis, University of Illinois, 1932. Typed.

Records titles of period from 1796 to 1832, omitting public documents, organization minutes, almanacs, and periodicals. Indicates 5 libraries where titles were examined, and lists card or printed catalogs where titles were found.

849. McMurtrie, Douglas C. Early printing in Dayton, Ohio. Dayton: Printing House Craftsmen's Club of Dayton and Vicinity, 1935. 30p.

Locates copies where known.

850. Wilkie, Florence. Early printing in Ohio, 1793-1820, with a check list of Ohio imprints for that period. M.S. thesis, Columbia University, 1933. 137 l. Typescript, unpublished.

Locates copies.

OKLAHOMA

851. Foreman, Carolyn T. Oklahoma imprints, 1835-1907; a history of printing in Oklahoma before statehood. Norman: Univ. of Oklahoma Press, 1936. 499p.

Locates copies when known.

OREGON

852. McMurtrie, Douglas C. Oregon imprints, 1847-1870. Eugene: Univ. of Oregon Press, 1950. 206p.

Locates 604 items (589 titles) in 114 collections.

PENNSYLVANIA

853. Carnegie Library of Pittsburgh. "Pittsburgh imprints, 1793-1849," comp. by Rose Demorest. Pittsburgh: The Library, 1943. 28p. Typed.

854. Doll, Eugene Edgar, and Funke, Anneliese M. The Ephrata cloisters; an annotated bibliography. Philadelphia: Carl Schurz Memorial Foundation, 1944. 139p. (Bibliographies on German American history, no. 3)

Locates copies of works produced by the printing press of the brotherhood, 1745-94.

855. Hildeburn, Charles Swift Riché. A century of printing. The issues of the press in Pennsylvania, 1685-1784. Philadelphia, 1885-86. 2v.

Lists 4,700 titles in 13 American libraries.

856. McMurtrie, Douglas C. The first printers of York, Pennsylvania, including the text of some of the imprints of the York press during the early days of the Revolutionary War. York: The Maple Press Co., 1940. 48p.

Locates copies of 11 titles.

857. Metzger, Ethel M. Supplement to Hildeburn's Century of printing, 1685-1775. With an introductory essay. Columbia University, Master's essay, [N. Y., 1930] 126 l. Typed. Photostat in New York Public Library.

Lists 476 titles not in Hildeburn and locates additional copies in 16 libraries. See Taylor for 1776-84, and Sealock for 1785-90.

858. Nolan, James B. The first decade of printing in Reading, Pennsylvania. Reading: Reading National Bank and Trust Co., 1930. 64p.

Bibliography covers 1788-1800, and shows holdings in public and private collections.

859. Reichmann, Felix, comp. Christopher Sower, Sr., 1694-1758, printer in Germantown, an annotated bibliography. Philadelphia: Carl Schurz Memorial Found., 1943. [79]p.

Occasionally locates copies.

860. Sealock, Richard B. "Publishing in Pennsylvania, 1785-1790. With a list of imprints not included in Evans' American bibliography." [N. Y.] 1935. 60p., 90 l. Typed. Photostat in New York Public Library.

Also gives additional locations for titles in Evans. List of 283 items with locations in 63 libraries.

861. Seidensticker, Oswald. The first century of German printing in America. 1728-1830.

Philadelphia: Schaefer & Koradi, 1893. 253p.

Locates copies in Pennsylvania Historical Society, German Pionier-Verein of Philadelphia, or private library of S. W. Pennypacker.

862. Shoemaker, Alfred Lewis. A check list of imprints of the German press of Northampton County, Pennsylvania, 1766-1905. Easton, Penn., 1943. 162p. (Northampton County Historical and Genealogical Society Publications, v. 4)

The location nearest Easton, Pa., is given for each title.

863. Taylor, Edith Stevens. "Supplement to Hildeburn's Century of printing, 1776-1784, with an introductory essay." N. Y., 1935. 155 l. Columbia University, Master's essay. Typed. Photostat in New York Public Library.

Lists 434 titles not in Hildeburn and locates copies in 25 libraries.

864. Thompson, David Wilson. Early publications of Carlisle, Pennsylvania, 1785-1835. Carlisle: The Sentinel, 1932. 133p.

Locates copies in 10 Pennsylvania, New York and Massachusetts libraries.

RHODE ISLAND

865. Alden, John Eliot, ed. Rhode Island imprints, 1727-1800. N. Y.: The Bibliographical Society of America, R. R. Bowker Co., 1949. 665p.

Locates copies in 273 public and private collections of 1,712 books, pamphlets and broadsides.

866. McMurtrie, Douglas C. "The beginning of printing in Rhode Island." Americana, 29 (1935), 607-29.

Locates a few rare items.

867. Rhode Island Historical Society. "Addenda to Rhode Island imprint list." Rhode Island Historical Society collections, 14 (1921), 87-96.

Supplement to "Rhode Island imprints... between 1727 and 1800," published in 1915. Locates copies in Rhode Island Historical Society, etc.

868. Rhode Island Historical Society. Rhode Island imprints; a list of books, pamphlets, newspapers and broadsides printed at Newport, Providence, Warren, Rhode Island, between 1727 and 1800. Providence, 1915. 88p.

Copies of 1,565 publications located in Rhode Island Historical Society, John Carter Brown Library, etc. Chronological.

SOUTH CAROLINA

869. McMurtrie, Douglas C. A bibliography of South Carolina imprints, 1731-1740." South Carolina historical and genealogical magazine, 34 (1933), 117-37. Reprinted. 1933.

Locates all known copies of 20 of the 42 titles printed on the Charles Town press.

870. McMurtrie, Douglas C. "Some 19th century South Carolina imprints, 1801-1820." South Carolina historical and genealogical magazine, 44 (1943), 87-106, 155-72, 228-46.

Locates about 225 titles in many libraries and collections.

871. Salley, Alexander S., Jr. "The first presses of South Carolina." Bibliographical Society of America proceedings and papers, 2 (1907-08), 28-69.

Locates copies of imprints to July 1, 1776.

872. Shearer, James F. "French and Spanish works printed in Charleston, South Carolina." Bibliographical Society of America papers, 34 (1940), 137-70.

Covers 1765-1886 period. Locates 68 titles in 39 libraries.

TENNESSEE

873. Historical Records Survey - Illinois. American Imprints Inventory. A check list of Tennessee imprints, 1793-1840. Chicago: Illinois Historical Records Survey, 1942. 285p. (American Imprints Inventory, no. 32)

Locates 797 titles in nearly 400 public and private collections.

874. Historical Records Survey - Tenn. American Imprints Inventory. Check list of Tennessee imprints, 1841-1850. Nashville: Tennessee Hist. Rec. Survey, 1941. 138 numb. l. (American Imprints Inventory, no. 20)

Locates 479 titles in about 300 libraries.

875. Historical Records Survey - Tenn. American Imprints Inventory. List of Tennessee imprints, 1793-1840, in Tennessee libraries. Nashville: Tennessee Hist. Rec. Survey, 1941. 97 numb. l. (American

Imprints Inventory, no. 16)

Lists 469 titles in 46 public and private collections.

876. McMurtrie, Douglas C. Early printing in Tennessee. With a bibliography of the issues of the Tennessee press, 1793-1830. Chicago: Chicago Club of Printing House Craftsmen, 1933. 141p.

Locates copies in 33 libraries or private collections.

TEXAS

877. Winkler, Ernest W., ed. A check list of Texas imprints, 1846-1860. Austin: Texas State Historical Association, 1949. 352p. (Published serially in Southwestern historical quarterly, v. 46-52 (1943-48)

About 1,300 entries are based on copies located in University of Texas Library, Texas State Library or some large non-Texas library. Locations are given for all copies consulted.

UTAH

878. McMurtrie, Douglas Crawford. The beginnings of printing in Utah, with a bibliography of the issues of the Utah press, 1849-1860. Chicago: John Calhoun Club, 1931. 91p.

Bibliography (p. 53-67) locates all known copies of 42 imprints.

VERMONT

879. Cooley, Elizabeth F. Vermont imprints before 1800; an introductory essay on the history of printing in Vermont, with a list of imprints, 1779-1799. Montpelier: Vermont Historical Society, 1937. 133p.

Locations for 508 imprints, 1779-99, in more than 30 libraries and private collections.

880. Rugg, Harold G. "The Dresden press." Dartmouth alumni magazine, 12 (1920), 796-814.

Lists first 32 imprints from first Vermont press, at Dresden (later Hanover), New Hampshire.

881. Rugg, Harold G. "Isaac Eddy, printer-engraver." In: Bibliographical essays: a tribute to Wilberforce Eames. [Cambridge: Harvard Univ. Press] 1924. p. 313-30.

P. 327-28: "Bibliography of Eddy's publications," 1814-16, locates copies in author's own collection, Tufts College, and American Antiquarian Society.

VIRGINIA

882. Cappon, Lester J. and Brown, Ira V. New Market, Virginia, imprints, 1806-1876. Charlottesville: Alderman Library, 1942. 36p. (Univ. of Va. bib. series, no. 5).

Locates imprints in 74 libraries.

883. Edmonds, Albert Sydney. "The Henkels, early printers in New Market, Virginia, with a bibliography." William and Mary College quarterly historical magazine, 2d ser., 18 (1938), 174-95.

Locates books and newspapers printed on Henkel press.

884. Frick, Bertha M. "A history of printing in Virginia, 1750-1783, with a list of Virginia imprints for that period." M. S. thesis, Columbia University, 1933. 127 l. Typescript, unpublished.

Locates copies.

885. Virginia State Library. Virginia imprint series. Richmond: The Library, 1946-1949. 3v.

Volumes published: No. 1, Preliminary check list for Abingdon, 1807-76; no. 4, Preliminary check list for Fredericksburg, 1778-1876; no. 9, Preliminary check list for Petersburg, 1786-1876. Based on WPA Imprints inventory list, with additions and corrections.

886. Wroth, Lawrence C. William Parks, printer and journalist of England and colonial America. With a list of the issues of his several presses and a facsimile of the earliest Virginia imprint known to be in existence. Richmond: William Parks Club, 1926. 70p.

Covers imprints, 1719-49, locating copies in 23 American and 4 English libraries.

WASHINGTON

887. Historical Records Survey - Wash. (State). American Imprints Inventory. A check list of Washington imprints, 1853-1876. Seattle: Washington Historical Records Survey, 1942. 89p. (American Imprints Inventory, no. 44)

Locates 214 titles in 96 libraries.

888. McMurtrie, Douglas C. "A record of

Washington imprints, 1853-1876, and some additional Washington imprints 1853-1876." Pacific Northwest quarterly, 34 (1943), 27-38. Reprinted.

Locates 18 imprints in 6 libraries. These are to supplement list of imprints in "A check list of Washington imprints, 1853-1876, ed. by Geraldine Beard." 1942.

WEST VIRGINIA

889. Historical Records Survey - West Va. American Imprints Inventory. A check list of West Virginia imprints, 1791-1830. Chicago: WPA Historical Records Survey, 1940. 62 numb. l. (American Imprints Inventory, no. 14)

Locates 106 titles in 166 libraries.

890. McMurtrie, Douglas C. West Virginia imprints; being a first list of books, pamphlets, and broadsides printed within the area now constituting the state of West Virginia, 1791-1830. Charleston, W. Va.: Charleston High School Print Shop, 1936. 24p.

Locates copies in 30 libraries.

WISCONSIN

891. Historical Records Survey - Wisconsin. American Imprints Inventory. A check list of Wisconsin imprints, 1833-1849, 1850-1854, 1855-1858, 1859-1863. Madison: Wis. Hist. Rec. Survey, 1942. 4v. (American Imprints Inventory, nos. 23-24, 41-42)

Volume 1 lists 569 titles in 175 libraries; v. 2 lists 551 titles in 300 libraries; v. 3 lists 724 titles in about 300 libraries; and v. 4 lists 713 titles in about 350 libraries.

892. [McMurtrie, Douglas C.] Early printing in Milwaukee. Milwaukee: Wisconsin Cuneo Press, 1930. 79p.

Summary of Milwaukee newspapers, p. 35-38; bibliography of Milwaukee imprints, 1836-59, p. 55-79. Locates copies, chiefly in Wisconsin Historical Society.

893. McMurtrie, Douglas C. Early printing in Wisconsin, with a bibliography of the issues of the press, 1833-1850. Seattle, Wash.: Frank McCaffrey, 1931. 220p.

Locates copies, chiefly in Wisconsin State Historical Society.

WYOMING

894. Historical Records Survey - Illinois. American Imprints Inventory. A check list of Wyoming imprints, 1866-1890. Chicago: Illinois Hist. Rec. Survey, 1941. 69 numb. l. (American Imprints Inventory, no. 18)

Locates 168 titles in 112 libraries.

895. McMurtrie, Douglas C. Pioneer printing in Wyoming. Cheyenne: Privately printed, 1933. 16p. (Reprinted from Annals of Wyoming, Jan. 1933)

Locates titles when known.

Latin America

896. Brown University, John Carter Brown Library. Books printed in Lima, 1585-1800. [Boston, 1908] 4p.

897. Brown University, John Carter Brown Library. Books printed in Lima and elsewhere in South America after 1800. Boston: Merrymount press, 1908. 8p.

Books listed for 1801-39, in John Carter Brown Library.

898. Brown University, John Carter Brown Library. Books printed in South America elsewhere than at Lima before 1801. [Boston, 1908] 1 l.

899. Cundall, Frank. "The press and printers of Jamaica prior to 1820." American Antiquarian Society proceedings, n. s. 26 (1916), 290-412. Reprinted. 1916. 126p.

Bibliography of Jamaica newspapers, almanacs, broadsides, and books locates copies in 8 American and 9 English libraries, and Institute of Jamaica.

900. Henry E. Huntington Library. Mexican imprints, 1544-1600, in the Huntington Library; an exhibition prepared and described by Henry R. Wagner. San Marino, 1939. 35p.

901. McMurtrie, Douglas C. Early printing on the Island of Antigua. With a facsimile of a... broadside of 1753, preserved in the Library of Congress. Evanston, Ill., 1943. 7p.

902. McMurtrie, Douglas C. The first printing in South America. Facsimile of the unique copy of the "Pragmatica sobre los diez dias del año," Lima, 1584, preserved in the John

Carter Brown Library. Providence: John Carter Brown Library, 1926. 8, [4]p.

903. U. S. Library of Congress. Colonial Printing in Mexico; catalog of an exhibition held at the Library of Congress in 1939 commemorating the four hundredth anniversary of printing in the new world. Wash.: Govt. Print. Off., 1939. 60p.

Chronologically arranged list, 1543-1821, of 85 items, with annotations.

904. Wagner, Henry R. "Sixteenth-century Mexican imprints." In: Bibliographical essays; a tribute to Wilberforce Eames. [Cambridge: Harvard Univ. Press], 1924, p. 249-68.

Locates 204 titles in 18 American libraries and 22 foreign collections.

Other countries

905. Clarke, J. F. "The first Bulgarian book." Harvard Library notes, 3 (1940), 295-302.

Survey of Bulgarian collection. See also Harvard Library notes, 4 (1941), 36.

906. Copinger, Harold Bernard. The Elzevir press; a handlist of the productions of the Elzevir presses at Leyden, Amsterdam, the Hague, and Utrecht. London: Grafton and Co., 1927. 142p.

Collection purchased by University of Michigan Library.

907. Doctrina Christiana. The first book printed in the Philippines, Manila, 1593. A facsimile of the copy in the Lessing J. Rosenwald Collection, Library of Congress, Washington, with an introductory essay by Edwin Wolf 2nd. [Wash.: Library of Congress, 1947] 50p., [76]p.

908. Goff, Frederick Richmond. Early Belgian books in the Rosenwald Collection of the Library of Congress. [n. p., 1947?] 246-256p. "Overdruk uit De Gulden passer, 25ᵉ Jaargang 1947, nrs. 3 en 4."

909. Lehmann-Haupt, Hellmut. "Russische buchholzschnitte, 1840-1850." In: Gutenberg-jahrbuch, 1932, p. 246-62.

Based largely on material in Rare Book Department of Columbia University Library.

910. McMurtrie, Douglas C. A Malta imprint of 1643; the apparently unique copy of which is preserved in the Library of Congress, Washington. Chicago: Privately printed, 1939. 7p.

Description and title page of I natali delle religiose militie, by G. Marulli.

911. McMurtrie, Douglas C. A memorandum on early printing on the Island of Malta, with bibliographical notes on issues of the early Maltese press represented in American libraries. Chicago: Privately printed, 1936. 12p.

Locates copies in Harvard University, New York Public Library and University of Michigan of imprints from 1647 to 1733.

912. New York Public Library. "French printing through 1650; a check list of books in the New York Public Library." New York Public Library bulletin, 40 (1936), 87-99, 335-46, 443-54, 505-22, 755-74. Reprinted with "A check list of mazarinades." 1938. 102p.

913. Van Patten, Nathan. Printing in Greenland with a list of Greenland imprints in the Krabbe library. Stanford University, Calif.: Stanford University Press, 1939. 40p.

The extensive Krabbe library on Greenland was acquired by Stanford University in 1937.

Illustrated books

914. Mather, Frank J. "A collection of early American illustrated books." Princeton University Library chronicle, 6 (1945), 99-126.

Includes article on early American book illustration by Sinclair Hamilton, donor of Princeton University Library collection of nearly 600 books.

915. New York Public Library. "Book illustration before Dürer; an exhibition." New York Public Library bulletin, 42 (1938), 94-103.

Lists 130 15th century books, including 8 manuscripts. All except 4, lent by the Pierpont Morgan Library, are held by New York Public Library.

916. New York Public Library. "Illustrated books of the past four centuries; a record of an exhibition held in the Print Gallery of the New York Public Library," by Frank Weitenkampf. New York Public Library bulletin, 23 (1919), 625-41, 717-38. Reprinted, 1920. 42p.

917. New York Public Library. The Spencer Collection of illustrated books. Rev. ed. N. Y.: The Library, 1928. 88p.

First edition appeared in Library's Bulletin, 18 (1914), 540-72. Reprinted, 44p.

Bookbinding

918. California, University, Library, Berkeley. Catalogue of the library presented by Henry D. Bacon. Sacramento: J. D. Young, Supt. State Printing, 1882. 22p. (Its: Bulletin, no. 3)

Consists of 1,410 volumes of English literature, bound by Bedford, Riviere, Hayday, and others.

919. Grolier Club Library. List of books and articles relating to bookbinding to be found in the library. [N. Y., 1907.] p. 117-184. (Reprinted from its Officers, committees... annual reports, etc., 1907.)

Lists 417 items.

920. Holmes, Thomas J. "The bookbindings of John Ratcliff and Edmund Ranger, seventeenth century Boston bookbinders." American Antiquarian Society proceedings, n. s. 38 (1928), 31-50.

Locations stated for surviving copies of bindings. Supplementary notes by Holmes appeared in the A. A. S. proceedings, n. s. 39 (1929), 291-306.

921. New York Public Library. "Binding styles; a foreword to an exhibition in the Spencer Room," by Philip Hofer. New York Public Library bulletin, 38 (1934), 607-18.

922. New York Public Library. "English publishers' bindings, 1800-1900; an exhibition in the New York Public Library." New York Public Library bulletin, 40 (1936), 655-64.

Drawn chiefly from New York Public Library collection.

923. Parrish, Morris L. "Variant bindings in the library at Dormy House." Colophon, pt. 17 (1934), 21-28.

Bindings of Victorian novels, a collection bequeathed to Princeton University Library.

924. Pierpont Morgan Library. A guide to an exhibition of armorial and related bookbindings 1500-1800. [N. Y.]: Pierpont Morgan Library, 1935. 71p.

Descriptive list of 149 examples from England, France and Italy.

925. Wead, Eunice. "Early binding stamps of religious significance in certain American libraries." The colophon, 20 (1935), [12p.]

Locates and describes some single blind-stamped 15th and 16th century bindings in 14 United States libraries.

926. Wead, Eunice. "Early binding stamps of religious significance in certain American libraries; a supplementary report." Studies in bibliography, papers of the Bibliographical Society of the University of Virginia, 2 (1949-50), 63-77.

Descriptions of blind-stamped bindings of 15th and 16th centuries, with locations.

Typography and book design

927. Boston Public Library. A list of books on the history and art of printing and some related subjects in the Public Library of the City of Boston and the libraries of Harvard College and the Boston Athenaeum. Published in commemoration of the two hundredth anniversary of the birth of Benjamin Franklin. Boston: The Library, 1906. 38p.

Includes all books on subject, in Harvard and Boston Public libraries, but only those in the Boston Athenaeum not found in first two.

928. Bullen, Henry L. Summary of the contents of the industrial graphic arts library and museum of the American Type Founders Company. Jersey City, 1933. 23p.

Most of material described now in Columbia University Library.

929. Butler, Pierce. "A typographical library: The John M. Wing Foundation of the Newberry Library." Bibliographical Society of America papers, 15 (1921), 73-87.

General description of the collection.

930. Carter, Constance. "The typography collection." Harvard Library notes, 3 (1936), 122-26.

In Harvard College Library.

931. Columbia University Library. "Five centuries of book design; a survey of styles in the Columbia Library," by Hellmut Lehmann-Haupt. Columbia University quarterly, 23 (1931), 176-98.

Description of examples in Columbia University Library.

932. Columbia University Library. "Typographic library," by C. C. Williamson. Columbia University quarterly, 33 (1941), 299-303.

Description of American Type Founders Library at Columbia.

933. Grolier Club. Gazette. V. 1, nos. 1-12, v. 2, nos. 1-2 (May 1921 - May 1936).

Contains many articles about the library.

934. Grolier Club. The Grolier Club and its iconographic collections, an address by Henry Watson Kent. N. Y., 1944. 28p.

935. Grolier Club. "The library," by Ruth S. Granniss. Grolier Club transactions, part 4 (1921), 51-68.

936. Grolier Club. The library. N. Y., 1925. 8p.

Brief descriptive account.

937. Grolier Club. A list of paintings and prints now displayed on the walls of the Grolier Club, comp. by Edward G. Kennedy. N. Y.: The Club, 1931. 60p. (Library pamphlet, no. 2)

938. Grolier Club. "The typographic collection of the Grolier Club and its classification," by Ruth S. Granniss. Printing art, 16 (1931), 17-22. Also appeared in Library journal, 36 (1911), 501-04.

939. Haykin, David Judson. "The Goudy collection." Library of Congress quarterly journal of current acquisitions, 1 (Jan.-March 1944), 63-65.

Brief description of an extensive collection of books, correspondence and memorabilia associated with Frederic W. Goudy.

940. McMurtrie, Douglas Crawford. The invention of printing; a bibliography. Chicago: Chicago Club of Printing House Craftsmen, 1942. 413p.

Lists 3,228 titles, with locations in American and European libraries.

941. Metropolitan Museum of Art. A guide to an exhibition of the arts of the book, by W. M. Ivins, Jr. N. Y., 1924. 96p.

Includes material from Museum, Pierpont Morgan Library, and private collections.

942. New Bedford Free Public Library. The William L. Sayer collection of books and pamphlets relating to printing, newspapers, and freedom of the press. New Bedford, Mass.: The Library, 1914-20. 2 pts.

A list of 563 titles.

943. New York Public Library. "Index to graphic arts printing processes," by H. Alan Steeves. New York Public Library bulletin, 47 (1943), 323-44. Reprinted. 24p.

"List is restricted to materials in the New York Public Library."

944. Rogers, Bruce. An account of the making of the Oxford lectern Bible. [Philadelphia, Pa.: Lanston Monotype Machine Comp., 1936?] 15p.

A copy of this Bible, specially prepared for Library of Congress, is in Rare Books Division.

945. Typothetae of the City of New York Library. Catalogue of the books in the library of the Typothetae of the City of New York. [N. Y.]: Printed for the Typothetae at the DeVinne Press, 1896. 176p.

946. U. S. Library of Congress. "The collection of Frederic and Bertha Goudy, a photostat record of cards drawn to form a preliminary check list." Wash., 1945. 40 l.

947. U. S. Library of Congress, General Reference and Bibliography Division. "Offset printing, with particular reference to the preparation of typescript copy for photolithographic reproduction." Wash., June 14, 1948. 6p. Typed.

948. Virginia State Library. "Finding list of books relating to printing, book industries, libraries and bibliography," comp. by Earl G. Swem. Virginia State Library bulletin, 5 (1912), 153-234.

Philosophy and Psychology

GENERAL

949. California, University, Library. A guide to the literature of aesthetics, by Charles M. Gayley. Berkeley: [State Print. Off.] 1890. 116p. (Univ. of California Library bulletin, no. 14)
   Drawn mainly from University of California Library collection, though locations not indicated.

950. Columbia University Library. A contribution to a bibliography of Henri Bergson. N. Y.: Columbia Univ. Press, 1913. 56p.
   90 books and articles by Bergson and 417 books and articles about him are listed; with a few exceptions, they may be found in Columbia University Library.

951. [Hoernlé, Reinhold F. A.] [Account of philosophical works presented to Harvard College Library by George H. Palmer]. Journal of philosophy, psychology and scientific methods, 17 (1920), 194-95.

952. Missouri, University, Library. The Thomas Moore Johnson collection, presented to the University of Missouri Library. Columbia: Univ. of Missouri, 1949. [77]p.

953. New York Public Library. "List of books in the New York Public Library relating to philosophy." New York Public Library bulletin, 12 (1908), 407-47, 464-516. Reprinted. 93p.

954. [New York University Library]. Hegel und die Hegelianer; ein bibliothek. Charlottenburg: Dr. Hellersberg Antiquariat & Verlag, [1927?] 39p.
   Lists 851 items, now in Washington Square Library, New York University.

955. Newberry Library. Thomas Taylor, The Platonist, 1758-1835; list of original works and translations, comp. by Ruth Balch. Chicago, 1917. 34p. (Special publications, no. 5)
   Indicates copies held by Newberry Library.

956. Southern California, University, School of Philosophy, Hoose Library of Philosophy. The Seeley Wintersmith Mudd Foundation special collection in the Hoose Library of Philosophy, School of Philosophy. [Los Angeles]: Univ. of Southern California, 1940. 39p.
   A collection of books mainly for philosophical research. Describes some of manuscripts, association books, and incunabula in collection.

957. U. S. Library of Congress. "Annual report on acquisitions; philosophy and religion." Library of Congress quarterly journal of acquisitions, 4 (Feb. 1947), 39-43; 5 (Feb. 1948), 45-52; 6 (Feb. 1949), 46-49.

958. U. S. Library of Congress, General Reference and Bibliography Division. "A list of philosophical periodicals published outside England and the U. S. A.," comp. by David Baumgardt. Wash., Mar. 1945. [50p.] Typed.

PSYCHOLOGY

959. Hardin, Floyd, comp. Child psychology; a bibliography of books in English. Denver, Colo.: Bibliographical Center for Research, 1938. 203 l. (Bibliographical Center for Research, Regional check list, no. 4)
   Locates copies in 20 Rocky Mountain region libraries.

960. National Research Council, Research Information Service. Union list of foreign

serials cited in Psychological index 1922, currently received in 114 libraries. Wash., 1925. 21 numb. l.

Shows locations for titles but does not indicate holdings.

961. New York Public Library. "Oneirocritica Americana," by Harry B. Weiss. New York Public Library bulletin, 48 (1944), 519-41, 642-53. Reprinted. 37p.

Based principally on collections of New York Public Library, American Antiquarian Society and Library of Congress; locations given.

OCCULT SCIENCES

962. Morgan, S. Rowland, comp. Index to psychic science; an introduction to systematized knowledge of psychical experience. Swarthmore, Penn., 1950. 117p.

Index to John William Graham collection of psychic science literature, Swarthmore College.

963. New York Public Library. "A calendar of cases of witchcraft in Scotland, 1510-1727," comp. by George Fraser Black. New York Public Library bulletin, 41 (1937), 811-47, 917-36; 42 (1938), 34-74. Reprinted. 102p.

964. New York Public Library. "List of works in the New York Public Library relating to witchcraft in Europe," comp. by George Fraser Black. New York Public Library bulletin, 15 (1911), 727-55. Reprinted. 31p.

965. New York Public Library. "List of works in the New York Public Library relating to witchcraft in the United States," comp. by George Fraser Black. New York Public Library bulletin, 12 (1908), 658-75. Reprinted. 18p.

966. New York Public Library. "List of works relating to Druids and Druidism," comp. by George Fraser Black. New York Public Library bulletin, 24 (1920), 11-24. Reprinted. 16p.

967. New York Public Library. "A list of works relating to lycanthropy [superstition of the Werewolf]," comp. by George Fraser Black. New York Public Library bulletin, 23 (1919), 811-15. Reprinted, 1920. 7p.

Locates copies in New York Public Library only, but list not limited to Library's holdings.

968. Winsor, Justin. The literature of witchcraft in New England. Worcester, Mass.: C. Hamilton, 1898. 25p. (Reprinted from American Antiquarian Society proceedings, n. s. 10 (1895), 351-73)

Locates copies of each title, when known.

ETHICS (Theoretical and Applied)

969. California, University, Library. Bibliographical references in ethology, by Thomas P. Bailey. Berkeley: University Press, 1899. 25p. (Univ. of California Library bulletin, no 13)

University of California holdings indicated.

970. Newberry Library. A check list of courtesy books in the Newberry Library, comp. by Virgil B. Heltzel. Chicago: The Library, 1942. 161p.

Lists 1,471 works composed or published before 1775.

971. U. S. Library of Congress, Division of Bibliography. Lotteries in the United States and foreign countries, comp. by Anne L. Baden. [Wash.] 1942. 16p. (Supplementary to the mimeographed list of June 6, 1934.)

PEACE AND WAR ETHICS

972. Brinton, Ellen Starr. "The Swarthmore College peace collection - a memorial to Jane Addams." American archivist, 10 (1947), 35-39.

Description of an extensive collection of printed and manuscript materials relating to peace.

973. Carnegie Endowment for International Peace Library. Education for world peace...; select list of books, pamphlets, and periodical articles, comp. by Mary Alice Matthews. [Wash., 1936] 37p.

Collection now a part of George Washington University Library.

974. Carnegie Endowment for International Peace Library. Peace and the peace movement; select list of references. Wash. [1924] 28 numb. l.

Collection now a part of George Washington University Library.

975. Carnegie Endowment for International Peace Library. Peace forces of today; select references to recent books and articles, comp. by Mary Alice Matthews. [Wash., 1934] 35p.

Collection now a part of George Washington University Library.

976. Carnegie Endowment for International Peace. Publications...with a list of depository libraries and institutions. Wash. [1920] 48p.

977. New York Public Library. "Plans for the organization of international peace, 1306-1789," comp. by Rudolf Hirsch. New York Public Library bulletin, 47 (1943), 569-80. Reprinted with revisions. 1943. 14p.

Lists 36 peace proposals, before 1789.

978. Swarthmore College Library. Guide to the Swarthmore College peace collection - a memorial to Jane Addams, comp. by Ellen Starr Brinton and others. Swarthmore, Penn.: The College, 1947. 72p.

979. Swarthmore College Library. Swarthmore college peace collection, a memorial to Jane Addams. Swarthmore, Penn., 1949. 16p. (Swarthmore College bulletin, v. 46, no. 3, Peace collection bulletin, no. 2)

Largely a check list of current peace periodicals being received in collection.

MARRIAGE AND DIVORCE

980. New York Public Library. "List of works in the New York Public Library relating to marriage and divorce." New York Public Library bulletin, 9 (1905), 466-513. Reprinted. 48p.

981. U. S. Library of Congress, Division of Bibliography. List of references...relating to divorces. Wash.: Govt. Print. Off., 1915. 110p.

982. U. S. Library of Congress, Division of Bibliography. Marriage and divorce, with special reference to legal aspects: a selected bibliography, comp. by Helen F. Conover. [Wash.] 1940. 55p.

Religion

GENERAL

983. Abbot, Ezra. "Literature of the doctrine of a future life." In: Alger, W. R. Critical history of the doctrine of a future life. Boston, 1880, p. 771-1008.

Locates copies in 9 American libraries.

984. Andover Theological Seminary Library. Catalogue of the library, by Oliver A. Taylor. Andover, 1838. 531p. Supplement, 1849. [7] p.

985. Boston Public Library. Catalogue of selected editions of the Book of common prayer both English and American, together with illuminated missals in manuscript, early printed Books of hours and other books of devotion, in the possession of private collectors in Boston or owned by the Boston Public or Harvard College Libraries, on exhibition at the Boston Public Library from August 1906 until February 1907. Boston: The Trustees of the Public Library, 1907. 62p.

Locations given for copies in Boston Public Library, Harvard College Libraries, and two private collections.

986. California State Library, Sutro Branch. Bibliography of books and pamphlets on the Protestant Reformation. San Francisco: The Library, 1940. 152 numb. l. (Its: Occasional papers. Bibliographical series, no. 1)

A catalog of books on the Protestant Reformation in the Sutro Branch.

987. California, University, Library. Catalogue of the theological library presented by Andrew S. Hallidie. Berkeley, 1886. 50p. (Its: Library bulletin, 7)

Lists about 550 titles of general theology.

988. Castañeda, Carlos E. "Sources for Spanish American church history." Catholic library world, 10 (1938), 99-102.

Description of Génaro Garcia collection of books and manuscripts in University of Texas Library.

989. Copinger, Walter Arthur, ed. Hand list of what is believed to be the largest collection in the world of editions of "The Imitation" of Thomas à Kempis. Consisting of a considerable number of mss., and over 1500 printed editions in fifty different languages, together with more than 120 works in connection with this work and its authorship. [Manchester? England], Privately printed, 1908. 98p.

Collection acquired by Harvard College Library in 1922.

990. Eames, Wilberforce. "Early New England catechisms; a bibliographical account of some catechisms published before the year 1800." American Antiquarian Society proceedings, n. s. 12 (1897), 76-182. Reprinted, 1898. 111p.

With few exceptions titles listed were in Lenox Library, now part of New York Public Library.

991. General Theological Library. Catalogue of the General Theological Library, Boston, Massachusetts; a dictionary catalogue of religion, theology, sociology and allied literature. Boston: Fort Hill Press [c1913] 313p.

Dictionary form, listing only books in English language.

992. Harvard University Library. Catalogue of a collection of works on ritualism and doctrinal theology, presented by John Harvey Treat, by William Coolidge Lane. Cambridge:

993 RELIGION

Harvard University Library, 1889. 29p. (Harvard University Library bibliographical contributions, no. 36.)

993. Jones, Matt B. "Notes for a bibliography of Michael Wigglesworth's 'Day of doom' and 'Meat out of the eater.'" American Antiquarian Society proceedings, n. s. 39 (1929), 77-84.

Notes on various editions, with locations of copies.

994. Matthews, C. D. "Reliques of the Rev. Dr. John G. Lansing." Moslem world, 30 (1940), 269-79.

Lists many items from collection in Denver Public Library.

995. Mead, Herman Ralph. A bibliography of George Berkeley, Bishop of Cloyne. Berkeley: Univ. of California Press, 1910. 46p. (Univ. of California Library bulletin, no. 17)

University of California's holdings on Bishop Berkeley (1685-1753) indicated.

996. New York Public Library. "Check list of works in the New York Public Library relating to the churches of Brooklyn." New York Public Library bulletin, 6 (1902), 50-52.

997. New York Public Library. "Check list of works relating to the churches and to the ecclesiastical history of the City of New York." New York Public Library bulletin, 5 (1901), 196-210.

998. New York Public Library. "Hannah More's cheap repository tracts in America," by Harry B. Weiss. New York Public Library bulletin, 50 (1946), 539-49, 634-41. Reprinted. 21p.

Locates copies of tracts published in America, 1797-1826, in 15 libraries.

999. New York Public Library. "List of periodicals in the New York Public Library, General Theological Seminary, and Union Theological Seminary relating to religion, theology, and church history." New York Public Library bulletin 9 (1905), 9-31, 50-72.

1000. Princeton Theological Seminary Library. Catalogue of the library of Princeton Theological Seminary. Part I. Religious literature. Princeton, N. J.: C. S. Robinson & Co., 1886. 453p.

1001. Richardson, Ernest Cushing, comp. A list of religious periodicals currently taken by Union, Princeton, Yale and Hartford Theological Seminaries. Wash., 1934. 31p.

Lists titles but not holdings of about 1,500 journals.

1002. Rockwell, William Walker. "Theological libraries in the United States." Religion in life, 13 (1944), 545-55.

General survey of resources, arranged by subjects and types of material.

1003. St. Clement's Church. Yarnall Library of Theology, comp. by Jos. Cullen Ayer. Philadelphia, 1933. 334p.

Catalog of over 9,000 volumes covering various fields of theology and related subjects. Library now deposited in Divinity School of Protestant Episcopal Church, Philadelphia.

1004. St. John, Wallace. The contest for liberty of conscience in England. Chicago: Univ. of Chicago Press, 1900. 153p.

Bibliography (p. 147-53) locates copies in Newberry Library, British Museum, and occasionally other libraries.

1005. Trinity College Library. A list of books from the library of the late Rev. Samuel Hart...added to the library of Trinity College. Hartford, Conn., 1917. 22p. (Trinity College bulletin, n. s. v. 14, no. 3)

Chiefly theology and classics.

1006. Trinity College Library. A list of pamphlets in the Trinity College library relating to the Bangorian controversy. Hartford, Conn., 1913. 23p. (Trinity College bulletin, n. s. v. 10, no. 3)

Controversy on relation of church and state. Pamphlets printed in London, 1716-24.

1007. Tuttle, Julius Herbert. "Writings of Rev. John Cotton." In: Bibliographical essays; a tribute to Wilberforce Eames. [Cambridge, 1924], p. 363-80.

Lists 77 titles, 1630-63, with locations.

1008. Union Theological Seminary Library (Richmond). Catalogue of the library belonging to the Union Theological Seminary in Prince Edward, Va. Richmond: J. Macfarlan, 1833. 107p.

Library now in Richmond, Virginia.

1009. U. S. Library of Congress, Division of Bibliography. Select list of references on a weekly rest day and Sunday legislation. Wash., Nov. 6, 1912. 30p.

1010. Vail, Robert W. G. "A check list of New England sermons." American Antiquarian Society proceedings, n. s. 45 (1935), 233-66. Preprinted, 1936. 36p.
Chronological list by states, 1634-1884, with locations in 30 public and private collections.

1011. Winship, George P. "Imitatio Christi." Harvard Library notes, 1 (1922), 187-90.
Account of Harvard College Library holdings, including Copinger collection.

1012. Yale University Library. Catalogue of an exhibition illustrating some phases of popular religious education before 1800, arranged by May Humphreys. [New Haven, 1914] 10p.

1013. Zion Research Library. Catalogue of the Zion Research Library, Brookline, Mass. [Boston: T. O. Metcalf Co., 1930] 168p.
Frequent supplements issued, 1930-37.

BIBLE

1014. American Antiquarian Society Library. "The Holy Bible in verse," by Charles L. Nichols. American Antiquarian Society proceedings, n. s. 36 (1926), 71-82. Reprinted.
Lists holdings of American Antiquarian Society and other libraries.

1015. American Bible Society Library. Catalogue of books contained in the library of the American Bible Society, embracing editions of the Holy Scriptures in various languages and other Biblical and miscellaneous works. N. Y.: American Bible Society's Press, 1863. 168p.
Appendix. 1870. [N. Y.? 1870] 36p. Contains books added to the Library since 1863.

1016. Baker University Library. The William Alfred Quayle collection of Bibles at Baker University, Baldwin City, Kansas, by Harriet Osborne. [Baldwin City] 1930. 12p.
Bequeathed to Baker University by the collector, Bishop Quayle.

1017. Bitzer, David R. "Materials available in the library of Union Theological Seminary, Richmond, Virginia, for the study of the text and canon of the New Testament." 1933. 374p. Dissertation, unpublished.

1018. Boston Public Library. "English Bibles in the library." More books, 11 (1936), 425-46; 12 (1937), 5-22, 185-212.
Description of most important versions of English Bible with special attention to Bibles owned by Boston Public Library.

1019. Chicago, University, Library. Catalogue of the Col. Grant Bible collection. [n. p., 19-] [382]p.
Contents: English folio Bibles 1535-1835 (191 items); miniature editions of the English Bible, 17 and 18 century, with those in Greek and Latin printed in Britain (106 items).

1020. Chicago, University, Dept. of New Testament and Early Christian Literature. The Rockefeller McCormick New Testament. Chicago: Univ. of Chicago Press [1932] 3v.
Facsimile edition.

1021. Clark, Kenneth W. A descriptive catalogue of Greek New Testament manuscripts in America. Chicago: Univ. of Chicago Press, [1937] 418p., 72 plates.
Locates manuscripts in 66 public and private libraries. Arranged by owners.

1022. Clark, Kenneth W. "Greek New Testament manuscripts in Duke University Library." Library notes, a bulletin issued for the Friends of Duke University Library, no. 16 (June 1946), 1-5.
Description of 7 manuscripts written from 11th century to about 1650.

1023. Cornell University Library. Catalogue of the Barnes Reference Library for Biblical study, presented by Alfred Cutler Barnes for the use of the Cornell University Christian Association; including all accessions to December 31, 1897. Ithaca, N. Y.: [Andrus & Church] 1898. 19p.

1024. Faye, Christopher Urdahl. A Bible exhibit at the University of Illinois Library, Urbana, 1934. 7p.
Lists 31 rare Bibles used in exhibit from University of Illinois Library.

1025. [General Theological Seminary]. "The Copinger collection. Library journal, 19 (1894), 17-18.
   Describes Copinger collection of Latin Bibles presented to the General Theological Seminary, New York City.

1026. [General Theological Seminary]. The gospel manuscripts of the General Theological Seminary, by Charles C. Edmunds and William H. P. Hatch. Cambridge: Harvard Univ. Press, 1918. 68p.
   Contents: The Hoffman ms.; Codex 2346; The Benton ms.

1027. Harrsen, Meta Philippine. The Nekcsei-Lipócz Bible, a fourteenth century manuscript from Hungary in the Library of Congress, Ms. Pre-accession 1; a study. Wash.: Library of Congress, 1949. 99p.

1028. Jewish Theological Seminary of America Library. Biblical manuscripts and books in the library of the Jewish Theological Seminary (mostly from the Sulzberger collection) N. Y., 1913. 11p.

1029. Michigan, University, Library. The minor prophets in the Freer collection and the Berlin fragment of Genesis, by Henry A. Sanders and Carl Schmidt. N. Y.: Macmillan, 1927. 436p. (University of Michigan studies, humanistic series, no. 21)
   Describes Washington manuscript of the Minor Prophets (in the Freer collection of the Smithsonian Institution) and the Berlin Fragment of Genesis now in Berlin State Library. Photostats are in Michigan University Library.

1030. Michigan, University, Library. The New Testament manuscripts in the Freer collection. N. Y.: Macmillan, 1918. 323p. (University of Michigan studies, humanistic series, v. 9)
   Freer collection is in Smithsonian Institution, Washington.

1031. Michigan, University, Library. The Old Testament manuscripts in the Freer collection. N. Y.: Macmillan, 1917. 357p. (University of Michigan studies, humanistic series, v. 8)
   Freer collection is in Smithsonian Institution, Washington.

1032. Michigan, University, William L. Clements Library. Some American Bibles. Ann Arbor: Univ. of Michigan, 1949. [10]p.
   Facsimiles of 8 early and rare Bibles in Clements Library.

1033. New York Public Library. "An exhibition of Bibles of ancient and moden times in various languages," by Victor Hugo Paltsits. New York Public Library bulletin, 27 (1923), 3-18. Reprinted. 18p.
   List with descriptions.

1034. New York Public Library. "The Pitcairn Bible." New York Public Library bulletin, 28 (1924), 443-52, 682-83. Reprinted. 14p.
   Bible, belonging to a Bounty mutineer, used on Pitcairn Island.

1035. Newberry Library. The history of the transmission of the English Bible; an exhibition in commemoration of the four-hundredth anniversary of the Coverdale Bible, the first printed English Bible, 1535-1935. Chicago: The Library [1935] 15p.

1036. Norlie, Olaf Morgan. The Norlie collection of English Bibles. Northfield, Minn.: Saint Olaf College, 1944. 129 numb. 1.
   "Report of...[the author's] Bible collection, now housed in the Saint Olaf College library."

1037. O'Callaghan, Edmund Bailey. A list of editions of the Holy Scriptures, and parts thereof, printed in America previous to 1860; with introduction and bibliographical notes. Albany: Munsell & Rowland, 1861. 415p.
   Locates copies in several private collections, especially Lenox Library. Now in New York Public Library.

1038. Parsons, Wilfrid. "First American editions of Catholic Bibles." U. S. Catholic Historical Society, Historical records and studies, 27 (1927), 89-98.
   A complete list of first editions of Bible in Catholic translations published in the United States, 1790-1860. Copies of all but one are in Riggs Library of Georgetown University.

1039. Pennsylvania, University, Library. A catalogue of the T. Edward Ross collection of Bibles presented to the University of Pennsylvania Library in memory of Lucien Bonaparte

Carpenter. Philadelphia: Univ. of Penn. Library, 1947. 95p.

1040. Pierpont Morgan Library. The Bible: manuscript and printed Bibles from the fourth to the nineteenth century: illustrated catalogue of an exhibition, December 1, 1947, to April 30, 1948. N. Y.: The Library, 1947. 48p., 16 plates.
Lists and describes 183 items.

1041. Prime, George Wendell. Fifteenth century Bibles. A study in bibliography. N. Y.: Anson Randolph & Co., 1888. 95p.
Gives locations of Bibles in United States and abroad when known.

1042. Rumball-Petre, Edwin A. R. America's first Bibles, with a census of 555 extant Bibles. Portland, Maine: Southworth-Anthoensen Press, 1940. 184p.
Locations shown for Christopher Saur, Robert Aitken, and Mathew Carey Bibles in institutional and private collections.

1043. U. S. Library of Congress. A catalog of Bible entries represented by Library of Congress printed cards issued to July 31, 1942. Ann Arbor: Edwards Bros., 1943. 249p.

1044. Wright, John. Early Bibles of America; being a descriptive account of Bibles published in the United States, Mexico, and Canada. 3rd ed., rev. & enl. N. Y.: T. Whittaker, 1894. 483p.
Appendices list owners of Eliot, Saur, and Aitken Bibles, so far as known.

1045. Wright, John. Historic Bibles in America. N. Y.: Thomas Whittaker, [c.1905]. 222p.
Indicates institutional and individual owners of Bibles described.

1046. Yale University Library. Catalogue of an exhibition of books, portraits, and facsimiles illustrating the history of the English translation of the Bible, arr. by Anna M. Monrad. [New Haven, 1911] 14p. (Reprinted from Librarian's report, 1910-11)

HYMNOLOGY

1047. Foote, Henry Wilder. Three centuries of American hymnody. Cambridge: Harvard Univ. Press, 1940. 418p.
Locates copies of some of hymnbooks in footnotes.

1048. Metcalf, Frank J[ohnson] American psalmody; or, titles of books, containing tunes printed in America from 1721 to 1820. N. Y.: C. F. Heartman, 1917. 54p. (Heartman's historical series, no. 27)
Locates copies in about two dozen libraries.

1049. Metcalf, Frank J. "Early hymn books printed in Washington, D. C." American collector, 5 (1928), 144-50.
Covers period from 1818 to 1830. Notes locations of known copies.

1050. Warrington, James. "A bibliography of church music books issued in Pennsylvania." Pennsylvania Germania, n. s. 1 (1912), 170-77, 262-68.
Locates copies when known.

MISSIONS

1051. Ackermann, Gertrude W. "Home missionary records." Minnesota history, 16 (1935), 313-18.
Description of American Home Missionary Society archives deposited in Chicago Theological Seminary Library.

1052. Ackermann, Gertrude W. "Some sources for Northwest history; home missionary records." Minnesota history, 16 (1935), 313-18.
Describes Minnesota material in archives of American Home Missionary Society at Chicago Theological Seminary. Filmslides in Minnesota Historical Society.

1053. Fisk University Library. American Missionary Association archives in Fisk University Library, by Arna Bontemps. Nashville, 1947. [12]p.
Description of letters and other papers for 1839-79, with several facsimiles.

1054. Missionary Research Library. Recommended titles on missions and related subjects, comp. by Hollis W. Hering. N. Y.: Committee of Reference and Counsel, 1925. 29p.

Based on collections in Missionary Research Library, New York City.

1055. Yale University Divinity School Day Missions Library. Catalogue of the Foreign Mission Library of the Divinity School of Yale University, comp. by George E. Day. New Haven: Tuttle, Morehouse and Taylor Press, 1895-1902. 6v. in 1.

CHRISTIAN CHURCHES AND SECTS

Baptist

1056. American Baptist Historical Society Library. Catalogue of the books and manuscripts in the library of the American Baptist Historical Society, June 1872 - [August, 1874]. [Philadelphia, 1872-74] 108, 40p.

Consists of the Catalogue published in 1872 with "Addenda."

1057. Colgate University. The Samuel Colgate Baptist historical collection, by Edward C. Starr. Hamilton, N. Y.: Colgate Univ., 1946. 11p.

Description of collection.

1058. Historical Records Survey - Florida. Inventory of the church archives of Florida: Baptist bodies. Jacksonville, Florida: Historical Records Survey, 1939-40. 11v.

Covers following associations: Black Creek, Lake County, Northeast Florida, Northwest Coast, Okaloosa, Orange Blossom, Palm Lake, Pinellas County, Seminole, Southwest, and Florida State Association of Old Line Baptist composed of Missionary Baptist Churches.

1059. Historical Records Survey - Georgia. Inventory of the church and synagogue archives of Georgia. Atlanta: Georgia Historical Records Survey, 1941. 2v.

Covers Atlanta Association of Baptist Churches and Fairburn Missionary Baptist Association.

1060. Historical Records Survey - Michigan. Calendar of the Baptist collection of Kalamazoo College, Kalamazoo, Michigan. Detroit: Michigan Historical Records Survey, 1940. 194p.

1061. Historical Records Survey - Missouri. Information concerning the manuscript depository collection of the Missouri Baptist Historical Society, Liberty, Missouri. St. Louis, 1941. 4p.

Reprinted (with additions) from "Guide to depositories of manuscript collections in the United States: Missouri."

1062. Historical Records Survey - Missouri. Inventory of the church archives of Missouri: Baptist bodies, Tebo Baptist Association. St. Louis: Missouri Hist. Records Survey, 1940. 55 numb. 1.

1063. Historical Records Survey - North Carolina. Inventory of the church archives of North Carolina; Southern Baptist Convention. Raleigh: N. C. Historical Records Survey, 1940-42. 7v.

Covers following associations: Allegany, Brunswick, Central, Flat River, Raleigh, Stanley, and Yancey.

1064. Historical Records Survey - New Jersey. Inventory of the church archives of New Jersey: Baptist bodies. Newark: Historical Records Survey, 1938. 289 numb. l.

-----. Seventh Day Baptist supplement. Newark: Historical Records Survey, 1939. 161 numb. l.

1065. Historical Records Survey - Rhode Island. Inventory of the church archives of Rhode Island: Baptist. Providence: Historical Records Survey, 1941. 231p.

1066. Historical Records Survey - Tennessee. Inventory of the church archives of Tennessee: Tennessee Baptist Convention. Nashville: Tennessee Historical Records Survey, 1939-42. 2v.

Covers Nashville and Ocoee Baptist Associations.

1067. Historical Records Survey - Virginia. Guide to the manuscript collections of the Virginia Baptist Historical Society. Supplement no. 1 - Index to obituary notices in the Religious herald, Richmond, Virginia, 1828-1938. Richmond, Va., Dec. 1940. 386p.

A volume [no. 3] of its Inventory of the Church archives of Virginia.

1068. Historical Records Survey - Virginia. Inventory of the church archives of Virginia:

Dover Baptist Association. Richmond: Virginia Historical Records Survey, 1939. 56 numb. l.

1069. Historical Records Survey - Virginia. Inventory of the church archives of Virginia: Negro Baptist Churches in Richmond. Richmond: Historical Records Survey of Virginia, 1940. 59 numb. l.

1070. Starr, Edward C. A Baptist bibliography; being a register of printed material by and about Baptists; including works written against the Baptists. Philadelphia: Judson Press, 1947. 240p.

Alphabetical by authors. Section A, only, included. Locations shown in 136 libraries.

1071. Starr, Edward C. "The Samuel Colgate Baptist historical collection." New York history, 19 (1938), 263-68. Reprinted.

Describes briefly collection of manuscripts and books at Colgate University; about 13,000 volumes relating to church history.

1072. Virginia Baptist Historical Society. "Bibliography of original Baptist Church records in the Virginia Baptist Historical Society, University of Richmond," comp. by Lester J. Cappon. University of Virginia Library annual report on historical collections, no. 7 (1936-37), 11-35.

Arranged by associations, counties and churches.

Christian Science

1073. Historical Records Survey - Arkansas. Inventory of the church archives of Arkansas: Church of Christ Scientist. Little Rock: Arkansas Historical Records Survey, 1941. 35 numb. l.

1074. Richart, Genevieve. "A list of authorized Christian Science literature in the Library of Congress." Wash., 1923. 70 numb. l. Typed.

Congregational

1075. Dexter, Henry M. Congregationalism of the last three hundred years, as seen in its literature. N. Y.: Harper, 1880. 716, 326p.

Appendix, p. 1-308: "Collections toward a bibliography of Congregationalism" locates copies in 33 American libraries. Author's own collection now in Yale University.

1076. Historical Records Survey - New Jersey. Inventory of the church archives of New Jersey: Congregational Christian churches. Newark: Historical Records Survey, 1941. 101 numb. l.

1077. Michigan, University, William L. Clements Library. Congregationalism in America, its beginnings as illustrated by an exhibition of its foundational books in the William L. Clements Library. Ann Arbor, 1947. 23p. (Bulletin, no. 48)

47 books selected from Library's collection of books on Congregationalism in New England.

1078. Yale University Library. Catalogue of an exhibition held in the Day Missions Library illustrating Congregationalism before 1800, comp. by Anna M. Monrad. [New Haven: Yale Univ. Press] 1915. 28p.

Disciples (Christian)

1079. Historical Records Survey - Wisconsin. Inventory of the church archives of Wisconsin: Disciples of Christ. Madison: Wisconsin Historical Records Survey, 1942. 83 numb. p.

Eastern Orthodox

1080. Basanoff, V. "Archives of the Russian church in Alaska in the Library of Congress." Pacific historical review, 2 (1933), 72-84.

Covers from 1762 to modern times.

1081. Historical Records Survey - New York (City) Inventory of the church archives in New York City: Eastern Orthodox Churches and the Armenian Apostolic Church in America. N. Y., 1940. 178 numb. l.

Evangelical

1082. Historical Records Survey - Michigan. Inventory of the church archives of Michigan: Evangelical and Reformed Church. Detroit: Michigan Historical Records Survey, 1941. 45 numb. l.

1083. Historical Records Survey - Michigan. Inventory of the church archives of Michigan: Evangelical Church, Michigan Conference.

Detroit: Michigan Historical Records Survey, 1941. 58 numb. l.

1084. Historical Records Survey - New Jersey. Inventory of the church archives of New Jersey: Evangelical Church. Newark: Historical Records Survey, 1941. 37 numb. l.

Huguenots

1085. Huguenot Society of America Library. Catalogue or bibliography of the library of the Huguenot Society of America, comp. by Julia P. M. Morand. N. Y., 1920. 351p. First edition, N. Y., 1890. 107p.

Lutheran

1086. Historical Records Survey - Connecticut. Inventory of the church archives of Connecticut: Lutheran. New Haven: Connecticut Historical Records Survey, 1941. 188p.

1087. Historical Records Survey - Delaware. Inventory of the church archives of Delaware: preprint of sections 22. Lutheran Church, and 29. Protestant Episcopal Church. Wilmington, Del., 1938. 43p.

1088. Historical Records Survey - New York (City). Inventory of the church archives in New York City: Lutheran Church. N. Y.: Historical Records Survey, 1940. 152 numb. l.

1089. Lutheran Historical Society Library. Catalogue of the Lutheran Historical Society's collection of books, pamphlets, manuscripts, photographs, etc., deposited in the Theological Seminary at Gettysburg, Pa. Philadelphia: The Society, 1890. 66p.

Consists of books, etc., by and about Lutherans and Lutheran Church in America.

1090. Wentz, A. R. "Collections of the Lutheran History Society." Pennsylvania history, 3 (1936), 66-69.

Brief description of materials on history of Lutheran Church, located in Library of Lutheran Historical Society at Theological Seminary, Gettysburg.

Mennonite

1091. Bender, Harold S. Two centuries of American Mennonite literature; a bibliography of Mennonitica Americana, 1727-1928. Goshen, Ind.: Mennonite Hist. Society, Goshen College, 1929. 181p.

Originally appeared in Mennonite quarterly review, 1927-28. Locates copies in 27 libraries.

1092. Friedmann, Robert. "The Mennonite historical library of Goshen College." American-German review, 9 (Dec. 1942), 12-14.

Includes a description of the library's manuscript materials.

1093. Mennonite Historical Library. Catalogue of the Mennonite Historical Library in Scottdale, Pennsylvania, comp. by John Horsch. Scottdale: Mennonite Publishing House, 1929. 88p.

Methodist

1094. [Cavender, Curtis H.] Catalogue of works in refutation of Methodism, from its origin in 1729, to the present time, comp. by H. C. Decanver [pseud.] 2d ed. N. Y., 1868. 55p.

Copies located in 4 libraries.

1095. Historical Records Survey - Illinois. Calendar of the Ezekiel Cooper collection of early American Methodist manuscripts, 1875-1839. Garrett Biblical Institute, Evanston, Illinois. Chicago, 1941. 97 numb. l.

1096. Historical Records Survey - Michigan. Inventory of the church archives of Michigan; African Methodist Episcopal Church, Michigan Conference. Detroit: Mich. Hist. Records Survey, 1940. 24 numb. l.

1097. Historical Records Survey - New York (City). Inventory of the church archives of New York City: The Methodist Church. N. Y.: Historical Records Survey, 1940. 216 numb. l.

1098. Trinity College Library. A list of the early editions and reprints of the General Convention journals, 1785-1814, in the library of Trinity College. [Hartford, Conn.] 1908. 8p. (Trinity College bulletin, n. s., v. 5, no. 2)

Moravian

1099. Historical Records Survey - North Carolina. Guide to the manuscripts in the archives of the Moravian Church in America, Southern Province, Winston-Salem, North Carolina. Raleigh, N. C.: N. C. Historical Records Survey, 1942. 136 numb. 1.

1100. Historical Records Survey - Wisconsin. Inventory of the church archives of Wisconsin: Moravian Church. Madison: Historical Records Survey, 1938. 57 numb. 1.

1101. Hulbert, Archer Butler. "The Moravian records." Ohio archaeological and historical quarterly, 18 (1909), 199-226.
  Describes Moravian libraries at Bethlehem, Pennsylvania.

Mormon

1102. New York Public Library. "List of works in the New York Public Library relating to the Mormons." New York Public Library bulletin, 13 (1909), 183-239. Reprinted. 57p.

Presbyterian and Reformed

1103. Historical Foundation of the Presbyterian and Reformed Churches. A great collection of Presbyterian and Reformed literature. Montreat, N. C.: The Foundation, 1944. 6p.
  Description of library of printed and manuscript materials possessed by Foundation.

1104. Historical Foundation of the Presbyterian and Reformed Churches. Survey of records and minutes in the Historical Foundation, comp. by Thomas H. Spence. Montreat, N. C.: Historical Foundation Publications, 1943. 46p.
  List of records and dates covered, geographically arranged.

1105. Historical Records Survey - Illinois. Inventory of the church archives of Illinois. Chicago: Illinois Historical Records Survey, 1941-42. 3v.
  Covers Presbytery of Cairo, Presbytery of Springfield, and Cumberland Presbyterian Church.

1106. Historical Records Survey - Michigan. Inventory of the church archives of Michigan: Presbyterian Church in the U. S. A. Detroit: Michigan Hist. Records Survey, 1940-41. 2v.
  Covers Presbyteries of Detroit and Flint.

1107. Historical Records Survey - New Jersey. Inventory of the church archives of New Jersey: Christian Reformed. Newark: Historical Records Survey, 1941. 39p.

1108. Historical Records Survey - New Jersey. Inventory of the church archives of New Jersey: Presbyterians. Presbyterian church in the U. S. A., United Presbyterian church of North America. Newark: Historical Records Survey, 1940. 562p.

1109. Historical Records Survey - New York (City) Inventory of the church archives of New York City: Presbyterian Church in the United States of America. N. Y.: Hist. Records Survey, 1940. 160 numb. 1.

1110. Historical Records Survey - New York (City) Inventory of the church archives of New York City: Reformed Church in America. N. Y.: Hist. Records Survey, 1939. 95 numb. 1.

1111. Historical Records Survey - West Virginia. Inventory of the church archives of West Virginia: The Presbyterian churches. Charleston: West Virginia Historical Records Survey, 1941. 301p.

1112. Holland Society of New York. Collections. N. Y., 1891-1915. 4v.
  Records of some Reformed Dutch churches in New York and New Jersey.

1113. Holland Society of New York. "Inventory and digest of early church records in the library." Holland Society of New York yearbook, (1912), 1-52.
  Includes 74 manuscript records of Dutch Reformed churches in America.

1114. Michigan, University, William L. Clements Library. The Presbyterian Church in America during the seventeenth and eighteenth centuries; an exhibition of books. Ann Arbor: Clements Library, 1947. 24p. (Bulletin, no. 49)
  26 books, 1613-1811, from Library's collection of history of Presbyterian Church in the United States.

1115. Presbyterian Historical Society Library. Catalogue of books in the library of the Presbyterian Historical Society. Philadelphia: J. B. Rodgers, 1865. 107p.

1116. Presbyterian Historical Society Library. Short title list of books printed in America before 1800, comp. by Thos. C. Pears, Jr. 1937. 141 l.
    Chronological list, 1662-1779, of theological literature in Society's library.

1117. Turner, Joseph Brown. "A catalogue of manuscript records in the possession of the Presbyterian Historical Society." Presbyterian Historical Society journal, 8 (March 1915), 13-22.

Protestant Episcopal

1118. Benton, Josiah Henry. The Book of common prayer and books connected with its origin and growth; catalogue of the collection of Josiah Henry Benton. 2d ed. prepared by William Muss-Arnolt. Boston: Privately printed, 1914. 142p.
    Collection now owned by Boston Public Library.

1119. Cameron, K. W. "Collections of Episcopal Church manuscripts." Protestant Episcopal church historical magazine, 10 (Dec. 1941), 402-07.
    Lists institutions and individuals having extensive collections of manuscripts.

1120. Historical Records Survey - Alabama. Inventory of the church archives of Alabama: Protestant Episcopal Church. Birmingham: Alabama Historical Records Survey, 1939. 106 numb. l.

1121. Historical Records Survey - Connecticut. Inventory of the church archives of Connecticut: Protestant Episcopal. New Haven: Connecticut Historical Records Survey, 1940. 309p.

1122. Historical Records Survey - District of Columbia. Inventory of church archives in the District of Columbia. Wash.: D. of C. Historical Records Survey, 1940. 2v.
    Volume 1, Protestant Episcopal Church, Diocese of Washington; v. 2, Washington Cathedral.

1123. Historical Records Survey - Maryland. Inventory of the church archives of Maryland: Protestant Episcopal Church, Diocese of Maryland. Baltimore: Md. Hist. Records Survey, 1940. 310p.

1124. Historical Records Survey - Massachusetts. A description of the manuscript collections in the Massachusetts Diocesan Library. Boston: Historical Records Survey, 1939. 81 numb. l.

1125. Historical Records Survey - Michigan. Inventory of the church archives of Michigan: Protestant Episcopal Church. Detroit: Mich. Hist. Records Survey, 1940. 3v.
    Covers Dioceses of Michigan, Northern Michigan, and Western Michigan.

1126. Historical Records Survey - Mississippi. Inventory of the church archives of Mississippi: Protestant Episcopal Church, Diocese of Mississippi. Jackson: Mississippi Historical Records Survey, 1940. 146 numb. l.

1127. Historical Records Survey - Nevada. Inventory of the church archives of Nevada. Protestant Episcopal Church. Reno: Nevada Historical Records Survey, 1941. 69 numb. l.

1128. Historical Records Survey - New Jersey. Inventory of the church archives of New Jersey: Protestant Episcopal, Diocese of New Jersey. Diocese of Newark. Newark: Historical Records Survey, 1940. 434p.

1129. Historical Records Survey - New York (City) Inventory of the church archives of New York City: Protestant Episcopal Church. N. Y.: N. Y. C. Historical Records Survey, 1940. 2v.
    Covers Dioceses of Long Island and New York.

1130. Historical Records Survey - N. Y. (State) Inventory of the church archives of New York State; exclusive of New York City: Protestant Episcopal Church. Albany: Historical Records Survey, 1939-41. 2v.
    Covers Dioceses of Western New York and Rochester.

1131. Historical Records Survey - Vermont. Inventory of the church archives of Vermont: Protestant Episcopal, Diocese of Vermont. Montpelier: Vt. Hist. Records Survey, 1940. 253p.

1132. Historical Records Survey - West Virginia. Inventory of the church archives of West Virginia: The Protestant Episcopal

Church. Wheeling: Diocese of West Virginia, 1939. 119p.

1133. Historical Records Survey - Wisconsin. Inventory of the church archives of Wisconsin: Protestant Episcopal Church. Madison: Wisconsin Hist. Records Survey, 1942. 2v.

Covers Dioceses of Eau Clair and Fond du Lac.

1134. Mampoteng, Charles. "The library and American church history." Historical magazine of the Protestant Episcopal Church, 5 (1936), 225-37.

Describes archival material bearing upon American church history held by General Theological Seminary, New York; also lists Episcopal Church periodicals available in library.

1135. New-York Historical Society. 250th anniversary of the Parish of Trinity Church in the City of New York. Catalogue of commemorative exhibition of historical treasures from the collections of the Parish of Trinity Church and of the New York Historical Society. N. Y.: The Society, 1947. 48p.

Includes views, manuscripts, books, pamphlets and broadsides.

1136. Pierpont Morgan Library. Catalogue of printed books illustrating the liturgy and history of the church. Loaned by Mr. J. Pierpont Morgan and exhibited in the Avery Library, Columbia University, on the occasion of the General Convention of the Protestant Episcopal Church, October 10 - November 8, 1913. [N. Y., 1913] 27p.

Catalog of 342 items.

1137. Pierpont Morgan Library. The four hundredth anniversary of the Book of Common Prayer. [N. Y.: The Library, 1949] [4]p.

Brief résumé of items exhibited September 1949 - January 1950.

1138. Stinnecke Maryland Episcopal Library. A catalogue of the Fathers and of works pertaining to patristic theology, in the library bequeathed by the Rt. Rev. W. R. Whittingham... bishop of Maryland, to his diocese... 1879. [Baltimore, 1883] 32p.

1139. Stinnecke Maryland Episcopal Library. A catalogue of the liturgies, liturgical works, books of private devotion, hymnals and collections of hymns, in the Stinnecke Maryland Episcopal library, the legacy of the Rt. Rev. W. R. Whittingham... bishop of Maryland, to his diocese. 1879. [Baltimore?]: Priv. print., 1881. 80p.

1140. Virginia, University, Library. "Parish records of the Diocese of Virginia, 1653-1900," comp. by Lester J. Cappon. University of Virginia Library annual report on historical collections, no. 4 (1933-34), 9-23.

List of registers, vestry books and other records in Virginia Diocesan Library, Virginia Historical Society, University of Virginia, Virginia State Library, and individual parishes.

1141. Virginia, University, Library. "Parish records of the Dioceses of southern Virginia and southwestern Virginia, 1648-1900," comp. by William Edwin Hemphill. University of Virginia Library annual report on historical collections, no. 5 (1934-35), 9-24.

List of parish records in offices of the Diocese of Southwestern Virginia (St. John's Parish House, Roanoke), University of Virginia, Virginia State Library, and individual parishes.

Quaker (Friends)

1142. Cadbury, Henry J. "Quaker books at Harvard." Friend, 110 (1937), 345-47.

1143. Edmunds, Albert J. "Quaker literature in the libraries of Philadelphia." The Westonian, 13 (1907), 182-203.

Descriptions with listing of outstanding titles.

1144. Elkins, Kimball C. "Quakeriana in the Harvard University Library." Harvard alumni bulletin, 39 (1937), 560-65. Reprinted in Friend, 110 (1937), 347-49.

1145. Hewett, Anna B. "The Quaker collection in the Haverford College Library." Special Libraries Council of Philadelphia and Vicinity bulletin, 11 (Jan. 1945), 1-4.

1146. Historical Records Survey - N. Y. (City) New York City church archives: Religious Society of Friends. Catalogue. Records in possession of, or relating to, the two New York yearly meetings of the Religious Society of Friends and their subordinate meetings, by John Cox. N. Y.: The Survey, 1940. 224 numb. l.

1147. Historical Records Survey - Rhode Island. Inventory of the church archives of Rhode Island: Society of Friends. Providence: Historical Records Survey, 1939. 80 numb. l.

1148. Mekeel, Arthur J. "Glimpses into Haverford Quakeriana." Friends Historical Association bulletin, 25 (1936), 12-21.

1149. Pennsylvania Historical Survey. Inventory of church archives: Society of Friends. Philadelphia, 1941. 397p.

1150. Philadelphia Friends' Library. Supplementary catalogue of books belonging to the Library of Friends of Philadelphia. From 1853 to 1873. Philadelphia: W. H. Pile, 1873. 73p.
 Library later merged with Friends' Select School.

1151. Philadelphia Library Association of Friends. Catalogue of books in Friends' Library, Cherry Street, below Fifth, Philadelphia. [Philadelphia]: J. Rakestraw, 1853. 82p.
 General collection, arranged by subjects.

1152. Swarthmore College Library. Catalogue of Friends' Historical Library of Swarthmore College, Swarthmore, Pa., 1893. [Swarthmore, 1893] 62p.

1153. Swarthmore College Library. Friends Historical Library of Swarthmore College. Swarthmore, Penn., n. d. [8]p.
 General description of collection.

1154. Thomas, Allen C. "Quaker books and Quakeriana in the library of Haverford College." Friends' Historical Society bulletin, 9 (1919), 27-32.

Roman Catholic

1155. American Catholic Historical Society Library. A list of some early American publications. American Catholic Historical Society records, 31 (1920), 248-56.
 Books and pamphlets, 1733-1809, relating to American Catholic history, in American Catholic Historical Society of Philadelphia Library.

1156. Bay, J. Christian. "Trappist library at Our Lady of Gethsemani, Kentucky." American collector, 4 (April 1927), 9-15.

1157. Benjamin, Mary A. "Madigan's great papal collection." The collector, 58 (Feb. - Mar. 1945), 41-44.
 Collection of 15 volumes of papal autographs held by Georgetown University.

1158. Bridgeport Public Library. Books by Catholic authors and other books of interest to Catholics in the Bridgeport Public Library and Reading Room, comp. by Frances E. Gleason. Bridgeport, Conn.: [Bridgeport Printing Co., 1941.] 181p.

1159. California State Library, Sutro Branch. Catalogue of works on the Catholic Church by Spanish, Portuguese and Spanish-American writers before 1800. San Francisco: The Library, 1941. 128p. (Its: Occasional papers, Bibliographical series no. 3, pt. 1-II).
 Catalog of books in Sutro Branch.

1160. Catholic Library Association, Oregon-Washington Regional Unit. Union list of Catholic periodicals in Catholic colleges of the Pacific Coast. [Portland? 1942]
 Locates holdings of 11 institutions.

1161. Chicago Public Library. Catholic reading list; a catalogue of books (in English) by Catholic authors in the Chicago Public Library. [Chicago]: Chicago Chapter of the Knights of Columbus, 1908. 55p.

1162. Cleveland Public Library. Books by Catholic authors in the Cleveland Public Library; a classified list, comp. by Emilie Louise Haley. [Cleveland]: The Library, 1911. 232p.

1163. District of Columbia Public Library. Books on Catholic subjects chiefly by Catholic authors, published 1930-1938. Wash.: The Library, 1938. 15p.
 Selected from Library's collection.

1164. District of Columbia Public Library. Catalogue of Catholic and other select authors in the Public Library of the District of

Columbia, comp. by Julia H. Laskey. 2d ed. [Washington] 1915. 120p. First edition issued 1911.

1165. Downing, Margaret B. "The James Dudley Morgan collection of L'Enfant papers." U. S. Catholic Historical Society historical records and studies, 14 (1920), 112-19.

Describes Morgan collection in Library of Congress.

1166. Ellis, John T. "A guide to the Baltimore Cathedral archives." Catholic historical review, 32 (1946), 341-60.

Brief description of records from second half of 18th century to 1921, to be found in archives collection. Also a list of files of archdiocesan newspapers in archives.

1167. Finotti, J. M. Bibliographia Catholica Americana; a list of works written by Catholic authors, and published in the United States. N. Y., 1872. 318p.

Locates copies in 9 libraries of titles issued from 1784 to 1820.

1168. Historical Records Survey - Mich. Inventory of the church archives of Michigan; Roman Catholic Church, Archdiocese of Detroit. Detroit: Michigan Historical Records Survey, 1941. 186p.

1169. Historical Records Survey - Nev. Inventory of the church archives of Nevada: Roman Catholic Church. Reno: Historical Records Survey, 1939. 49 numb. 1.

1170. Historical Records Survey - N. H. Inventory of the Roman Catholic Church records in New Hampshire. Manchester, 1938. 127 numb. 1.

1171. Historical Records Survey - N. Y. (City) Inventory of the church archives in New York City: Roman Catholic Church, Archdiocese of New York. N. Y., 1941. 181p.

1172. Historical Records Survey - Ohio. Inventory of the church archives of Ohio: Roman Catholic Church, Parishes of the Catholic Church, Diocese of Cleveland. Columbus, Ohio: The Survey, 1942. 447p.

1173. Historical Records Survey - Wis. Inventory of the church archives of Wisconsin: Roman Catholic Church, Diocese of La Crosse. Madison, 1942. 237p.

1174. Holweck, F. G. "The historical archives of the archdiocese of St. Louis." St. Louis Catholic historical review, 1 (Oct. 1918), 24-39.

A list of more important papers to be found in collection of Catholic Historical Society of St. Louis.

1175. Lallou, William L. "The archives of the American Catholic Historical Society (Philadelphia)." Catholic historical review, 1 (1915), 193-95.

Lists about 25 valuable works in library of Society.

1176. Louisville Free Library. Some books in the Louisville Free Public Library of interest to Catholic readers. Louisville: Federation of Catholic Societies, 1914. 86p.

1177. Meehan, Thomas F. "Early Catholic weeklies." U. S. Catholic Historical Society historical records and studies, 28 (1937), 237-55.

Locates copies in libraries of St. Louis University, Notre Dame University, Villanova College, Georgetown University, and Dominican House of Studies.

1178. Merrill, William S. Catholic authorship in the American colonies before 1784. [Wash., 1917]. 18p. (Reprint from Catholic historical review, 3 (1917), 308-25.)

Supplements Finotti, covering earlier period, before 1784. Often locates copies.

1179. Middleton, Thomas Cooke. Catholic periodicals published in the United States. From the earliest in 1809 to the close of the year 1892. Philadelphia: Villanova College, Penn., 1908. 24p.

Supplementary to list published in Records of the American Catholic Historical Society of Philadelphia for Sept. 1893. Gives location of numbers in some cases.

1180. O'Connor, Thomas F. "Catholic archives in the United States." Catholic historical review, 31 (Jan. 1946), 414-30.

Review of principal ecclesiastical and institutional archives in various states.

1181. Parsons, Wilfrid. Early Catholic

Americana, a list of books and other works by Catholic authors in the United States, 1729-1830. N. Y.: Macmillan Co., 1939. 282p.

More comprehensive than Finotti. Locates copies of 1,187 items in about 30 libraries.

1182. Parsons, Wilfrid. A list of Catholic books printed in the United States, 1729-1830. Wash.: Riggs Library, Georgetown University, 1937. 103 numb. l.

"A compilation of titles copied directly from books on the shelves of the Riggs Memorial Library of Georgetown University."

1183. St. Charles' Seminary. "Index of historical pamphlets in the library of St. Charles Seminary, Overbrook, Pa." American Catholic Historical Society of Philadelphia record, 13 (March 1902), 60-119.

Lists 700 pamphlets concerning history of Church, particularly in Philadelphia.

1184. Thomas, Sister Ursula. "The Catholic Church on the Oklahoma frontier; a critical bibliography." Mid-America, 20 (1938), 186-207.

Collections and manuscript sources for study of Catholic Church are located in 7 libraries in Oklahoma, and 9 outside the state.

1185. Trenton Public Library. Catholic catalogue, including Catholic authors and also certain works of Protestant authors which have special interest for Catholics. Trenton: Council no. 155, Knights of Columbus, 1908. 63p.

1186. U. S. Library of Congess, Division of Bibliography. "List of references on John Henry Newman." Wash., Nov. 16, 1921. 17p. Typed.

1187. Yates, Garard F. "The Talbot collection, Georgetown University." Catholic library world, 16 (1945), 118-20, 125.

Brief description of collection of 62 items presented to University by Mary Benjamin. Includes autographs of saints, and other Catholic documents.

Shaker

1188. Grosvenor Library. Shaker literature in the Grosvenor Library; a bibliography. Buffalo: The Library, 1940. [65]-119p. (Grosvenor Library bulletin, v. 22, no. 4, June 1940)

1189. MacLean, John Patterson. A bibliography of Shaker literature, with an introductory study of the writings and publications pertaining to Ohio believers. Columbus, O.: F. J. Heer, 1905. 71p.

Lists locations in 33 libraries. MacLean Library acquired in part by Library of Congress.

1190. New York Public Library. "List of works in the New York Public Library relating to Shakers." New York Public Library bulletin, 8 (1904), 550-59. Reprinted. 10p.

1191. Winter, E. C. "Shaker literature in the Grosvenor Library; a bibliography." Grosvenor Library bulletin, 22 (June 1940), 66-119.

Unitarian

1192. Historical Records Survey - N. J. Inventory of the church archives of New Jersey: Unitarian Church. Newark: Historical Records Survey, 1940. 32 numb. l.

Universalist

1193. Historical Records Survey - Mass. An inventory of Universalist archives in Massachusetts. Boston: Historical Records Survey, 1942. 489p.

Minor sects

1194. Historical Records Survey - Mich. Inventory of the church archives of Michigan: Church of the Nazarene, Michigan District Assembly. Detroit: Mich. Hist. Records Survey, 1942. 50 numb. l.

1195. Historical Records Survey - Mich. Inventory of the church archives of Michigan: Pilgrim Holiness Church, Michigan District. Detroit: Michigan Historical Records Survey, 1942. 27 numb. l.

1196. Historical Records Survey - N. J. Inventory of the church archives of New Jersey: Baha'i Assemblies. Newark: Historical Records Survey, 1940. 26 numb. l.

1197. Historical Records Survey - Wis. Inventory of the church archives of Wisconsin:

Assemblies of God. Madison: Wisconsin Historical Records Survey, 1942. 73 numb. l.

1198. Historical Records Survey - Wis. Inventory of the church archives of Wisconsin: Church of the United Brethern in Christ. Madison: Wis. Hist. Records Survey, 1940. 136 numb. l.

U.S. Church Archives

1199. Allison, William Henry. Inventory of unpublished material for American religious history in Protestant Church archives and other repositories. Wash.; Carnegie Inst., 1910. 254p. (Carnegie Inst. of Wash. Publ., 137).

Locates material primarily in archives of governing bodies of various Protestant churches, missionary societies, theological seminaries, colleges and historical collections.

1200. Avery, Mary. "Survey of Seattle church archives." Pacific Northwest quarterly, 28 (April 1937), 163-91.

Describes holdings and condition of archives of 275 Seattle churches.

1201. Connecticut State Library. List of church records on deposit at Connecticut State Library. Hartford, 1942. 10p. (Connecticut State Library bulletin, no. 18)

1202. Deutsch, Herman J., ed. "Survey of Spokane church archives." Pacific Northwest quarterly, 28 (1937), 383-403.

Describes holdings and condition of archives of 158 Spokane churches.

1203. Historical Records Survey - Mich. Inventory of the church archives of Michigan: Dearborn churches. Detroit: Mich. Hist. Records Survey, 1940. 54 numb. l.

1204. Historical Records Survey - Mich. Inventory of the church archives of Michigan: Salvation Army in Michigan. Detroit: Mich. Hist. Records Survey, 1942. 49 numb. l.

1205. Historical Records Survey - N. J. Inventory of the church archives of New Jersey: The Salvation Army, Jersey City. Newark: Historical Records Survey, 1940. 34 numb. l.

1206. Historical Records Survey - Okla. Inventory of the church archives of Oklahoma: Bryan County. Oklahoma City, 1937. 24p.

1207. Historical Records Survey - Utah. Inventory of the church archives of Utah. Salt Lake City: Utah Hist. Records Survey, 1940-41. 3v.

V. 1, History and bibliography of religion; v. 2, Baptist Church; v. 3, Smaller denominations.

1208. Historical Records Survey - Wash. "Inventory of the church archives of Washington: Survey of Everett, Yakima, and Wenatchee Church archives." Pacific Northwest quarterly, 30 (1939), 417-36.

1209. Historical Records Survey - W. Va. A preliminary bibliography relating to churches in West Virginia, Virginia, Kentucky and Southern Ohio. Charleston, W. Va.: Hist. Rec. Sur., 1940. 15 numb. l.

1210. New York State Library. "Church records, originals or typewritten copies added to the New York State Library to June 30, 1921." New York State Library bulletin, 760 (1922), 85-97.

1211. Oberlin College Library. "Letters and papers of Charles Grandison Finney in the Oberlin College Library; a calendar and index." Oberlin, Ohio, 1939. 3v. Typed.

Records about 2,700 items, 1817-75, relating to activities of famous evangelist.

1212. Spence, Thomas, Jr., Peterson, Virgil V., and O'Connor, Thomas F. "Church archives and history." American Association for State and Local History bulletins, 1 (1946), 257-304.

Three papers describing church records of Historical Foundation of the Presbyterian and Reformed Churches, Mormons and Roman Catholic Church in the United States.

1213. Sweet, William M. "Church archives in the United States." Church history, 8 (1939), 43-53.

Lists depositories of archives of many denominations.

NON-CHRISTIAN RELIGIONS

Buddhism

1214. New York Public Library. "Buddhism; a list of works in the New York Public Library," comp. by Ida Augusta Pratt. New York Public Library bulletin, 20 (1916), 114-80. Reprinted. 78p.

Judaism

1215. Adler, Elkan N. Catalogue of Hebrew manuscripts in the collection of Elkan Nathan Adler. Cambridge, England: University Press, 1921. 228p.

A collection of over 4,000 items acquired in 1923 by Jewish Theological Seminary, New York.

1216. Boston Public Library. Judaica, a selected reading list of books in the Public Library of the city of Boston. Boston: The Trustees, 1934. 140p.

1217. Cohen, Boaz. "The library of the Jewish Theological Seminary of America." Jewish forum, 17 (1934), no. 1 and 2.

1218. Ezekiel, Jacob. Catalogue of books bequeathed to the Hebrew Union College by Jacob Ezekiel, Cincinnati, Ohio, 1892. [Cincinnati, O., 1901] 14p.

1219. Halper, Benzion. Descriptive catalogue of Genizah fragments in Philadelphia. Philadelphia: Dropsie College, 1924. 235p.

Descriptions of 487 items in Dropsie College Library, University of Pennsylvania, and Young Men's Hebrew Association

1220. Historical Records Survey - Col. Inventory of the church archives of Colorado: Jewish bodies. Denver: Colorado Historical Records Survey, 1941. 34 numb. l.

1221. Historical Records Survey - La. Inventory of the church and synagogue archives of Louisiana: Jewish congregations and organizations. University, La.: Dept. of Archives, La. State Univ., 1941. 183p.

1222. Historical Records Survey - Mich. Inventory of the church and synagogue archives of Michigan: Jewish bodies. Detroit: Michigan Historical Records Survey, 1940. 65 numb. l.

1223. Historical Record Survey - Miss. Inventory of the church and synagogue archives of Mississippi: Jewish congregations and organizations. Jackson: B'nai B'rith, 1940. 41 numb. l.

1224. Historical Records Survey - Tenn. Inventory of the church and synagogue archives of Tennessee: Jewish congregations. Nashville: Tennessee Historical Records Survey, 1941. 55 numb. l.

1225. Historical Records Survey - Wis. Inventory of the church archives of Wisconsin; Jewish congregations. Madison, 1942. 64p.

1226. Illinois, University, Library. Books of Jewish interest in the Library of the University of Illinois. Urbana: University of Illinois, 1913. 20p. (Univ. of Illinois bulletin, 11 (1913), no. 3)

"List is restricted to bound books and pamphlets."

1227. Jewish Theological Seminary. Biblical manuscripts and rare prints (mostly from Sulzberger Collection) N. Y., 1914. 15p.

1228. Jewish Theological Seminary. "The library" [of the Jewish Theological Seminary], by Alexander Marx. In: Jewish Theological Seminary of America. Semicentennial volume. N. Y., 1939, ch. 8, p. 87-120.

1229. Jewish Theological Seminary. "The library of the Jewish Theological Seminary of America," by Alexander Marx. In: Jewish Theological Seminary of America register, 1940-1941. N. Y., 1940, p. 43-75.

Contains a history of library and description of outstanding acquisitions.

1230. John Hopkins University Library. Catalogue of the Leopold Strouse rabbinical library giving a list of the accessions by annual gift from Mr. Strouse during the years 1896, 1897, 1898 and 1899. Baltimore, 1900. 28p.

Total collection numbers 2,500 volumes.

1231. Kaplan, Mitchell M. Panorama of ancient letters; four and a half centuries of Hebraica and Judaica; bibliographical notes and descriptions of 1,000 rare books and manuscripts... presented to New York University. N. Y., 1942. 316p.

1232. Lesser, Isaac. Catalogue of the Lesser library, comp. by Cyrus Adler. Philadelphia: [E. Hirsch & Co.] 1883. 65p.
Collection now held by Hebrew Education Society, Philadelphia.

1233. Marx, Alexander. Polemical manuscripts in the library of the Jewish Theological Seminary of America. N. Y., 1929, p. 248-78. ("Reprinted from the A. S. Freidus memorial volume.")
Collection of 20 unpublished Hebrew treatises and 10 in other languages.

1234. Metcalf, Keyes D. "Jewish collections in American libraries." Journal of Jewish bibliography, 3 (Jan.-Apr., 1942), 5-14.
Descriptions of principal American collections.

1235. Nemoy, Leon. "The Alexander Kohut memorial collection of Judaica." Yale University Library gazette, 2 (1927), 17-25.
Describes entire Hebrew collection at Yale.

1236. Nemoy, Leon. "Hebrew and kindred manuscripts in the Yale University Library." Journal of Jewish bibliography, 1 (July, 1939), 107-10.

1237. Nemoy, Leon. "The Shalom Asch library." Yale University Library gazette, 18 (1944), 55-63.
A collection of Hebrew and Yiddish books and manuscripts.

1238. New York College of the City of New York Library, Davison Library of Judaica. Special list of books in medieval Hebrew poetry and liturgy. N. Y., 1948. 34p.

1239. New York Public Library. "List of anti-Semitic and of Jewish-Christian (Conversionist) periodicals in the New York Public Library." New York Public Library bulletin, 7 (1903), 30-31.

1240. New York Public Library. "List of works in the New York Public Library relating to the history and condition of the Jews in various countries," comp. by Daniel Carl Haskell. New York Public Library bulletin, 17 (1913), 537-86, 611-64, 713-64, 781-834. Reprinted, with index, 1914. 278p.

1241. New York University Library. The Solomon Rosenthal collection of Hebraica, ed. by Abraham I. Katsh. [N. Y.] 1942. 53, [21]p.
A list of 496 titles in Washington Square Library, New York University.

1242. Roback, Abraham A. "The Yiddish collection in the Harvard Library." Harvard alumni bulletin, 31 (1929), 843-53.

1243. Rosenbach, Abraham S. Wolf. "An American Jewish bibliography, being a list of books and pamphlets by Jews, or relating to them, printed in the United States from the establishment of the press in the colonies until 1850." American Jewish Historical Society publications, no. 30 (1926), 1-486.
Locates copies in 28 American libraries.

1244. Schapiro, Israel. The Hebrew collections of the Library of Congress, [n. p., 1917] p. 355-59. (Reprinted from the Journal of the American Oriental Society, v. 36. 1917.)

1245. Stern-Taeubler, Selma. "Acquisitions." American Jewish archives, 1 (Jan. 1949), 53-64.
A list of recent accessions to American Jewish Archives in Hebrew Union College, Cincinnati.

1246. Texas, University, Library. The Abraham I. Schecter collection of Hebraica and Judaica; a check list of the Judaica with other related materials in the University of Texas Library. Austin: The Library, 1939-43. 2v.
V. 1, a check list of the books in the Hebrew language, comp. by Ralph Hagedorn. 1,500 titles; v. 2, a list of books printed in roman, plus the books of Jewish interest or content classified in the Dewey decimal classification. 1,700 titles.

1247. [U. S. Library of Congress. "Catalog of Hebraica." Wash.] 6 v. Typed, with additions in handwriting.
Approximately 30,000 titles through 1944 in Hebraic Section, Orientalia Division. Material to 1928 also in two separate catalogs, typed, with additions in handwriting.

1248. Wolfson, Harry A. "Hebrew books in Harvard." Harvard alumni bulletin, 34 (1932), 886-97.

RELIGION

1249. Yale University Library. Catalogue of Hebrew and Yiddish manuscripts and books from the library of Sholem Asch, presented to Yale University, comp. by Leon Nemoy. New Haven: Yale University Library, 1945. 69p.

1250. Yale University Library. Check list of an exhibition of Judaica and Hebraica held at the Sterling Memorial Library, Yale University, comp. by Leon Nemoy. New Haven: [Yale Univ. Press] 1933. 23p.

1251. Zionist Archives and Library of Palestine Foundation Fund. Palestine and Zionism: a three year cumulation, January 1946 - December 1948: an author and subject index to books, pamphlets and periodicals, ed. by Sophie A. Udin. N. Y.: Zionist Archives, 1949. 469p.

Books indexed are in Zionist Archives and Library.

Mohammedanism

1252. New York Public Library. "The Koran in Slavonic; a list of translations." New York Public Library bulletin, 41 (1937), 95-102. Reprinted. 10p.

1253. New York Public Library. "A list of works in the New York Public Library, relating to Muhammadanism." New York Public Library bulletin, 15 (1911), 211-46.

Social Sciences

SOCIOLOGY

1254. Boston Public Library. A list of books on social reform in the Public Library of the City of Boston. Boston: The Library, 1898. 58p. (Reprinted from Boston Public Library monthly bulletin, 3 (1898), 157-84, 203-37)

1255. Chicago Public Library. The social sciences; finding list, Chicago Public Library. [Chicago]: The Library, 1914. 371p.

1256. Locke, Edwin. "FSA." U. S. camera. 1 (1941), 20-27.
Description of the sociological and economic survey of America made by the Farm Security Administration, now in the Library of Congress.

1257. Minnesota, University, Library. Periodical subscription list... social sciences. [Minneapolis, 1936] 2v. in 1.

1258. New York Public Library. "Check list of works relating to the social history of the City of New York--its clubs, charities, hospitals, etc.,--in the New York Public Library." New York Public Library bulletin, 5 (1901), 261-93.

1259. New York Public Library. "Economic and sociological periodicals in the New York Public Library." New York Public Library bulletin, 27 (1923), 27-52; 28 (1924), 743-62; 29 (1925), 66-101, 147-63, 815-26, 866-72; 30 (1926), 28-49, 449-68, 717-27, 881-91; 31 (1927), 35-62, 843-75, 940-63.

1260. New York Public Library. "List of books and some articles in periodicals in the New York Public Library, relating to political rights, constitutions, and constitutional law," prep. by A. R. Hasse. New York Public Library bulletin, 8 (1904), 22-36, 52-88, 103-38, 155-98.

1261. Public affairs information service bulletin... a cooperative clearing house of public affairs information... N. Y.: H. W. Wilson, I (1915) - to date.
Based largely on material in New York Public Library.

1262. Russell Sage Foundation Library. Bulletin. No. 1-165. N. Y., 1913-45.
Contains brief bibliographies on social work and related subjects.

1263. Stearns, Bertha-Monica. "Reform periodicals and female reformers, 1830-1860." American historical review, 37 (1932), 678-99.
Locates titles but not holdings.

1264. U. S. Department of Labor Library. "National economic councils: a list of references." U. S. Bureau of Labor Statistics monthly labor review, 32 (1931), 1249-58.

1265. U. S. Department of Labor Library. Recent references on social welfare and the Constitution. Wash., 1936. 5p.

1266. U. S. Library of Congress, Division of Bibliography. Select list of references on Anglo-Saxon interests; 2d issue, with additions. Wash.: Govt. Print. Off., 1906. 22p.

1267. U. S. Library of Congress, Division of Bibliography. Youth movements in the United States and foreign countries, including a section on the National Youth Administration, comp. by Ann Duncan Brown. [Wash.] 1936. 46p.

1268. Virginia State Library. "Finding list of the social sciences, political science, law, and education," comp. by Earl G. Swen. Virginia State Library bulletin, 3 (1910), 1-352.

STATISTICS

General

1269. John Crear Library. List of publications of the Canadian Bureau of Statistics in the John Crerar Library. Chicago, 1937. 20p. (Reference list, no. 37)

1270. U. S. Library of Congress, Division of Bibliography. A selected list of books on statistical methods and their application, comp. by Helen F. Conover. [Wash.] 1938. 23p. [Supplementary list] Jan. 13, 1941. 18p.

1271. U. S. Library of Congress. General Reference and Bibliography Division. "Statistical and other books of reference concerning the United States," comp. by Frances Cheney. Wash., Dec. 1, 1944. 45p. Typed.

Demography - population

1272. Arizona Statewide Archival and Records Project. Guide to public vital statistics records in Arizona. Phoenix: Historical Records Survey Program, 1941. 62p.

1273. Historical Records Survey - Ala. Guide to public vital statistics in Alabama. Prelim. ed. Birmingham: Alabama Historical Records Survey, 1942. 73 numb. 1.

1274. Historical Records Survey - Ala. Guide to vital statistics records in Alabama: church archives. Birmingham: Alabama Hist. Rec. Survey, 1942. 237 numb. 1.

1275. Historical Records Survey - Ark. Guide to vital statistics records in Arkansas: church records. Little Rock: Historical Records Survey, 1942. 620p.

1276. Historical Records Survey - Cal. A guide to church vital statistics records in California: San Francisco and Alameda Counties: six denominations. San Francisco: Northern California Historical Records Survey, 1942. 63 numb. 1.

1277. Historical Records Survey - Cal. Guide to public vital statistics records in California. San Francisco: Northern California Historical Records Survey, 1941. 2v.
V. 1, birth records; v. 2, death records.

1278. Historical Records Survey - Col. Guide to vital statistics records in Colorado. Denver: Colorado Historical Records Survey, 1942. 2v.
V. 1, public archives; v. 2, church archives.

1279. Historical Records Survey - Conn. Guide to vital statistics in the church records of Connecticut. New Haven: Connecticut Historical Records Survey, 1942. 190p.

1280. Historical Records Survey - Fla. Guide to public vital statistics records in Florida. Jacksonville: Florida Historical Records Survey, 1941. 70 numb. 1.

1281. Historical Records Survey - Fla. Guide to supplementary vital statistics from church records in Florida. Prelim. ed. Jacksonville: Florida Historical Records Survey, 1942. 3v.
V. 1, Alachu; v. 2, Gilchrist; v. 3, Orange

1282. Historical Records Survey - Ga. Guide to public vital statistics records in Georgia. Atlanta: Ga. Hist. Records Survey, 1941. 73 numb. 1.

1283. Historical Records Survey - Id. Guide to vital statistics records in Idaho: state and county. Boise: Idaho Hist. Records Survey, 1942. 47 numb. 1.

1284. Historical Records Survey - Ill. Guide to church vital statistics records in Illinois. Prelim. ed. Chicago: Illinois Historical Records Survey, 1942. 359p.

1285. Historical Records Survey - Ill. Guide to public vital statistics records in Illinois. Chicago: Ill. Hist. Records Survey, 1941. 138 numb. 1.

1286. Historical Records Survey - Ind. Guide to public vital statistics records in Indiana. Indianapolis: Indiana Historical Records Survey, 1941. 265 numb. 1.

1287. Historical Records Survey - Iowa. Guide to public vital statistics in Iowa. Des Moines:

Iowa Historical Records Survey, 1941. 113 numb. l.

1288. Historical Records Survey - Kan. Guide to public vital statistics records in Kansas. Topeka: Kansas Historical Records Survey, 1942. 262 numb. l.

1289. Historical Records Survey - Ky. Guide to public vital statistics records in Kentucky. Louisville: Kentucky Historical Records Survey, 1942. 257p.

1290. Historical Records Survey - La. Guide to public vital statistics records in Louisiana. New Orleans: Louisiana State Board of Health, 1942. 79p.

1291. Historical Records Survey - Mass. Guide to the public vital records in Massachusetts. Boston: Historical Records Survey, 1942. 342p.

1292. Historical Records Survey - Mich. Vital statistics holdings by government agencies in Michigan. Detroit: Mich. Hist. Records Survey, 1941-42. 4v.
Covers birth, marriage, death, and divorce records.

1293. Historical Records Survey - Mich. Vital statistics holdings of church archives in Michigan: Wayne County. Detroit: Michigan Historical Records Survey, 1942. 151p.

1294. Historical Records Survey - Minn. Guide to church vital statistics records in Minnesota: baptisms, marriages, funerals. St. Paul: Hist. Records Survey, 1942. 253 numb. l.

1295. Historical Records Survey - Minn. Guide to public vital statistics records in Minnesota. St. Paul: Minn. Hist. Records Survey, 1941. 142 numb. l.

1296. Historical Records Survey - Miss. Guide to vital statistics records in Mississippi. Jackson: Mississippi Historical Records Survey, 1942. 2v.
V. 1, public archives; v. 2, church archives.

1297. Historical Records Survey - Mo. Guide to public vital statistics: records in Missouri. St. Louis: Missouri Historical Records Survey, 1941. 120p.

1298. Historical Records Survey - Mo. Guide to vital statistics: church records in Missouri. St. Louis: Missouri Historical Records Survey, 1942. 236p.

1299. Historical Records Survey - Mont. Guide to public vital statistics in Montana. Bozeman: Hist. Rec. Survey, Montana State College, 1941. 85p.

1300. Historical Records Survey - Mont. Inventory of the vital statistics records of churches and religious organizations in Montana, 1942. Bozeman: Mont. Hist. Records Survey, 1942. 117 numb. l.

1301. Historical Records Survey - Neb. Guide to public vital statistics records in Nebraska. Lincoln: Neb. Hist. Rec. Survey, 1941. 94 numb. l.

1302. Historical Records Survey - Nev. Guide to public vital statistics records in Nevada. Reno, 1941. 26 numb. l.

1303. Historical Records Survey - N. H. Guide to church vital statistics records in New Hampshire. Prelim. ed. Manchester: New Hampshire Historical Records Survey, 1942. 104 numb. l.

1304. Historical Records Survey - N. J. Guide to vital statistics records in New Jersey. Newark, 1941-42. 2v.
V. 1, public archives; v. 2, church archives.

1305. Historical Records Survey - N. M. Guide to public vital statistics records in New Mexico. Albuquerque: New Mexico Historical Records Survey, 1942. 135p.

1306. Historical Records Survey - N. Y. (City) Guide to vital statistics records in the City of New York: churches. N. Y., 1942. 5v.
Separate volume for each borough.

1307. Historical Records Survey - N. Y. (State) Guide to public vital statistics records in New York State (including New York City). Albany, 1942. 3v.
V. 1, birth records; v. 2, marriage records; v. 3, death records.

1308. Historical Records Survey - N. Y. (State) Guide to vital statistics records of churches in New York State (exclusive of New York City). Albany, 1942. 2v.

1309. Historical Records Survey - N. C. Guide to vital statistics records in North Carolina. Raleigh: N. C. Hist. Records Survey, 1942. 62p.
   Covers public vital statistics.

1310. Historical Records Survey - N. D. Guide to church vital statistics records in North Dakota. Bismarck: North Dakota Historical Records Survey, 1942. 150p.

1311. Historical Records Survey - N. D. Guide to public vital statistics records in North Dakota. Bismarck: North Dakota Historical Records Survey, 1941. 77p.

1312. Historical Records Survey - Okl. Guide to public vital statistics records in Oklahoma. Oklahoma City: Oklahoma Historical Records Survey, 1941. 85 numb. 1.

1313. Historical Records Survey - Ore. Guide to public vital statistics records in Oregon. Portland: Oregon Historical Records Survey, 1942. 80p.

1314. Historical Records Survey - R. I. Guide to church vital statistics records in the state of Rhode Island. Providence, 1942. 171p.
   "Supplement to Guide to the public vital statistics records..."

1315. Historical Records Survey - R. I. Guide to the public vital statistics records: births, marriages, deaths in the state of Rhode Island and Providence plantations. Providence, 1941. 280p.

1316. Historical Records Survey - S. D. Guide to public vital statistics records in South Dakota. Mitchell: S. D. Hist. Records Survey, 1942. 82 numb. 1.

1317. Historical Records Survey - Tenn. Guide to church vital statistics in Tennessee. Nashville, Tenn.: War Services Section, 1942. 510p.

1318. Historical Records Survey - Tenn. Guide to public vital statistics in Tennessee. Nashville: Tennessee Historical Records Survey, 1941. 146 numb. 1.

1319. Historical Records Survey - Tex. Guide to public vital statistics records in Texas. San Antonio: State Bureau of Vital Statistics, 1941. 177p.

1320. Historical Records Survey - Utah. Guide to public vital statistics of Utah. Salt Lake City: Utah Historical Records Survey, 1941. 54p.

1321. Historical Records Survey - Wash. (State) Guide to church vital statistics records in Washington. Prelim. ed. Seattle: Washington Historical Records Survey, 1942. 93p.

1322. Historical Records Survey - Wash. (State) Guide to public vital statistics records in Washington. Seattle: Washington Historical Records Survey, 1941. 131p.

1323. Historical Records Survey - W. Va. Guide to church vital statistics records in West Virginia. Charleston: West Virginia Historical Records Survey, 1942. 278p.

1324. Historical Records Survey - W. Va. Inventory of public vital statistics records in West Virginia: births, deaths and marriages. Charleston: West Virginia Historical Records Survey, 1941. 76p.

1325. Historical Records Survey - Wis. Guide to church vital statistics records in Wisconsin. Madison: Wisconsin Historical Records Survey, 1942. 257 numb. 1.

1326. Historical Records Survey - Wis. Guide to public vital statistics records in Wisconsin. Madison: Wisconsin Historical Records Survey, 1941. 247 numb. 1.

1327. Historical Records Survey - Wy. Guide to public vital statistics records in Wyoming. Cheyenne, 1941. 31 numb. 1.

1328. Historical Records Survey - Wy. Guide to vital statistics records in Wyoming: church archives. Prelim. ed. Cheyenne: Wyoming Historical Records Survey, 1942. 62 numb. 1.

1329. Hutchinson, Edward Prince. Guide to the official population data and vital statistics of Sweden, comp. by Edward P. Hutchinson. Wash., 1942. 72p.
   Based upon Library of Congress collection.

1330. Hutchinson, Edward Prince. Preliminary report of the population collection in the Library of Congress. [Wash.] 1940. 12 l.

1331. Population index, v. 1 (Jan. 20, 1935) - to date.
Bibliography of population literature, based primarily upon Library of Congress collections.

1332. U. S. Library of Congress, Census Library Project. "Bibliography." In: United Nations. Statistical Office. Demographic yearbook, 1948. Lake Success, N. Y., 1949. (United Nations Publ., sales no.: 1949 XIII 1.), p. 549-596.
"Citations to available official publications containing census and other demographic statistics for each political area."

1333. U. S. Library of Congress, Census Library Project. Catalog of United States census publications, 1790-1945, prep. by Henry J. Dubester. Wash.: Govt. Print. Off., 1949. 320p.
Library of Congress call numbers included.

1334. U. S. Library of Congress, Census Library Project. General censuses and vital statistics in the Americas. Wash.: Govt. Print. Off., 1943. 151p.

1335. U. S. Library of Congress, Census Library Project. National censuses and vital statistics in Europe, 1918-1939; an annotated bibliography, prep. by Henry J. Dubester. Wash.: Govt. Print. Off., 1948. 215 p. 1940-48 Supplement. Wash., 1948. 48p.

1336. U. S. Library of Congress, Census Library Project. National censuses and vital statistics in France between two world wars, 1921-1942; a preliminary bibliography. Wash., 1945. 22p.

1337. U. S. Library of Congress, Census Library Project. National censuses and vital statistics in Germany after the first world war, 1918-1944. Wash., 1946. 37p.

1338. U. S. Library of Congress, Census Library Project. National censuses and official statistics in Italy since the first world war, 1921-1944; a preliminary bibliography. Wash., 1945. 58p.

1339. U. S. Library of Congress, Census Library Project. Population censuses and other official demographic statistics of British Africa; an annotated bibliography, prep. by Henry J. Dubester. Wash.: Govt. Print. Off., 1950. 78p.

1340. U. S. Library of Congress, Census Library Project. Recent censuses in European countries; a preliminary list. [Wash.] 1942. 49p.
Locates holdings in Library of Congress or U. S. Department of Commerce, when available in either library.

1341. U. S. Library of Congress, Census Library Project. State censuses; an annotated bibliography of censuses of population taken after the year 1790 by states and territories of the United States, prep. by Henry J. Dubester. Wash.: Govt. Print. Off., 1948. 73p.

1342. U. S. Library of Congress, Division of Bibliography. "List of references on the mountain whites." Wash., Sept. 12, 1935. 26p. Typed.

1343. War Services Program - La. Guide to vital statistics records of church archives in Louisiana. New Orleans: Louisiana State Board of Health, 1942. 2v.
V. 1, Protestant and Jewish churches; v. 2, Roman Catholic churches.

POLITICAL SCIENCE

General

1344. Dartmouth College Library. "The Rosenstock-Huessy library." Dartmouth College Library bulletin, 2 (June 1938), 191-95.
Material of political and sociological importance through World War I in Dartmouth College Library. In German, for most part.

1345. Henry E. Huntington Library. "Papers of Francis Lieber," by Charles B. Robson. Huntington Library bulletin, 3 (1933), 135-55.
Description of Lieber papers in Huntington Library and an appraisal of Lieber's contributions in political and social sciences from 1827 to 1872.

1346. U. S. Library of Congress. Catalogue of

works relating to political economy and the science of government, in the Library of Congress. Arranged by subject-matters. Wash.: Govt. Print. Off., 1869. 65p.

1347. U. S. Library of Congress, Division of Bibliography. "A list of references on the flag of the United States (supplementing previous lists)," comp. by Florence S. Hellman. Wash., Aug. 25, 1941. 17p. Typed.

1348. U. S. Library of Congress, Division of Bibliography. A selected list of recent books on modern political systems, comp. by Grace H. Fuller. Wash., June 26, 1936. 26p.

1349. Weber, Hilmar H. "Some notes on the Stolberg collection." Harvard alumni bulletin, 36 (1934), 798-808.

Describes collection of 2,500 volumes in political science, acquired for Harvard College Library.

Form of state

1350. Carnegie Endowment for International Peace. Referendum on war. [Wash., 1938] 8p.

Collection now a part of George Washington University Library.

1351. Elkins, Kimball C. "Utopias." Harvard Library notes, 3 (1935), 46-50.

Describes Francis G. Peabody collection, Harvard College Library.

1352. U. S. Library of Congress, Division of Bibliography. A list of references on mandates. [Wash., 1924] 31p.

1353. U. S. Library of Congress, Division of Bibliography. Nationalism: a selected list of writings since 1918, with a section on economic nationalism. [Wash.] 1934. 22p.

1354. U. S. Library of Congress, Division of Bibliography. Select list of references on the initiative, referendum and recall. Wash.: Govt. Print. Off., 1912. 102p.

1355. U. S. Library of Congress, Division of Bibliography. Selected list of recent writings on internationalism (superstate), comp. by Anne L. Baden. [Wash., 1933] 30p.

1356. U. S. Library of Congress, General Reference and Bibliography Division. World government, a list of selected references, comp. by Helen F. Conover. [Wash.] 1947. 11 l.

1357. U. S. Library of Congress, Reading Rooms. An annotated and selected list of books about democracy. Wash., 1941. 26p.

Internal relations

1358. Los Angeles Public Library, Municipal Reference Library. The prevention and control of race riots. Los Angeles, 1944. 12 numb. l. (Social adjustment bibliographies, no. 1)

Most of material is in Municipal Reference Library.

1359. Schroeder, Theodore. Free speech bibliography, including every discovered attitude toward the problem, covering every method of transmitting ideas and of abridging their promulgation upon every subject-matter. N. Y.: H. W. Wilson Co., 1922. 247p.

Locates copies in 5 libraries.

1360. U. S. Library of Congress, Division of Bibliography. A selected list of references on freedom of speech and the press (supplementary to typewritten list of April 14, 1930), comp. by Grace Hadley Fuller. [Wash.] 1938. 27p.

1361. U. S. Library of Congress, European Affairs Division. Freedom of information, a selective report on recent writing. Wash., 1949. 153p.

Locates copies by call numbers when in Library of Congress.

1362. U. S. Library of Congress, General Reference and Bibliography Division. "Interracial relationships in the United States: a selected list of references," comp. by Helen F. Conover. Wash., Apr. 2, 1945. 21p. Typed.

1363. U. S. Library of Congress, General Reference and Bibliography Division. "Ideas of liberty: a list of writings by American authors since 1920," comp. by Helen F. Conover. Wash., Dec. 1945. 28p. Typed.

1364. U. S. Library of Congress, General Reference and Bibliography Division. "Race relations: selected references for the study of the integration of minorities in American labor," comp. by Helen F. Conover. Wash., Apr. 1944. 38p. Typed.

Suffrage and elections

1365. U. S. Library of Congress, Division of Bibliography. A list of books (with references to periodicals) relating to proportional representation. Wash.: Govt. Print. Off., 1904. 30p.

1366. U. S. Library of Congress, Division of Bibliography. List of references on primary elections, particularly direct primaries. Wash.: Govt. Print. Off., 1905. 25p.

1367. U. S. Library of Congress, Division of Bibliography. List of references on the electoral college with emphasis on the substitution of direct vote by the people for the electoral college. Wash., Jan. 18, 1937. 17p.

1368. U. S. Library of Congress, Division of Bibliography. List of references on the popular election of senators. Wash.: Govt. Print. Off., 1904. 39p. Additional references. Wash.: Govt. Print. Off., 1911. p. 43-55.

1369. U. S. Library of Congress, Division of Bibliography. Select list of references on corrupt practices in elections. Wash.: Govt. Print. Off., 1908. 12p.

Immigration and colonization

1370. Friedrich, Gerhard. "A new supplement to Seidensticker's American-German bibliography." Pennsylvania history, 7 (Oct. 1940), 213-24.

Lists 77 additional titles to be found either in Juniata College (Huntingdon, Pa.) or collection of W. E. Swigart (Huntingdon, Pa.)

1371. Helbig, Richard E. "German American researches; the growth of the German American collection of the New York Public Library during 1906-1907; its importance for historical and literary studies." German-American annual, n. s. 6 (Sept.-Oct. 1908), 257-85.

Description of the collection; includes a "list of [German] newspapers and periodicals received gratis."

1372. Pan American Union, Columbus Memorial Library. Mexicans in the United States; a bibliography. Wash.: Pan American Union, 1942. 14p. (Bibliographic series, no. 27)

1373. Qualey, Carlton C. "A hunt for Norwegian-American records." Norwegian-American studies and records, 7 (1933), 95-120.

Description of Norwegian-American Historical Association's program for collecting records relating to Norwegians in America.

1374. Smith, Charles Wesley. "A contribution toward a bibliography of Morris Birkbeck and the English settlement in Edwards County, Illinois, founded by Morris Birkbeck and George Flower, 1817-1818." Illinois State Historical Library publications, 10 (1906), 165-77.

Locates copies in several United States libraries.

1375. Union Saint-Jean-Baptiste d'Amérique, Bibliothèque. Catalogue de la Bibliothèque de l'Union, deuxième édition. Woonsocket, R. I., 1935. 302p. First edition, 1917.

Catalog of books, manuscripts and brochures on history of Canada and the United States and their relations with France.

1376. U. S. Library of Congress, Division of Bibliography. Immigration in the United States: a selected list of references, comp. by Anne L. Baden. Wash., 1943. 94p.

1377. U. S. Library of Congress, Division of Bibliography. A list of books (with references to periodicals) on immigration. 3d issue, with additions. Wash.: Govt. Print. Off., 1907. 157p.

1378. U. S. Library of Congress, Division of Bibliography. List of books (with references to periodicals) relating to the theory of colonization, government of dependencies, protectorates, and related topics. 2d ed. with additions. Wash.: Govt. Print. Off., 1900. 156p.

1379. U. S. Library of Congress, Division of Bibliography. List of references on American immigration, including Americanization, effect of European war, etc. [Wash.] 1918. 28 l.

1380. U. S. Library of Congress, Division of Bibliography. A list of books relating to the Germans in the United States. Wash.: Govt. Print. Off., 1904. 32p.

1381. U. S. Library of Congress, Division of Bibliography. Select list of references on Chinese immigration. Wash.: Govt. Print. Off., 1904. 31p.

1382. U. S. Library of Congress, General

Reference and Bibliography Division. Japanese in the United States, a selected list of references, comp. by Helen D. Jones. Wash., 1946. 36p.

1383. U. S. Library of Congress, General Reference and Bibliography Division. Non-self governing areas with special emphasis on mandates and trusteeships: a selected list of references, comp. by Helen F. Conover. Wash., 1947. 2v. (467p.)

1384. U. S. Library of Congress, Reading Room. "Y Cymry yn America; the Welsh in America; references to literature available in the Library of Congress." Wash., 1935. 18 numb. 1. Typed.

Negroes

1385. Atlanta University Library. Harlem on review; exhibition of printed materials from the Harold Jackman collection. Atlanta, Ga., [1943][7]p.
The Jackman collection, in the Atlanta University Library, "consists of all forms of source materials dealing with the life and history of the Negro."

1386. Bontemps, Arna. "Special collections of Negroana." Library quarterly, 14 (1944), 187-206.
Describes 4 large collections in detail and several smaller collections briefly.

1387. Dunlap, Mollie E. "Special collections of Negro literature in the United States." Journal of Negro education, 4 (Oct. 1935), 482-89.
Locates special collections of Negro literature in 9 libraries and 7 private collections.

1388. Frazier, E. Franklin. "The Booker T. Washington papers." Library of Congress quarterly journal of current acquisitions, 2 (Oct. - Dec. 1944), 23-31.
Description of collection deposited in Library of Congress.

1389. Grinstead, S. E., comp. A select, classified, and briefly annotated list of two hundred fifty books by or about the Negro, published during the past 10 years. Nashville, Tenn.: Fisk University, 1939. Unpaged.
Based on Negro collection in Fisk University Library.

1390. Hampton Normal and Agricultural Institute, Collis P. Huntington Library. A classified catalogue of the Negro collection in the Collis P. Huntington Library. Hampton Institute, Va., 1940. 255, [35]p.

1391. Henderson, Rose. "The Schomburg collection of Negro history and literature." Southern workman, 63 (1934), 327-34.
Collection in New York Public Library.

1392. Howard University, Carnegie Library. A catalogue of books in the Moorland Foundation. Wash.: The University, 1939. 6 pts. in 1 v.

1393. Lewinson, Paul. A guide to documents in the National Archives for Negro studies. Wash., 1947. 28p. (American Council of Learned Societies, Committee on Negro Studies publications, no. 1)

1394. Louisville Free Public Library. Some books and pamphlets, music, magazines and newspapers by Negro writers, composers and editors in the Colored Department of the Louisville Free Public Library. Louisville, Ky.: The Library, 1921. 12p. Supplementary list. Louisville, 1922. 4p.

1395. Martin, Thomas P. "Sources of Negro history in the Manuscript Division of the Library of Congress." Journal of Negro history, 19 (1934), 72-76.

1936. Mock, James R. "The National Archives with respect to the records of the Negro." Journal of Negro history, 23 (1938), 49-56.

1397. New York Public Library. "List of works relating to the American Colonization Society, Liberia, Negro colonization, etc., in the New York Public Library." New York Public Library bulletin, 6 (1902), 265-69.

1398. Porter, D. B. "A library on the Negro." American scholar, 7 (Winter, 1938), 115-17.
Describes Howard University Library's resources on Negro.

1399. St. Louis Public Library. The American Negro; a selected list of books, comp. by Norma Klinge and George-Anna Tod. [St. Louis]: The Library, 1923. 14p.

1400. Thompson, Edgar T. and Thompson, Alma Macy. Race and region; a descriptive bibliography compiled with special reference to the relations between whites and Negroes in the U. S. Chapel Hill: Univ. of North Carolina Press, 1949. 194p.

Indicates holdings of Duke University, University of North Carolina and North Carolina College (Durham).

1401. U. S. Library of Congress. 75 years of freedom; commemoration of the 75th anniversary of the proclamation of the 13th amendment to the Constitution of the United States. The Library of Congress. [Wash.: Govt. Print. Off., 1943] 108p.

"The contribution of the American Negro to American culture was the theme of a series of exhibits and concerts in the Library of Congress commencing on December 18th, the 75th anniversary of the proclamation of the Thirteenth amendment, which ended slavery in the United States." - p.v.

1402. U. S. Library of Congress, Division of Bibliography. List of discussions of the fourteenth and fifteenth amendments, with special reference to Negro suffrage. Wash.: Govt. Print. Off., 1906. 18p.

1403. U. S. Library of Congress, Division of Bibliography. Select list of references on the Negro question. 2d issue with additions. Wash.: Govt. Print. Off., 1906. 61p.

Foreign relations

1404. Bemis, Samuel Flagg and Griffin, Grace Gardner. Guide to the diplomatic history of the United States, 1775-1921. Wash.: Govt. Print. Off., 1935. 979p.

Some locations are given throughout the book; pt. 2 includes "a comprehensive summary of the manuscripts and archival collections of the United States and of the major foreign countries which deal with the relations between the United States and those countries."

1405. Benson, Nettie Lee. "Washington: symbol of the United States in Mexico, 1800-1823." University of Texas Library chronicle, 2 (Spring, 1947), 175-82.

Periodicals of Mexico, 1800-23, and their attitudes toward the United States. Based on University of Texas collection.

1406. New York Public Library. "Japanese-American relations: a list of works in the New York Public Library," comp. by Dorothy Purviance Miller. New York Public Library bulletin, 25 (1921), 47-54, 89-102, 157-71, 326-47. Reprinted. 67p.

1407. Pan American Union, Columbus Memorial Library. Bibliography on the Monroe Doctrine... in the library of the Pan American Union. [Wash., 1924] 23 numb. l.

1408. Pan American Union, Columbus Memorial Library. Recent trends in inter-American relations; a bibliography. Wash.: The Union, 1939, 52p. (Bibliographic series, No. 21)

All works listed are in Columbus Memorial Library.

1409. Pan American Union, Columbus Memorial Library. Selected list of books and magazine articles on inter-American relations. Wash., 1934. 20 numb. l. (Bibliographic series, no. 7. 2d ed.)

1410. Pennsylvania Historical Survey. Calendar of Joel R. Poinsett papers in the Henry D. Gilpin collection. Philadelphia: Hist. Soc. of Pennsylvania, 1941. 264p.

613 items of personal letters and documents relating to history of American diplomacy, 1794-1851, in Historical Society of Pennsylvania Library.

1411. Peterson, Clarence S., comp. American-Scandinavian diplomatic relations, 1776-1876. [Baltimore?] 1948. 92p.

Calendar of documents in Library of Congress, National Archives, and private collections.

1412. U. S. Library of Congress, Division of Bibliography. Foreign relations of the United States: a bibliographical list. Wash., May 21, 1929. 24p. [Supplementary list] Apr. 9, 1935. 23p.

1413. U. S. Library of Congress, Division of Bibliography. List of recent books on foreign relations of the United States (supplementary to mimeographed lists of 1929 and 1935), comp. by Helen F. Conover. [Wash.] 1940. 55p.

1414. U. S. Library of Congress, Division of Bibliography. List of references on the

Monroe doctrine. Wash.: Govt. Print. Off., 1919. 122p.

1415. U. S. Library of Congress, Division of Bibliography. A selected list of references on the diplomatic and trade relations of the United States with the Union of Soviet Socialist Republics, 1919-1935, comp. by Helen F. Conover. Wash., 1935. 29p.

1416. U. S. Library of Congress, Division of Bibliography. United States relations with Mexico and Central America, with special reference to intervention: a bibliographical list. Wash., Nov. 13, 1928. 30p.

1417. U. S. Library of Congress, Legislative Reference Service. List of references on American-Japanese relations from July 1, 1939 to December 1941. [Wash., 1942] 12p.

1418. U. S. National Archives. President Roosevelt and international cooperation for war and peace; an exhibit of Franklin D. Roosevelt library materials and Federal records. Wash., 1945. 12p.

Legislatures and legislation

1419. Griffin, Appleton Prentiss Clark. List of books, etc., treating of the United States Senate. [Wash.: Govt. Print. Off., 1906] 11p. (59th Cong., 1st sess. Senate. Doc. 303)
In Library of Congress.

1420. Hasse, Adelaide R. Index of economic material in documents of the states of the United States: California, 1849-1904. [Wash.: Carnegie Institution of Washington, 1908.] 316p.
Unless otherwise indicated, material indexed is in New York Public Library.

1421. Hasse, Adelaide R. Index of economic material in documents of the states of the United States: Delaware, 1789-1904. [Wash.]: Carnegie Institution of Washington, 1910. 137p.
Unless otherwise indicated, material indexed is in New York Public Library.

1422. Hasse, Adelaide R. Index of economic material in documents of the states of the United States: Illinois, 1809-1904. [Wash.]: Carnegie Institution of Washington, 1909. 393p.
Unless otherwise indicated, material indexed is in New York Public Library.

1423. Hasse, Adelaide R. Index of economic material in documents of the states of the United States: Kentucky, 1792-1904. [Wash.]: Carnegie Institution of Washington, 1910. 452p.
Unless otherwise indicated, material indexed is in New York Public Library.

1424. Hasse, Adelaide Rosalie. Index of economic material in documents of the states of the United States: Maine, 1820-1904. [Wash.]: Carnegie Institution of Washington, 1907. 95p.
Unless otherwise indicated, material indexed is in New York Public Library.

1425. Hasse, Adelaide R. Index of economic material in documents of the states of the United States: Massachusetts, 1789-1904. [Wash.]: Carnegie Institution of Washington, 1908. 310p.
Unless otherwise indicated, material indexed is in New York Public Library.

1426. Hasse, Adelaide R. Index of economic material in documents of the states of the United States: New Hampshire, 1789-1904. [Wash.]: Carnegie Institution of Washington, 1907. 66p.
Unless otherwise indicated, material indexed is in New York Public Library.

1427. Hasse, Adelaide R. Index of economic material in documents of the states of the United States: New Jersey, 1789-1904. [Wash.]: Carnegie Institution of Washington, 1914. 705p.
Unless otherwise indicated, material indexed is in New York Public Library.

1428. Hasse, Adelaide R. Index of economic material in documents of the states of the United States: New York, 1789-1904. [Wash.]: Carnegie Institution of Washington, 1907. 553p.
Unless otherwise indicated, material indexed is in New York Public Library.

1429. Hasse, Adelaide R. Index of economic material in documents of the states of the United States: Ohio, 1787-1904. [Wash.]: Carnegie Institution of Washington, 1912. 2v.
Unless otherwise indicated material indexed is in New York Public Library.

SOCIAL SCIENCES

1430. Hasse, Adelaide R. Index of economic material in documents of the states of the United States: Pennsylvania, 1790-1904. [Wash.]: Carnegie Institution of Washington, 1919-22. 1v. in 3pts.

Unless otherwise indicated, material indexed is in New York Public Library.

1431. Hasse, Adelaide Rosalie. Index of economic material in documents of the states of the United States: Rhode Island, 1789-1904. [Wash.]: Carnegie Insitution of Washington, 1908. 95p.

Unless otherwise indicated, material indexed is in New York Public Library.

1432. Hasse, Adelaide R. Index of economic material in documents of the states of the United States: Vermont, 1789-1904. [Wash.]: Carnegie Institution of Washington, 1907. 71p.

Unless otherwise indicated, material indexed is in New York Public Library.

1433. Jenkins, William S. Supplement check list of legislative journals of the states of the United States of America. Boston: Nat. Assoc. of State Libraries, 1943. 107p.

Locates some unique copies and manuscripts. Supplementary information to the "Check list" - not a revision.

1434. John Crerar Library. Guide to the serial and periodical publications in Great Britain. Parliament. Sessional papers. 1914-1933, preliminary edition, comp. by Ruby Lane Taylor. Chicago, 1934. 53p. (Reference list 30)

1435. Tennessee State Library, Legislative Reference Dept. Index of legislative reference material. Nashville: McQuiddy Printing Co., 1915. 85p.

1436. Texas State Library. Finding-list of books on political science, law and allied topics, prep. by John Boynton Kaiser. Austin: Austin Print. Co., 1911. 51p. (Texas Library and Historical Commission. Legislative Reference Section. Bulletin, no. 1)

A catalog of books in Texas State Library on political and social sciences and law. Excludes United States and state documents.

1437. U. S. Congress, House Library. Index of congressional committee hearings in the library of the United States House of Representatives prior to Jan. 3, 1943. Wash.: Govt. Print. Off., 1944. 399 p.

-----. Supplemental index to Congressional committee hearings, January 3, 1943 to Jan. 3, 1947, comp. by Elizabeth M. Shumaker. Wash.: Govt. Print. Off., 1947. 63p.

1438. U. S. Congress, Senate Library. Catalogue of the library of the United States Senate. Wash.: Govt. Print. Off., 1924. 1,210p. Supersedes various earlier catalogs: 1895, 1901, 1906, 1908, 1910, 1912, 1914, 1916, 1918, 1920, 1922.

1439. U. S. Congress, Senate Library. Index of congressional committee hearings (not confidential in character) prior to January 3, 1935 in the United States Senate Library. Wash.: Govt. Print. Off., 1935. 1,056p. Supplements were printed in 1937 (148p.), and 1939 (270p.)

1440. U. S. Library of Congress, Division of Bibliography. "Apportionment of members of the House of Representatives: a list of references." Wash., Sept. 17, 1928. 25p. Typed.

1441. U. S. Library of Congress, Division of Bibliography. "The Congress of the United States: a bibliographical list." Wash., Dec. 21, 1926. 42p. Typed.

1442. U. S. Library of Congress, Division of Bibliography. List of references on one chamber and two chamber legislatures (supplementary to the list in Special Libraries, March, 1914), comp. by Grace H. Fuller. Wash., Apr. 3, 1937. 15p.

1443. U. S. Library of Congress, Division of Bibliography. "List of references on senators from Ohio." Wash., May 31, 1922. 29p. Typed.

1444. U. S. Library of Congress, Division of Bibliography. "Women in the Congress of the United States: a list of references." Wash., Feb. 7, 1941. 22p. Typed.

1445. U. S. Library of Congress, Legislative Reference Service. The organization of Congress; a select, annotated bibliography on the organization, procedure and reorganization of Congress, comp. by William R. Tansill. Wash.: Govt. Print. Off., 1945. 22p.

1446. U. S. National Archives. Preliminary inventory of the records of the Senate Committee on Appropriations: Subcommittee on Inquiry in re Transfer of Employees, 1942, comp. by Theodore J. Cassady and Harold E. Hufford. Wash., 1948. 8p. (Preliminary inventory, no. 12)

1447. U. S. National Archives. Preliminary inventory of the records of the United States Senate, comp. by Harold E. Hufford and Watson G. Caudill. Wash., 1950. 284p. (Preliminary inventory, no. 23)

Political parties

1448. Massachusetts Historical Society. Historical index to the [Timothy] Pickering papers, ed. by Harriet E. Green. Boston, 1896. 580p. (The Society's collections, 6th series, v. 8).

A collection of manuscripts about history of the Federalist party, now in Massachusetts Historical Society.

1449. New York Public Library. "Political parties in the United States, 1800-1914; a list of references," comp. by Alta Claflin. New York Public Library bulletin, 19 (1915), 647-718. Reprinted. 74p.

1450. U. S. Library of Congress, Division of Bibliography. List of works relating to political parties in the United States. Wash.: Govt. Print. Off., 1907. 29p.

1451. U. S. Library of Congress, Division of Bibliography. A selected list of references on the history of political parties in the United States, comp. by Grace H. Fuller. Wash., May 14, 1936. 43p.

ECONOMICS

General

1452. Columbia University Library. That these treasures shall endure. [N. Y.] Columbia Univ. Press, n. d. 12p.

General statement, with little detailed information, on Edwin R. A. Seligman economic history collection.

1453. Georgetown University, School of Foreign Service. The political economy of total war. Wash.: School of Foreign Service, Georgetown University [1942] 128p.

Cover title: Syllabus for two courses of study of one term each on the political economy of total war, including an essay on geopolitics... Bibliography by Legislative reference service, Library of Congress.

1454. Harvard University, Bureau for Economic Research in Latin America. Economic literature of Latin America, a tentative bibliography. Cambridge: Harvard Univ. Press, 1935-36. 2v.

Appendix B: Notes on collections of Latin American economic literature in leading libraries.

1455. Harvard University, Graduate School of Business Administration, Baker Library. "The Adam Smith collection at the Harvard School of Business Administration." Business Historical Society bulletin, 19 (1945), 26-28.

1456. Harvard University, Graduate School of Business Administration, Baker Library. The Vanderblue Memorial collection of Smithiana, by Charles J. Bullock. Boston: The Library, 1939. 68p. (Kress Library of Business and Economics, publication, no. 2)

Catalog of Adam Smith collection in Baker Library.

1457. Harvard University Library. Guides to the Harvard libraries, no. 1: Economics and business, by Arthur H. Cole. Cambridge: Harvard University Library, 1947. 64p.

Also published as Guide to the Harvard libraries for the use of research workers in business and economics. Cambridge, 1947.

1458. Hill, Edwin C. "A priceless treasure of business." Nation's business, 18 (Sept. 1930), 33-35, 164, 166.

Brief description of Seligman collection of business books at Columbia University.

1459. John Crerar Library. A catalogue of French economic documents from the sixteenth, seventeenth and eighteenth centuries. Chicago: The Library, 1918. 104p.

A collection of 1,471 items in John Crerar Library.

1460. [John Crerar Library] NRA, the new deal for business and industry; a bibliography, May-August, 1933, together with a list of official publications of other new governmental agencies, compiled for the John Crerar Library by Jerome K. Wilcox. Chicago: American Library Association, 1933. 78p.

Lists material in John Crerar Library and University of Chicago's School of Commerce and Administration library.

1461. New York Public Library. "Check list of works in the New York Public Library on the theory of value." New York Public Library bulletin, 6 (1902), 171-73.

1462. New York Public Library. "Check list of works in the New York Public Library relating to the financial and commercial history of Brooklyn." New York Public Library bulletin, 6 (1902), 46-49.

1463. New York Public Library. "Check list of works relating to the financial and commercial history, etc., of the City of New York in the New York Public Library." New York Public Library bulletin, 5 (1901), 42-59.

1464. New York Public Library. "Economic and social aspects of war; a selected list of references," comp. by William Nathaniel Seaver. New York Public Library bulletin, 19 (1915), 167-78. Reprinted. 14p.

1465. Pan American Union, Columbus Memorial Library. Current Latin American periodicals relating to economic subjects in the library of the Pan American Union. Wash.: The Union, 1938. 36 numb. l. (Bibliographic series, no. 20)

1466. Seligman, Edwin Robert Anderson. Curiosities of early economic literature. San Francisco: Priv. print. by John Henry Nash, 1920. 26p.

Seligman collection described is now in Columbia University Library.

1467. Stanford University, Hoover Library. Industrial relations in Germany, 1914-1939; annotated bibliography of materials in the Hoover Library on War, Revolution, and Peace and the Stanford University Library, comp. by Waldo Chamberlin. Stanford University: Stanford Univ. Press [1942] 403p.

Lists 1,720 items.

1468. U. S. Dept. of Commerce Library. Price sources; index of commercial and economic publications currently received in the libraries of the Department of Commerce which contain current market commodity prices, comp. by Elizabeth M. Carmack. Wash.: Govt. Print. Off., 1931. 320p.

1469. U. S. Dept. of Labor Library. Reconstruction: a preliminary bibliography, comp. by Laura A. Thompson. [Wash., 1918] 57 numb. l. Supplementary list of references. Wash., 1919. 52 numb. l.

1470. U. S. Library of Congress, Division of Bibliography. The business situation, 1929-1931, and its recovery: a select list of references. Wash., Oct. 12, 1931. 31p.

1471. U. S. Library of Congress, Division of Bibliography. Economic conditions in the United States, a list of recent references. Wash., Sept. 19, 1932. 32p.

1472. U. S. Library of Congress, Division of Bibliography. "The economic policy of Soviet Russia, with special reference to the five-year plans: a bibliographical list," comp. by Helen F. Conover. Wash., Mar. 24, 1939. 19p. Typed.

1473. U. S. Library of Congress, Division of Bibliography. Select list of references on economic reconstruction, including reports of the British Ministry of Reconstruction. Wash.: Govt. Print. Off., 1919. 47p.

1474. U. S. National Archives. Preliminary list of published and unpublished reports of the National Resources Planning Board, 1933-1943, comp. by Lester W. Smith and others. Wash., 1946. 138p. (Special report, no. 3)

1475. U. S. Treasury Dept. Library. National wealth and national income in the United States and foreign countries, 1935-42; selected list of references, comp. by Wanda M. Johnson. Wash., 1943. 79p. Supplement. Wash., 1945. 78p.

Unless otherwise indicated, material is in Treasury Library.

Money and banking

1476. Bender, John E. "The William A. Porter collection." University of Pennsylvania Library chronicle, 5 (1937), 36-41.

Manuscripts relating to legal history of

Second Bank of the United States, in University of Pennsylvania Library.

1477. Cole, Arthur H. "The Bancroft collection." Business Historical Society bulletin, 9 (1935), 93-96.
  A collection of printed and manuscript material in Baker Library, Harvard School of Business Administration, relating to "South Sea Bubble" in 18th century.

1478. New York Public Library. "The Bank for International Settlements; a list of references," comp. by Rollin Alger Sawyer. New York Public Library bulletin, 36 (1932), 229-42. Reprinted. 16p.

1479. New York Public Library. "The Federal Reserve Banking System; a bibliography," comp. by Rollin Alger Sawyer. New York Public Library bulletin, 32 (1928), 34-48, 93-126, 180-94, 221-47. Reprinted. 106p. "Supplement number one," appeared in the Bulletin, 35 (1931), 229-38, 477-98. Reprinted. 32p.
  Shows New York Public Library's holdings.

1480. New York Public Library. "List of works in the New York Public Library relating to bimetallism, gold and silver standards, etc." New York Public Library bulletin, 9 (1905), 344-87. Reprinted. 44p.

1481. New York Public Library. "List of works in the New York Public Library relating to money and banking." New York Public Library bulletin, 12 (1908), 192-228, 239-82, 295-331, 346-99. Reprinted. 170p.

1482. New York Public Library. "Social credit; a reading list," comp. by Rollin Alger Sawyer. New York Public Library bulletin, 40 (1936), 411-18. Reprinted. 10p.

1483. New York Public Library. "The world depression, 1929- . A list of books and pamphlets," comp. by William Wayne Shirley. New York Public Library bulletin, 37 (1933), 970-90, 1040-68. Reprinted, with additions and revisions, 1934.

1484. Pinkett, Harold T. "Records in the National Archives relating to the Civilian Conservation Corps." Social service review, 22 (March 1948), 46-53.

1485. U. S. Farm Credit Administration Library. A selected list of references on the Farm Credit Administration, comp. by Robert Haven Willey. Wash., 1935. 56p.

1486. U. S. Library of Congress, Division of Bibliography. Branch, group, and chain banking: a list of recent writings, comp. by Anne L. Baden. Wash., Apr. 15, 1937. 30p.

1487. U. S. Library of Congress, Division of Bibliography. Federal and state control of banking, with special reference to guaranty of deposits: a bibliographical list of writings, comp. by Anne L. Baden. [Wash., 1932] 32p.

1488. U. S. Library of Congress, Division of Bibliography. Inflation: a selected list of recent references, comp. by Grace Hadley Fuller. [Wash.] 1942. 46p.

1489. U. S. Library of Congress, Division of Bibliography. Inflation: a supplementary list of references, comp. by Florence S. Hellman, [Wash.] 1943. 43p.

1490. U. S. Library of Congress, Division of Bibliography. Inflation and deflation of the currency; a list of references. [Wash., 1933] 20p.

1491. U. S. Library of Congress, Division of Bibliography. List of books with references to periodicals, relating to postal savings banks. Wash.: Govt. Print. Off., 1908. 23p.

1492. U. S. Library of Congress, Division of Bibliography. A list of recent references on bankruptcy in the U. S. (Supplementing list of January 2, 1940), comp. by Grace Hadley Fuller. [Wash.] 1941. 23p.

1493. U. S. Library of Congress, Division of Bibliography. A list of references on tax exemption of securities, comp. by Florence S. Hellman. [Wash.] 1942. 17p. Supplementary to mimeographed lists, 1931 and 1938 (same title)

1494. U. S. Library of Congress, Division of Bibliography. A list of the more important books in the Library of Congress on banks and banking. Wash.: Govt. Print. Off., 1904. 55p.

1495. U. S. Library of Congress, Division of Bibliography. A list of works relating to the first and second banks of the United States, with chronological list of reports, etc., contained in the American state papers and in the Congressional documents. Wash.: Govt. Print. Off., 1908. 47p.

1496. U. S. Library of Congress, Division of Bibliography. Select list of books with references to periodicals, relating to currency and banking, with special regard to recent conditions. Wash.: Govt. Print. Off., 1908. 93p.

1497. U. S. Library of Congress, Division of Bibliography. Select list of references on the monetary question, comp. by H. H. B. Meyer, and W. A. Slade. Wash.: Govt. Print. Off., 1913. 247p.

1498. U. S. Library of Congress, Division of Bibliography. Selected list of references on bankruptcy in the U. S., with special reference to bankruptcy legislation, 1929-1939, comp. by Grace Hadley Fuller. [Wash.] 1940. 48p.

1499. U. S. Library of Congress, General Reference and Bibliography Division. Money and banking: a selected list of references, comp. by Helen F. Conover. Wash., 1946. 14 l.

1500. U. S. Library of Congress, Legislative Reference Service. Building and loan associations, a bibliography, by W. H. Gilbert. [Wash., 1941] 58 l.

1501. U. S. National Archives. Preliminary check list of records of the Division of Insolvent National Banks of the Bureau of the Comptroller of the Currency 1865-1945, comp. by Lyle J. Holverstott, Maxcy R. Dixon and J. Eric Maddox. [Wash., 1946] 14p. (Preliminary check list, no. 45)

1502. U. S. Securities and Exchange Commission Library. Complete list of material; revised to December 1, 1939. [Wash., 1939] 341p. Supplement, no. 1, Wash., 1940. 12p.

1503. Wall, Alexander J. "The Landauer lottery collection." New-York Historical Society quarterly bulletin, 16 (1932), 87-91.
   Collection, held by New York Historical Society, consists of lottery cards and advertisements.

Natural resources

1504. New York Public Library. "Nationalization of coal mines; a list of references in the New York Public Library," comp. by Rollin Alger Sawyer. New York Public Library bulletin, 24 (1920), 297-305. Reprinted. 11p.

1505. U. S. Library of Congress, Division of Bibliography. Conservation of natural resources in the United States, a selected list of recent references, comp. by Anne L. Baden. [Wash.] 1942. 59p. Earlier ed. [Wash. 1934] 65p.

1506. U. S. Library of Congress, Division of Bibliography. List of references on water rights and the control of waters. Wash.: Govt. Print. Off., 1914. 111p. Supplement. 1931. 26p.

1507. U. S. Library of Congress, Division of Bibliography. Select list of references on the conservation of natural resources in the United States. Wash.: Govt. Print. Off., 1912. 110p.

1508. Washington State Library. Select list of references on conservation of natural resources, comp. by Josephine Holgate. Olympia, Wash., 1911. 37p.

Cooperation

1509. Detroit Public Library. Consumer problems and cooperation in the United States; a selected list of references. [Detroit]: The Library, 1937. 25p.

1510. U. S. Library of Congress, Division of Bibliography. Cooperation in the United States and foreign countries: a list of bibliographies, comp. by Anne L. Baden. Wash., 1943. 35p.

1511. U. S. Library of Congress, Division of Bibliography. A selected list of recent books and pamphlets on cooperation in the United States and foreign countries, comp. by Grace Hadley Fuller. Wash., Dec. 1937. 50p. [Supplementary list] June 22, 1939. 44p.

Socialism and collectivism

1512. Columbia University Library. Brook farm, 1841-1847, an exhibition to commemorate the centenary of its founding. Check list and historical introduction compiled from the

exhibition notes, written by Arthur Eugene Bestor, Jr. ... Rev. ed., with check list of items newly added to the exhibit, and a reference list of important books not on display. N. Y., 1941. 11p. (Columbia University Libraries, Exhibition notes no. 1, 2d ed.)
Includes some loaned material.

1513. U. S. Library of Congress, General Reference and Bibliography Division. "Communal settlements in the United States; a selected list of references," comp. by Helen Dudenbostel Jones. Wash., 1947. 74 l. Typed.

1514. U. S. Library of Congress, General Reference and Bibliography Division. "German Communists, 1925-1945: a selected list of references," comp. by David Baumgardt. Wash., 1949. 15p. Typed.

Public finance

1515. Massachusetts State Library. Bibliography of works on taxation, January, 1898, prep. by Ellen M. Sawyer. [Boston]: Wright & Potter Printing Co., [1898] 25p.
A list of works in Library on taxation in the United States and foreign countries.

1516. New York Public Library. "Check list of American federal documents relating to finance in the New York Public Library." New York Public Library bulletin, 6 (1902), 287-92. Reprinted with "Check list of American municipal official documents relating to finance." 41p.

1517. New York Public Library. "Check list of American official documents relating to finance in the New York Public Library." New York Public Library bulletin, 6 (1902), 315-27. Reprinted with "Check list of American federal documents relating to finance." 41p.

1518. New York Public Library. "Check list of foreign government documents on finance in the New York Public Library." New York Public Library bulletin, 5 (1901), 457-86.

1519. New York Public Library. "Henry George and the single tax; a list of references to material in the New York Public Library," comp. by Rollin Alger Sawyer. New York Public Library bulletin, 30 (1926), 481-503, 571-98, 685-716. Reprinted. 90p.
A list of George's manuscripts, printed works, and a representative collection of critical writings in New York Public Library.

1520. New York Public Library. "War taxation, 1914-1917; list of references to material in the New York Public Library," comp. by Morris Kolchin. New York Public Library bulletin, 21 (1917), 459-70. Reprinted. 14p.

1521. U. S. Library of Congress, Division of Bibliography. Defense financing: a selected list of references, comp. by Grace Hadley Fuller. [Wash.] 1941. 40p. A supplementary list of references. [Wash.] 1942. 45p.

1522. U. S. Library of Congress, Division of Bibliography. Federal income tax in the United States: a selected list of recent references, comp. by Helen F. Conover. [Wash.] 1942. 27p. Supplementary to lists of Dec. 10, 1931, July 9, 1934, and June 8, 1937.

1523. U. S. Library of Congress, Division of Bibliography. Inheritance taxation, a list of recent references. Wash., 1940. 38p.

1524. U. S. Library of Congress, Division of Bibliography. List of recent references on the income tax. Wash.: Govt. Print. Off., 1921. 96p. Supplements list issued in 1907.

1525. U. S. Library of Congress, Division of Bibliography. List of references on exemptions from taxation (exclusive of tax exempt securities). Wash., May 24, 1932. 13p. [Supplementary list] comp. by Florence S. Hellman. Feb. 28, 1941. 31p. Typed.

1526. U. S. Library of Congress, Division of Bibliography. List of references on lotteries in the United States and foreign countries, with emphasis on their use as a means of raising governmental revenue, comp. by Anne L. Baden. [Wash.] 1934. 30p.

1527. U. S. Library of Congress, Division of Bibliography. "List of references relating to debts of southern states incurred for railroads and internal improvements." Wash., 1910. 28p. Typed.

1528. U. S. Library of Congress, Division of Bibliography. "List of works relating to collection of debts of foreign countries." Wash., 1907. 25p. Typed.

1529. U. S. Library of Congress, Division of Bibliography. Sales tax in the United States and foreign countries; a selected list of references, comp. by Anne L. Baden. [Wash.] 1942. 61p.

1530. U. S. Library of Congress, Division of Bibliography. Select list of references on the budget of foreign countries. Wash.: Govt. Print. Off., 1904. 19p.

1531. U. S. Library of Congress, Division of Bibliography. Select list of works relating to taxation of inheritances and of incomes; United States and some foreign countries. Wash.: Govt. Print. Off., 1907. 86p. Additional references. 1911. p. 87-144.

1532. U. S. Library of Congress, Division of Bibliography. A selected list of recent references on inheritance taxation in the United States and foreign countries, comp. by Ann Duncan Brown. [Wash., 1935] 47p.

1533. U. S. Library of Congress, Division of Bibliography. A selected list of references on the cost of government in the United States: federal, state, county and municipal, comp. by Grace Hadley Fuller. Wash., Oct. 1934. 38p. [Supplementary list] 1940. 40p.

1534. U. S. Library of Congress, Division of Bibliography. A selected list of references on the federal budget, comp. by Grace Hadley Fuller. [Wash.] 1940. 17p.

1535. U. S. Library of Congress, Division of Bibliography. State taxation: a bibliographical list of recent writings. Wash., June 13, 1932. 52p.

1536. U. S. Library of Congress, Division of Bibliography. Tariff revision, 1929: a bibliographical list. [Wash.] 1929. 25p.

1537. U. S. Library of Congress, Division of Bibliography. Taxation of natural resources, with special reference to severance taxes: a bibliographical list of writings, comp. by Anne L. Baden. [Wash.] 1940. 17p.

1538. U. S. Library of Congress, Legislative Reference Service. Bibliography on federal taxation. [Wash., 1942.] 21p.

1539. U. S. Library of Congress, Reading Room. "A list of references on the sales tax." [Wash., 1932] 29 numb. l. Typed.

1540. U. S. National Archives. Preliminary inventory of the land-entry papers of the General Land Office, comp. by Harry B. Yoshipe and Philip P. Browder. Wash., 1949. 77p. (Preliminary inventory, no. 22)
Collection located in National Archives.

1541. U. S. National Archives. Preliminary inventory of the records of the United States Direct Tax Commission for the District of South Carolina, comp. by Jane Greene. Wash., 1948. 8p. (Preliminary inventory, no. 14)

1542. Virginia State Library. "A bibliography of taxation in Virginia since 1910," comp. by Wilmer L. Hall. Virginia State Library bulletin, 16 (1925), 1-38.
"With a few specified exceptions all the matter listed is in the State Library." Limited to literature relating directly to Virginia from 1910 to 1925.

Tariff

1543. New York Public Library. "A check list of works in the New York Public Library relating to corn laws." New York Public Library bulletin, 6 (1902), 191-200.

1544. U. S. Library of Congress, Division of Bibliography. Brief list of references on the tariff question: pro and con. Wash., May 9, 1922. 11p. [Supplementary list] Jan. 21, 1928. 27p.

1545. U. S. Library of Congress, Division of Bibliography. A list of books (with references to periodicals) on mercantile marine subsidies, by A. P. C. Griffin. 3d ed. with additions. Wash.: Govt. Print. Off., 1906. 140p. Additional references relating to mercantile marine subsidies. Wash.: Govt. Print. Off., 1911. 141-164p.

1546. U. S. Library of Congress, Division of Bibliography. List of references on reciprocity. 2d ed. Wash.: Govt. Print. Off., 1910. 137p.

1547. U. S. Library of Congress, Division of Bibliography. List of works on the tariffs of foreign countries. General; Continental tariff union; France; Germany; Switzerland; Italy;

Russia; Canada. Wash.: Govt. Print. Off., 1906. 42p.

1548. U. S. Library of Congress, Division of Bibliography. Select list of references on the British tariff movement (Chamberlain's plan). 2d issue, with additions. Wash.: Govt. Print. Off., 1906. 60p.

1549. U. S. Library of Congress, Division of Bibliography. Select list of references on wool, with special reference to the tariff. Wash.: Govt. Print. Off., 1911. 163p.

1550. U. S. Tariff Commission Library. Reciprocal trade; a current bibliography; selected list of references. 3d ed. Wash., 1937. 282p. Supplement to the 3d ed., Wash., 1940. 232p.

1551. U. S. Tariff Commission. The tariff: a bibliography. Wash.: Govt. Print. Off., 1934. 980p. Earlier edition: A list of books and pamphlets relating to the tariff. [Wash., 1932] 48p.

Production and economic organization

1552. Carnegie Library of Pittsburgh. Literature of the coal industry, 1920-1925, comp. by E. H. McClelland. Pittsburgh: The Library, 1921-26. (1920-23 reprinted from Coal industry, 1921-24; 1924-25 reprinted from Coal trade bulletin, 1925-26)

1553. Guthrie, Chester L. "The United States Grain Corporation records in the National Archives." Agricultural history, 12 (1938), 347-54.

1554. New York Public Library. "A list of works in the New York Public Library, relating to prices." New York Public Library bulletin, 6 (1902), 115-59.

1555. St. Louis Public Library. Furs and fur bearers of the United States and Canada, a list of books and articles on the technology and romance of the subject, comp. by Edith Varney. [St. Louis]: The Library, 1929. 10p. (Reprinted from the Library's Monthly bulletin, April 1929)

1556. U. S. Library of Congress, Division of Bibliography. The effect of war on the cost of living: a selected list of references, comp. by Ann Duncan Brown. Rev. ed. [Wash.] 1942. 32p.

1557. U. S. Library of Congress, Division of Bibliography. List of books, with references to periodicals, relating to trusts. 3d ed., with supplementary select list to 1906. Wash.: Govt. Print. Off., 1907. 93p.

1558. U. S. Library of Congress, Division of Bibliography. Maintenance of resale prices in the United States; a bibliographical list, comp. by Anne L. Baden. [Wash., 1930] 19p.

1559. U. S. Library of Congress, Division of Bibliography. Petroleum industry of the United States; a selected list of recent references, comp. by Anne L. Baden. [Wash.] 1942. 60p.

1560. U. S. Library of Congress, Division of Bibliography. Select list of references on sugar, chiefly in its economic aspects. Wash.: Govt. Print. Off., 1910. 238p.

1561. U. S. Library of Congress, Division of Bibliography. Select list of references on the cost of living and prices. Wash.: Govt. Print. Off., 1910. 107p. Additional references. Wash.: Govt. Print. Off., 1912. 120p.

1562. U. S. Library of Congress, Division of Bibliography. A selected list of references on economic planning, with a section on economic councils, comp. by Florence S. Hellman. Wash., Oct. 24, 1935. 39p.

1563. U. S. Library of Congress, Division of Bibliography. Water power in the United States; a selected list of references, comp. by Anne L. Baden. [Wash.] 1929. 40p. Supplement. 1933. 28p.

1564. U. S. Library of Congress, General Reference and Bibliography Division. Cartels, combines and trusts; a selected list of references, comp. by Frances Cheney. Wash., 1944. 123p.

1565. U. S. Library of Congress, General Reference and Bibliography Division. "Coal and fuel utilization in the U. S. S. R.: a selected list of references," comp. by Elizabeth A. Gardner. Wash., Dec. 6, 1948. 15p. Typed.

1566. U. S. Library of Congress, Legislative

Reference Service. Bibliography on full employment. Wash.: Govt. Print. Off., 1945. 56p. (79th Cong., 1st sess. Senate Committee print. no. 2)

1567. U. S. Library of Congress, Legislative Reference Service. Cartels and international patent agreements; a selected and annotated bibliography with index of commodities, comp. by Leisa Bronson. Wash., 1943. 49p.

1568. U. S. Library of Congress, Legislative Reference Service. The war production program. Selected documentation on the economics of war. Wash.: Division of Information, War Production Board, 1942. 31p.
Lists 142 titles available in Library of Congress.

1569. U. S. Library of Congress, Reading Room. "A list of references on economic planning." [Wash., D. C., 1933] 22 (i. e. 23) numb. l. Typed.
Library of Congress call numbers are indicated when available.

1570. U. S. Tariff Commission Library. Raw materials bibliography; general references to selected raw materials and basic economic resources. Wash., 1939. 85 numb. l.

LABOR

General

1571. Black, J. William. References on the history of labor and some contemporary labor problems. Oberlin, Ohio, 1893. 43p. (Oberlin College Library bulletin, v. 1, no. 2)

1572. Illinois, University, Institute of Labor and Industrial Relations. University of Illinois library resources in labor and industrial relations. [Urbana]: The Institute, 1949. 141 numb. l.
Survey and listing of resources in field, held by University of Illinois Library.

1573. Los Angeles Public Library, Municipal Reference Library. Veteran employment in public service. 1945. 7 numb. l. (Social adjustment bibliographies, no. 3)

1574. Michigan, University, Library. "The Labadie labor collection," by Roland C.

Stewart. Michigan alumnus quarterly review, 53 (1946), 247-53. Reprinted.

1575. Pan American Union, Columbus Memorial Library. Bibliography on labor and social welfare in Latin America. Wash.: Pan American Union, Division of Labor and Social Supervision, 1944. 76 numb. l.
Based on holdings of Pan American Union Library.

1576. Steele, Helen M. "The Library of the United States Department of Labor, Washington, D. C." Special libraries, 41 (1950), 93-97.
Description of resources and organization.

1577. U. S. Bureau of Labor Library. References to material on industrial diseases in the Library of the United States Bureau of Labor. Wash., 1912. 30 numb. l.

1578. U. S. Department of Labor. Employment of the physically handicapped: selected references, comp. by Helen M. Steele and Lola A. Wyckoff. Wash.: U. S. Dept. of Labor, 1948. 68p.

1579. U. S. Department of Labor. "Labor banks in the United States: a list of references," comp. by Laura A. Thompson. U. S. Bureau of Labor Statistics monthly labor review, 23 (1926), 661-70.

1580. U. S. Department of Labor. "Recent references on convict labor," comp. by Edna L. Stone. U. S. Bureau of Labor Statistics monthly labor review, 21 (1925), 867-86.

1581. U. S. Department of Labor Library. "Absenteeism in industry: a list of references," comp. by Edna L. Stone and Carolyn Cox. U. S. Bureau of Labor Statistics monthly labor review, 25 (1927), 190-97.

1582. U. S. Department of Labor Library. Frances Perkins: a bibliographical list. [Wash. 1937] 17p.
Supplemented by Frances Perkins: a bibliographical list, 1937-1945. Wash., 1945. 12p.

1583. U. S. Department of Labor Library. Labor and industry: list of periodicals and newspapers in U. S. Department of Labor Library (arranged by country). [Wash., 1919] 23 numb. l.

1584. U. S. Department of Labor Library. "List of labor papers and journals... received currently." U. S. Bureau of Labor Statistics monthly labor review, 8 (June 1919), 334-53.

1585. U. S. Department of Labor Library. List of references on the Kansas Court of Industrial Relations, comp. by Laura A. Thompson. [Wash., 1921] 10 numb. l.
   Supplementary list, issued 1922. 5 numb. l. Superseded by U. S. Bureau of Labor Statistics bulletin 322, p. 39-51.

1586. U. S. Department of Labor Library. Monthly statistics of employment, wages and hours, issued currently by state labor departments. [Wash., 1938] 6p. Revised ed., 1939.

1587. U. S. Department of Labor Library. "The older worker in industry: list of references." U. S. Bureau of Labor Statistics monthly labor review, 29 (1929), 237-42.

1588. U. S. Department of Labor Library. The public contracts (Walsh-Healey) acts: selected references, comp. by Eleanor M. Mitchell. Wash., 1940. 16p.

1589. U. S. Department of Labor Library. Recent literature on collective bargaining, comp. by Laura A. Thompson. [Washington, 1919] 9 numb. l.

1590. U. S. Department of Labor Library. "Workers' leisure: a selected list of references." U. S. Bureau of Labor Statistics monthly labor review, 24 (1927), 637-47.

1591. U. S. Federal Works Agency Law Library. War public works; a compilation of statutes, executive orders, regulations, and other documents relating to the construction, financing, operation, and maintenance of community facilities under the Lanham Act, as amended, comp. by Minnie Wiener. Wash.: Govt. Print. Off., 1943. 171p.

1592. U. S. Library of Congress, Division of Bibliography. "Andrew Furuseth: a bibliographical list," comp. by Grace H. Fuller. Wash., Dec. 3, 1942. 19p. Typed.

1593. U. S. Library of Congress, Division of Bibliography. List of references on prison labor. Wash.: Govt. Print. Off., 1915. 74p.

1594. U. S. Library of Congress, Division of Bibliography. Machinery in industry, with special emphasis upon its effects on labor: a selected list of writings, comp. by Anne L. Baden. [Wash. 1934] 28p.

1595. U. S. Library of Congress, Division of Bibliography. Select list of references on workingmen's insurance: general, United States, Great Britain, Germany, France, Belgium. Wash.: Govt. Print. Off., 1908. 28p.

1596. U. S. Library of Congress, Legislative Reference Service. Labor in wartime (April 1941-March 1942); selected and annotated bibliography on labor problems and policies in a wartime economy. Wash., 1942. 92p.

1597. U. S. National Archives. Preliminary inventory of the records of the Maritime Labor Board, comp. by Caroline W. Hiatt and Salvatore D. Nerboso. Wash., 1949. 7p. (Preliminary inventory, no. 20)

1598. U. S. National Archives. Preliminary inventory of the records of the National War Labor Board. Wash., 1943. 16p. (Preliminary inventory, no. 5)

1599. U. S. National Archives. Preliminary inventory of the War Labor Policies Board records, comp. by Mary Walton Livingston and Leo Pascal. Wash., 1943. 22p. (Preliminary inventory, no. 4)

1600. Wisconsin State Historical Society Library. Collections on labor and socialism in the Wisconsin State Historical Library. Madison: The Society, 1915. 14p. (Bulletin of information, no. 77)

Pensions, wages and insurance

1601. Bureau of Railway Economics Library. Pensions in railway service; references. Wash., 1932. 42 numb. l.

1602. New York Public Library. "Check list of works in the New York Public Library on wages, etc." New York Public Library bulletin, 6 (1902), 174-90.

1603. New York Public Library. "The minimum wage; a preliminary list of selected references, prep. by Charles Clarence

Williamson. New York Public Library bulletin, 17 (1913), 665-71. Reprinted. 9p.

1604. New York Public Library. "The Social Security Act; a selected reading list," comp. by Gilbert A. Cam. New York Public Library bulletin, 41 (1937), 292-98. Reprinted. 9p.

1605. New York Public Library. "The Townsend Plan; a selected list of references." New York Public Library bulletin, 40 (1936), 321-26. Reprinted. 8p.

1606. U. S. Department of Labor Library. "Employee stock ownership in the United States: a selected bibliography." U. S. Bureau of Labor Statistics monthly labor review, 24 (1927), 1366-75.

1607. U. S. Department of Labor Library. Government annuities in Canada and New Zealand: a list of references. Wash., 1934. 5p.

1608. U. S. Department of Labor Library. The guaranteed annual wage and other proposals for steadying the worker's income: selected references, comp. by Laura A. Thompson. Wash., 1945. 19p.

1609. U. S. Department of Labor Library. List of references on minimum wage for women in the United States and Canada, comp. by Edna L. Stone. Wash., 1925. 42p. (U. S. Women's Bureau bulletin, no. 42) Supplement, Wash., 1939. 9p.

1610. U. S. Department of Labor Library. "Old-age pensions in Canada: a list of references." U. S. Bureau of Labor Statistics monthly labor review, 28 (1929), 430-35.

1611. U. S. Department of Labor Library. "Profit sharing and labor copartnership: a list of recent references." U. S. Bureau of Labor Statistics monthly labor review, 16 (1923), 859-71. Supplemented by Profit-sharing: selected references, 1923-1939, comp. by Ruth Fine. Wash., 1939. 18p.

1612. U. S. Department of Labor. "Public old-age pensions in Australia and New Zealand: a list of references. U. S. Bureau of Labor Statistics monthly labor review, 28 (1929), 678-83.

1613. U. S. Department of Labor Library. "Public old-age pensions in the United States; a list of references," comp. by Edna L. Stone. U. S. Bureau of Labor Statistics monthly labor review, 22 (1926), 1414-22; 28 (1929), 1161-75; 34 (1932), 738-46.

1614. U. S. Department of Labor Library. Public old-age pensions in the United States: references 1932 to 1934, comp. by Edna L. Stone. [Wash., 1934] 10 l.

1615. U. S. Department of Labor Library. Recent references on minimum wage in the United States. [Wash., 1936] 5p.
Supplements List of References on minimum wage for women in the United States and Canada, 1925.

1616. U. S. Department of Labor Library. The Townsend old-age pension plan: list of references. Wash., 1936. 8p.

1617. U. S. Department of Labor Library. Unemployment insurance and reserves in the United States: a selected list of references. Wash., 1935. 54p. (U. S. Bureau of Labor Statistics bulletin, no. 611)

1618. U. S. Federal Security Agency Library. Selected readings on group insurance, prep. by Ruth K. Bray. Wash.: The Library, 1948. 13p.

1619. U. S. Federal Security Agency Library. Some basic readings in social security. Wash.: Govt. Print. Off., 1947. 94p. (Publication, no. 28) Supplement in press, 1950.

1620. U. S. Library of Congress, Division of Bibliography. Group Insurance: a bibliographical list of recent writings. Wash., Nov. 27, 1935. 25p.

1621. U. S. Library of Congress, Division of Bibliography. Health insurance in the United States and foreign countries: a bibliographical list, comp. by Helen F. Conover. Wash., Apr. 23, 1938. 49p.

1622. U. S. Library of Congress, Division of Bibliography. "A list of recent references on life insurance." Wash., May 25, 1934. 15p. Typed. [Supplementary list] Oct. 26, 1938. 26p. Typed.

1623. U. S. Library of Congress, Division of

Bibliography. List of recent references on unemployment insurance and reserves (supplementary to previous lists) [Wash.] 1934. 22p.

1624. U. S. Library of Congress, Division of Bibliography. List of references on profit sharing and bonus systems. Wash., Feb. 12, 1920. 24p. [Supplementary list] comp. by Grace H. Fuller, June 21, 1938. 54p.

1625. U. S. National Archives. Preliminary check list of the records of the Wage and Hour Division of the Department of Labor, 1938-1942, comp. by Ernst St. Aubin. [Wash.] 1946. 6p.

1626. U. S. Social Security Board Library. Some basic readings in social security. Wash.: Govt. Print. Off., 1947. 94p. (Social Security Board Library publication, no. 28, rev.)

A revision, up to June 1, 1946, of the 1942 edition.

Hours of work

1627. Bureau of Railway Economics. List of references relating to the eight-hour working day and to limitations of working hours in the United States, with special reference to railway labor. [Wash.] 1917. 30 numb. l.

1628. Bureau of Railway Economics. List of references to books and articles on the Adamson Law of September 1916. [Wash.] 1917. 19 numb. l.

1629. Bureau of Railway Economics Library. Six-hour day, a list of references. Wash., 1936. 17 numb. l.

1630. U. S. Department of Labor Library. "Five-day week and other recent proposals for a shorter work week: a list of references." U. S. Bureau of Labor Statistics monthly labor review, 32 (1931), 501-18.

1631. U. S. Department of Labor Library. "The five-day week in industry: a list of references." U. S. Bureau of Labor Statistics monthly labor review, 24 (1927), 20-24.

1632. U. S. Department of Labor Library. Hours of work in relation to output: an annotated list of references, comp. by Laura A. Thompson. [Wash., 1920] 13p.

1633. U. S. Library of Congress, Division of Bibliography. List of books, with references to periodicals, relating to the eight-hour working day and to limitation of working hours in general. Wash.: Govt. Print. Off., 1908. 24p.

Capital and labor relations

1634. Bureau of Railway Economics. Some references to material on the development of relations between railroad managements and railroad employees that emphasize cooperation. April 22, 1924. [Wash., 1924] 29, 22, 111 numb. l.

Copies located in 6 libraries.

1635. Detroit Public Library. Labor relations in the automobile industry, a bibliography, comp. by Roberta McBride. Detroit: The Library, 1950. 64p.

1636. Lovett, Robert W. "The Thompson Products collection." Business Historical Society bulletin, 23 (1949), 191-95.

About 50,000 pages of documents in Baker Library, Harvard, from Thompson Products, Inc., Cleveland, Ohio, concerning labor-management-government relations.

1637. Princeton University, Dept. of Economics and Social Institutions, Industrial Relations Section Library. Subject index of the library of Industrial Relations Section. Rev. November, 1945. Princeton: Industrial Relations Section, 1945. 46 numb. l.

1638. Stanford University, Graduate School of Business. Subject index and list of periodicals of the library of the Division of Industrial Relations, Graduate School of Business, Stanford University. [Stanford University] 1938. 42p.

1639. Stanford University, Hoover Library. Industrial relations in wartime: Great Britain, 1914-1918, an annotated bibliography of materials in the Hoover Library on War, Revolution, and Peace, by Waldo Chamberlin. Stanford University, 1940. 239p.

1640. U. S. Department of Labor Library. "Union-management cooperation: a selected bibliography." U. S. Bureau of Labor Statistics monthly labor review, 25 (1927), 936-43.

1641. U. S. Library of Congress, Division of Bibliography. Select list of references on industrial arbitration. Wash.: Govt. Print. Off., 1903. 15p.

Employers' liability

1642. Connecticut State Library. Employers' liability and workmen's compensation; list of references to material in the Connecticut State Library. Hartford: The Library, 1913. 27p. (Connecticut State Library bulletin, no. 5)

1643. U. S. Library of Congress, Division of Bibliography. Select list of references on employers' liability and workmen's compensation. Wash.: Govt. Print. Off., 1911. 196p.

1644. U. S. Library of Congress, Division of Bibliography. Select list of works relating to employers liability. Wash.: Govt. Print. Off., 1906. 25p.

Labor unions

1645. Barnett, George E. A trial bibliography of American trade union publications. Baltimore: Johns Hopkins Press, 1904. 112p. (Johns Hopkins University studies in historical and political science, series 22, nos. 1-2).

Alphabetical list, with locations in Johns Hopkins University, U. S. Department of Labor, John Crerar Library, Library of Congress, and central offices of unions or federations.

1646. Barnett, George E., ed. A trial bibliography of American trade-union publications. 2d ed. Baltimore: Johns Hopkins Press, 1907. 139p.

Locates copies in Johns Hopkins University, U. S. Department of Labor, John Crerar Library, Library of Congress, or the union office.

1647. Reynolds, Lloyd George and Killingworth, Charles T. Trade union publications: the official journals, convention proceedings and constitutions of international unions and federations, 1850-1941. Baltimore: Johns Hopkins Press, 1944-45. 3v.

Based upon Johns Hopkins University collection.

1648. Special Libraries Association, Social Sciences Group, Industrial Relations Subgroup. Union list of trade union publications. Ithaca: N. Y. State School of Labor and Industrial Relations, Cornell University, 1950? In progress.

To record holdings of 12 to 15 libraries.

1649. U. S. Dept. of Labor Library. List of American trade union journals and labor papers currently received by the Department of Labor Library. Wash., 1939-1950.

Issued approximately every two years.

1650. U. S. Dept. of Labor Library. Maintenance-of-membership and other measures for union security; selected references, 1941-1945, comp. by Edna L. Stone: Wash., 1945. 12p.

Labor disputes

1651. Bureau of Railway Economics. List of references on the right to strike, comp. by Mary B. Ladd. [Boston, 1919] 15p. Reprint from Special libraries, 10 (Dec. 1919), 255-68.

Union list of material in the Bureau of Railway Economics Library, Library of Congress, and Department of Labor Library.

1652. New York Public Library. "Sit-down strikes; a reading list," comp. by George E. Pettengill. New York Public Library bulletin, 41 (1937), 481-86. Reprinted. 5p.

1653. U. S. Dept. of Agriculture Library. Farmers' and farm laborers' strikes and riots in the U. S. Wash., 1935. 83p.

1654. U. S. Dept. of Labor Library. Conciliation and arbitration in industrial disputes; a selected list of recent references. [Wash., 1938] 15p.

1655. U. S. Department of Labor Library. Injunctions in labor disputes: list of recent references. Wash., 1931. 8p. (Supplements bibliography in U. S. Bureau of Labor Statistics monthly labor review, Sept. 1928.)

1656. U. S. Dept. of Labor. "Injunctions in labor disputes: select list of recent references," comp. by Laura A. Thompson. U. S. Bureau of Labor Statistics monthly labor review, 27 (1928), 631-50.

1657. U. S. Library of Congress, Division of Bibliography. Select list of books (with references to periodicals) on labor, particularly relating to strikes. Wash.: Govt. Print. Off., 1903. 65p.

1658. U. S. Library of Congress, Division of Bibliography. Select list of references on boycotts and injunctions in labor disputes. Wash.: Govt. Print. Off., 1911. 69p.

Unemployment

1659. Chicago, University, Library. Unemployment and relief documents; a bibliography of source materials. Chicago: Public Administration Service, 1934. 18p.

Compiled by Document Section of the University of Chicago libraries, supplemented by the staff of the Children's Bureau of the U. S. Department of Labor. Material from 1929 to 1934 not copyrighted and not issued by trade publishers.

1660. U. S. Dept. of Labor Library. Recent literature on unemployment, with particular reference to causes and remedies, comp. by Laura A. Thompson. [Wash., 1921] 35 numb. l.

1661. U. S. Library of Congress, Division of Bibliography. A list of references on the unemployment situation in the United States, 1929-1930. Wash., Sept. 22, 1930. 11p. [Supplementary list] July 21, 1932. 34p. [Supplementary list] Aug. 14, 1934. 41p.

1662. U. S. Library of Congress, Division of Bibliography. Unemployment and unemployment relief in foreign countries: a list of recent references (supplementing previous mimeographed lists). [Wash.] 1934. 23p.

1663. U. S. Library of Congress, Division of Bibliography. Unemployment relief measures in the United States: a list of recent references. Wash., Sept. 26, 1931. 26p.

Child labor

1664. U. S. Dept. of Labor. "Children in street trades in the United States: a list of references," comp. by Laura A. Thompson. [Wash.]: Govt. Print. Off., 1925. 12p. (Reprint from U. S. Bureau of Labor Statistics monthly labor review, 21 (1925), 1261-72.)

1665. U. S. Dept. of Labor. "Federal control of child labor: a list of references," comp. by Laura A. Thompson. U. S. Bureau of Labor Statistics monthly labor review, 20 (1925), 71-101.

1666. U. S. Dept. of Labor. References on child labor and minors in industry, 1916-1924, comp. by Laura A. Thompson. Wash.: Govt. Print. Off., 1925. 153p. (U. S. Children's Bureau, publication, no. 147)

Supplements Bureau publication no. 18 on child labor, issued 1916.

1667. U. S. Library of Congress, Division of Bibliography. List of books (with references to periodicals) relating to child labor. Wash.: Govt. Print. Off., 1906. 66p.

1668. U. S. Library of Congress, Division of Bibliography. List of references on child labor. Wash.: Govt. Print. Off. 1916. 161p. (U. S. Children's Bureau, Industrial series, no. 3, Bureau publications, no. 18)

LAW

Law library catalogs

1669. Alabama Supreme Court Library. Catalogues of the Supreme Court Library and of the State Library, comp. by J. M. Riggs. Montgomery: Brown Printing Co., 1902. 248p., 301p.

1670. Allegheny County Law Library. Catalogue of the Allegheny County Law Library, Pittsburgh, Pa., Circulating Department, by J. Oscar Emerich. Pittsburgh, Penn., 1912. 144p. Supplement. 1913. 6p.

1671. American Patent Law Association Library. Catalogue of the library. Wash.: Byron S. Adams, 1922. 32p.

1672. Association of the Bar of the City of New York Library. Catalogue of the library of the Association of the Bar of the City of New York. N. Y.: J. J. Little & Co., 1892. 1,135p.

Lists about 40,000 volumes.

1673. Boston Social Law Library. Catalogue of the Social Law Library in Boston. 3d ed. Boston: Printed for the Proprietors, 1865. 281p.

1674. California State Library, Law Department. Catalogue of the California State Library, Law Department, by Talbot H. Wallis. Sacramento: James J. Ayers, Supt. State

Printing, 1886. 655p. Supplemental catalogue of the Law Department... including accessions from 1886 to 1893. Sacramento: A. J. Johnston, 1893. 169p.

1675. Catalogue of an exhibit of the early laws of the several states in the Union, consisting of the colonial laws, the first territorial laws, and the first laws of each of the states represented. Arranged by the New Jersey State Bar Association on the occasion of the fifty-fourth annual meeting of the American Bar Association. Atlantic City, Sept. 1931. 16p.
"With very few exceptions, and these are noted... the books were found in... the Bar Association of the City of New York."--Pref.

1676. Chicago Law Institute Library. Index-catalogue of the library of the Chicago Law Institute to December 31, 1901. Chicago: Chicago Law Institute, 1902. 700p. First annual supplement, 1903. 27p.

1677. Chicago Law Institute Library. Subject index, January 1, 1902 - December 31, 1943. [Chicago]: The Institute [1944] 495p.
A cumulative catalog, taking the place of all previous issues. Books on "substantive law."

1678. Colorado Supreme Court Library. Catalogue of the Supreme Court library of the state of Colorado, 1910. [Denver, 1910] 232p.

1679. Connecticut State Library. "List of law reports, digests, and statutes in the Connecticut State Library." Connecticut State Library, Report of the State Librarian, for the year ended September 30, 1904. Hartford, 1905. p. 38-153.

1680. Delaware State Library. Catalogue of the law books contained in the Delaware State Library. Milford: Milford Chronicle Publishing Co., [1914] 318p.

1681. District of Columbia Bar Association Library. Catalogue of the library of the Bar Association of the District of Columbia. Washington: Judd & Detweiler, 1912. 114p. Earlier edition issued 1891. 55p.

1682. Equitable Life Assurance Society of the United States. Catalogue of the law library of the Equitable Life Assurance Society. N. Y.: Baker & Godwin, 1880. 330p.

1683. Essex County Bar Association (Newark, New Jersey) Library. Catalogue of the law library of the Essex County Bar Association. [Rochester, N. Y.: Lawyers Co-operative Publishing Co.] 1941. 83p. Suppl. to the 1941 catalogue... 1943. [Newark, A. W. Cross, 1943] 1v. Bound with main work.

1684. Essex County Law Library [Salem, Mass.] Catalogue of the library of the Essex County Law Library Association, comp. by Frank V. Wright. Salem: A. N. Webb and Co., 1897. 424p.

1685. Fall River Law Library [Fall River, Mass.] Catalog of the Fall River Law Library, prep. by Nicholas Hatheway. St. Paul, Minn.: West Publishing Co., 1907. 75p.

1686. Georgia State Law Library. Catalogue of the Law Library of the State of Georgia. Atlanta: James P. Harrison and Co., 1879. 183p.

1687. Harvard University, Law School Library. Catalogue of the library of the Law School of Harvard University. Cambridge: The Law School, 1909. 2v.
"Contains only the books on the American and English common law."

1688. Henry E. Huntington Library. Checklist of American laws, charters, and constitutions of the 17th and 18th centuries in the Huntington Library, comp. by Willard O. Waters. San Marino, Calif., 1936. 140p. (Huntington Library lists, no. 1)

1689. Illinois Supreme Court, Law Library. Subject index of Supreme Court Law Library, comp. by R. H. Wilkin. Chicago: Severinghaus [1921] 187p.

1690. Indiana Law Library. Catalogue of the Indiana State Law Library, by John C. McNutt. Indianapolis: W. B. Burford, 1898. 725p.

1691. Indiana Supreme Court, Law Library. Catalogue and subject index of Indiana Supreme Court Law Library. [Indianapolis, 1940] 645p.

1692. Indianapolis Bar Association. Catalog of the law library of Indianapolis Bar Association, by Gladys Wells Ringer. Indianapolis: Bobbs-Merrill Co., 1935. 328p. Cumulative supplement. 1939. 120p.

1693. Iowa State University Library. Catalogue of the Hammond historical law collection, in the Law Library of the State University of Iowa, comp. by Frank H. Noble. Iowa City: The University, 1895. 52p.

Lists 1,237 items dealing with the Civil War period and the history of common law.

1694. Kansas State Library. Catalogue of the Law Department. Topeka, 1932. 528p. Supplement, 1934. Topeka, 1935. 23p.

1695. Law Association of Philadelphia Library. Catalogue of the library of the Law Association of Philadelphia... founded A. D. 1802. Philadelphia: H. B. Ashmead, 1861. 113p.

1696. Law Library Association of St. Louis. A catalogue of the books in the library of the Law Library Association of St. Louis. St. Louis: Nixon-Jones Printing Co., 1895. 762p.

1697. Lawrence Law Library. Catalogue [of] Lawrence Law Library, May 1, 1914. [Lawrence, Mass.: Wood Press], 1914. 72p.

1698. Library Company of the Baltimore Bar. A catalog of the books in the "Horwitz addition" of the Library Company of the Baltimore Bar. Baltimore: Daily Record, 1937. 237p.

About 2,500 volumes, directed toward legal biography, history, jurisprudence, criminology, sociology and fiction.

1699. Library Company of the Baltimore Bar. A subject index of the books in the library of the Library Company of the Baltimore Bar 1797-1840, by Andrew H. Mettee. Baltimore, 1930. 816p.

1700. Louisiana State Bar Association Library. Catalogue of the library of the Louisiana Bar Association, to June, 1911, prep. by Stephen A. Mascaro. New Orleans, La.: E. P. Andree Printing Co., 1911. 242p. Supplements, 1928-30.

1701. Louisiana State Library, Law Department. Catalogue of the Louisiana State Library, Law Department, comp. by Albertine F. Phillips. [New Orleans] 1905. 199p.

1702. Maine State Library (Augusta). Catalogue of the law books. Waterville: Waterville Sentinel Pub. Co., 1916. 70p.

1703. Maryland State Library. Catalogue of the Maryland State Library, Law Department, by L. H. Gadd. Annapolis: Maryland Republican Steam Print, 1895. 379p.

1704. Michigan State Library, Law Department. Catalogue of the Michigan State Library, Law Department, comp. by S. Arthur Tomlinson. Lansing: R. Smith & Co., 1896. 685p.

1705. Minnesota State Library. Law book catalogue of the Minnesota State Library to December 31, 1902, prep. by Charlotte A. Dure. St. Paul: Pioneer Press Co., 1903. 620p.

1706. Missouri State Library, Law Department. Catalog of the Law Department of the Missouri State Library, comp. by George E. Smith and A. J. Menteer. Jefferson City, Mo., 1915. 436p.

1707. Montana State Library, Law Department. Catalogue. Helena: State Pub. Co., 1898. 80p.

1708. New York Law Institute. Catalogue of the books in the library of the New York Law Institute. N. Y.: Martin's Steam Printing House, 1874. 614p.

Lists 17,000 volumes.

1709. New York State Library, Law Library. Catalogue of the New York State Library; subject index of the Law Library, from its foundation to Dec. 31, 1882, prep. by Stephen B. Griswold. Albany: Weed, Parsons & Co., 1883. 251p. Supplements issued in 1894 and 1905.

1710. New York Supreme Court, Appellate Division, Fourth Department, Law Library. Catalogue, by Irwin Taylor. Rochester, 1907. 459p.

1711. North Carolina Supreme Court Library. Catalogue of the Supreme Court Library, prep. by R. H. Bradley. Raleigh: E. M. Uzzell & Co., 1914. 162p.

1712. North Carolina Supreme Court Library. Condensed catalog of the Supreme Court Library... 1942. Raleigh, 1942. 47p.

Earlier editions: Catalogue of the Supreme Court Library, by R. H. Bradley. Raleigh: J. Daniels, 1892. 69p. "A guide to the textbooks, law reviews, and state and federal reports and codes" in the Library.

1713. North Dakota State Law Library. Catalogue of the North Dakota State Law Library, by E. F. Porter. Bismarck: Tribune, State Printers, 1901. 43p.

1714. Ohio Supreme Court Law Library. Index-catalogue of the Law Library of the Supreme Court of Ohio, by Edward Antrim. Columbus: F. J. Heer Printing Co., 1914. 592p. Supplemental index-catalogue. 1917. 57 l.

1715. Oregon Supreme Court Library. Author and subject lists of text-books in the library. Salem, Ore.: Willis S. Duninay, 1913. 321p.

1716. Pennsylvania Historical Society Library. The Charlemagne Tower collection of American colonial laws. [Philadelphia] 1890. 298p.

Collection of laws prior to 1800.

1717. Pennsylvania State Library. Catalogue of law books of the Pennsylvania State Library, prep. by William Wallace Chisholm. [Harrisburg]: W. S. Ray, 1899. 964p.

1718. Pennsylvania State Library. "Check list of laws and statutes of Pennsylvania from 1714 to 1901 in the Pennsylvania State Library." In: Report of the State Librarian of Pennsylvania for 1904, p. 103-20.

1719. Philadelphia Free Library. Catalogue of the exhibits of the Hampton L. Carson collection of books, documents, portraits and autograph letters illustrative of the growth of the common law. [Philadelphia]: Free Library of Philadelphia, 1930. 54p.

1720. San Francisco Law Library. Catalogue of the San Francisco Law Library, comp. by F. P. Deering. San Francisco: [C. A. Murdock and Co.] 1888. 304p.

More than 26,000 volumes listed.

1721. U. S. Circuit Court of Appeals Library. Catalogue. New Orleans, 1933. 157p.

1722. U. S. Dept. of Justice Library. Catalogue of the library of the Department of Justice, to September 1, 1904, by James A. Finch, librarian. Wash.: Govt. Print. Off., 1904. 1,135p.

Pt. 1, general index; pt. 2, subject index; pt. 3, U. S. government publications.

1723. U. S. Library of Congress. Catalogue of law books in the Library of Congress. Arranged by subject-matters. Wash.: Govt. Print. Off., 1869. 305p.

1724. U. S. Patent Office. Catalogue of books in the Law Library of the United States Patent Office. Wash.: Govt. Print. Off., 1883. 62p.

1725. U. S. Solicitor of the Treasury Library. Catalogue. Wash.: Govt. Print. Off., 1894. 91p.

1726. Washington State Library. Catalog and check list of session laws, statutes and compilations of the Washington State Law Library. Olympia, 1914. 192p.

1727. West Virginia State Library. Index catalogue of the West Virginia State Library, law books only. Charleston, W. Va.: [Tribune Print. Co.] 1920. 567p.

1728. West Virginia, University. "Bibliography of Virginia and West Virginia legal publications in library of College of Law, West Virginia University." West Virginia law quarterly, 26 (Nov. 1919), 43-57.

1729. Wisconsin State Library. Subject-index to the law books in the Wisconsin State Library, by John R. Berryman. Madison: Democrat Printing Co., 1905. 639p.

1730. Worcester County Law Library. Catalogue of the Worcester County Law Library. 1881. Worcester, Mass.: C. Hamilton, 1881. 67p.

1731. Wyoming State Library. Catalogue of the law books in the Wyoming State Library. Cheyenne: Daily Sun Book and Job Printing House, 1891. 28p.

1732. Yale University Law Library. The William Blackstone collection in the Yale Law Library; a bibliographical catalogue, by Catherine Spicer Eller. [New Haven]: Yale Univ. Press, 1938. 113p. (Yale Law Library publications, no. 6)

Latin American law

1733. Pan American Union, Columbus Memorial Library. A selected list of Latin American periodicals containing laws and legal information. Wash., 1942. 27p. (Bibliographic series, no. 28)

1734. U. S. Library of Congress, Law Library. Guide to the law and legal literature of Argentina, Brazil, and Chile, by E.M. Borchard. Wash.: Govt. Print, Off., 1917. 523p.

1735. U. S. Library of Congress, Law Library. A guide to the law and legal literature of Bolivia, by Helen L. Clagett. Wash.: Library of Congress, 1947. 110p. ([U. S.] Library of Congress. [Latin American series, no. 12])

1736. U. S. Library of Congress, Law Library. A guide to the law and legal literature of Colombia, by Richard C. Backus and Phanor J. Eder. Wash.: Govt. Print. Off., 1944. 222p.

1737. U. S. Library of Congress, Law Library. A guide to the law and legal literature of Cuba, the Dominican Republic and Haiti, by Crawford M. Bishop and Anyda Marchant. Wash., 1944. 276p.

1738. U. S. Library of Congress, Law Library. A guide to the law and legal literature of Ecuador, by Helen L. Clagett. Wash., 1947. 100p. ([U. S.] Library of Congress. Latin American series, no. 18)

1739. U. S. Library of Congress, Law Library. A guide to the law and legal literature of Mexico, by John T. Vance and Helen L. Clagett. Wash.: The Library, 1945. 269p.

1740. U. S. Library of Congress, Law Library. A guide to the law and legal literature of Paraguay, by Helen L. Clagett. Wash.: Library of Congress, 1947. 59p. ([U. S.] Library of Congress. [Latin American series, no. 14])

1741. U. S. Library of Congress, Law Library. A guide to the law and legal literature of Peru, by Helen L. Clagett. Wash., 1947. 188p. ([U. S.] Library of Congress. Latin American series, no. 20)

1742. U. S. Library of Congress, Law Library. A guide to the law and legal literature of the Mexican states, by Helen L. Clagett. Wash.: Library of Congress, 1947. 180p. ([U. S.] Library of Congress. [Latin American series, no. 13])

1743. U. S. Library of Congress, Law Library. A guide to the law and legal literature of Uruguay, by Helen L. Clagett. Wash.: Library of Congress, 1947. 123p. ([U. S.] Library of Congress. Latin American series, no. 26)

1744. U. S. Library of Congress, Law Library. A guide to the law and legal literature of Venezuela, by Helen L. Clagett. Wash., 1947. 128p. ([U. S.] Library of Congress. Latin American series, no. 16)

1745. U. S. Library of Congress, Law Library. Legal codes of the Latin American republics. Wash.: Library of Congress, 1942. 95p. [U. S. Library of Congress. Latin American series, no. 1]

Other foreign law

1746. Hummel, Arthur W. "Books on Korean law." Library of Congress quarterly journal of current acquisitions, 4 (Aug. 1947), 7-8.
Collection presented to Library of Congress by Korean government officers.

1747. Massachusetts State Library. Catalogue of the laws of foreign countries in the State Library of Massachusetts, 1911, prep. by Ellen M. Sawyer. Boston: Wright & Potter, 1911. 311p.

1748. New York Public Library. "List of works in the New York Public Library relating to Muhammadan law, prep. by Ida A. Pratt. New York Public Library bulletin, 11 (1907), 8-17. Reprinted. 10p.

1749. Northwestern University, Law School. Preliminary catalogue of the Gary collection of continental law. Chicago, 1904. 34p. (Northwestern University, School of Law, quarterly bulletin, ser. 2, no. 4)

1750. Stern, William B. "A bibliography of books and articles on Mohammedan law in the English language." Law library journal, 43 (Feb. 1950), 16-21.
Locates copies in 12 libraries.

1751. Taracanzio, Timothy A. "The Russian collection of the Harvard Law School Library." Harvard alumni bulletin, 37 (1935), 750-56.

1752. U. S. Bureau of Foreign and Domestic Commerce. "Finding list," bibliography of modern Chinese law in Library of Congress. Comp. and ed. July-Dec. 1944 by China Legal Section, Far Eastern Unit, Bureau of Foreign & Domestic Commerce, Dept. of Commerce. [Wash.: China American Council of Commerce & Industry, 1944] 48 l.

1753. U. S. Dept. of Justice Library. Catalogue of foreign books (in languages other than English) in the library of the Department of Justice. Wash.: Govt. Print. Off., 1900. 77p.
Arranged by subjects.

1754. U. S. Library of Congress. The Paul Krueger collection of books on Roman and general law in the Library of Congress. [Wash.]: The Library, 1934. 244 l.
Consists of about 4,691 volumes, purchased in 1931.

1755. U. S. Library of Congress. [Signor Otto Lange collection of Roman law] Wash., Jan. 20, 1921. 9p. Typed.
Copy of Library of Congress order sheets.

1756. U. S. Library of Congress, Law Library. The bibliography of international law and continental law, by Edwin M. Borchard. Wash.: Govt. Print. Off., 1913. 93p.

1757. U. S. Library of Congress, Law Library. Early Spain; provisional union list and desiderata of the Law Library. Wash., 1935. 143p.
Locations in 55 libraries of early Spanish legal publications.

1758. U. S. Library of Congress, Law Library. Guide to the law and legal literature of France, by George Wilfred Stumberg. Wash.: Govt. Print. Off., 1931. 242p.

1759. U. S. Library of Congress, Law Library. Guide to the law and legal literature of Germany, by E. M. Borchard. Wash.: Govt. Print. Off., 1912. 226p.

1760. U. S. Library of Congress, Law Library. Guide to the law and legal literature of Spain, prep. by Thomas W. Palmer, Jr. Wash.: Govt. Print. Off., 1915. 174p.

General

1761. American Association of Law Libraries. Law libraries in the United States and Canada. 4th ed. [Chicago]: Commerce Clearing House, 1948. 70p.
Directory, arranged by states, indicating number of volumes in each library.

1762. Ames Foundation. A bibliography of early English law books, comp. by Joseph Henry Beale. Cambridge: Harvard Univ. Press, 1926. 304p.
Locates copies in 7 American and various English libraries.

1763. Anderson, Robert Bowie. "The Law School Library in Langdell Hall." Harvard Library notes, 3 (1940), 326-32.

1764. Anderson, Robert Bowie. A supplement to Beale's bibliography of early English law books. Cambridge: Harvard Univ. Press, 1943. 50p.
Lists additional titles in Harvard Law School Library, not recorded by Beale, and corrections in Beale's entries.

1765. Association of the Bar of the City of New York. Association of the Bar of the City of New York: the first quarter-century of its library, by Wm. James Courtnald Berry. N. Y., 1896? 134p.

1766. Association of the Bar of the City of New York. Handbook of the library... containing a brief sketch of its history and present contents. N. Y., 1921. 22p. (Its Bulletin, no. 8, November 1921.)

1767. Bates, Albert Carlos. Connecticut statute laws. A bibliographical list of editions of Connecticut laws from the earliest issues, to 1836. [Hartford: Case, Lockwood & Brainard Co.], 1900. 120p.
Copies located in 19 libraries.

1768. Beale, Joseph Henry. A bibliography of early English law books, compiled for the Ames Foundation. Cambridge: Harvard Univ. Press, 1926. 304p.
Based primarily on holdings of Harvard Law School Library.

1769. Beardsley, Arthur S. "University of Washington Law Library attains 100,000 volume mark." Law library journal, 37 (May 1944), 43-56.

Description of resources.

1770. Benedict, Russell. Illustrated catalogue of acts and laws of the Colony and State of New York and of the other original colonies and states, constituting the collection made by Hon. Russell Benedict... to be sold... February 27, 1922... by... the American Art Association. [Greenwich, Conn.: Condé Nast Press, 1922] 262p.

Locates copies in 45 libraries.

1771. California Supreme Court. Index to the records of the Supreme Court of California, on file in the State Library. Sacramento: A. J. Johnston, Supt. State Printing, 1891. 213p.

1772. Cowley, John D. A bibliography of abridgments, digests, dictionaries, and indexes of English law to the year 1800. London: Quaritch, 1932. 196p. [Selden Society publication].

Lists 330 titles and locates copies in 7 American and 17 British libraries.

1773. Dockweiler, J. F. "The Nation's principal repository of legal literature." American Bar Association journal, 24 (May 1938), 404-06.

Describes Library of Congress Law Library.

1774. [Gray, Roland] A catalogue of books belonging to John Chipman Gray, Boston. [Cambridge: Riverside Press] 1904. 175p.

Many volumes subsequently presented to Harvard University. Mainly law.

1775. Greenwood, Jane L. "Bibliography of legal treatises of the District of Columbia." Law library journal, 39 (Feb. 1946), 1922.

Locates material in Library of Congress.

1776. Harvard Law School Association. The centennial history of the Harvard Law School, 1817-1917. [Boston]: The Association, 1918. 412p.

A description of the Library of the Harvard Law School, and a bibliography of books and articles pertaining to the Law School, most of which are in the Law School Library.

1777. Harvard University, Law School Library. Harvard Law Library information bulletin, 1 (1947) - to date.

Contains lists of accessions.

1778. Harvard University, Law School Library. Harvard Law School. The treasure room to be built in Langdell Hall. [Boston: Printed by Court Square Press, Inc., 1947]. 30p.

Contains a brief account of collections destined for treasure room.

1779. Harvard University, Law School Library. A list of selected books from the tercentennial exhibition of the Harvard Law School Library. Cambridge: Harvard Univ. Press, 1936. 18p.

A list of 164 books selected for exhibition.

1780. Henry E. Huntington Library. Legal manuscripts and printed books: a sequence illustrating the development of English and American law. [San Marino, 1935] 30p.

1781. Henry E. Huntington Library. A selection of legal manuscripts and printed books for the visit of the State Bar of California. San Marino, Calif., 1934. 26p.

1782. James, Eldon R. "The Harvard Law School Library." Law library journal, 26 (1934), 157-61.

1783. James, Eldon R. A list of legal treatises printed in the British colonies and the American states before 1801. Cambridge: Harvard University Press, 1934. p. 159-211. (Reprint from Harvard legal essays.)

Based on Harvard Law School holdings but lists items from other sources.

1784. Little, Eleanor N. "The Treasure Room of the Law School Library." Harvard Library bulletin, 3 (1949), 148-51.

In Harvard University.

1785. McMurtrie, Douglas C. A bibliography of Kentucky statute law, 1792-1830." Filson Club history quarterly 9 (1935), 95-120.

Locates 79 titles in 29 American libraries.

1786. Martin, Wm. H. "Some Virginia law books in a Virginia law office." Virginia law register, n.s., 12 (1926), 13-19, 74-84, 141-51, 193-202, 279-89, 321-30, 385-400, 478-90.

Treats of Virginia statute law compilations, revisions, codes, etc. Locates copies.

1787. New York Law Institute. The New York Law Institute library. N. Y., 1918. 19p.
   A brief history and description of resources.

1788. New York State Library, Law Library. Some rare and interesting law books in the New York State library. Albany: Univ. of the State of New York, 1922. p. 82-103. (Reprinted from the Report of the Director of the New York State Library, 1919.)

1789. New York University, presentation and initial showing of a collection of ancient English legal documents, dating from the thirteenth century, the gift to New York University of Moses H. Grossman, LL.D., in honor of Frederick Brown, Esq. N. Y., 1930. 8p.

1790. Pulling, Arthur C. "Harvard Law School Library." Law library journal, 43 (1950), 1-11.

1791. Pulling, Arthur C. "The Harvard Law School Library - recent accessions." Harvard law review, 58 (1945), 1248-52.

1792. Pulling, Arthur C. "The library and the use of its facilities." Harvard Law School bulletin, 7 (October, 1949), 6-7.
   Harvard Law School Library.

1793. Pulling, Arthur C. "The Treasure Room." In: Harvard Law School year book, Cambridge: Harvard University [1949], 182-83.
   Relates to Harvard Law School Library.

1794. Rauch, John G. and Armstrong, Nellie C. A bibliography of the laws of Indiana, 1788-1827, beginning with the Northwest Territory. Indianapolis: Indiana Library and Historical Department, 1928. 77p. (Indiana Historical collections, v. 16)
   Locates copies examined in 8 libraries.

1795. Schwerin, Kurt. "The Elbert H. Gary library of law, Northwestern University and its foreign and international law sections." Illinois libraries, 32 (1950), 168-72.
   Description of 140,000 volume collection.

1796. Sotheby, Wilkinson & Hodge. Catalogue of the valuable and extensive library formed by George Dunn. [London]: Dryden Press, J. Davy & Sons, [1913-17]. 4 pts.
   Lots 1-355 (early manuscripts and printed books relating to English law, sold at Sotheby's Feb. 1913) acquired by Harvard Law School.

1797. U. S. Library of Congress. "Annual report on acquisitions: Law." Library of Congress quarterly journal of acquisitions, 3 (Aug. 1946), 14-29; 4 (Aug. 1947), 40-54; 5 (Aug. 1948), 28-40; 6 (Aug. 1949), 50-62; 7 (Aug. 1950), 44-58.

1798. U. S. Library of Congress. Centennial of the Law Library, 1832-1932; an exhibit of books, prints, and manuscripts in honor of the Supreme Court of the United States and the American Bar Association on the occasion of the laying of the cornerstone of the Supreme Court building, October 13, 1932. Wash.: Govt. Print. Off., 1932. [6]p.

1799. U. S. Library of Congress, Law Library. Account of its activities and the more important accessions for the fiscal year, June 30, 1930 - June, 1941. Wash.: Govt. Print. Off., 1931-1942. 12v.

1800. U. S. Library of Congress, Law Library. Anglo-American legal bibliographies; an annotated guide, by William L. Friend. Wash.: U. S. Govt. Print. Off., 1944. 166p.
   Lists 298 titles, alphabetically by author.

1801. Williamson, Roland. The Law Library in the Capitol, Washington, D. C. Wash.: J. Byrne and Co., 1929. 281p.
   Six lectures describing use and contents of Law Library of Congress, the "Supreme Court Library."

1802. Yale University, School of Law Library. Yale law library manual. [New Haven]: Yale Univ. Press, 1937. 74p. (Yale Law Library publication, no. 5)
   Includes a description of law collection.

International law

1803. Carnegie Endowment for International Peace Library. Intervention; select list of references on intervention in its relation to international law and the protection of foreign loans and investments. [Wash., 1938] 14p.
   Collection now a part of George Washington University Library.

1804. Childs, James B. "Latin American treaty collections." Inter-American bibliographical review, 3 (Winter, 1943-44), 197-205.
A list of Latin American treaty collections by country, based on Library of Congress collection.

1805. Council on Foreign Relations. The Library of the Council on Foreign Relations. N. Y., [1946?] 11p.
Description of object and scope of library.

1806. Holland Society of New York Library. Catalogue of the works of Grotius and of books relating to him, presented to the Holland Society of New York by its President, Robert B. Roosevelt... October 1890. N. Y.: The Society, 1890? 28p.
Now on deposit at Columbia University. A reprint of the original (bookseller's) catalog.

1807. Michigan, University, William L. Clements Library. The ter-centenary of Hugo Grotius' "De jure belli ac pacis" 1625-1925. Ann Arbor, 1925. 4p. (Bulletin, no. 6)
Catalog of an exhibition.

1808. Myers, Denys Peter. Manual of collections of treaties and of collections relating to treaties. Cambridge: Harvard Univ. Press, 1922. 685p.
Items in Harvard University Library unless otherwise indicated.

1809. Olivart, Ramón de Dalman, Marqués de. Bibliographie du droit international; catalogue d'une bibliographie de droit international et sciences auxiliares. 2d ed. Paris: A. Pedone, 1905-10. 4v. and supplement.
Collection now in Harvard Law School Library.

1810. Savord, Ruth. "Library service in international relations." Special libraries, 31 (1940), 46-51.
Describes work and collections of library of Council on Foreign Relations, New York City.

1811. United Nations Conference on International Organization, San Francisco, 1945. UNCIO conference library. Short title classified catalog, June 1, 1945... [San Francisco, 1945] 66 numb. 1.
"Compiled by the General Reference and Bibliography Division, the Library of Congress."

1812. U. S. Dept. of State Library. Catalogue. [Wash., 1830] 150p.

1813. U. S. Dept. of State Library. Catalogue of the works relative to the law of nations and diplomacy in the library of the Department of State, June 30, 1886. Wash.: Govt. Print. Off., 1887. 111p. A-C (No more published) First edition, 1881. 87p.

1814. U. S. Dept. of State Library. Catalogue of treaties, 1814-1918. Wash.: Govt. Print. Off., 1919. 716p.

1815. U. S. Dept. of State Library. Catalogue of works relating to the law of nations and diplomacy in the library of the Department of State of the United States. Part 1. October 1897. [A-Byn] Wash.: Department of State, 1897. 110p. (No more published.)

1816. U. S. Dept. of State Library. A list of books received at the library of the Department of State. [Wash., 1886-87] 11v. in 1. Continued under slightly different title, 1892-1906. 32v. in 4.

1817. U. S. Library of Congress. Division of Bibliography. Disarmament, with special reference to naval limitation: a bibliographical list. Wash., Dec. 11, 1929. 40p. Recent references. Dec. 15, 1934. 42p.

1818. U. S. Library of Congress, Division of Bibliography. Freedom of the seas: a bibliographical list. Wash., Jan. 13, 1930. 37p.

1819. U. S. Library of Congress, Division of Bibliography. The League of Nations: a selected list of recent references; comp. by Ellen Fay Chamberlin. [Wash., 1933] 46p.

1820. U. S. Library of Congress, Division of Bibliography. A list of recent references on neutrality, with a section on maritime neutrality and the freedom of the seas, comp. by Helen F. Conover. [Wash.] 1941. 26p.

1821. U. S. Library of Congress, Division of Bibliography. List of references on international arbitration. Wash.: Govt. Print. Off., 1908. 151p.

1822. U. S. Library of Congress, Division of Bibliography. List of references on international courts with special reference to the Permanent Court of International Justice. Wash., Oct. 10, 1923. 27p.

1823. U. S. Library of Congress, Division of Bibliography. A list of references on recognition in international law and practice. Wash.: Govt. Print. Off., 1904. 18p.

1824. U. S. Library of Congress, Division of Bibliography. List of references on the Permanent Court of International Justice. Wash., Oct. 25, 1923. 21p. 11 supplements issued, 1926-37.

1825. U. S. Library of Congress, Division of Bibliography. List of references on the treaty-making power. Wash.: Govt. Print. Off., 1920. 219p.

Lists 1,010 references.

1826. U. S. Library of Congress, Division of Bibliography. List of references on the United States consular service, with appendix on consular systems in foreign countries. Wash.: Govt. Print. Off., 1905. 27p.

1827. U. S. Library of Congress, Division of Bibliography. "List of references on the Washington conference on the limitation of armaments, 1921-1922." Wash., Dec. 27, 1922. 24p. Typed. [Supplementary list] Feb. 28, 1925. 14p. Typed.

1828. U. S. Library of Congress, Division of Bibliography. Military government: list of references, comp. by Grace Hadley Fuller. Wash., 1944. 14p. Supplementary... Wash., 1946. 17p.

1829. U. S. Library of Congress, General Reference and Bibliography Division. The League of Nations, intellectual cooperation program; a list of references. Wash., 1945. 20p.

1830. U. S. Library of Congress, General Reference and Bibliography Division. "Luther H. Evans: writings and addresses on UNESCO." Wash., June 2, 1949. 6p. Typed.

1831. U. S. Library of Congress, General Reference and Bibliography Division. United Nations Educational, Scientific and Cultural Organization (UNESCO) a selected list of references, comp. by Helen D. Jones. Wash., 1948. 56p.

1832. U. S. Library of Congress, Legislative Reference Service. Selected references on international federations. [Wash., 1942] 12 l.

Constitutional law and history

1833. Chicago, University, Library. Official publications relating to American state constitutional conventions. N. Y.: H. W. Wilson, 1936. 91p.

Based primarily on holdings of Chicago libraries, Library of Congress, and New York Public Library. Locates copies not found in these institutions in about 40 other libraries.

1834. Ford, Paul Leicester. Pamphlets on the Constitution of the United States, published during its discussion by the people, 1787-1788. Brooklyn, 1888. 451p.

Contains bibliography with location of copies in 13 libraries.

1835. Henry E. Huntington Library. The Constitution of the United States; an exhibition on the 150th anniversary of its formation, exhibition and notes by Max Farrand and David Davies. San Marino: The Library, 1937. 25p. Reprinted 1948.

Based on materials from Huntington Library, with 2 exceptions.

1836. Mugridge, Donald H. "Neither slavery nor involuntary servitude..." Library of Congress quarterly journal of current acquisitions, 5 (Aug. 1948), 12-18.

Describes copy of 13th amendment to the Constitution received by Library of Congress, signed by President Lincoln and all members of Congress voting for passage.

1837. Newberry Library. A list of documentary material relating to state constitutional conventions, 1776-1912, comp. for use in the Newberry library by Augustus Hunt Shearer. Chicago, 1915. 37 numb. l. (Newberry Library bulletin, no. 4)

1838. Newberry Library. A list of official publications of American state constitutional conventions, 1776-1916, comp. by Augustus Hunt Shearer. Chicago: [The Library] 1917. 39p. (Newberry Library bulletin, no. 6)

A revision of and addition to its Bulletin no. 4. Items are located in Newberry Library or one of 4 other Chicago libraries.

1839. U. S. Constitution Sesquicentennial Commission. Broadsides relating to the ratification of the Constitution and the formation of the government of the United States from historical societies and libraries. Wash., 1937. 12p.

Describes and locates 78 broadsides.

1840. U. S. Federal Security Agency Library. Federal grants-in-aid in health-education-social security, selected references, 1938-1948, prep. by Ruth Bray. Wash.: The Library, 1948. 19p.

1841. U. S. Library of Congress, Division of Bibliography. The bill of rights, a list of references, comp. by Grace Hadley Fuller. Wash., 1940. 21p.

1842. U. S. Library of Congress, Division of Bibliography. Federal aid to specific activities in the United States: a selected list of recent writings. Wash., Jan. 31, 1935. 44p.

1843. U. S. Library of Congress, Division of Bibliography. "List of references on present day constitutions, politics and government of the new or changed governments of the world." Wash., May 22, 1922. 22p. Typed. [Supplementary list] Mar. 15, 1932. 47p. Typed.

1844. U. S. Library of Congress, Division of Bibliography. List of references on the modification or repeal of the eighteenth amendment. [Wash., 1930] 16p. Supplement. 1932. 18p.

1845. U. S. Library of Congress, Division of Bibliography. Select list of books on the Constitution of the United States. Wash.: Govt. Print. Off., 1903. 14p.

1846. U. S. Library of Congress, Division of Bibliography. Select list of references on impeachment. 2d. ed. with additions. Wash.: Govt. Print. Off., 1912. 38p.

1847. U. S. Library of Congress, Division of Bibliography. A selected list of recent references on the Constitution of the United States, comp. by Grace Hadley Fuller. [Wash.] 1940. 50p.

1848. U. S. Library of Congress, Division of Bibliography. A selected list of references on the Bill of Rights, comp. by Grace H. Fuller. Wash., Apr. 3, 1940. 21p.

1849. Virginia State Library. "A bibliography of the conventions and constitutions of Virginia, including references to essays, letters and speeches in the Virginia newspapers," by Earl G. Swem. Virginia State Library bulletin, 3 (1910), 353-441.

Most of material listed is in Virginia State Library.

Criminal law

1850. U. S. Library of Congress, Division of Bibliography. Capital punishment: a bibliographical list. [Wash.?] 1931 23p.

1851. U. S. Library of Congress, Division of Bibliography. A list of recent references on lynching and lynch law, comp. by Ann Duncan Brown. [Wash.] 1940. 16p.

1852. U. S. Library of Congress, Division of Bibliography. Select list of references on capital punishment. Wash.: Govt. Print. Off., 1912. 45p.

Martial law

1853. U. S. Library of Congress, Division of Bibliography. List of references on embargoes. Wash.: Govt. Print. Off., 1917. 44p.

Private law

1854. Massachusetts State Library. Hand-list of legislative sessions and session laws, statutory revisions, compilations, codes, etc., and constitutional conventions of the United States and its possessions and of the several states to May, 1912, prep. by Charles J. Babbitt. [Boston, 1912]. 634p.

Material is in Massachusetts State Library unless otherwise located in text.

1855. U. S. Library of Congress, Legislative Reference Service. Sources of information on legislation of 1937-1938-1939; a bibliographical list of published material received in the Library of Congress reporting legislative bills and enactments of 1937, 1938, 1939. Wash.: Govt. Print. Off., 1938-40. 3v.

PUBLIC ADMINISTRATION

Central government administration

1856. Chicago Joint Reference Library. Periodicals currently received; a list of 676 periodicals in public administration and related fields. Chicago: The Library, 1944. 40 numb. l.

1857. Greer, Sarah. A bibliography of civil service and personnel administration. N. Y.: McGraw-Hill Book Company, Inc., 1935. 143p.
Based on material in library of Institute of Public Administration, New York City.

1858. Greer, Sarah. A bibliography of public administration. N. Y.: National Institute of Public Administration, 1926. 238p.
Based on material in library of the Institute.

1859. Grieder, Elmer M. "The Littauer Center Library: a few notes on its origin." Harvard University Library notes, 4 (1942), 97-104.
Library on public administration, Harvard University.

1860. Institute of Public Administration. A bibliography of public administration. Part 1 - General literature, by Sarah Greer. N. Y.: The Institute, Columbia University, 1933. 90p.
Part 2 not published. Based on material in library of Institute.

1861. U. S. Civil Service Commission Library. A bibliography of public personnel administration literature. Wash.: The Library, 1949. 7v.
Comprehensive bibliography superseding all earlier lists issued by Library.

1862. U. S. Civil Service Commission Library. Personnel literature. Wash.: The Library, 1941 - to date.
Monthly record of material received by Civil Service Commission Library.

1863. U. S. Library of Congress, Division of Bibliography. A list of recent references on governmental accounting and budgeting: national, state, county, municipal, comp. by Florence S. Hellman. [Wash.] 1940. 33p.

1864. U. S. Library of Congress, Division of Bibliography. A list of references on the civil service and personnel administration in the United States: federal, state and local (a supplementary list of references), comp. by Ann Duncan Brown. [Wash.] 1942. 107p. Supplements 1936 list, 91p., and 1939 list, 55p.

1865. U. S. Library of Congress, Division of Bibliography. "A list of references on the Civil Service in Great Britain," comp. by Ann D. Brown. Wash., June 22, 1937. 18p. Typed.

1866. U. S. Library of Congress, Division of Bibliography. Select list of references on old age and civil service pensions. Wash.: Govt. Print. Off., 1903. 18p.

1867. U. S. Library of Congress, Division of Bibliography. Selected list of references on military pensions and bounties of the United States, comp. by Anne L. Baden. [Wash., 1933] 51p. [Recent references] comp. by Florence S. Hellman. Nov. 4, 1939. 19p. Typed.

1868. U. S. Library of Congress, Division of Bibliography. Selected list of references on the regulation and control of radio broadcasting in the United States and foreign countries, comp. by Anne L. Baden. [Wash.? 1933] 34p.

1869. U. S. Library of Congress, Division of Bibliography. Selected list of writings on the control of the liquor traffic in the United States and foreign countries, comp. by Anne L. Baden. [Wash.] 1933. 55p.

1870. U. S. Library of Congress, General Reference and Bibliography Division. Renegotiation of war contracts; a selected list of references, comp. by Grace Hadley Fuller. [Wash.] 1944. 18p.

1871. U. S. National Archives. Preliminary inventory of records of the United States Secret Service, comp. by Lyle J. Holverstott. Wash., 1949. 16p. (Preliminary inventory, no. 16)

Local government: county, city, town

1872. Chicago Municipal Reference Library. Catalogue of the Chicago Municipal Library, 1908. Chicago: Bureau of Statistics and Municipal Library, 1908. 149p.

1873. Chicago Municipal Reference Library. Index to municipal legislation; a cumulative, alphabetical, subject index of municipal ordinances, proposed or adopted by city councils, boards of aldermen, city commissions and similar bodies, as recorded in their printed official proceedings and journals, comp. by Frederick Rex. Chicago: The Library, 1937. 250 numb. 1.

1874. Chicago Public Library. Check list of books and pamphlets on municipal government found in the free public libraries of Chicago. Issued in connection with the International Municipal Congress and Exposition, Chicago, September 18th to 30th, 1911. [Chicago]: The Library, 1911. 44p.

Locates copies in Chicago Public Library, John Crerar and Newberry libraries.

1875. Chicago, University, Library. Chicago and Cook County; a union list of their official publications, including the semi-official institutions. Chicago: Univ. of Chicago, 1934. 230 numb. 1.

A list of publications of local governments within limits of Chicago and Cook County, exclusive of archival mss. Gives holdings of University of Chicago, Chicago Public Library, John Crerar Library and Municipal Reference Library.

1876. Detroit Public Library. Municipal affairs; books and articles in the Detroit Public Library. Detroit, 1902. 44p.

1877. Greer, Sarah. A bibliography of police administration and police science. N. Y.: Institute of Public Administration, Columbia University, 1936. 152p.

Based on material in library of Institute.

1878. Illinois, University, Library. Municipal codes, charters and ordinances in the University of Illinois Library (rev. Apr. 1944), by Nelle M. Signor. Urbana, 1944. 19 numb. 1.

1879. Illinois, University, Library. Municipal documents and other publications on municipal government in the University of Illinois Library, by Mabel L. Conat and Marian Leatherman. [Urbana]: The University [1917] 49p. (University of Illinois bulletin, v. 14, no. 37, May 14, 1917)

1880. Los Angeles Public Library, Municipal Reference Library. The government of metropolitan areas. 1947. 27, 6p. (Social adjustment bibliographies, no. 4)

Most of material is in Municipal Reference Library.

1881. Michigan State Library. References to books and periodicals in the Michigan State Library relating to municipal affairs. [Lansing?] n. d. 23p.

Classified list.

1882. New York Public Library. "Check list of general municipal documents of New York City, and of New York State documents, and other papers, relating to the City in the New York Public Library." New York Public Library bulletin, 5 (1901), 5-19.

1883. New York Public Library. "Check list of general serial municipal documents of Brooklyn in the New York Public Library." New York Public Library bulletin, 6 (1902), 12-19.

1884. New York Public Library. "Check list of works relating to fires and the Fire Department of the City of New York in the New York Public Library." New York Public Library bulletin, 5 (1901), 147-50.

1885. New York Public Library. "List of city charters, ordinances, and collected documents in the New York Public Library." New York Public Library bulletin, 16 (1912), 631-719, 799-871, 885-947; 17 (1913), 7-78, 255-96, 313-59. Reprinted with slight variation of title. 383p.

1886. New York Public Library. "A list of works on county government, including county publications; references to material in the New York Public Library," comp. by Rollin Alger Sawyer. New York Public Library bulletin, 19 (1915), 433-70. Reprinted. 40p.

1887. Signor, Nelle. "Municipal reference collection, University of Illinois Library." Special libraries, 35 (1944), 493-94.

General description of types of publications found in Municipal Reference collection.

1888. U. S. Library of Congress, Division of Bibliography. County government and its reorganization in the United States: a bibliographical list of recent writings, comp. by Anne L. Baden. [Wash., 1934.] 31p.

1889. U. S. Library of Congress, Division of Bibliography. A list of recent references on county government in the United States, comp. by Florence S. Hellman. [Wash.] 1940. 13p.

1890. U. S. Library of Congress, Division of Bibliography. "List of references on county government." In: James, Herman G. County government in Texas. [Austin, Tex.]: Univ. of Texas [1925] p. 103-18.
Library of Congress call numbers listed.

1891. U. S. Library of Congress, Division of Bibliography. Politics and government in the District of Columbia with special reference to suffrage: a list of recent references, comp. by Ann Duncan Brown. Wash., 1940. 14p.

1892. U. S. Library of Congress, Division of Bibliography. Select list of books on municipal affairs, with special reference to municipal ownership. With appendix: Select list of state documents. Wash.: Govt. Print. Off., 1906. 34p.

1893. U. S. Library of Congress, Division of Bibliography. Select list of references on commission government for cities. Wash.: Govt. Print. Off., 1913. 70p.

1894. U. S. Library of Congress, Division of Bibliography. A selected list of references on municipal government in the United States, comp. by Ann Duncan Brown. [Wash.] 1938. 57p.

Government, U. S. and state

1895. Graves, William Brooke, and others. American state government and administration; a state by state bibliography of significant general and special works, comp. by W. Brooke Graves, Norman J. Small and E. Foster Dowell. Chicago: Council of State Governments, 1949. 79p.
Compiled in Legislative Reference Service, Library of Congress.

1896. Graves, William Brooke, comp. Reorganization of the executive branch of the Government of the United States; a compilation of basic information and significant documents, 1912-1948. Wash., 1949. 425p. ([U. S.] Library of Congress. Legislative Reference Service. Public affairs bulletin, no. 66)
Selected references, p. 401-12, in Library of Congress.

1897. Historical Records Survey - Wis. Inventory of state archives of Wisconsin. Treasury Department. Madison, Wis.: The Survey, 1942. 232p.

1898. Historical Records Survey - Wis. Inventory of state archives: Wisconsin. Banking Department. Madison: Wis. Hist. Rec. Survey, 1942. 325 numb. l.

1899. John Crerar Library. Bibliographical guides, directories, and authority lists for studying the New Deal, comp. by Jerome K. Wilcox. Chicago, 1935. 11p. (Reference list 31)

1900. John Crerar Library. Bibliography of official rosters, state manuals, state yearbooks, etc., currently issued, comp. by Jerome K. Wilcox. Chicago, 1930. 28p. (Reference list, no. 7)

1901. New York Public Library. "Reorganization of the administrative agencies of the United States Government," a selective reading list, comp. by Gilbert A. Cam. New York Public Library bulletin, 41 (1937), 909-14. Reprinted. 6p.

1902. U. S. Geological Survey Library. Bibliographical list. [Wash.] 1935-36. no. 1-5.

1. A list of references on the United States Geological Survey and its work, comp. by James T. Rubey, rev. ed. 1935. 29p.
2. References on the Federal Emergency Administration of Public Works and its work, including the Public Works Housing Division, comp. by James T. Rubey, rev. ed. 1936. 47p.
3. A suggestive list of references on federal regulation of the petroleum industry since August 19, 1933 with special reference to the Petroleum Administration, comp. by James T. Rubey and William H. Heers, rev. ed. 1935. 39p.
4. A suggestive list of references on the United States Soil Erosion Service and its work, comp. by James T. Rubey, rev. ed. 1935. 8p.

5. Some recent references (since 1928) on national and state planning in the United States, comp. by Harold Merrill and others. 1935. 24p.

1903. U. S. Library of Congress, Division of Bibliography. Centralization in the government of the United States, including state rights; a selected list of references. Wash., 1940. 18p.

1904. U. S. Library of Congress, Division of Bibliography. A list of recent writings on state government and its reorganization, with a section on interstate compacts, comp. by Anne L. Baden. Wash., Oct. 1, 1935. 44p.

1905. U. S. Library of Congress, Division of Bibliography. List of references on the reorganization of the executive departments. Wash., Nov. 10, 1925. 25p. [Supplementary list] comp. by Anne L. Baden. Feb. 1, 1932. 21p. [Supplementary list] comp. by Florence S. Hellman. Apr. 1936. 46p.

1906. U. S. Library of Congress, Division of Bibliography. List of works relating to the Supreme Court of the United States. Wash.: Govt. Print. Off., 1909. 124p.

1907. U. S. Library of Congress, Division of Bibliography. Presidential terms, lists of references. Wash., 1940. 10, 10, 16p.

1908. U. S. Library of Congress, Division of Bibliography. "Select list of references on the departments of the United States government." Wash., May 15, 1911. 54p. Typed. "Supplementary list"... May 19, 1915. 15p.

1909. U. S. Library of Congress, Division of Bibliography. A selected list of references on the constitutional powers of the president of the United States including powers recently delegated, comp. by Florence S. Hellman. [Wash., 1933] 30p.

1910. U. S. Library of Congress, Division of Bibliography. A selected list of references on the New Deal, comp. by Florence S. Hellman. [Wash.] 1940. 71p.

1911. U. S. Library of Congress, Division of Bibliography. The Supreme Court issue: a selected list of references, comp. by Florence S. Hellman. Wash., Mar. 9, 1938. 42p.

1912. U. S. Library of Congress, General Reference and Bibliography Division. Presidential inaugurations: a selected list of references. Wash., 1949. 58p.

1913. U. S. National Archives. A list of Federal agencies terminated since 1933 and agencies now having custody of their records, comp. by Guy A. Lee, 1945; rev. by Seymour J. Pomrenze. Wash., 1948. 15p.

1914. U. S. Treasury Dept. Library. Index-reference catalogue of the Library of the Treasury Department. Wash.: Govt. Print. Off., 1891. 517p.

National governments, foreign

1915. U. S. Library of Congress, Division of Bibliography. Select list of books on the cabinets of England and America. Wash.: Govt. Print. Off., 1903. 8p.

1916. U. S. Library of Congress, General Reference and Bibliography Division. The governments of the major foreign powers; a bibliography, comp. by Helen F. Conover. [Wash.] 1945. 45p.

WELFARE AND SOCIAL ACTIVITIES

General

1917. American Foundation for the Blind. Books about the blind. A bibliographical guide to literature relating to the blind, by Helga Lende. N. Y.: American Foundation for the Blind, Inc., 1940. 215p.

Based mainly on the book collection in the American Foundation for the Blind library.

1918. Chicago, University, Library. Private civic and social service agencies of Chicago; a union list of their reports and publications. Chicago: Univ. of Chicago Bookstore, 1936. 243p.

Lists holdings of 5 Chicago libraries.

1919. Milhollen, Hirst. "The American Red Cross collection of photographs and negatives." Library of Congress quarterly journal of current acquisitions, 2 (Oct. - Dec. 1944), 32-38.

Description of a collection of 50,000 photographs, for period from 1900 to 1933, relating to Red Cross, now in Library of Congress.

1920. New York Public Library. "Check list of works in the New York Public Library relating to the charities, missions, etc., of Brooklyn." New York Public Library bulletin, 6 (1902), 61-63.

1921. New York Public Library. "List of works in the New York Public Library relating to beggars, mendicants, tramps, vagrants, etc." New York Public Library bulletin, 10 (1906), 279-89. Reprinted. 11p.

1922. U. S. Department of Labor Library. Laws relating to "mothers' pensions" in the United States, Canada, Denmark and New Zealand. Wash., 1919. 316p. (U.S. Children's Bureau publication, no. 63)
Bibliography: p. 267-316.

1923. U. S. Library of Congress, Division of Bibliography. A selected list of recent references on federal and state grants-in-aid including a section on education, comp. by Grace Hadley Fuller. [Wash.] 1940. 28p.

1924. Volta Bureau Library. Periodicals devoted to the interests of the deaf, by Fred De Land. [Wash.: Volta Bureau, 1913] 16p.
Lists holdings of Volta Bureau.

Political associations

1925. Columbia University Library. An exhibition of selections from the Edwin Patrick Kilroe collection of Tammaniana, Low Memorial Library, December 1942 - February 1943. [N. Y., 1943] 12p.

Criminology

1926. New York Public Library. "List of works in the New York Public Library relating to criminology," comp. by Daniel Carl Haskell. New York Public Library bulletin, 15 (1911), 259-317, 350-71, 379-446, 463-501, 515-57, 567-621, 635-714. Reprinted. 362p.

1927. St. Louis Public Library. Crime waves and criminals; an outline of social divergence and abnormality; a selected list of books to be found in the St. Louis Public Library, comp. by Lucius H. Cannon. [St. Louis] The Library, 1925. 24p. (Reprinted from the Library's Monthly bulletin, April 1925)

1928. Social Science Research Council. A guide to material on crime and criminal justice... prepared by Augustus Frederick Kuhlman for the Committee on Survey of Research on Crime and Criminal Justice of the Social Science Research Council. N. Y.: H. W. Wilson Co., 1929. 633p.
Union list of material in 13 libraries.

1929. Thomas, Elizabeth. Criminology; a college library resources check list. Stillwater: Okla. A. & M. College, 1948. 27p. (Okla. A. & M. College bulletin, v. 45, no. 1)
A check list of books on criminology at Oklahoma Agricultural & Mechanical College.

1930. U. S. Library of Congress, Division of Bibliography. Crime and criminal justice: a bibliography of bibliographies and a selected list of recent books, 1937-1939, comp. by Helen F. Conover. [Wash., 1940] 52p.

1931. U. S. Library of Congress, Division of Bibliography. Select list of recent references on crime and criminal justice. Wash., Feb. 1935. 27p.

1932. U. S. National Archives. Preliminary check list of the records of the Attorney General's Advisory Committee on Crime, 1934-1938, comp. by Helen Beach. [Wash., 1946] 3p. (Preliminary check list, no. 38)

1933. Wigmore, John Henry. A preliminary bibliography of modern criminal law and criminology. Chicago: Northwestern University, 1909. 128p. (Gary Library of Law, Northwestern University Law School, Bulletin, no. 1)

Secret societies

1934. Birdsong, Robert E. "Check list of Rosicrucian literature in the Library of Congress, comp. 1937-1947." [n. p., 1947] 1v. (unpaged) Typewritten.

1935. Freemasons, Chicago Scottish Rite Library. Catalogue of Chicago Scottish Rite Library, 1925. [Chicago, 1925] 116p. Supplement, 1927. 35p.

1936. Freemasons, District of Columbia Grand Lodge Library. Classified catalogue. Wash.: R. Beresford, 1886-94. 56p.

1937. Freemasons, Grand Lodge of Iowa

Library. Catalogue of the works on freemasonry and kindred subjects in the library of the Grand Lodge of Iowa, A. F. & A. Masons. 5th ed. (1849, '54, '73), June 1883. To which is prefixed a separate catalogue of the Bower collection, by T. S. Parvin. Iowa City: Republican Pub. Co., 1883. 135p.

1938. Freemasons, U. S. Scottish Rite, Supreme Council for the Southern Jurisdiction Library. The Taylor collection in the library of the Supreme Council, 33°. Wash., 1905. 98p.

1939. Freemasons, U. S. Scottish Rite, Supreme Council Southern Jurisdiction Library. Libraries of the Supreme Council of the 33d degree for the Southern Jurisdiction of the United States at Washington. N. Y.: J. J. Little & Co., 1884. 267p.

1940. [Gassett, Henry]. Catalogue of books on the Masonic institution in public libraries of twenty-eight states of the union: anti-Masonic in arguments and conclusions. Boston: Camrell & Moore, 1852. 270p.

"Catalogue of books," p. 125-260, lists holdings of libraries by states.

1941. Hamilton, Milton Wheaton. "Anti-Masonic newspapers, 1826-1834." Bibliographical Society of America papers. 32 (1939), 71-97. Reprinted.

Lists only New York state papers, with files located in many American libraries.

1942. Masonic Library Association of Allegheny County, Pa. Catalogue of the library of the Masonic Library Association of Allegheny County, comp. and arr. by Agnes M. Elliott. Pittsburgh: Eichbaum Press, 1897. 54p.

1943. Odd Fellows, Independent Order of, Library. Catalogue of books in the library of the Independent Order of Odd-fellows of the City of Baltimore. Classified and alphabetically arranged by titles. Baltimore: W. J. C. Dulany Co., 1893. 288p.

Insurance

1944. Insurance Library Association of Boston. A catalogue of the library of the Insurance Library Association of Boston; to which is added a sketch of the history and work of the association, together with other information; comp. and arranged by Henry E. Hess. [Boston: F. Wood] 1899. 267p. Supplement. 1903. 71p.

1945. Insurance Society of New York. Newsletter, (1915), to date.

Each issue contains a list of "Additions to the library," formerly entitled "New books."

1946. National Bureau of Casualty and Surety Underwriters Library. Annual index to current literature dealing with casualty insurance, suretyship and related subjects received in the library... 1927-1931. N. Y., 1928-32. 5 numbers.

Now the Association of Casualty and Surety Executives.

1947. U. S. Library of Congress, Division of Bibliography. Government control of insurance in the United States and foreign countries; a selected list of recent writings, comp. by Anne L. Baden. [Wash., 1940] 49p.

1948. U. S. Library of Congress, Division of Bibliography. List of works relating to government regulation of insurance. United States and foreign countries. 2d ed. Wash.: Govt. Print. Off., 1908. 67p.

EDUCATION

General

1949. California, University, Library. Catalogue of books in the pedagogical section of the University Library, rev. ed. Berkeley: [State Print. Off.] 1895. 80p.

1950. Columbia University Library. Books on education in the libraries of Columbia University, ed. by C. A. Nelson. N. Y.: [Knickerbocker Press], 1901. 435p. (Its Library bulletin, no. 2.)

Lists 13,500 titles. Collection now in Teachers College Library.

1951. Currier, Thomas F. "Educational collections in Widener Library." Harvard alumni bulletin, 29 (1927), 570-73.

Gifts of Charles H. Thurber and George A. Plimpton to Harvard University.

1952. Graves, F. P. The Maria Hosmer

Penniman Memorial Library of Education. [Philadelphia, 1920] 43p. (Reprinted from University of Pennsylvania bulletin, 20 (1920)

Describes collection of education books now in University of Pennsylvania School of Education Library.

1953. Harvard University Library. Exhibit of books and documents from the library... to illustrate selected aspects of the history of education. Cambridge: Harvard Univ. Press, 1936. 30p.

1954. John Crerar Library. The official state educational directories; a bibliography, comp. by Jerome K. Wilcox. Chicago, 1931. 15p. (Reference list, no. 12)

1955. New York Public Library. "Check list of works in the New York Public Library relating to the schools of Brooklyn." New York Public Library bulletin, 6 (1902), 55-59.

1956. New York Public Library. "Check list of works relating to the schools, and to the educational history of the City of New York in the New York Public Library." New York Public Library bulletin, 5 (1901), 233-60.

1957. Pennsylvania, University, Library. Some new accessions to the Penniman Memorial Library of Education, University of Pennsylvania, by Thomas Woody. Philadelphia: [The University] 1928. 43p.

1958. Philadelphia Board of Public Education, Pedagogical Library. Catalogue of the Pedagogical Library, comp. by Lillian Ione MacDowell. Philadelphia: Walther Printing House, 1907. 525p.

1959. Smith, Henry Lester and Painter, William T. Bibliography of literature on education in countries other than the United States of America (Jan. 1. 1919 to Dec. 31, 1924). Bloomington, Ind.: Bureau of Cooperative Research, Indiana Univ., 1937. 139p. (Bulletin of the School of Education, Indiana Univ., v. 14, no. 1)

Includes references to material in Indiana University Library only.

1960. Taylor, Louise M. "Education collections of the Harvard College Library." Harvard teachers record, 5 (1935), 15-23.

"The article presents detailed evidence as to the value of the great collections."

1961. Thursfield, Richard Emmons. Henry Barnard's American journal of education. Baltimore: Johns Hopkins Press, 1945. 359p. (Johns Hopkins University studies in historical and political science, ser. 63, no. 1)

Appendix II, p. 327-29, describes Henry Barnard manuscript collection in Washington Square Library, New York University.

1962. U. S. Office of Education. Bibliography, no. 1-76. Wash., 1931-45.

Subject lists based upon Office of Education Library collections.

1963. U. S. Office of Education Library. Bibliography of current research studies in education. [Wash., 1928] 112p. Supplementary list no. 1. [Wash., 1928] 45p.

1964. U. S. Office of Education Library. Bibliography of education, 1911-12. Wash., 1915. 151p. (U. S. Bureau of Education bulletin, no. 30. 1915)

1965. U. S. Office of Education Library. Bibliography of research studies in education, 1926-27 - 1939-40. Wash.: Govt. Print. Off., 1929-41. 14v. (U. S. Office of Education bulletin, 1928, no. 22; 1929, no. 36; 1930, no. 23; 1931, no. 13; 1932, no. 16; 1933, no. 6; 1934, no. 7; 1935, no. 5; 1936, no. 5; 1937, no. 6; 1938, no. 5; 1939, no. 5; 1940, no. 5; 1941, no. 5)

1966. U. S. Office of Education Library. Bibliography on education during the depression; particularly emphasizing economies, by Martha R. McCabe. Wash.: U. S. Office of Education, 1934. 33p. (Office of Education circular, no. 118)

1967. U. S. Office of Education Library. Doctors' theses in education: a list of 797 theses deposited with the Office of Education and available for loan, by Ruth A. Gray. Wash.: Govt. Print. Off., 1935. 69p. (U. S. Office of Education pamphlet, no. 60)

1968. U. S. Office of Education Library. Library circular, no. 1 - 9. Wash., 1912.

"Monthly record of current educational publications." After 1912 issued as Education Bureau bulletins.

1969. U. S. Office of Education Library. Library facilities of the Office of Education. Wash.: Dept. of the Interior, Office of Education [1937] 18p.

1970. U. S. Office of Education Library. Library leaflet, no. 1-36. [Wash.: Govt. Print. Off., 1919-29] 36v.

1. List of references on rural life and culture. 1919. 7p.
2. List of references on education tests and measurements. 1919. 18p.
3. List of references on play and playgrounds. 1919. 11p.
4. List of references on economic value of education. 1919. 7p.
5. List of references on junior high school. 1919. 15p.
6. Stories for young children. 1919. 8p.
7. List of references on vocational education. 1919. 16p.
8. List of references on teachers' salaries. 1919. 16p.
9. List of references on project method in education. 1919. 8p.
10. List of references on education for citizenship. 1920. 16p.
11. List of references on consolidation of schools. 1920. 8p.
12. List of references on educational surveys. 1920. 16p.
13. List of references on use of pictures in education. 1920. 12p.
14. Milam, C. H. What libraries learned from the war. 1922. 6p.
15. List of references on vocational education. 1922. 20p.
16. List of references on rural life and culture. 1922. 10p.
17. List of references on project method in education. 1923. 9p.
18. List of references on visual education. 1923. 11p.
19. List of references on education of women in the United States. 1923. 7p.
20. List of references on junior high school. 1923. 15p.
21. List of references on home economics. 1923. 21p.
22. List of references on secondary education in the United States. 1923. 10p.
23. Bibliography of all-year schools and vacation schools in the United States. 1923. 15p.
24. List of references on money value of education. 1924. 7p.
25. List of references on vocational education. 1924. 20p.
26. List of references on rural life and culture. 1924. 12p.
27. List of references on junior high school. 1924. 11p.
28. List of references on higher education. 1924. 31p.
29. List of references on play and playgrounds. 1924. 13p.
30. List of references on education for citizenship. 1925. 16p.
31. List of references on student self-government and honor-system. 1925. 6p.
32. List of references on vocational guidance. 1925. 11p.
33. List of references on vocational guidance. 1927. 22p.
34. List of references on secondary education. 1927. 22p.
35. List of references on higher education. 1927. 40p.
36. McCabe, M. R. List of references on vocational guidance. 1929. 21p.

1971. U. S. Office of Education Library. List of educational research studies in city school systems. Wash., 1930-36. 6v. (U. S. Office of Education circular, 18, 42, 72, 128, 143, 161)

1972. U. S. Office of Education Library. List of educational research studies of state departments of education and state educational associations. Wash., 1931-36. 6v. (U. S. Office of Education circular, 31, 44, 63, 127, 141, 160)

1973. U. S. Office of Education Library. Planning for post-war education in the United States; an annotated list of recent references. Wash., 1943. 8p. Supplement. Wash., 1945. 17p.

1974. U. S. Office of Education Library. Record of current educational publications. Wash.: Govt. Print. Off., 1912-32. 115v. Monthly to 1921, irregular to end of 1930, and quarterly after 1931.

1975. Yale University Library. Check list of an exhibition of the rarer books and manuscripts given to the Penniman memorial library of education of Yale University by James Hosmer Penniman, comp. by Mary Withington. New Haven: University Library, 1921. 39p.

Teachers and teaching methods

1976. U. S. Bureau of Education Library. List of references on mothers' clubs and parent-teacher associations. Wash.: Govt. Print. Off., 1913-14. 2v.

1977. U. S. Office of Education Library. "Bibliography of research studies in the training and professional status of teachers." U. S. Office of Education bulletin, 13 (1931), 184-224.

1978. U. S. Office of Education Library. List of references on moving pictures in education. Wash., 1914. 4p.

1979. U. S. Office of Education Library. List of references on play and playgrounds. Wash.: Govt. Print. Off., 1913-24. 5v.
Issued 1913, 1914, 1916, 1919, 1924, the latter two as Library leaflet, no. 3, 29.

1980. U. S. Office of Education Library. List of references on student self-government. Wash.: Govt. Print. Off., 1914. 6p.

1981. U. S. Office of Education Library. List of references on teachers' pensions. Wash., 1914. 7p.

Textbooks

1982. Currier, Thomas F. "School books." Harvard Library notes, 2 (1925), 76-78.
In Harvard College Library.

1983. New York Public Library. "The hornbook; foreword by James C. McGuire to a list of the collection of hornbooks given by him to the New York Public Library." New York Public Library bulletin, 31 (1927), 891-98. Reprinted. 10p.
List with descriptions of 33 English hornbooks, p. 893-98.

1984. Partch, Clarence E. "Century-old textbooks in the Rutgers Library." Rutgers University Library journal, 1 (1937), 17-21.

1985. Plimpton, George A. "The hornbook and its use in America." American Antiquarian Society proceedings, n. s. 26 (1916), 264-72.
Description of a collection now in Columbia University.

1986. U. S. Library of Congress, European Affairs Division. Textbooks, their examination and improvement; a report on international and national planning and studies. Research and bibliography by Helen F. Conover, Oct. 1948. Wash., 1948. 155p.
Bibliography, p. 10-14, locates titles available in Library of Congress and other Washington, D. C., libraries.

Vocational education and guidance

1987. B'nai B'rith Group Vocational Guidance Service, Philadelphia. Choosing a career; a selected list of material on occupations and careers available at the Free Library of Philadelphia. Enlarged by the Library staff. Philadelphia: Free Library, 1946. 27p.
A subject list of books available at the Free Library of Philadelphia.

1988. Cleveland Public Library. Index to vocational literature. Cleveland, 1937. 156 numb. l.

1989. Evanston Public Library. Careers and occupations; recent books and pamphlets in the Evanston Public Library on more than 400 vocations. [Evanston, Ill.] 1936. 201 numb. l.

1990. Iowa State College Library. Vocations; a selected bibliography of material in the Iowa State College Library. [Ames, 1941] 25 numb. l.

1991. Philadelphia Free Library. Choosing a career; a selected list of material on occupations and careers available at the Free Library of Philadelphia. Philadelphia: The Library, 1946. 27p.
Classified list of books, pamphlets, periodicals, and government publications.

1992. U. S. Library of Congress, Division of Bibliography. "Select list of references on industrial and technical education." Wash., Nov. 17, 1911. 28p. Typed.

1993. U. S. Office of Education Library. List of references on vocational education. Wash., 1914-24. 4v.

Issued 1914, 1919, 1922, 1924, the last three as Library leaflet, no. 7, 15, 25.

1994. U. S. Office of Education Library. List of references on vocational guidance. [Wash., 1914-29] 4v.

Issued 1914, 1925, 1927, 1929, the last three as Library leaflet, no. 32, 33, 36.

Secondary education

1995. Holmes, Pauline. "Boston Public Latin School memorabilia in the Harvard College Library." Harvard alumni bulletin, 37 (1935), 834-39.

1996. U. S. Office of Education Library. List of references on secondary education in the United States. Wash.: Govt. Print. Off., 1913-27. 4v.

Issued 1913, 1915, 1923, 1927, the latter two as Library leaflet, no. 22, 34.

Colleges and universities

1997. Cole, Eva Alice. "A check list of biographical directories and general catalogues of American colleges." New York genealogical and biographical record, 46 (1915), 51-57. Reprinted 1915. 7p.

152 titles, representing 123 American and Canadian colleges or universities. All titles are in either the Columbia University Library or supplied by the U. S. Bureau of Education Library.

1998. Columbia University Library. Columbiana: a bibliography of manuscripts, pamphlets and books relating to the history of King's College, Columbia College, Columbia University. Published on the one hundred and fiftieth anniversary of King's College, comp. by Charles Alexander Nelson. [N. Y.]: Columbia University, 1904. 48p.

1999. Dana, Maria Trumbull. "Benjamin Silliman manuscripts." Yale University Library gazette, 6 (1932), 74-83.

Describes 5 items recently presented to Library, giving "an interesting picture of Yale at the end of the eighteenth century," through diaries and books belonging to Benjamin Silliman.

2000. Davis, Andrew M. An analysis of the early records of Harvard College, 1636-1750. Cambridge: Harvard University Library, 1895. 21p. (Harvard University Library bibliographical contributions, no. 50)

2001. Dexter, Franklin Bowditch. Biographical sketches of the graduates of Yale College with annals of the College history, October 1701 - September 1815. N. Y.: H. Holt & Co., 1885-1912. 6v.

Locates copies of alumni publications in 12 libraries.

2002. Hartwell, Edith. "The Founders' Room." University of Pennsylvania Library chronicle, 4 (1936), 51-57.

Description of collection pertaining to early history of University of Pennsylvania.

2003. Harvard University. The Harvard University archives; a pamphlet prepared for the information of officers of instruction and administration. 3d. ed. [Cambridge] 1947, 10p.

Brief description of archival material collected and requested by Archives Department of Harvard University Library.

2004. Harvard University Library. A few notes concerning the records of Harvard College, by Andrew M. Davis. Cambridge: Library of Harvard University, 1888. 14p. (Harvard University Library bibliographical contributions, no. 27)

Lists and describes some records and the main collections in Harvard College Library.

2005. Lane, William Coolidge. "Early Harvard broadsides." American Antiquarian Society proceedings, n. s. 24 (1914), 264-304.

List of broadsides, 1642-1810, with locations of copies in 20 libraries.

2006. Lewis, William Ditto. "The University of Delaware and its predecessors; a bibliography." Delaware notes, 17th ser. (1944), 111-125.

Based on University of Delaware Library collection.

2007. Lowe, John Adams. Williamsiana; a bibliography of pamphlets and books relating to the history of Williams College, 1793-1911. Williamstown, 1911. 37p.

2008. Mathews, Albert. "Notes on the Harvard College records, 1636-1800."

Colonial Society of Massachusetts publications, 14 (1913), 312-18.

2009. Morison, Samuel E. "Inventory of the Harvard University archives, to 1800." In: Harvard College in the seventeenth century. Cambridge: Harvard Univ. Press, 1936, Appendix F, p. 662-81.

2010. New York University Library. New York University Collection: an address prepared for the Washington Square College Book Club of New York University, by Theodore Francis Jones. N. Y., 1938. 34p.

2011. Schneider, Herbert and Schneider, Carol, eds. Samuel Johnson, president of King's College; his career and writings. N. Y.: Columbia Univ. Press, 1929. 4v.
Bibliography (v. 4, p. 283-361) gives locations.

2012. Shipton, Clifford K. "The collections of the Harvard University archives." Harvard Library bulletin, 1 (1947), 176-84.

2013. Shipton, Clifford K. "The Harvard University archives." College and research libraries, 3 (1941), 51-56.

2014. Sibley, John Langdon. Biographical sketches of graduates of Harvard University in Cambridge, Massachusetts... 1642-1725. Cambridge: C. W. Sever, 1873-1945. 7v.
Often locates copies of publications of alumni.

2015. U. S. Library of Congress. Catalog Division. A list of American doctoral dissertations printed in [1912-]38. Received in the Catalog Division from [1912-] September 1939. Wash.: Govt. Print. Off., 1913-39. 27v.

2016. U. S. Library of Congress, General Reference and Bibliography Division. "Earnings of college graduates, a selective bibliography," by Kathrine Oliver Murra. In: U. S. Advisory Commission on Service Pay. Career compensation for the uniformed forces. Wash.: Govt. Print. Off., 1948. p. 56-65.
Library of Congress call numbers listed.

2017. U. S. Office of Education Library. "List of college and student publications currently received by the libraries in the District of Columbia." U. S. Bureau of Education, Report of the Commissioner of Education, 1 (1909), 551-56.
Represents 4 libraries.

2018. U. S. Office of Education Library. List of references on higher education. Wash., 1913-29. 4v.
Issued 1913, 1924, 1927, 1929, the second and third as Library leaflet 28, 35, and the last in 3 parts.

2019. Virginia, University, Library. "A bibliography of the unprinted official records of the University of Virginia," comp. by William Edwin Hemphill. University of Virginia Library annual report on historical collections, no. 6 (1935-36), 9-30.
List of records beginning in 1814, indicating locations in various divisions of the University.

2020. Walton, Clarence E. An historical prospect of Harvard College, 1636-1936. Boston: Society for the Preservation of New England Antiquities, 1936. 48p.
Tercentenary exhibition of Harvard College Library.

2021. Winship, George Parker. Brown University broadsides. Providence, 1913. 7p.

2022. Young, Malcolm O. Amherstiana; a bibliography of Amherst College. Amherst College, Mass., 1921. 40p.
Based on Amherst College Library collection.

Special aspects

2023. Henry E. Huntington Library. Learning for ladies (1508-1895), a book exhibition at the Huntington library, by Merle E. Curti. San Marino, Calif., 1936. 15p.

2024. Newberry Library. A preliminary checklist of American writing manuals and copybooks to 1850, comp. by Ray Nash. Chicago: Newberry Library, 1950. 72p.
Lists 274 items, with locations in 13 public and private collections.

2025. U. S. Library of Congress. Sources of information for fundamental education with special reference to education for literacy; a preliminary report by Kathrine Oliver Murra.

Prepared for the Libraries Section of UNESCO. Wash., 1948. 81, 123p.

2026. U. S. Office of Education Library. List of courses of study for elementary and secondary schools, 1930-1935, by Edith A. Wright. Wash.: U. S. Office of Education, 1935. 46p. (U. S. Office of Education circular, no. 139)

2027. U. S. Office of Education Library. List of references on Maria Montessori and her methods. Wash.: Govt. Print. Off., 1913-14. 2v.

2028. U. S. Office of Education Library. List of references on rural schools and rural school teaching. Wash., 1914. 5p.

2029. U. S. Office of Education Library. List of references on the economic value of education. [Wash.: Govt. Print. Off., 1913-24] 4v.
Issued 1913, 1915, 1919, 1924, the last two as Library leaflet, no. 4, 24.

COMMERCE AND COMMUNICATION

General

2030. Detroit Public Library. Government ownership and operation of electric utilities; a selected list of references. [Detroit]: The Library, 1936. 21p.

2031. U. S. Library of Congress, Division of Bibliography. Business cycles: a selected list of references, comp. by Helen F. Conover. [Wash.] 1939. 41p.

2032. U. S. Library of Congress, Division of Bibliography. Government ownership of public utilities; a bibliographical list. Wash., Mar. 12, 1935. 25p.

2033. U. S. Library of Congress, Division of Bibliography. List of references on federal control of commerce and corporations. 3d. ed. Wash.: Govt. Print. Off., 1913. 164p.
References of a general character on interstate commerce.

2034. U. S. Library of Congress, Division of Bibliography. List of references on federal control of commerce and corporations; special aspects and applications. Wash.: Govt. Print. Off., 1914. 104p.

2035. U. S. Library of Congress, Division of Bibliography. A list of references on transportation, with a section on the problem of motor and rail competition and coordination in the United States, comp. by Ellen Fay Chamberlin. [Wash., 1933] 22p.

2036. U. S. Library of Congress, Division of Bibliography. Public utilities: a list of recent references with special reference to rates and regulations. [Wash., 1928] 68p. Supplementary lists, May 26, 1931. 36p.; Nov. 3, 1934. 47p.

2037. U. S. Securities and Exchange Commission Library. List of references on public utilities. [Wash., 1936] 220p.
"This bibliography covers all books which have been printed in the United States; periodicals only from 1921; and some foreign material." "References marked with an asterisk are available in the Securities and Exchange Commission Library."

2038. U. S. Tariff Commission. Index of foreign commercial and economic periodicals currently received in departmental and other institutional libraries located at Washington, D. C., comp. by Carlton C. Rice. Wash.: Govt. Print. Off., 1926. 88p.
Represents 30 libraries. Classified list.

Domestic and foreign trade

2039. John Crerar Library. List of city chambers of commerce, etc., buyers' guides; industrial and manufacturing directories, comp. by Jerome K. Wilcox. Chicago, 1931. 19p. (Reference list 13) Supplement 1. Chicago, 1931. 2p.

2040. U. S. Library of Congress, Division of Bibliography. A list of bibliographies on foreign commerce, comp. by Florence S. Hellman. [Wash.] 1934. 46p.

2041. U. S. Library of Congress, Division of Bibliography. "List of government publications containing current statistics on foreign commerce (including year books of statistical abstracts)." Wash., Nov. 21, 1914. 26p. Typed.

2042. U. S. Library of Congress, General Reference and Bibliography Division. "Foreign information services (exclusive of the U. S.):

a list of serial references for the period July 1, 1945 - March 15, 1946," comp. by Elizabeth A. Gardner. Wash., 1946. 3 pts. Typed.

Contents: I. General, 26p.; II. Individual countries (Albania-Canada), p. 27-65; III. Great Britain, 6p.

2043. U. S. National Archives. Preliminary inventory of the records of the Federal Trade Commission, comp. by Estelle Rebec. Wash., 1948. 7p. (Preliminary inventory, no. 7)

Postal service

2044. Boston Philatelic Society. Catalogue of books on philately in the Public Library of the City of Boston. Derby, Conn.: D. H. Bacon, 1903. 31p.

2045. Carnegie Library of Pittsburgh, American Philatelic Society. Books in the library of the American Philatelic Society. Pittsburgh: The Library, 1910. 20p.

Library of Society is now housed in Carnegie Library of Pittsburgh.

2046. Harwell, Richard Barksdale. "Confederate cover discovery." American philatelist, 60 (April 1947), 545-57.

Study of covers in 1,900 letters from Vice-President of Confederacy Alexander H. Stephens' correspondence in Emory University Library.

2047. Tower, William H. "A philatelic medley." Princeton University Library chronicle, 5 (1943), 14-26.

Tower stamp collection added to Princeton University Library.

2048. U. S. Library of Congress. Postage stamps; a selective check list of books on philately in the Library of Congress. [Wash.: Govt. Print. Off., 1940] 60p.

An international list geographically arranged.

2049. U. S. Library of Congress, Division of Bibliography. "List of references on the postal money order service." In: U. S. Post Office Dept. The United States postal money-order system. Wash., 1915. p. 125-56.

Library of Congress call numbers included.

2050. U. S. Library of Congress, Division of Bibliography. "List of works relating to second-class mail matter," comp. by A. P. C. Griffin. In: U. S. Postal Commission Report. Wash.: Govt. Print. Off., 1907. p. 843-62. (59th Cong., 2d sess. House. Doc. 608)

2051. U. S. Library of Congress, Division of Bibliography. Select list of references on parcels post. Wash.: Govt. Print. Off., 1911. 39p.

2052. U. S. Library of Congress, Division of Bibliography. "Select list of references on the postal service of the United States." Wash., Oct. 24, 1911. 31p. Typed. [Supplementary list] May 17, 1923. 32p. Typed. [Supplementary list] Mar. 9, 1931. 45p. Typed.

Telephone

2053. U. S. Library of Congress, Division of Bibliography. "A selected list of recent references on the telephone in the United States (with special reference to its economic and social conditions)." Wash., Aug. 6, 1934. 36p. Typed. [Supplementary list] Aug. 13, 1935. 13p. Typed.

Railroads

2054. Brayer, Herbert O. "The Pliny Fiske collection of railroad and corporation finance." Princeton University Library chronicle, 6 (1945), 171-78.

Survey of collection in Princeton University Library.

2055. Bureau of Railway Economics. Government ownership of railways. A list of publications, 1917-1929. Wash., 1929. 98p. (Its Bulletin, special series, no. 49. Supplement to no. 62, Old Series, rev. 1917.) Suppl, 1930-1937. Wash. 1938. 111 numb. l.; suppl, 1938-Nov. 1, 1939. Wash., 1939. 24 numb. l.

2056. Bureau of Railway Economics. List of publications pertaining to government ownership of railways. [Wash., 1917] 100p. (Its Bulletin, no. 62, revised, Misc. ser. no. 16, rev. to Jan. 1917) Suppl., 1917-1929. Wash., 1929. 98p.

2057. Bureau of Railway Economics. Railway economics; a collective catalogue of books in fourteen American libraries, prepared by the

Bureau. Chicago: Univ. of Chicago Press, [1912]. 446p.
   Gives statement of files.

2058. Bureau of Railway Economics Library. Albert Fink, October 27, 1827-April 3, 1897, a bibliographical memoir of the father of railway economics and statistics in the United States. Wash., 1927. 23 numb. l.

2059. [Bureau of Railway Economics Library] The Baltimore and Ohio Railroad Company and its subsidiaries; a bibliography, comp. by Edmund Arthur Freeman. [Wash., 1927] 378 numb. l.
   Locates copies in 60 libraries.

2060. Bureau of Railway Economics Library. Bibliography of the Nashville, Chattanooga & St. Louis Railway. Wash., 1922. 29 numb. l.

2061. Bureau of Railway Economics Library. The Camden and Amboy Railroad and Transportation Company, a bibliography, prep. by Douglas R. Stephenson. [Wash.] 1947. 54 numb. l.

2062. Bureau of Railway Economics Library. Canadian Pacific Railway Company, a trial bibliography. Wash., 1928. 94 numb. l.

2063. Bureau of Railway Economics Library. Chicago and North Western Railway Company, a centennial bibliography, comp. by Helen R. Richardson. Wash., 1948. 168 numb. l.

2064. Bureau of Railway Economics Library. Consolidation of railroads in Great Britain; a list of references chronologically arranged. Wash., 1938. 30 numb. l.

2065. Bureau of Railway Economics Library. Cost of railroad transportation - a bibliographical memorandum of some of the reports and discussions of this subject. Wash., 1941. 148 numb. l.

2066. Bureau of Railway Economics Library. Disaster relief by railroads, 1906-1930; a list of references (chronologically arranged). Wash., 1930. 30 numb. l.

2067. Bureau of Railway Economics Library. Financial structure of railroads in the United States, 1933-1935. A list of references chronologically arranged. Wash., 1935. 20 numb. l.

2068. Bureau of Railway Economics Library. Illinois Central Railway System - a centennial bibliography, comp. by Helen R. Richardson. Wash.: Printed for Illinois Central System by McArdle Print. Co., 1950. 255p.

2069. Bureau of Railway Economics Library. List of references on maximum railway passenger fares. [Wash., 1915] 13 numb. l.

2070. Bureau of Railway Economics Library. List of references on the Delaware and Hudson Company. Wash., 1923. 45 numb. l.

2071. Bureau of Railway Economics Library. A list of references on the Norfolk and Western Railway. Wash., 1924. 52 numb. l.

2072. Bureau of Railway Economics Library. A list of references on the proposed consolidation of railroads, chronologically arranged. Wash., 1923. 29 numb. l.

2073. Bureau of Railway Economics Library. List of references on the use of railroads in war. Wash., 1915. 34 l.
   Locates copies.

2074. Bureau of Railway Economics Library. List of references on valuation of steam railways. Chicago: American Railway Engineering Association, 1916. 154p. (American Railway Engineering Association bulletin, 18 (1916), no. 190)

2075. Bureau of Railway Economics Library. A list of references to literature relating to the Union Pacific system. Wash., 1922. 299 numb. l.

2076. Bureau of Railway Economics Library. A list of references to recent material on some railroad holding companies. Wash., 1931. 64 numb. l.

2077. Bureau of Railway Economics Library. Nationalization of railways, 1939-1949; a list of references, comp. by Helen R. Richardson. Wash., 1949. 30 numb. l.

2078. Bureau of Railway Economics Library. Organization of railways; some material published from 1920-1929. Wash., 1929. 26 numb. l.

2079. Bureau of Railway Economics Library.

The Pan American Railway, 1879-1927; some references chronologically arranged. Wash., 1928. 20 numb. l.

2080. Bureau of Railway Economics Library. Pick-up and delivery service in the United States and Canada, 1933-1937, a list of references chronologically arranged. Wash., 1936. 32 numb. l.

2081. Bureau of Railway Economics Library. Pooling in the United States, 1920-1939, a list of references. Wash., 1939. 81 numb. l.

2082. Bureau of Railway Economics Library. Railroad bibliographies - a trial checklist, August, 1938. Wash., 1938. 71p.
In three parts: I. Bibliographies, bibliographical memoranda and lists compiled by Bureau of Railway Economics Library; II. Bibliographies, bibliographical memoranda and lists compiled by others; III. Index of compilers and subjects. Suppl., 1949. 14 numb. l.

2083. Bureau of Railway Economics Library. Railroad consolidation, a list of references. Wash., 1930. 83p.

2084. Bureau of Railway Economics Library. Railroad conventions, 1823-1889; memorandum listing their proceedings and other publications chronologically by dates of conventions. Wash., 1945. 32 numb. l.

2085. Bureau of Railway Economics Library. Railroad economics - a trial check list. [Wash., 1938] 71 numb. l.

2086. Bureau of Railway Economics Library. Railroads and geology in the United States, an exhibit of reports and other material in the library, showing their inter-relations for 130 years. Wash., 1938 29 numb. l.

2087. Bureau of Railway Economics Library. Railroads and national defense in the United States. Wash.: The Library, 1941. 62 numb. l.

2088. Bureau of Railway Economics Library. Railroads in New York City, 1813-1899; a list of references, chronologically arranged. Wash., 1939. 74p.

2089. Bureau of Railway Economics Library. Railroads in New York City, 1900-1939; a list of references, chronologically arranged. Wash., 1939. 56p.

2090. Bureau of Railway Economics Library. The railroads' library. Wash., 1942. 23p.
Description of resources of Bureau of Railway Economics Library.

2091. Bureau of Railway Economics Library. Railroads of Iowa, prep. by Harry L. Eddy. [Wash., 1947] 30 numb. l.
List of material in Bureau's Library.

2092. Bureau of Railway Economics Library. Railway hospital service in North America - memorandum listing references to material on the subject in BRE Library. [Wash., 1944] 21 numb. l.

2093. Bureau of Railway Economics Library. Scandinavian railways, 1934-1940 - a brief list of references, chronologically arranged. [Wash., 1940] 16p.

2094. Bureau of Railway Economics Library. Store door delivery; a list of references, chronologically arranged. Wash., 1933. 30 numb. l.

2095. Bureau of Railway Economics Library. Trial bibliography on New York, New Haven and Hartford Railroad. Wash., 1915. 244 numb. l.

2096. "Deposit of Illinois Central Railroad Company records in the Newberry Library, Chicago." Business Historical Society bulletin, 19 (Nov. 1945), 173-75.
Description of extensive collection, printed and manuscript, 1851-1906, deposited in Newberry Library.

2097. Harvard University, Graduate School of Business Administration, Baker Library, Kress Library of Business and Economics. The pioneer period of European railroads. Boston: Baker Library [1946] 71p. (Publication, no. 3)
Contains list of items relating to European railroad development, published in 1848 or earlier, which are available in the Baker and other Harvard libraries.

2098. Harvard University, Graduate School of Business Administration, Baker Library.

"The Samuel M. Felton collection." Business Historical Society bulletin, 1 (October - November, 1926), 8-13.
    About 2,500 books and pamphlets, chiefly pertaining to early United States railroading, in Baker Library, Harvard University.

2099. Illinois Railroad and Warehouse Commission Library. Catalogue. Springfield: Jefferson's Print. Co., 1912. 188p.

2100. New York Public Library. "Check list of publications on American railroads before 1841," comp. by Thomas R. Thomson. New York Public Library bulletin, 45 (1941), 3-68, 533-84, 859-940; 46 (1942), 865-909. Reprinted. 250p.
    Lists 2,671 items and locates copies in 35 cooperating libraries.

2101. New York Public Library. "List of works in the New York Public Library relating to government control of railroads, rates regulations, etc." New York Public Library bulletin, 10 (1906), 184-209. Reprinted. 26p.

2102. Newberry Library. Deposit of Illinois Central Railroad Company records in the Newberry Library, Chicago. Chicago, 1945. 4p.
    Brief account of records, 1851-1906, deposited with Library.

2103. Newberry Library. Guide to the Burlington archives in the Newberry Library, 1851-1901, comp. by Elisabeth Coleman Jackson and Carolyn Curtis. Chicago: The Library, 1949. 374p.
    Catalog and guide to more than 1,000,000 letters, 1,500 bundles of miscellaneous material, and 2,000 volumes of ledgers, accounts and operating books.

2104. Stanford University Library. Catalogue of the Hopkins Railway Library, by Frederick J. Teggart. Palo Alto, 1895. 231p. (Publications of the Library, v. 1)

2105. Traffic Club of Chicago. Historical collection of the Traffic Club of Chicago; a complete catalogue of documents, books, and pictures, articles in scrapbooks and articles in frames, on display in the rooms of the club. Chicago: The Club, 1919. 36p.
    Lists 970 items relating to railroad, canal boat, stage and other forms of transportation.

2106. U. S. Library of Congress, Division of Bibliography. A list of books, with references to periodicals, relating to railroads in their relation to the government and the public. Wash.: Govt. Print. Off., 1907. 131p.
    List of works relating to government regulation and government ownership of railroads.

2107. U. S. Library of Congress, Division of Bibliography. Railways in the United States: a bibliographical list, comp. by Ellen Fay Chamberlin. [Wash., 1933] 38p.

2108. U. S. Library of Congress, Division of Bibliography. Select list of books on railroads in foreign countries. Government regulation: General; Continental Europe; International freight agreement; Great Britain; France; Germany; Belgium; Switzerland; Italy; Austria-Hungary; Russia. Wash.: Govt. Print. Off., 1905. 72p.

2109. U. S. Library of Congress, Division of Bibliography. Select list of references on the valuation and capitalization of railroads. Wash.: Govt. Print. Off., 1909. 28p.

Waterways

2110. Bureau of Railway Economics. An economic survey of inland waterway transportation in the United States. Wash., 1930. 238p. (Its Bulletin, Special series, no. 56)
    Bibliography, p. 227-38.

2111. Bureau of Railway Economics Library. The St. Lawrence seaway; an official transcript of cards in catalog of Bureau of Railway Economics Library, arranged chronologically. Wash., 1941. 61 numb. l.

2112. New York Public Library. "American interoceanic canals; a list of works in the New York Public Library," comp. by John Christian Frank. New York Public Library bulletin, 20 (1916), 11-81. Reprinted, with an author index, 90p.

2113. Ochs, Robert D. The historical source material in the Illinois and Michigan Canal Office, Lockport, Illinois. Lockport, 1937. 109p.
    Lists and describes maps, field reports, legal documents, letter books, commissioners' reports, leases, and other material concerning the canal from 1822 to date. About 10,000 items.

2114. U. S. Library of Congress. List of books and of articles in periodicals relating to interoceanic canal and railway routes (Nicaragua; Panama, Darien, and the Valley of the Atrato; Tehuantepec and Honduras; Suez Canal), by Hugh A. Morrison, Jr. Wash.: Govt. Print. Off., 1900. 174p. (56th Cong., 1st sess. Senate doc. 59)

Lists 863 books and pamphlets and 1,176 periodical articles. Items not in Library of Congress frequently located elsewhere.

2115. U. S. Library of Congress, Division of Bibliography. The St. Lawrence navigation and power project; a list of recent references, comp. by Ann Duncan Brown. Wash., 1940. 11p. Supplement. 1942. 28p.

2116. U. S. Library of Congress, Division of Bibliography. Select list of references on inland waterways of Europe. Washington Barracks, D. C.: Press of the Engineer School, 1910. 75p. (Occasional papers, Engineer School, U. S. Army, no. 38)

2117. U. S. Library of Congress, Division of Bibliography. Waterways in the United States: a selected list of recent references, comp. by Grace Hadley Fuller. [Wash.] 1938. 43p.

Ocean and air transport

2118. American Association of Port Authorities. Bibliographic notes on ports and harbors, including lists by the Library of Congress. Part I. Place bibliography and general titles. Part II. Subject bibliography, comp. by Perry Young. New Orleans: American Association of Port Authorities, 1926. 188p.

Locates copies in Library of Congress.

2119. Brown, Karl. "Materials of maritime interest in the New York Public Library." American Neptune, 1 (Oct. 1941), 381-90.

A general description of both practical materials and rarities.

2120. Harvard University, Graduate School of Business Administration, Baker Library. "East Indiamen and clipper ships." Business Historical Society bulletin, 2 (May, 1928), 3-10.

Pertains to Gordon Dexter collection, in Baker Library, Harvard University.

2121. Harvard University, Graduate School of Business Administration, Baker Library. "Shipping papers of James Hunnewell." Business Historical Society bulletin, 8 (1934), 63-66.

Describes papers relating to Hawaiian shipping in the middle of the 19th century now in Baker Library, Harvard School of Business Administration.

2122. Harvard University, Graduate School of Business Administration, Baker Library. "Sources for maritime history." Business Historical Society bulletin, 6 (September, 1932), 8-12.

In Baker Library, Harvard University.

2123. Harvard University, Graduate School of Business Administration, Baker Library. "The Suez Canal, an achievement of enthusiasm and diplomacy." Business Historical Society bulletin, 3 (June, 1929), 1-8.

Collection of material on Canal presented to Baker Library, Harvard University.

2124. New York Public Library. "The Atlantic Neptune," by Robert Lingel. New York Public Library bulletin, 40 (1936), 571-603.

Locates copies in 18 institutions, American and foreign.

2125. Pellett, Mirl Edison. Water transportation; a bibliography, guide, and union catalogue... with the cooperation of thirty-four North American libraries. N. Y.: H. W. Wilson, 1931. v. 1. (685p.)

Locates 5,700 titles on harbors, ports and port terminals in 35 cooperating libraries and 74 government documents depository libraries.

2126. U. S. Library of Congress, Division of Aeronautics. Aeropolitics; a selective bibliography on the influence of aviation on society, comp. by Arthur G. Renstrom. Wash., 1948. 31p.

Based on Library of Congress collection.

2127. U. S. Library of Congress, Division of Bibliography. List of references on ship subsidies, 1915-1922. Wash., May 12, 1922. 12p.

2128. U. S. Library of Congress, Division of Bibliography. List of references on shipping and shipbuilding. Wash.: Govt. Print. Off., 1919. 303p.

2129. U. S. Library of Congress, Division of Bibliography. List of works relating to deep waterways from the Great Lakes to the Atlantic Ocean, with some other related works. Wash.: Govt. Print. Off., 1908. 59p.

2130. U. S. Library of Congress, Division of Bibliography. Selected list of writings on the American Merchant Marine, including subsidies, comp. by Anne L. Baden. Wash., Jan. 18, 1936. 46p.

2131. U. S. Library of Congress, Division of Bibliography. Shipping question; a list of recent writings. Wash., Jan. 27, 1928. 34p.

Local transit

2132. Boston Elevated Railway Company Library. Reference list of literature on urban electric railways, indexed by cities, compiled from reports by railroad commissions, public service commissions, legislative commissions, investigating commissions, electric railway companies, transportation experts and others, with classified index. June, 1927. [Boston: E. L. Grimes Printing Co., 1927] 151p.

All references are to books in Boston Elevated Railway Company Library.

2133. Chicago Municipal Reference Library. Proposed subways in the city of Chicago; a list of references to material on file in the Municipal Reference Library (chronologically arranged), comp. by Frederick Rex. [Chicago, 1932] 15 numb. 1.

2134. New York Public Library. "Check list of works relating to street railways, rapid transit, etc., in the City of New York in the New York Public Library." New York Public Library bulletin, 5 (1901), 160-62.

2135. U. S. Federal Works Agency Library. Bibliography on automobile parking in the United States, comp. by Frances Mahoney. Wash.: Public Roads Administration, 1946. 47p.

Lists 1,035 titles compiled from material in libraries of Federal Works Agency and Public Roads Administration.

2136. U. S. Library of Congress, Division of Bibliography. Motor transport in the United States: a bibliographical list, comp. by Ellen Fay Chamberlin. [Wash., 1933] 21p.

2137. U. S. Library of Congress, Division of Bibliography. Urban transportation in the United States; street-railways, subways, taxis, trolley-buses, etc.: a bibliographical list, comp. by Ellen Fay Chamberlin. [Wash., 1933] 15p.

CUSTOMS AND FOLKLORE

Women

2138. Bell, Martha S. "Collection of writings by Virginia women." College and research libraries, 7 (1946), 343-45.

Description of 840-volume collection, representing 300 authors, in Randolph-Macon Woman's College Library.

2139. Boston Public Library. Catalogue of the Galatea collection of books relating to the history of woman. Boston, 1898. 34p. (Reprinted from Boston Public Library monthly bulletin, 3 (1898), 67-102.)

Catalog of over 1,000 volumes given to the Boston Public Library by Thomas Wentworth Higginson.

2140. [John Crerar Library] La femme et le féminisme. Collection de livres, périodiques etc. sur la condition sociale de la femme et le mouvement féministe. Faisant partie de la bibliothèque de M. et Mme. C. V. Gerritsen (Dr. Aletta H. Jacobs) à Amsterdam. Paris: V. Giard & Brière, 1900. 240p.

Collection much enlarged, acquired by John Crerar Library, 1904.

2141. New York Public Library. "List of works in the New York Public Library relating to woman." New York Public Library bulletin, 9 (1905), 528-84. Reprinted. 57p.

2142. New York Public Library. "Women in the making of America." New York Public Library bulletin, 45 (1941), 468-72. Reprinted. 7p.

Classified list of biographies.

2143. North Carolina, University, Woman's College, Library. The woman's collection; a bibliography of material in all matters pertaining to women's interests added to the Women's College Library of the University of North Carolina, 1937-43, comp. by Minnie Middleton Hussey and Roseanne Hudson.

Greensboro: Library, Woman's College, University of North Carolina, 1944. 121p. 1944-45 supplements. 1945-46. 2v. 1946 Supplement. 1947. 40p.

2144. Northwestern University Library. Biblioteca femina, assembled by Grace Thompson Seton, chairman of Letters of the National Council of Women of the United States, inc., 1933-1939. [n. p. 1940?] 41 numb. 1.

Collection of works by women authors in Northwestern University Library.

2145. Stearns, Bertha-Monica. "Early western magazines for ladies." Mississippi Valley historical review, 18 (1931), 319-30.

Locates titles.

2146. U. S. Library of Congress, Division of Bibliography. "Women as physicians in the United States: a selected list of books and pamphlets," comp. by Ann D. Brown. Wash., Oct. 16, 1940. 32p. Typed.

Folklore

2147. Harvard University Library. Catalogue of English and American chap-books and broadside ballads in Harvard College Library, by Charles Welsh and William H. Tillinghast. Cambridge: Harvard University Library, 1905. 171p. (Harvard University Library bibliographical contributions, no. 56)

Lists 2,461 titles in 23 classes.

2148. New York Public Library. "A catalogue of the American, English, and foreign chapbooks in the New York Public Library," comp. by Harry B. Weiss. New York Public Library bulletin, 39 (1935), 3-34, 105-26, 181-92, 789-810. Reprinted, 1936. 80p.

Lists 1,171 items, covering period from 1750 to 1850.

2149. New York Public Library. "The folkways of Brazil, a bibliography," comp. by Rex Gorham, ed. by Karl Brown. New York Public Library bulletin, 47 (1943), 255-72, 427-35; 48 (1944), 435-40, 501-11. Reprinted. 67p.

Based on holdings of New York Public Library; locates books not in that Library.

2150. New York Public Library. "A preliminary check list of American chapbooks," by Harry B. Weiss. New York Public Library bulletin, 49 (1945), 587-96.

Locates copies in 10 libraries.

2151. Newberry Library. The Arthurian legend; a check list of books in the Newberry Library, comp. by Jane D. Harding. Chicago: The Library, 1933. 120p. Supplement. 1938. 90p.

Includes texts and critical works.

2152. Nitze, William Albert. "The Newberry collection of Arthuriana." Modern philology, 30 (1932), 1-4. Reprinted. 4p.

Brief sketch of Arthuriana in Newberry Library, Chicago.

2153. Thayer, Gordon Woods. "The John G. White collection at the Cleveland Public Library." College and research libraries, 6 (1945), 219-23.

Description of a major collection of folklore and orientalia.

Miscellany

2154. New York Public Library. "A bibliography of etiquette books published in America before 1900," comp. by Mary Read Bobbitt. New York Public Library bulletin, 51 (1947), 687-720. Reprinted. 35p.

Locates copies in 82 libraries.

2155. New York Public Library. "List of works in the New York Public Library relating to Gipsies." New York Public Library bulletin, 10 (1906), 358-67. Reprinted. 10p.

2156. Princeton University Library. A list of Christmas books in the Princeton University Library. Princeton, 1942. 31p.

Science

GENERAL

2157. American Association of Museums. Handbook of American museums. Wash.: The Association, 1932. 779p.
Contains data on libraries, in museums and historical societies.

2158. Anderson, Henry J. Catalogue of the library of the late Henry James Anderson, comprising a fine collection of scientific and mathematical works and many valuable manuscripts... to be sold by auction... October 1879... Geo. A. Leavitt & Co., Auctioneers. N. Y., 1879. 86p.
Scientific and mathematical works (nos. 704-1134, p. 48-73) were bought for Columbia University.

2159. Bay, Jens Christian. "Bibliotheca Thordarsoniana. A private collection of scientific and technological literature." Bibliographical Society of American papers, 23 (1929) pt. 1, p. 1-17.
Describes collection of 25,000 books in the Thordarson Library, since acquired by University of Wisconsin. See also Hagedorn below.

2160. California Academy of Sciences. Catalogue of the library. [San Francisco, 1889] 91p. (Reprinted from its Proceedings, 2d ser., v. 1 (1889).
Arranged by types of publications and subjects.

2161. Carnegie Library of Pittsburgh. Men of science and industry; a guide to the biographies of scientists, engineers, inventors and physicians, in the Carnegie Library of Pittsburgh. Pittsburgh: The Library, 1915. 189p.

2162. Carnegie Library of Pittsburgh. Science and technology; a record of literature recently added to the Carnegie Library of Pittsburgh. Pittsburgh: The Library, 1946 - to date. Quarterly.
"A reprint of material from the card catalogues of the library."

2163. Freemasons, U. S. Scottish Rite, Supreme Council Southern Jurisdiction Library. The Busby collection in the library of the Supreme Council, 33º, Washington, D. C. Wash.: [Wilkens-Sheiry Printing Co.] 1907. 82p.
A collection of technical and scientific books donated by William Busby.

2164. Hagedorn, Ralph. "Bibliotheca Thordarsoniana: the sequel." Bibliographical Society of America papers, 44 (1950), 29-54.
Survey of the extensive Chester H. Thordarson collection of rare books acquired by University of Wisconsin Library. Collection relates to "development of British scientific thought and technological evolution," broadly interpreted.

2165. John Crerar Library. A list of glossaries in the fields of science and technology, comp. by Bernice Simpson. Chicago, 1936. 40p. (Reference list 36).

2166. John Crerar Library. A selected and annotated list of new scientific and technical reference books published mainly by foreign and lesser known American publishers, comp. by H. Einar Mose. Chicago, 1931. 26p. (Reference list 16).

2167. John Crerar Library. Sources of

current reviews of scientific and technical books, comp. by Jerome K. Wilcox. Chicago, 1930. 13p. (Reference list, no. 6).

2168. Leikind, Morris C. "Robert Kastor's portraits of scientists." Library of Congress quarterly journal of current acquisitions, 4 (Aug. 1947), 9-11.

Collections of 194 pen-and-ink sketches of contemporary scientists, received by Library of Congress.

2169. Linda Hall Library, 1946-1948. Kansas City, Mo., 1949. 37p.

Survey of Library's collections, chiefly in science and technology, arranged by subject fields.

2170. Metropolitan Museum of Art Library. Bibliography of museums and museology, by William Clifford. N. Y., 1923. 98p.

Based on Metropolitan Museum collection.

2171. National Research Council. Research Information Service. Handbook of scientific and technical societies and institutions of the United States and Canada, 4th ed. Wash.: The Council, 1942. 389p. (National Research Council bulletin, no. 106)

Includes brief data on libraries.

2172. New York Public Library. "Scientific and technical dictionaries of the Spanish and English languages," comp. by José Sanchez and Samuel Baig. New York Public Library bulletin, 48 (1944), 619-38. Reprinted. 22p.

Most titles are located in New York Public Library, Engineering Societies Library of New York, or Library of Congress.

2173. San Francisco Public Library. Catalogue of books in the classes of natural science and useful arts. San Francisco: [Press of the Stanley-Taylor Co.] 1899. [105]-262p.

Paged continuously with its Catalogue no. 9 (Foreign literature).

2174. Simons, Corinne Miller. "The Lloyd Library and Museum - a brief history of its founders and resources." College and research libraries, 2 (1941), 245-47.

2175. Simons, Corinne Miller. "Lloyd Library and Museum; a history of its

resources." Special Libraries, 34 (Dec. 1943), 481-86.

Brief description of resources.

2176. Spratt, Hereward Philip. Libraries for scientific research in Europe and America. London: Grafton, 1936. 227p.

Describes collections and facilities for scientific research available in 33 United States libraries, p. 128-211.

2177. U. S. Library of Congress. "Annual report on acquisitions; Science." Library of Congress quarterly journal of acquisitions, 3 (Aug. 1946), 28-45; 4 (Aug. 1947) 62-66; 5 (Aug. 1948), 51-55.

2178. U. S. Library of Congress, Division of Bibliography. "The administration of research: a selective bibliography," prep. by Kathrine O. Murra and Helen D. Jones. In: U. S. President's Scientific Research Board. Science and public policy. Wash.: Govt. Print. Off., 1947. v. 3, p. 253-324.

Locates copies principally in Library of Congress, but occasionally in 6 other libraries.

2179. U. S. Library of Congress, General Reference and Bibliography Division. "Bibliography: books and articles on scientific and political aspects of atomic energy," comp. by Morris Leikind. In: U. S. Congress, Senate, Special Committee on Atomic Energy. Atomic energy act of 1946. [Wash.: Govt. Print. Off., 1946] p. 90-125. (79th Cong., 2d sess. Senate. Rept. 1211)

2180. U. S. Library of Congress, General Reference and Bibliography Division. Fiscal and budgetary phases of research; a selected list of references, comp. by Helen Dudenbostel Jones. Wash., 1949. 33p.

2181. U. S. Library of Congress, General Reference and Bibliography Division. The social impact of science: a select bibliography, with a section on atomic power. Wash.: Govt. Print. Off., 1945. 51p. (79th Cong., 1st sess. Senate, Subcommittee monograph no. 3)

2182. U. S. Library of Congress, Legislative Reference Service. Atomic energy: significant references covering various aspects of the subject, arranged topically, comp. by

Janie E. Mason. v. 1+, 1946 - date. Washington, 1946 - date. Monthly.
Title varies.

2183. Virginia State Library. "Finding list of the books in science, medicine, agriculture, technology, military and naval science," comp. by Earl G. Swem. Virginia State Library bulletin, 4 (1911), 73-501.

HISTORY

2184. Babson Institute Library. A descriptive catalogue of the Grace K. Babson collection of the works of Sir Isaac Newton and the materials relating to him in the Babson Institute Library. N.Y.: Herbert Reichner, 1950. 230p.
Lists over 600 items: first editions, works from Newton's library, manuscripts, portraits, etc., in library at Babson Park, Mass.

2185. Buffalo Museum of Science. Milestones of science: a reference list of epochal books in the collection of the Museum. Buffalo, N.Y.: Buffalo Museum of Science, 1941. 30 numb. 1.

2186. California, University, History of Science Club. Exhibition of first editions of epochal achievements in the history of science... on display at the University Library. Berkeley, 1934. 48p.
Titles not in the University of California Library are starred.

2187. Harvard University Library. "The Sarton collection in the history of science." Harvard Library bulletin, 4 (1950), 276-77.
In Harvard College Library.

2188. Heindel, Richard H. "Historical manuscripts in the Academy of Natural Sciences, Philadelphia." Pennsylvania history, 5 (1938), 30-32.
Brief description of some of miscellaneous letters in Academy's collections (1744-1870).

2189. Henry E. Huntington Library. Science and the new world (1526-1800) an exhibition to illustrate the scientific contributions of the new world and the spread of scientific ideas in America, by Theodore Hornberger, San Marino: The Library, 1937. 18p.

2190. Historical Records Survey - Mass. Calendar of the letters of Charles Robert Darwin to Asa Gray. Boston: Historical Records Survey, 1939. 148p.

2191. John Crerar Library. A list of books on the history of science. January, 1911, prep. by Aksel G. S. Josephson. Chicago: The Library, 1911. 297p. Supplement, December 1916. 1917. 139p.

2192. John Crerar Library. A list of books on the history of science. 2d supplement, prep. by Reginald B. Gordon. Chicago: The Library, 1941. 12p.

2193. John Crerar Library. Subject bibliography to histories of scientific and technical subjects. Chicago, 1933-1944. 3v. (Reference list 28, 49, 55)

2194. Kilgour, Frederick G. "The first century of scientific books in the Harvard College Library." Harvard Library notes, 3 (1939), 217-25.

PERIODICALS (General Science)

2195. American Chemical Society, Cincinnati Section. Union list of scientific and technical periodicals in the libraries of greater Cincinnati, comp. and ed. by Bernard Gessiness. Cincinnati: The Section, 1948. 120p.
Gives holdings of 58 public and industrial libraries. 3,200 titles.

2196. Bolton, Henry Carrington. A catalogue of scientific and technical periodicals, 1665-1895; together with chronological tables and a library check list. 2d ed. Wash.: Smithsonian Institution, 1897. 1,247p. (Smithsonian miscellaneous collections, v. 40)
Represents 133 libraries, but exact holdings not shown.

2197. Carnegie Library of Pittsburgh. Scientific, technical and trade periodicals currently received by the Carnegie Library of Pittsburgh. Pittsburgh: The Library, 1940. 34p.

2198. Cobb, Ruth. "Periodical bibliographies and abstracts for the scientific and technological journals of the world." National Research Council bulletin, 1 (1920), 131-54.

Shows locations in 9 government libraries in Washington.

2199. Drury, Francis K. W., ed. Technical and scientific serials in the libraries of Providence, 1920. Providence, R. I., [1921] 63p.

Lists 2,500 titles in 10 libraries.

2200. Duke University Library. Check list of scientific periodicals and of selected serials in the libraries of Duke University, ed. by Mrs. V. G. Watkins. Durham: The Library, 1944. 125p.

2201. Indiana Academy of Science. "A catalogue of scientific periodical literature on file in various libraries of the state," by Howard James Banker and Will Scott. Indiana Academy of Science proceedings, (1911), 445-73.

Gives holdings of 11 libraries in Indiana.

2202. Indiana Academy of Science. "Report of the Committee on 'A list of the scientific and technical serials in the libraries of the state of Indiana.'" Indiana Academy of Science proceedings, (1913), 237-364.

Lists holdings of 19 libraries.

2203. Indiana Academy of Science Library. Periodical literature currently received by the Library of the Indiana Academy of Science, comp. by Nellie M. Coats. Indianapolis, 1935. 18 numb. l.

2204. Lloyd Library and Museum of Botany, Pharmacy and Materia Medica. Catalogue of the periodical literature in the Lloyd Library, by Walter H. Aiken and Sigmund Waldbott. Cincinnati, 1936. 103p. (Lloyd Library bulletin, no. 34)

List of 2,200 titles, with holdings.

2205. Louisiana State University Library. List of scientific and technical serials in the Louisiana State University Library. Baton Rouge, 1949. 89p.

2206. Pan American Union, Columbus Memorial Library. Journals dealing with the natural, physical and mathematical sciences published in Latin America; a tentative directory, by Katherine Lenore Morgan. Wash.: Pan American Union, Division of Intellectual Cooperation, 1944. 62 numb. l.

Based upon holdings of Pan American Union Library.

2207. [Special Libraries Association, Minnesota Chapter] Checklist of a selected list of continental European scientific serials in Twin City libraries. [Minneapolis] 1944. 6p.

2208. U. S. Library of Congress, Selected list of European scientific and technical journals... Compiled from the Library of Congress union list of European journals in the District of Columbia [by] M. Sanchez. Wash. 1942. 23p.

MATHEMATICS

2209. American Mathematical Society. "Catalogue of the library." American Mathematical Society bulletin, 52 (1946), no. 5, pt. 2, 173p.

Records about 11,600 volumes deposited in Columbia University Library. New edition of 1932 catalog.

2210. Cornell University Library. Special lists. No. 1, Mathematics. Ithaca, 1883. 92p. (Reprinted from Cornell University Library bulletin, 1 (1882-83), 60-76, 95-108, 127-40, 155-80, 205-12)

2211. Denver Public Library. Higher mathematics: a selected list of recent books in the Science and Engineering Department. Denver: The Library, 1943. 8p.

2212. Frick, Bertha M. "The David Eugene Smith Mathematical Library of Columbia University." Osiris; studies on the history and philosophy of science, 1 (1936), 79-86.

2213. Frick, Bertha M. "The first Portuguese arithmetic." Scripta mathematica, 11 (1945), 327-39.

Item described now in Columbia University Library.

2214. Illinois, University, Library. "A list of mathematical books in America, published before and including 1850 which are in the library of the University of Illinois." Urbana, 1938. 18 numb. l. Typed.

Two supplementary lists inserted at end.

2215. Karpinski, Louis C. Bibliography of

mathematical works printed in America through 1850. Ann Arbor: Univ. of Michigan Press, 1940. 697p.

Locates 2,998 titles in over 100 libraries.

2216. Karpinski, Louis C. "Colonial American arithmetics." In: Bibliographical essays: a tribute to Wilberforce Eames. [Cambridge: Harvard University Press.] 1924, p. 242-48.

Lists 29 titles, 1556-1775, with locations in 8 libraries.

2217. Michigan, University, William L. Clements Library. Mathematica Americana; a guide to an exhibition. Ann Arbor, 1935. 7p. (Bulletin, no. 23)

Books from Library's collection.

2218. New York Public Library. "List of works on the history of mathematics (including works printed before 1800) in the New York Public Library." New York Public Library bulletin, 7 (1903), 464-95.

2219. Plimpton, George A. "The history of elementary mathematics in the Plimpton Library." Science, 68 (1928), 390-95.

Describes collection now in Columbia University.

2220. Simons, Lao Genevra. Bibliography of early American texbooks on algebra published in the colonies and the United States through 1850. N. Y.: Scripta mathematica, Yeshiva College, 1936. 68p.

Locates 71 treatises in 50 libraries.

2221. Smith, David Eugene. Addenda to Rara arithmetica which described in 1908 such European arithmetics printed before 1601 as were then in the library of the late George Arthur Plimpton. Boston: Ginn, 1939. 52p.

Lists collection now in Columbia University Library.

2222. Smith, David Eugene. "Among my autographs." A series of 29 articles which appeared in 16 numbers of the American mathematical monthly, 28-29, (February 1921- December 1922).

Describes collection of autographed letters of famous mathematicians in David Eugene Smith Library at Columbia University.

2223. Smith, David Eugene. "The first printed arithmetic (Treviso, 1478)." Isis, 6 (1924), 311-31.

Item described now in Plimpton collection, Columbia University Library.

2224. Smith, David Eugene. "In the surnamed chosen chest." American mathematical monthly, 32 (1925), 287-94, 393-97, 444-50.

Describes David Eugene Smith Library at Columbia University: association copies, orientalia, and numismatica mathematica.

2225. Smith, David Eugene. Mathematical portraits and pages. London: Ginn and Co., 1916. 21p.

Material described now in Smith collection, Columbia University Library.

2226. Smith, David Eugene. Rara arithmetica; a catalogus of the arithmetics written before the year MDCI, with a description of those in the library of George Arthur Plimpton of New York. Boston: Ginn, 1908. 507p.

Most of titles described are in the Plimpton collection, now in the Columbia University Library. Lists over 550 works in about 1,200 editions.

2227. Smith, David Eugene, and Seely, Caroline E. Union list of mathematical periodicals. Wash.: Govt. Print. Off., 1918. 60p. (U. S. Bureau of Education bulletin, no. 9. 1918.)

Lists holdings of 52 libraries.

2228. Yale University, Sheffield Scientific School Library. Catalogue of the Hillhouse mathematical library...; and of other mathematical books belonging to the Sheffield Scientific School. [New Haven, 1870] 44p. (Appendix to the fifth annual report of the Sheffield Scientific School)

ASTRONOMY

2229. Brasch, Frederick E. "Bibliography of Kepler's works." In: History of Science Society. Johann Kepler, 1571-1630. Baltimore: Williams and Wilkins, 1931, p. 86-133.

Based upon Library of Congress holdings.

2230. Brasch, Frederick E. "The first edition of Copernicus' De revolutionibus." Library of Congress quarterly journal of current acquisitions, 3 (May 1946), 1922.

Description of copy acquired by Library of Congress.

2231. Haraszti, Zoltán. "Rara astronomica." More books, 3 (1928), 285-95.
Describes some recent and rare additions to the Bowditch collection in Boston Public Library.

2232. Harvard University Library. "Valuable gifts to the library." Harvard alumni bulletin, 29 (1927), 502-04.
Astronomical books presented to Harvard University from libraries of Robert W. Willson and Harcourt Amory.

2233. Holden, Edward Singleton. Catalogue of the Library of the Lick Observatory of the University of California. Sacramento, 1891. 122p.
Part 1, to July 1, 1890. No more published.

2234. John Crerar Library. Pluto, the ninth planet: a bibliography, comp. by Jerome K. Wilcox. Chicago, 1932. 12 p. (Reference list 24).

2235. Michigan, University, Library. "Astronomical and mathematical rarities in the University of Michigan Library," by Louis C. Karpinski. Michigan alumnus, 25 (1919), 592-97. Reprinted. 6p.
Incunabula and 16th century works.

2236. National Research Council, Research Information Service. List of manuscript bibliographies in astronomy, mathematics and physics. Wash., 1923. 14p. (Reprint and circular series, no. 41)
Locates unpublished bibliographies and card catalogs of subjects indicated.

2237. U. S. Hydrographic Office Library. Catalogue of books in the library of the United States Hydrographic Office. January, 1875. Wash.: Govt. Print. Off., 1875. 182p.
Arranged by subjects and types of material.

2238. U. S. National Archives. List of climatological records in the National Archives. Wash., 1942. 160p. (Special lists, no. 1)

2239. U. S. National Archives. Preliminary check list of the records of the Naval Observatory 1840-1929, comp. by Kenneth F. Bartlett and James R. Masterson. [Wash., 1946] 6p. (Preliminary checklist, no. 42)

2240. U. S. Naval Observatory. "Printed treasures in the Library of the United States Naval Observatory," by Grace O. Savage. U. S. Naval Institute proceedings, 56 (1930), 977-79.
Describes collection of 36,000 volumes and 8,000 pamphlets.

2241. U. S. Naval Observatory Library. Catalogue... Part 1, - Astronomical bibliography, by Edward S. Holden. Wash.: Govt. Print. Off., 1879. 10p.
"A list of all the indexes to scientific periodicals relating to astronomy, geodesy, optics, and mathematics which are in the Library... together with a list of... works on scientific bibliography."

2242. Wroth, Lawrence Counselman. Some American contributions to the art of navigation, 1519-1802. Providence: Associates of the John Carter Brown Library, 1947. 41p.

2243. Wroth, Lawrence Counselman. The way of a ship; an essay on the literature of navigation science. Portland, Me.: Southworth-Anthoensen Press, 1937. 91p.
Describes an exhibition of books from collection in John Carter Brown Library.

2244. Yale University Library. "A Library of nautical Americana and early books on navigation," by Thomas C. Mendenhall, 2d. Yale University Library gazette, 24 (1949), 70-73.
Description and list of collection, dated 1471-1551, acquired by Yale University Library.

PHYSICS

2245. Brasch, Frederick E. "Two important manuscripts by Albert Einstein." Library of Congress quarterly journal of current acquisitions, 2 (Feb. 1945), 39-48.
Acquired by Library of Congress.

2246. Carnegie Library of Pittsburgh. "Literature on the use of the X-ray," comp. by Victor S. Polansky. Heat treating and forging, 16 (1930), 876-80, 1011-14.
Material available in Carnegie Library of Pittsburgh.

2247. John Crerar Library. A bibliography on noise; from material found in the John Crerar Library. Chicago, 1932. 21p. (Reference list 18)

2248. New York Public Library. "Ultraviolet rays; a list of references to material in the New York Public Library," comp. by William Berthold Behrens. New York Public Library bulletin, 19 (1915), 495-512. Reprinted. 20p.

2249. U. S. Library of Congress, General Reference and Bibliography Division. "A list of writings by and about Petr L. Kapitsa," comp. by Morris C. Leikind. Wash., Feb. 27, 1947. 5p. Typed.

2250. Virginia, University, Adolph Lomb Optical Library. Catalogue of the ... library. Charlottesville: Alderman Library, 1947. 203p. (Univ. of Virginia bibliographical series, no. 7)
    Books on history and development of modern optical science.

CHEMISTRY

2251. American Chemical Society. List of periodicals abstracted by Chemical abstracts, with key to library files. Columbus: Ohio State Univ., 1946. 209p.
    Locates copies in 280 cooperating libraries.

2252. Armstrong, Eva V. "Edgar Fahs Smith and his memorial collection." General magazine and historical chronicle, 41 (1939), 274-83.
    Relates to history of chemistry. Collection in University of Pennsylvania Library.

2253. Armstrong, Eva V. Playground of a scientist. Philadelphia, 1949. 26p. Reprinted from Scientific monthly, 42 (1936), 339-48, and General magazine and historical chronicle, 44 (1941)
    Describes Smith collection of books on chemistry in University of Pennsylvania Library.

2254. Armstrong, Eva V. "Some incidents in the collection of the Edgar Fahs Smith Memorial Library." Journal of chemical education, 10 (1933), 356-68.
    Relates to history of chemistry. Collection in University of Pennsylvania Library.

2255. Armstrong, Eva V. Some treasures in the Edgar Fahs Smith Memorial Collection. [Philadelphia, 1933] 12p. Reprinted from General magazine and historical chronicle, 35 (1939)
    Relates to history of chemistry. Collection in University of Pennsylvania Library.

2256. Carnegie Library of Pittsburgh. Metal corrosion and protection; references to books and magazine articles. 2d ed. rev. and enl. Pittsburgh: The Library, 1909. 64p. (Reprinted from its Monthly bulletin, July 1909) Supplement in Proceedings of the Engineers Society of Western Pennsylvania, 31 (1915), 193-222.

2257. Carnegie Library of Pittsburgh. Sodium nitrate industry of Chile; references to books and magazine articles. Pittsburgh: The Library, 1908. 11p. (Reprinted from its Monthly bulletin, March 1908.)

2258. Carnegie Library of Pittsburgh. Waterglass; a bibliography, comp. by Morris Schrero. Pittsburgh: The Library, 1922. 87p.

2259. Colorado State College Library. Current serials in chemistry; a study of the titles held in Colorado and Wyoming libraries, with a supplement including titles of serials in chemistry and a union list of holdings, by James G. Hodgson. [Fort Collins] 1945. 14, 51 numb. 1. (Library bulletin, no. 17, Dec. 1945)
    Holdings located in 17 Colorado and 1 Wyoming library.

2260. Fulton, John F. and Peters, Charlotte H. Works of Joseph Priestley, 1733-1804; preliminary short title list. New Haven: Laboratory of Physiology, Yale University School of Medicine, 1937. 20p.
    Locates copies in 29 American and English libraries.

2261. Gates, Elizabeth. Union list of chemical periodicals in the Cincinnati libraries, Cincinnati: Univ. of Cincinnati. 1925. 58p. (Univ. of Cincinnati studies, ser. 2, v. 11, pt. 2)
    Lists holdings of 11 libraries.

2262. Grosvenor Library. Chemistry bibliography; a check list of periodical holdings and standard chemical reference tools to be found in the libraries of the chemical plants and in the public libraries of Buffalo and the Niagara frontier. Buffalo, N. Y.: The Library, 1936. 52 numb. l.

2263. Hodgson, James Goodwin. Current serials in chemistry; a study of the titles held in Colorado and Wyoming libraries, with a supplement including titles of serials in chemistry and a union list of holdings. Fort Collins: Colorado A. and M. College, 1945. 14, 51 numb. l.

2264. Killeffer, D. H. "A great American chemical library." Chemical and engineering news, 27 (August 15, 1949), 2322-26.
   Description of the library of Chemists' Club of New York, a research library of 55,000 volumes, which has absorbed the library of the American Chemical Society. Includes a list of periodicals.

2265. National Research Council, Research Information Service. List of manuscript bibliographies in chemistry and chemical technology. Wash., 1922. 17p. (Reprint and circular series, no. 36) ("Reprinted from the Journal of industrial and engineering chemistry, v. 14, no. 12, Dec. 1922.")
   Locates unpublished bibliographies and card catalogs.

2266. New England Association of Chemistry Teachers Library. Catalog of the library and museum belonging to the New England Association of Chemistry Teachers, including the Williams memorial section of the Association library and the Williams memorial section of the Association exhibits. April, 1915. [Boston, 1915] 18p.
   Collection deposited in Boston University. A list of 379 volumes, of which about 300 are on chemistry.

2267. New York Public Library. "Selenium: 1817-1925; a list of references in the New York Public Library," comp. by Marion Foster Doty. New York Public Library bulletin, 30 (1926), 440-48, 525-55, 599-629, 728-37, 793-824. Reprinted. 114p.

2268. Pennsylvania, University, Library. The story of the Edgar Fahs Smith memorial collection in the history of chemistry, by E. V. Armstrong. [Philadelphia]: Univ. of Pennsylvania, 1937. 21p.

2269. Purdue University Library. A guide to chemical literature, specially prepared for use in the libraries of Purdue University, part 1, organic chemistry, comp. by Betty J. Pearce. [Lafayette, Ind.] Purdue University Library, 1942. 14p.
   Classified and annotated list of basic reference material in each division of chemistry available in Purdue University Library.

2270. Reid, Winnifred and Fulton, John F. "The bicentenary exhibition of Joseph Priestley." Yale University Library gazette, 8 (1933), 63-73.
   Describes Yale University Library's holdings of works and memorabilia relating to Joseph Priestley.

2271. Remick, A. E. "A survey of Detroit's chemical library facilities." Detroit chemist, 7 (1935), 114-18.

-----. "A revision of the survey of Detroit's library facilities." Detroit chemist, 8 (1936), 250-52, 254-56, 258.
   Lists holdings of 10 Detroit libraries of chemical journals abstracted by Chemical abstracts.

2272. Special Libraries Association, Chemistry Section. Union list of journals, proceedings, annuals and other serials in the chemical libraries of the Chemistry Section - Science - Technology Division of the Special Libraries Association, ed. by Hester A. Wetmore. Rahway, N. J.: J. Merck & Co., 1935. 317 l.
   Lists holdings of 49 libraries.

2273. Special Libraries Association, Chemistry Section. Union list of scientific periodicals in the chemical libraries of the Chemistry Section, Science-Technology Group of the Special Libraries Association. 2d. ed. rev. by Betty Joy Cole. N. Y.: The Association [1939] 77p.
   Lists about 1,000 titles in 68 libraries.

2274. Taggart, W. T. "The Edgar Fahs Smith Memorial Library on the history of chemistry." University of Pennsylvania Library chronicle, 1 (1933), 31-37.

2275. West, Clarence Fay and Hull, Callie.

"Check list of chemical periodicals in the libraries of the South." Journal of chemical education, 7 (1930), 2449-98.

Lists holdings of 59 libraries in 13 Southern states of "journals currently covered by Chemical abstracts."

2276. Wilson, William J. "Catalogue of Latin and vernacular alchemical manuscripts in the United States and Canada." Osiris, 6 (1939), 1-836. Issued also separately: Brugis: Ex Officina Sanctae Catharinae, 1939. 836p.

Locates and describes in detail 79 manuscripts in 31 libraries or collections.

GEOLOGY

2277. American Geographical Society. A catalogue of geological maps of South America, by Henry B. Sullivan. N. Y.: American Geographical Society, 1922. 191p. (Research series, no. 9)

Union list of maps in the U. S. Geological Survey, Pan American Union, Army War College, Library of Congress, and American Geographical Society.

2278. Brooklyn Public Library. Earthquakes and volcanoes; a list of books with references to periodicals in the Brooklyn Public Library. 2d ed., enl. Brooklyn: Eagle Press, 1909. 28p.

2279. Carnegie Library of Pittsburgh. Mica; references to books and magazine articles. Pittsburgh: The Library, 1908. 18p. (Reprinted from its Monthly bulletin, Oct. 1908.)

2280. Carnegie Library of Pittsburgh. Sand, its occurence, properties, and uses; a bibliography. Pittsburgh: The Library, 1918. 72p.

2281. Hardwicke, Robert Etter. Petroleum and natural gas bibliography. Being the result of an effort to compile and classify the items of literature in English for which copyrights have been issued, but including many other published items which have been catalogued by the Library of Congress, as well as a few items of general interest not found in the Library of Congress, all of which fall within a comprehensive definition of book literature, as distinguished from periodical literature... but including... references to all articles, notes and comments relating to petroleum and natural gas appearing in the legal periodicals published in the United States. Austin: University of Texas, 1937. 167p.

2282. John Crerar Library. Rare earths and minor metals, 1935-1940, comp. by R. B. Gordon. Chicago, 1941. 18p. (Reference list 48)

2283. National Research Council, Division of Geology and Geography. List of manuscript bibliographies in geology and geography, comp. by Homer P. Little. Wash., 1922. 17p. (Reprint and circular series of the Nat. Res. Counc., no. 27)

Locates unpublished bibliographies and card catalogs.

2284. New York Public Library. "List of works in the New York Public Library relating to the geology, mineralogy, and palaeontology of New Jersey," comp. by George Fraser Black. New York Public Library bulletin, 20 (1916), 501-25. Reprinted, with index. 36p.

2285. Roberts, Joseph K. Annotated geological bibliography of Virginia. Richmond, Va.: Dietz Press, 1942. 726p. (Univ. of Virginia Bibliographical series, no. 2)

Records 2,568 titles and references, giving locations in 12 libraries in or near Virginia.

2286. U. S. Coast and Geodetic Survey. Original topographic and hydrographic sheets registered in the archives of the U. S. Coast and Geodetic Survey. Wash.: Govt. Print. Off., 1883. 70p.

2287. U. S. Engineer School Library. Geology of the Mississippi Valley south of Cairo, the climate of the Mississippi Valley, its change in the past and predictions for the future; a bibliography of books and articles on the subjects in English, prep. by Henry E. Haferkorn. [Wash.] Army War College, 1927.

Appendix II. p. 107-16, in U. S. Engineer School Library. The Mississippi River and valley; bibliography, mostly non-technical. Fort Humphreys, Va.: The Library, 1931. 116p. Locates copies, chiefly in Library of Congress.

2288. U. S. Engineer School Library. Sand movement and beaches; including references, on bars, bays, coast changes, currents, erosion, estuaries, shorelines, tides, waves and wave action; with an index; a bibliography, prep. by H. E. Haferkorn. Fort Humphreys, Va.: Engineer School, 1929. 114p.

Locates copies in Engineer School Library and Library of Congress.

2289. U. S. Geological Survey. Geologic literature of North America, 1785-1928, by John Milton Nickles. Wash.: Govt. Print. Off., 1923-31. 3v. (Its Bulletin, no. 746, 747, 823).

Based upon Survey's Library.

2290. U. S. Geological Survey. Bibliography of North American geology, 1929-1939, by Emma M. Thom. Wash.: Govt. Print. Off., 1944. 1,546p. (Its Bulletin, no. 937)

Based upon Survey's Library.

2291. U. S. Geological Survey. Bibliography of North American geology, 1940-1947. Wash.: Govt. Print. Off., 1942-49. 4v. (Its Bulletin, no. 938, 949, 952, 958)

Biennial supplement to two preceding works. Based upon Survey's Library.

2292. U. S. Geological Survey. Bibliography of photo-mapping and allied subjects, comp. by Eric Haquinius and E. A. Shuster, Jr. [Wash.] 1929. 84 l.

2293. U. S. Library of Congress, Division of Bibliography. "A list of recent references on anthracite coal, with special reference to Pennsylvania," comp. by Florence S. Hellman. Wash., July 7, 1938. 24p. Typed.

2294. U. S. Library of Congress, General Reference and Bibliography Division. Weather in relation to war; a list of references, comp. by Grace Hadley Fuller. [Wash.] 1943. 24p.

2295. U. S. Weather Bureau Library. Selected bibliography on meteorology and related subjects. Wash., 1943. 31p.

PALEONTOLOGY

2296. U. S. Geological Survey. A classed and annotated bibliography of fossil insects, by Samuel Hubbard Scudder. 2d ed. Wash.: Govt. Print. Off., 1890. 101p. (Its Bulletin 69)

BIOLOGY AND ANTHROPOLOGY

2297. Altsheler, Brent. Natural history index-guide; an index to 3,365 books and periodicals in libraries. 2d ed. rev. & enl. N. Y.: H. W. Wilson, 1940. 583p.

Gives locations of some rare books listed in Bibliography, p. 455-583.

2298. Boston Society of Natural History Library. Catalogue of the library of the Boston Society of Natural History. Boston: Freeman & Bolles, 1837. 27p.

2299. Illinois State Museum of Natural History. Report on the progress and condition. Springfield: Illinois State Journal Co., 1912. 557p.

P. 52-445, "Catalogue of the Library of the Illinois State Museum of Natural History."

2300. Johnson, Duncan Starr and Barnhart, J. H. List of biological serials in the libraries of Baltimore, 1901. Baltimore: Johns Hopkins Press, 1902. 41p.

Gives holdings of 10 libraries.

2301. Metcalf, Jessie L. A check list of periodicals and other serials in the biological sciences in the Detroit Public Library and libraries of Wayne University. Detroit: Wayne University, Dept. of Biology, 1941. 64p.

2302. Minnesota, University, Library. Check list of periodicals and serials in the biological and allied sciences available in the Library of the University of Minnesota and its vicinity. Minneapolis: The University, 1925. 126p. (Minn. Univ. bibliographical series, no. 2)

Lists holdings of University of Minnesota, Mayo Clinic, Hennepin County Medical Library, and Ramsey County Medical Library.

2303. National Research Council, Research Information Service. List of manuscript bibliographies in the biological sciences. Wash., 1923. 51p. (Reprint and circular series, no. 45)

Locates unpublished bibliographies and card catalogs of biological sciences.

2304. Special Libraries Association, Biological Sciences Group. Directory of biological sciences libraries in the Special Libraries Association. N. Y.: The Group, 1942. 71p.

Describes 156 libraries in the United States, including their services and subject specialties.

2305. Trinity College Library. The Russell collection of books on natural history in Trinity College Library. Hartford: The College, 1913. 28p. (Trinity College bulletin, n. s., vol. 10, no. 2.)

2306. Wistar Institute of Anatomy and Biology. List of biological serials, exclusive of botany in the libraries of Philadelphia. Philadelphia, 1909. 61p. (Wistar Institute bulletin, no. 2)
Lists holdings of 6 libraries.

Anthropology

2307. Currier, Margaret. "The Peabody Museum Library." Harvard Library bulletin, 3 (1949), 94-101.
Library of archaeology and anthropology, Harvard University.

2308. Currier, Margaret. "Peabody Musem Library at Harvard University." Museum news, 19 (Apr. 1, 1949), 7-8.

2309. Denver Public Library. Cliff dwellers and cliff dwellings of North America; a selected bibliography, comp. by Louise Guerber. [Denver, 1925] 21p.

2310. New York Public Library. "A list of works relating to the aborigines of Australia and Tasmania," comp. by George Fraser Black. New York Public Library bulletin, 17 (1913), 876-929. Reprinted. 56p.

2311. Redfield, Robert. "Research materials in middle American ethnology, with special reference to Chicago libraries." College and research libraries, 3 (1942), 311-25.
Description of resources of Chicago libraries, with union list of major sources in Newberry, Field Museum, and University of Chicago.

2312. Ripley, William Z. Selected bibliography of the anthropology and ethnology of Europe. Boston: Public Library, 1899. 160p.
Includes works on these subjects in Boston Public Library.

2313. Saville, Marshall H. "Bibliography of the anthropology of Ecuador." In his: Antiquities of Manabi, Ecuador. A preliminary report. N. Y., 1907. v. 1, p. 121-35.
Locates copies in Museum of the American Indian (New York).

2314. Tucker, Sara Jones. "Archival material for the anthropologist in the National Archives, Washington, D. C." American anthropologist, 44 (1941), 617-44.

BOTANY

2315. Atwood, Alice Cary. Catalogue of the botanical library of John Donnell Smith presented in 1905 to the Smithsonian Institution. Wash., 1908. 94p. (National Museum, Contributions from the United States National Herbarium, v. 12, pt. 1)
1,600 bound volumes consisting chiefly of works relative to systematic botany.

2316. [Brooklyn Botanic Garden.] "Books and manuscripts illustrating the history of botany." Brooklyn Botanic Garden record, 24 (1935), 159-94.
Lists and describes 186 important items in Brooklyn Botanic Garden Library, gathered for an exhibit.

2317. Brooklyn Botanic Garden Library. "List of current periodicals on file in the Brooklyn Botanic Garden Library, August 1, 1916." Brooklyn Botanic Garden record, 5 (1916), 131-40.
A union list, including 6 other New York City libraries.

2318. Harvard University, Arnold Arboretum Library. Catalogue, comp. by Ethelyn Maria Tucker. Cambridge: Cosmos Press, 1914-33. 3v. (Publication, no. 6)

2319. Kelly, Howard Atwood. Catalogue of the mycological library of Howard A. Kelly, comp. by Louis C. C. Krieger. Baltimore, 1924. 260p.
Collection presented in 1928 to University of Michigan Library. Over 7,000 titles.

2320. Linder, David H. "The Farlow Herbarium and Library." Harvard alumni bulletin, 38 (1936), 1049-54.
For cryptogamic botany; Harvard University.

2321. Lloyd Library and Museum of Botany, Pharmacy and Materia Medica. Bibliographical contributions from the Lloyd Library. Cincinnati: Lloyd Library, 1911-18. 3v.

V. 1, bibliography relating to the floras; v. 2-3, bibliography relating to botany, exclusive of floras. A catalog of Lloyd Library's botanical holdings, including periodicals in botany, pharmacy, chemistry, entomology, and natural science.

2322. McKelvey, Susan D. "The Arnold Arboretum." Harvard alumni bulletin, 38 (1936), 464-71.
Includes description of library at Harvard University.

2323. Missouri Botanical Garden Library. "The Sturtevant Prelinnean library of the Missouri Botanical Garden." Missouri Botanical Garden seventh annual report, (1896), 123-209. Reprinted, 1896.
A catalog of collection of early herbals, natural histories, and medical botanies given by E. Lewis Sturtevant to Missouri Botanical Garden.

2324. Missouri Botanical Garden Library. "A supplementary catalogue of the Sturtevant Prelinnean library," by C. E. Hutchings. Missouri Botanical Garden fourteenth annual report, (1903), 233-316.
Supplementary list of additions to Sturtevant Prelinnean library, received since 1896.

2325. Robinson, Benjamin L. "The Gray Herbarium." Harvard alumni bulletin, 31 (1929), 906-11.
In Harvard University. Includes description of library.

2326. Swingle, Walter T. Chronologic list of the dissertations of Charles Linnaeus, 1743 to 1776, with reference to the libraries in the United States containing original editions of these dissertations. Prepared and photographed... United States Department of Agriculture. Wash., 1923. 54 l.
186 entries. Locates copies in 9 libraries.

2327. Thaxten, Roland. "The Farlow Library and Herbarium of Cryptogamic Botany." Harvard alumni bulletin, 29 (1927), 679-86.
In Harvard University.

2328. U. S. Dept. of Agriculture. A bibliography of plant genetics. Wash.: Govt. Print. Off., 1934. 552p. (Miscellaneous publication 164)

ZOOLOGY

2329. Allen, Francis Pitcher. A check list of periodical literature and publications of learned societies of interest to zoologists in the University of Michigan libraries. Ann Arbor: Univ. of Mich. Press, 1935. 83p. (Museum of Zoology, Univ. of Michigan circular, no. 2)

2330. American Entomological Society. Catalogue of works in the library of the American Entomological Society. Philadelphia: The Society, 1868. 32p. [With its Transactions. Philadelphia, 1867-68. v. 1]

2331. Carnegie Library of Pittsburgh. "List of books on ornithology contained in the Carnegie Library of Pittsburgh." Cardinal, 2 (1929), 133-80; 3 (1934), 185-96. Reprinted.

2332. Coues, Elliott. "List of faunal publications relating to North American ornithology." In his: Birds of the Colorado Valley. U. S. Geological survey of the territories. Misc. pub. no. 11, p. 567-784. Wash., 1878.
Nearly all in Library of Congress.

2333. Field Museum of Natural History, Edward E. Ayer Ornithological Library. Catalogue., by John Todd Zimmer. Chicago, 1926. 2v. (Field Museum of Natural History publication, 239-40. Zoological series, v. 16)
Ornithological books and periodicals owned by the Library.

2334. Gudger, Eugene Willis. "Notes on certain books of unusual interest in the Blackford collection of the Brooklyn Museum." Brooklyn Insitute of Arts and Sciences, Brooklyn Museum science bulletin, 3 (1925), 167-72.
A list of 30 books from Blackford collection, on fishes and fishing.

2335. Harvard University, Museum of Comparative Zoology. [Cambridge?, 1936] 89p.
Compiled by Museum staff on occasion of Tercentenary of Harvard University. Includes library of museum.

2336. John Crerar Library. A select bibliography of hibernation in mammals, comp. by H. Einar Mose. Chicago, 1930. 32p. (Reference list 8)

2337. John Crerar Library. State lists of birds, a bibliography, comp. by Jerome K. Wilcox. Chicago, 1932. 23p. (Reference list 23)

2338. Michigan, University, William L. Clements Library of American History. Ichthyologia et herpetologia Americana; a guide to an exhibition illustrating the development of knowledge of American fishes, amphibians, and reptiles. Ann Arbor: Univ. of Mich. Press, 1936. 22p. (Bulletin, no. 25)
Description of 46 items, 1551-1817.

2339. New York Public Library. "Check list of works on fish and fisheries in the New York Public Library." New York Public Library bulletin, 3 (1899), 296-312, 334-48.

2340. Palmer, T. S. "Deane collection of portraits of ornithologists: the development of an idea." Science, 100 (1944), 288-90.
Describes collection of portraits of ornithologists in Library of Congress.

2341. Phillips, John C. American game mammals and birds; a catalogue of books, 1582 to 1925, sport, natural history, and conservation. Boston: Houghton, Mifflin Co., 1930. 638p.
Most of titles are from Charles Sheldon Library belonging now to Yale University.

2342. Thayer, Evelyn and Keyes, Virginia. Catalogue of a collection of books on ornithology in the library of John E. Thayer. Boston: Privately Printed, 1913. 186p.
Library later presented to Harvard University.

Medicine

GENERAL

2343. Carnegie Library of Pittsburgh. "Bibliography of ophthalmia neonatorum (purulent conjunctivitis of the new-born.)" News notes of California libraries, 9 (1919), 687-733.
Based on Carnegie Library of Pittsburgh collection, with additions from printed bibliographic sources.

2344. Carnegie Library of Pittsburgh. Industrial accidents; a select list of books. Pittsburgh: The Library, 1910. 12p.

2345. Carnegie Library of Pittsburgh. Lampblack; a bibliography. Pittsburgh: The Library, 1919. 8p.

2346. John Crerar Library. Amebic dysentery bibliography, 1934 to July 1935, comp. by Ella M. Salmonsen. Chicago, 1935. 33p. (Reference list 33)

2347. John Crerar Library. A list of books, pamphlets and articles on cremation, including the collection of the Cremation Association of America, ed. by H. Einar Mose. Chicago, 1940. 65p. First edition issued in 1918.

2348. John Crerar Library. List of references on dinitrophenol, weight reduction diet, 1885-1934, comp. by Ella M. Salmonsen. Chicago, 1934. 11p. (Reference list 29)

2349. John Crerar Library. List of references on maggot therapy, by Ella M. Salmonsen. Chicago, 1936. 15p. (Reference list 35)

2350. John Crerar Library. Phobias, comp. by Ella M. Salmonsen. Chicago, 1939. [17p.] (Reference list 43)

2351. John Crerar Library. A selected list of books on military medicine and surgery. September 24, 1917. Chicago: The Library, 1917. 58p.

2352. John Crerar Library. The therapeutic value of music, by Ella M. Salmonsen. Chicago, 1941. 13p. (Reference list 47)

2353. New York Academy of Medicine Library. Dental bibliography; a reference index to the literature of dental science and art as found in the libraries of the New York Academy of Medicine and Bernhard Wolf Weinberger, comp. by Bernhard Wolf Weinberger. 2d ed. [N. Y., c1929-32], 2v. in 1. 262p.
Pt. 1, a reference index; pt. 2, a subject index.

2354. New York Public Library. "Occupational therapy: one means of rehabilitation," by Emily G. Davis. New York Public Library bulletin, 48 (1944), 383-99. Reprinted. 19p.
A selected list of books and articles from material in New York Public Library.

2355. U. S. Bureau of Labor Statistics Library. Books and periodicals on accident and disease prevention in industry in the library of the Bureau of Labor Statistics. [Wash.: Govt. Print. Off., 1916] 23p.

2356. U. S. Department of Labor Library. The national health program and medical care in the United States: selected recent references, comp. by Ruth Fine. Wash., 1940. 25p. Supplement, 1941. 8p.

2357. U. S. Library of Congress, Division of Bibliography. List of references on the drug habit and traffic. Wash., May 1, 1926.

35p. [Supplementary list] June 12, 1929. 18p.

2358. U. S. Library of Congress, Division of Bibliography. Medical care in the United States and foreign countries, with special reference to socialization: selected list of recent writings, comp. by Anne L. Baden. [Wash.] 1935. 45p. Supplement. 1938. 26p.

2359. U. S. Library of Congress, Division of Bibliography. Safety measures: a list of recent references on accident prevention in its various aspects, comp. by Anne L. Baden. [Wash.] 1942. 56p.

2360. U. S. Library of Congress, Science and Technology Project. Radioactive manganese, iron, cobalt, copper, zinc and strontium; a selected bibliography of recent literature with special reference to biological and medical applications, comp. by Morris C. Leikind and Mabel H. Eller. [Wash.] 1948. 17p.

CATALOGS AND SURVEYS OF COLLECTIONS

2361. Boston University, School of Medicine Library. Library catalogue of the Boston University School of Medicine. Boston: Boston University School of Medicine, 1878. 70p.

2362. Dock, George. The medical library of the University of Michigan. Brooklyn, 1905. 9p. (Reprinted from the Medical library and historical journal, 3 (July 1905), no. 3)
   Description of the collection.

2363. Fitz, Reginald. "A glimpse of the Medical School Library." Harvard alumni bulletin, 35 (1933), 409-12.
   Harvard University.

2364. Fulton, John F. The Harvey Cushing collection of books and manuscripts. N. Y.: Schuman's, 1943. 205p.
   Short-title catalog of Harvey Cushing collection of medical books in medical library of Yale University.

2365. Harvard University, Medical School Library. "The Magratti library of legal medicine." Harvard alumni bulletin, 36 (1934), 957-59.
   In Harvard Medical School.

2366. Holt, Anna C. "The Warren Library of the Harvard Medical School Library." Harvard University Library notes, 4 (1942), 89-94.
   Collection of medical books assembled by five generations of Warrens.

2367. Jones, Harold Wellington. "The value of special collections in medical libraries." Medical Library Association bulletin, 30 (Oct. 1941), 40-55.
   Tabulation of special collections in American medical libraries, p. 51-55.

2368. Meinecke, Bruno. "Medical collections at the University of Michigan." Medical Library Association bulletin, 30 (1941), 85-89.
   Brief description of some rare and interesting medical books at the University of Michigan.

2369. New York College of Pharmacy. Catalogue of the library of the College of Pharmacy of the City of New York. N. Y., 1891. 86p. Supplement. 1900.
   College of Pharmacy now affiliated with Columbia University.

2370. New York Public Library. "Check list of works relating to the health, vital statistics, etc., of the City of New York in the New York Public Library." New York Public Library bulletin, 5 (1901), 141-46.

2371. Simons, Corinne Miller. "Eclectic books presented to Lloyd Library." National eclectic medical quarterly, 39 (Sept. 1947), 20-23; 39 (Dec. 1947), 13-16.
   Describes additions to eclectic medical collection at Lloyd Library.

2372. Simons, Corinne Miller. "World's largest collection of eclectic publications." National eclectic medical quarterly, 36 (March 1945), 7-9.
   Describes eclectic medical collection in Lloyd Library, Cincinnati.

2373. Society of the New York Hospital. Catalogue of the books belonging to the library. N. Y.: Craighead, 1845. 194p. Supplements 1-6 issued 1861-86.
   Collection now in New York Academy of Medicine.

2374. Stiles, Charles Wardell and Hassall, Albert. Index-catalogue of medical and veterinary zoology. Wash.: Govt. Print. Office, 1920. 886p. (U. S. Hygienic Laboratory bulletin, no. 114)

"Represents the combined card catalogues of the Zoological Division of the U. S. Bureau of Animal Industry and of the Division of Zoology, Hygienic Laboratory, U. S. Public Health Service."

2375. Texas, University, Library. "The anesthesia collection at the University of Texas Medical Branch library, Galveston," by Chauncey D. Leake. University of Texas Library chronicle, 2 (Fall, 1946), 117-24.

2376. U. S. Army Medical Library. The Army Medical Library author catalog. Wash., 1948 - to date.

Annual record of monographic material received by the Army Medical Library.

2377. U. S. Army Medical Library. Congresses; tentative chronological and bibliographical reference list of national and international meetings of physicians, scientists and experts. Wash.: Govt. Print. Off., 1938. 288p. (Reprinted from Surgeon-General's Office Library Index-catalogue, 4th series, v. 3, p. 1-288.) First addition to reference list of congresses. Index-catalogue, 4th series, 4 (1939), 29-51. Reprinted.

2378. U. S. Army Medical Library. Index-catalogue. Wash.: Govt. Print. Off., 1880-95. 16v. 2d ser. Wash., 1896-1916. 21v. 3d ser. Wash., 1918-[1932]. 10v. 4th ser. Wash., 1936-50. 11v. Discontinued with 4th series, v. 11 (MH-MZ).

2379. U. S. Army Medical Library, Reference Division. American medical books; a selected list of 135 titles. Wash., 1949. 9 l.

2380. U. S. Bureau of Animal Industry. Index-catalogue of medical and veterinary zoology, pt. 1 - 10, authors A-Mysh, by Albert Hassall, and Margie Potter. Wash.: Govt. Print. Off., 1932-48. v. 1-10.

Revision of work of same title, by C. W. Stiles and Albert Hassall, pub. 1902-12, in Bureau of Animal Industry bulletin, no. 39.

2381. U. S. Library of Congress. "Army Medical Library catalog cards. (April-December 1948)." Supplement to the Cumulative catalog of Library of Congress printed cards, 1948. Wash.: Library of Congress, 1948. v. 3, p.[2909]-3058.

"Substitute for the Medical card series which was discontinued on April 1, 1948."

2382. U. S. National Archives. Preliminary inventory of the records of the Bureau of Medicine and Surgery, comp. by Kenneth F. Bartlett. Wash., 1948. 18p. (Preliminary inventory, no. 6)

2383. U. S. National Archives. Report of a survey of medical records created by the federal government. Wash., 1945. 180p.

2384. Yale University School of Medicine, Yale Medical Library. The Harvey Cushing collection of books and manuscripts, comp. by Margaret Brinton and Henrietta T. Perkins. N. Y.: Schuman's, 1943. 207p.

PERIODICALS

2385. Garrison, Fielding Hudson. The medical and scientific periodicals of the 17th and 18th centuries with a revised catalogue and check-list. Baltimore: Johns Hopkins University, 1934. (Reprinted from Bulletin of the Institute of the History of Medicine, 2 (July 1934), 285-343)

Indicates titles listed in the Union list of serials in the United States and Canada and in Index catalogue of the Surgeon General's Library.

2386. Grosvenor Library. "Medical periodicals in Buffalo libraries." Grosvenor Library bulletin, 1 (1919), 9-21.

Represents 3 libraries, with statement of holdings - University of Buffalo Medical School, Gratwick Laboratory, and Grosvenor Library.

2387. Medical Library Association. Check list of U. S. A. and Canadian holdings of German medical and dental periodicals, 1939-1948. Wash.: The Association, 1949. 136p.

Union list for 39 libraries.

2388. New York State Library. Medical serials. 2d ed., comp. by Ada Bunnell. Albany: Univ. of the State of New York, 1910. 153p. (Bibliography bulletin, no. 47)

Catalog of Medical Department of the New York State Library.

2389. Pan American Sanitary Bureau Library. Medical and public health journals from Latin America received by the library of the Pan American Sanitary Bureau. Wash.: The Bureau [1935] 14 numb. 1.

2390. Special Libraries Association. Union list of serials in the medical and biological libraries in the Los Angeles area, ed. by Hazel Dean. Los Angeles, 1950. In preparation.

2391. U. S. Army Medical Library. "Check list of recent foreign periodicals in the Army Medical Library." Medical Library Association bulletin, 34 (1946), 34-36.
  Includes 85 titles begun since 1939 outside Americas and Great Britain.

2392. U. S. Army Medical Library. Current list of medical literature. Wash., July 1950 - to date.
  Monthly record covering 1,225 journals.

2393. U. S. Army Medical Library. Dental journals currently received in the Army Medical Library. Wash., 1949. 10 l.
  Lists 248 titles.

2394. U. S. Army Medical Library. Journals on neurology, psychology, and psychiatry currently received in the Army Medical Library. Wash., 1949. 15 l.
  Lists 190 titles.

2395. U. S. Army Medical Library. Journals on tropical medicine and related subjects, selected from titles received in the Army Medical Library 1947-1948. n. p., n. d. 3 l.
  Lists 41 titles.

2396. U. S. Army Medical Library. List of abbreviations for serial publications referred to in the fourth series of the Index-catalogue. Wash., 1948. 138p. (Reprinted from v. 10, 4th series, Index-catalogue of the Library of the Surgeon General's Office.)

2397. U. S. Army Medical Library. Medicofilm service of the Army Medical Library; its purposes and plan of operation; together with a list of more than 4000 abbreviated titles of medical periodicals currently received by this Library, September 1940. Wash.: The Library, 1940. 26p.

2398. U. S. Army Medical Library. New books and serials. Wash.: The Library, 1947 - to date.
  Issued irregularly -- usually two numbers each month.

2399. U. S. Army Medical Library. Periodicals currently received in Army Medical Library. Wash., 1940. 61p.

2400. U. S. Army Medical Library. State and county medical and dental society journals received in the Army Medical Library. Wash., 1948. 7 l.
  Lists 165 titles.

2401. Yale University Library. "List of medical serials in the libraries of Connecticut, May, 1919." [New Haven, 1919] 92p. (Reprinted from Connecticut State Medical Society proceedings, (1919), 163-256.)
  Represents 13 libraries.

HISTORY

2402. Briscoe, Ruth Lee. "A history of the [Medical] Library of the University of Maryland, 1813-1938." University of Maryland College of Medicine bulletin, 23 (Oct. 1938), 44-57.
  Historical survey of Library's collections.

2403. Columbia University, Teachers College Library. The Adelaide Nutting historical nursing collection. N. Y.: Teachers College, 1929. 68p.

2404. Cushing, Harvey. A bio-bibliography of Andreas Vesalius. N. Y.: Schuman's, 1943. 229p.
  Copies located in numerous American libraries.

2405. Doe, Janet. A bibliography of the works of Ambroise Paré: premier chirurgien & conseiller du Roy. Chicago: Univ. of Chicago Press, 1937. 265p.
  Locates copies in about 230 American and foreign libraries.

2406. Fitz, Reginald. "The Medical School Library - its first hundred years." Harvard Library notes, 3 (1939), 262-70. "Part II." Ibid, 3 (1940), 307-16.
  Harvard University.

2407. Harrington, Thomas F. The Harvard Medical School; a history, narrative and documentary, 1782-1905. N. Y., Chicago: Lewis Publishing Co., 1905. 3v.

Includes Medical Library.

2408. Henry E. Huntington Library. Medical knowledge in Tudor England as displayed in an exhibition of books and manuscripts, introduction and notes by Sanford V. Larkey. [San Marino, 1932] 31p.

2409. Holt, Anna C. "The Library of the Harvard Medical School, 1847 and 1947." Harvard Library bulletin, 2 (1948), 32-43.

2410. Insurance Company of North America. The historical collection of the Insurance Company of North America, by M. J. McCosker. Philadelphia, 1945. 173p.

Description of collections of marine paintings and ship models, and pictures, models and specimens of early American fire-fighting equipment; also early records and historical documents owned by company and loaned to other institutions in the United States.

2411. Keynes, Geoffrey. A bibliography of the writings of William Harvey, M. D., discoverer of the circulation of the blood. Cambridge: Cambridge Univ. Press, 1928. 67p.

Copies located in Philadelphia College of Physicians, New York Academy of Medicine, U. S. Surgeon-General's Library, and British collections.

2412. Luckhardt, A. B. "Medical history collections in United States and Canada; Dr. William Beaumont collection of the University of Chicago." Bulletin of the history of medicine, 7 (May 1939), 535-63.

2413. Savage, J. E. "The historical collection in the library of the School of Medicine of the University of Maryland." University of Maryland School of Medicine bulletin, 23 (Oct. 1938), 58-62.

2414. U. S. Army Medical Library. "The collection of Arabic medical literature in the Army Medical Library, with a check list of Arabic manuscripts," by Claudius F. Mayer. Bulletin of the history of medicine, 11 (1942), 201-16.

2415. U. S. Army Medical Library. Texts illustrating the history of medicine in the library of the Surgeon General's Office, U. S. Army, arranged in chronological order. Wash.: Govt. Print. Off., 1912. 89-178p. Reprinted from Index-catalogue of the Surgeon General's Office, v. 17, 2d ser.

2416. Yale University School of Medicine, Yale Medical Library. The centennial of surgical anesthesia; an annotated catalogue of books and pamphlets bearing on the early history of surgical anesthesia, exhibited at the Yale Medical Library, October 1946, comp. by John F. Fulton and Madeline E. Stanton. New York: H. Schuman, 1949. 102p.

Locates copies in 30 collections.

INCUNABULA AND EARLY PRINTING

2417. Boston Medical Library. A catalogue of the medieval and renaissance manuscripts and incunabula in the Boston Medical Library, comp. by James F. Ballard. Boston, 1944. 246p.

Lists 52 manuscripts and 674 incunabula. Supersedes 1929 Catalogue of medical incunabula, and other earlier lists. Supplement in press.

2418. College of Physicians of Philadelphia Library. Catalogue of incunabula. [N. Y.: P. B. Hoeber, 1923] 96p. Reprinted from Annals of medical history, 5 (1923), 45-76.

Lists 337 titles.

2419. College of Physicians of Philadelphia Library. "Census of incunabula in the Library of the College of Physicians of Philadelphia, 1938." Transactions and Studies of the College of Physicians of Philadelphia. 4th series, 6 (1938), 159-93.

Lists 409 editions of medical incunabula, of which 126 are undated.

2420. Fisch, Max H. Nicolaus Pol Doctor 1494. N. Y.: Pub. for Cleveland Medical Library Assoc. by Herbert Reichner, 1947. 246p.

Lists books and manuscripts from Nicolaus Pol's library now in Cleveland Medical Library, Yale University Medical Library, etc.

2421. Garrison, Fielding Hudson. "Progress in the cataloguing of medical incunabula, with a revised check list of the incunabula in the

Army Medical Library, Washington, D. C." New York Academy of Medicine bulletin, 2d ser., 6 (1930), 365-435.

2422. Henry E. Huntington Library. "Incunabula medica in the Huntington Library," comp. by Herman Mead. Huntington Library bulletin, no. 1 (1931), 107-51.

532 items from incunabula collection.

2423. Jones, Harold W. "List of books and periodicals printed before 1840 selected from the possession of the Army Medical Library and referring to Central-and South-American medicine." Inter-American Bibliographical and Library Association proceedings, 3 (1940), 78-82.

Lists 54 titles in the Army Medical Library.

2424. Klebs, A. C. "Incunabula lists. I. Herbals." "Bibliographical Society of America papers, 11 (1917), 75-92; 12 (1918), 41-57.

List of 15th century herbals located in the United States.

2425. McCulloch, Champe C. "A check list of medical incunabula in the Surgeon General's Library, Washington." Annals of medical history, 1 (1917), 301-15.

A check list of 28,000 rare volumes of medical incunabula now in U.S. Army Medical Library.

2426. McMurtrie, Douglas C. "Early Kentucky medical imprints, with a bibliography to 1830." Kentucky State Historical Society register, 31 (1933), 256-70. Reprinted.

Locates copies in 26 libraries and private collections.

2427. Mayer, Claudius F. "Bio-bibliography of XVI century medical authors." Wash.: Govt. Print. Off., 1941. Fasc. 1, Abarbanel-Alberti, S. In: U. S. Surgeon-General's Office, Index Catalogue, 4th series, v. 6, p. 1-52.

Locates copies where known, in American and European libraries.

2428. Medical Society of the County of Kings (Brooklyn) Library. A descriptive list of the medical incunabula in the library of the Medical Society, comp. by Charles Frankenberger. N. Y., 1924. 8p. (Reprint from Annals of medical history, v. 6, p. 131-33.)

Lists 23 items of 15th century works.

2429. Medical Society of the County of Kings (Brooklyn) Library. An index of the incunabula and other printed medical publications to the year 1600 now in the library... Brooklyn... Jan. 1, 1912. [Brooklyn: Brooklyn Eagle Press, 1912.] 20p. (Reprint from Medical Library Association of Brooklyn 8th annual report.)

Indexes 15th and 16th century material in Society's Library.

2430. New York Academy of Medicine. Catalogue of an exhibition of early and later medical Americana, by Archibald Malloch. N. Y., [1927]. 64p.

Includes a number of reproductions and some borrowed material. Lists 95 items.

2431. New York Academy of Medicine. "Catalogue of an exhibition of medical manuscripts and incunabula." New York Academy of Medicine bulletin, 5 (1929), 278-92.

2432. Texas, University, Library. "Two studies on the herbal: I. The herbal in pharmacy and medicine, by C. C. Albers; II. The herbal in poetry, by Thomas P. Harrison, Jr." University of Texas chronicle, 1 (1945), 14-29.

Material is in University of Texas Library unless otherwise noted.

2433. U. S. Army Medical Library. A catalogue of incunabula and manuscripts in the Army Medical Library, by Dorothy M. Schullian and Francis E. Sommer. N. Y.: Henry Schuman [1950] 361p.

Pt. 1, incunabula and early western manuscripts; pt. 2, oriental manuscripts.

2434. U. S. Army Medical Library. "Collection of incunabula and early medical prints in the library of the Surgeon General's Office, U. S. Army." In: U. S. Surgeon-General's Office Library. Index-catalogue, Wash., 1932, 3d ser., v. 10, p. 1415-36

Technology

GENERAL

2435. Carnegie Library of Pittsburgh. Technical book review index. Chicago: Index Office, 1915; 2 nos. Pittsburgh: Carnegie Library of Pittsburgh, 1917-1929. 12v.

Book reviews appearing in scientific, technical and trade journals currently received in Technology Department, Carnegie Library of Pittsburgh.

2436. Carnegie Library of Pittsburgh. Technical indexes and bibliographies appearing serially. Pittsburgh: The Library, 1910. 17p. (Reprinted from its Monthly bulletin, June 1910.)

A list of serials currently received by Carnegie Library of Pittsburgh.

2437. Denver Public Library. List of technical books in the Denver Public Library. [Denver, 1924] p. 37-325.

2438. Detroit Public Library. Industrial arts; selected list. [Detroit] The Library, 1914. 64p.

"Limited to publications which have appeared since 1909."

2439. Detroit Public Library. Tools of victory for the battle of production. [Detroit]: The Library, 1942. 100p.

Bibliography of technical literature.

2440. Engineering Societies Library. Catalogue of technical periodicals, libraries in the City of New York and vicinity, comp. and ed. by Alice Jane Gates, with the cooperation of a committee of the New York Library Club. N.Y.: United Engineering Society, 1915. 110p.

Lists holdings of 7 libraries.

2441. Franklin Institute Library. Catalogue of the library of the Franklin Institute of the State of Pennsylvania, for the Promotion of the Mechanic Arts. Philadelphia: Franklin Institute, 1876. 472p.

2442. John Crerar Library. A check list of recent industrial surveys; part 1, general; part 2, surveys of states, counties or sections of the U.S.; part 3, surveys of cities, comp. by Jerome K. Wilcox. Chicago, 1931. 13, 41p. (Reference lists no. 14, 15)

2443. John Crerar Library. Check list of the official publications of the Century of Progress International Exposition and its exhibitors, 1933, comp. by Jerome K. Wilcox. Chicago, 1933-35. 2v. (Reference list 27, 32)

2444. John Crerar Library. A list of books on industrial arts. October, 1903. Chicago: The Library, 1904. 249p.

2445. John Crerar Library. A list of books on the history of industry and the industrial arts, comp. by A. G. S. Josephson. Chicago: The Library, 1915. 486p.

2446. Lilly Research Laboratories. A list of the serial holdings in the library of the Lilly Research Laboratories. [Indianapolis]: Eli Lilly and Co., 1941. 28 numb. l. (Bulletin, no. 5)

2447. National Carbon Company. Technical periodicals; complete record of technical periodicals in the Cleveland libraries. Cleveland, Ohio, 1916. 22p.

Represents holdings of 10 libraries.

2448. New York Public Library. "Catalogue of the William Barclay Parsons Collection," comp. by Karl Brown. New York Public Library bulletin, 45 (1941), 95-108, 585-658. Reprinted, with index. 108p.

Relates to general engineering, transportation and communication, military and naval art and science.

2449. New York Public Library. New technical books. A selected list of books on industrial arts and engineering, recently added to the library. Quarterly. I (1915) - to date.

2450. Special Libraries Association, Science-Technology Group. Union list of technical periodicals in two hundred libraries of the Science-Technology Group of the Special Libraries Association. 3d ed., comp. by Elizabeth G. Bowerman. N. Y.: The Association, 1947. 285p.

Lists about 5,000 titles.

2451. U. S. Library of Congress, Division of Bibliography. A selected list of recent references on industrial research, comp. by Florence S. Hellman. Wash., Nov. 27, 1939. 37p.

2452. U. S. Library of Congress, Division of Bibliography. "A selected list of references on fairs and expositions, 1928-1939," comp. by Florence S. Hellman. Wash., June 11, 1938. 49p. Typed.

2453. U. S. Library of Congress, General Reference and Bibliography Division. "Patent relations of employers and employees, with special reference to government employees: a list of references," comp. by Helen Dudenbostel Jones. In: U. S. Dept. of Justice. Investigation of government patent practices and policies, report and recommendations of the Attorney General to the President. Wash.: Govt. Print. Off. [1947] v. 3, p. 315-28.

ENGINEERING

General

2454. American Society of Civil Engineers. Catalogue of the library, 1900-02. N. Y.: The Society, 1901-1903. 2v.

The library was incorporated in Engineering Societies Library in 1917.

2455. Carnegie Library of Pittsburgh. Engineering ethics. Pittsburgh: The Library, 1917. 17p. (Reprinted from its Monthly bulletin, February 1917)

2456. Conklin, Dorothy G. "The Engineering Library." [Harvard University] Harvard Library notes, 1 (1923), 240-42.

2457. Cooper Union Library. A guide to the literature on the history of engineering available in the Cooper Union Library. N. Y.: Cooper Union, 1946. 46p. (Engineering and science series, no. 28)

2458. Engineering index. N. Y.: Engineering Index, Inc., 1884 - to date.

Beginning with 1919, based on Engineering Societies Library collection, and all material indexed is held by that library.

2459. Engineering Societies Library. Bibliography on pallets used in modern materials handling. N. Y.: The Library, 1949. 15p. (Engineering Societies Library bibliographies, no. 4)

2460. Engineering Societies Library. Bibliography on precision investment casting by the lost wax processes. N. Y.: The Library, 1949. 15p. (Engineering Societies Library bibliographies, no. 3)

2461. Engineering Societies Library. Bibliography on prestressed reinforced concrete. N. Y.: The Library, 1948. 25p. (Engineering Societies Library bibliographies, no. 2)

2462. Engineering Societies Library. Technical publications received by the Engineering Societies Library and reviewed by the Engineering Index Service, 1929-46. N. Y.: Engineering Index Service, 1929-46. 5 numbers.

Reprints of lists of periodicals appearing in annual volumes of Engineering Index.

2463. John Crerar Library. Reference list on mineral wool, by Jerome K. Wilcox. Chicago, 1930. 8p. (Reference list 1.)

2464. Michigan, University, Library. Catalogue of engineering books in the library of the University of Michigan. Ann Arbor: Register Pub. Co. [1890] 36p.

2465. New York Public Library. "Asbestos; a list of references to material in the New

York Public Library," comp. by William Burt Gamble. New York Public Library bulletin, 33 (1929), 664-87, 756-69, 806-35. Reprinted. 72p.

2466. New York Public Library. "Engineering books available in America prior to 1830," comp. by Ralph R. Shaw. New York Public Library bulletin, 37 (1933), 38-61, 157-60, 209-22, 301-10, 539-55. Reprinted. 69p.
Locates copies in numerous libraries.

2467. Nicholson, Natalie N. "The Engineering Library at Harvard University." Harvard Library bulletin, 1 (1947), 387-90.

2468. Purdue University Library. A manual of the William Freeman Myrick Goss Library of the history of engineering and associated collections, by W. M. Hepburn. Lafayette: Purdue University, Engineering Experiment Station, 1947. 218p.

2469. Texas Engineers Library. Printed catalog; accessions, Jan. 1943 - Aug. 31, 1947. College Station, Tex.: The Library, 1948. 245p.

2470. U. S. Army, Corps of Engineers. Catalogue of the library of the Engineer Department, United States Army. Wash., 1881. 819p.

2471. U. S. Engineer Dept. Library. Catalogue of the library of the Engineer Department, United States Army. Wash., 1881. 819p.
Pt. 1, authors; pt. 2, subjects.

2472. Yale University Library. Finding list of engineering serials in the libraries of New Haven. 3d ed. [New Haven, 1922] 60p. Earlier editions 1910 and 1914.
Lists 576 titles, with statement of 6 libraries' holdings.

Mechanical

2473. American Society of Mechanical Engineers. Catalog of transactions and periodicals in the library of the American Society of Mechanical Engineers. N. Y., 1904. 32p.
Now merged with Engineering Societies Library.

2474. Carnegie Library of Pittsburgh. Bibliography on blast cleaning with metallic abrasives, comp. by Ralph Hopp. Pittsburgh: The Library, 1941. 25p. (Reprinted from Heat treating and forging, 27 (1941), 280, 289-90, 328-32.)
Material available in the Carnegie Library of Pittsburgh.

2475. Carnegie Library of Pittsburgh. Sintering of iron ore and blast-furnace flue dust; a bibliography, comp. by Leo Filar. Pittsburgh: The Library, 1944. 31p. (Reprinted from Blast furnace and steel plant, 31 (1943), 1262-69.)
Material available in Carnegie Library of Pittsburgh.

2476. Carnegie Library of Pittsburgh. Steam turbines; references to books and magazine articles. Pittsburgh: The Library, 1904. 23p.

2477. Carnegie Library of Pittsburgh. "Water softening." Carnegie Library of Pittsburgh monthly bulletin, 9 (1904), 165-72.
A list of references on water softening, from periodicals in Carnegie Library of Pittsburgh.

2478. Engineering Societies Library. Bibliography on machinery foundations; design, construction, vibration elimination. N. Y.: The Library, 1950. 18p. (Engineering Societies Library bibliographies, no. 5)

2479. John Crerar Library. Gages, 1938-1942, a bibliography, comp. by Reginald B. Gordon. Chicago, 1942. 16p. (Reference list 52)

2480. Longyear, E. J., Company. Bibliography of diamond drilling. 3d ed. Minneapolis: The Company, 1948. 52p. Supplement. 1949. 6p.
Prepared with assistance of Engineering Societies Library and nearly all references held by that library.

Electrical

2481. American Institute of Electrical Engineers. A catalogue of periodical publications in the library of the American Institute of Electrical Engineers. N. Y.: The Institute, 1904. 26p.
Now merged with Engineering Societies Library.

2482. American Institute of Electrical Engineers Library. Catalogue of the Wheeler gift of books, pamphlets and periodicals in the library of the American Institute of Electrical Engineers, ed. by William D. Weaver. N. Y.: The Institute, 1909. 2v.

A catalog of about 7,000 books published before 1886. Library of the Institute was consolidated in 1909 with those of the American Society of Mechanical Engineers and American Institute of Mining Engineers to form Engineering Societies Library.

2483. Bureau of Railway Economics Library. Electrification of railways, a list of references to material published 1926 - March 1929 inclusive. Wash., 1929. 135 numb. l.

2484. Columbia Broadcasting System Reference Library. Radio and television bibliography. 6th ed. N. Y.: The Library, 1942. 96p.

Books, pamphlets and articles on radio and television, in Reference Library of the CBS.

2485. Hellman, Florence S., comp. "The Muscle Shoals project: a bibliographical list with index." In: U. S. Congress, House, Committee on Military Affairs. Muscle Shoals; hearings. Wash.: Govt. Print. Off., 1927. Pt. 4, p. 1373-90.

2486. John Crerar Library. Electrical insulation, 1941-43; a bibliography, by Reginald B. Gordon. Chicago: The Library, 1944. 32 numb. l. (Reference list, no. 53)

2487. John Crerar Library. Magnetic recording, 1900-1949, comp. by Carmen Wilson. Chicago, 1950. Unpaged. (Bibliography, no. 1)

Lists 339 references.

2488. New York Public Library. "List of works in the New York Public Library relating to illumination." New York Public Library bulletin, 12 (1908), 686-734. Reprinted. 49p.

2489. New York Public Library. "List of works on electricity in the New York Public Library." New York Public Library bulletin, 6 (1902), 426-64, 481-519; 7 (1903), 6-29. Reprinted. 100p.

2490. Northwestern University, Technological Institute Library. Bibliography on high frequency and dielectric induction heating. Evanston, 1946. 97 numb. l.

2491. Northwestern University, Technological Institute Library. Selected bibliography on radar. Evanston, 1946. 39 numb. l.

2492. Philadelphia International Electrical Exhibition, 1884. Subject catalogue of the Memorial library of the International Electrical Exhibition, held under the auspices of the Franklin Institute, September - October, 1884. Philadelphia: Burk & McFetridge, 1884. xcviip.

Collection now in Franklin Institute.

2493. U. S. Library of Congress, Division of Bibliography. Muscle Shoals: a bibliographical list of recent references. [Wash. 1931] 31p.

2494. U. S. Library of Congress, Division of Bibliography. Radio and radio broadcasting; a selected list of references, comp. by Anne L. Baden. [Wash.] 1941. 109p.

Mining

2495. American Institute of Mining Engineers. A catalogue of periodical publications in the library of the Institute. N. Y., 1904. 47p.

Now merged with Engineering Societies Library.

2496. California State Mining Bureau Library. Catalogue of the library of the California State Mining Bureau, San Francisco, Cal. September 1, 1892. Sacramento: A. J. Johnston, Supt. State Printing. 1892. 149p.

2497. Carnegie Library of Pittsburgh, Technology Dept. Non-metallic inclusions in iron and steel, comp. by Lois F. McCombs and Morris Schrero. Pittsburgh: Mining and Metallurgical Advisory Boards, 1935. 308p. (Mining and metallurgical investigations. Cooperative bulletin 70)

2498. Columbia University, School of Mines, Library. Catalogue of the books and pamphlets in the library of the School of Mines of Columbia College July 1st, 1875. N. Y.: J. W. Amerman, 1875. 399p.

2499. John Crerar Library. State mining directories and key indexes to the mineral resources of each state: a bibliography, comp. by Jerome K. Wilcox. Chicago, 1932. 39p. (Reference list 22) Supplement no. 1. 2p.

2500. U. S. Bureau of Mines. Bibliography of petroleum and allied substances. Wash.: Govt. Print. Off., 1918 - to date.
Annual bibliography issued in Bureau's Bulletin series.

2501. U. S. Engineer School Library. Petroleum pipeline activities; a bibliography. Fort Belvoir, Va., 1947. 121p.

Military and naval

2502. Northwestern University, Technological Institute Library. Bibliography on the atomic bomb. Evanston, Ill.: Northwestern University, 1945. 13p.

2503. U. S. Library of Congress, Division of Bibliography. A list of books on marine engineering, naval architecture and shipbuilding. Wash., 1940. 9p.

2504. U. S. Library of Congress, Division of Bibliography. "List of references on the economic and statistical aspects of shipbuilding in Great Britain and the United States, 1930-1940," comp. by Helen F. Conover. Wash., Feb. 17, 1941. 24p. Typed.

Railroad and road

2505. American Society of Civil Engineering. "Highway engineering; roads and pavements; a subject catalog of the books and pamphlets in the Engineering Societies Library, December 1921." American Society of Civil Engineers proceedings, 48 (Jan. 1922), 57-91.

2506. American Society of Civil Engineers Library. Index to the library of the American Society of Civil Engineers... part 1. Railroads. N. Y.: The Society, 1881. 189p.
Now in Engineering Societies Library.

2507. Bureau of Railway Economics. A check list of railway periodicals showing files in the library of the Bureau of Railway Economics. Wash., 1924. 112p.

2508. Bureau of Railway Economics. List of references on grade crossings. [Wash., 1915] 27 numb. l.

2509. Bureau of Railway Economics Library. Container cars - a transcript of entries from the catalog of the Bureau of Railway Economics Library. Wash., [1940] 14 numb. l.

2510. Bureau of Railway Economics Library. Gages of railroads in Asia. Wash., 1945. 26 numb. l.

2511. Bureau of Railway Economics Library. List of references on railway motor cars, rev. ed. [Wash.] 1925. 62 numb. l.

2512. Bureau of Railway Economics Library. Railroad car building industry; a list of references in the Bureau of Railway Economics Library, chronologically arranged, with indications of some other locations, prep. by Douglas R. Stephenson. [Wash., 1946] 18 numb. l.

2513. Carnegie Library of Pittsburgh. Airbrakes; references to books and magazine articles. Pittsburgh: The Library, 1915. 55p. (Reprinted from its Monthly bulletin, July 1915)

2514. Carnegie Library of Pittsburgh. "Pennsylvania Turnpike; a bibliography," comp. by Victor S. Polansky. In: Harper, Frank C., Pennsylvania turnpike; the twenty-first century highway, 1942. p. 70-72.

2515. Carnegie Library of Pittsburgh. Road dust preventives; references to books and magazine articles. Pittsburgh: The Library, 1916. 39p.

2516. New York Public Library. "List of works in the New York Public Library relating to bridges and viaducts." New York Public Library bulletin, 9 (1905), 295-329.

2517. U. S. Library of Congress, Division of Bibliography. "Bibliography; select list of references on national aid to road building in the United States." In: U. S. Congress, Joint Gommittee on Federal Aid in the Construction of Post Roads. Federal aid to good roads. Wash.: Govt. Print. Off., 1915. p. 293-313. (63d Cong., 3d sess. House. Doc. 1510)

2518. Washington State Library. Roads; select list of references on roads. Olympia, Wash., 1912. 41p.

Canal

2519. Gaul, John James. Reclamation, 1902-1938: a supplemental bibliography. [Denver, Colo., 1939] 98 numb. l. (Bibliographical Center for Research regional check list, no. 6)

"List of serials showing locations in the region," leaves xv-xxvi.

Hydraulic

2520. Carnegie Library of Pittsburgh. Floods and flood protection; references to books and magazine articles. Pittsburgh: The Library, 1908. 48p. (Reprinted from its Monthly bulletin, July 1908) Supplement. Pittsburgh: The Library, 1911. 16p. (Reprinted from its Monthly bulletin, Oct. 1911.)

2521. Carnegie Library of Pittsburgh. "References to flood literature." Report of flood commission of Pittsburgh, Pa. 1 (1912), 397-432.

A list of references to material in Carnegie Library of Pittsburgh.

2522. New York Public Library. "List of works in the New York Public Library relating to hydraulic engineering." New York Public Library bulletin, 11 (1907), 512-62, 565-626. Reprinted. 102p.

2523. Seattle Public Library. Harbors and docks; a list of books and references to periodicals in the Seattle Public Library. [Seattle] 1913. 40p. (Reference list, no. 5)

Geographical arrangement.

2524. U. S. Engineer School Library. American literature on dams, a bibliography, comp. by Alvan W. Clark. Fort Belvoir, Va., 1948. 182p.

2525. U. S. Library of Congress, Division of Bibliography. Bibliography on flood control. Wash.: Govt. Print. Off., 1928. 83p. (70th Cong., 1st sess. House. Committee on Flood Control, Committee document 4)

2526. U. S. Library of Congress, Division of Bibliography. The St. Lawrence navigation and power project, a list of recent references, comp. by Ann Duncan Brown. [Wash.] 1942. 28p.

2527. U. S. Light-house Board Library. Index-catalogue of the library of the Lighthouse Board. Wash.: Govt. Print. Off., 1886. 116 numb. l.

Sanitary

2528. Carnegie Library of Pittsburgh. Air conditioning; references to books and magazine articles. Pittsburgh: Carnegie Library, 1914. 58p. (Reprinted from its Monthly bulletin, Nov. 1914)

2529. Carnegie Library of Pittsburgh. Bibliography of smoke and smoke prevention, comp. by E. H. McClelland. Pittsburgh: Univ. of Pittsburgh, 1913. 164p. (Pittsburgh, University, Mellon Institute of Industrial Research, Smoke investigation bulletin, no. 2)

Starred items are in Carnegie Library of Pittsburgh.

2530. Carnegie Library of Pittsburgh. Refuse and garbage disposal. Pittsburgh: The Library, 1909. 39p. (Reprinted from its Monthly bulletin, Jan. 1909)

All items mentioned in Carnegie Library of Pittsburgh.

2531. Carnegie Library of Pittsburgh. Sewage disposal and treatment; references to books and magazine articles. Pittsburgh: The Library, 1910. 96p. (Reprinted from its Monthly bulletin, Nov. 1910.)

2532. Carnegie Library of Pittsburgh. Smoke prevention; references to books and magazine articles. Pittsburgh: The Library, 1907. 20p. (Reprinted from its Monthly bulletin, May 1907.)

2533. Claremont College Library. Special collection on the water problems of southern California. Claremont, California: The Library, 1935-38. 3 nos.

Description, by groups of material, of collection of 4,000 items in Claremont College Library.

2534. John Crerar Library. List of references on dust explosions, by Ella M. Salmonsen. Chicago, 1936. 10p. (Reference list 34)

2535. John Crerar Library. Radiant (panel) heating, 1940-1945, comp. by Inge B. Jorgensen. [Chicago, 1945] 10p. (Reference list 56)

2536. Massachusetts Institute of Technology Library. A subject list of theses in civil and sanitary engineering in the Institute library; a 25 year record, 1913-1938, prep. by Ralph R. McNay. Cambridge, Mass., 1939. 68 numb. 1.

Limited to theses written at Massachusetts Institute of Technology.

2537. New York Public Library. "List of works on city wastes and street hygiene in the New York Public Library." New York Public Library bulletin, 16 (1912), 731-83.

2538. Princeton University Library. History of the art of illumination. Princeton: The Library, 1916. 7p.

Catalog of an exhibition.

2539. Trinity College Library. Sanitary science, a list of books in the Trinity College Library acquired chiefly through the J. Ewing Mears Foundation on Sanitary Science. Hartford, Conn., 1914. 33p. (Trinity College bulletin, n. s., v. 11, no. 2)

Automotive

2540. Carnegie Library of Pittsburgh. The gyroscope; reference to books and magazine articles. Pittsburgh: The Library, 1917. 23p. (Reprinted from its Monthly bulletin, May 1917)

2541. Detroit Public Library. "Catalog of the Salomons-Bendix collection presented to the Detroit Public Library in 1945 by R. L. Polk and Company." [Detroit: Automotive History Collection, Detroit Public Library, 1945] 20p. Typewritten.

Listing of automotive material, largely French and English imprints prior to 1900.

2542. New York Public Library. "Automobile tires; a list of references in the New York Public Library," comp. by Marcia Babcock Konstanzer. New York Public Library bulletin, 27 (1923), 124-46. Reprinted. 35p.

2543. New York Public Library. "List of works relating to storage batteries, 1900-1915," comp. by George S. Maynard. New York Public Library bulletin, 19 (1915), 365-99. Reprinted. 37p.

2544. U. S. Library of Congress, Division of Bibliography. Automobile industry: selected list of recent writings, comp. by Anne L. Baden. Wash., Oct. 6, 1938. 74p.

AERONAUTICS

2545. Brockett, Paul. Bibliography of aeronautics. Wash.: Smithsonian Institution, 1910. 940p. (Smithsonian miscellaneous collections. v. 55. Publication 1920)

Locates copies in Smithsonian Institution, Library of Congress, and other Washington libraries, as well as in many foreign libraries.

2546. Eells, Richard. "The Library of Congress." Air affairs, 3 (Autumn, 1949), 139-45.

Discussion of Library of Congress aeronautical collection.

2547. Eells, Richard. The national air collection. [n. p., 1947] [4] p.

"Reprinted from November, 1947 U. S. air services." Based on Library of Congress holdings.

2548. Henry E. Huntington Library. Conquest of the air: the evolution of aeronautics to 1883, an exhibition, prep. by Lyle H. Wright. San Marino: The Library, 1941. 16p.

2549. Illinois, University, Library. List of books and pamphlets in the library on aeronautics, comp. by Margaret Hutchins. [Urbana, 1917] 18 l. Typed.

Includes books on meteorology, kites and military subjects.

2550. Institute of Aeronautical Sciences. Aeronautical readers guide; a catalogue of selected aeronautical books in the Paul Kollsman library. N. Y.: Pub. for the Aeronautical Archives by the Inst. of Aeronautical Sciences, Sept. 1940-June 1941. v. 1, no. 1-4. (Absorbed by Journal of Aeronautical sciences: Aeronautical review section.)

2551. Institute of the Aeronautical Sciences. Exhibition of early American children's books of aeronautical interest. Dime novels about flying machines. Aviation fiction for boys and girls from the Bella C. Landauer Aeronautical Collection. N. Y.: The Institute, 1942. 14p.

Collection held by the Institute.

2552. John Crerar Library. Airplanes vs.

transmission of disease, by Ella M. Salmonsen. Chicago, 1942. 3p. (Reference list 50)

2553. John Crerar Library. The use of windmills in aeronautics, a bibliography, comp. by Jerome K. Wilcox. Chicago, 1930. 4p. (Reference list 5)

2554. McFarland, Marvin and Renstrom, Arthur. "The papers of Wilbur and Orville Wright." Library of Congress quarterly journal of current acquisitions, 7 (Aug. 1950), 22-34.
Description of 30,000-piece manuscript collection received by Library of Congress.

2555. Maggs Bros., London, booksellers. Aerostation. London, 1940. 114p.
Collection acquired by Denver Public Library.

2556. Maggs Bros., London, booksellers. A descriptive catalogue of books and engravings illustrating the evolution of the airship and the aeroplane. London: Courier Press, 1920. 170p.
Entire collection of 1,494 items bought by Huntington Library.

2557. Michelmore, G. W. Catalogue of an aeronautic and railroad library formed by an English collector. N. Y.: Anderson Galleries, 1919. 50p.
Acquired en bloc by Henry E. Huntington Library.

2558. New York Public Library. "History of aeronautics; a selected list of references to material in the New York Public Library," comp. by William Burt Gamble. New York Public Library bulletin, 40 (1936), 27-48, 120-38, 347-66, 455-75, 616-39, 704-26, 878-99, 939-54, 1037-48; 41 (1937), 49-55, 137-45, 335-57, 427-34, 487-505, 571-95, 635-62, 703-32. Reprinted, 1938. 325p. An earlier "List of works in the New York Public Library relating to aeronautics," appeared in the Bulletin, 12 (1908), 628-43, and was reprinted. 16p.

2559. Northwestern University, Technological Institute Library. Selected bibliography on rockets and jet propulsion. Evanston: Northwestern Univ. Library, 1945. 25 numb. 1.

2560. Renstrom, Arthur George. Air cargo. [n. p., 1943] 6p. (Reprinted from Aeronautical engineering review, October, 1943. V. 2, no. 10)
Prepared in Library of Congress, Division of Aeronautics.

2561. Renstrom, Arthur George, comp. Postwar aviation... A selective bibliography on peacetime plans and problems. [n. p., 1944] 2 pts. in 1 v. (Reprinted from Aeronautical engineering review, December, 1943. V. 2, no. 12; pt. 2: Reprinted from Aeronautical engineering review, January, 1944. V. 3, no. 1.)
Based on Library of Congress collections.

2562. Renstrom, Arthur George, comp. Principal U. S. investigations in aeronautics, 1918-37. N. Y., 1938. 8p. ("Reprinted from Air law review, official journal of the American academy of air law and the American section of the International committee on radio, vol. IX, no. 1, January, 1938." p. 65-73.)
Reports, investigations, hearings, etc., pertaining to aeronautics. Available in Library of Congress.

2563. St. Louis Public Library. Aeronautics; a list of books and articles. [St. Louis]: The Library, 1928. 26p. (Reprinted from Monthly bulletin of the St. Louis Public Library, n. s., v. 26, no. 6, June 1928.)

2564. Sanborn, Ruth A. "The aviation collection at the Business School Library." Harvard Library bulletin, 2 (1948), 266-70.
In Harvard University, Graduate School of Business Administration, Baker Library.

2565. Seattle Public Library. List of books on aeronautics in the Seattle Public Library, Technology Division. [Seattle, Wash., 1931] 60p.
A collection of more than 3,000 volumes, classified, with author index.

2566. Smithsonian Institution Library. A list of the books forming the Langley aeronautical collection deposited in the Library of Congress by the Smithsonian Institution, March 1930. Wash., 1930. 69p.
Photographic reproduction of catalog cards, 21 to a page, of the collection.

2567. U. S. Civil Aeronautics Administration

Library. Selected references on airports. [Wash., 1943] 14p.

2568. U. S. Civil Aeronautics Administration Library. Selected references on wood in airplane manufacture. [Wash., 1943] 8p.

2569. U. S. Engineer School Library. Aerial photography; bibliography of available material, prep. by Henry E. Haferkorn. Wash.: Engineer School, 1918. 2v.

2570. U. S. Library of Congress. "Annual report on acquisitions: Aeronautics." Library of Congress quarterly journal of acquisitions, 3 (Aug. 1946), 41-43; 4 (Aug. 1947), 25-31; 5 (Aug. 1948), 21-27; 6 (Aug. 1949), 37-49; 7 (Aug. 1950), 37-43.

2571. U. S. Library of Congress. "Maggs collection of aeronautics." [Wash., 1935] 204 numb. l. Typed.
Consists of Tissandier, Hoernes, Silberer and Maggs collections, purchased by Library of Congress, 1930.

2572. U. S. Library of Congress, Division of Aeronautics. Aeronautic Americana; a bibliography of books and pamphlets on aeronautics published in America before 1900, by N. H. Randers-Pehrson and A. G. Renstrom. N. Y.: Institute of the Aeronautical Sciences, 1943. 40p.
Union list, locating copies in 47 libraries.

2573. U. S. Library of Congress, Division of Aeronautics. The aeronautical index... A subject and author index to aeronautical periodicals and technical reports. 1938-to date. N. Y.: Institute of the Aeronautical sciences, 1939-to date.
Prepared from card index of books received by Library of Congress, Division of Aeronautics, and articles appearing in other publications.

2574. U. S. Library of Congress, Division of Aeronautics. Aeronautics in Alaska: a list of references, comp. by Arthur G. Renstrom. Wash., 1944. 39p.

2575. U. S. Library of Congress, Division of Aeronautics. Bibliography on skin friction and boundary flow, comp. by A. F. Zahm and C. A. Ross. Wash., 1932. 46 l.

2576. U. S. Library of Congress, Division of Aeronautics. A check list of aeronautical periodicals and serials in the Library of Congress, prep. by Arthur G. Renstrom. Wash., 1948. 129p.

2577. U. S. Library of Congress, Division of Aeronautics. Check list of state aeronautical publications. Wash., 1942. 14p.

2578. U. S. Library of Congress, Division of Aeronautics. Recent references on air freight and express. [Wash., 1943?] 11p. Supplementary list. [Wash., 1943] 17p.

2579. U. S. Library of Congress, Division of Aeronautics. United States aviation policy; a selective bibliography, comp. by Arthur G. Renstrom. Wash., 1947. 58p.

2580. U. S. Library of Congress, Division of Bibliography. Bibliography on gliding and soaring flight. [Elmira, N. Y. 1934] 13 l.

2581. Zahm, Albert F. "The Division of Aeronautics in the Library of Congress." National aeronautics, 17 (Nov. 1939), 7, 43.

HOME ECONOMICS

2582. Bitting, Katherine (Golden). Gastronomic bibliography. San Francisco, Calif., 1939. 718p.
Many of the books listed are now in the Bitting Collection, Rare Books Division, Library of Congress.

2583. Carnegie Library of Pittsburgh. Electric heating and cooking; references to books and magazine articles. Pittsburgh: The Library, 1910. 14p. (Reprinted from its Monthly bulletin, Jan. 1910)

2584. Lincoln, Waldo. "Bibliography of American cookery books, 1742-1860." American Antiquarian Society proceedings, n. s. 39 (1929), 85-225. Reprinted. 145p.
Chronological list of 492 titles, with locations in 23 libraries.

2585. New York Public Library. "An annotated list of bibliographies of cookery books," comp. by James E. Gourley. New York Public Library bulletin, 41 (1937), 696-700.

2586. New York Public Library. "Dehydrated foods; a list of references to material in the New York Public Library," comp. by Perrie Jones. New York Public Library bulletin, 21 (1917), 645-55. Reprinted. 13p.

2587. New York Public Library. "Regional American cookery, 1884-1934; a list of works on the subject," comp. by James E. Gourley. New York Public Library bulletin, 39 (1935), 452-60, 543-60. Reprinted, 1936. 36p.
   Locates copies in 13 libraries.

2588. New York Public Library. "The Whitney cookery collection," by Lewis M. Stark. New York Public Library bulletin, 50 (1946), 103-26. Reprinted. 26p.
   Lists 218 books and manuscripts on cookery, in New York Public Library.

2589. Pennell, Elizabeth (Robins). "My cookery books." Boston and N. Y.: Houghton, Mifflin Co., 1903. 171p.
   Collection now in Library of Congress.

2590. U. S. Office of Education Library. List of references on home economics. Wash., 1913-23. 3v.
   Issued 1913, 1914, 1923, the last as Library leaflet 21.

AGRICULTURE

General

2591. John Crerar Library. Hydroponics, a bibliography, comp. by Kanardy L. Taylor. Chicago, 1937. 11p. (Reference list 38)

2592. New Bedford Free Public Library. A collection of books, pamphlets, log books, pictures, etc., illustrating whales and the whale fishery, contained in the Free Public Library, New Bedford, Mass. 2d ed. [New Bedford, 1920.] 24p. First ed. published 1907.

2593. Swem, Earl G., ed. A contribution to the bibliography of agriculture in Virginia. Richmond: D. Bottom, Supt. of Public Printing, 1918. 35p. (Virginia State Library bulletin, v. 11, nos. 1-2)

2594. U. S. Bureau of Agricultural Engineering. Agricultural engineering; a selected bibliography, comp. by Dorothy W. Graf. Wash., 1937. 373p.

2595. U. S. Dept. of Agriculture. The influence of weather on crops: 1900-1930; a selected and annotated bibliography. Wash.: Govt. Print. Off., 1931. 246p. (Miscellaneous publication 118)

2596. U. S. Dept. of Agriculture Library. Agricultural library notes, v. 1-17, no. 6, Jan. 1926 - June, 1942. Wash., 1926-42. 17v.
   Continued by Bibliography of agriculture.

2597. U. S. Dept. of Agriculture Library. Agriculture in defense, v. 1 (no. 1-37), Oct. 17, 1941 - June 26, 1942. [Wash., 1941-42]
   "A series of abstracts of current publications received in the library."

2598. U. S. Dept. of Agriculture Library. Bibliographical bulletin. No. 1-10, July 1943 - Feb. 1949. Wash., 1943-49. 10v.

   1. Bibliography on lice and man with particular reference to wartime conditions. July 1943. 106p.
   2. A summary of the literature on milkweeds (Asclepias spp.) and their utilization. Oct. 15, 1943. 41p.
   3. Bibliography on the Japanese in American agriculture. Jan. 1944. 61p.
   4. List of bulletins of the agricultural experiment stations for the calendar years 1941 and 1942. Sept. 1944. 70p.
   5. Bibliography on butter oil. July 1944. 40p.
   6. Bibliography on dehydration of food. June 1945. 120p.
   7. Bibliography on cork oak. April 1946. 66p.
   8. Bibliography on aviation and economic entomology. April 1947. 186p.
   9. Review of literature on chinchona disease, injuries and fungi. December 1947. 70p.
   10. The technical literature of agricultural motor fuels including physical and chemical properties, engine performance, economics, patents, and books. Feb. 1949. 259p.

2599. U. S. Dept. of Agriculture Library. Bibliographical contributions, no. 1-35. Wash., 1919-39.

1. A check list of publications of the Department of Agriculture on the subject of plant pathology, 1837-1913. June 1919. 38p. (superseded by no. 8)
2. Check list of publications of the state agricultural experiment stations on the subject of plant pathology, 1876-1920. 179p. April 1922. (superseded by no. 16)
3. Check list of publications issued by the Bureau of Plant Industry, United States Department of Agriculture, 1901-1920 and by the divisions and offices which combined to form this bureau, 1862-1901. Jan. 1921. 127p.
4. Bibliography on the preservation of fruits and vegetables in transit and storage, with annotations. June 1922. 76p.
5. Index to some sources of current prices. April 1943. 124p.
6. Partial list of publications on dairying issued in the United States, 1900 to June 1923. August 1923. 236p.
7. Bibliography on the marketing of agricultural products. June 1924. 133p. (Superseded by U. S. Dept. of Agr. Misc. cir. 35)
8. Author and subject index to the publications on plant pathology issued by the U. S. Department of Agriculture up to January 1, 1925. June 1925. 158p.
9. World food supply; a selected bibliography. June 1925. 68p. (Supplemented by Agricultural economics bibliography, no. 82)
10. Refrigeration and cold storage; a selected list of references covering the years 1915-1924 and the early part of 1925. Oct. 1925. 58p.
11. List of manuscript bibliographies and indexes in the U. S. Department of Agriculture including serial mimeographed lists of current literature. Jan. 1926. 38p.
12. Peat, a contribution towards a bibliography of the American literature through 1925. Sept. 1926. 95p.
13. A classified list of soil publications of the United States and Canada. June 1927. 549p.
14. List of the publications on soils issued by the U. S. Department of Agriculture, 1844-1926. May 1927. 63p.
15. List of the publications on soils issued by the state agricultural experiment stations of the United States through 1926. July 1927. 81p.
16. Author and subject index to the publications on plant pathology issued by the state agricultural experiment stations up to December 1, 1927. June 1928. 261p.
17. Bibliography on ice cream up to and including the year 1926. March 1928. 291p.
18. Agricultural and home economics extension in the United States; a selected list of references. Sept. 1928. 56p.
19. Cattle, sheep and goat production in the range country; a selected list of publications issued by the U. S. Department of Agriculture and the agricultural colleges, experiment stations, and departments of agriculture of the seventeen range states. Oct. 1928. 78p.
20. Check list of publications on entomology issued by the U. S. Department of Agriculture through 1927, with subject index. Jan. 1930. 261p.
21. List of publications on apiculture contained in the U. S. Department of Agriculture and in part those contained in the Library of Congress. May 1930. 218p.
22. George Washington and agriculture; a classified list of annotated references. 2d ed. Feb. 1936. 77p.
23. Agriculture of the American Indians, classified list of annotated historical references. May 1932. 89p.
24. Selected references on the history of English agriculture. 2d ed. Oct. 1939. 105p.
25. References on the significance of the frontier in American history. Oct. 1935. 63p.
26. Selected references on the history of agriculture in the United States. 2d ed. Jan. 1939. 43p.
27. A list of American economic histories. 2d ed. April 1939. 43p.
28. References on the mountaineers of the Southern Appalachians. Dec. 1935. 148p.
29. References on agricultural museums. August 1936. 43p.
30. References on the Great Lakes-Saint Lawrence Waterway Project. 2d ed. Dec. 1940. 189p.

2600 TECHNOLOGY

31. References on economic history as a field of research and study. Oct. 1936. 83p.
32. References on agricultural history as a field for research. Dec. 1937. 41p.
33. References on American colonial agriculture. Sept. 1938. 101p.
34. References on agriculture in the life of the Nation. Jan. 1939. 73p.
35. A guide for courses in the history of American agriculture. Sept. 1939. 192p.

2600. U. S. Dept. of Agriculture Library. Bibliography of agriculture, 1 (July 1942) - to date. Wash.: Govt. Print. Off., 1942 - to date.

Volumes 1-2 issued in sections. Supersedes: Agricultural economics literature, Current literature in agricultural engineering, Entomology current literature, Plant science literature, Forestry current literature, List of agricultural experiment station publications received by the Library, Cotton literature, Soil conservation literature.

2601. U. S. Dept. of Agriculture Library. Bulletin. Wash.: Govt. Print. Off., 1894-1912. 76 nos.

"Consists of the quarterly accessions to the Department library, except the following: No. 2, Periodicals and society publications currently received... 1894; No. 9, List of publications of the U. S. Department of Agriculture from 1841 to June 30, 1895, inclusive. 1896; No. 16, References to the literature of the sugar beet... comp. by Claribel R. Barnett. 1897; No. 18, Bibliography of poultry; comp. by Emma B. Hawks. 1897; No. 20, Reference list of publications relating to edible and poisonous mushrooms; comp. by Josephine A. Clark. 1898; No. 24, List of publications relating to forestry in the department library. 1898; No. 37, Catalogue of the periodicals and other serial publications in the library... 1901; No. 37, Suppl. No. 1 (1901-1905) 1907; No. 41, List of references to publications relating to irrigation and land drainage; comp. by Ellen A. Hedrick. 1902; No. 42, Catalogue of the publications relating to botany in the library... 1902; No. 55, Catalogue of the publications relating to entomology in the library... 1906; No. 75, List of periodicals currently received in the library of the U. S. Dept. of Agriculture... 1909; No. 76, Catalogue of publications relating to forestry in the library of the U. S. Dept. of Agriculture... 1912."

2602. U. S. Dept. of Agriculture Library. Library lists. Wash., 1942-49. No. 1-49.

1. Selected list of American agricultural books, rev. ed., April 1947. 40p.
2. Farm tenancy in the United States, 1940-1945, rev. ed., August 1946. 84p.
3. Rationing, July 1942. 60p.; Suppl., Feb. 1943. 51p.
4. Agricultural labor in the United States, July 1941 - February 1943. April 1943. 59p.
5. A preliminary list of Latin American periodicals and serials. August 1943. 195p.
6. Rehabilitation of low-income farmers. August 1943. 56p.
7. Agricultural credit; publications of Federal Government and state agricultural colleges. March 1944. 41p.
8. Selected references on Thomas Jefferson and his contributions to agriculture. April 1944. 7p.
9. Land settlement. June 1944. 167p.
10. Guayule. July 1944. 61p. (Supersedes Soil conservation bibliography, no. 4)
11. Cold storage lockers and locker plants. August 1944. 32p.
12. Bibliography on the poultry industry in countries other than Canada and the United States. Sept. 1944. 113p.
13. Vanilla: culture, processing and economics. Feb. 1945. 28p.
14. Safety of life; farm and home safety, 1941-44, list of references. April 1945. 21p.
15. Victory gardening in the United States; a list of references to publications designed to aid the gardener. June 1945. 32p.
18. Partial list of United States farm papers received in the U. S. Department of Agriculture Library. Oct. 1945. 6p. Rev. ed., March 1949. 2p.
19. The farmhouse. Oct. 1945. 124p. Supplement. Sept. 1947. 40p.
20. Sesame. Nov. 1945. 18p.
21. Land transfer and titles, 1920-1945. Dec. 1945. 41p.
22. Inheritance of farm real estate, 1920-1945. Jan. 1946. 34p.
23. Forest credit in the United States, 1930-1945. March 1946. 10p.
24. Effects of temperature and humidity on cellulosic materials with special reference to tire cord. March 1946. 9p.

25. Available bibliographies and lists, rev. ed. Sept. 1948. 1p.
26. School lunches. May 1946. 66p.
27. Fertilizer use and crop yields. July 1946. 67p.
28. Audio-visual aids as means of communications. August 1946. 4p.
29. The mango. October 1946. 62p.
30. Classification scheme of the Bibliography of agriculture, Oct. 1946. 25p.
31. Rice hulls and rice straw, 1907-1944. Dec. 1946. 28p.
32. The mangosteen. Dec. 1946. 29p.
33. Personnel administration publications. Jan. 1947. 6p.
34. Economic aspects of forest-fire protection and damage. Jan. 1947. 48p.
35. Landscape gardening for the rural community in the United States. April 1947. 46p.
36. The forest resources of Mississippi. May 1947. 31p.
37. Marketing fruits and vegetables, 1942-46. Oct. 1947. 166p.
38. Farm migration, 1940-45. Sept. 1947. 51p.
39. Rural reading list. Oct. 1947. 39p.
40. Mississippi Delta, its economy and land use. Jan. 1948. 154p.
41. Bibliography on cooperation in agriculture. June 1948. 178p.
42. Packaging and prepackaging of fresh fruits and vegetables, July 1946 - Dec. 1947. April 1948. 30p. (Supplements Library list 37)
43. Marketing of dairy products, 1936-40. June 1948. 75p.
44. Cellulose-water relations, selected bibliography with special reference to swelling of cotton and to its utilization in water-resistant fabrics. March 1949. 63p.
45. Educational exhibits. March 1949. 6p.
46. Rural community organization. May 1949. 51p.
47. Crop and livestock insurance, 1941-48. June 1949. 14p. (Supplements Agric. economics bibliography 67 and Economic library list 24)
48. Bibliography on extension research, November 1943 through December 1948, classified and annotated. July 1949. 19p.
49. Physical risks in farm production, selected references, 1930-1948. August 1949. 29p.

2603. U. S. Office of Education Library. List of references on rural life and culture. [Wash.] Govt. Print. Off., 1913-24. 5v.
    Issued 1913, 1914, 1919, 1922, 1924, the last three as Library leaflet 1, 16, 26.

Library catalogs and surveys

2604. Horticultural Society of New York. "The library, 1924-1939; its extraordinary character, its possibilities, and its needs," by Edwin De T. Bechtel. Horticultural Society of New York monthly bulletin, (October 1939), 5-11.
    General description of Society's library with list of its rare books.

2605. Illinois Dept. of Agriculture Library. Catalogue of the library of the Illinois Department of Agriculture. 1884. Springfield: H. W. Rokker's Publishing House, 1884. 59p.
    Dictionary catalog.

2606. Massachusetts Horticultural Society Library. Catalogue of the library of the Massachusetts Horticultural Society. Cambridge: University Press, 1918-20, 587p.
    Pt. 1, alphabetical list of authors and titles; pt. 2, subject catalog.

2607. Massachusetts Horticultural Society Library. Selected catalog of the library. Rev. ed., comp. by Dorothy S. Manks, Boston, 1936. 64p. Supplement. Boston, 1942. 32p.

2608. Massachusetts State Board of Agriculture Library. Classification and catalogue of the library of the Massachusetts State Board of Agriculture, prep. and arr. by Frederick H. Fowler. Boston: Wright & Potter Printing Co., 1899. 127p.

2609. Pennsylvania Horticultural Society Library. Catalog of the library. The Pennsylvania Horticultural Society. Philadelphia: The Society, 1941. 161p.

Periodicals

2610. Purdue University Library. List of journals in agriculture, biology, chemistry, and related subjects in the libraries of Purdue University, comp. by Esther M. Schlundt and others. Lafayette, Ind.: Purdue University Agricultural Experiment Station and Purdue University Library, 1940. 42p.
    Alphabetical list, showing holdings.

2611. Stuntz, Stephen Conrad. List of the agricultural periodicals of the United States and Canada published during the century July 1810 to July 1910. Wash.: Govt. Print. Off., 1941. 190p. (U. S. Dept. of Agric. Misc. publ., no. 398)

Based primarily on periodicals in U. S. Department of Agriculture Library or the Library of Congress. Indicates holdings in Department of Agriculture Library.

2612. U. S. Dept. of Agriculture Library. List of periodicals currently received in the library of the United States Department of Agriculture, June 1, 1936, comp. by Elizabeth G. Hopper. Wash.: Govt. Print. Off., 1936. 337p. (U. S. Dept. of Agriculture, Miscellaneous publication, no. 245)

Supersedes lists issued 1901, 1909, and 1922. Revision in progress.

2613. U. S. Office of Experiment Stations. Experiment station record, v. 1-95. Sept. 1889 - Dec. 1946. Wash.: Govt. Print. Off., 1890-1948. 95v.

2614. U. S. Office of Experiment Stations. List of bulletins of the agricultural experiment stations in the United States from their establishment to the end of 1920. Wash., 1924. 185p. (U. S. Dept. of Agriculture, departmental bulletin 1199)

Biennial supplements issued from 1921 to 40. 10v. Material listed in U. S. Department of Agriculture Library.

History

2615. Edwards, Everett E. Bibliography of the history of agriculture in the United States. Wash.: Govt. Print. Off., 1930. 307p. (U. S. Dept. of Agriculture, Misc. Pub. 84).

"Work... has been done in the Bureau of Agricultural Economics Library, the U. S. Dept. of Agriculture Library, and the Library of Congress."

2616. Harvard University, Graduate School of Business Administration, Baker Library. "Agricultural records in the Baker Library." Business Historical Society bulletin, 9 (1935), 60-63.

A survey of manuscripts in Baker Library on agriculture in the United States, 1762-1925.

2617. "The McCormick Historical Association." Business Historical Society bulletin, 10 (Nov. 1936), 76-78.

Brief description of materials in Association's Library (Chicago), relating to agricultural history, McCormick family, Virginia, etc.

2618. True, Rodney H. "Some pre-revolutionary agricultural correspondence." Agricultural history, 12 (1938), 107-17.

Letters in Yale University Library written by American colonists from 1749 to 1769, to Jared Eliot of Connecticut.

2619. Virginia State Library. "A list of manuscripts relating to the history of agriculture in Virginia... now in the Virginia State Library," comp. by Earl G. Swem. Virginia State Library bulletin, 6 (1913), 1-20.

Economics

2620. Kulsrud, Carl J. "The archival records of the Agricultural Adjustment Program." Agricultural history, 22 (July 1948), 197-204.

Describes records in National Archives.

2621. U. S. Dept. of Agriculture. Bibliography on land settlement. Wash.: Govt. Print. Off., 1934. 492p. (Miscellaneous publication 172)

2622. U. S. Dept. of Agriculture. Bibliography on land utilization, 1918-36. Wash.: Govt. Print. Off., 1938. 1,508p. (Miscellaneous publication 284)

2623. U. S. Dept. of Agriculture. Bibliography on the marketing of agricultural products. Wash.: Govt. Print. Off., 1925. 56p. (Miscellaneous circular 35)

2624. U. S. Dept. of Agriculture. Bibliography on the marketing of agricultural products. Wash.: Govt. Print. Off., 1932. 351p. (Miscellaneous publication 150)

2625. U. S. Dept. of Agriculture. Rural standards of living; a selected bibliography. Wash.: Govt. Print. Off., 1931. 84p. (Miscellaneous publication 116)

2626. U. S. Dept. of Agriculture Library. Agricultural economics bibliographies, 1938-42. Nos. 1-97.

Some early numbers are out of date, superseded by later issues, or do not show holdings. Still pertinent are the following:

1. Agricultural economics; a selected list of references. Rev. Jan. 1938. 26p.
2. Flour milling and bread making; selected list of references. Rev. April 1931. 24p.
12. Government control of export and import in foreign countries. Feb. 1926. 126p.
15. Alabama; an index to the state official sources of agricultural statistics. March 1926. 96p. (Useful for historical studies)
17. Farm youth; a selected list of references to literature issued since January 1920. Oct. 1926. 40p. (Supplemented by no. 65)
18. Price fixing by governments 424 B. C. - 1926 A. D.; a selected bibliography, including some references on the principles of price fixing, and on price fixing by private organizations. Oct. 1926. 149p. (See also no. 79 and no. 86)
19. The apple industry in the United States; a selected list of references on the economic aspects of the industry together with some references on varieties. June 1927. 170p.
20. Bounties on agricultural products; a selected bibliography. July 1927. 128p.
21. Oklahoma; an index to the State official sources of agricultural statistics... including a list of the unofficial sources of Oklahoma agricultural statistics. Aug. 1927. 460p. (Useful for historical studies)
23. Control of production of agricultural products by governments; a selected bibliography. Dec. 1927. 88p.
24. The poultry industry; a selected list of references on the economic aspects of the industry, 1920-1927. Feb. 1928. 106p.
25. Taxation and the farmer; a selected and annotated bibliography. June 1928. 190p.
26. Labor requirements of farm products in the United States; a list of references to material published since 1922. April 1929. 62p.
28. The strawberry industry in the United States; a selected list of references on the economic aspects of the industry. September 1929. 52p.
30. Large scale and corporation farming; a selected list of references. Nov. 1929. 87p. (Supplemented by no. 69)
31. California; an index to the State sources of agricultural statistics. (Useful for historical studies.)
   Part I. - Fruits, vegetables and nuts; an index to the official sources. Sections 1 and 2, Jan. 1930. 724p.
   Part II. - Crops other than fruits, vegetables and nuts; an index to the official sources. June 1930. 430p.
   Part III. - Livestock and livestock products; an index to the official sources. Jan. 1931. 371p.
   Part IV. - Land, farm property, irrigation, and miscellaneous items; an index to the official sources. April 1931. 128p.
   Part V. - An index to some unofficial sources. Feb. 1930. 69p.
33. Wheat; cost of production, 1923-1930. References relating to the United States and some foreign countries. Jan. 1931. 33p.
35. Switzerland; a guide to official statistics on agriculture, population, and food supply. March 1932. 341p.
36. The grape industry; a selected list of references on the economic aspects of the industry in the United States, 1920-1931. March 1932. 161p.
38. List of State official serial publications containing material on agricultural economics. July 1932. 222p. (Out of date; indicates ownership of serials listed, however.)
39. Greece; a guide to official statistics of agriculture, population, and food supply. Oct. 1932. 142p.
40. Barter and scrip in the United States. Feb. 1933. 43p.
41. The domestic allotment plans for the relief of agriculture. Feb. 1933. 48p.
42. Measures taken by foreign countries to relieve agricultural indebtedness. March 1933. 57p.
43. Part-time farming; a brief list of recent references. Feb. 1933. 20p. (Superseded by no. 77)
44. Uses for cotton; selected references in the English language. Nov. 1932. 43p. (Supplemented by no. 91)
45. State measures for the relief of agricultural indebtedness in the United States, 1932 and 1933. March 1933. 64p.

47. Farm mortgages in the United States; selected references... January 1928 - April 1933. May 1933. 86p.
48. Price analysis; selected references on supply and demand curves and related subjects, Jan. 1928 - June 1933. Sept. 1933. 98p.
49. Rumania; a guide to official statistics of agriculture, population, and food supply. Oct. 1933. 216p.
50. Agricultural relief; a selected and annotated bibliography. Aug. 1933. 382p. (Supersedes no. 27)
51. Business and agriculture, 1920-1933; a partial bibliography of material on the interdependence of business and agriculture. Nov. 1933. 151p.
52. The American farm problem. April 1934. 13p.
53. State measures for the relief of agricultural indebtedness in the United States, 1933 and 1934. June 1934. 402p.
54. Measures of major importance enacted by the 73d Congress, March 9 to June 16, 1933 and January 3 to June 18, 1934. Nov. 1934. 55p.
55. List of periodicals containing prices and other statistical and economic information on fruits, vegetables and nuts. Jan. 1935. 238p.
56. Consumption of fruits and vegetables in the United States; an index to some sources of statistics. Jan. 1935. 125p.
57. Economic development of the cotton-textile industry in the United States, 1910-1935. Sept. 1935. 137p.
58. Price studies of the U. S. Department of Agriculture showing demand-price, supply-price, and price-production relationships. Oct. 1935. 38p.
60. Valuation of real estate, with special reference to farm real estate. Dec. 1935. 350p. (Supersedes no. 29)
61. Financing American cotton production and marketing in the United States. Nov. 1935. 45p.
62. Livestock financing in the United States; selected references to material published 1915-1935. Dec. 1935. 57p. (Supersedes no. 7)
63. Government control of cotton production in the United States, 1933-1935; a selected list of references. Jan. 1936. 59p.
64. Agricultural labor in the United States, 1915-1935; a selected list of references. Dec. 1935. 493p. (Supplemented by nos. 72 and 95)
65. Farm youth in the United States; a selected list of references to literature issued since October 1926. June 1936. 196p. (Supplements no. 17)
66. Measures of major importance enacted by the 74th Congress, January 3 to August 26, 1935 and January 3 to June 20, 1936. July 1936. 209p.
67. Crop and livestock insurance; a selected list of references to literature issued since 1898. Nov. 1936. 264p.
68. Incidence of the processing taxes under the Agricultural Adjustment Act; a selected list of references. Jan. 1937. 46p.
69. Large scale and corporation farming; a selected list of references. April 1937. 121p. (Supplements no. 30; supersedes no. 46)
70. Farm tenancy in the United States, 1918-1936; a selected list of references. June 1937. 302p. (Supersedes no. 59; supplemented by no. 85)
71. List of periodicals containing prices and other statistical and economic information on dairy products. Oct. 1937. 114p.
72. Agricultural labor in the United States, 1936-1937; a selected list of references. March 1938. 205p. (Supplements no. 64; supplemented by no. 95)
73. Income; selected references on the concept of income and methods of obtaining income statistics. May 1938. 48p.
74. The soybean industry; a selected list of references on the economic aspects of the industry in the United States, 1900-1938. Oct. 1938. 474p.
75. The tobacco industry; a selected list of references on the economic aspects of the industry, 1932 - June 1938. Sept. 1938. 337p.
76. Agricultural relief measures relating to the raising of farm prices - 75th Congress, January 5, 1937 to June 16, 1938. Feb. 1939. 109p.
77. Part-time farming in the United States; a selected list of references. Feb. 1939. 272p. (Supersedes no. 43)
78. Rural psychology; a partial list of references. March 1939. 76p.

79. Price fixing by government in the United States, 1926-1939; a selected list of references on direct price fixing of agricultural products by the Federal and State governments. July 1939. 214p. (See also no. 18 and no. 86)
80. The peanut industry; a selected list of references on the economic aspects of the industry, 1920-1939. Nov. 1939. 238p.
81. Transportation of agricultural products in the United States, 1920-June 1939; a selected list of references relating to the various phases of railway, motor, and water carrier transportation. Part I. General transportation and transportation of agricultural products. November 1939; Part II. Highway, rail, and water transportation. November 1939; Part III. Index to Parts I and II. Nov. 1939. 812p.
82. The world food supply; a partial list of references, 1925-1939. Dec. 1939. 164p.
83. Land classification; a selected bibliography. March 1940. 95p.
84. Agricultural relief measures relating to the raising of farm prices - 74th Congress, January 3, 1935 to June 20, 1936. April 1940. 75p.
85. Farm tenancy in the United States, 1937-1939; a selected list of references, April 1940. 160p. (Supplements no. 70)
86. Price fixing by government in foreign countries, 1926-1939; a selected list of references on direct price fixing of agricultural products by foreign governments. July 1940. 631p. (See also no. 18 and no. 79)
87. Corn in the development of the civilization of the Americas; a selected and annotated bibliography. Sept. 1940. 195p.
88. Cotton linters; selected references in English, 1900 - July 1940. Oct. 1940. 39p.
89. Anthropology and agriculture; selected references on agriculture in primitive cultures. Nov. 1940. 134p.
90. The sampling method in social and economic research; a partial list of references. Jan. 1941. 155p.
91. Uses for cotton; selected references in the English language, 1933 - July 1940. Feb. 1941. 129p. (Supplements no. 44)
92. Agricultural relief measures relating to the raising of farm prices - 73d Congress, March 9, 1933 to June 18, 1934. Sept. 1941. 80p.
93. War and agriculture in the United States, 1914-1941; selected references. Jan. 1942. 43p.
94. Tax delinquency on rural real estate, 1928-1941; selected references. Jan. 1942. 314p.
95. Agricultural labor in the United States, 1938-June 1941; a selected list of references. Feb. 1942. 268p. (Supplements nos. 64 and 72)
96. Distribution of farm income by size; a selected bibliography. Feb. 1942. 103p.
97. The dairy industry in the United States, 1940-1941; selected references on the economic aspects of the industry. Feb. 1942. 133p. (Supplements Economic library list no. 11)

2627. U. S. Dept. of Agriculture Library. Agricultural economics literature. Wash., 1927-42. v. 1-16.
Continued by Bibliography of agriculture.

2628. U. S. Dept. of Agriculture Library. Economic library lists. Wash., 1939-41. No. 1-28.

1. State trade barriers; selected references, rev. ed. June 1940. 60p.
2. The frozen food industry; selected references, January 1937 to March 1939. April 1939. 14p.
3. High drafting in cotton spinning; selected references. April 1939. 12p.
4. Egg auctions; selected references. July 1939. 20p.
5. Acts administered by Agricultural Marketing Service. Oct. 1939. 9p.
6. Periodicals relating to shipping. Oct. 1939. 14p.
7. Electrical properties of cotton; some references to the literature, 1931-date. Nov. 1939. 3p.
8. Sea Island cotton; selected references. Nov. 1939. 13p.
9. Cotton picking machinery; a short list of references. March 1940. 19p.
10. The tomato industry in Puerto Rico and

Cuba; a short list of references. June 1940. 12p.

11. The dairy industry in the United States; selected references on the economic aspects of the industry. July 1940. 59p. (Supplemented by Agricultural economics bibliography, no. 97)

12. Planning for the farmer; a short reading list of free and inexpensive material. July 1940. 5p.

13. Indirect flood damages; a list of references. August 1940. 16p.

14. Relocation of farm families; selected references on settler relocation. Sept. 1940. 46p.

15. Homestead tax exemption in the United States; a selected list of references. Oct. 1940. 23p.

16. Maté; a list of references. Oct. 1940. 9p.

17. Exhibits; a selected list of references. Nov. 1940. 12p.

18. Food and cotton stamp plans; a selected list of references. Nov. 1940. 26p.

19. The banana industry in tropical America with special reference to the Caribbean area, 1930-1940; a selected list of references. Jan. 1941. 30p.

20. The sunflower, its cultivation and uses; a selected list of references. April 1941. 18p.

21. Delta County, Colorado; a selected list of references. April 1941. 13p.

22. Relation of environmental factors to cotton fiber length; selected references in English, 1915-1939. April 1941. 12p.

23. Almonds; selected references on the industry, 1929 to 1940. May 1941. 13p.

24. Crop and livestock insurance, 1937-1940; a selected list of references. June 1941. 38p.

25. Imperial County, California; a selected list of references. June 1941. 77p.

26. Economic aspects of farm tractor operation; selected references, 1935-March 1941. June 1941. 52p.

27. Leake and Union counties, Mississippi; a selected list of references. June 1941. 15p.

28. Okfuskee County, Oklahoma; a selected list of references. June 1941. 13p.

2629. U. S. Dept. of Agriculture Library. Farmers' response to prices. Wash., 1933. 26p.

2630. U. S. Dept. of Agriculture Library. Food control during forty-six centuries. Wash., 1922. 20p.

2631. U. S. Dept. of Agriculture Library. Freight rates and agriculture. Wash., 1927. 36p.

2632. U. S. Dept. of Agriculture Library. Long-time agricultural programs in the U. S. Wash., 1927. 21p.

2633. U. S. Dept. of Agriculture Library. Meat industry in the U. S. Wash., 1928. 24p.

2634. U. S. Library of Congress, Legislative Reference Service. Agriculture in a war economy (April 1941 - March 1942); selected and annotated bibliography on agricultural problems and policies in a wartime economy. Wash., 1942. 81p.

Animal culture

2635. Homsher, Lola M. "The Wyoming Stock Growers' Association records in University of Wyoming Library." Mississippi Valley historical review, 33 (Sept. 1946), 279-88.

2636. Kahn, Herman. "Records in the National Archives relating to the range cattle industry, 1865-1895." Agricultural history, 20 (1946), 187-90.

2637. New York Public Library. "List of works in the New York Public Library relating to fishing and fish culture." New York Public Library bulletin, 13 (1909), 259-307. Reprinted. 49p.

2638. William and Mary College Library. The Peter Chapin collection of books on dogs; a short-title list, by Howard M. Chapin. Williamsburg, Va., 1938. 131p. (College of William and Mary bulletin, v. 32, no. 7, Nov. 1938).
    Lists 1,993 titles.

2639. Wisconsin, University, College of Agriculture Library. A list of the publications on apiculture contained in the Dr. Charles C. Miller Memorial Apicultural Library. Madison, Wis., 1936. 283p.

Plant culture

2640. Arents, George. Books, manuscripts and drawings relating to tobacco... on exhibition at the Library of Congress. [Wash.: Govt. Print. Off., 1938] 113p.
Collection now in New York Public Library.

2641. Arents, George. "Early literature of tobacco." South Atlantic quarterly. 37 (April 1938), 97-107. N. Y.: Priv. print., for the Lib. of Congress, 1938. 13p.
Collection described now in New York Public Library.

2642. Brooks, Jerome E., ed. Tobacco; its history illustrated by the books, manuscripts, and engravings in the library of George Arents, Jr. N. Y.: Rosenbach Co., 1937-46. 5v.
Catalog of collection now in New York Public Library.

2643. New York Public Library. "Gardens & gardening; a selected list of books... to accompany an exhibition of garden books." New York Public Library bulletin, 31 (1927), 163-77, 384-410. Reprinted. 48p.

2644. Pan American Union, Columbus Memorial Library. Selected bibliography on tobacco, comp. by W. W. Garner. Wash.: The Union, 1933. 25 numb. l.

2645. Potter, Alfred C. "Some early books on tobacco." Harvard Library notes, 3 (1936), 101-18.
In Harvard College Library.

2646. San Bernardino Free Public Library. Citrus fruits and their culture. San Bernardino, Calif., 1913. [24]p.
Bibliography of special collection of literature on citrus fruits in San Bernardino Public Library.

2647. Seattle Public Library. Bibliography on soy beans. [Seattle, 1932?] 46 numb. l.
"Includes material... published from 1890 to 1931, with the exception of (1) patent literature, (2) material on the agricultural phases of the subject."

2648. U. S. Dept. of Agriculture Library. Cotton literature; selected references. Wash., 1931-42. 12v.
Continued by Bibliography of agriculture.

2649. U. S. Dept. of Agriculture Library. Plant science literature. [Wash., 1935-42] 15v.
Preceded by Botany current literature and Agronomy current literature; superseded by Bibliography of agriculture, section D, plant science.

2650. U. S. Library of Congress, General Reference and Bibliography Division. "Date production in the United States: a selected list of references," comp. by Elizabeth A. Gardner. Wash., Feb. 1, 1946. 11p. Typed.

Forestry

2651. Carnegie Library of Pittsburgh. Trees and forestry; a selected list of the more important books in the Library. Pittsburgh: The Library, 1917. 18p. (Reprinted from its Monthly bulletin, May 1917.)

2652. Historical Records Survey - Fla. A list of the materials in the Austin Cary memorial forestry collection in the University of Florida. Tallahassee: Florida Historical Records Survey, 1941. 47p.
Material on forestry and conservation.

2653. Minnesota Historical Society, Forest Products History Foundation. Preliminary inventory of manuscript material dealing with the history of the forest products industry. [St. Paul, 1947] 24p.
A union list, by states, of collections in various depositories.

2654. Pinkett, Harold T. "Records of research units of the United States Forest Service in the National Archives." Journal of forestry, 45 (1947), 272-75.

2655. U. S. Dept. of Agriculture Library. Effects of fire on forests; a bibliography. Wash., 1938. 130p.

2656. U. S. Dept. of Agriculture Library. Farm forestry; a list of references. Wash., 1938. 26p.

2657. U. S. Dept. of Agriculture Library. Forest recreation; a bibliography. Wash., 1938. 129p.

2658. U. S. Dept. of Agriculture Library. Forestry; some books and bulletins in English; a bibliography. 2d ed. Wash., 1937. 26p.

2659. U. S. Forest Service. Shelterbelts for the prairies; an annotated bibliography of the more important references. 1943. Wash., 1943. 21p.

2660. U. S. Forest Service Library. Cooperative marketing of forest products; a bibliography. Wash., 1939. 22p.

2661. U. S. Forest Service Library. Forestry current literature; an index of books and periodicals on forestry and related subjects received in the Forest Service Library. Wash., 1910-1940.
  Superseded by Bibliography of agriculture. Section E. Forestry.

2662. U. S. Forest Service Library. Precipitation and climate, particularly as they affect the western states. A bibliography. [Wash.] 1935. 16p.

2663. U. S. Forest Service Library. A union check list of forestry serials. [Wash., 1936.] 146p.

2664. U. S. Library of Congress, Division of Bibliography. A selected list of recent references on the lumber industry of the United States and Canada, comp. by Florence S. Hellman. Wash., May 16, 1939. 34p.

2665. U. S. National Archives. Preliminary inventory of the records of the Forest Service, comp. by Harold T. Pinkett. Wash., 1949. 17p. (Preliminary inventory, no. 18)

Soil conservation

2666. Carnegie Library of Pittsburgh. "Bibliography of physical properties and bearing value of soils." American Society of Civil Engineers proceedings, 43 (1917), 1192-1240. "Supplement," comp. by Morris Schrero. American Society of Civil Engineers proceedings, 57 (1931), 871-921.
  References are to items in Carnegie Library of Pittsburgh.

2667. U. S. Dept. of Agriculture Library. Soil conservation bibliographies. Wash., 1940-42. No. 1-4.

  1. Wind erosion and sand dune control; a selected list of references. June 1940. 66p.
  2. Personnel administration and personnel training, selected list of references. August 1940. 59p.
  3. Infiltration of water into the soil. Oct. 1940. 76p.
  4. Guayule; a list of references. 1942. 53p.

2668. U. S. Dept. of Agriculture Library. Soil conservation literature. March-April, 1937 - May-June, 1942. Wash., 1937-42. 6v.
  Continued in Bibliography of agriculture.

2669. U. S. Dept. of Agriculture Library. Soil conservation service library lists. Wash., 1941. 2 nos.

  1. Orchard erosion control. 1941. 8p.
  2. Economic and social aspects of soil conservation. 1941. 24p.

2670. U. S. Library of Congress, Division of Bibliography. A list of references on the United States Civilian Conservation Corps, comp. by Ann Duncan Brown. [Wash.] 1936. 26p.
  Contains 365 references.

2671. U. S. National Archives. Preliminary inventory of the records of the Civilian Conservation Corps, comp. by Harold T. Pinkett. Wash., 1948. 16p. (Preliminary inventory, no. 11)

2672. U. S. National Archives. Record group 114. Records of Soil Conservation Service; Preliminary check list of records of Soil Conservation Service 1928-42, comp. by Guy A. Lee and Freeland F. Penney. Wash., 1947. 45p.

2673. Yenawine, Wayne S. "Civilian Conservation Corps camp papers; a check list of papers published before July 1, 1937." Urbana, 1938. 385 numb. l. Typewritten thesis.
  Locates holdings only in University of Illinois Library.

BUSINESS

General

2674. Cole, Arthur H. "The Business School

Library and its setting." Harvard Library bulletin, 1 (1947), 332-38.
In Harvard University.

2675. Cole, Arthur H. "Corporation material in the Business School Library." Harvard University Library notes, 4 (1941), 46-53.
In Harvard University.

2676. Dartmouth College, Amos Tuck School of Business Administration. Reading list on business administration. 5th rev. ed. Hanover, N. H.: The College, 1947. 59p.

2677. Eaton, Charles C. "The corporations collection." Harvard Business School Alumni Association bulletin, 6 (1930), 99-101.
In Harvard Graduate School of Business Administration.

2678. Engineering Societies Library. Filing systems for engineering offices; a selected list of references. N. Y.: The Library, 1948. 6p. (Engineering Societies Library bibliographies, no. 1)

2679. Harvard University, Graduate School of Business Administration, Baker Library. "The C. A. Moore donation." Business Historical Society bulletin, (Sept. 1926), 3-8.
Describes collection of 50,000 books, 20,000 pamphlets, in Baker Library, Harvard University.

2680. Harvard University, Graduate School of Business Administration, Baker Library. "Collection of photographs of contemporary business leaders." Business Historical Society bulletin, 9 (1935), 47-48, 64-66, 81-82, 98.
In Baker Library, Harvard University.

2681. Harvard University, Graduate School of Business Administration, Baker Library. The growth of the Baker Library. Boston: Harvard Graduate School of Business Administration, [1940] 8p.
Harvard Graduate School of Business Administration.

2682. Harvard University, Graduate School of Business Administration, Baker Library. A guide to Baker Library. Cambridge, 1931. 16p.
In Harvard Graduate School of Business Administration.

2683. Harvard University, Graduate School of Business Administration, Baker Library. "Special collections of the Business Library." Harvard alumni bulletin, 26 (1924), 465-66.

2684. John Crerar Library. Time and motion study, 1933-1939, comp. by Constance A. Strandel. Chicago, 1940. 31p. (Reference list 46)

2685. Kehl, Mary Margaret. Union list of services in thirty-four libraries in Manhattan. N. Y.: Special Libraries Association, 1934. 12 numb. l.
A list of 118 business services with brief descriptive notes.

2686. Meixell, Granville. The trade catalog collection; a manual with source lists. N. Y.: Special Libraries Association, 1934. 53 numb. l.
Describes Columbia University collection.

2687. Meyer, Herman Henry Bernard, comp. List of references on scientific management as the basis of efficiency, with special reference to the government service. Wash.: Govt. Print. Off., 1920. 22p.
Library of Congress call numbers listed.

2688. New York Public Library. "Scientific management; a list of references in the New York Public Library," comp. by Walter Vail Brown. New York Public Library bulletin, 21 (1917), 19-43, 83-136. Reprinted. 81p.

2689. New York Public Library. "Shorthand books in the New York Public Library," comp. by Karl Brown and D. C. Haskell. New York Public Library bulletin, 36 (1932), 243-49, 439-57, 521-30, 562-86, 646-52, 703-20, 779-86, 842-49; 37 (1933), 69-76, 148-56, 223-35, 311-24, 526-38, 633-44, 699-714, 800-21, 902-26, 991-1006, 1069-1076; 38 (1934), 24-55, 115-42, 183-207, 281-96, 475-512, 563-96, 647-94, 746-95, 866-96. Reprinted, with additions and corrections, 1935. 644p.

2690. Newark Free Public Library. Business books: 1920-1926; an analytical catalog of 2600 titles. N. Y.: H. W. Wilson Co., 1927. 592p.
"Supp. to '2400 business books and guide to business literature, 1920.'" Based on Newark Free Public Library collection.

2691. Newark Free Public Library. 2400 business books, and guide to business literature, by Linda N. Morley and Adelaide C. Kight. 3d ed. N. Y.: H. W. Wilson Co., 1920. 456p.

Based on Newark Free Public Library collection.

2692. Special Libraries Association, Illinois Chapter. "List of service holdings in special libraries in Chicago area." Illinois libraries, 31 (1949), 461-89.

Lists business services and similar publications held by 90 libraries.

2693. U. S. Dept. of Labor Library. Seniority in industrial relations: a selected list of references, comp. by Laura A. Thompson. Wash., 1944. 21p. Supplementary list of references. [Wash., 1944] 1p.

2694. U. S. Dept. of Labor Library. Seniority in promotion and discharge: a list of references. Wash., 1939. 8p.

Revision of 1938 list.

2695. U. S. Library of Congress, Division of Bibliography. Bibliography on standardization. Wash.: Govt. Print. Off., 1932. 19p. (U. S. Bureau of Standards, Miscellaneous publications, no. 136)

2696. U. S. Library of Congress, Division of Bibliography. Instalment plan: a selected list of references, comp. by Anne L. Baden. [Wash.] 1941. 41p.

2697. U. S. Library of Congress, Legislative Reference Service. Small business bibliography. Wash.: Govt. Print. Off., 1941. 49p. (77th Cong., 1st sess. Senate Committee print no. 4)

History

2698. Ayres, Frank C. "The Business Historical Society, Inc." Harvard Business School Alumni Association bulletin, 5 (1929), 197-98.

Describes some of collections deposited by Society in Baker Library, Harvard University.

2699. Barck, Dorothy C. "New York Historical Society." Business Historical Society bulletin, 8 (Jan. 1934), 1-5.

Describes materials on business history held by the New York Historical Society.

2700. Business Historical Society bulletin, 1 (1926), to date.

Numerous short articles and lists descriptive of materials relating to business history, chiefly in Baker Library, Graduate School of Business Administration, Harvard University.

2701. Cole, Arthur H. "Acquisition of material from the Poor Publishing Company." Business Historical Society bulletin, 16 (1942), 83-84.

Extensive papers of Poor Publishing Company, Wellesley Hills, Mass.; presented to Harvard Graduate School of Business Administration.

2702. Cole, Arthur H. "Business manuscripts: collection, handling, and cataloguing." Library quarterly, 8 (1938), 93-113.

A paper based on collections and procedures of Baker Library, Harvard Graduate School of Business Administration.

2703. Cole, Arthur H. "Early days of the Business School Library." Harvard Library notes, 3 (1939), 270-77.

In Harvard University.

2704. Cole, Arthur H. "Kress library of business and economics." Harvard Library notes, 3 (1940), 316-19.

In Baker Library, Harvard University.

2705. [Cole, Arthur H.] Kress Library of Business and Economics 1938 - 1949. Boston: Harvard Graduate School of Business Administration, [1950]. 8p.

In Harvard Graduate School of Business Administration.

2706. Corning, Howard. "The collections of the Business Historical Society at the Baker Library." Harvard alumni bulletin, 31 (1929), 564-69.

In Harvard University.

2707. Corning, Howard. "The Essex Institute of Salem." Business Historical Society bulletin, 7 (Oct. 1933), 1-5.

Survey of materials in the Institute for research in business history.

2708. Eckler, Albert R. "Collection of company records in Baker Library." Harvard Business School Association bulletin, 11 (1935), 192-93.

2709. Field, Alston G. "The collection of business records in western Pennsylvania." Business Historical Society bulletin, 8 (June 1934), 57-63.

Describes collections deposited in Historical Society of Pennsylvania.

2710. Garrison, Curtis W. "Economic material in the Pennsylvania archives and other depositories." Business Historical Society bulletin, 8 (Dec. 1934), 97-101.

Chiefly a brief description of early 19th century records on business and economic history, deposited in State Library of Pennsylvania.

2711. Glidden, Sophia H. "Silks, velvets and spices." Business Historical Society bulletin, 2 (January, 1928), 8-12.

Papers of Israel Thorndike, in Baker Library, Harvard University.

2712. Harvard University, Graduate School of Business Administration, Baker Library. "The Aldrich Library." Harvard alumni bulletin, 30 (1927), 285.

In Harvard Graduate School of Business Administration.

2713. Harvard University, Graduate School of Business Administration, Baker Library. "The Baldwin collection." Business Historical Society bulletin, 5 (May 1931), 1-5.

Loammi Baldwin papers, in Baker Library, Harvard University.

2714. Harvard University, Graduate School of Business Administration, Baker Library. "The Barberini collection of the Business Historical Society." Harvard alumni bulletin, 32 (1929), 62-66.

In Baker Library, Harvard University.

2715. Harvard University, Graduate School of Business Administration, Baker Library. "Business letters from the Apache country." Business Historical Society bulletin, 3 (February, 1929), 1-6.

Records of Bigelow, Kennard and Company, Boston, in Baker Library, Harvard University.

2716. Harvard University, Graduate School of Business Administration, Baker Library. "The business manuscripts in Baker Library." Harvard Business School Alumni Association bulletin, 9 (1933), 119-21.

In Harvard University.

2717. Harvard University, Graduate School of Business Administration, Baker Library. "Business papers of a great Roman family." Business Historical Society bulletin, 3 (Sept. 1929), 1-9.

Description of 87 volumes of account books and other business records, 1618-1816, of Barberini and Sciarra-Colonna families.

2718. Harvard University, Graduate School of Business Administration, Baker Library. "The flowing bowl." Business Historical Society bulletin, 2 (November, 1928), 1-7.

George C. Dempsey collection, on history of liquor, in Baker Library, Harvard University.

2719. Harvard University, Graduate School of Business Administration, Baker Library. The Kress Library of Business and Economics. Catalogue, covering material published through 1776, with data upon cognate items in other Harvard libraries. Boston: Baker Library [1940] 414p.

2720. Harvard University, Graduate School of Business Administration, Baker Library. List of business manuscripts in Baker Library, prep. by Margaret R. Cusick. Boston: The Library, 1932. 112p.

Lists and describes 508 collections.

2721. Harvard University, Graduate School of Business Administration, Baker Library. "Medici manuscripts." Harvard Business School Alumni Association bulletin, 4 (1927), 7-8.

In Baker Library, Harvard University.

2722. Harvard University, Graduate School of Business Administration, Baker Library. "The motion picture industry." Business Historical Society bulletin, 4 (October, 1930), 1-4.

Documents of firm of Raff & Gammon, in Baker Library, Harvard University.

2723. Harvard University, Graduate School of Business Administration, Baker Library. "New England's business history." Business Historical Society bulletin, 4 (November, 1930), 1-5.

Source materials in Baker Library, Harvard University.

2724. Harvard University, Graduate School of Business Administration, Baker Library. "Original manuscripts of the Medici." Business Historical Society bulletin, 1 (November, 1927), 1-6.
In Baker Library, Harvard University.

2725. Harvard University, Graduate School of Business Administration, Baker Library. "A record of colonial craftsmanship." Business Historical Society bulletin, 2 (March, 1928), 1-9.
Manning collection of American craftsmanship, in Baker Library, Harvard University.

2726. Harvard University, Graduate School of Business Administration, Baker Library. "A unique library acquisition." Harvard alumni bulletin, 27 (1924), 133-35.
Briggs-Stabler papers, 1800-40, relating to surveying along frontiers, canals, railroads; in Baker Library, Harvard University. See also Business Historical Society bulletin, 6 (May 1932), 6-12; 6 (Nov. 1932), 6-13; 7 (Jan. 1933), 1-5.

2727. Harvard University, Graduate School of Business Administration, Kress Library of Business and Economics. The Kress Library of Business and Economics, founded upon the collection of books made by Herbert Somerton Foxwell. Boston: Baker Library, Harvard Graduate School of Business Administration, 1939. 53p. (The Kress Library of Business and Economics publication, no. 1)
Describes collection of early economic and business literature in Baker Library.

2728. Hedges, James Blaine. "The Brown papers; the record of a Rhode Island business family." American Antiquarian Society proceedings, 51 (1942), 21-36.
One collection of Brown papers is in John Carter Brown Library; another is in library of Rhode Island Historical Society.

2729. Hidy, Muriel E. "The George Peabody papers." Business Historical Society bulletin, 12 (1938), 1-6.
Business papers, 1830-57, in Essex Institute, Salem, Mass.

2730. Historical Records Survey, Ohio. Inventory of business records, The D. Connelly Boiler Company. The J. B. Savage Company. Cleveland, Ohio, 1941. 104p.

A steam boiler and a printing business whose records are in the collections of Western Reserve University.

2731. Hussey, Miriam. "Business manuscripts in the library of the Historical Society of Pennsylvania." Business Historical Society bulletin, 10 (June 1936), 48-51.
Description of records of particular interest for Philadelphia business history of all periods.

2732. Johansen, Dorothy O. "The Simeon G. Reed collection of letters and private papers." Pacific Northwest quarterly, 27 (1936), 54-65.
Describes and classifies letters, papers and records now in Reed College Library. "Basic materials for economic studies of the development of the Pacific Northwest in... transportation, industry and agriculture."

2733. Johnson, Edgar A. J. "The Kress Library of Business and Economics." Harvard alumni bulletin, 41 (1938), 219-23.
In Harvard Graduate School of Business Administration.

2734. Larsen, Henrietta M. "The records of a flour milling firm of Rochester, New York." Business Historical Society bulletin, 11 (1937), 108-10.
Records of Moseley and Motley, a firm founded in mid-19th century; in Baker Library, Harvard University.

2735. Loehr, Rodney C. "Business history material in the Minnesota Historical Society." Business Historical Society bulletin, 14 (Feb. 1940), 21-28.
Description of archival and manuscript records chiefly relating to Minnesota.

2736. Pennsylvania, University, Wharton School of Finance and Commerce, Industrial Research Department. The Wetherill papers, 1762-1899; being the collection of business records of the store and white lead works founded by Samuel Wetherill in the late eighteenth century, by Miriam Hussey. Philadelphia: Univ. of Pennsylvania, Industrial Research Dept., 1942. 121p.

2737. Perry, Josepha M. "Samuel Snow, tanner and cordwainer." Business Historical Society bulletin, 19 (1945), 183-95.
Records of Samuel Snow, of North Berwick, Me., in Baker Library, Harvard University.

2738. Pike, Charles B. "Chicago Historical Society." Business Historical Society bulletin, 8 (May 1934), 37-41.

Describes some collections of interest for business history in Chicago Historical Society.

2739. Quenzel, Carrol H. "West Virginia University collection of historical manuscripts." Business Historical Society bulletin, 8 (Mar. 1934), 21-23.

Describes resources for business research.

2740. "Records of a universal science." Business Historical Society bulletin, 3 (1929), 6-14.

Description of Dale library of weights and measures now in Columbia University.

2741. Thompson, R. T. "Colonel Neilson: salt merchant." Rutgers University Library journal, 1 (Dec. 1937), 11-16.

Description of collection of Neilson papers deposited in Rutgers University Library.

2742. Vail, R. W. G. "The American Antiquarian Society." Business Historical Society bulletin, 7 (Dec. 1933), 1-5.

Survey of American Antiquarian Society's materials for business history.

2743. Virginia, University, Library. "A check list of bound business records in the manuscript collections of the Alderman Library, University of Virginia," comp. by Francis L. Berkeley, Jr. University of Virginia Library annual report on historical collections, no. 8 (1937-38). 17-45.

Lists ledgers and similar manuscripts for about 50 Virginia counties, arranged by counties.

2744. Withington, Mary C. "The Nathaniel and Thomas Shaw papers." Yale University Library gazette, 1 (1927), 47-52.

Account books, ledgers, and letters of New London, Conn., merchants, now in Yale University Library.

Transportation

2745. Bureau of Railway Economics Library. A proposed department of transportation - a bibliographical memorandum, prep. by Douglas R. Stephenson. [Wash., 1946] 12 numb. l.

2746. Haines, Donal Hamilton. The transportation library of the University of Michigan; its history and needs. Ann Arbor, Mich., 1929. 14p.

2747. Harvard University, Graduate School of Business Administration, Baker Library. "The Joseph P. Day gift." Business Historical Society bulletin, 1 (Dec. 1926), 15-16.

Pamphlets on United States transportation, in Baker Library, Harvard University.

2748. Historical Records Survey. Calendar of the Stevens family papers, Lieb Memorial Library, Stevens Institute of Technology, Hoboken, New Jersey. Newark: Historical Records Survey, 1940-41. 3v.

Papers cover period from 1664 to 1777, and relate chiefly to development of transportation in the United States.

2749. Historical Records Survey. Ship registers and enrollments of Boston and Charlestown: v. 1, 1789-1795. Boston: National Archives Project, 1942. 248p.

2750. Historical Records Survey. Ship registers and enrollments of Bristol-Warren, Rhode Island, 1773-1939. Providence: National Archives Project, 1941. 435p.

2751. Historical Records Survey. Ship registers and enrollments of Machias, Maine, 1780-1930. Rockland: National Archives Project, 1942. 2v.

2752. Historical Records Survey. Ship registers and enrollments of New Orleans. University: Hill Memorial Library, Louisiana State Univ., 1941-42. 6v.

2753. Historical Records Survey. Ship registers and enrollments of Newport, Rhode Island, 1790-1939. Providence: National Archives Project, 1938-41. 2v.

2754. Historical Records Survey. Ship registers and enrollments of Providence, Rhode Island, 1773-1939. Providence: National Archives Project, 1941. 2v.

2755. Historical Records Survey. Ship registers and enrollments Saco, Maine, 1791-1915. Rockland, Me. National Archives Project, 1942. 108 l.

2756. Historical Records Survey. Ship registers and enrollments port of Marshfield, Oregon, 1873-1941. Portland, 1942. 78 l.

2757. Historical Records Survey. Ship registers and enrollments port of Portland, Oregon, 1867-1941. Portland, 1942. 280 l.

2758. Historical Records Survey. Ship registers of Dighton-Fall River, Massachusetts, 1789-1938. Boston: National Archives Project, 1939. 178 numb. l.

2759. Historical Records Survey. Ship registers of New Bedford, Massachusetts. Boston: National Archives Project, 1939-41. 3v.

2760. Historical Records Survey. Ship registers of Port of Philadelphia, Pennsylvania. Philadelphia, 1942. v. 1, A-D. 293p.

2761. Historical Records Survey. Ship registers of the District of Barnstable, Massachusetts, 1814-1913. Boston: The Survey, 1938. 173p.

2762. Historical Records Survey. Ship registers of the District of Plymouth, Massachusetts, 1789-1908. Boston: National Archives Project, 1939. 218p.

2763. Historical Records Survey. Ship registries and enrollments, port of Eureka, California, 1859-1920. San Francisco, 1941. 166 numb. l.

2764. Hitchcock, Jeannette M. "The Hopkins Transportation Library." College and research libraries, 2 (1940), 60-62, 75.
   General description of Stanford University's transportation library.

Accounting

2765. American Institute of Accountants. Accountants' index. A bibliography of accounting literature to December, 1920. [N. Y.]: American Institute of Accountants, 1921. 1,578p.
   "Supplements published from time to time." Materials listed are in Institute's library.

2766. American Institute of Accountants Library. Library catalogue, January 1919. [N. Y.: American Institute of Accountants, c. 1919.] 237p.

2767. American Telephone and Telegraph Company. Catalogue. Accounting library. N. Y.: American Telephone and Telegraph Comp., 1914. v. 1, 76p.
   No more published. A catalog of books, periodicals and pamphlets in Accounting Library of the Company.

2768. Bureau of Railway Economics Library. American railway accounting, a bibliography. Wash.: Railway Accounting Officers Association, 1926 - to date.
   An annual bibliography, reprinted from Railway accounting procedure.

2769. Bureau of Railway Economics Library. A list of references on American railway accounting. Wash., 1924. 159 numb. l.

2770. Columbia University Library. Exhibition of selected books and manuscripts from the Montgomery Library of Accountancy. [N. Y.]: Columbia University, 1937. 24p.

2771. Columbia University Library. The Montgomery Library of Accountancy: A check list of books, printed before 1850, in the Montgomery Library of Accountancy at Columbia University. N. Y.: Columbia Univ. Press, 1927-30. 2v.

2772. Hatfield, Henry R. and Littleton, A. C. "A check-list of early bookkeeping texts." Accounting review, 7 (1932), 194-206.
   Locates copies in American Institute of Accountants and in a private collection now owned by St. John's University.

Advertising, etc.

2773. Carnegie Library of Pittsburgh. Trade-names index; with definitions and sources from a card file in the Technology Department of the Carnegie Library of Pittsburgh, and a bibliography of sources of trade-names and trade-marks. N. Y.: Special Libraries Association, 1941. 178p.

2774. Harvard University, Graduate School of Business Administration, Baker Library. "A short history of trade cards." Business Historical Society bulletin, 5 (April, 1931), 1-6.
   Collections in Baker Library, Harvard University.

2775. Landauer, Bella C. Early American

trade cards from the collection of Bella C. Landauer. N. Y.: W. E. Rudge, 1927. 25p.
Now in New-York Historical Society.

2776. New York Public Library. Summary of patents and trade marks on file in the Patent Division. N. Y.: The Library, 1943. 7p.
Listed by country.

2777. U. S. Library of Congress, Division of Bibliography. "Containers and closures: a selected list of recent references," comp. by Anne L. Baden. Wash., Sept. 15, 1942. 34p. Typed.

2778. U. S. Library of Congress, Division of Bibliography. "Public relations: a selected list of references," comp. by Helen G. Dudenbostel. Wash., May 20, 1940. 34p. Typed. [Supplementary list] 1940-1943, comp. by Helen F. Conover. Jan. 18, 1944. 4p. Typed. [Supplementary list] 1944-1946. Feb. 27, 1947. 5p. Typed.

2779. U. S. Library of Congress, Division of Bibliography. Selected list of recent references on advertising including its economic and social effects, comp. by Anne L. Baden. Wash., May 9, 1940. 38p.

2780. U. S. Patent Office. Catalogue of the library of the Patent Office. Wash., 1878. 717p. Catalogue of additions. Wash., 1883. 452p.; 1889. 438p.

CHEMICAL TECHNOLOGY

2781. Carnegie Library of Pittsburgh. "Bibliography on decolorizing of glass," comp. by Morris Schrero and F. C. Flint. American Ceramic Society bulletin, 16 (1937), 236-46.
Material listed is in Technology Department, Carnegie Library of Pittsburgh.

2782. Carnegie Library of Pittsburgh. Books on the heat treatment of steel, comp. by E. H. McClelland. Pittsburgh: The Library, 1928. 12p. (Reprinted from Forging, stamping, heat treating, 13 (1927), 369-71)
Material available in Carnegie Library of Pittsburgh.

2783. Carnegie Library of Pittsburgh. Brick manufacture and brick laying; references to books and magazine articles. Pittsburgh: Carnegie Library, 1912. 33p. (Reprinted from its Monthly bulletin, Jan. 1912)

2784. Carnegie Library of Pittsburgh. By-product coking; references to books and magazine articles. Pittsburgh: The Library, 1915. 40p. (Reprinted from its Monthly bulletin, May 1915) Supplement, May 1915-June 1921. Pittsburgh: The Library, 1921. 18p.

2785. Carnegie Library of Pittsburgh. Case-hardening. Pittsburgh: Carnegie Library, 1918. 10p. (Reprinted from its Monthly bulletin, March 1918)

2786. Carnegie Library of Pittsburgh. Manganese steel, a bibliography, comp. by E. H. McClelland and Victor S. Polansky with preface by Sir Robert Hadfield. Pittsburgh: The Library, 1926. 60p. (Reprinted from Blast-furnace and steel plant, Dec. 1924, Aug. and Sept. 1926, and in part from Forging-stamping-heat treating, Feb. 1925)

2787. Carnegie Library of Pittsburgh. Pickling of iron and steel; a bibliography, comp. by Victor S. Polansky. Pittsburgh: The Library, 1924. 44p. (Reprinted from Blast-furnace and steel plant and Forging-stamping-heat treating, 1924.)

2788. Carnegie Library of Pittsburgh. "Pickling of iron and steel; a bibliography, revised," comp. by Victor S. Polansky. In: Imhoff, Wallace C. Pickling of iron and steel. Pittsburgh: Penton Pub. Co., 1929. p. 147-82.

2789. Carnegie Library of Pittsburgh. Stainless steel and stainless iron; a list of references to material in Carnegie Library of Pittsburgh, comp. by Victor S. Polansky. Pittsburgh: The Library, 1923. 21p.

2790. Carnegie Library of Pittsburgh, Technology Dept. Enamel bibliography and abstracts, 1928 to 1939, inclusive, with subject and co-author indexes; comp. by E. H. McClelland. Columbus, Ohio: American Ceramic Society, 1944. 352p.

2791. Carnegie Library of Pittsburgh, Technology Dept. Tin-plate manufacture, a bibliography, comp. by V. S. Polansky. Pittsburgh: The Library, 1941. 31p. (Reprinted from Blast-furnace and steel plant, Feb., April 1941.)

TECHNOLOGY

2792. Carnegie Library of Pittsburgh, Technology Dept. Zinc coating (hot galvanizing); a bibliography, comp. by Victor S. Polansky. Pittsburgh: The Library, 1936. 110p.

2793. Denver Public Library. A selected list of books on metals, compiled by Margery Bedinger. [Denver] 1943. 30p.

2794. Houghten, Mattie L., comp. List of books in Library of Congress on oil shale industry and development (periodical references not included). Wash.: Research Branch, Bureau of Ships, Navy Dept., 1945. 6 l. ([U. S.] Bureau of Ships. Technical literature research series, no. 35)

2795. John Crerar Library. A list of English, French and German periodicals on brewing, distillation, wine and other alcoholic beverages, comp. by Jerome K. Wilcox. Chicago, 1933. 9p. (Reference list 26)

2796. Massachusetts Institute of Technology Library. M.I.T. Library annual (1948), ed. by Vernon D. Tate and Margaret P. Hazen. Cambridge, Mass.: The Institute, 1949. 84p.

Includes descriptions of Arthur Rotch Memorial Library and Gaffield collection, pertaining to glass industry.

2797. New York Public Library. "Chemistry and manufacture of writing and printing inks; a list of references in the New York Public Library," comp. by William Burt Gamble. New York Public Library bulletin, 29 (1925), 579-91, 625-77, 706-41. Reprinted, 1926. 105p.

2798. New York Public Library. "Insulating oil (1900-1925); a list of references in the New York Public Library," comp. by Arthur W. Fyfe, Jr. New York Public Library bulletin, 30 (1926), 892-907, 935-88. Reprinted. 71p.

2799. New York Public Library. "List of works in the New York Public Library relating to ceramics and glass." New York Public Library bulletin, 12 (1908), 577-614. Reprinted. 38p.

2800. New York Public Library. "Starches, 1811-1925; a list of references dealing with the chemistry and technology of starches, dextrins, and amylases," comp. by Robert Walton. New York Public Library bulletin, 31 (1927), 12-34, 97-140, 178-221, 411-41, 464-523, 572-617, 639-90, 718-87. Reprinted. 160p.

Locates copies in 11 libraries outside New York Public Library.

2801. Pacific Coast Gas Association Library. Catalogue. [San Francisco] 1916. 109p.

2802. Sinclair Refining Company. Classified catalog, technical and general library. N. Y., 1939. 158p.

2803. Tulsa Public Library, Technical Dept. Petroleum bibliography. Tulsa, Okla., 1942-49. No. 1-31.

A list of books and references on petroleum in Tulsa Public Library.

2804. U. S. Library of Congress, Division of Bibliography. List of references on dyestuffs chemistry, manufacture, trade. Wash.: Govt. Print. Off., 1919. 186p.

2805. U. S. Library of Congress, Division of Bibliography. Select list of books, with references to periodicals, relating to iron and steel in commerce. Wash.: Govt. Print. Off., 1907. 24p.

2806. U. S. Library of Congress, Division of Bibliography. "A selected list of references on the copper industry 1914-1941," comp. by Helen F. Conover. Wash., July 22, 1941. 29p. Typed.

MANUFACTURES

2807. Associated Knit Underwear Manufacturers of America. References on the knit goods industry. Published by the Knit goods manufacturers of America, comp. by Bibliography Division of the Library of Congress. Utica, N. Y., 1920. 34p.

2808. Carnegie Library of Pittsburgh. "Chromium plating; a list of references," comp. by Victor S. Polansky. Brass world and platers' guide, 22 (1926), 272-73.

Material available in Carnegie Library of Pittsburgh.

2809. Carnegie Library of Pittsburgh. Electric driving in rolling-mills and foundries;

references to books and magazine articles. Pittsburgh: The Library, 1907. 15p. (Reprinted from its Monthly bulletin, Nov. 1907).

2810. Carnegie Library of Pittsburgh. Rolling-mill rolls, a bibliography, comp. by Victor S. Polansky. Pittsburgh: The Library, 1929. 59p. (Reprinted from Blast-furnace and steel plant, March-June 1929.)

2811. Carnegie Library of Pittsburgh. Seamless tubing; a bibliography, comp. by Victor S. Polansky. [Pittsburgh]: The Library, 1928. 78p. (Reprinted from Blast-furnace and steel plant, Feb.-April, Oct. 1927, May, July 1928.)

2812. Carnegie Library of Pittsburgh, Technology Dept. Iron and steel wire; a bibliography, comp. by Ralph H. Phelps. Pittsburgh: The Library, 1936. 68p.

2813. Clark, Frederick C. "Foreign paper trade periodicals. A list of American subscribers maintaining permanent files." Paper, 21 (Oct. 3, 1917), 90, 92, 94, 96, 98, 100.
Locates files in public and private collections.

2814. John Crerar Library. Bakelite, a bibliography, comp. by Jerome K. Wilcox. Chicago, 1931. 26p. (Reference list 10)

2815. John Crerar Library. Cellophane, a bibliography, comp. by Jerome K. Wilcox. Chicago, 1931. 12p. (Reference list 11)

2816. John Crerar Library. The state industrial and manufacturing directories; a bibliography, by Jerome K. Wilcox. Chicago, 1932. 15p. (Reference list, no. 21)

2817. Lincoln, Jonathan Thayer. "Material for a history of American textile machinery; the Kilburn-Lincoln papers." Journal of economic and business history, 4 (1932), 268-80.
In Baker Library, Harvard University.

2818. Meyer, Herman H. B., comp. "Paper manufacture; a bibliography." Paper trade journal, 72 (Mar. 24, 1921), 56-66; (Mar. 31), 50-58, 68; (Apr. 7), 48-60.
Based on Library of Congress collection.

2819. New York Public Library. "Hand-spinning and hand-weaving; a list of references in the New York Public Library," comp. by William Burt Gamble. New York Public Library bulletin, 26 (1922), 381-96, 499-521. Reprinted. 41p.

2820. New York Public Library. "List of works in the New York Public Library relating to electric welding," comp. by William Burt Gamble. New York Public Library bulletin, 17 (1913), 375-95. Reprinted. 23p.

2821. New York Public Library. "List of works in the New York Public Library relating to oxy-acetylene welding." New York Public Library bulletin, 18 (1914), 1049-78. Reprinted. 34p.

2822. New York Public Library. "List of works in the New York Public Library relating to the development and manufacture of typewriting machines," comp. by William Burt Gamble. New York Public Library bulletin, 17 (1913), 697-712. Reprinted. 18p.

2823. St. Louis Public Library. The shoe industry; a list of books and articles; comp. by Cecile Pajanovitch. [St. Louis]: The Library, 1923. 9p. (Reprinted from Monthly bulletin of the St. Louis Public Library, n. s., v. 21, no. 9, Sept. 1923.)

2824. U. S. Library of Congress, Division of Bibliography. "Bibliography on textile machinery," prep. by H. H. B. Meyer. In: U. S. Bureau of Foreign and Domestic Commerce. The cotton-spinning machinery industry. Wash.: Govt. Print. Off., 1916. P. 91-98. (Miscellaneous series, no. 37)

2825. U. S. Library of Congress, Division of Bibliography. "List of references on the cotton industry and trade." Wash., May 5, 1911. 42p. Typed. [Supplementary list] Dec. 13, 1916. 29p. Typed.

2826. U. S. Library of Congress, Division of Bibliography. Steel and the steel industry; a selected list of recent references, comp. by Anne L. Baden. [Wash.] 1942. 64p.

2827. U. S. Library of Congress, Legislative Reference Service. Synthetic and reclaimed rubber; a select and annotated list of references prepared for the Office for Emergency Management, by L. E. Beane. Wash., 1943. 53p. (War service bulletin, H-4)

2828 TECHNOLOGY

2828. U. S. National Archives. Inventory of the records of the Rubber Survey Committee, August - September 1942, comp. by Philip P. Brower. Wash., 1947. 21p. (Inventories of World War II records, no. 1)

BUILDING

2829. Portland Cement Association Library. Catalog of books, periodicals and pamphlets in the library of the Portland Cement Association. Chicago, 1918. 59p.

Fine Arts

GENERAL

2830. American Library Association, Art Reference Round Table. A union list of holdings of foreign art periodicals published 1939-46, comp. by Ruth E. Schoneman. Chicago, 1950. [44]p.

2831. Boston Museum of Fine Arts. Bibliographies of Indian art, by Amanda K. Coomaraswamy. Boston, 1925. 54p. ("Partly reprinted with additions from pts. 1, 2 and 4 of the Catalogue of the Indian collections in the Museum of Fine Arts.")
Most of the references are in the Library of the Museum of Fine Arts.

2832. Chicago Public Library Omnibus Project. Subject index to literature on Negro art, selected from the Union catalog of printed materials on the Negro in the Chicago libraries. Chicago: The Library, 1941. 49p.

2833. Denver Public Library. African Negro art; books of interest in connection with the exhibition of the Denver Art Museum on Art of Africa. Denver: The Library, 1945. 4p.

2834. Harvard University Library. Guides to the Harvard libraries, no. 2: Fine arts, by E. Louise Lucas. Cambridge: The Library, 1949. 54p.

2835. Henry E. Huntington Library. The art collections, a preliminary handbook of the art gallery and the Arabella D. Huntington memorial art collection. San Marino, 1940. 55p.

2836. Hispanic Society of America. Handbook, museum and library collections. N. Y., 1938. 442p. (Hispanic notes and monographs) Ch. 10, manuscript maps; ch. 11, prints; ch. 12, manuscripts and books.

2837. Hofer, Philip. "The Graphic Arts Department: an experiment in specialization." Harvard Library bulletin, 1 (1947), 252-53.
Description of Harvard College Library Department.

2838. Johnson, E. D. H. "Special collections at Princeton: V. The works of Thomas Rowlandson." Princeton University Library chronicle, 2 (Nov. 1940), 7-[20]
Survey of collection of prints, books illustrated by Rowlandson, and books about Rowlandson.

2839. Louisville Free Public Library. Catalog of art in the Louisville Free Public Library, paintings, statuary, etchings, prints, photographs, and bronze tablets. Louisville, 1928. 41p.

2840. Lucas, E. Louise. "A decade in the Fogg Museum Library." Harvard Library notes, 3 (1938), 195-97.
Description of Harvard University art library.

2841. Montignani, John Brommer. Books on Latin America and its art in the Metropolitan Museum of Art Library. N. Y., 1943. 63p.

2842. New York Public Library. "American art auction catalogues, 1785-1942; a union list," by A. Harold Lancour. New York Public Library bulletin, 47 (1943), 3-43, 99-110, 354-62, 395-416, 439-517, 635-54, 709-84, 896-921; 48 (1944), 157-226. Reprinted with revisions and additions, 1944. 377p.
Lists over 7,000 catalogs of art objects, with locations in 21 libraries.

FINE ARTS

2843. New York Public Library. "A checklist of the editions of Leonardo da Vinci's works in college and public libraries in the United States," comp. by Maureen Cobb Mabbott. New York Public Library bulletin, 38 (1934), 911-18. Reprinted. 10p.

Locates copies in 21 American and foreign libraries.

2844. New York Public Library. "Christ in art," by Frank Weitenkampf. New York Public Library bulletin, 24 (1920), 207-12. Reprinted. 8p.

Description of a collection of 20,000 pictures in New York Public Library.

2845. New York Public Library. "Pennsylvania Dutch folk art and architecture, a selective annotated bibliography," comp. by Saro John Riccardi. New York Public Library bulletin, 46 (1942), 471-83.

Lists 138 titles in New York Public Library.

2846. New York Society Library. A classified catalogue with critical notes of the works on art in the Green Alcove of the New York Society Library, selected and presented by Robert Lenox Kennedy. N. Y., 1879. 48p.

2847. Sheets, Marian L. "Library of anthropology, Denver Art Museum." Special Libraries, 36 (1945), 194-97.

Describes collection in Library of Department of Indian Art, Denver Art Museum.

2848. Smith, Robert Chester and Wilder, Elizabeth, eds. A guide to the art of Latin America. Wash.: [Govt. Print. Off.] 1948. 480p. ([U. S.] Library of Congress. Latin American series, no. 21)

In Library of Congress, unless otherwise located in one of 30 other libraries.

2849. Stohlman, W. Frederick. "Special collections at Princeton; I. The Marquand Art Library." Princeton University Library chronicle, 1 (1939), 9-[14]

Short sketch of history of growth of Marquand Art Library.

2850. U. S. Library of Congress. "Annual reports on acquisitions: Fine arts." Library of Congress quarterly journal of current acquisitions, 4 (Nov. 1946), 29-40.

2851. U. S. Library of Congress, Division of Bibliography. "List of references on pottery." Wash., Apr. 25, 1921. 10p. Typed. [Supplementary list] Oct. 18, 1938. 31p. Typed.

2852. U. S. Library of Congress, Hispanic Foundation. Bibliography of the fine arts in the other American republics. [Wash., 1941] 12p.

2853. U. S. Library of Congress, Hispanic Foundation. The fine and folk arts of the other American republics; a bibliography of publications in English. Wash., 1942. 18p.

2854. U. S. Library of Congress, Prints and Photographs Division. The colonial art of Latin American, a collection of slides and photographs, prep. by Robert C. Smith. Wash., 1945. 43p.

Includes bibliographies.

2855. Virginia State Library. "Finding list of books relating to music, fine arts and photography," comp. by Earl G. Swem. Virginia State Library bulletin, 5 (1912), 235-80.

LANDSCAPE ARCHITECTURE AND CITY PLANNING

2856. Boston Public Library. The Codman collection of books on landscape gardening. Also a list of books on trees and forestry. Boston: The Library, 1899. 26p. (Reprinted from the Boston Public Library's Monthly bulletin, 3 (1898), 371-85)

2857. Bullock, Helen D. "The personal and professional papers of Frederick Law Olmsted." Library of Congress quarterly journal of current acquisitions, 6 (Nov. 1948), 8-15.

Papers of a landscape architect and city planner, 30,000 items, for period from 1819 to 1923.

2858. Detroit Public Library. A list of references in the Detroit Public Library on Michigan's development, prepared for the Michigan State Planning Commission. [Detroit]: The Library, 1935. 73p.

2859. Hubbard, Mrs. Theodora (Kimball). Classified selected list of references on city planning. Boston: National Conference on

City Planning, 1915. 48p.
Locates copies in 5 libraries on the East Coast.

2860. Kimball, Theodora. "The library of the School of Landscape Architecture at Harvard University." Special libraries, 4 (1923), 165-68.

2861. Los Angeles Public Library, Municipal Reference Library. Planning for Los Angeles. 1945. 11 numb. 1. (Social adjustment bibliographies, no. 2)

2862. Manwaring, Elizabeth W. "A collection of books on English landscape gardening." Yale University Library gazette, 22 (1948), 81-86.
Brief description of books on English landscape gardening at Yale University and elsewhere.

2863. New York Public Library. "Check list of works on landscape gardening and parks in the New York Public Library." New York Public Library bulletin, 3 (1899), 506-17.

2864. New York Public Library. "Check list of works relating to parks, monuments, etc., in the City of New York in the New York Public Library." New York Public Library bulletin, 5 (1901), 163-66.

2865. New York Public Library. "Select list of works relating to city planning and allied subjects." New York Public Library bulletin, 17 (1913), 930-60. Reprinted. 35p.
List of about 600 classified titles.

2866. New York Public Library. "Selected list of references bearing on the city plan of New York." New York Public Library bulletin, 17 (1913), 396-408. Reprinted. 15p.

2867. New York Public Library. "Slum clearance in the United States; a selected reading list," comp. by Gilbert A. Cam. New York Public Library bulletin, 42 (1938), 551-60. Reprinted. 12p.

2868. New York Public Library. "War memorials; a list of references in the New York Public Library," comp. by Frank Weitenkampf. New York Public Library bulletin, 23 (1919), 499-506. Reprinted. 10p.

2869. Oregon State Library. City planning; a selective bibliography of material in the Oregon State Library. [Salem, 1934] 10p.

2870. St. Louis Public Library. National parks, national monuments and national forests; a selective list of books and articles. [St. Louis: The Library], 1931. 28p. (Reprinted from Monthly bulletin of the St. Louis Public Library, n. s., v. 29, no. 7, July 1931.)

2871. U. S. Library of Congress, Division of Bibliography. List of references on regional, city and town planning, with special reference to the Tennessee Valley project, comp. by Florence S. Hellman. [Wash.] 1933. 46p.

2872. U. S. National Resources Committee. Classified guide to material in the Library of Congress covering urban community development. Wash.: National Resources Committee, 1936. 102p.

2873. Walker, Ella K. "City planning; bibliography of material in the University of California and Oakland and Berkeley public libraries." Berkeley City Club civic bulletin, 2 (March 14, 1914), 117-52.

ARCHITECTURE

2874. "Archives of colonial architecture." American magazine of art, 21 (1930), 464-65.
Describes archives in Division of Fine Arts at Library of Congress, consisting of photographic records of American colonial architecture.

2875. Boston Public Library. Catalogue of books relating to architecture, construction and decoration in the Public Library of the City of Boston. 2d ed., with an additional section on city planning. Boston: The Library, 1914. 535p. (Subject catalogue, no. 10) First edition. 1894. 150p.

2876. Boston Public Library. An index to the pictures and plans of library buildings to be found in the Boston Public Library, by James Lyman Whitney. 2d, enl. ed. Boston: The Trustees, 1899. 31p. (Reprinted from the Library's Monthly bulletin, August 1899)

2877. Columbia University Library, Avery Architectural Library. Catalogue of the Avery

Architectural Library. A memorial library on architecture, archaeology, and decorative art. N. Y.: Columbia College Library, 1895. 1139p.

2878. Columbia University Library, Avery Architectural Library. House plan books prior to 1890 in the Avery Library, by Talbot F. Hamlin. N. Y.: Columbia University, 1938. 51p.

Arranged by country, with chronological index. A list of architectural books containing plans and elevations of houses, published as aids to the builder.

2879. Connecticut State Library. Connecticut houses: a list of manuscript histories. Hartford, 1942. 47 l. (Connecticut State Library bulletin, no. 17). Earlier editions in Connecticut State Library bulletin, no. 7 and 16, and in Report of the State Librarian for the two years ending June 30, 1930, p. 77-115.

2880. Cornell University Library. "Works relating to architecture in Cornell University Library." Cornell University Library bulletin, 1 (1882), 24-41.

2881. Curtis, Nathaniel Cortlandt. The Ricker Library; a familiar talk to students of architecture in the University of Illinois. Urbana: The University, 1920. 77p. (Univ. of Illinois bulletin, v. 12, no. 29)

"A list of general works on architecture selected from the catalogue of the Ricker Library..." p. 53-75, includes old and rare books.

2882. Detroit Public Library. Architecture, a list of books in the Detroit Public Library. [Detroit]: The Library, 1925. 72p.

2883. General Society of Mechanics and Tradesmen Library. Catalogue of the J. Morgan Slade Library and other architectural works in the Apprentices' Library. N. Y.: J. J. Little & Co., 1892. 24p.

2884. Hamlin, Talbot F. Greek revival architecture in America. N. Y.: Oxford Univ. Press, 1944.

Bibliography (p. 383-409) is based almost entirely on holdings of Avery Architectural Library, Columbia University.

2885. Henry E. Huntington Library. English eighteenth-century architecture: an exhibition, by William A. Parish. San Marino: The Library, 1941. 16p.

2886. Hitchcock, Henry Russell. American architectural books; a list of books, portfolios and pamphlets on architecture and related subjects published in America before 1895. 3d rev. ed. Minneapolis: Univ. of Minnesota Press, 1946. 130p.

Locates 1,461 editions in 131 libraries.

2887. John Crerar Library. The diorama; a bibliography, comp. by Jerome K. Wilcox. Chicago, 1933. 7p. (Reference list 25)

2888. Kimball, Fiske. "Some architectural designs of Benjamin Henry Latrobe." Library of Congress quarterly journal of current acquisitions, 3 (May, 1946), 8-13.

Describes collection of drawings, 1795-99, received by Library of Congress.

2889. National Society of the Colonial Dames of America - Connecticut. Connecticut houses, a list of manuscript histories of early Connecticut homes. Hartford: The State, 1931. 39p. (Conn. State Library bulletin, no. 16)

A list of 655 manuscript histories "permanently on deposit" in Connecticut State Library.

2890. Peabody Institute Library. Books on architecture, decoration and furniture in the library of the Peabody Institute. Baltimore, 1920. 23p.

2891. St. Louis Public Library. The old St. Louis riverfront; an exhibition of architectural studies in the historic area of the Jefferson National Expansion Memorial. [St. Louis? 1938] 19p.

2892. St. Louis Public Library. Selected titles from the Steedman collection of works on architecture and allied arts. [St. Louis: The Library] 1930. 8p. (Reprinted from Monthly bulletin of the St. Louis Public Library, n. s., v. 28, no. 7, July-Aug. 1930.)

2893. Smith, Edward Robinson. "Architectural books." Architectural review, 7 (1900), 113-17, 137-42; 8 (1901), 39-43, 99-102.

Description of important material in Avery Library, Columbia University.

2894. Smith, Edward Robinson. "The Henry

Ogden Avery architectural library of Columbia University, New York." Royal Institute of British Architects journal, ser. 3, 21 (1913-14), 497-512.

2895. Smith, Edward Robinson. "Special collections in American libraries: the Henry O. Avery Memorial Library of Architecture and Allied Arts, Columbia University." Library journal, 28 (1903), 277-85.

2896. U. S. Federal Housing Administration Library. Remodeling and modernization of urban dwellings, 1942-1946; a selected list of periodical references, comp. by Ruth L. Mushabac. Wash.: Federal Housing Administration, 1946. 12 numb. l.

2897. U. S. Library of Congress. Historic American Buildings Survey; catalog of the measured drawings and photographs of the survey in the Library of Congress, March 1, 1941. [Wash.: Govt. Print. Off., 1941] 470p.

2898. U. S. Library of Congress, Division of Bibliography. A list of recent references on community centers, comp. by Grace H. Fuller. Wash., Feb. 2, 1939. 19p.

2899. U. S. Library of Congress, Division of Bibliography. A list of recent references on housing with special reference to housing projects and slum clearance, comp. by Ann Duncan Brown. [Wash., 1934] 35p.

2900. U. S. Library of Congress, General Reference and Bibliography Division. "Recent books and periodical articles on library architecture," comp. by Thomas S. Shaw. [Wash.] 1947. 22 l. Typed.

2901. VanDerpool, James Grote. "S. A. H. microfilm project: preliminary report and listings of special works." Society of Architectural Historians journal, 8 (1949), 68-85.

Lists key architectural books, 15th to 19th centuries, available in Avery Library, Columbia University.

2902. Wall, Alexander J. "Books on architecture printed in America, 1775-1830." In: Bibliographical essays: a tribute to Wilberforce Eames. [Cambridge: Harvard Univ. Press], 1924, p. 299-311.

Locates copies in 32 libraries.

NUMISMATICS

2903. American Numismatic Society Library. Catalogue of the numismatic books in the library. New York, 1883. 31p.

Also includes important periodicals in field.

2904. Bowker, Howard Franklin. A numismatic bibliography of the Far East; a check list of titles in European languages. N. Y.: American Numismatic Society, 1943. 144p. (Numismatic notes and monographs, 101)

Lists 910 items and 71 catalogs with locations in 14 public and private collections.

2905. Essex Institute. Oriental numismatics; a catalog of the collection of books relating to the coinage of the East, presented to the Essex Institute, Salem, Massachusetts, by John Robinson. Salem, 1913. 102p.

Lists 506 titles.

2906. Hall, W. S. "United States coins in the Princeton University Library coin collection." Princeton University Library chronicle, 6 (1945), 138-40.

2907. New York Public Library. "List of works in the New York Public Library relating to numismatics," comp. by Daniel Carl Haskell. New York Public Library bulletin, 17 (1913), 981-1049; 18 (1914), 59-86, 149-75, 404-28. Reprinted. 195p.

2908. Newark Museum. Numismatics; a list of books and pamphlets in the Frank I. Liveright collection. Newark, N. J.: The Museum, 1939. 15p.

DRAWING

2909. Gallatin, Albert E. Aubrey Beardsley; catalogue of drawings and bibliography. N. Y.: Grolier Club, 1945. 141p.

Collection of original Beardsley drawings presented to Princeton University Library.

2910. [Harvard University Library] A catalogue of the works illustrated by George Cruikshank, and Isaac and Robert Cruikshank in the library of Harry Elkins Widener, by A. S. W. Rosenbach. Philadelphia: Priv. printed, 1918. 279p.

Collection now owned by Harvard University.

2911. Mather, Frank Jewett, Jr. "A statistical survey of the Meirs Cruikshank collection." Princeton University Library chronicle, 4 (Feb.-Apr. 1943), 50-52.
  Collection of books, prints, drawings, paintings, and letters in Princeton University Library.

2912. Mather, Frank Jewett, Jr. "Winslow Homer as a book illustrator, with a descriptive checklist." Princeton University Library chronicle, 1 (1939), 15-32.
  Includes a check list of 75 titles in either Princeton University Library or named private collections.

2913. Metropolitan Museum of Art. Japanese illustrated books. N. Y.: The Museum Press, 1941. 20 plates.

2914. Morse, Willard S. and Brincklé, Gertrude. Howard Pyle; a record of his illustrations and writings. Wilmington, Del.: The Wilmington Society of Fine Arts, 1921. 242p.
  Howard Pyle collection record is owned by Wilmington Society of Fine Arts and housed in Wilmington (Del.) Institute Free Library.

2915. New York Public Library. "American drawing books," by Carl W. Drepperd. New York Public Library bulletin, 49 (1945), 795-812. Reprinted 1946 with revisions and additions. 20p.
  Locates copies in 6 libraries.

2916. Newberry Library. Checklist of the C. L. Ricketts calligraphy collection acquired by the Newberry Library, June 1941. [Chicago, 1941?] 58 1.

2917. Newberry Library. "Rare printed manuals of calligraphy, Italian and American, in the Newberry Library," by Stanley Morison. The Newberry Library bulletin, 2d ser., no. 1 (July 1948), 12-24.

2918. Pierpont Morgan Library. Collection, J. Pierpont Morgan, drawings by the old masters, formed by C. Fairfax Murray. . London, [1905]-1912. 4v.
  Lists and reproduces 814 drawings.

2919. Pierpont Morgan Library. Drawings by Giovanni Battista Piranesi; illustrated catalogue of an exhibition, January 10, 1949, to March 19, 1949. N. Y.: [The Library], 1949. 28p., 16 plates.

2920. Princeton University Library. "Meirs collection of Cruikshankiana." In: Princeton University Library classed list. Princeton, 1920. v. 6, p. 3565-83.

2921. Richardson, Mary H. "Drawings of Clifford Kennedy Berryman." Library of Congress quarterly journal of current acquisitions, 3 (Feb. 1946), 6-10.
  Collection of about 1,200 sketches by American political cartoonist, presented to Library of Congress.

2922. San Francisco Art Association. Catalogue of the loan exhibition of drawings and etchings by Rembrandt from the J. Pierpont Morgan collection. With a preface, bibliography and explanatory notes, by J. Nilsen Laurvik... February-March 1920. [San Francisco], 1920. 62p., plates.
  Catalog of 401 items, 384 etchings and 17 drawings.

DECORATION AND DESIGN

2923. Detroit Public Library. Furniture: a list of books in the Detroit Public Library, Fine Arts Department. [Detroit] 1929. 65p.

2924. Grand Rapids Public Library. List of books on furniture. Grand Rapids, Mich.: The Library, 1927. 143p.
  Lists Grand Rapids Public Library's holdings.

2925. Indiana State Library. Early American furniture; an annotated selective list of books, comp. by Marie J. LaGrange. Indianapolis: Indiana State Library, 1939. 12 numb. 1.

2926. John Crerar Library. Reference list on decalcomania, by Jerome K. Wilcox. Chicago, 1930. 4p. (Reference list 2)

2927. National Academy of Design. Catalogue of the library. N. Y.: J. J. O'Brien & Son, 1898. 24p.

2928. New York Public Library. "Bibliography of English Regency furniture, interiors and architecture, 1795-1830; an annotated and selective list of references exemplifying the taste of the Prince Regent, later George IV, King of England," comp. by Saro John Riccardi. New York Public Library bulletin, 44 (1940), 319-25. Reprinted. 8p.

Items not in New York Public Library are located in other New York City libraries.

2929. New York Public Library. "List of books on needlework." New York Public Library bulletin, 3 (1899), 365-70.

2930. New York Public Library. "List of works in the New York Public Library relating to furniture and interior decoration." New York Public Library bulletin, 12 (1908), 531-62. Reprinted. 32p.

2931. New York Public Library. "Plant forms in ornament; a selective list of titles in the New York Public Library and certain other libraries in New York City," comp. by Muriel Frances Baldwin. New York Public Library bulletin, 37 (1933), 511-25, 613-32, 715-41. Reprinted. 59p.

2932. New York Public Library. "Schoolroom decoration; a list of references," comp. by Rachel H. Beall. New York Public Library bulletin, 20 (1916), 897-900. Reprinted. 6p.

Locates copies in New York Public Library, Newark (N. J.) Public Library, Pratt Institute, and Columbia University Teachers College.

2933. Pennsylvania Museum and School of Industrial Art Library. The Library of the Pennsylvania Museum's School of Industrial Art. Catalogue, 1931. [Philadelphia], 1931. 133p.

2934. Rhode Island School of Design Library. The library, Rhode Island School of Design, by Evelyn Chase. Providence, 1942. 30p.

History and description of library of 15,000 books, 20,000 mounted pictures, 13,000 lantern slides, etc.

2935. U. S. Library of Congress, Division of Bibliography. Handicrafts: a selected list of recent books and pamphlets, comp. by Helen F. Conover. Wash., Apr. 20, 1939. 37p.

Costume

2936. Boston Public Library. Costume; a selected list of books in the Public Library of the city of Boston. Boston: The Library, 1928. 48p.

2937. Brooklyn Public Library. A reading and reference list on costume. Rev. ed. Brooklyn: The Library, 1932. Published also as part of Traphagen, Ethel. Costume design and illustration. N. Y.: John Wiley and Sons, 1932. 2d ed. p. 165-223.

2938. Detroit Public Library, Fine Arts Department. Costume; a list of books. Detroit: The Library, 1928. 56p.

2939. [Harzberg, Hiler] Catalogue of the Hiler costume library. Paris: [Lecram Press, 1927] 70p.

Collection now held by Queens Borough Public Library.

2940. Hiler, Hilaire and Hiler, Meyer. Bibliography of costume; a dictionary catalog of about eight thousand books and periodicals. N. Y.: H. W. Wilson, 1939. 911p.

Gives Library of Congress card number for each title cataloged in Library of Congress.

2941. Meyers, Charles Lee, comp. Bibliography of colonial costume, compiled for the Society of Colonial Wars in the state of New Jersey. [N. Y., c1923] 36p.

Includes section on "Books in Library of Congress..."

2942. Monro, Isabel Stevenson and Cook, Dorothy E. Costume index; a subject index to plates and illustrated text. N. Y.: H. W. Wilson, 1937. 338p.

Locates copies of more than 600 works in 33 libraries.

2943. New York Public Library. "Some early costume books," by Karl Küp. New York Public Library bulletin, 40 (1936), 926-32.

Works described in Spencer collection, New York Public Library.

2944. Salmagundi Club. Catalogue of the costume books in the library of the Salmagundi Club, New York. [N. Y.], 1906. [36]p.

A general collection.

2945. Western Reserve Historical Society. The Charles G. King collection of books on costume. Cleveland, O., 1914. 48p. (Western Reserve Historical Society. Tract, no. 93.)

PAINTING

2946. Addison, Agnes, ed. Portraits in the University of Pennsylvania. Philadelphia: Univ. of Pennsylvania Press, 1940. 67p.

2947. American Antiquarian Society Library. Checklist of the portraits in the library of the American Antiquarian Society, by Frederick L. Weis. Worcester, Mass.: The Society, 1947. 76p. (Reprinted from the American Antiquarian Society proceedings, n. s. 56 (1946), 55-128)

2948. Henry E. Huntington Library. Catalogue of British paintings in the Henry E. Huntington Library and Art Gallery, by C. H. Collins Baker. San Marino, 1936. 100p. 50 pl.
    Bibliographical references interspersed.

2949. Henry E. Huntington Library. Catalogue of William Blake's drawings and paintings in the Huntington Library, by C. H. Collins Baker. San Marino: The Library, 1938. 42p. and 24 pages of plates.

2950. Lincoln, Waldo. Checklist of the portraits in the American Antiquarian Society. Worcester, Mass.: The Society, 1924. 14p.
    Lists 62 portraits owned by Society.

2951. New-York Historical Society. List of 500 portraits of men made in New York City, 1900-1942 by Pirie MacDonald, photographer of men, in the collections of the New-York Historical Society. [N. Y.: The Society, 1943] 23p.

2952. Swem, E. G. Catalog of portraits in the library and other buildings of William and Mary College. Williamsburg, 1936. 62p. (College of William and Mary bulletin, v. 30, no. 6, April 1936).

2953. Weber, Carl J. A thousand and one fore-edge paintings; with notes on the artists, bookbinders, publishers, and other men and women connected with the history of a curious art. Waterville, Maine: Colby College Press, 1949. 194p.
    Appendix A, p. 131-83: "A list of a thousand-and-one fore-edge paintings in American libraries and collections." In 56 locations.

ENGRAVING

2954. "American wood engravers, the Drake collection." American magazine of art, 23 (1931), 424.
    Describes value of Drake collection of American wood engravings, in Library of Congress, to students of art.

2955. Boston Public Library. The Tosti engravings. [Boston, 1871] 24p. Supplement, 1873. 21p.
    Portion of collection of 10,000 prints owned by Boston Public Library.

2956. Columbia University Library. The William Barclay Parsons railroad prints; an appreciation and a check list. N. Y.: Columbia Univ. Library, 1935. 58p.
    A historical collection owned by Columbia University Library.

2957. Dudley, Laura H. "Florentine woodcuts." Harvard Library notes, 1 (1921), 123-30.
    Describes collection in Harvard College Library of examples of Florentine book illustration of 15th century.

2958. Grolier Club. Chronological exhibition of mezzotints from von Siegen to Barney, exhibited at the Grolier Club, New York annual meeting, 1918. [N. Y.: DeVinne Press, 1918.] 78p.
    Drawn mainly from the Pierpont Morgan Library collection.

2959. Henry E. Huntington Library. Lithographs by Honoré Daumier; an exhibition of French political and social cartoons, 1832-1865, prep. by William A. Parish. San Marino: The Library, 1948. 21p.

2960. Hispanic Society of America. Woodcuts from fifteenth-century books in the library. [N. Y.] 1931. 2 pts.

2961. Irwin, Theodore. Catalogue of the library and a brief list of the engravings and etchings belonging to Theodore Irwin, Oswego, N. Y. N. Y.: [J. J. Little & Co.], 1887. 534p.
    Now in Pierpont Morgan Library.

2962. "List of prints from the Chalcographie du Louvre, and from the German Reichsdruckerei: Kupferstiche and Holzschmitte alter Meister in Nachbildungen." In: U. S. Library of Congress. Report of the Librarian of Congress... for the fiscal year ending June 30, 1905. Wash.: Govt. Print. Off., 1905. p. 223-310.

"A collection of engravings selected by the Minister of Education, of the French government, from the prints in the Chalcographie du Louvre, and presented to the Library of Congress" and "A collection of fac-similes of copper and wood engravings of the old masters presented by the German government to the Library of Congress."

2963. Los Angeles Public Library. Catalogue of the collection of Japanese prints owned by the Los Angeles Public Library, comp. by Judson D. Metzgar. n. p., 1930. 43, 36 numb. l.

2964. Massachusetts Institute of Technology. The Forbes collection of whaling prints at the Francis Russell Hart Nautical Museum. Cambridge: Mass. Inst. of Tech., 1941. 14p.

Includes over 1,000 whaling prints presented to Massachusetts Institute of Technology.

2965. Metropolitan Museum of Art. A catalogue of Italian Renaissance woodcuts, by William M. Ivins. Boston: Merrymount Press, 1917. 65p.

2966. New York Public Library. "CCL; an exhibition of good prints." New York Public Library bulletin, 44 (1940), 395-404. Reprinted. 11p.

Lists and describes 96 prints, from 15th to 20th centuries.

2967. New York Public Library. Catalogue of the work of Kitagawa Utamaro, 1735-1806, in the collections of the New York Public Library, by Massey Trotter. N. Y.: The Library, 1950. 25p.

Lists and describes 130 prints.

2968. New York Public Library. "Currier and Ives, printmakers to the American people; a catalogue of an exhibition." New York Public Library bulletin, 35 (1931), 3-18. Reprinted. 19p.

Drawn from collections of Harry T. Peters and New York Public Library.

2969. New York Public Library. "Fifteenth and sixteenth century prints in the collection of the New York Public Library." New York Public Library bulletin, 38 (1934), 919-33.

An enlarged and revised issue of "Old prints in the Prints Division," in the Bulletin, 22 (1918), 255-64. Reprinted, with revisions and additions, 1935. 46p. For further description, see "Fifteenth and sixteenth century prints," Bulletin, 40 (1936), 564.

2970. New York Public Library. A handbook of the S. P. Avery collection of prints and art books in the New York Public Library. N. Y.: De Vinne Press [1901?] 84p. A "Supplement: additions of prints, 1901-1920," appeared in Bulletin, 24 (1920), 719-36, and was reprinted (1921). 22p.

2971. New York Public Library. "John Greenwood; an American-born artist in eighteenth-century Europe, with a list of his etchings and mezzotints," comp. by Frank Weitenkampf. New York Public Library bulletin, 31 (1927), 623-34. Reprinted. 27p.

2972. New York Public Library. "List of works in the New York Public Library relating to prints and their production," by Frank Weitenkampf. New York Public Library bulletin, 19 (1915), 847-935, 959-1002. Supplement, 21 (1917), 605-10. Reprinted, 1916. 162p.; Supplement. 8p.

2973. New York Public Library. "One hundred notable American engravers, 1683-1850; list of prints on exhibition." New York Public Library bulletin, 32 (1928), 139-74. Reprinted. 38p.

2974. Nordbeck, Theodore M. "The 'Noh' dance prints." Harvard Library notes, 3 (1938), 158-59.

In Harvard College Library.

2975. Parker, Alice Lee. "The Whistler material in the Rosenwald collection." Library of Congress quarterly journal of current acquisitions, 3 (Oct. 1945), 63-66.

Whistler letters and manuscripts received by Library of Congress.

2976. Parsons, Arthur J. "The Division of Prints of the Library of Congress." Print collector's quarterly, 3 (1913), 310-35.

2977. Pennell, Joseph and Pennell,

Elizabeth R. "The Pennell Whistleriana in the Library of Congress." American magazine of art, 12 (1921), 293-305.

2978. Penrose, Boies. "Prints and drawings in the collections of the Historical Society of Pennsylvania." Pennsylvania magazine of history, 66 (1942), 140-60.

2979. Philadelphia Free Library. Checklist of books and contributions to books by Joseph and Elizabeth Robins Pennell, by Victor Egbert; issued in connection with a Pennell exhibition. [Philadelphia, 1945] 29 numb. l.

2980. Philadelphia Museum of Art. William Blake, 1757-1827; a descriptive catalogue of an exhibition... selected from collections in the United States, by Elizabeth Mongan and Edwin Wolf. Philadelphia: The Museum, 1939. 175p.

Locates copies of Blake's works in 10 public and 36 private collections.

2981. Pierpont Morgan Library. Die holzschnitte im besitz der The Pierpont Morgan Library in New York, mit einleitung von L. W. Schreiber; mit 33 abbildungen. Strassburg: J. H. E. D. Heitz, 1929. 10p. 33 facsims. (Einblattdrucke des fünfzehnten jahrhunderts, 71. bd.)

2982. Pierpont Morgan Library. Exhibition of etchings by Rembrandt from the J. Pierpont Morgan collection, held at the New York Public Library, November 1, 1917 to March 31, 1918. N. Y., 1917. 8p.

Lists 155 items.

2983. Pittsburgh Etching Club. Catalogue of an exhibition of a selection of etchings by Rembrandt, from the T. Harrison Garrett collection, deposited in the Library of Congress at Washington. Carnegie Institute... February 3 to 24, 1911. [Pittsburgh? 1911] [5]p.

2984. Thies, Louis. Catalogue of the collection of engravings bequeathed to Harvard College by Francis Calley Gray. Cambridge: Welch, Bigelow, and Co., 1869. 530p.

2985. U. S. Library of Congress. "Annual report on acquisitions: prints and photographs." Library of Congress quarterly journal of acquisitions, 5 (Nov. 1947), 48-54; 6 (Nov. 1948), 37-44; 7 (Nov. 1949), 45-51.

2986. U. S. Library of Congress. Joseph Pennell memorial exhibition; catalogue. Wash.: [Govt. Print. Off.] 1927. 46p.

Includes books, periodicals, and catalogs; etchings, lithographs, drawings, pastels, and water colors; selective bibliography. Items borrowed from non-Library of Congress collections indicated.

2987. U. S. Library of Congress. The Noyes collection of Japanese prints, drawings, etc., presented by Crosley Stuart Noyes. Wash.: Govt. Print. Off., 1906. 32p. (Reprinted from Report of the Librarian of Congress, 1906.)

2988. U. S. Library of Congress, Prints and Photographs Division. Catalog of the Gardiner Greene Hubbard collection of engravings, comp. by A. J. Parsons. Wash.: Govt. Print. Off., 1905. 517p.

2989. U. S. Library of Congress, Prints and Photographs Division. The Joseph and Elizabeth Robins Pennell collection of Whistleriana shown in Division of Prints, Library of Congress, ... catalogue compiled by Joseph and Elizabeth Robins Pennell. Wash.: Govt. Print. Off., 1921. 65p.

2990. U. S. Library of Congress, Prints and Photographs Division. Selective checklist of prints and photographs recently cataloged and made available for reference, lots 2280-2984. [Wash.] 1949. 58p.

"Lots 1-2279 are mainly of a special character, such as photographs made or assembled by the Farm Security Administration and the Office of War Information."

2991. Vanderbilt, Paul. "Prints and photographs of Nazi origin." Library of Congress quarterly journal of current acquisitions, 6 (Aug. 1949), 21-27.

Description of collection of about 18,500 photographs, relating to Hermann Göring and his associates, held by Library of Congress.

2992. Weitenkampf, Frank. A bibliography of William Hogarth. Cambridge: Library of Harvard University, 1890. 14p. (Harvard University Library. Bibliographical contributions, no. 37.)

2993. Wroth, Lawrence Counselman and Adams, Marion. American woodcuts and engravings, 1670-1800. Providence: Associates

of the John Carter Brown Library, 1946. 44p.
Catalog of an exhibition held in Library.

PHOTOGRAPHY

2994. Columbia University Library. A catalogue of the Epstean Collection on the history and science of photography and its applications especially to the graphic arts. N. Y.: Columbia Univ. Press, 1937. [110]p. Authors and short title index, Epstean collection. Corrected, with additions, to May 1, 1938. [N. Y., 1938] 31 l. Accessions, May 1938-Dec. 1941, with addenda, 1942... [N. Y.]. 1942. 29 l.

2995. Gaul, John J., comp. A checklist of photography, listing the more important holdings in the Rocky Mountain region, together with a few unlocated titles. Denver, Colo., 1937. 12 l. (Bibliographical Center for Research checklist, no. 1)

2996. Magurn, Ruth S. "Collection of Spanish photographs in the Fogg Museum." Fogg Museum bulletin, 5 (1935), 12-15.
At Harvard University.

2997. New York Public Library. "Color photography; a list of references in the New York Public Library," comp. by William Burt Gamble. New York Public Library bulletin, 28 (1924), 475-98, 557-77, 611-56, 688-719. Reprinted. 123p.
Lists 2,355 books and periodical articles, from 1761 to 1923.

2998. U. S. Library of Congress, Division of Bibliography. A selected list of recent references on photography and its applications, comp. by Ann Duncan Brown. [Wash.] 1941. 35p.

2999. U. S. Library of Congress, Photograph Section. Index of microfilms, series A, lots 1-1737. [Wash.] 1945. 26 l.
"An alphabetical index to the principal subjects of the first 100 reels of microfilm copies of documentary photographs."

MUSIC

General

3000. Albrecht, Otto E. "Eighteenth-century music in the University Library." University of Pennsylvania Library chronicle, 5 (1937), 13-24.

3001. Apel, Willi. "The collection of photographic reproductions at the Isham Memorial Library, Harvard University." Journal of Renaissance and baroque music, 1 (1946), 68-73, 144-48.

3002. Boston Public Library. Catalogue of the Allen A. Brown collection of music in the Public Library of the City of Boston. Boston: The Library, 1910-16. 4v.

3003. California, University, Library. Catalog of the music library. Los Angeles, 1947.
Musical scores, the collection of the Federal Music Project in Los Angeles, transferred to the University Library, 1942.

3004. Carnegie Library of Pittsburgh. Catalogue of the Karl Merz musical library, held by the Academy of Science and Art... for the Carnegie Free Library of Pittsburgh. Pittsburgh: Foster, 1892. 26p.
Collection now housed in Carnegie Library of Pittsburgh.

3005. Chicago Public Library. Music. Catalog of the collection of instrumental and vocal scores in the Chicago Public Library. [Chicago]: The Library, 1923. 269p. Supplement I, comprising the additions made since... 1923. Chicago: The Library, 1926. 39p.

3006. Colby College Library. Hardy music at Colby; a check-list compiled with an introduction, by Carl J. Weber. Waterville, Me.: The Library, 1945. 22p. (Colby College monograph, no. 13)
A list of all music mentioned by Thomas Hardy, a copy of which is in the Colby College Library.

3007. Day, Cyrus Lawrence and Murrie, Eleanore Boswell. English songbooks, 1651-1702; a bibliography. Oxford: University Press, 1940. 439p.
Locates 252 secular songbooks in 7 American and 15 British libraries.

3008. Denver Public Library, Art and Music Department. Music education; an annotated bibliography. Denver: The Library, 1944. 11p.

3009. Evanston Public Library. Catalogue of the Sadie Knowland Coe music collection and other musical literature in the Evanston Public Library, comp. by Gertrude L. Brown. Evanston, Ill., 1916. 126p.

Collection includes 1,600 music scores, 400 pieces of sheet music, 572 pianola rolls, etc.

3010. Goff, Frederick R. "Early music books in the rare books division of the Library of Congress." Music Library Association notes, 6 (Dec. 1948), 58-74. Reprinted 1949. 16p.

List and description of individual items.

3011. Henry E. Huntington Library. Catalogue of music in the Huntington Library, printed before 1801, by Edythe N. Backus. San Marino: The Library, 1949. 773p. (Huntington Library list, no. 6)

3012. Heyer, Anna Harriet. A check-list of publications of music. Ann Arbor: School of Music, Univ. of Michigan, 1944. 49p.

Locates source material in field of music (periodicals, historical collections and collected editions of works of individual composers) in 113 libraries in the United States.

3013. Hill, Richard S. "Music from the collection of Baron Horace de Landau." Library of Congress quarterly journal of current acquisitions, 7 (Aug. 1950), 11-21.

Description of collection of early and rare works in music acquired by Library of Congress.

3014. Historical Records Survey. List of the letters and manuscripts of musicians in the William Andrews Clark Memorial Library (University of California at Los Angeles). Los Angeles: Southern California Historical Records Survey, 1940. 12 numb. l.

3015. Illinois, University, Library, Music Library. Sampling of important holdings, ed. by Jay Allen. Urbana, 1948. 33 l.

Listing of titles under three main headings: "Music," "Musical literature," and "Source material."

3016. Laciar, S. L. "Edwin A. Fleisher music collection." Library journal, 58 (1933), 369-70.

Description of "probably the largest and most complete library of orchestral music in the world," now housed in the Free Library of Philadelphia.

3017. Los Angeles Public Library. A bibliography of early music (c.1240-c.1725) in the Music Department of the Los Angeles Public Library. Los Angeles, 1941. 88 numb. l.

3018. Louisville Free Public Library. Music scores and books about music in the Louisville Free Public Library. Louisville, Ky.: The Library, 1915. 74p.

3019. McColvin, Lionel R. and Reeves, Harold. Music libraries: their organization and contents, with a bibliography of music and musical literature. London: Grafton and Co., 1937-38. 2v.

Volume 2, p. 274-92, gives general surveys of 34 music libraries in the United States.

3020. Meyer-Baer, Kathi. "The music collection of Duke University Library." Library notes, a bulletin issued for the Friends of Duke University Library, no. 21 (Jan. 1949), 1-5.

General survey of Library's holdings, listing major titles.

3021. Miller, Dayton C. Catalogue of books and literary material relating to the flute and other musical instruments. Cleveland, 1935. 120p. (The Dayton C. Miller collection relating to the flute II).

Now in Library of Congress.

3022. New York Public Library. Catalogue of orchestral music in the collection of the Musical Library, Circulation Department... New York Public Library. [N. Y., 1943] 134 numb. l.

3023. New York Public Library. "Index to opera plots; an index to the stories of operas, operettas, ballets, etc., from the 16th to the 20th century," comp. by Waldemar Rieck. New York Public Library bulletin, 30 (1926), 12-27, 110-34, 164-200, 233-57. Reprinted, 1927. 102p.

3024. New York Public Library. "List of works in the New York Public Library relating to folk songs, folk music, ballads, etc." New York Public Library bulletin, 11 (1907), 187-226. Reprinted. 40p.

3025. New York Public Library. "Portuguese music: a list of recent accessions to the Music Division of the New York Public Library. New York Public Library bulletin, 26 (1922), 359-62.

3026. New York Public Library. "Selected list of works in the New York Public Library relating to the history of music." New York Public Library bulletin, 12 (1908), 32-67. Reprinted. 36p.

3027. Oakland Public Library. Sacred and secular music list, including the Vesper, Hughes and Dow gifts. [Oakland, Calif.:] The Library, 1937. 62p.

Arranged by types of music.

3028. Pearson, Constance. Bibliography of folk songs of the world, based on books available in Public Library at Los Angeles and Doheny Library at the University of Southern California. [Los Angeles, 1943] 26 numb. l.

3029. Peoria Public Library. List of music and books on music and musicians in the Peoria Public Library. [Peoria, Ill.: Duroc Press, 1915] 55p.

3030. Philadelphia Free Library. The Edwin A. Fleisher music collection in the Free Library of Philadelphia. Philadelphia: Priv. printed, 1933-45. 2v.

3031. St. Louis Public Library. Miniature scores in the St. Louis Public Library, comp. by Elizabeth B. Platt. St. Louis, 1930. 6p.

3032. San Francisco Public Library. Finding list of music and the literature of music. San Francisco, 1912. 53p.

3033. U. S. Library of Congress. "Annual reports on acquisitions: music." Library of Congress quarterly journal of current acquisitions, 5 (Nov. 1947), 35-47; 6 (Nov. 1948), 28-36; 7 (Nov. 1949), 34-44.

3034. U. S. Library of Congress, Division of Music. Catalogue of early books on music (before 1800), by Julia Gregory. Wash.: Govt. Print. Off., 1913. 312p.

3035. U. S. Library of Congress, Division of Music. Catalogue of early books on music (before 1800). Supplement (books acquired by the Library 1913-1942), by Hazel Bartlett. With a list of books on music in Chinese and Japanese. Wash., 1944. 143p.

Lists about 500 items, supplementing the Gregory catalog of 1913.

3036. U. S. Library of Congress, Division of Music. Catalogue of opera librettos printed before 1800, prepared by O. G. T. Sonneck. Wash.: Govt. Print. Off., 1914. 2v.

Lists about 6,000 works.

3037. U. S. Library of Congress, Division of Music. Dramatic music (class M1500, 1510, 1520); catalogue of full scores, comp. by O. G. T. Sonneck. Wash.: Govt. Print. Off., 1908. 170p.

3038. U. S. Library of Congress, Division of Music. An exhibit of music, including manuscripts and rare imprints prepared for the sixtieth annual convention of the Music Teachers National Association held in Washington, D. C., on December 28, 29 and 30, 1938. Wash.: Govt. Print. Off., 1939. 61p.

3039. U. S. Library of Congress, Division of Music. Orchestral music (class M1000-1268) catalogue. Scores. Wash.: Govt. Print. Off., 1912. 663p.

3040. U. S. Library of Congress, Orientalia Division. Books on East Asiatic music in the Library of Congress printed before 1800. [Wash.: Govt. Print. Off., 1945] 121-33p. ("Reprinted from the Supplement to the Catalogue of early books on music, 1944")

Contents: Works in Chinese, comp. and annotated by K. T. Wu; Works in Japanese, comp. and annotated by Shio Sakanishi.

3041. Vogel, Emil, comp. Bibliography of "Italian secular vocal music printed between the years 1500-1700," rev. and enl. by Alfred Einstein. Music Library Association notes, 2 (1945), 185-200, 275-90; 3 (1945-46), 51-66, 154-69, 256-71, 363-78; 4 (1946-47), 41-56, 201-16, 301-16; 5 (1947-48), 65-96, 277-308; 385-96; 537-48.

Locations chiefly in European collections but American library holdings shown occasionally.

3042. Werner, Eric. Manuscripts of Jewish music in the Eduard Birnbaum collection. Cincinnati, 1944. 32p.

Collection in Hebrew Union College, Cincinnati.

Individual composers - general

3043. Beethoven, Ludwig van. Beethoven letters in America; fac-similies with commentary by O. G. Sonneck. N. Y.: Beethoven Association, 1927. 213p.

Locates 35 Beethoven letters and notes in America.

3044. Boston Public Library. Beethoven 1770-1827, a selected bibliography prepared in connection with the Beethoven centenary festival, Boston, March 22-29, 1927. [Boston: The Library, 1927] [32]p.

3045. Campbell, Frank C. "Schubert song autographs in the Whittall collection." Library of Congress quarterly journal of current acquisitions, 6 (Aug. 1949), 3-8.

Description of group of Schubert manuscripts in Library of Congress.

3046. Simon, H. "Clementi manuscripts at the Library of Congress." Musical quarterly, 28 (1942), 105-14.

Describes manuscripts and single sheets in Library of Congress Clementi material.

3047. Spivacke, Harold. "The Brahms and Chausson manuscripts presented by Mr. Fritz Kreisler." Library of Congress quarterly journal of current acquisitions, 6 (May 1949), 57-62.

Autograph scores of Brahm's Concerto for violin, Opus 77, and Chausson's Poème for violin and orchestra, Opus 25.

3048. Spivacke, Harold. "Paganiniana." Library of Congress quarterly journal of current acquisitions, 2 (Oct.-Dec. 1944), 49-67. Reprinted. 19p.

Description of a collection of Nicolò Paganini documentary and pictorial material and musical manuscripts acquired by Library of Congress.

3049. Waters, Edward N. "A Brahms manuscript: the Schicksalslied." Library of Congress quarterly journal of current acquisitions, 3 (May 1946), 14-18.

Brahms manuscript acquired by Library of Congress.

3050. Waters, Edward N. "Liszt's Soirées de Vienne." Library of Congress quarterly journal of current acquisitions, 6 (Feb. 1949), 10-19.

Original manuscript received by Library of Congress.

American music

3051. Brown University Library. Series of old American songs, reproduced in facsimile from original or early editions in the Harris collection of American poetry and plays. Providence: The Library, 1936. 50 facsim.

3052. California, University, Department of Music. Check list of California songs (Archive of California Folk Music) - part 1. Texts in print. Berkeley, 1940. 160 numb. l.

University of California holdings indicated.

3053. Cleveland Public Library. Index to Negro spirituals. [Cleveland]: The Library, 1937. 149 numb. l.

3054. Denver Public Library, Art and Music Department. A selected list on American folksongs and ballads. Denver: The Library, 1942. 7p.

3055. Eichhorn, Hermene and Mathis, Treva. North Carolina composers as represented in the holograph collection. Greensboro: Woman's College Library, Univ. of North Carolina, 1945. 39p.

A guide to original music manuscripts of some of leading composers of North Carolina, collected in Library of the Woman's College of the University of North Carolina.

3056. Fisk University Library. Selected items from the George Gershwin memorial collection of music and musical literature, founded by Carl Van Vechten. Nashville, Tenn.: The Library, 1947. 32p.

Lists some of books, music, autographs, pictures, etc., in collection at Fisk University Library.

3057. Grosvenor Library. "Transportation in American popular songs: a bibliography of items in the Grosvenor Library." Grosvenor Library bulletin, 27 (June 1945), 61-106.

3058. Historical Records Survey. District of Columbia. A bibliographical index of musicians in the United States of America from colonial times. Wash.: Music Division, Pan American Union, 1941. 439p.

3059. Indiana State Library. Indiana music collection. Music by Indiana composers and about Indiana, available for circulation in the Indiana Division of the State Library. [Indianapolis, 1942] 13 numb. 1.

3060. Johnson, H. Earle. "Notes on sources of musical Americana." Music Library Association notes, 5 (March 1948), 169-77.
   Brief survey of American library resources in field.

3061. Jordan, Philip D. "Some sources for Northwest history: Minnesota sheet music." Minnesota history, 26 (1945), 52-54.
   Describes Minnesota Historical Society's music collection.

3062. Los Angeles Public Library. Latin American music in the Los Angeles Public Library; a list of scores and books. [Los Angeles] 1943. 71 numb. 1.

3063. McCusker, Honor. "Fifty years of music in Boston; the Dwight collection of musical letters." More books, 12 (1937), 341-59, 397-408, 451-62.
   Describes over 200 letters about musical history of Boston from the 1840's to the 1890's, from Dwight collection in Boston Public Library.

3064. Mott, Margaret M. "A bibliography of song sheets: sports and recreations in American popular songs: part I." Music Library Association notes, 2d ser., 6 (1949), 379-418.
   Based primarily upon Grosvenor Library holdings, supplemented by Library of Congress, etc.

3065. Muller, Joseph, comp. The star spangled banner; words and music issued between 1814-1864; an annotated bibliographical list with notices of the different versions, texts, variants, musical arrangements, and notes on music publishers in the United States. Illustrated with 108 portraits, facsimiles, etc. N. Y.: G. A. Baker & Co., 1935. 223p.
   "Based chiefly on materials collected by Joseph Muller and acquired by Library of Congress in 1935."

3066. Music Library Association, Southern California Chapter. California music: a checklist of the holdings of Southern California libraries, comp. by Olive T. Sprong. [Los Angeles] 1949. 19 numb. 1.

3067. New York Public Library. "The folk music of the Western Hemisphere; a list of references in the New York Public Library," comp. by Julius Mattfeld. New York Public Library bulletin, 28 (1924), 799-830, 864-89. Reprinted, with additions, 1925. 74p.
   Classified by type.

3068. New York Public Library. "A hundred years of grand opera in New York, 1825-1925; a list of records," comp. by Julius Mattfeld. New York Public Library bulletin, 29 (1925), 695-702, 778-814, 873-914. Reprinted, 1927. 107p.

3069. Rau, Albert George and David, Hans Theodore. A catalogue of music by American Moravians, 1742-1842, from the archives of the Moravian church at Bethlehem, Pa. Bethlehem: Moravian Seminary and College for Women, 1938. 120p.

3070. Sonneck, Oscar George Theodore. "The star spangled banner" (revised and enlarged from the "Report" on the above and other airs, issued in 1909). Wash.: Govt. Print. Off., 1914. 115p.
   Based on Library of Congress collection.

3071. Strunk, W. O. State and resources of musicology in the United States. Wash.: American Council of Learned Societies, 1932. 76p. (American Council of Learned Societies bulletin, no. 19)
   Discussion of library and other resources in musicology, with a union list of 45 outstanding publications: periodicals, standard historical works, and critical reprints of older music. Holdings of 57 libraries recorded.

3072. U. S. Library of Congress, Division of Music. A bibliography of early secular American music (18th century) by Oscar George Theodore Sonneck. Rev. and enl. by William Treat Upton. Wash.: The Library, 1945. 617p.
   Locates copies.

3073. U. S. Library of Congress, Division of

Music. Bibliography of Latin American folk music, comp. by Gilbert Chase. [Wash.: The Library] 1942. 141p.
Lists 1,143 items by country.

3074. U. S. Library of Congress, Division of Music. Catalog of phonograph records; selected titles from the Archive of American Folk Song issued to January 1943. Wash.: Govt. Print. Off., 1947-48. 16p. (6th and 7th issues.)

3075. U. S. Library of Congress, Division of Music. Folk music of the United States and Latin America; combined catalog of phonograph records. Wash.: The Library, 1948. 47p.
"This catalog lists 107 records, containing 341 titles... selected as among the best and most representative of over 10,000 records in the collection of the Archive of American Folk Song."

3076. U. S. Library of Congress, Division of Music. A guide to Latin-American Music, by Gilbert Chase. Wash., 1945. 274p.

3077. U. S. Library of Congress, Division of Music. Archive of American Folk Song. Check-list of recorded songs in the English language in the Archive of American Folk Song to July, 1940. Wash.: [The Library] 1942. 3v.

3078. Upton, William Treat. "Eighteenth century American imprints in the Society's Dielman collection of music." Maryland historical magazine, 35 (1940), 374-81.
Description of 18th century American imprints in collection of Maryland Historical Society.

Individual American composers

3079. Fisk University Library. Selected items from the George Gershwin memorial collection of music and musical literature founded by Carl Van Vechten. Nashville, Tenn.: The Library [1947] 32p.

3080. Philadelphia Free Library. The musical works of William Henry Fry, in the collections of the Library Company of Philadelphia, by William Treat Upton. Philadelphia, 1946. 33p.

3081. Sonneck, Oscar George Theodore. Catalogue of first editions of Edward MacDowell. Wash.: Library of Congress, 1917. 89p. Supplement... containing notes on Columbia's copies of MacDowell first editions. N. Y.: Columbia Univ. Music Library, 1943. 14 numb. l.

3082. U. S. Library of Congress, Division of Music. Catalogue of first editions of Edward MacDowell (1861-1908) by O. G. Sonneck. Wash.: Govt. Print. Off., 1917. 89p.

3083. U. S. Library of Congress, Division of Music. Catalogue of first editions of Stephen C. Foster (1826-1864), by Walter R. Whittlesey and O. G. Sonneck. Wash.: Govt. Print. Off., 1915. 79p.
Title catalog, with indexes by authors, publishers, and first lines.

3084. Waters, Edward N. "Gershwin's Rhapsody in Blue." Library of Congress quarterly journal of current acquisitions, 4 (May, 1947), 65-66.
Original manuscript presented to Library of Congress.

3085. Waters, Edward N. "New Loeffleriana." Library of Congress quarterly journal of current acquisitions, 1 (Apr.-June, 1944), 6-14.
Collection of material relating to Charles Martin Loeffler (1861-1935), American composer.

AMUSEMENTS

Theater, moving pictures, etc.

3086. Academy of Motion Picture Arts and Sciences. Check-list of material in Academy Library. Hollywood, Calif.: The Academy, 1936. 34 numb. l.
Gives periodical holdings as well as titles of books.

3087. Boston Public Library, Allen A. Brown Collection. A catalogue of the Allen A. Brown collection of books relating to the stage in the Public Library of the City of Boston. Boston: The Library, 1919. 952p.
About 3,500 volumes relating to drama and stage, with special emphasis on history of the theater.

3088. Cleveland Public Library. Index to folk dances, drills, singing games and rhythms. Cleveland: The Library, 1937. 104 numb. l.

3089. Davis, Harry. "Roland Holt theatre collection." Carolina play-book, 9 (1936), 43-46.
Describes collection in University of North Carolina Dramatic Museum.

3090. Fox Film Corporation. Catalogue of the stories and plays owned by Fox Film Corporation. Los Angeles: Times-Mirror Press, 1935. 326p. Earlier edition, 1931. 222p.

3091. Gilder, Rosamond and Freedley, George. Theatre collections in libraries and museums; an international handbook. N. Y.: Theatre Arts, 1936. 182p.
Pages 9-57 describe outstanding United States collections.

3092. Hall, Edward B. Concerning the theatre collection at Harvard College; its early beginnings and growth. [Cambridge?] 1930. 7p.

3093. Hall, Edward B. "Recent accessions to the theatre collection." Harvard alumni bulletin, 32 (1930), 1039-45.
In Harvard College Library.

3094. [Hall, Edward B.] The Rogers memorial room. Cambridge: Cosmos Press, 1935. 31p.
Describes collection, in Harvard College Library, of (1) memorabilia relating to composer John Barnett (1802-90) and (2) events and figures of historical significance in theater from 1850 to 1930.

3095. Hall, Lillian A. "Lawrence Barrett." Harvard Library notes, 3 (1936), 129-32.
Manuscripts pertaining to Barrett in Harvard College Library's theater collection.

3096. Hall, Lillian A. "Notes from the theatre collection." Harvard Library notes, 3 (1935), 86-89.
In Harvard College Library.

3097. Hall, Lillian A. "Some early black-face performers and the first minstrel troupe." Harvard Library notes, 1 (1920), 39-45.
Based on theatre collection, Harvard College Library.

3098. Hall, Lillian A. "The theatre collection at Harvard." Harvard alumni bulletin, 29 (1927), 1074-83.

3099. Hall, Lillian A. "Theatre collection Harvard College." Special libraries, 31 (March 1940), 81-83.

3100. Harvard University Library. "Theatre and drama." Harvard Library notes, 2 (1925), 78-83.
Resources of Harvard College Library.

3101. Harvard University Library, Theatre collection. Catalogue of dramatic portraits in the Theatre collection, by Lillian A. Hall. Cambridge: Harvard Univ. Press, 1930-34. 4v. Covers A-R.

3102. Illinois, University. Visual Aids Service... motion picture film, radio transcriptions. Champaign, Ill.: The Service, 1949. 315p.

3103. McLeod, Malcolm. "Some items in the theatre collection." Harvard Library notes, 1 (1920), 33-35.
In Harvard College Library.

3104. Magriel, Paul David. A bibliography of dancing; a list of books and articles on the dance and related subjects. N. Y.: H. W. Wilson, 1936. 229p. 1st-3rd supplements, 1936-39. N. Y.: H. W. Wilson, 1938-40. 3v.
Indicates locations of rare books in Library of Congress, New York Public Library, Boston Public Library or Harvard College Library.

3105. Michigan, University, Audio-Visual Education Center. Motion pictures, filmstrips, slides, recordings, exhibits. Ann Arbor, 1949. 264p. (Michigan, University, Official publication, v. 50, no. 94, May 24, 1949)

3106. [National Broadcasting Co., Inc., Literary Rights Division.] A catalogue of dramatic scripts. [N. Y., 1934]. No paging.
Scripts of dramatic programs owned by NBC.

3107. New York Public Library. "Catalogue of the Becks collection of prompt books in the New York Public Library." New York Public Library bulletin, 10 (1906), 100-48. Reprinted. 49p.

3108. New York Public Library. "The development of scenic art and stage machinery; a list of references in the New York Public Library," comp. by William Burt Gamble. New York Public Library bulletin, 23 (1919), 369-401, 439-56, 527-34, 559-82, 643-66, 739-63. Reprinted. 128p.; revised and enlarged edition, 1928. 231p.

3109. New York Public Library. "Pageants in Great Britain and the United States; a list of references," comp. by Caroline Hill Davis. New York Public Library bulletin, 20 (1916), 753-91. Reprinted. 43p.

Locates some items in Library of Congress, Columbia University, and Russell Sage Foundation.

3110. New York Public Library. "The Robinson Locke dramatic collection." New York Public Library bulletin, 29 (1925), 307-22. Reprinted. 25p.

3111. Pinthus, Kurt. "The world's largest theater library." Library of Congress, quarterly journal of current acquisitions, 1 (Oct.-Dec., 1943), 32-39.

Brief survey of Library of Congress' extensive collection of theater materials.

3112. San Antonio Public Library. Circusana; a guide book to the Harry Hertzberg circus collection. San Antonio, Texas: The Library [1943] 47p.

3113. Shaw, Robert G. "John Gilbert's plays and playbills." Harvard Library notes, 1 (1920), 27-30.

Relates to theatre collection, Harvard College Library.

3114. U. S. Library of Congress. "Bequest of Harry Houdini." Wash., [Aug. 14, 1928?] 40p. Typed.

Incomplete list.

3115. U. S. Library of Congress, Division of Bibliography. "The circus: a bibliographical list." Wash., Feb. 11, 1928. 40p. Typed.

3116. U. S. Library of Congress, Division of Bibliography. "List of references on pageants, with separate sections on Elizabethan pageants, pageants based on Shakespeare's plays and on costuming for pageants." Wash., 1916. 45p. Typed.

3117. U. S. Library of Congress, Division of Bibliography. Moving pictures in the United States and foreign countries; a selected list of recent writings, comp. by Anne L. Baden. [Wash.] 1940. 67p.

3118. Walls, Howard Lamarr. Motion picture incunabula in the Library of Congress, by Howard L. Walls. [N. Y., 1944] 155-58p. (Reprinted from the Journal of the Society of Motion Picture Engineers, v. 42, March, 1944)

3119. Warren, Katherine. "John Moore's prompt-books." Harvard Library notes, 1 (1920), 38-39.

In theatre collection, Harvard College Library.

Chess

3120. Allen, George. Catalogue of the chess collection of the late George Allen. Philadelphia, 1878. 89p.

Now in Philadelphia Library Company. Collection comprised about 1,000 printed volumes, 250 letters, and 50 engravings and photographs.

3121. Brooklyn Public Library. "The checker and chess collection." Brooklyn Public Library bulletin, 4th ser., 1 (1922), 113-18, 138-48, 162-74.

3122. Buschke, Albrecht. "Chess libraries in America." Princeton University Library chronicle, 2 (1941), 147-[52]

Emphasis is on collection presented to Princeton University Library by Eugene B. Cook.

3123. Gambet, Adrien. "The J. C. J. Wainwright chess collection." Harvard Library notes, 1 (1922), 191-95.

In Harvard College Library.

3124. Princeton University Library. "Cook chess collection." In: Princeton University Library classed list. Princeton, 1920. v. 6, p. 3585-3608.

3125. Quaritch, firm, booksellers. Catalogue of rare and valuable works relating to the history and theory of the game of chess, being the greater portion of the famous library formed by J. W. Rimington-Wilson. London, 1929. 96p.

Many books listed acquired for White collection, Cleveland Public Library.

3126. Rimington-Wilson, J. W. Catalogue of the famous chess library... the property of the late R. H. Rimington-Wilson... which will be sold by auction by Sotheby and Company. London, 1928. [56]p.

Many of these books acquired for White collection, Cleveland Public Library.

Playing cards

3127. Harvard University Library. "The Thorndike playing cards." Harvard alumni bulletin, 38 (1936), 728-29.

Collection in Harvard College Library.

3128. Harvard University Library. "Whitney collection of playing cards." Harvard alumni bulletin, 30 (1927), 183-88.

In Harvard College Library.

Athletics

3129. Henderson, Robert W., comp. Early American sport; a chronological check-list of books published prior to 1860 based on an exhibition held at the Grolier Club. N. Y.: Grolier Club, 1937. [135]p.

Locates copies in 21 public and private collections.

3130. Henry E. Huntington Library. Sporting books in the Huntington Library, comp. by Lyle H. Wright. San Marino, Calif., 1937. 132p. (Huntington Library lists, no. 2)

3131. New York Public Library. "Bibliography of boxing, a chronological check list of books in English published before 1900," comp. by Paul Magriel. New York Public Library bulletin, 52 (1948), 263-88. Reprinted. 28p.

"The largest part... was compiled from the collections of the New York Public Library and the Library of Congress." Locates copies in 30 libraries.

3132. New York Public Library. "List of works in the New York Public Library on sport in general, and on shooting in particular." New York Public Library bulletin, 7 (1903), 164-86, 201-34. Reprinted. 57p.

3133. New York Public Library. "The modern Olympics; a list of references," comp. by Karl Brown. New York Public Library bulletin, 43 (1939), 405-31. Reprinted. 29p.

3134. New York Public Library. "The Spalding baseball collection." New York Public Library bulletin, 26 (1922), 86-127. Reprinted. 44p.

A catalog of collection on baseball and other sports.

3135. Pierpont Morgan Library. Sports and pastimes from the fourteenth through the eighteenth century; illustrated guide to an exhibition, March 25, 1946 - June 29, 1946. N. Y.: [The Library], 1946. 47p.

133 items: illuminated manuscripts, printed books, engravings and drawings.

3136. Racquet and Tennis Club. A guide to the library. N. Y., 1942. 43p.

Describes, by subject, special collections of books "of a sporting nature" contained in Club library.

3137. U. S. Library of Congress, Division of Bibliography. Judo, Jiu-Jitsu, and hand-to-hand fighting: a list of references, comp. by Helen D. Jones. Wash., 1943. 18p.

3138. Wynne, Marjorie G. "The Wagstaff sporting books and manuscripts." Yale University Library gazette, 20 (1945), 6-14.

A gift of 13 manuscript titles and 3 sporting periodicals given to Yale University Library.

Fishing

3139. Albee, Louise Rankin. The Bartlett collection; a list of books on angling, fishes, and fish culture in the Harvard College Library. Cambridge, Mass.: Harvard University Library, 1896. 180p. (Harvard Univ. Library bibliographical contributions, no. 51)

3140. Fearing, Daniel B. "An angling library and some of its treasures." American Fisheries Society transactions, 45 (March 1916), 53-75. Reprinted. 1916.

Collection later presented to Harvard University.

3141. [Fearing, Daniel B.] A catalogue of an exhibition of angling books. N. Y.: Grolier Club [1911] 59p.

Collection now in Harvard College Library.

3142 FINE ARTS

3142. Fearing, Daniel B. Check list of books on angling, fish, fisheries, fish-culture, etc. N. Y., 1901. 138p.

    Collection now in Harvard College Library.

3143. [Fearing, Daniel B.] The making of an angling library and a short account of its treasures. [Santa Barbara, Calif.: D. H. Schauer, 1915] 20 1.

    Collection now in Harvard College Library.

3144. Princeton University Library. Freshwater angling; fifty books and other material tracing its development; an exhibition. [Princeton, 1946] 24p.

3145. Westwood, Thomas. Bibliotheca piscatoria. Catalogue of the library of Thomas Westwood, esq. ... For sale by J. W. Bouton. N. Y., 1873. 46p.

    Collection acquired by Lenox Library; now in New York Public Library.

Linguistics

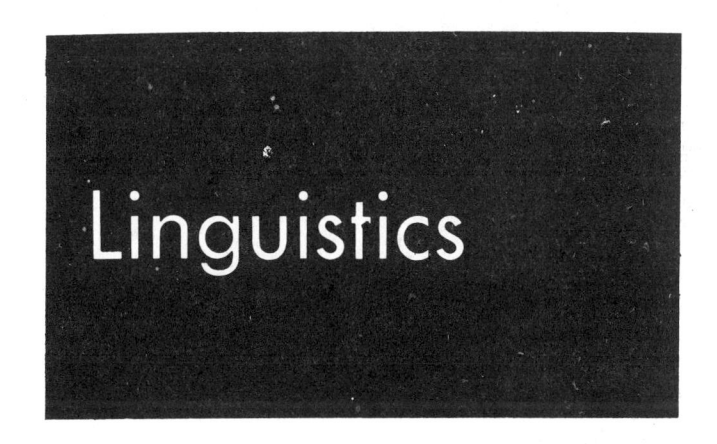

GENERAL

3146. Krebs, Emil. Verzeichnis der bücherei des verstorbenen legationsrates Krebs... Alphabetisch nach sprachen geordnet, diese in sich möglichst nach inhalt (wörterbücher, grammatiken, chrestomathien, sprachführer, literatur in der sprache und literatur über das land.). [Berlin, 1931?] 236p.
Collection now in Library of Congress.

3147. New York Public Library. List of grammars, dictionaries, etc., of the languages of Asia, Oceanica, Africa in the New York Public Library. N. Y.: The Library, 1909. 201p. Reprinted from individual lists relating to these three groups, which appeared in the Bulletin, 13 (1909), 319-78, 391-432, 443-86.

3148. New York Public Library. "List of works in the New York Public Library relating to international and universal languages." New York Public Library bulletin, 12 (1908), 644-57. Reprinted. 14p.

3149. New York Public Library. "The literature of slang," comp. by William Jeremiah Burke. New York Public Library bulletin, 40 (1936), 1013-22; 41 (1937), 19-28, 113-24, 313-20, 681-95, 785-97, 851-74, 937-59; 42 (1938), 333-42, 497-507, 564-82, 645-55. Reprinted, 1939. 180p. A section of an earlier list on criminology, entitled, "Language of criminals," appeared in Bulletin, 15 (1911), 350-51, 710-11.

3150. [Pargellis, Stanley]. A chart of comparative holdings in linguistics. n. p., n. d.
Statistics of holdings by languages of 23 leading American libraries.

3151. Plimpton, George A. "Grammatical manuscripts and early printed grammars in the Plimpton Library." American Philological Association transactions, 64 (1933), 150-78.
Describes collection now in Columbia University.

3152. St. Louis Public Library. Books containing American local dialects; a series of lists. St. Louis, 1914. 16p.

3153. Shapiro, Karl Jay. A bibliography of modern prosody. Baltimore: Johns Hopkins Press, 1948. 36p.
Based upon Library of Congress collection.

3154. Sotheran, H. & Co. Attempt at a catalogue of the library of the late Prince Louis-Lucien Bonaparte, by Victor Collins. [London] 1894. 718p. Part 2, Index of authors, [Chicago]: Newberry Library, 1902. 107p.
Collection on European languages and dialects acquired by Newberry Library, 1901; totals 13,699 titles.

3155. U. S. Library of Congress, Division of Bibliography. Foreign language-English dictionaries, a selected list, comp. by Grace Hadley Fuller. [Wash.] 1942. 132p.
Lists 1,133 items.

3156. U. S. Library of Congress, Division of Bibliography. Foreign language-English dictionaries: a supplementary list of references, comp. by Grace Hadley Fuller. [Wash.] 1944. 42p.
Lists 362 items.

GERMANIC LANGUAGES

3157. California, University, Library. A list of first editions and other rare books in the

Weinhold library, comp. by W. R. R. Pinger. Berkeley: University Press, 1907. 143p. (Univ. of California Library bulletin, no. 16)

Collection of 8,500 titles on German philology.

3158. Guild, Edward Chipman. A classified list of the German dialect collection, established by Edward C. Guild, comp. and annotated by the donor. Brunswick, Me., 1898. p. 329-48. (Bowdoin College Library, Bibliographical contributions, no. 8)

A collection held by Bowdoin College.

3159. Pennsylvania, University, Library. Opening of the Bechstein Germanic library; addresses, University of Pennsylvania, March 21, 1896. [Philadelphia: Press of A. C. Leeds, 1896] 61p.

Collection relating to Germanic philology.

3160. Schilling, Hugo K. "The Weinhold library." University of California chronicle, 8 (1905-06), 144-50.

Description of German philology collection purchased by University of California.

3161. Starch, Taylor. "Frisian books in the Harvard Library." Harvard alumni bulletin, 32 (1930), 1047-50.

ROMANCE LANGUAGES

3162. Adams, George C. S. and Woodard, Clement M. A census of French and Provencal dialect dictionaries in American libraries. Lancaster, Pa.: Lancaster Press, 1937. 17p. (Linguistic Society of America special publications)

Gives locations in 45 libraries for titles listed in Wartburg's Bibliographie des dictionnaires patois. 1934. Also lists 200 items in collections not listed by Wartburg.

3163. Blondheim, David S. Catalogue of the library of the late David S. Blondheim. [Wash.: Mimeoform Service, 1935] 68 l.

Philological collection, mainly for Romance languages, acquired by Louisiana State University library.

3164. Born, Lester K. "The manuscripts of the major grammatical works of John of Garland." American Philological Association transactions, 69 (1938), 259-73.

Original manuscripts are in foreign libraries. Library of Congress has complete photostatic copies of the 13 manuscripts.

3165. Boston Public Library. Concise bibliography of Spanish grammars and dictionaries, from the earliest period to the definitive edition of the Academy's dictionary, 1490-1780, by William I. Knapp. Boston: The Library, 1884. 8p. (Bibliographies of special subjects, no. 2)

Locates copies in Boston Public Library and several foreign libraries.

3166. Cornell University Library. Catalogue of the Rhaeto-Romanic collection presented to the Library by Willard Fiske. Ithaca, 1894. 32p. "Additions." Cornell University Library bulletin, 3 (1896), 235-36.

Books in the Romansch language to be found in the Cornell University Library.

3167. Rogers, Francis M. "The libraries for Romance languages and literatures." Harvard Library bulletin, 4 (1950), 271-76.

In Harvard College Library.

SLAVIC LANGUAGES

3168. U. S. Library of Congress, General Reference and Bibliography Division. The study and teaching of Slavic languages; a selected list of references, comp. by John T. Dorosh. Wash., 1949. 97p.

3169. U. S. Library of Congress, Reading Room. A preliminary check list of Russian dictionaries published in the U. S. S. R., 1917-1942, comp. by George A. Novossiltzeff. Wash., 1944. 143 numb. l.

SEMITIC LANGUAGES

3170. New York Public Library. "Bibliography of the modern South Arabic languages," by Wolf Leslau. New York Public Library bulletin, 50 (1946), 607-33.

Lists 195 titles chronologically.

3171. New York Public Library. "Bibliography of the Semitic languages of Ethiopia," by Wolf Leslau. New York Public Library bulletin, 49 (1945), 287-302, 375-90, 438-55, 516-29, 597-606. Reprinted. 94p.

Nearly all books and articles listed are in the New York Public Library; other sources are indicated.

MALAY-POLYNESIAN, ETC.

3172. Churchill, William. "The Fale 'ula Library; a collection of literature relating to the philology and geography of the South Seas." American Geographical Society bulletin, 41 (1909), 305-43.

Catalog of a private collection, but indicates those in the American Geographical Society's library.

3173. Newberry Library, Edward E. Ayer Collection. Checklist of Philippine linguistics, comp. by Doris Welch. Chicago: The Library, 1950. In press.

3174. Newberry Library, Edward E. Ayer Collection. Hawaiian language, comp. by Ruth Lapham Butler. [Chicago: The Library, 1941?] [33p.]

A list of 301 items of Hawaiian linguistic material.

AMERICAN INDIAN

3175. Newberry Library, Edward E. Ayer Collection. A bibliographical check list of North and Middle American Indian linguistics in the Edward E. Ayer collection, comp. by Ruth Lapham Butler. Chicago: The Library, 1941. 2v.

3176. Pennsylvania, University, University Museum Library. Catalogue of the Berendt linguistic collection, by Daniel Garrison Brinton. [Philadelphia]: Dept. of Archaeology and Paleontology, 1900. 32p. (Reprinted from Pennsylvania University, Free Museum of Science and Art bulletin, 2 (1900), 203-34)

Deals with Mexican and Central American Indian languages.

3177. Pilling, James Constantine. Bibliography of the Algonquian languages. Wash.: Govt. Print. Off., 1891. 614p. (U. S. Bureau of American Ethnology. Bulletin, no. 3)

Locates "copies seen."

3178. Pilling, James Constantine. Bibliography of the Athapascan languages... Wash.: Govt. Print. Off., 1892. 125p. (U. S. Bureau of American Ethnology. Bulletin, no. 14)

Locates copies seen in the United States and British Museum.

3179. Pilling, James Constantine. Bibliography of the Chinookan languages (including the Chinook jargon). Wash.: Govt. Print. Off., 1893. 81p. (U. S. Bureau of American Ethnology. Bulletin, no. 15)

Locates copies seen in the United States and British Museum.

3180. Pilling, James Constantine. Bibliography of the Eskimo Language. Wash.: Govt. Print. Off., 1887. 116p. (U. S. Bureau of American Ethnology. Bulletin, no. 1)

Locates copies seen in the United States and British Museum.

3181. Pilling, James Constantine. Bibliography of the Iroquoian languages. Wash.: Govt. Print. Off., 1888. 208p. (U. S. Bureau of American Ethnology. Bulletin, no. 6)

Locates copies seen in the United States and British Museum.

3182. Pilling, James Constantine. Bibliography of the Muskhogean languages. Wash.: Govt. Print. Off., 1889. 114p. (U. S. Bureau of American Ethnology. [Bulletin, no. 9])

Locates copies seen in the United States and British Museum.

3183. Pilling, James Constantine. Bibliography of the Salishan languages. Wash.: Govt. Print. Off., 1893. 86p. (U. S. Bureau of American Ethnology. Bulletin, no. 16)

Locates copies seen in the United States and British Museum.

3184. Pilling, James Constantine. Bibliography of the Siouan languages. Wash.: Govt. Print. Off., 1887. 87p. (U. S. Bureau of American Ethnology. Bulletin, no. 5)

Locates copies seen in the United States and British Museum.

3185. Pilling, James Constantine. Bibliography of the Wakashan languages. Wash.: Govt. Print. Off., 1894. 70p. (U. S. Bureau of American Ethnology. Bulletin, no. 19)

Locates copies seen in the United States and British Museum.

3186. U. S. Bureau of American Ethnology

Library. "Catalogue of linguistic manuscripts in the library of the Bureau of Ethnology," by James C. Pilling. In: U. S. Bureau of American Ethnology annual report, 1879-80. p. 553-77. Wash., 1881.

OTHER LANGUAGES

3187. New York Public Library. "Aleutian manuscript collection," by Avrahm Yarmolinsky. New York Public Library bulletin, 48 (1944), 671-80. Reprinted. 12p.

Appends a list of 42 titles relating to Aleut language.

3188. Thayer, Gordon W. "West African languages." Harvard Library notes, 1 (1923), 238-40.

In Harvard College Library.

Literature

GENERAL LITERATURE

Poetry

3189. Auslander, Joseph and Kilmer, Kenton. "Citadel: poetry in the national library." Saturday review of literature, 25 (Apr. 25, 1942), 3-4.

Description of the Library of Congress poetry collections, printed and manuscript.

3190. Morrison, Hugh Alexander. Guide to the poetry of the world war. [Wash.] 1921. 376 l. Typed.

"Poems by French and other foreign authors are included whenever English translations have appeared." Based on Library of Congress collection.

Drama

3191. Columbia University Library. List of books chiefly on the drama and literary criticism, ed. by George H. Baker. N. Y., 1897. 64p. (Columbia University Library bulletin, no. 1)

Material on drama and literary criticism in Columbia University Library.

3192. New York Public Library. "Foreign plays in English; a list of translations in the New York Public Library," comp. by Daniel Carl Haskell. New York Public Library bulletin, 24 (1920), 61-92, 219-61. Reprinted. 86p.

Fiction

3193. Boston Public Library. A chronological index to historical fiction; including prose fiction, plays and poems. 2d and enl. ed. Boston: The Library [1875] 32p.

3194. Chicago Public Library. Historical novels: a bibliography, comp. by Ruth Utter. [Chicago: The Library] 1940. 43 l.

3195. Goodrich, Nathaniel Lewis. "Prose fiction; a bibliography." Bulletin of bibliography, 4 (1906-07), 118-21, 133-36, 153-55; 5 (1907-08), 11-13, 38-39, 54-55, 78-79.

Mainly in New York State Library; otherwise locations indicated where copies were seen.

3196. Mercantile Library Association of the City of New York. Catalogue of novels, tales, and works in foreign languages, in the New York Mercantile Library, September 1, 1861. N. Y.: Baker & Godwin, 1861. 92p.

3197. New Orleans Public Library. A partial list of fiction in the New Orleans Public Library; a selected list catalogued by author and title with annotations. New Orleans, La.: New Orleans Public Library, 1911. 56p.

3198. Peoria Public Library. List of English fiction, French fiction and juveniles. Peoria, Ill.: H. S. Hill Printing Co., 1894. 106p. Supplement... May, 1894 to December, 1904. Peoria: E. Hine & Co., 1904. 62p.

3199. Philadelphia Free Library, Wagner Institute Branch. A contribution to the classification of works of prose fiction; being a classified and annotated dictionary catalogue of the works of prose fiction in the Wagner Institute Branch of the Free Library of Philadelphia: [G. V. Baird] 1904 [1905] 308p. (Free Library of Philadelphia, bulletin, no. 5)

3200. Virginia State Library. "Finding list of fiction," comp. by Earl G. Swem. Virginia State Library bulletin, 2 (1909), 229-75.

Miscellany

3201. Boston Public Library. Catalogue of books in foreign languages in the Boston Public Library, Lower hall, Central department, 3d ed., May, 1881. Boston: Printed by order of the Trustees, 1881. 32p.

3202. Brockton Public Library. List of foreign books, including volumes in the French, German, Hebrew, Swedish and Yiddish languages in the Brockton Public Library. Brockton, Mass., 1915. 30p.

3203. Chicago Public Library. [Lists of books, in foreign languages added to the Chicago Public Library, 1938-1948. Chicago: The Library, 1938-48.] 41 issues.

Includes Czech, Slovak, French, Hungarian, Polish, Spanish, Yiddish, Danish, Norwegian, German, Modern Greek, Hebrew, Italian, Lithuanian, Netherland, Swedish, Russian, Ukrainian, Portuguese, and Yugoslav books.

3204. Colby College Library. Catalogue of a sentimental exhibition of books in the Colby College Library. Waterville, Me., 1948. 12p.

Catalog of 100 association books owned by Colby College Library.

3205. Columbia University Library. The bookshelf of Brander Matthews. N. Y.: Columbia Univ. Press, 1931. 114p.

The books and papers of Brander Matthews were bequeathed to the Columbia University Library.

3206. Donovan, Frank Pierce. The railroad in literature. Boston: Railway and Locomotive Historical Society, Baker Library, Harvard Business School, 1940. 138p.

Based on Library of Congress holdings, listing fiction, poetry, songs, biography, etc.

3207. Faxon, Frederick W. Literary annuals and gift-books; a bibliography with a descriptive introduction. Boston: Boston Book Co., 1912. 140p.

Supplemented by C. L. Goold's Literary annuals, 1928. Locates copies of about 2,000 volumes of English and American annuals in 11 libraries.

3208. Goold, Clarissa L. "Literary annuals and gift-books; their value in library collections, with a list supplementing F. W. Faxon's Literary annuals and gift-books... (1912)." Columbia University, Master's essay, October, 1928. 76p. Typescript.

Lists titles and editions not in Faxon, and locates additional copies of titles included in Faxon.

3209. James, A. E. "Literary annuals and gift-books." Rutgers University library journal, 1 (June 1938), 14-21.

Includes "a supplementary check list of literary annuals based upon the holdings of the Rutgers University Library," p. 16-21.

3210. Michigan, University, William L. Clements Library. Facsimiles and forgeries; a guide to a timely exhibition. Ann Arbor, 1934. 14p. (Bulletin, no. 21)

Famous forgeries in the Clements Library, dating from 1493 to 1863.

3211. Michigan, University, William L. Clements Library. "You may fool all the people some of the time..."; a guide to an ever-timely exhibition. Ann Arbor, 1941. 22p. (Bulletin, no. 35)

Concerned with historical hoaxes or falsehoods.

3212. New York Public Library. "Catalogue of literary annuals and gift books in the New York Public Library." New York Public Library bulletin, 6 (1902), 270-75.

3213. Packard, Frederick C. "The Harvard vocarium discs." Harvard Library bulletin, 3 (1949), 441-45.

Discussion and list of collection of phonograph recordings of readings of poetry, drama, etc., in Harvard College Library.

3214. U. S. Library of Congress, Division of Bibliography. "List of references on handwriting (examination, authentication, detection of forgery, etc.)" Wash., Dec. 30, 1920. 26p. Typed.

3215. U. S. Library of Congress, Division of Bibliography. "List of references on wit, humor, laughter, satire, etc." Wash., July 16, 1915. 21p. Typed.

3216. Vermont, University, Library. University of Vermont. Catalogue of the library of George Perkins Marsh. Burlington: The University, 1892. 742p.

Of importance for Romance languages and Scandinavian literature. Presented to University in 1883.

3217. Virginia State Library. "Finding list of books in some of the classes of language and literature," comp. by Earl G. Swem. Virginia State Library bulletin, 7 (1914), 265-326.

3218. Virginia State Library. "A list of some books on debating," comp. by Earl G. Swem. Virginia State Library bulletin, 8 (1915), 5-30.

AMERICAN LITERATURE

Poetry

3219. Brown University Library. The Anthony memorial; catalogue of the Harris collection of American poetry, with biographical and bibliographical notes by John C. Stockbridge. Providence, 1886. 320p.

3220. Damon, Samuel Foster. "The Negro in early American songsters." Bibliographical Society of America papers, 28 (1934), 132-63.

Bibliography, p. 154-63, is a list of songsters in Brown University's Harris collection of American poetry and plays, published in or before 1830, and containing Negro songs.

3221. Ford, Worthington C. "The Isaiah Thomas collection of ballads." American Antiquarian Society proceedings, n. s. 33 (1923), 34-112. Reprinted. 1924. 81p.

List of 302 American and English ballads, mainly printed in Boston, received by the American Antiquarian Society in 1814 from Isaiah Thomas.

3222. Harris, Caleb Fiske. Index to American poetry and plays in the collection of C. Fiske Harris. Providence, 1874. 171p.

Collection now in Brown University Library.

3223. Jantz, Harold S. "The first century of New England verse." American Antiquarian Society proceedings, n. s. 53 (1943), 219-508.

"Bibliography of early New England verse," p. 391-508, locates copies in 14 American libraries and British Museum of extant manuscripts and unique or very rare early imprints.

3224. New York Public Library. "Early American poetry to 1820; a list of works in the New York Public Library," comp. by John Christian Frank. New York Public Library bulletin, 21 (1917), 517-72. Reprinted. 58p.

3225. New York Public Library. "Gilder poetry collection," by L. M. Stark. New York Public Library bulletin, 52 (1948), 341-54.

Lists collection of 300 volumes of American and English poetry, now in New York Public Library, chiefly for period from 1880 to 1909.

3226. Porter, Dorothy B. North American Negro poets, a bibliographical checklist of their writings, 1760-1944. Hattiesburg, Miss.: The Book Farm, 1945. 90p. (Heartman's historical series, no. 70)

Locates titles in 25 libraries or collections.

3227. Rudolph, E. L. Confederate broadside verse; a bibliography and finding list of Confederate broadside ballads and songs. New Braunfels, Tex.: Book Farm, 1950. 119p.

Locates copies of 318 items in 24 libraries.

3228. U. S. Library of Congress. Recent American poetry and poetic criticism; a selected list of references, comp. by Allen Tate. Wash., 1943. 13 l.

3229. U. S. Library of Congress, Division of Music. Twentieth century poetry in English, contemporary recordings of the poets reading their own poems; catalog of phonograph records. Wash.: Reference Dept., Library of Congress, 1949. 12p.

3230. U. S. Library of Congress, General Reference and Bibliography Division. Sixty American poets, 1896-1944: selected... by Allen Tate. A preliminary check list by Frances Cheney. Wash., 1945. 188p.

Locates copies of works and also manuscript collections.

3231. Wegelin, Oscar. Early American poetry; a compilation of the titles of volumes of verse and broadsides by writers born or residing in North America north of the Mexican border. 2d ed. N. Y.: Peter Smith, 1930. 239p.

Volume 1, 1650-1799, lists 1,379 titles. Locations frequently given, chiefly in American Antiquarian Society and Brown University.

Drama

3232. Atkinson, Fred Washington. "American drama in Atkinson collection. Part I, 1756-1830. March 1, 1918." 134 l. Typed.
Collection acquired by University of Chicago Library in 1921.

3233. Hill, Frank Pierce. American plays printed 1714-1830; a bibliographical record. Stanford University: Stanford Univ. Press, 1934. 152p.
Locations indicated in 10 libraries. Arranged by authors, with 347 numbered entries.

3234. Michigan, University, William L. Clements Library. The Clements Library presents an exhibition of early American drama. Ann Arbor, 1947. 3p. (Bulletin, no. 51)
List of 51 titles, 1609-1864.

3235. Michigan, University, William L. Clements Library. Early American drama; a guide to an exhibition in the William L. Clements Library, arr. by Ada P. Booth. Ann Arbor: The Library, 1945. 18p. (Bulletin, no. 45)
Plays selected from Ely collection of American drama in Clements Library. Lists and describes 18 items, 1609-1818.

3236. New York Public Library. "List of American dramas in the New York Public Library," comp. by Daniel Carl Haskell. New York Public Library bulletin, 19 (1915), 739-86. Reprinted, 1916. 63p.

3237. U. S. Library of Congress, Copyright Office. Dramatic compositions copyrighted in the United States, 1870 to 1916. Wash.: Govt. Print. Off., 1918. 2v.

3238. Warren, Katherine. "American plays." Harvard Library notes, 1 (1920), 35-38.
In theatre collection, Harvard College Library.

Fiction

3239. Brown, Herbert Ross. The sentimental novel in America, 1789-1860. Durham, N. C.: Duke Univ. Press, 1940. 407p.
Locations are sometimes indicated in footnotes throughout the book.

3240. California State Library. "Fiction in the State Library having a California coloring." News notes of California libraries, 9 (1914), 228-42. Supplementary list, ibid, 13 (1918), 874-78.

3241. California State Library. "Fiction in the State Library having a California coloring, compiled by the California Department." News notes of California libraries, 21 (April 1926), 101-27.

3242. Johnson, James Gibson. Southern fiction prior to 1860: an attempt at a first-hand bibliography. Charlottesville, Va.: Michie Co., 1909. 126p.
Locates many items.

3243. McVoy, Lizzie Carter and Campbell, Ruth Bates. A bibliography of fiction by Louisianians and on Louisiana subjects. [Baton Rouge: Louisiana State Univ. Press, 1935] 87p. (Louisiana State Univ. studies, no. 18)
"The greater portion can be located in the combined libraries of Baton Rouge and New Orleans."

3244. New York Public Library. "The Beadle Collection" of dime novels given to the New York Public Library [by Frank P. O'Brien] New York Public Library bulletin, 26 (1922), 555-628. Reprinted. 99p.
Description and catalog.

3245. Newberry Library. American novels with an American setting printed before 1880; a check list of books in the library August 1941. [Chicago, 1941] 36 l.

3246. Raddin, George Gates, Jr. An early New York library of fiction; with a checklist of the fiction in H. Caritat's circulating library, no. 1 City Hotel, Broadway, New York, 1804. N. Y.: H. W. Wilson Co., 1940. 113p.
Locates copies of works listed in 26 American libraries, and several foreign and private collections.

3247. U. S. Library of Congress, Reading Room. "A list of fiction in the Library of Congress by American authors or published in America, 1775-1800." [Wash., 1936] 22 numb. l. Typed.

3248. Wilson, Louis Round. "Fiction with

North Carolina setting." North Carolina review, (June 2, 1912), 3.

Locates over 100 titles in University of North Carolina Library.

3249. Wright, Lyle H. American fiction, 1774-1850: a contribution toward a bibliography. Rev. ed. San Marino, Calif., 1948. 355p. (Huntington Library publications)

Locations of 2,772 titles given in 19 public or institutional libraries and 2 private collections. Earlier edition issued 1939.

Miscellany

3250. Albany Institute and Historical and Art Society Library. Albany authors; a list of books written by Albanians contained in the collection of the Albany Institute and Historical and Art Society, 1902. [Albany, N. Y.? 1902?] 107p.

3251. Buffalo, University, Lockwood Memorial Library. A selection of books and manuscripts in the Lockwood Memorial Library of the University of Buffalo. N. Y., 1935. 60p.

Consists mainly of the writings of important American literary figures: Emerson, Hawthorne, Longfellow, Lowell, Thoreau, Whitman, Woodrow Wilson, etc.

3252. Connecticut Historical Society. Publications by Connecticut authors, exhibited by the Connecticut Historical Society and the Watkinson Library. Hartford, 1935. 28p.

3253. Denver Public Library. Colorado writers, comp. by Lorene L. Scott. Denver: The Library, 1939. 31p.

3254. Duke University Library. Checklist of the Paul Hamilton Hayne library. Durham, 1930. 109p. (Duke University Library bulletin, no. 2, July 1930)

Lists over 1,800 books, pamphlets and periodicals; strong in literature of the Old South prior to 1875.

3255. Engstfeld, Caroline P. Bibliography of Alabama authors. 2d ed. Birmingham: Howard College, 1923. 48p. (Howard College bulletin, v. 81, June 1923, special issue)

Based on Birmingham Public Library and Alabama Department of Archives and History collections.

3256. Fayer, Margaret L. "Abernethy collection at Middlebury College." Special libraries, 36 (1945), 15-17.

A collection of American literature, 7,000 books and 1,000 manuscripts, with much material on Thoreau.

3257. Harwell, Richard Barksdale. Confederate belles-lettres; a bibliography and a finding list of the fiction, poetry, drama, songsters, and miscellaneous literature published in the Confederate States of America. Hattiesburg, Miss.: Book Farm, 1941. 79p.

Copies located in 29 libraries.

3258. Indianapolis Public Library. A list of books by Indiana authors in the Indianapolis Public Library. [Indianapolis]: Daily Echo Press [1915?] 12p.

3259. Lammers, Sophia J. A provisional list of Nebraska authors. Lincoln: Univ. of Nebraska, 1918. 60p. (Bibliographical contributions from the Library of the University of Nebraska, no. 5)

3260. Leisy, Ernest. "Materials for investigations in American literature." Studies in philology, 23 (1926), 90-115.

Lists important collections of Americana in American libraries.

3261. Middlebury College Library. A check list of books in the Julian Willis Abernethy library of American literature, Middlebury College, comp. by Harriet Smith Potter. [Middlebury, Vt., 1930] (Middlebury College bulletin, 25 (Oct. 1930), no. 2)

A collection of about 7,000 volumes.

3262. Middlebury College Library. A check list, Abernethy library of American literature, comp. by Viola C. White. Middlebury, Vt.: Middlebury College Press, 1940. 291p.

3263. New York Public Library. "American letter-writers, 1698-1943," by Harry B. Weiss. New York Public Library bulletin, 48 (1944), 959-82; 49 (1945), 33-61. Reprinted. 54p.

Locates copies of books about letter-writing in 28 libraries.

3264. New York University Library. Index to early American periodical literature. N. Y.: Pamphlet Distributing Co., 1941-42. 5 pamphlets; No. 1. The list of periodicals indexed;

No. 2. Edgar Allan Poe; No. 3. Walt Whitman; No. 4. Ralph Waldo Emerson; No. 5. French fiction.

Selected portions of card index to early American periodicals at New York University, Washington Square Library.

3265. Porter, Dorothy B. "Early American Negro writings; a bibliographical study." Bibliographical Society of America papers, 39 (1945), 192-268.

Lists all known published materials written by American Negroes before 1835. Locations given in 37 libraries.

3266. Thompson, Ralph. American literary annuals and gift books, 1825-1865. N. Y.: H. W. Wilson, 1936. 183p.

Lists and describes about 230 titles, with location of copies in 19 libraries.

3267. Turner, Lorenzo Dow. Anti-slavery sentiment in American literature prior to 1865. Wash.: Association for the Study of Negro Life and History, Inc., 1929. 188p.

Locates copies of rare items in Bibliography, p. 153-82, in 13 libraries.

3268. U. S. Library of Congress, Division of Bibliography. "List of references on John Chapman, 1775-1847, 'Johnny Appleseed'." Wash., July 3, 1935. 4p. Typed.

3269. Werner, William L. "Fred Lewis Pattee: author, scholar, teacher." Headlight on books at Penn State, 17 (1948), 1-16.

Includes a selection of representative titles from "The Pattee collection: library of American literature," at Pennsylvania State College. Collection numbers about 2,000 volumes.

3270. Wilcox, Fannie M. "Texas state author collection." American Library Association bulletin, 24 (1930), 561-62.

Description of a collection of books by Texas authors in Texas State Library.

3271. Wisconsin State Historical Society Library. Bibliography of Wisconsin authors; being a list of books and other publications, written by Wisconsin authors, in the library of the State Historical Society of Wisconsin, by Emma Alethea Hawley. Madison: Democrat Printing Co., 1893. 263p.

3272. Wroth, Lawrence C. An American bookshelf, 1755. Philadelphia: Univ. of Pennsylvania Press, 1934. 191p.

Copies located in some "Appendices" and in "Notes" at end of each chapter.

Individual authors

ABBOTT, JACOB

3273. Weber, Carl J., comp. A bibliography of the published writings of Jacob Abbott. Based primarily upon the Abbott collection in the Colby College Library and supplemented by the Jacob Abbott books in a score of other libraries. Waterville, Me.: Colby College Press, 1948. 155p. (Colby College monograph, no. 14)

ALDRICH, THOMAS BAILEY

3274. Winship, George P. "The Aldrich collection of books." Harvard alumni bulletin, 22 (1920), 852-54.

Thomas Bailey Aldrich memorial collection, Harvard College Library.

ANDERSON, SHERWOOD

3275. Newberry Library. "The Anderson papers." The Newberry Library bulletin, 2d ser., no. 2 (Dec. 1948), 64-70.

Description of Sherwood Anderson personal papers in Newberry Library.

BARLOW, JOEL

3276. U. S. Library of Congress, Division of Bibliography. "Joel Barlow, 1754-1812: a bibliographical list." Wash., May 15, 1935. 26p. Typed.

BRYANT, WILLIAM CULLEN

3277. Spivey, Herman E. "Manuscript resources for the study of William Cullen Bryant." Bibliographical Society of America papers, 44 (1950), 254-68.

Describes 18 collections in various institutions.

CONNOLLY, JAMES BRENDAN

3278. Marriner, Ernest Cummings. Jim Connolly and the fishermen of Gloucester: an appreciation of James Brendan Connolly at eighty. Waterville, Me.: Colby College Press, 1949. 77p. (Colby College monograph, no. 15)

Bibliography, p. 47-77, based on collection in Colby College Library.

COOPER, JAMES FENIMORE

3279. Columbia University Library. An exhibition of first editions of James Feminore Cooper, gift of Leonard Kebler. N. Y.: The Library, 1946. 5p.

CRANE, STEPHEN

3280. Dartmouth College Library. A Stephen Crane collection, by Herbert F. West. Hanover, N. H.: The Library, 1948. 30p.

DELAND, MARGARET

3281. Humphry, James, III. "The works of Margaret Deland, together with a check-list of eighty of her works now in the Colby College Library." Colby College quarterly, ser. 2, no. 8 (Nov. 1948), 134-40.

DICKINSON, EMILY

3282. [Whicher, George F.] Emily Dickinson... a bibliography. 2d ed. Amherst, Mass.: Jones Library, 1930. 63p.

All except 16 titles are in Jones Library, Amherst, Mass.

EMERSON, RALPH WALDO

3283. Gohdes, Clarence. "Noted Emerson collection comes to Duke." Library notes, a bulletin issued for the Friends of Duke University Library, no. 21 (Jan. 1949), 9-10.

Carroll A. Wilson collection of first editions, English editions, and autograph letters acquired by Duke University Library.

FRENEAU, PHILIP

3284. Paltsits, Victor Hugo. A bibliography of the separate & collected works of Philip Freneau, together with an account of his newspapers. N. Y.: Dodd, Mead & Co., 1903. 96p.

Copies located in 14 libraries.

FROST, ROBERT

3285. Dartmouth College Library. Fifty years of Robert Frost; a catalogue of the exhibition held in Baker Library, ed. by Ray Nash. Hanover, N. H.: Dartmouth College Library, 1944. 14p.

GRISWOLD, RUFUS W.

3286. McCusker, Honor. "The correspondence of R. W. Griswold." More books, 16 (1941), 105-16, 152-56, 190-96, 286-89; 18 (1943), 57-68, 323-33. (To be continued in the Boston Public Library quarterly)

Lists over 1,200 letters and manuscripts in Boston Public Library, giving a picture of literary set of New York and Philadelphia in 1840's.

HARTE, FRANCIS BRET

3287. Historical Records Survey, California. Calendar of the Francis Bret Harte letters in the William Andrews Clark Memorial Library (University of California at Los Angeles). Los Angeles: Southern California Historical Records Survey, 1942. 36 numb. l.

HAWTHORNE, NATHANIEL

3288. Buffalo, University, Library. A catalogue of an exhibition of first editions, association books, autograph letters, and manuscripts of Nathaniel Hawthorne. Buffalo: The Library, 1937. 19p.

Drawn from the Library's own holdings and the private collection of W. T. H. Howe.

3289. New York Public Library. "List of books, etc., by and relating to Nathaniel Hawthorne, prepared as an exhibition to commemorate the centenary of his birth," by Victor Hugo Paltsits. New York Public Library bulletin, 8 (1904), 312-22. Reprinted. 11p.

HEARN, LAFCADIO

3290. Harvard University Library. "The Frances Blackler Kennedy memorial collection of Lafcadio Hearn," by Harris Kennedy. Harvard University Library notes, 4 (1941), 38-45.

HOWELLS, WILLIAM DEAN

3291. Hamlin, Arthur T. "The Howells collection." Harvard Library notes, 3 (1938), 147-53.

Contains unpublished letters of Mark Twain, Henry James and John Hay.

IRVING, WASHINGTON

3292. Eaton, Vincent L. "The Leonard Kebler gift of Washington Irving first editions." Library of Congress quarterly journal of current acquisitions, 5 (Feb. 1948), 9-16.

Description of collection of early editions and manuscripts of Irving received by Library of Congress.

3293. Hispanic Society of America. Washington Irving diary, Spain, 1828-1829, ed. from the manuscript in the library of the Society by Clara Louisa Penney. N. Y.: The Society, 1926. 142p. (Hispanic notes and monographs)

3294. New York Public Library. "Catalogue of the Seligman collection of Irvingiana; list of manuscripts and other material by or about Washington Irving given by Mrs. Isaac N. Seligman and Mr. George S. Hellman." New York Public Library bulletin, 30 (1926), 83-109. Reprinted as The Seligman Collection of Irvingiana. 31p.

3295. New York Public Library. "The Hellman collection of Irvingiana," by Robert William Glenroie Vail. New York Public Library bulletin, 33 (1929), 207-19. Reprinted. 15p.

A catalog of manuscripts and printed works.

3296. New York Public Library. "Washington Irving--a bibliography," comp. by William Robert Langfeld. New York Public Library bulletin, 36 (1932), 415-22, 487-94, 561-71, 627-36, 683-89, 755-78, 828-41. Reprinted. 1933. 90p.

Locates copies in public and private collections.

3297. Williams, Stanley T. "The Irving manuscripts." Yale University Library gazette, 1 (1927), 35-38.

Letters, notebooks and first editions in Yale University Library.

JAMES, WILLIAM

3298. Colby College Library. The centenary of William James, January 11, 1842-1942. Waterville, Me.: The Library, 1942. 7p.

Catalog of an exhibition.

3299. Perry, Ralph B. "The James collection." Harvard University Library notes, 4 (1942), 74-79.

Extensive collection of family letters of William, Henry and other Jameses from 1816 to 1915 in Harvard College Library.

JEWETT, SARAH ORNE

3300. Walton, Clarence E. "The Jewett collection." Harvard alumni bulletin, 35 (1933), 474-76.

Books belonging to Jewett family (including Sarah Orne Jewett), presented to Harvard College Library.

3301. Weber, Clara Carter and Weber, Carl J., comps. A bibliography of the published writings of Sarah Orne Jewett. Waterville, Me.: Colby College Press, 1949. 105p. (Colby College monograph, no. 18)

Descriptions of first editions are taken from copies in Colby College Library; other listings are from various sources.

LELAND, CHARLES GODFREY

3302. Jackson, Joseph. A bibliography of the works of Charles Godfrey Leland. Philadelphia, 1927. 129p. Reprinted from Pennsylvania magazine of history and biography, 49-51 (1925-27).

Locates copies in Free Library of Philadelphia, Historical Society of Pennsylvania or University of Pennsylvania. Periodicals not located.

LINDSAY, VACHEL

3303. Dartmouth College Library. The George Matthew Adams Vachel Lindsay collection; a note and descriptive list, by Herbert F. West. Hanover, N. H.: Dartmouth College Library, 1945. 11p.

LOWELL, JAMES RUSSELL

3304. Livingston, Luther Samuel. A bibliography of the first editions in book form of the writings of James Russell Lowell, comp. largely from the collection formed by the late Jacob Chester Chamberlain, with assistance from his notes and memoranda. N. Y.: Privately printed, 1914. 136p. (The Chamberlain bibliographies)

Sometimes locates copies elsewhere.

3305. Potter, Alfred C. "James Russell Lowell's library." Harvard Library notes, 3 (1935), 57-60.

Discussion of collection of books from Lowell's library, acquired by Harvard University.

MACLEISH, ARCHIBALD

3306. U. S. Library of Congress, Division of Bibliography. "Writings of Archibald MacLeish (supplementing "A Catalogue of the First Editions of Archibald MacLeish," by Arthur Mizener, 1938)," comp. by Florence S. Hellman. Wash., July 9, 1942. 18p. Typed. General Reference and Bibliography Division. [Supplementary list] Dec. 13, 1944. 11p. Typed.

3307. U. S. Library of Congress, General Reference and Bibliography Division. "Archibald MacLeish: writings in anthologies." Wash., Dec. 7, 1944. 10p. Typed.

3308. Yale University Library. A catalogue of the first editions of Archibald MacLeish; prepared for an exhibition of his works held in the Yale University Library, comp. by Arthur Mizener. [New Haven]: Yale University Library, 1938. 30p.

MAJOR, CHARLES

3309. Hepburn, William Murray. "The Charles Major manuscripts in the Purdue University Libraries." Indiana quarterly for bookmen, 2 (July 1946), 71-81.

MELVILLE, HERMAN

3310. Briggs, Walter B. "The Herman Melville manuscripts." Harvard Library notes, 3 (1938), 172-73.

In Harvard College Library.

3311. Sealts, Merton M., Jr. "Melville's reading; a check-list of books owned and borrowed." Harvard Library bulletin, 2 (1948), 141-63, 378-92; 3 (1949), 119-30, 268-77, 407-21; 4 (1950), 98-109.

Locates copies in 27 public and private collections.

MOORE, JULIA A.

3312. Greenly, Albert H. "The sweet singer of Michigan bibliographically considered." Bibliographical Society of America papers, 39 (1945), 91-118.

"Check list of the published works of Julia A. Moore: and selected references to her": p. 112-18. Locates copies in Library of Congress.

MORLEY, CHRISTOPHER

3313. Sargent, Ralph M. "Dear Chris." Haverford review, 3 (Winter 1944), 22-25.

Account of collection of Christopher Morley's literary correspondence, presented to Haverford College Library.

NORTON, CHARLES ELIOT

3314. Winship, George P. "The Norton collection in the library." Harvard alumni bulletin, 23 (1921), 706-07.

Charles Eliot Norton, in Harvard College Library.

O'NEILL, EUGENE

3315. McAneny, Marguerite L. "Eleven manuscripts of Eugene O'Neill." Princeton University Library chronicle, 4 (1943), 86-89.

Describes 11 original manuscripts of plays of Eugene O'Neill presented to Princeton University Library.

3316. U. S. Library of Congress, Division of Bibliography. "Eugene O'Neill: a list of recent references," comp. by Ann D. Brown. Wash., Feb. 28, 1940. 15p. Typed.

PHILLIPS, WENDELL

3317. U. S. Library of Congress, Division of Bibliography. "Wendell Phillips (1811-1884): a bibliographical list." Wash., June 15, 1931. 11p. Typed.

POE, EDGAR ALLAN

3318. Columbia University Library. Material by and about Edgar Allan Poe to be found in the library of Columbia University, prep. by Clara W. Bragg. [N. Y.]: Columbia University Library, 1909. 18p.

Lists 135 titles.

3319. Enoch Pratt Free Library. Edgar Allan Poe, letters and documents in the Enoch Pratt

Free Library, by Arthur H. Quinn and Richard H. Hart. N. Y.: Scholars' Facsimiles and Reprints, 1941. 84p.

Reprints 41 important items from Amelia F. Poe collection of 298 items.

3320. Heartman, Charles F. A bibliography of first printings of the writings of Edgar Allan Poe. Hattiesburg, Miss.: Book Farm, 1940. 264p.

Chronologically arranged. Copies located in institutional and private collections.

3321. Heartman, Charles F. and Canny, James R. A bibliography of first printings of the writings of Edgar Allan Poe. Rev. ed. Hattiesburg, Miss.: Book Farm, 1943. 294p. (Heartman's historical series, no. 53)

First published under title: A census of first editions and source materials by Edgar Allan Poe in American collections, comp. by Charles F. Heartman and Kenneth Rede. Metuchen, N. J., 1932. Locates copies in several libraries.

3322. New York Public Library. "Edgar Allan Poe; an exhibition on the centenary of his death, October 7, 1849; a catalogue of the first editions, manuscripts, autograph letters from the Berg collection," by John D. Gordan. New York Public Library bulletin, 53 (1949), 471-91. Reprinted. 23p.

3323. Ostrom, John Ward. Check list of letters to and from Poe. Charlottesville: Alderman Library, 1941. 57p. (Univ. of Virginia bibliographical series, no. 4)

Locates originals of 734 letters, when known, with an index by libraries, referring to individual letters.

ROBERTS, ELIZABETH MADDOX

3324. Tate, Allen. "The Elizabeth Maddox Roberts papers." Library of Congress quarterly journal of current acquisitions, 1 (Oct.-Dec. 1943), 29-31.

Collection received by Library of Congress.

ROBINSON, EDWIN ARLINGTON

3325. Adams, Léonie. "The Lédoux collection of Edwin Arlington Robinson manuscripts." Library of Congress quarterly journal of current acquisitions, 7 (Nov. 1949), 9-13.

Description of collection presented to the Library of Congress.

3326. Colby College Library. Edwin Arlington Robinson at Colby College. Waterville, Me.: The Library, 1944. 4p.

3327. New York Public Library. "Edwin Arlington Robinson, a descriptive list of the Lewis M. Isaacs collection of Robinsoniana." New York Public Library bulletin, 52 (1948), 211-33. Reprinted. 25p.

Collection in New York Public Library.

ROWSON, SUSANNA HASWELL

3328. Vail, R. W. G. Susanna Haswell Rowson, the author of Charlotte Temple. Worcester: American Antiquarian Society, 1933. 116p. (Reprinted from American Antiquarian Society proceedings, n. s. 42 (1932), 47-160)

Copies of biographical references and 252 works by Susanna Haswell Rowson, published 1791-1887, located in 52 public and private collections.

SANDBURG, CARL

3329. U. S. Library of Congress, Division of Bibliography. "Carl Sandburg: a bibliography," comp. by Thomas S. Shaw. Wash., Oct. 27, 1948. 62p. Typed.

SHAPIRO, KARL JAY

3330. Enoch Pratt Free Library. Bibliography of the work of Karl Jay Shapiro, by Louise Quesnel and William Webster. Rev. ed. Baltimore: The Library, 1950. 13p.

Complete listing of published verse and prose.

STEIN, GERTRUDE

3331. Gallup, Donald. "The Gertrude Stein collection." Yale University Library gazette, 22 (1947), 21-32.

Describes manuscripts, letters, and book collection of Miss Stein, now in Yale University Library.

3332. Yale University Library. A catalogue of the published and unpublished writings of Gertrude Stein, exhibited in the Yale University Library, 22 February to 29 March 1941, comp. by Robert Bartlett Haas and Donald Clifford Gallup. New Haven: The Library, 1941. 64p.

Most of material now in Yale University Library.

TAGGARD, GENEVIEVE

3333. Dartmouth College Library. "Taggard collection." Dartmouth College Library bulletin, 4 (Feb. 1947), 87-91.

Brief description of collection of books, poems and articles by and about Genevieve Taggard.

TARKINGTON, BOOTH

3334. Princeton University Library. An exhibit of Booth Tarkington's works in the Treasure Room. March/April, 1946. Princeton, N. J., 1946. 11p.

THOREAU, HENRY DAVID

3335. Wade, Joseph Sanford. A contribution to a bibliography from 1909 to 1936 of Henry David Thoreau. [N. Y.? 1939] p. [163]-203. ("Reprinted from Journal of the New York Entomological Society, v. 47, June, 1939, p. 163-203.")

At the Library of Congress "most of the actual checking and completion of citations was performed."

TWAIN, MARK

3336. Morse, Willard Samuel. A check list of the Mark Twain collection assembled by the late Willard S. Morse, prep. by Ellen K. Shaffer and Lucille S. J. Hall. Offered for sale by Dawson's Book Shop. [Los Angeles] 1942. 92 numb. l.

Collection given to Yale University Library in 1942.

3337. U. S. Library of Congress, Division of Bibliography. "List of writings by Mark Twain translated into certain foreign languages." Wash., July 12, 1939. 14p. Typed.

WHEATLEY, PHILLIS

3338. Heartman, Charles F. Phillis Wheatley (Phillis Peters): a critical attempt and a bibliography of her writings. N. Y., 1915. [49]p. (Heartman's historical series, no. 7)

Copies located in 14 libraries. Chronological list of 43 items, 1770-1915.

WHITMAN, WALT

3339. Detroit Public Library. An exhibition of the works of Walt Whitmen, including books, manuscripts, letters, portraits, association items. Detroit: Sponsored by Friends of the Detroit Public Library, Inc., 1945. 48p.

3340. Duke University Library. Catalogue of the Whitman collection in the Duke University Library, comp. by Ellen Frances Frey. Durham: Duke University Library, 1945. 148p.

3341. Duke University Library. The Trent collection in the rare book room of the Duke University Library, in honor of Mary Duke Trent, Sarah Elizabeth Trent, Rebecca Grey Trent. Durham: Duke University [1943?] 7p.

Collection consists of materials relating to Walt Whitman. Described more fully in 1945 Catalogue of the Whitman collection, ed. by Frey.

3342. Wells, Carolyn and Goldsmith, Alfred F. A concise bibliography of the works of Walt Whitman, with a supplement of fifty books about Whitman. Boston: Houghton Mifflin Company, 1922. 106p.

Library of Congress has all items listed.

3343. Williams, Stanley T. "The Adrian Van Sinderen collection of Walt Whitman." Yale University Library gazette, 15 (1941), 49-53.

638 Whitman items, in Yale University Library.

WHITTIER, JOHN GREENLEAF

3344. Currier, Thomas Franklin. A bibliography of John Greenleaf Whittier. Cambridge: Harvard Univ. Press, 1937. 692p.

Locations frequently mentioned for rarer items.

3345. Essex Institute. "The John Greenleaf Whittier centenary exhibition." Essex Institute historical collections, 44 (1908), 123-46.

Lists first editions and manuscripts exhibited.

WOLFE, THOMAS

3346. Little, Thomas. "The Thomas Wolfe

collection of William B. Wisdom." Harvard Library bulletin, 1 (1947), 280-87.

WOODBERRY, GEORGE E.

3347. New York Public Library. "A list of writings by and about George Edward Woodberry," comp. by R. R. Hawkins. New York Public Library bulletin, 34 (1930), 279-96.
  Items in New York Public Library indicated.

CANADIAN LITERATURE

CARMAN, BLISS

3348. Morse, William I. Bliss Carman; bibliography. Windham, Conn.: Hawthorn House, 1941. 86p.
  Based on a collection of which greater part was subsequently presented to Harvard College Library.

ENGLISH LITERATURE

Poetry

3349. Boston Public Library, Moulton Library. A list of the books forming the gift of Louise Chandler Moulton to the Public Library of the City of Boston. Boston, 1909. 26p.
  The greater part of gift consists of English verse.

3350. Boys, R. C. "Finding list of English poetical miscellanies, 1700-48, in selected American libraries." Journal of English literary history, 7 (1940), 144-62.
  Locates 523 titles in 37 libraries or collections.

3351. Brown, Carleton Fairchild and Robbins, Rossell Hope. The index of Middle English verse. N. Y.: Columbia Univ. Press, 1943. 785p.
  Lists locations of manuscripts.

3352. Case, Arthur E. A bibliography of English poetical miscellanies, 1521-1750. Oxford: Bibliographical Society, 1935. 386p.
  Lists 225 items, with locations of copies in Harvard, Yale, Huntington, and occasionally other American libraries.

3353. Collmann, Herbert L., ed. Ballads and broadsides, chiefly of the Elizabethan period and printed in black-letter, most of which were formerly in the Heber collection and are now in the library at Britwell Court, Buckinghamshire. Oxford, 1912. 287p.
  Acquired by Henry E. Huntington Library.

3354. Grosvenor Library. Catalogue of poetry in the English language, in the Grosvenor Library. [Buffalo, N. Y.]: The Library, 1902. 123p.
  Lists 3,542 volumes and 296 pamphlets.

3355. Holmes, Thomas James, and Thayer, Gordon W., comps. English ballads and songs in the John G. White collection of folk lore and orientalia of the Cleveland Public Library and in the Library of Western Reserve University. Cleveland: The Library Club, 1931. 85p.
  Includes translations into other languages. Indicates locations in one or both of above-mentioned libraries.

3356. Kahrl, George M. "The poetry room." Harvard Library notes, 3 (1935), 10-12.
  Modern English and American poetry, Harvard College Library.

3357. Newberry Library. English poetry. Chicago [1918-20] 2v.

3358. Palmer, George Herbert. A Herbert bibliography; being a catalogue of a collection of books relating to George Herbert gathered by George Herbert Palmer. Cambridge: Harvard University Library, 1911. 19p. (Harvard University Library, Bibliographical contributions, no. 59)
  Collection presented to Harvard Library.

3359. St. Louis Public Library. Contemporary British and American poets; an annotated guide to critical and biographical material, comp. by Grace Rodger and Yvonne Walter. [St. Louis]: The Library, 1929. 14p. (Reprinted from Monthly bulletin of the St. Louis Public Library, n. s. 27 (March 1929), 75-86)

3360. Vogt, George M. "Coleridge and Wordsworth." Harvard Library notes, 2 (1925), 31-33.
  Books and manuscripts presented to Harvard College Library by Norton Perkins.

3361. Wellesley College Library. A catalogue

of early and rare editions of English poetry, collected and presented to Wellesley College by George Herbert Palmer, with additions from other sources. Boston: Houghton Mifflin, 1923. 613p.

Drama

3362. Bowers, Fredson. A supplement to the Woodward & McManaway check list of English plays 1641-1700. Charlottesville: Bibliographical Society of the University of Virginia, 1949. 22p.

3363. Chicago, University, Library. A rough check-list of the University of Chicago libraries' holdings in seventeenth century editions of plays in English. [Chicago: Univ. of Chicago, 1941] 26 numb. l.

3364. Greg, Walter Wilson. A bibliography of the English printed drama to the Restoration. London: Bibliographical Society, 1939. 349p.

Volume 1, Stationers' records plays to 1616, nos. 1-349. Indicates locations in 17 American libraries.

3365. Henry E. Huntington Library. Catalogue of the Larpent plays in the Huntington Library, comp. by Dougald MacMillan. San Marino, 1939. 442p. (Huntington Library lists, no. 4) "Additions and corrections." Huntington Library quarterly, 6 (1943), 491-94.

A list of 2,502 plays collected by John Larpent, official Examiner of Plays in Great Britain, between 1737 and Jan. 1824. Now in Huntington Library.

3366. Henry E. Huntington Library. Tudor drama; an exhibition selected from source materials in the Huntington Library. San Marino, 1932. 27p.

3367. Leach, Howard S. Union list of collections of English drama in American libraries. Princeton: Princeton University Library, 1916. 12p. (Reprint from American Library Institute proceedings, (1916), 72-81)

Lists 78 of the large collections, locating copies in 70 libraries.

3368. New York Public Library. "The Bible in English drama; an annotated list of plays dealing with Biblical themes, including translations from other languages," comp. by Edward Davidson Coleman. New York Public Library bulletin, 34 (1930), 695-714, 785-817, 839-82; 35 (1931), 31-50, 103-27, 167-88. Reprinted, 1931. 212p.

3369. New York Public Library. "The Jew in English drama; an annotated bibliography," comp. by Edward Davidson Coleman. New York Public Library bulletin, 42 (1938), 827-50, 919-32; 43 (1939), 45-52, 374-78, 443-58; 44 (1940), 361-72, 429-44, 495-504, 543-68, 620-34, 675-98, 777-88, 845-66. Reprinted, 1943. 237p.

3370. Pennsylvania, University, Library. Quartos of old English plays in the library. [Philadelphia.] 1907. 7p. (Reprinted from Pennsylvania, University, General Alumni Society, Alumni register, February 1907.)

List of 17th century plays.

3371. Pierpont Morgan Library. English drama from the mid-sixteenth to the later eighteenth century; catalogue of an exhibition, October 22, 1945-March 2, 1946. [N.Y.: The Library, 1945] 95p.

3372. Potter, Alfred Claghorn. A bibliography of Beaumont and Fletcher. Cambridge: Harvard University Library, 1890. 20p. (Harvard University Library, Bibliographical contributions, no. 39)

3373. Sotheby, Wilkinson and Hodge. Chatsworth Library; Kemble-Devonshire collection of English plays and playbills consisting mainly of plays, etc., prior to 1640. London [1914]. 32p.

Acquired en bloc by the Huntington Library.

3374. Woodward, Gertrude L. & McManaway, James. A checklist of English plays 1641-1700. Chicago: Newberry Library, 1945. 155p.

Locates copies in 16 American libraries. Copies of three-fourths of 1,340 items are in Folger and Huntington libraries, and one-half are in Harvard and Yale.

Fiction

3375. Black, Robert K. The Sadleir-Black Gothic collection. Charlottesville: Bibliographical Society of the University of Virginia, University of Virginia Library, 1949. 15p.

An address, giving details of collection of Gothic novels in the University of Virginia Library.

3376 LITERATURE

3376. Bond, Richmond P. "English novels." Harvard Library notes, 2 (1928), 195-98.
Lists 300 titles, chiefly 1750-1850, in Harvard College Library.

3377. Brooklyn Library. Catalogue of English prose fiction including juveniles and translations. Compl. & revised ed., July, 1894. Brooklyn, 1894. 254p.
Now part of Brooklyn Public Library.

3378. Chicago Public Library. A finding list of novels, stories and other forms of prose fiction in English for adults. Chicago: The Library, 1922. 301p. Suppl. I, 1927. 78p.

3379. Henry E. Huntington Library. The English novel; an exhibition of manuscripts and first editions, Chaucer to Conrad, 3d ed. San Marino: Huntington Library, 1939. 26p.

3380. [Hunter College Library]. A remarkable collection of books illustrating the history of the English novel, tale and prose romance, 1686-1850. On sale by C. A. Stonehill, Jr., London, 1937. Catalogue No. 134. 64p.
Collection acquired by Hunter College, New York City.

3381. Ingpen and Stonehill. A remarkable collection of books illustrating the history of the English novel, tale, and prose romance, 1600-1850. London, 1928. 72p. (Catalogue, no. 7, new series)
English novel, 765 lots, acquired en bloc by Harvard College Library.

3382. Mendenhall, J. C. "The Singer Memorial." University of Pennsylvania Library chronicle, 2 (1934), 13-18.
Collection of English 18th century fiction in the University of Pennsylvania Library.

3383. Mercantile Library Association of the City of New York. Catalogue of English prose fiction in the Mercantile Library of the City of New York, to July, 1876. N. Y.: Allen & Co., 1876. 123p.

3384. Parrish, Morris L. "Adventures in reading and collecting Victorian fiction." Princeton University Library chronicle, 3 (Feb. 1942), 33-[44].
Relates to collection bequeathed to Princeton University Library.

3385. Parrish, Morris L. Charles Kingsley and Thomas Hughes; first editions... in the library at Dormy House, Pine Valley, New Jersey. London: Constable & Co., 1936. [166]p.
Collection bequeathed to Princeton University Library.

3386. Parrish, Morris L. Victorian lady novelists: George Eliot, Mrs. Gaskell, the Brontë Sisters. First editions in the library at Dormy House, Pine Valley, New Jersey. London: Constable & Co., 1933. 160p.
Collection bequeathed to Princeton University Library.

3387. Parrish, Morris L. and Miller, Elizabeth V. Wilkie Collins and Charles Reade; first editions (with a few exceptions) in the library at Dormy House, Pine Valley, New Jersey. London: Constable and Co., 1940. 354p.
Collection bequeathed to Princeton University Library.

3388. Portland Public Library. Catalogue of English prose fiction, in the Portland Public Library of Portland, Maine. Portland: Smith & Sale, 1904. 122p.

3389. San Francisco Public Library. English prose fiction, including translations. 2d ed. San Francisco, 1905. 175p.

Miscellany

3390. Akron University, Bierce Library. The Albert I. Spanton collection of English and American literature; bibliography and list of donors. Akron, O.: The Library, 1943. 34p.
Books bearing on English renaissance, Shakespeare, and definitive editions of English and American writers, in the Akron University Library.

3391. Church, Elihu Dwight. A catalogue of books, consisting of English literature and miscellanea, including many original editions of Shakespeare forming a part of the library of E. D. Church, comp. by George Watson Cole. N. Y.: Dodd, Mead & Co., 1909. 2v.
Now in Henry E. Huntington Library. Other locations sometimes shown.

3392. Clark, William Andrews. The library of William Andrews Clark, Jr. Early English

literature, 1519-1700. San Francisco: J. H. Nash, 1920-25. 4v.
Now in University of California, Los Angeles.

3393. Clark, William Andrews. The library of William Andrews Clark, Jr. Index to authors and titles. San Francisco: J. H. Nash, 1922-30. 2v.
Now in University of California, Los Angeles.

3394. Clark, William Andrews. The library of William Andrews Clark, Jr. Modern English literature. San Francisco: J. H. Nash, 1920-28. 4v.
Now in University of California, Los Angeles.

3395. Franklin, E. M. "Wrenn Library." Texas monthly, 2 (1928), 668-78.
General description of Wrenn Library, University of Texas.

3396. Harvard University Library. "In memory of Lionel Harvard." Harvard Library notes, 2 (1926), 91-103.
About 350 titles, nondramatic English literature, 17th century, acquired for Harvard College Library.

3397. Harvard University Library. "The Murdock books." Harvard Library notes, 3 (1935), 17-20.
Chiefly English literature, 18th and 19th centuries, Harvard College Library.

3398. Henry E. Huntington Library. Checklist or brief catalogue... [English literature to 1640], comp. under the direction of George Watson Cole. N. Y.: Priv. print., 1919. 455p. Additions and corrections, July 1919-June 1920. N. Y.: Priv. print., 1920. 461-570p.
Books by British authors, and books printed in Great Britain or Ireland regardless of nationality of author, to 1640.

3399. Henry E. Huntington Library. "Some Victorian forged rarities, by Roland Baughman." Huntington Library bulletin, no. 9 (1936), 91-117.
Huntington Library has 54 of 55 Wise forgeries investigated by Carter and Pollard.

3400. New York Public Library. "First fruits, an exhibition of first editions of first books by English authors in the Henry W. and Albert A. Berg collection," by John D. Gordan. New York Public Library bulletin, 53 (1949), 159-72, 227-47. Reprinted. 36p.
Chronologically arranged, 1590-1888.

3401. New York Public Library. "Macpherson's Ossian and the Ossianic controversy; a contribution towards a bibliography," by George Fraser Black. New York Public Library bulletin, 30 (1926), 424-39, 508-24. Reprinted. 41p.

3402. Pforzheimer, Carl. The Carl H. Pforzheimer Library, English literature 1475-1700. N. Y.: Priv. print. [The Morrill Press] 1940. 3v.
Important books in English literature, rarities and unique copies.

3403. Pierpont Morgan Library. Original manuscripts and drawings of English authors from the Pierpont Morgan Library on exhibition at the New York Public Library, December 8 to March 1, 1924-1925. [N. Y.: Priv. Print. for the Pierpont Morgan Library by Bruce Rogers and W. E. Rudge, 1925] 54p.

3404. Plimpton, George A. The education of Chaucer, illustrated from the schoolbooks in use in his time. London: Oxford Univ. Press, 1935. 176p.
Based on manuscripts in Plimpton collection now in Columbia University Library.

3405. Princeton University Library. "[The Parrish collection of Victorian literature]" Princeton University Library chronicle, 8 (1946), 1-50.
This whole issue of Chronicle describes collection, with separate articles on Kingsley, Dickens, Hardy, Bulwer-Lytton, and Trollope holdings.

3406. Ratchford, Fannie E., ed. Letters of Thomas J. Wise to John Henry Wrenn; a further inquiry into the guilt of certain nineteenth-century forgers. N. Y.: Knopf, 1944. 591p.
"List of 19th-century English forgeries in the Wrenn Library, with the dates they were acquired and the prices Wrenn paid for them." p. 378-83.

3407. Rugg, Harold G. "Modern authors in New England libraries." College and research libraries, 6 (1944), 54-57.

A report of holdings of 27 libraries for 79 modern American and English writers.

3408. Shelley, Philip A. "A token of the season." Headlight on books at Penn State, 14 (1944), 1-36.

A check list of an exhibition of annuals, foreign and American, at Pennsylvania State College Library, drawn partly from Library's holdings and partly from compiler's private collection.

3409. Sper, Felix. The periodical press of London, theatrical and literary (excluding the daily newspaper), 1800-1830. Boston: Faxon, 1937. 58p.

Locates copies in 27 American and several English libraries.

3410. Texas, University, Library. A catalogue of the library of the late John Henry Wrenn, comp. by Harold B. Wrenn, ed. by Thomas J. Wise. Austin: Univ. of Texas, 1920. 5v.

A collection of 5,300 volumes of English and American literature.

3411. Texas, University, Library. Certain nineteenth century forgeries; an exhibition of books and letters at the University of Texas, June 1 - Sept. 30, 1946, described by Fannie E. Ratchford. [Austin, 1946] 57p.

Relates to Thomas J. Wise forgeries of Victorian authors.

3412. Thorpe, James. "English and American literature in the McCormick collection; some bibliographical notes." Princeton University Library chronicle, 10 (Nov. 1948), 16-40.

In Princeton University Library.

3413. Todd, William B. "The number, order, and authorship of the Hanover pamphlets attributed to Chesterfield." Bibliographical Society of America papers, 44 (1950), 224-38.

Locates copies of pamphlets, printed in 1743, attributed to Lord Chesterfield.

3414. Transylvania College Library. The Welsh collection. Lexington, Ky., 1923. 13p. (Transylvania College bulletin supplement, v. 15, no. 10, Nov. 1923)

List of general collection of 92 book rarities, chiefly pertaining to English literature.

3415. Troxell, Gilbert McCoy. "The Ganson Goodyear Depew memorial collection." Yale University Library gazette, 1 (1927), 53-55.

439 volumes and pamphlets by and about Thackeray and Kipling.

3416. Troxell, Gilbert McCoy. "The Parsons gifts." Yale University Library gazette, 15 (1940), 41-43.

Lists outstanding books by 11 authors from collection of recent English and American writers: Machen, Cabell, Hergesheimer, Wister, Bullen, Coppard, Grahame, Hawkins, Hewlett, Morgan and Weyman.

3417. U. S. Library of Congress. "Annual reports on acquisitions: British belles-lettres." Library of Congress quarterly journal of current acquisitions, 4 (Aug. 1947), 32-34.

3418. Walker, John W., firm, London. Catalogue of English literature of the seventeenth and eighteenth centuries. London: J. W. Walker, 1926. [38]p. (Catalogue, no. 12, 1926)

Pamphlets and a few books, mainly from Earl of Essex's library, acquired by Huntington Library.

3419. White, William Augustus. Catalogue of early English books, chiefly of the Elizabethan period; collected by William Augustus White and catalogued by Henrietta C. Bartlett. N. Y.: Pynson Printers, 1926. 170p.

Occasionally locates copies in Folger and Huntington libraries.

3420. Yale University, Elizabethan Club. The year book of the Elizabethan Club. New Haven: The Club, 1933. 102p.

"Check list of the rare books in the Library," p. 58-88.

Individual authors

BACON, FRANCIS

3421. Livingston, Dorothy F. and Patton, Mollie M. "Contribution to a bibliography of Francis Bacon; editions before 1700 in Yale libraries." In: Papers in honor of Andrew Keogh. New Haven, 1938, p. 95-143.

3422. U. S. Library of Congress; Division of Bibliography. "A selected list of references on Francis Bacon, Viscount St. Albans (1561-1626)." Wash., Dec. 6, 1930. 5p. Typed.

BAILEY, PHILIP JAMES

3423. Peckham, Morse. "American editions of Festus, a preliminary survey." Princeton University Library chronicle, 8 (1947), 177-84.

Lists all editions of Festus by Philip J. Bailey found in Boston Public, New York Public, Philadelphia Free, Library of Congress, and libraries of Princeton, Harvard, Yale and University of Pennsylvania.

3424. Peckham, Morse. "A Bailey collection." Princeton University Library chronicle, 7 (1946), 149-54.

Describes books, letters and material relating to Philip J. Bailey, author of Festus, in Princeton University Library.

BEERBOHM, MAX

3425. Gallatin, Albert E. Sir Max Beerbohm; bibliographical notes. Cambridge: Harvard Univ. Press, 1944. 121p.

Based on Gallatin collection, subsequently presented to Harvard College Library.

BLAKE, WILLIAM

3426. Keynes, Geoffrey. A bibliography of William Blake. N. Y.: Grolier Club, 1921. 516p.

Locates rarer items.

BOSWELL, JAMES

3427. Isham, Ralph Heyward. The private papers of James Boswell, from Malahide Castle, in the collection of Lt.-Col. Ralph Heyward Isham; a catalogue, by Frederick A. Pottle and Marion S. Pottle. London: Oxford Univ. Press, 1931. 231p.

Now in Yale University Library.

3428. Pottle, Frederick Albert. The literary career of James Boswell, esq.; being the bibliographical materials for a life of Boswell. Oxford: Clarendon Press, 1929. 335p.

Copies located and described.

BROME, RICHARD

3429. Cook, Elizabeth. "The plays of Richard Brome." More books, 22 (1947), 285-301.

Describes complete set of Brome's plays in Boston Public Library.

BROWNING, ROBERT

3430. Armstrong, A. Joseph. Browning the world over, etc. Waco, Texas: Baylor University, 1933. (Baylor bulletin, 36, nos. 3-4, p. 5-190)

"A bibliography of foreign Browningiana," p. 95-187, locates only those books which are in the Baylor University Browning collection.

3431. Baker, Frank Sheaffer, comp. "A Browning bibliography: Elizabeth Barrett, Robert Browning in the Harvard College Library, Wellesley College Library, Boston Public Library." 1932. 108 numb. l. Typed.

3432. Baylor University. Baylor University's Browning collection and other Browning interests, by A. J. Armstrong. Waco, Texas, 1927. 43p. (Baylor bulletin, v. 30, no. 4, Dec. 1927)

3433. Baylor University Library. Browningiana in Baylor University, comp. by Aurelia E. Brooks. [Waco, Texas: Baylor University, 1921] 405p. (Baylor University bulletin, v. 24, nos. 5-6)

An author, title and subject bibliography of items by and about Browning in Baylor University Library.

BUNYAN, JOHN

3434. New York Public Library. "The pilgrim's progress; John Bunyan, his life and times, 1628-1928," comp. by Charles Flowers McCombs. New York Public Library bulletin, 32 (1928), 786-809. Reprinted. 26p.

Catalog of an exhibition drawn from New York Public Library and Pierpont Morgan Library.

3435. Newberry Library. Catalogue of John Bunyan, his work and his time. An exhibition of books and prints in commemoration of the 300th anniversary of his birth, 1628-1928. Chicago, 11p.

BURNEY, FANNY

3436. U. S. Library of Congress, Division of Bibliography. "Fanny Burney (Madame Frances D'Arblay) 1752-1840; a bibliographical list." Wash., Nov. 21, 1930. 15p. Typed.

BUTLER, SAMUEL

3437. Hoppe, A. J. A bibliography of the writings of Samuel Butler (author of "Erewhon") and of writings about him, with some letters from Samuel Butler to the Rev. F. G. Fleay, now first published. London: Office of "The Bookman's journal," [1925] 184p.

Gives a few American locations.

3438. Humphry, James, III. "Samuel Butler: author of Erewhon." Colby Library quarterly, ser. 2, no. 9 (Feb. 1949), 141-45.

Brief description of some titles in collection of single works by Samuel Butler, given to Colby College Library.

3439. Williams College, Chapin Library. Catalogue of the collection of Samuel Butler of Erewhon in the Chapin Library. Portland, Maine: Southworth-Anthoensen Press, 1945. 35p.

BYRON, GEORGE GORDON

3440. Henry E. Huntington Library. Byron, 1788-1938; an exhibition, prep. by Ricardo Quintana. San Marino: The Library, 1938. 15p.

Describes 30 items of Byroniana in Huntington Library.

3441. Steffan, T. G. "Byron autograph letters in the library of the University of Texas." Studies in philology, 43 (1946), 682-99.

Lists 74 letters and other manuscripts.

3442. Texas, University, Library. A descriptive catalogue of an exhibition of manuscripts and first editions of Lord Byron, comp. and annotated by R. H. Griffith and H. M. Jones. Austin: Univ. of Texas Press, 1924. 106p.

Most of items exhibited were drawn from University of Texas Library; owners' names are indicated for remainder.

3443. Texas, University, Library. Lord Byron and his circle; a calendar of manuscripts in the University of Texas Library, comp. by Willis W. Pratt. Austin, 1947. 60p.

Contains 293 entries.

CARLYLE, THOMAS

3444. Michigan, University, Library. A catalogue of the Dr. Samuel A. Jones Carlyle collection, with additions from the general library; comp. by Mary Eunice Wead. Ann Arbor: University of Michigan, 1919. 119p.

Jones collection of Carlyleana was purchased en bloc by University of Michigan Library.

CARROLL, LEWIS

3445. Columbia University Library. Catalogue of an exhibition at Columbia University to commemorate the one hundredth anniversary of the birth of Lewis Carroll (Charles Lutwidge Dodgson), 1832-1898. N. Y.: Columbia Univ. Press, 1932. 153p.

Includes loaned material.

3446. Harvard University Library. The Harcourt Amory collection of Lewis Carroll in the Harvard College Library, comp. by Flora V. Livingston. Cambridge, Mass.: Priv. print., 1932. 190p.

3447. Parrish, Morris L. A list of the writings of Lewis Carroll in the library at Dormy House, Pine Valley, New Jersey. [Philadelphia] 1928. 148p. Supplementary list. [Philadelphia] 1933. [116] p.

Collection bequeathed to Princeton University Library.

3448. Williams, Sidney Herbert and Madan, Falconer. A handbook of the literature of the Rev. C. L. Dodgson (Lewis Carroll). London: Oxford Univ. Press, 1931. 336p.

Locates copies in American and English libraries.

COLERIDGE, SAMUEL TAYLOR

3449. Harvard University Library. "Scribblings and marginalia." Harvard Library notes, 3 (1936), 132-35.

Coleridge annotations and marginalia, Harvard College Library.

CONRAD, JOSEPH

3450. Keating, George T. A Conrad memorial library, the collection of George T. Keating. N. Y.: Doubleday, Doran & Co., 1929. 448p.

Now in Yale University Library.

3451. Yale University Library. A Conrad memorial library; addresses delivered at the opening of the exhibition of Mr. George T. Keating's Conrad collection... with a check list of Conrad items supplementary to Mr. Keating's published catalogue, by James T. Babb. New Haven: Yale University Library, 1938. 40p. (Yale University Library gazette, 13 (1938), no. 1)

CROWNE, JOHN

3452. Winship, George Parker. The first Harvard playwright. Cambridge: Harvard Univ. Press, 1922. 22p.

A bibliography of Restoration dramatist John Crowne.

CUNNINGHAME GRAHAM, R. B.

3453. Dartmouth College Library. The Herbert Faulkner West collection of R. B. Cunninghame Graham, presented in memory of "Don Roberto" to the Dartmouth College Library in August nineteen hundred and thirty-eight, comp. by Herbert Faulkner West. [Hanover]: Priv. print. [Dartmouth Printing Co.] 1938. 20p.

DEFOE, DANIEL

3454. [Hutchins, Henry C.] "Defoe at Yale." Yale University Library gazette, 22 (1948), 99-115.

Describes the Yale Defoe collection, Defoeana and Defoe's library at Yale.

3455. Hutchins, Henry C. Robinson Crusoe and its printing, 1719-1731. A bibliographical study. N. Y.: Columbia Univ. Press, 1925. 201p.

Locates copies.

3456. Hutchins, Henry C. "Robinson Crusoe at Yale." Yale University Library gazette, 11 (1936), 17-36.

A survey of 650 volumes in the library, most of them bearing the name of Robinson Crusoe.

3457. James, Margaret A. and Tucker, Dorothy F. "Daniel Defoe, journalist." Business Historical Society bulletin, 2 (January, 1928), 2-6.

Commercial pamphlets in Baker Library, Harvard University.

DICKENS, CHARLES

3458. Clark, William Andrews. The library of William Andrews Clark, Jr. Cruikshank and Dickens. San Francisco: J. H. Nash, 1921-23. 2v.

Now in University of California, Los Angeles.

3459. Eckel, John C. Prime Pickwicks in parts, census with complete collation, comparison and comment... with a foreword by A. Edward Newton. N. Y.: Edgar H. Wells & Co., 1928. 91p.

Locates original copies of the Posthumous papers of the Pickwick Club in institutional and private collections.

3460. [Harvard University Library] A catalogue of the writings of Charles Dickens in the library of Harry Elkins Widener, by A. S. W. Rosenbach. Philadelphia: Privately printed, 1918. 111p.

Collection now in Harvard University.

3461. Henry E. Huntington Library. "The Dickens letters in the Huntington Library," by Franklin P. Rolfe. Huntington Library quarterly, 1 (1938), 335-63.

A survey of over 1,350 letters to, from, or pertaining to Charles Dickens.

3462. New York Public Library. "Charles Dickens; his life as traced by his works," comp. by Cortes W. Cavanaugh. New York Public Library bulletin, 33 (1929), 291-319. Reprinted. 31p.

3463. Parrish, Morris L. A list of the writings of Charles Dickens. [Philadelphia, 1938] 18 unnumb. p.

Compiled from collection at Dormy House, Pine Valley, N. J.; bequeathed to Princeton University Library.

3464. Philadelphia Free Library. The life and works of Charles Dickens, 1812-1870; an exhibition from the collection of William M. Elkins, Esq. of Philadelphia, held at the Free Library, June-July, 1946, by John H. Powell. Philadelphia: The Library, 1946. 58p.

Material described now owned by Free Library of Philadelphia.

DONNE, JOHN

3465. Keynes, Geoffrey. A bibliography of Dr. John Donne, Dean of Saint Paul's. Cambridge: Cambridge Univ. Press, 1932. 195p.

Copies located in Harvard, Huntington, R. B. Adam Library, and English collections.

DRYDEN, JOHN

3466. Boston Public Library. "The plays of John Dryden." More books, 8 (1933), 1-13, 45-59, 89-100.

"A list of Dryden's plays in the Boston Public Library," p. 100.

3467. Osborn, James Marshall. Macdonald's bibliography of Dryden; an annotated check list of selected American libraries. [1942] 69-98, 197-212p. Reprinted from Modern philology, 39 (1941), no. 1-2.

Copies located in 10 libraries.

EDGEWORTH, MARIA

3468. Slade, Bertha Coolidge. Maria Edgeworth, 1767-1849; a bibliographical tribute. London: Constable, 1937. 253p.

Copies located in American and English libraries.

EVELYN, JOHN

3469. Keynes, Geoffrey. John Evelyn; a study in bibliophily & a bibliography of his writings. N. Y.: Grolier Club, 1937. 308p.

Locates copies in Henry E. Huntington Library and occasionally in other American libraries.

FIELDING, HENRY

3470. Cross, Wilbur Lucius. "The Fielding collection." Yale University Library gazette, 1 (1927), 31-34.

Describes a collection of 2,000 volumes given to Yale University Library by Frederick Dickson.

3471. Cross, Wilbur Lucius. The history of Henry Fielding. New Haven: Yale Univ. Press, 1918. 3v.

Bibliography (v. 3, p. [287]-366) locates copies in Yale Library and occasionally other libraries.

GOLDSMITH, OLIVER

3472. Balderston, Katharine Canby. A census of the manuscripts of Oliver Goldsmith. N. Y.: E. B. Hackett, 1926. 73p.

Locates manuscripts in America and England.

3473. Scott, Temple. Oliver Goldsmith, bibliographically and biographically considered based on the collection of material in the library of W. M. Elkins, Esq. N. Y.: Bowling Green Press, 1928. 368p.

Collection now owned by Free Library of Philadelphia.

GRAY, THOMAS

3474. Northup, Clark Sutherland. A bibliography of Thomas Gray. New Haven: Yale Univ. Press, 1917. 296p. (Cornell studies in English...[I]).

Locates books in 8 American libraries.

HARDY, THOMAS

3475. Colby College Library. "Books from Hardy's Max Gate Library." Colby Library quarterly, 2 (Aug. 1950), 246-54.

Annotated list of 50 titles from Thomas Hardy's library, now owned by Colby College Library.

3476. Colby College Library. A century of Thomas Hardy; catalogue of a centennial exhibition, Colby College Library. [Fairfield, Me.: Galahad Press, 1940] 14p.

3477. Colby College Library. The first hundred years of Thomas Hardy, 1840-1940; a centenary bibliography of Hardiana, by Carl J. Weber. Waterville, Me.: Colby College Library, 1942. 276p.

Based primarily on material in Colby College Library.

3478. Colby College Library. Hardy at Colby; a check-list of the writings by and about Thomas Hardy now in the library of Colby College, comp. by Carl J. Weber. Waterville, Me.: Colby College Library, 1936. 152p.

3479. Colby College Library. The jubilee of Tess, 1891-1941; catalogue of an exhibition in commemoration of the fiftieth anniversary of the publication of Tess of the D'Urbervilles, by Thomas Hardy. Waterville, Me.: The Library, 1941. 62p.

Books in Colby College Library.

3480. Yale University Library. Thomas Hardy, O. M. 1840-1928, catalogue of a memorial exhibition of first editions, autograph letters and manuscripts, by Richard L. Purdy. New Haven, 1928. 41p.

"Items not otherwise designated are from the Yale Library."

HOLCROFT, THOMAS

3481. New York Public Library. "A bibliography of Thomas Holcroft," by Elbridge Colby. New York Public Library bulletin, 26 (1922), 455-92, 664-86, 765-87.

Indicates copies in New York Public Library and occasionally in other libraries.

HOUSMAN, ALFRED EDWARD

3482. Dillard, Henry B. "The manuscript poems of Alfred Edward Housman." Library of Congress quarterly journal of current acquisitions, 5 (Feb. 1948), 7-8.

Acquired by Library of Congress.

3483. Housman, A. E. A Shropshire lad, ed. with notes and bibliography by Carl J. Weber. Waterville, Me.: Colby College Press, 1946. 133p.

Bibliography lists about 80 editions in Colby College Library.

HOWELL, JAMES

3484. Vann, William Harvey. Notes on the writings of James Howell. [Waco, Tex.: Baylor University Press, 1924] 71p.

Locates copies in 9 American and 9 British libraries.

JOHNSON, SAMUEL

3485. Harvard University Library. "A Johnson exhibition." Harvard Library notes, 3 (1935), 20-29.

Drawn from first editions and autograph letters of Samuel Johnson in Harvard College Library.

3486. Yale University Library. A catalogue of an exhibition of first editions of the works of Samuel Johnson in the library of Yale University, by Allen T. Hazen and Edward L. McAdam, Jr. New Haven, 1935. 32p.

KEATS, JOHN

3487. Harvard University Library. "John Keats." Harvard Library notes, 1 (1921), 78-81.

Account of exhibitions, Harvard College Library.

LAMB, CHARLES

3488. Finch, Jeremiah Stanton. "Charles Lamb's 'Companionship... in almost solitude' " Princeton University Library chronicle, 6 (1945), 179-99.

Lists the Lamb manuscripts in the Scribner Lamb collection at Princeton University Library.

3489. Finch, Jeremiah Stanton. "The Scribner Lamb collection." Princeton University Library chronicle, 7 (1946), 133-48.

Describes rare editions and autograph manuscripts of Charles and Mary Lamb in collection given to Princeton University Library.

3490. Texas, University, Library. Charles Lamb, 10 February 1775-27 December 1834; an exhibition of books and manuscripts in the Library of the University of Texas. Austin: Univ. of Texas, 1935. 7p.

LEAR, EDWARD

3491. Field, William B. O. Edward Lear on my shelves. [Munich]: Privately printed, 1933. 455p.

Based on a collection subsequently presented to Harvard College Library.

LEECH, JOHN

3492. Field, William B. O. John Leech on my shelves. [Munich] 1930. 313p.

Based on collection presented to Harvard College Library.

MARLOWE, CHRISTOPHER

3493. Tannenbaum, Samuel A. Christopher Marlowe (a concise bibliography). N. Y.: Scholars' Facsimiles and Reprints, 1937. 95p. (His Elizabethan bibliographies, no. 1)

Supplement 1. N. Y.: The Author, 1937. 5p.
Supplement. N. Y.: The Author, 1947. 99p.

"Materials... gathered almost wholly from... the New York Public Library and... the library of Columbia University."

MARTINEAU, HARRIET

3494. New York Public Library. "Harriet Martineau, a bibliography of her separately printed books, comp. by Joseph B. Rivlin." New York Public Library bulletin, 50 (1946), 387-408, 476-98, 550-72, 789-808, 838-56, 888-908; 51 (1947), 26-48. Reprinted. 150p.

Lists works in New York Public Library and locates other copies and editions in 118 libraries.

MEREDITH, GEORGE

3495. Yale University Library. A catalogue of the Altschul collection of George Meredith in the Yale University Library, comp. by Bertha Coolidge. [Boston] 1931. 195p.

MILTON, JOHN

3496. Fletcher, Harris Francis. Contributions to a Milton bibliography, 1800-1930. Urbana: Univ. of Illinois, 1931. 166p. (Univ. of Illinois studies in language and literature, v. 16, no. 1)

"A list of addenda to Stevens's Reference guide to Milton." List represents material found in University of Illinois Library.

3497. Fletcher, Harris Francis. John Milton's complete poetical works. Urbana: Univ. of Illinois Press, 1943-48. 4v.

"List of copies used for collation," with locations, in front of each volume.

3498. Magoun, Francis P., Jr. "Miltoniana." Harvard Library notes, 2 (1925), 49-56.

In Harvard College Library.

3499. Witherspoon, A. M. "A new Milton gift." Yale University Library gazette, 20 (1945), 33-35.

Describes a first edition of tractate "Of education," by Milton.

MORE, THOMAS

3500. Sullivan, Frank and Sullivan, Majie Padberg. Moreana, 1478-1945; a preliminary check list of material by and about Saint Thomas More. Kansas City, Mo.: Rockhurst College, 1946. [175]p.

Locates manuscripts but not printed material.

POPE, ALEXANDER

3501. Colby College Library. "The Pope collection at Colby," by Frederick A. Pottle. Colby Library quarterly, ser. 1, no. 7 (June 1944), 106-16.

3502. Griffith, Reginald Harvey. Alexander Pope; a bibliography. Austin: Univ. of Texas, 1922-27. v. 1, pt. 1-2.

Many of the items listed are from the Wrenn Library, University of Texas, but other locations are frequently indicated.

3503. Lefferts, Marshall Clifford. Alexander Pope; notes towards a bibliography of early editions of his writings; a catalogue of Marshall C. Lefferts's great collection of first and later editions of the works of Alexander Pope, with the autograph manuscript of An essay on man. Offered for sale by Dodd, Mead & Co., N. Y. [Cedar Rapids, Ia.: Torch Press, 1910] 50p.

Collection acquired by Harvard University.

3504. Ratchford, Fanny E. "The Pope bicentennial exhibition." University of Texas Library chronicle, 1 (Summer, 1944), 1-9.

ROBERTSON, THOMAS WILLIAM

3505. U. S. Library of Congress, Division of Bibliography. "Thomas William Robertson, 1829-1871: a bibliographical list." Wash., Apr. 20, 1928. 9p. Typed.

ROSSETTI, DANTE GABRIEL

3506. Duke University Library. Dante Gabriel Rossetti, an analytical list of manuscripts in the Duke University Library, ed. by P. F. Baum. Durham: Duke Univ. Press, 1931. 122p.

RUSKIN, JOHN

3507. French, Robert D. "The R. B. Adam collection of Ruskin." Yale University Library gazette, 4 (1929), 1-7.

Describes Ruskiniana in Yale University Library.

3508. Hogan, Charles Beecher. "The Yale collection of the manuscripts of John Ruskin." Yale University Library gazette, 16 (1942), 61-69.

3509. Roberts, Ethel D. "The Ruskin collection at the Wellesley College Library." Library journal, 47 (1922), 75-76.

3510. Thorp, Willard. "The Ruskin manuscripts." Princeton University Library chronicle, 1 (1940), 1-10.

Ruskin manuscripts, letters and sketchbooks, formerly part of Brantwood collection, now in Princeton University Library.

SANDYS, GEORGE

3511. Bowers, Fredson and Davis, Richard Beale. "George Sandys: a bibliographical catalogue of printed editions in England to 1700." New York Public Library bulletin, 54 (1950), 159-81, 223-44, 280-86.

Locates copies in 15 American and 5 English collections.

SCOTT, WALTER

3512. Henry E. Huntington Library. "The Scott letters in the Huntington Library." Huntington Library quarterly, 2 (1939), 319-52.

102 letters of Sir Walter Scott giving additions and corrections to Grierson's listings in his The Letters of Sir Walter Scott.

3513. U. S. Library of Congress, Division of Bibliography. "A list of the American editions of the writings of Sir Walter Scott in the Library of Congress." Wash., Aug. 16, 1916. 12p. Typed. [Supplementary list] July 3, 1931. 6p. Typed.

SHAKESPEARE, WILLIAM

3514. Bartlett, Henrietta Collins and Pollard, Alfred W. A census of Shakespeare's plays in quarto, 1594-1709, rev. and extended. New Haven: Yale Univ. Press, 1939. 165p. 1st ed. 1916. 153p.

Locates and describes every known copy of each edition.

3515. Bartlett, Henrietta Collins. "First editions of Shakespeare's quartos." Library, ser. 4, 16 (1935), 166-72.

Supplements Bartlett and Pollard's Census of Shakespeare's plays. Locates copies.

3516. Bartlett, Henrietta Collins. Mr. William Shakespeare, original and early editions of his quartos and folios; his source books and those containing contemporary notices. New Haven: Yale Univ. Press, 1922. 217p.

Locations shown for 15 libraries and collections in America, and many British sources.

3517. Boston Public Library. Catalogue of the Barton collection, Boston Public Library. In two parts: pt. I. Shakespeare's works and Shakespeariana; pt. II. Miscellaneous. [Boston]: The Library, [1878-] 88. 2v.

Records about 12,000 volumes.

3518. Boston Public Library. Catalogue of the works of William Shakespeare, original and translated, together with the Shakespeariana embraced in the Barton collection of the Boston Public Library, by James Mascarene Hubbard. [Boston]: The Library, 1880. 227p.

3519. Boston Public Library. Shakespeare tercentenary, 1616-1916; an exhibition, free lectures, selected list of working editions, and works relating to Shakespeare, offered by the Public Library of the City of Boston. Boston: The Trustees, 1915. 44p.

3520. Charlton, Henry Buckley. "The Folger Shakespeare Memorial Library." John Rylands Library bulletin, 27 (1942), 70-73.

Describes history and some of resources of Folger Library.

3521. Ellesmere, Francis Egerton. A catalogue, bibliographical and critical, of early English literature, forming a portion of the library at Bridgewater House. London: T. Rodd, 1837. 366p.

Collection now in possession of Henry E. Huntington Library.

3522. Folger Shakespeare Library. The Folger Shakespeare Library, Washington. [Wash.]: Published for the Trustees of Amherst College, 1933. 36p.

A general description of Library's collections.

3523. Folger Shakespeare Library. The Folger Shakespeare Library; a brief description. [Amherst, Mass.?]: Published for the Trustees of Amherst College, 1949. 13p.
Includes general description of collections.

3524. Folger Shakespeare Library. The Folger Shakespeare Memorial Library, administered by the Trustees of Amherst College; a report on progress, 1931-1941, by Joseph Quincy Adams. [Amherst, Mass.]: Pub. for the Trustees of Amherst College, 1942. 61p.
Lists accessions for decade, under 6 appropriate headings.

3525. Harvard University Library. "The Shakespeare quartos." Harvard Library notes, 2 (1928), 185-95.
In Harvard College Library.

3526. Harvard University Library. "The Shakespeare shelves." Harvard Library notes, 1 (1923), 258-67.
In Harvard College Library.

3527. Jaggard, Wm. Shakespeare bibliography; a dictionary of every known issue of the writings of our national poet and of recorded opinion thereon in the English language. Stratford-on-Avon: Shakespeare Press, 1911. 729p.
Copies located in 6 American libraries.

3528. [Livingston, Luther Samuel] The four folios of Shakespeare's plays... together with a census of known perfect copies of the first folio. [N. Y., 1907] 32p.

3529. Meyer, Herman Henry Bernard. A brief guide to the literature of Shakespeare. Chicago: American Library Association, 1915. 61p.
Includes Library of Congress card numbers.

3530. New York Public Library. Catalogue of an exhibition of Shakespeareana, comp. by Henrietta Collins Bartlett. N. Y.: The Library, 1916. 161p.

3531. Plimpton, George A. The education of Shakespeare, illustrated from the schoolbooks in use in his time. N. Y.: Oxford Univ. Press, 1933. 140p.
Based on Plimpton collection now owned by Columbia University.

3532. Rosenbach, A. S. W. A description of the four folios of Shakespeare, 1623, 1632, 1663-4, 1685 in the original bindings... gift to the Free Library of Philadelphia. Philadelphia, 1945. 18p.
Gives facsimile reproductions of original title pages.

3533. St. Louis Public Library. "Guide to the literature of Shakespeare in the St. Louis Public Library." St. Louis Public Library monthly bulletin, n. s. 14 (1916), 77-135.

3534. Schelling, F. E. "The Horace Howard Furness Memorial." University of Pennsylvania Library chronicle, 1 (1933), 6-7.
Description of 12,000-volume collection of Shakespearian and Elizabethan literature in University of Pennsylvania Library.

3535. Schelling, F. E. "Shakespeare books in the library of the Furness Memorial." University of Pennsylvania Library chronicle, 3 (1935), 33-41.

3536. Shakespeare, William. Notes & additions to the census of copies of the Shakespeare first folio, by Sidney Lee. London, N. Y.: H. Frowde, 1906. 30p. (Reprinted from The Library, 2d ser. 7 (1906), 113-39)
Locates copies in American and British libraries or collections.

3537. Shakespeare, William. Shakespeare's comedies, histories, and tragedies; being a reproduction in facsimile of the first folio edition, 1623, from the Chatsworth copy... with introduction and census of copies by Sidney Lee. Oxford: Clarendon Press, 1902. 908p. V. 2 is "A supplement... containing a census of extant copies." Oxford, 1902. 45p.
The supplement lists 158 copies, and locates 152 copies.

3538. Smith, Robert Metcalf. The Shakespeare folios and the forgeries of Shakespeare's handwriting in the Lucy Packer Linderman Memorial Library of Lehigh University, with a list of original folios in American libraries, by Robert Metcalf Smith. Bethlehem, Pa., 1927. 47p.
Describes copies of the 4 folios of Shakespeare in Lehigh University Library, and all known copies in America; also the 2 forgeries from the pen of William Ireland, now in Lehigh University Library.

3539. Virginia State Library. "Finding list of collected works of Shakespeare and Shakespeareana," comp. by Earl G. Swem. Virginia State Library bulletin, 1 (1908), 293-308.

3540. Whicher, George F. "Shakespeare for America." Atlantic monthly, 147 (1931), 759-68.

Description of Folger Shakespeare Library.

3541. White, William Augustus. Catalogue of early English books, chiefly of the Elizabethan period, collected by William A. White, and catalogued by Henrietta C. Bartlett. [N. Y., 1926] 170p.

Some Shakespeare items from collection went to Harvard, remaining material to Princeton and the New York Public Library.

3542. Winsor, Justin. A bibliography of the original quartos and folios of Shakespeare, with particular reference to copies in America. Boston: J. R. Osgood, 1876. 109p.

Locates copies in 7 public and private collections.

3543. Winsor, Justin. Halliwelliana; a bibliography of the publications of James Orchard Halliwell-Phillipps. Cambridge, Mass.: University Press; J. Wilson & Son, 1881. 30p. (Harvard University Library, Bibliographical contributions, no. 10)

Based on Harvard College Library, Boston Athenaeum and Boston Public Library holdings. Chiefly relating to Shakespeare.

SHAW, GEORGE BERNARD

3544. Kelling, Lucile. "The Henderson collection of GBS." Antiquarian bookman, 6 (1950), 1193-94.

Description of collection relating to George Bernard Shaw in University of North Carolina Library.

3545. Yale University Library. "The Henderson memorial collection of Shaw," ed. by Andrew Keogh. Yale University Library gazette, 12 (1937), 31-42.

Collection of Shaviana now in Yale University Library.

SHELLEY, PERCY BYSSHE

3546. Texas, University, Library. An account of an exhibition of books and manuscripts of Percy Bysshe Shelley. Austin: Univ. of Texas, 1935. 40p.

Some works and manuscripts by Shelley from the Texas University Library collection.

SOUTHEY, ROBERT

3547. New York Public Library. "First and rare editions of Southey in the library," by Nelson Nichols. New York Public Library bulletin, 26 (1922), 3-5.

Lists 25 editions, 1810-50, held by New York Public Library.

SPENSER, EDMUND

3548. Johnson, Francis R. A critical bibliography of the works of Edmund Spenser printed before 1700. Baltimore: Johns Hopkins Press, 1933. 61p.

Based principally upon Spenser collection of Tudor and Stuart Club of Johns Hopkins University.

STEVENSON, ROBERT LOUIS

3549. [Harvard University Library] A catalogue of the books and manuscripts of Robert Louis Stevenson in the library of the late Harry Elkins Widener, with a memoir by A. S. W. Rosenbach. Philadelphia: Privately printed, 1913. 266p.

Collection now owned by Harvard University.

3550. Literary Anniversary Club. Catalogue of the Stevenson exhibition under the auspices of the Literary Anniversary Club... displayed in the San Francisco Public Library. [San Francisco] 1932. 22p.

Locates copies in 18 private libraries, some of which have since been deposited in public institutions.

SWIFT, JONATHAN

3551. Hubbard, Lucius Lee. Contributions toward a bibliography of Gulliver's travels to establish the number and order of issue of the Motte editions of 1726 and 1727, their relative accuracy and the source of the changes made in the Faulkner edition of 1735, with a list of editions in a private collection and twenty-five plates. Chicago: W. M. Hill, 1922. 189p.

Locates copies in Harvard, Yale, Boston Public Library, etc. Hubbard collection now in University of Michigan.

3552. Landa, Louis A. and Tobin, James Edward. Jonathan Swift; a list of critical studies...; to which is added, Remarks on some Swift manuscripts in the United States by Herbert Davis. N. Y.: Cosmopolitan Science and Art Service Co., 1945. 62p. (Eighteenth century bibliographical pamphlets)

Pages 7-16 briefly describe 5 collections of Swiftiana in America.

3553. Ratchford, Fannie E. "Jonathan Swift: a bicentennial exhibition." University of Texas Library chronicle, 2 (1946), 17-20.

Brief description of some Swift books selected from collections at University of Texas Library.

3554. Texas, University, Library. An exhibition of printed books at the University of Texas, October 19 - December 31, 1945... Jonathan Swift 1667-1745. [Austin: Univ. of Texas, 1945?] 48p.

TENNYSON, ALFRED

3555. Texas, University, Library. An exhibition of manuscripts and printed books at the University of Texas, October 1-30, 1942: Alfred, Lord Tennyson, 1809-1892, by Fannie E. Ratchford. [Austin? 1942] 20p.

Drawn from Wrenn, Aitken, and Stark collections at University of Texas.

THACKERAY, WILLIAM MAKEPEACE

3556. New York Public Library. "William Makepeace Thackeray, 1811-1863," by John D. Gordan. New York Public Library bulletin, 51 (1947), 259-96. Reprinted. 39p.

Material from Berg collection "for an exhibition of Thackeray's work as seen in first editions, association copies, manuscripts, autograph letters and original drawings."

3557. Parrish, Morris L. Catalogue of an exhibition of the works of William Makepeace Thackeray, together with books, articles and catalogues referring to Thackeray. Philadelphia, 1940. 95 unnumb. p.

Collection bequeathed to Princeton University Library.

3558. Van Duzer, Henry Sayre. A Thackeray library; first editions and first publications, portraits, water colors, etchings, drawings and manuscripts, collected by Henry Sayre Van Duzer; a few additional items are included, forming a complete Thackeray bibliography; with twenty-three illustrations. N. Y.: Privately printed, 1919. 198p.

Occasionally locates copies elsewhere than in author's collection.

THOMPSON, FRANCIS

3559. Boston College Library. An account of books and manuscripts of Francis Thompson, edited by Terence L. Connolly, Chestnut Hill, Mass.: Boston College [1937] 79p.

Describes Thompsoniana in the Boston College Library.

THOMSON, JAMES

3560. Tregaskis, James, bookseller. "Thomson's Seasons; a remarkable collection of Thomson's Seasons from 1723 to 1908, comprising examples of the work of the most famous eighteenth and nineteenth century book illustrators...," by James Tregaskis, Bookseller, London. In: "Caxton Head" catalogue. London, 1911. p. 65-71.

Acquired by Columbia University Library, 1912.

TROLLOPE, ANTHONY

3561. Booth, Bradford A. "The Parrish Trollope collection." Trollopian, 1 (Summer 1945), 11-19.

Collection bequeathed to Princeton University Library.

3562. Parrish, Morris L. Chronology of the writings of Anthony Trollope. [Philadelphia, 1936] 5 unnumb. p.

Compiled from collection at Dormy House, Pine Valley, N. J., bequeathed to Princeton University Library.

3563. Wilson, Carroll A. "Morris L. Parrish: Trollope collector." Trollopian, 1 (Summer 1945), 5-10.

Relates to collection bequeathed to Princeton University Library.

WALPOLE, HORACE

3564. Harvard University Library. "From Mr. Horatio Walpole's library." Harvard Library notes, 2 (1925), 23-29.

Description of a collection of books from

Horace Walpole's private library, now owned by Harvard University.

3565. Hazen, Allen Tracy. A bibliography of Horace Walpole. New Haven: Yale Univ. Press, 1948. 189p.

Locates copies in institutional and personal collections.

3566. Tucker, Mildred M. "The Merritt Walpole collection." Harvard Library notes, 3 (1935), 41-45.

Survey of a collection of books by and about Horace Walpole, and Walpole manuscripts presented to Harvard College Library.

WALTON, IZAAK

3567. Oliver, Peter. A new chronicle of the compleat angler. N.Y.: Paisley Press, 1936. 301p.

284 editions chronologically arranged, 1653-1935. Locations in 9 collections, public and private.

WILDE, OSCAR

3568. Clark, William Andrews. The library of William Andrews Clark, Jr. Wilde and Wildeiana. San Francisco: J. H. Nash, 1922-31. 5v.

Now in University of California, Los Angeles.

3569. Conway, William E. "The Oscar Wilde collection at the Clark Memorial Library." Book Club of California quarterly news-letter, 12 (1947), 78-79.

WORDSWORTH, WILLIAM

3570. Connecticut College for Women, Palmer Library. An exhibition of first and other early editions of the works of William Wordsworth... with a few autographs and manuscripts lent from the personal library of Professor John Edwin Wells. New London: The Library, 1938. 8 numb. 1.

3571. Cornell University Library. The Cornell Wordsworth collection; a brief account together with a catalogue of the exhibition held in the University Library on the occasion of the centenary of Wordsworth's death. Ithaca, N.Y.: Cornell Univ. Press, 1950. 42p.

3572. Cornell University Library. The Wordsworth collection formed by Cynthia Morgan St. John and given to Cornell University by Victor Emanuel; a catalogue, comp. by Leslie Nathan Broughton. Ithaca, 1931. 124p.

3573. Cornell University Library. The Wordsworth collection formed by Cynthia Morgan St. John and given to Cornell University by Victor Emanuel; a supplement to the catalogue, comp. by Leslie Nathan Broughton. Ithaca: Cornell Univ. Press, 1942. 87p.

3574. Dunklin, Gilbert T. "The George McLean Harper papers." Princeton University Library chronicle, 11 (Winter 1950), 89-94.

Survey of collection, in Princeton University Library, relating mainly to Wordsworth.

3575. New York Public Library. "William Wordsworth, 1770-1850; an exhibition." New York Public Library bulletin, 54 (1950), 333-48. (To be continued.)

Drawn from Berg collection, New York Public Library.

3576. Patton, Cornelius Howard. The Amherst Wordsworth collection; a descriptive bibliography. [Amherst, Mass.] Trustees of Amherst College, 1936. 304p.

"Other Wordsworth collections," p. 273-90.

3577. Winship, George P. "Oxford vs. Harvard." Harvard Library notes, 2 (1925), 33-37.

Wordsworth holdings of Harvard College Library.

YEATS, WILLIAM BUTLER

3578. Yale University Library. A catalogue of English and American first editions of William Butler Yeats; prepared for an exhibition of his works held in the Yale University Library, comp. by William M. Roth. New Haven, 1939. 104p.

Lists all of Yeats's, first editions and some periodicals to which he contributed.

YOUNG, EDWARD

3579. Pettit, Henry. "Further additions to the check-list of Young's 'Night-thoughts' in America." Bibliographical Society of America papers, 44 (1950), 192-95.

Locations of 145 editions of Edward Young's Night-thoughts.

GERMAN LITERATURE

Drama

3580. Johns Hopkins University Library. Fifty years of German drama; a bibliography of modern German drama, 1880-1930, based on the Loewenberg collection. Baltimore: Johns Hopkins Press, 1941. 111p.

Collection in Johns Hopkins University Library.

Fiction

3581. Boston Public Library. Works of fiction in the German language in the Public Library of the City of Boston. Boston: The Library, 1905. 164p.

3582. Snider, Helen Griffith. "A bio-bibliographical list of the Lincke collection of the University of Chicago, A-H (exclusive of translations)" Chicago, 1942. 721p. (M.A. thesis, University of Chicago. Typed.)

A popular circulating-library collection of about 15,000 volumes of 18th and 19th century German fiction and foreign fiction in German translation.

Miscellany

3583. Boston Public Library. "The Sears-Freiligrath Library of German literature," by Margaret Munsterberg. More books, 16 (1941), 179-89.

A survey and description of collection of 1,700 volumes of German literature, especially poetry, in the Boston Public Library.

3584. Buffalo Public Library. Books in German. Deutsche bucher in der Buffalo Oeffentlichen Bibliothek. Buffalo, 1908. 156p.

3585. Cleveland Public Library. Katalog der deutschen bücher. Cleveland: Verlaghause der Evangelischen Gemeinschaft, 1885. 96p.

3586. Detroit Public Library. Katalog der bücher in deutscher sprache. Detroit: Druck von J. Bornman & Son [1904] 169p.

3587. Faber du Faur, Curt von. "The Faber du Faur library." Yale University Library gazette, 20 (1945), 1-6.

Description of a German literature collection, emphasizing 17th century, now in Yale University Library.

3588. Goodnight, Scott Holland. German literature in American magazines prior to 1846. Madison, Wis., 1907. 264p. (Univ. of Wis. bulletin, no. 188, Philology and literature series, v. 4, no. 1)

Lists periodicals and holdings in Wisconsin State Historical Library.

3589. Heuser, Frederick W. J., ed. First editions of the German romantic period in American libraries. N.Y.: Modern Language Association of America, 1942. 48p.

Covers major German authors born between 1770 and 1790. Copies of works located in 98 libraries.

3590. Loacker, E. M. "Germanic libraries at the University of California at Los Angeles." Modern language forum, 25 (June 1940), 82-84.

3591. Morgan, Bayard Quincy. A bibliography of German literature in English translation. Madison, 1922. 708p. (University of Wisconsin studies in language and literature, no. 16)

Copies located in 7 libraries.

3592. Morgan, Bayard Quincy. A critical bibliography of German literature in English translation, 1481-1927; with supplement embracing the years 1928-1935. 2d ed. Stanford University: Standord Univ. Press, 1938. 773p.

Locations shown for Library of Congress, Boston Public Library, Harvard, Columbia, Newberry, New York Public Library, Stanford, University of California, University of Wisconsin, and British Museum.

3593. Peoria Public Library. Katalog deutscher bücher in der Peoria oeffentlichen bibliothek, Peoria, Illinois. [Peoria] E. Hine & Co. [1900] 48p.

Author and title catalog of German books in Peoria Public Library.

3594. U.S. Library of Congress. "Annual reports on acquisitions: German language and literature." Library of Congress quarterly journal of acquisitions, 4 (Aug. 1947), 35-39.

Individual authors

GOETHE, JOHANN WOLFGANG VON

3595. Chicago, University, Library. The Wieboldt-Heinemann Goethe collection. "A checklist of titles by and about Johann Wolfgang von Goethe... presented to the library of the University of Chicago." Chicago, 1945. 8, 26 1. Typed.

3596. Schneider, Heinrich. "Goethe autographs at Harvard." Harvard Library bulletin, 3 (1949), 371-85.

3597. Schreiber, Carl Frederick. The William A. Speck collection of Goethana. [New Haven? 1916] xiip. (Collections of Yale University, no. 3)

3598. Speck, William A. "The Goethe medals and medallions in Yale University Library." Yale University Library gazette, 1 (1926), 17-20.
Describes collection of 215 medals and medallions of Goethe and his contemporaries.

3599. Yale University Library. Goethe's works, with the exception of Faust; a catalogue compiled by members of the Yale University Library staff, ed. by Carl Frederick Schreiber. New Haven: Yale Univ. Press, 1940. 239p.
A catalog of the William A. Speck Collection of Goetheana in the Yale University Library.

HEINE, HEINRICH

3600. Weber, Hilmar H. "Heinrich Heine." Harvard Library notes, 3 (1935), 71-80.
In Kirschstein collection, Harvard College Library.

3601. Weigand, Hermann John. "Heine manuscripts at Yale: their contribution concerning him as man and artist." Studies in philology, 34 (1937), 65-90.

3602. Weigand, Hermann John. "The Kohut-Rutra collection of Heineana." Yale University Library gazette, 8 (1933), 46-49.
Collection of 400 volumes by and about Heine, in Yale University Library.

HOFMANNSTHAL, HUGO VON

3603. [Jacoby, Karl] Hugo von Hofmannsthal. Bibliographie. Berlin: Maximilian Gesellschaft, 1936. 182p.
Based on collection subsequently presented to Harvard College Library. Lists works by and about Hugo von Hofmannsthal, Austrian poet and dramatist.

LESSING, GOTTHOLD

3604. Weber, Hilmar H. "The Reisinger Lessing collection." Harvard Library notes, 3 (1938), 161-63.
In Harvard College Library.

MANN, THOMAS

3605. Angell, Joseph W. "The Thomas Mann collection." Yale University Library gazette, 13 (1938), 41-45.
Describes Mann collection in the Library.

SCANDINAVIAN LITERATURE

Icelandic literature

3606. Barnason, Gudrun. "The Schofield memorial." Harvard Library notes, 2 (1931), 247-64.
Describes Kristjánsson collection of Icelandic books, Harvard College Library.

3607. Cawley, F. Stanton. "Ultima Thule at Harvard." Harvard Alumni bulletin, 33 (1931), 1100-03.
Icelandic books.

3608. Cornell University Library. Catalogue of Runic literature forming a part of the Icelandic collection, comp. by H. Hermannsson. London: Oxford University Press, 1918. 105p.

3609. Cornell University Library. Catalogue of the Icelandic collection bequeathed by Willard Fiske, comp. by Halldór Hermannsson. Ithaca, 1914. 755p. Additions, 1913-1926, comp. by Halldór Hermannsson. Ithaca, 1927. 284p. Additions, 1927-1942, comp. by Halldór Hermannsson. Ithaca, 1943. 295p.

3610. Elkins, Kimball C. "The Icelandic periodicals." Harvard Library notes, 2

(1931), 265-67.
Collections in Harvard College Library.

3611. Hermannsson, Halldór. The ancient laws of Norway and Iceland; a bibliography. Ithaca: Cornell University Library, 1911. 83p. (Islandica, v. 4)
Based on Cornell University Library holdings.

3612. Hermannsson, Halldór. Bibliographical notes. Ithaca: Cornell Univ. Press, 1942. 91p. (Islandica, v. 29)
Contents: Book illustration in Iceland, titles and nicknames of Icelandic books, translations into Icelandic, and additions to bibliographies of 16th and 17th century Icelandic books. Based on Cornell University collection.

3613. Hermannsson, Halldór. Bibliography of the Eddas. Ithaca: Cornell University Library, 1920. 95p. (Islandica; an annual relating to Iceland and the Fiske Icelandic collection in Cornell University Library, v. 13)
Based on Cornell University collection.

3614. Hermannsson, Halldór. Bibliography of the Icelandic sagas and minor tales. Ithaca: Cornell University Library, 1908. 126p. (Islandica; an annual relating to Iceland and the Fiske Icelandic collection in Cornell University Library, v. 1) The sagas of Icelanders, a supplement to Bibliography of the Icelandic sagas and minor tales. Ithaca: Cornell Univ. Press, 1935 (Islandica, v. 24)

3615. Hermannsson, Halldór. Bibliography of the mythical-heroic sagas. Ithaca: Cornell University Library, 1912. 73p. (Islandica; an annual relating to Iceland and the Fiske Icelandic collection in Cornell University Library, v. 5)
Based on Cornell University collection.

3616. Hermannsson, Halldór. Bibliography of the sagas of the kings of Norway and related sagas and tales. Ithaca: Cornell University Library, 1910. 75p. (Islandica; an annual relating to Iceland and the Fiske Icelandic collection in Cornell University Library, v. 3)
Based on Cornell University collection.

3617. Hermannsson, Halldór. Icelandic authors of today, with an appendix giving a list of works dealing with modern Icelandic literature. Ithaca: Cornell University Library, 1913. 69p. (Islandica; an annual relating to Iceland and the Fiske Icelandic collection in Cornell University Library, v. 6)
Based on Cornell University holdings.

3618. Hermannsson, Halldór. Icelandic books of the 16th century (1534-1600). Ithaca: Cornell Univ. Library, 1916. 72p. (Islandica, v. 9)
Based on Cornell University collection.

3619. Hermannsson, Halldór. Icelandic books of the 17th century, 1601-1700. Ithaca: Cornell Univ. Library, 1922. 121p. (Islandica, v. 14)
Based on Cornell University collection.

3620. Hermannsson, Halldór. The Northmen in America. Ithaca, N. Y.: Cornell University Library, 1909. 94p. (Islandica; an annual relating to Iceland and the Fiske Icelandic collection in Cornell University Library, v. 2)
Based on Cornell University collection.

3621. Hermannsson, Halldór. Old Icelandic literature; a bibliographical essay. Ithaca: Cornell Univ. Press, 1933. 50p. (Islandica, v. 23)
Based on Cornell University collection.

3622. Hermannsson, Halldór. The periodical literature of Iceland down to the year 1874. N. Y.: Cornell Univ. Library, 1918. 100p. (Islandica, v. 11)
Based on Cornell University collection.

3623. Hermannsson, Halldór. The sagas of the kings (Konuga sögur) and the mythical-heroic sagas (Fornalder sögur). Two bibliographical supplements. Ithaca: Cornell Univ. Press, 1937. 84p. (Islandica, v. 26)
"The first bibliography... supplements the Bibliography of the sagas of the kings of Norway... The second supplements the Bibliography of the mythical-heroic sagas..." - Pref. Based on Cornell University collection.

3624. Maurer, Konrad von. Katalog der bibliothek des verstorbenen universitäts professors Konrad von Maurer. Munich: Junge & Sohn, 1903. 304, 106p.
Now in Harvard University Library. Over 9,000 items, notably in Icelandic literature and philology and in Germanic law and philology.

Other Scandinavian literature

3625. Benson, Adolph Burnett. "The Scandinavian collection." Yale University Library gazette, 8 (1933), 49-53.
Description of Yale's Scandinavian materials.

3626. Benson, Adolph Burnett. "Swedish rarities in the Yale University Library." American Swedish monthly, 29 (July 1935), 5-8.

3627. Carlson, William H. "Scandinavian collections in the libraries of the United States." Scandinavian studies and notes, 15 (1939), 217-38. Supplemented by "Some further notes on Scandinaviana in the libraries of the United States." Scandinavian studies, 16 (1941), 291-303.
Describes 27 outstanding American collections.

3628. Chicago Public Library. Danish-Norwegian, Swedish; recent Scandinavian books added to the Chicago Public Library. [Chicago] 1942. 172p.

3629. Chicago Public Library. Scandinavian books, Danish-Norwegian-Swedish. [Chicago]: The Library, 1929. 172p.

3630. Harvard University Library. "Swedish books and books relating to Sweden in the Harvard College Library, March 1929." 185p. Typed.

3631. Minneapolis Public Library. Finding list of the Minneapolis Public Library Scandinavian literature, 3d ed. Minneapolis: University Press, 1908. 47p. Supplement, 1908-1912. Minneapolis: Index Press, 1913. 35p.

3632. Pierpont Morgan Library. The first editions of Hans Christian Andersen, the king of the fairy tales, with Hilaire Belloc's essay. [Edinburgh: Turnbull & Spears, 19-?] 31p.
List of 98 items, including autograph manuscripts now in Pierpont Morgan Library.

FRENCH LITERATURE

Drama

3633. Forest, H. U. "Hurlburt Memorial French collection." University of Pennsylvania Library chronicle, 5 (1937), 75-79.
Collection of French drama.

3634. U. S. Library of Congress. A list of French plays, 1789-1860, purchased by the Library of Congress in 1930. [Wash., 1930] 157 l.
Collection of about 2,500 items.

Fiction

3635. Boston Public Library. Works of fiction in the French language, together with translations from the French, in the Bates Hall of the Public Library of the City of Boston. Boston: The Library, 1892. 104p.

3636. Jones, Silas Paul. A list of French prose fiction from 1700-1750. N. Y.: H. W. Wilson, 1939. 150p.
Locates copies occasionally in America, and gives several European sources.

3637. Lowell City Library. French fiction in the Lowell City Library. Lowell, Mass., 1916. 45p.

3638. Mercantile Library Association of the City of New York. Finding list of French prose fiction in the Mercantile Library of the City of New York. February, 1888. [N. Y.]: The Library, 1888. 76p.

3639. Webb, Willard. "A bibliography of fiction concerned with the history of France," prep. by Willard Webb. Wash.: Library of Congress, 1927. 48 l. Photostat from typewritten copy.
The novels listed are arranged in three groups: 1. Chronological; 2. alphabetical by title; 3. alphabetical by author.

3640. Williams, Ralph Coplestone. Bibliography of the seventeenth-century novel in France. N. Y.: Century Co., 1931. 355p.
Locates copies in Library of Congress and several foreign libraries.

Miscellany

3641. California, University, Library. The dedication of the library of French thought. Berkeley: Univ. of California, 1918. 40p.
Description of 2,500-volume collection covering French literature, philosophy, and

science, originally exhibited at Panama-Pacific International Exposition and subsequently presented to the University of California.

3642. Detroit Public Library. List of French books. [Detroit] 1925. 76p.

3643. Hawkins, Richmond L. "The manuscripts of the Roman de la Rose in the libraries of Harvard and Yale Universities." Romanic review, 19 (1928), 1-24.

3644. Morize, André. "Two shelves of rarities." Harvard Library notes, 2 (1925), 6-9.
  French literature, 16th and 17th centuries, from the library of Edward Moura, in Harvard College Library.

3645. New York Public Library. "A bibliography of modern Provençal in the English language, 1840-1940," comp. by Alphonse V. Roche. New York Public Library bulletin, 46 (1942), 379-88. Reprinted. 10p.
  Most of works listed are in New York Public Library. Locations are given for others.

3646. New York Public Library. "A check list of mazarinades in the New York Public Library," prep. by Horace E. Hayden. New York Public Library bulletin, 41 (1937), 29-41. Reprinted with "French printing through 1650," 1938. 102p.

3647. New York Public Library. "Provençal literature and language, including the local history of southern France; a list of references in the New York Public Library," comp. by Daniel Carl Haskell. New York Public Library bulletin, 25 (1921), 372-400, 445-75, 537-69, 675-736, 753-85, 808-62; 26 (1922), 11-52, 128-53, 200-22, 397-434, 522-36, 632-41, 687-732, 788-837, 863-822, 947-1005, 1033-1086. Reprinted, with additions and index, 1925. 885p.

3648. Salmagundi Club Library. Revised catalogue of the J. Sanford Saltus collection of Louis XVII books in the library of the Salmagundi Club. New York. [N. Y.: D. Taylor & Co.] 1908. [22]p.
  Now in French Institute Library, New York.

3649. U. S. Library of Congress. "Toinet collection of French literature acquired by purchase by the Library of Congress, 1929." [Wash., 1929] 142 l. Typed.

Individual authors

BEAUMARCHAIS, PIERRE A. C. DE

3650. New York Public Library. "Editions of Beaumarchais available for study in New York City," comp. by Harriet Dorothea Macpherson. New York Public Library bulletin, 29 (1925), 13-28. Reprinted. 18p.
  Locates copies in 6 libraries.

BOSSUET, JACQUES BENIGUE

3651. Shaw, Gertrude M. "Harvard's Bossuet." Harvard Library notes, 2 (1925), 60-62. See also Harvard Library notes, 2 (1926), 90.

LAFONTAINE, JEAN DE

3652. New York Public Library. "The Fragonard plates for the 'Contes et Nouvelles' of La Fontaine," by Edwin Wolf, 2nd. New York Public Library bulletin, 53 (1949), 107-20. Reprinted. 16p.
  Locates copies in Library of Congress, National Art Gallery, Boston Museum of Fine Arts, Metropolitan Museum of Art, and a private collection.

MOLIÈRE, JEAN BAPTISTE

3653. Harvard University Library. Catalogue of the Molière collection in the Harvard College Library, comp. by Thomas Franklin Currier and Ernest Lewis Gay. Cambridge: Harvard University Library, 1906. 148p. (Harvard University Library, bibliographical contributions, no. 57)

MONTAIGNE, MICHEL E. DE

3654. Buffum, Imbrie. "Special collections at Princeton: II. The LeBrun collection of Montaigne." Princeton University Library chronicle, 1 (Feb. 1940), 11-[16]
  Survey of collection presented to Princeton University Library.

3655. Wright, Charles H. C. "The Bôcher collection of editions of Montaigne and Molière." Harvard Library notes, 2

(1925), 9-11.
   In Harvard College Library.

MONTESQUIEU, CHARLES DE S.

3656. New York Public Library. "Montesquieu: a bibliography," comp. by David C. Cabeen. New York Public Library bulletin, 51 (1947), 359-83, 423-30, 513-19, 545-65, 593-616. Reprinted. 87p.
   Locates all editions of Montesquieu's works in New York Public Library and Columbia University Libraries.

ROUSSEAU, JEAN JACQUES

3657. Hawkins, Richmond L. "The manuscripts of Jean-Jacques Rousseau at Harvard University." Romanic review, 20 (1929), 209-21.

3658. [Pierpont Morgan Library]. La collection Jean-Jacques Rousseau de la bibliothèque de J. Pierpont Morgan... lettres, notes manuscrites et éditions, par Albert Schinz. Paris: E. Champion [1925] 59p., 3 facsims. (Smith College studies in modern languages, v. 7, no. 1, Oct. 1925)

VOLTAIRE, FRANÇOIS M. A.

3659. Morehouse, Andrew R. "The Voltaire collection in the Rare book room." Yale University Library gazette, 17 (1943), 66-79.
   400 works by and about Voltaire now in rare book room of Yale University Library.

ITALIAN LITERATURE

Miscellany

3660. Baumgartner, Leona and Fulton, John F. A bibliography of the poem Syphilis Sive Morbus Gallicus by Girolamo Francastoro of Verona. New Haven: Yale Univ. Press, 1935. 157p.
   Editions located in 68 American and foreign libraries.

3661. Boston Public Library. Collezione dei libri italiani moderni che trovansi nella Libreria pubblica della città di Boston. Boston: Pubblicata degli amministratori, 1922. 108p.
   "Books published since 1900, arranged under subjects with author index and fiction title index."

3662. Carter, Constance. "The Italian literature collection." Harvard Library notes, 3 (1935), 81-86.
   In Harvard College Library.

3663. Durkin, Joseph T. "A rich source collection for Catholic scholars of the Risorgimento: the Henry Nelson Gay materials of Harvard University." Catholic historical review, 29 (1943), 347-56.

3664. "Gay Risorgimento collection." Harvard Library notes, 2 (1931), 243-46.

3665. Grolier Club. Catalogue of an exhibition of original and early editions of Italian books. N. Y.: Grolier Club, 1902? 99p.
   Material exhibited now in Wellesley College Library, part of Plimpton collection.

3666. Harvard University Library. "Rappresentazioni sacre." Harvard Library notes, 1 (1921), 130-32.
   Collection of 16th century editions in Harvard College Library.

3667. New York Public Library. Catalogo dei libri italiani che trovansi presso il Dipartimento de Circolazione. N. Y., 1912. 31p.
   Classified list of about 1,350 titles.

3668. Salvemini, Gaetono. "The H. Nelson Gay Risorgimento collection in the Harvard College Library." Harvard alumni bulletin, 37 (1935), 629-31.

3669. Scott, Mary Augusta. Elizabethan translations from the Italian. Boston: Houghton Mifflin Co., 1916. 558p.
   Locates copies of 394 Elizabethan translations from the Italian and 72 Italian and Latin publications in English.

3670. Shields, Nancy Catching. Italian translations in America. N. Y.: Institute of French Studies, 1931. 410p.
   Bibliography of 1,383 Italian translations published in the United States from 1751 to 1928. Arranged chronologically, with locations given in various libraries.

3671. U. S. Library of Congress. "Accademia

della Crusca collection," [purchased by the Library of Congress in 1914][Wash., 1914] 44, 6 numb. 1. Typed.

1,134 titles (1,800 volumes) priced.

3672. Wellesley College Library. Catalogue of the Frances Taylor Pearsons Plimpton collection of Italian books and manuscripts in the library of Wellesley College, comp. by Margaret Hastings Jackson. Cambridge: Harvard Univ. Press, 1929. 434p.

Collection specialized in 14th to 16th century period.

3673. Wood, Marjorie P. "The Gay Risorgimento collection." Harvard Library notes, 3 (1935), 6-9.

In Harvard College Library.

Individual authors.

DANTE, ALIGHIERI

3674. Boston Public Library. Dante; a list of books in the Public Library of the city of Boston, prepared in commemoration of the six hundredth anniversary of the poet's death, 1321-1921. Boston: The Library, 1921. 59p.

3675. Cambridge Public Library. List of books on Dante in the Cambridge Public Library. Cambridge, Mass., 1921. 12p.

3676. Cornell University Library. Catalogue of the Dante collection presented by Willard Fiske, comp. by Theodore W. Koch. Ithaca: The Library, 1898-1950. 2v. Additions 1898-1920, comp. by Mary Fowler. Ithaca, 1921. 152p.

3677. Dante Society. "Additions to the Dante collection in the Harvard College Library," by William Coolidge Lane. (In the Society's Annual reports, 10 (1891), 15-31; 11 (1892), 55-72; 12 (1893), 25-39; 13 (1894), 1-16; 14 (1895), 37-54; 16 (1897), 35-82; 17 (1900), 15-34; 23 (1905), 1-109; 27 (1909), 1-28; 35 (1917), 1-46.)

3678. Duke University Library. "The Henry Bellamann Dante collection," by A. H. Gilbert. Library notes, a bulletin issued for the Friends of Duke University Library, no. 16 (May 1946), 14-15.

About 300 volumes, including translations of Divine comedy into various languages, early editions, and critical works.

3679. Koch, Theodore Wesley. "Dante in America: a historical and bibliographical study." Dante Society annual report, 15 (1896), 75-150.

Copies located in 11 libraries.

3680. Koch, Theodore Wesley. A list of Danteiana in American libraries, supplementing the catalogue of the Cornell collection. Boston: Ginn & Co., 1901. 67p. (Reprint from the 18th Annual report of the Dante Society.)

Copies located in 20 American libraries.

3681. Lane, William Coolidge. The Dante collections in the Harvard College and Boston Public Libraries. Cambridge, Mass.: Harvard University Library, 1890. 116p. (Harvard University Library, Bibliographical contributions, no. 34)

3682. Laws, A. C. Dante collection at the University of Pennsylvania. Philadelphia: Stern, 1901. 12p. Reprinted from Pennsylvania Library Club's Occasional papers, 10 (1901).

3683. Michigan, University, Library. The Walter Library, by Benjamin Parsons Bourland. [Ann Arbor, 1900] 7p. (Reprinted from Michigan alumnus, 6 (1900), 196-202)

List of Dante books.

3684. Newberry Library. Dante, his work, his time and his influence; a select list of books prepared in connection with an exhibit in commoration of the six hundredth anniversary of the poet's death, 1321-1921. Chicago: The Library [1921] 11p.

PETRARCH, FRANCESCO

3685. Cornell University Library. Catalogue of the Petrarch collection bequeathed by Willard Fiske, comp. by Mary Fowler. Ithaca: Cornell Univ. Press, 1916. 547p.

VINCI, LEONARDO DA

3686. Mabbott, Maureen C. A check list of the editions of Leonardo da Vinci's works in college and public libraries in the United States. N. Y.: N. Y. Public Library, 1935. 10p. ("Reprinted from the Bulletin of the New York Public Library of November 1934.")

Locates copies in 21 libraries.

SPANISH, PORTUGUESE AND LATIN AMERICAN LITERATURE

Drama

3687. Hispanic Society of America. A collection of Spanish dramatic works presented to the Library of Congress by the Hispanic Society of America. N. Y., 1938. 3v.

3688. Michigan, University, Library. Index of Spanish drama, comp. by Francis W. Allen. Ann Arbor, Mich., 1937. 235 numb. 1.
Author and title index of about 7,000 Spanish plays in University of Michigan Library.

3689. Oberlin College Library. The Spanish drama collection in the Oberlin College Library, a descriptive catalogue. Author list, by Paul Patrick Rogers. Oberlin, Ohio: Oberlin College, 1940. 468p. A supplementary volume containing reference lists, by Paul Patrick Rogers. Oberlin, 1946. 157p.
Records 7,530 items, 1675-1924.

Fiction

3690. Bourland, Caroline B. The short story in Spain in the seventeenth century, with a bibliography of the novela from 1576 to 1700. Northampton: Smith College, 1927. 215p.
Copies located in Hispanic Society, New York Public Library, Boston Public Library, Harvard and various foreign libraries.

3691. Chandler, Frank Wadleigh. Romances of roguery; an episode in the history of the novel. Part 1: The picaresque novel in Spain. N. Y.: Columbia Univ. Press, 1899. 483p. (Columbia University studies in literature, v. 2)
Bibliography, p. 399-469, locates copies in Boston Public Library (Ticknor collection), and several foreign libraries.

3692. Pan American Union, Columbus Memorial Library. Latin America in fiction; a bibliography of books in English for adults, comp. by A. Curtis Wilgus. Wash.: Pan American Union, 1941. 35p. (Bibliographic series, no. 26)

3693. Zellars, W. C. Bibliography of the Spanish historical novel during the first half of the nineteenth century. Albuquerque: Univ. of New Mexico Press, 1929. 16p. (University of New Mexico bulletin, Language series, 2, no. 1, Sept. 1929.)
Copies located in 13 American libraries.

Miscellany

3694. Arizona, University, Library. Mexican writers; a catalogue of books in the University of Arizona Library, prepared by Estelle Lutrell. Tucson, 1920. 83p. (Univ. of Arizona record, v. 13, no. 5)

3695. Boston Public Library. Catalogue of the Spanish Library and of the Portuguese books bequeathed by George Ticknor together with the collection of Spanish and Portuguese literature in the General Library, by James Lyman Whitney. Boston, 1879. 476p.

3696. California State Library, Sutro Branch. Catalogue of Mexican pamphlets in the Sutro collection (1623-1816). San Francisco: The Library, 1939. 99p. (1817-1920). 1939. p. 100-84. (1821). 1939. p. 185-277. (1822). 1939. p. 278-384. (1823-1826). 1940. p. 385-488. (1827-1842). 1940. p. 489-781 (3v.) (1853-1888). 1940. p. 887-963. Supplement (1605-1828), 2v. 1941. 198p. (1623-1888). 65p. Supplement (1829-1887). 1941. p. 199-290. Author index. San Francisco, 1941. 65 numb. 1.

3697. Catholic University of America Library. Bibliographical and historical description of the rarest books in the Oliveira Lima collection at the Catholic University of America, comp. by Ruth E. V. Holmes. Wash., 1926. 367p.
Describes 209 items in detail.

3698. Crawford, J. P. W. "The Rennert Library." General magazine and historical chronicle, 295 (1927), 484-89.
Collection of Spanish classical literature, particularly Lope de Vega, in University of Pennsylvania Library.

3699. Crawford, J. P. W. "The Spanish and Italian collections." University of Pennsylvania Library chronicle, 1 (1933), 15-21.

3700. Green, O. H. "The J. P. Wickersham Crawford memorial collection." University of Pennsylvania Library chronicle, 7 (1939), 55-59.
Collection of Spanish literature, with emphasis on Spanish Renaissance.

3701. Keniston, Hayward, comp. Periodicals in American libraries, for the study of the Hispanic languages and literatures. N. Y.: Hispanic Society of America, 1927. [68p.]

About 760 titles, with holdings shown in 23 libraries.

3702. Palha, Fernando. Catalogue de la bibliothèque de M. Fernando Palha. Lisbon: Libanio da Silva, 1896. 4v. in 2.

Greater part of collection now in Harvard University Library.

3703. Spell, Jefferson Rea. "Mexican literary periodicals of the twentieth century." Modern Language Association publications, 54 (1939), 835-52.

Locates files in 5 Mexican and 3 United States libraries, and compiler's collection.

3704. Spell, Jefferson Rea. "Spanish-American literary periodicals." University of Texas Library chronicle, 1 (Fall, 1944), 3-6.

3705. U. S. Library of Congress. "Portuguese collection." [Wash., 1929] 120 l. Typed.

List of 2,100 volumes and pamphlets acquired through Maggs Bros., 1928.

3706. U. S. Library of Congress, Hispanic Foundation. Latin American belleslettres in English translation, a selective and annotated guide, by James A. Granier. 2d ed. Wash., 1943. 33p.

3707. Watkinson Library of Reference. Books on Spain and Spanish literature in the Watkinson Library. Hartford, Conn., 1927. 15p. (Its Bulletin, no. 1)

3708. Yale University Library. Spanish American literature in the Yale University Library; a bibliography, by Frederick Bliss Luquiens. New Haven: Yale Univ. Press, 1939. 335p.

Lists 5,668 items, arranged by country.

Individual authors

CERVANTES, MIGUEL DE

3709. Aguilera, Francisco. "Further additions to the Cervantes collection." Library of Congress quarterly journal of current acquisitions, 4 (Nov. 1946), 7-9.

3710. Aguilera, Francisco. "The Kebler addition to the Don Quixote collection." Library of Congress quarterly journal of current acquisitions, 2 (Oct.-Dec. 1944), 11-22.

Description of a collection of early editions of Don Quixote acquired by the Library of Congress. Supplementary references appearing in the Library of Congress quarterly journal of current acquisitions include Edwin B. Knowles, Jr.'s, "A rare Quixote edition," 3 (Feb. 1946), 3-5; and Francisco Aguilera's "Further additions to the Kebler collection," 4 (Nov. 1946), 7-9.

3711. Hispanic Society of America. Exhibition of books relating to Miguel de Cervantes Saavedra. Tercentenary (April fifteenth to May first). N. Y.: The Society, 1916. 23pl.

3712. Hispanic Society of America. Urrabieta Vierge and illustrators of Don Quixote (19th and 20th centuries); an exhibition from books in the library of the Hispanic Society of America. N. Y.: The Trustees, 1934. 36p.

3713. Jackson, William A. "The Carl T. Keller collection of Don Quixote." Harvard Library bulletin, 1 (1947), 306-310.

In Harvard College Library.

3714. New York Public Library. "Cervantes literature in the New York Public Library; catalogue of editions of Don Quixote, and of other works by and relating to Miguel de Cervantes Saavedra." New York Public Library bulletin, 3 (1899), 259-65.

3715. Serís, Homero. La colección Cervantina de la Sociedad hispánica de América. Urbana: Univ. of Illinois, 1920. 158p. (Univ. of Illinois studies in language and literature, v. 6, no. 1)

FERNANDEZ DE LIZARDI, J. J.

3716. California State Library, Sutro Branch. An annotated bibliography of the poems and pamphlets of J. J. Fernandez de Lizardi: the first period (1808-1823). San Francisco: The Library, 1940. 179 numb. l. (Its: Occasional papers. Mexican history series, no. 2, pt. 1)

A detailed list and description of the Lizardi works in the Sutro Branch.

3717. Nickerson, Mildred E. "José Joaguín Fernández Lizardi." Harvard Library notes, 3 (1935), 89-93.

Collection of novels, poetry, pamphlets, etc., in Harvard College Library by or relating to Lizardi, Mexican writer of early 19th century.

3718. Radin, Paul. "An annotated bibliography of the poems and pamphlets of Fernández de Lizardi (1824-1827)." Hispanic American historical review, 26 (1946), 284-91.

Locates copies in University of California (Bancroft), Harvard, University of Texas, and Yale. (Part 3 of California State Library Sutro Branch's Occasional papers, Mexican history series, no. 2, parts 1 and 2.)

3719. Spell, J. R. "Fernandez de Lizardi: a bibliography." Hispanic American historical review, 7 (1927), 490-507.

Locates copies in Bancroft Library (California), Hispanic Society, University of Texas, and several Mexican libraries.

GÓNGORA Y ARGOTE, LUIS DE

3720. Hispanic Society of America. Góngora in the library of the Hispanic Society of America. N. Y.: The Society, 1927. 4 pts.

Bibliographical descriptions of certain editions in Library.

ISIDORE OF SEVILLE

3721. Brown, Robert Benaway. The printed works of Isidore of Seville. [Lexington] 1949. 32p. (Univ. of Kentucky Libraries occasional contributions, no. 5)

Locates copies in various American and European libraries.

GREEK AND LATIN LITERATURE

3722. Bates, W. N. "A scholar's library of Aristotle." University of Pennsylvania Library chronicle, 6 (1938), 16-18.

Brief description of Charles W. Burr collection.

3723. Harvard University Library. "Aesopian imitations." Harvard Library notes, 1 (1923), 242-48.

List of 18th century English items in Harvard College Library.

3724. Harvard University Library. "Smyth Classical Library." Harvard Library bulletin, 44 (1942), 506-27.

In Harvard College Library.

3725. Hendrickson, G. L. "The Marston Juvenals." Yale University Library gazette, 12 (1938), 71-88.

Collection of manuscripts, editions and translations of poet Juvenal in Yale University Library.

3726. Horace. Quintus Horatius Flaccus; editions in the United States and Canada, as they appear in the Union Catalog of the Library of Congress. [Oakland, Calif.]: Mills College. 1938. 240p.

Locates 2,723 editions in about 125 libraries.

3727. McKenzie, Kenneth. "Some remarks on a fable collection." Princeton University Library chronicle, 5 (1944), 137-49.

Describes a collection of over 600 books and pamphlets of and about fables in Princeton University Library.

3728. Morgan, Morris Hicky. A bibliography of Persius. Cambridge: Harvard University Library, 1909. 90p. (Harvard University Library, Bibliographical contributions, no. 58). Earlier ed., 1893.

A collection of 1,029 titles received by Harvard University.

3729. Munsterberg, Margaret. "The bi-millenial anniversary of Horace." More books, 10 (1935), 245-58.

Describes Boston Public Library's holdings of books by and about Horace.

3730. Nelen, Eleanor W. "Aesops in the Library of Congress." Horn book, 14 (Sept.-Oct. 1938), 311-15.

3731. New York Public Library. "A Vergilian exhibition held at the New York Public Library." New York Public Library bulletin, 34 (1930), 491-528. Reprinted, with title, Bimillennivm Vergilianvm, LXX. A. C.-A. D. MCMXXX. 40p.

Includes catalog of exhibition. Owners shown, if work is not in New York Public Library.

3732. Newberry Library. Virgil; an exhibition of early editions and facsimiles of manuscripts commemorating the two-thousandth anniversary of his birth, 70 B. C.-1930 A. D. Chicago: The Library, 1930. 10p.

The 63 items exhibited are from Newberry Library collection.

3733. Oldfather, William Abbott. "Bibliographical notes on the Fables of Avianus." Bibliographical Society of America papers, 15 (1921), 61-72.

Notes of additional editions and translations, with American locations, supplementing Hervieux's Les fabulistes latins, which lists only European locations.

3734. Oldfather, William Abbott. Contributions toward a bibliography of Epictetus. [Urbana]: University of Illinois, 1927. 201p. (University of Illinois bulletin, 25, no. 12.)

Locates copies in about 23 libraries.

3735. Pauli, A. F. "Our most recent gift - the Wadsworth collection." Wesleyan University Library about books, 12 (Mr.-Je. 1942), 1-4.

Describes 4,000-volume collection on classical languages and literature.

3736. Phillips Academy, Oliver Wendell Holmes Library. Catalogue of the Charles H. Forbes collection of Vergiliana in the Oliver Wendell Holmes Library of Phillips Academy, Andover, Mass. [Andover, Mass.: Andover Press] 1931. 107p.

3737. Princeton University Library. A preliminary catalogue of the Horace collection presented to the Library of Princeton University by Robert Wilson Patterson. Princeton: The Library, 1917. 93p.

3738. Swan, Marshall W. "Seneca: texts and translations." More books, 20 (1945), 347-54.

Describes finest editions and translations of Seneca's works to be found in Boston Public Library.

3739. U. S. Library of Congress, Union Catalog Division. Horace; a chronological checklist of entries in the Union Catalog of the Library of Congress, British Museum, and Bibliothèque Nationale, comp. by Ernest Kletsch. Wash., 1935. 64 l.

3740. Wood, Marjorie P. "The Herbert Weir Smyth collection." Harvard Library notes, 3 (1938), 145-46.

In Harvard College Library. Primarily Greek and Latin classics.

3741. Yale University Library. An exhibition of manuscripts and books illustrating the transmission of the classics from ancient times to 1536. Selected for the Library and the Department of Classics by T. E. Marston and E. T. Silk. [New Haven: Yale Univ. Press, 1947] [18]p.

CELTIC LITERATURE

3742. Chicago Public Library. Irish books in the Chicago Public Library, 1942. [Chicago, 1942] 18p.

3743. Harvard University Library. "Breton literature, linguistics and folklore in the Library of Harvard College, May 30, 1931." [Cambridge, 1931] 34 numb. l. Typed. "Supplement. titles added, 1931-38." 16 numb. l. Typed.

3744. Robinson, Fred N. "Celtic books at Harvard: the history of a departmental collection." Harvard Library bulletin, 1 (1947), 52-65.

SLAVIC LITERATURE

3745. Babine, Alexis Vasilievich. The Yudin Library. Wash.: Judd and Detweiler, 1905. 40p.

A collection of 80,000 volumes of Russian and other Slavic literature, acquired by the Library of Congress in 1907.

3746. Chicago Public Library. Latvian books. [Chicago]: The Library, 1929. 63p.

3747. Chicago Public Library. Russian literature, including Ukrainian, comp. by John J. Schmidt. [Chicago]: The Library, 1918. 88p.

A catalog of about 2,250 volumes in Russian section of Chicago Public Library.

3748. Cleveland Public Library. Katalog dziel polskich. [Cleveland] 1912. 77p.

3749. Cole, Toby. "Guide to Russian collections in American libraries." New York Public Library bulletin, 51 (1947), 644-50.

Gives number of volumes in Russian and

number of periodicals, serials and newspapers currently received, and subjects well represented in the holdings of 80 libraries.

3750. Cornell University Library. "The Schuyler collection." Cornell University Library bulletin, 1 (1886), 301-15.
Collection of Russian literature, folklore, history, etc.

3751. Heifetz, Anna (Sherman) "Bibliography of Chekhov's works translated into English and published in America." Bulletin of bibliography, 13 (1929), 172-76.
Locates copies in Library of Congress, Columbia University and New York Public Library.

3752. Larson, Cedric. "Slavica rara." American scholar, 8 (1939), 375-77.
Describes briefly Slavic collections of about 200,000 pieces in Library of Congress.

3753. New York Public Library. "Chekhov in English, a list of works by and about him," comp. by Anna Heifetz. New York Public Library bulletin, 53 (1949), 27-38, 72-93. Reprinted. 35p.
Most of 368 items are in New York Public Library. Locations given for remainder.

3754. New York Public Library. "Lermontov in English, a list of works by and about the poet, 1814-1841-1941," comp. by Anna Heifetz. New York Public Library bulletin, 46 (1942), 775-90. Reprinted. 17p.
209 entries, all but 25 in New York Public Library; remainder in Library of Congress or Harvard College Library.

3755. New York Public Library. "Pushkin in English; a list of works by and about Pushkin, 1792-1837-1937," ed. by Avrahm Yarmolinsky. New York Public Library bulletin, 41 (1937), 530-59. Reprinted. 32p.

3756. New York Public Library. Spis Polskich ksiazek; Polish book list. [N. Y.]: The Library, 1915. 31p.
Polish books in Library's Circulation Department.

3757. New York Public Library. "Tolstoi in English, 1878-1929; a list of works by and about Tolstoi available in the New York Public Library," comp. by Antonina Yassukovich.
New York Public Library bulletin, 33 (1929), 531-65. Reprinted. 37p.

3758. Palmieri, Aurelio. Rarità bibliografiche russe nella Biblioteca del Congresso in Washington. Roma: Tipografia Pontificia Nell' Instituto Pio ix, 1917. 8p.
"Estratto dal Bessarione, rivista di studi orientali."

3759. Pennsylvania, University, Library. A catalogue of the Russian books presented to the University of Pennsylvania by Charlemagne Tower. Saint-Petersburg, 1902. 138p.
"Classified list in Russian (p. 1-69); alphabetical list translated into English (p. [73]-138)."

3760. Polish Roman Catholic Union of America, Archives and Museum. Polonica in English; annotated catalogue of the Archives and Museum of the... Union, by Alphonse S. Wolanin. Chicago: The Union, 1945. 186p.
Describes books in Union's reference library.

3761. U. S. Library of Congress, Division of Bibliography. "Maksim Gor'kii (Aleksei Maksimovich Peshkov, 1868-1936): a bibliographical list," comp. by Florence S. Hellman. Wash., Apr. 20, 1939. 68p. Typed.

3762. U. S. Library of Congress, Division of Bibliography. "Mikhail IUr'evich Lermontov: a bibliographical list in English," comp. by Helen F. Conover. Wash., Apr. 13, 1938. 9p. Typed.

3763. U. S. Library of Congress, Division of Bibliography. "Pushkin: a bibliography of works in English available in the Library of Congress." Wash., Sept. 9, 1936. 7p. Typed.

3764. U. S. Library of Congress, General Reference and Bibliography Division. "Russian belles-lettres in English translation: a selected list." Wash., July 30, 1946. 18p. Typed.

3765. U. S. Library of Congress, Processing Department. Monthly list of Russian Accessions, 1 (April 1948) - to date.

3766. Yale University Library. Catalogue of Slavica in the Library of Yale University, comp. by Joel Sumner Smith. [Leipzig]:

Privately printed, 1896. 106p.
List of 908 items.

ORIENTAL LANGUAGES AND LITERATURE

Semitic languages and literature

3767. Harvard University, Semitic Museum. "Catalogue of Arabic mss. in Semitic Museum obtained in 1907," comp. by James R. Jewett. [Cambridge, 1907?] 230p. ms. copy.

3768. Hitti, Philip K. and others. Descriptive catalog of the Garrett collection of Arabic manuscripts in the Princeton University Library. Princeton: Princeton Univ. Press, 1938. 668, 56p.

3769. New York Public Library. "List of dramas in the New York Public Library relating to the Jews, and of dramas in Hebrew, Judeo-Spanish, and Judeo-German; together with essays on the Jewish stage," prep. by A. S. Friedus. New York Public Library bulletin, 11 (1907), 18-51. Reprinted. 34p.

3770. New York Public Library. "List of works in the New York Public Library relating to Arabic poetry." New York Public Library bulletin, 12 (1908), 7-31. Reprinted. 25p.

3771. Root, Elizabeth de W. "The Arabic collection in the library of the Hartford Seminary Foundation." Connecticut Library Association bulletin, 10 (April 1943), 9, 11.
Description of collection of over 3,000 printed books and 1,200 manuscripts, including 1,000 volumes in various editions and languages, of Arabian Nights.

Indic languages and literature

3772. Brown, W. N. "New acquisitions of Sanskrit manuscripts." University of Pennsylvania Library chronicle, 3 (1935), 58-61.

3773. Cutts, Elmer. "A basic bibliography for Indic studies." American Council of Learned Societies bulletin, 28 (May, 1939), 109-69.
Locates material in Library of Congress and 40 other libraries.

3774. Emeneau, Murray B. A union list of printed Indic texts and translations in American libraries. New Haven: American Oriental Society, 1935. 540p. (American oriental series, v. 7)
Locates texts in 15 libraries.

3775. Poleman, Horace I. "Facilities for Indic studies in America: a survey." American Council of Learned Societies bulletin, no. 28 (1939), 27-107.
Lists, by states, all museums, libraries and institutions having Indic material, and describes collections.

3776. Weber, Albrecht Friedrich. Katalog der bibliothek des verstorbenen professors des sanskrit an der Universität zu Berlin. [Gütersloh: Gedruckt bei C. Bertelsmann, 1902?] 117p.

Chinese, Japanese, etc.

3777. Asakawa, Kanichi. "The evolution of Japanese culture." Yale University Library gazette, 9 (1934), 29-37.
A collection of 300 items, chiefly in written form, given to Yale University Library by Yale Association of Japan.

3778. Beal, Edwin G., Jr. and Kuroda, Andrew Y. "The Japanese collection of Otto Karow." Library of Congress quarterly journal of current acquisitions, 6 (Nov. 1948), 3-7.
About 3,200 volumes, chiefly devoted to linguistics and literature, acquired by the Library of Congress.

3779. Bodde, Derk. "Our new Chinese collection." University of Pennsylvania Library chronicle, 7 (1939), 60-65; 12 (1944), 38-43.
A description of books on China written in Western languages, and books in Chinese, in the University of Pennsylvania Library.

3780. Britton, Roswell S. Fifty Shang inscriptions. Princeton: Princeton University Library, 1940. [78]p.
Readings of Princeton collection of Shang-Anyang divination inscriptions.

3781. Chicago Art Institute, Ryerson Library. Descriptive catalogue of Japanese and Chinese illustrated books in the Ryerson Library of the Art Institute of Chicago, by Kenji Toda. Chicago: [Lakeside Press] 1931. 466p. Supplement... Index of the titles in Chinese and Japanese characters and errata. [Chicago, 1933]

3782. Chicago, University, Library. Western translations of Chinese books in the University of Chicago libraries. [1943] 7 l. Typed.

3783. Ch'iu, A. K'ai-ming. A classified catalogue of Chinese books in the Chinese-Japanese library of the Harvard-Yenching Institute at Harvard University. Cambridge, 1938-40. 3v.

3784. Columbia University Library. "The gift from the Imperial Household of Japan, in the Japanese collection, Columbia University," by Ryusaku Tsunoda. Columbia University quarterly, 25 (1933), 293-302.

Describes collection of 5,594 volumes of books and manuscripts, beginning with 8th century A.D.

3785. Gardner, Charles S. A union list of selected Chinese books in American libraries. Wash.: American Council of Learned Societies, 1932. 50p.

Copies located in 9 libraries.

3786. Harvard University Library. A guide to Chinese-Japanese Library of Harvard University, under the auspices of the Harvard-Yenching Institute. Cambridge, 1932. 24p.

A survey of the 71,036 volumes of Chinese, and 3,835 volumes of Japanese books in the library.

3787. Hobbs, Cecil C. "Burma's gift to America." Library of Congress quarterly journal of current acquisitions, 7 (Feb. 1950), 7-10.

Description of 600-volume collection of Burmese literature presented to Library of Congress.

3788. Hummel, Arthur W. "An ancient Chinese manuscript." Library of Congress quarterly journal of current acquisitions, 3 (Aug. 1946), 6.

6th century scroll received by Library of Congress.

3789. Hummel, Arthur W. "Chinese, Japanese, and other east Asiatic books in the Library of Congress." Amerasia, 1 (1937), 410-14.

3790. John Crerar Library. Catalogue of East Asiatic books on arts and sciences, collected by Dr. Berthold Laufer in 1908-1910, for the John Crerar Library... 825 works in 14,055 volumes. [Wash., 1914]

Original manuscript in John Crerar Library.

3791. Newberry Library. Descriptive account of the collection of Chinese, Tibetan, Mongol, and Japanese books in the Newberry Library, by Berthold Laufer. Chicago: The Library [1913] 42p. (Newberry Library publications, no. 4)

Collection acquired by University of Chicago Library in 1943. Includes manuscripts and early printed books.

3792. U. S. Library of Congress, Orientalia Division. Chinese, Japanese and other East Asiatic books added... 1919/20 - 1939/40. Wash.: Govt. Print. Off., 1920-1941. 21v. in 3.

3793. U. S. Library of Congress, Orientalia Division. Title index to independent Chinese works in the Library of Congress, 3d ed. Wash., 1932. 2v.

Contains 13,419 entries.

3794. Williams, Frederick Wells and Price, Francis W. The best hundred books on China; a finding list of books in English, selected and annotated. New Haven: Yale University Library, 1924. 20p.

In Yale University Library.

Miscellany

3795. American Oriental Society Library. Catalogue of the library of the American Oriental Society, ed. by Elizabeth Strout. New Haven: Yale University Library, 1930. 308p.

Collection on permanent deposit in Yale University Library. Deals with the history and culture of Oriental nations, and works on Oriental languages and literatures.

3796. Astor Library. Catalogue of books in the Astor Library relating to the languages and literature of Asia, Africa and the oceanic islands. N. Y., 1854. 424p.

Now in New York Public Library.

3797. Brill, firm, booksellers. Oriental literature of the large library of the late Gabriel Ferrand. Leiden, 1938. 48p.

Many books listed acquired for White collection, Cleveland Public Library.

3798. Columbia University. Firdausi Celebration, 935-1935; addresses... a bibliography of the principal manuscripts and printed editions of the Shāh-nāmah in certain leading public libraries of the world, ed. by David Eugene Smith. N. Y.: McFarlane, Warde, McFarlane, 1936. 138p.

Copies of Iranian poet's works located in American libraries.

3799. New York Public Library. "List of works in the New York Public Library relating to the oriental drama." New York Public Library bulletin, 10 (1906), 251-56.

3800. U. S. Library of Congress. "Annual reports on acquisitions: Orientalia." Library of Congress quarterly journal of current acquisitions, 3 (Feb. 1946), 16-48; 4 (Feb. 1947), 17-38; 5 (Feb. 1948), 22-44; 6 (Feb. 1949), 25-45; 7 (Feb. 1950), 17-42.

JUVENILE LITERATURE

3801. American Antiquarian Society. Exhibit of American children's books printed before 1800. Worcester, Mass.: The Society, 1928. 14p.

3802. Bates, Albert Carlos. The history of the Holy Jesus; a list of editions of this once popular children's book. Hartford, 1911. 14p.

Locates copies where known of editions from 1745 to 1814.

3803. Blanck, Jacob Nathaniel, comp. Harry Castlemon, boys' own author; appreciation and bibliography. N. Y.: R. R. Bowker Co., 1941. 142p.

"The books described are located in the collection of J. K. Lilly, Jr., who, more than any other person, collaborated in the production of the bibliography; and in the Rare book collection of the Library of Congress under whose direction the book was compiled." - Pref.

3804. Blanck, Jacob Nathaniel. Peter Parley to Penrod; a bibliographical description of the best-loved American juvenile books. N. Y.: R. R. Bowker Co., 1938. 153p.

Locations in Library of Congress frequently indicated.

3805. Boston Public Library. A bibliography of books written by children of the twentieth century, by Kathleen B. Landrey. Boston: The Library, [1937] 13p. (Reprinted from More books, April 1937)

3806. Carnegie Library of Pittsburgh. Catalogue of books in the Children's Department of the Carnegie Library of Pittsburgh. 2d ed. Pittsburgh: The Library, 1920. 2v.

V. 1, author and title list; v. 2, subject index.

3807. Carnegie Library of Pittsburgh. Stories to tell to children: a selected list for use by libraries, schools, clubs, and radio with a special listing of stories and poems for holiday and music programs. 6th ed. Pittsburgh: The Library, 1949. 96p.

Selected from material in Carnegie Library of Pittsburgh.

3808. Harvard University Library. "Children's books." Harvard Library notes, 2 (1925), 57-59.

In Harvard College Library.

3809. Jordan, Alice M. "Early children's books." More books, 15 (1940), 185-91.

Describes and lists purchase of 50 early children's books for Boston Public Library, with explanation of their contribution to history of literature for children.

3810. New Haven Free Public Library. Books for young people in the... Library. New Haven, Conn.: The Library, 1898. 66p.

Includes reference lists on legal holidays, books in juvenile collection, and books for young people selected from adult collection.

3811. New York Public Library. "The juvenilia of Mary Belson Elliott; a list with notes," comp. by Philip D. Jordan. New York Public Library bulletin, 39 (1935), 869-81. Reprinted with additions and revisions by Daniel C. Haskell, 1936. 18p.

Locates copies of 144 titles in 16 American and British libraries.

3812. New York Public Library. "Samuel Wood and Sons, early New York publishers of children's books," by Harry B. Weiss. New York Public Library bulletin, 46 (1942), 755-71. Reprinted. 18p.

Check list based principally on collections of New York Public Library, Wilbur M. Stone, and A. S. W. Rosenbach. A few locations in Library of Congress.

3813. New York Public Library. "Something about Simple Simon," by Harry B. Weiss. New York Public Library bulletin, 44 (1940), 461-70.

Includes "preliminary check list, by titles, of publications containing 'Simple Simon,' mostly in the New York Public Library."

3814. Nolen, Eleanor W. "National library builds a children's book collection." Horn book, 14 (July-Aug. 1938), 246-48.

3815. Pan American Union, Columbus Memorial Library. Children's books in English on Latin America. Wash.: Pan American Union, 1941. 41, 7p. (Bibliographic series, no. 25)

"Books not in the Pan American Union Library were examined at the Library of Congress."

3816. Rosenbach, A. S. W. Early American children's books; with bibliographical descriptions of the books in his private collection. Portland, Maine: Southworth Press, 1933. 354p.

Collection of 816 titles presented to Free Library of Philadelphia.

3817. San Francisco Public Library. Finding list of the juvenile department. San Francisco, 1896. 63p. Supplemental catalogue. San Francisco, 1900. 28p.

3818. Stone, Wilbur Macey. "The history of Little Goody Two-Shoes." American Antiquarian Society proceedings, n. s. 49 (1939), 333-70.

Bibliography, p. 357-70, locates 108 English and 66 American editions, 1765-1850, in 10 public and private collections.

3819. Stone, Wilbur Macey. The Thumb Bible of John Taylor. Brookline, Mass.: The LXIVMOS, 1928. 68p.

An attempt toward a list of editions, 1614-1810, p. 48-68, and location of copies in America and England.

3820. U. S. Library of Congress, General Reference and Bibliography Division. "Children's literature and reading: a selected list of references in English, French, Portuguese, and Spanish," comp. by Elizabeth A. Gardner. Wash., July 29, 1946. 19p. Typed.

3821. Weiss, Harry B. Little Red Riding Hood, a terror tale of the nursery, including... a preliminary check list of English and American editions of Little Red Riding Hood. Trenton, N. J., 1939. 19p.

Locates copies in several public and private collections.

Geography and Maps

GENERAL

3822. American Geographical Society. Current geographical publications; additions to the research catalogue of the American Geographical Society. N. Y.: The Society, 1938 - to date.

3823. American Geographical Society. Early topographical maps:... as illustrated by the maps of the Harrison collection, by John C. Wright. N. Y.: The Society, 1924. 38p. (Library series, no. 3)
Collection in American Geographical Society.

3824. American Geographical Society. Research catalogue. N. Y., 1940. 26 rolls of 16 mm. microfilm.
Contains 113,000 entries for books, articles, government publications of geographical interest, and distinctive maps received by the Society, 1923-40. Additions listed in Society's Current geographical publications, 1938 - to date.

3825. American Scientific Congress. Catalogue of an exhibition of maps in National Academy of Sciences building... comprising some 400 maps and other materials related to the programs of section iii, geological sciences, and section viii, history and geography, arranged by Lawrence Martin... upon the occasion of the Eighth American Scientific Congress at Washington, D. C., May 10-18, 1940. Wash.: Govt. Print. Off. (Library branch) 1940. 14p.
Drawn from Library of Congress and other Washington libraries.

3826. Arkansas Geological Survey, State Map Library. Catalog of maps available in the State Map Library; maps mounted, indexed, filed and catalogued by employees on WPA project. [Little Rock, Ark.] 1939. 78p.

3827. Atkinson, Geoffroy. La littérature géographique française de la renaissance; répertoire bibliographique... Description de 524 impressions d'ouvrages publiés en française avant 1610, et traitant des pays et des peuples non européens, que l'on trouve dans les principales bibliothèques de France et de l'Europe occidentale. Paris: Picard, 1927. 563p. Supplement. Paris: Picard, 1936. 87p.
Lists some American locations, though principally European.

3828. Bibliographie géographique internationale. Paris: Association de Géographes Francais, 1891-1949. 57v.
Titles published in the United States since 1923 (v. 23 - to date) supplied by American Geographical Society and are available in Society's library.

3829. California State Library. List of printed maps contained in the Map Department. Sacramento: A. J. Johnston, Supt. State Printing, 1899. 43p. (Its: Special bulletin, no. 1)

3830. Chicago, University, Library. Atlases in libraries of Chicago; a bibliography and union check list. Chicago, 1936. 244p.
Lists world atlases and atlases of Orient, Americas, and Europe; also travel guides.

3831. Eames, Wilberforce. A list of editions of Ptolemy's geography, 1475-1730. N. Y., 1886. 45p. Reprinted from Sabin's Dictionary, v. 16.
Locates all known copies.

3832. Harris, Chauncy D. and Fellman,

Jerome D. A comprehensive checklist of serials of geographic value. Part I. Geographic serials proper. Chicago: Univ. of Chicago, Dept. of Geography, 1949. 100 numb. l. Preliminary edition. Revised edition in preparation.

"A Chicago-centered union list indicating the complete holdings of the Univ. of Chicago Library... and the holdings of other libraries insofar as necessary to obtain a complete set of each listed serial."

3833. Harvard University, Institute of Geographical Exploration. The catalogue of the collection of Joseph T. Tower, Jr. ... in the Institute of Geographical Exploration, Harvard University. [Boston: Merrymount Press] 1933. 136p.

Old and rare books, maps and documents relating to discovery and exploration in Northern Polar region and adjacent areas in North America.

3834. Hawley, Edith J. Roswell. "Bibliography of literary geography." Bulletin of bibliography, 10 (1918-19), 34-38, 58-60, 76, 93-94, 104-05.

In New York Public Library or Library of Congress.

3835. Hispanic Society of America. Facsimiles of portolan charts belonging to the Hispanic Society of America. N. Y., 1916. 8p., 16 facsim.

3836. Hispanic Society of America. Portolan charts, their origin and characteristics with a descriptive list of those belonging to the Hispanic Society of America, by Edward Luther Stevenson. N. Y., 1911. 76p.

3837. Karpinski, Louis C. Cartographical collections in America. Imago mundi, 1 (1935), 62-64.

An account of leading collections on cartography in American libraries.

3838. Kimball, LeRoy E. "James Wilson of Vermont, America's first globe maker." American Antiquarian Society proceedings, n. s. 48 (1938), 29-48.

Wilson globes from 1811 to 1850, and several undated globes, located in 10 public and private collections.

3839. LeGear, Clara E. "The Division of Maps at the Library of Congress." Education, 60 (Dec. 1939), 220-24.

Describes collections of maps and charts in Library of Congress.

3840. Lewis, William Ditto. "Catalogue of the maps in the Christopher Ward collection at the University of Delaware." Delaware notes, 22d ser. (1949), 67-88.

Lists and describes in detail 71 maps in the collection.

3841. Martin, Lawrence. "A rare Agnese atlas." Library of Congress quarterly journal of current acquisitions, 1 (Oct.-Dec. 1943), 25-28.

Description of a Battista Agnese manuscript atlas, c. 1543, acquired by Library of Congress.

3842. Mayhew, Dorothy F. "The Tower collection at the Institute of Geographical Exploration." Harvard alumni bulletin, 35 (1933), 982-84.

Collection of books, maps, and documents pertaining to discovery and exploration, presented to Harvard Universtiy.

3843. Mendenhall, Thomas C., 2d. "English voyages." Yale University Library gazette, 19 (1945), 57-61.

Lists 64 titles on English voyages for an exhibition, at Yale University Library, of books owned by Henry C. Taylor or by Yale University.

3844. Michigan, University, William L. Clements Library. Atlases of the sixteenth and seventeenth centuries [by Louis C. Karpinski] Ann Arbor, 1924. 4p. (Bulletin, no. 4)

Description of an exhibition.

3845. Mix, David·E. E. Catalogue of maps and surveys. Albany, N. Y., 1859. 375p.

Lists holdings of New York (State) Secretary of State, State Engineer, Comptroller, and State Library.

3846. New England History Teachers' Association. A catalogue of the collection of historical material at Simmons College, Boston. 2d ed. Boston: Houghton Mifflin, 1912. 33p.

Collection of maps, charts, atlases and pictures.

3847. New York Public Library. "Catalogue of the De Bry collection of voyages, in the New York Public Library." New York Public Library bulletin, 8 (1904), 230-43. Reprinted. 14p.

3848. New York Public Library. "General atlases of geography (ancient and modern) in the New York Public Library." New York Public Library bulletin, 4 (1900), 63-69.

3849. New York Public Library. "List of maps of the world in the New York Public Library exhibited in the Lenox Branch on the occasion of the visit of members of the eighth International Geographical Congress, 13-15 September, 1904." New York Public Library bulletin, 8 (1904), 411-22.

3850. New York Public Library. "Maps: how to make them and read them; a bibliography of general and specialized works on cartography," by Walter W. Ristow. New York Public Library bulletin, 47 (1943), 381-86. Reprinted. 8p.

3851. New York Public Library. "Periodicals relating to geography in the New York Public Library, and Columbia University Library." New York Public Library bulletin, 2 (1898), 92-95.

Chiefly of historical interest.

3852. New York Public Library. Ptolemaeus, Claudius. Geography of Ptolemy. Translated and ed. by Edward Luther Stevenson. N. Y.: The Library, 1932. 167p. Facsimiles, including maps.

Maps are reproductions, with two exceptions, from Codex Ebnerianus, owned by New York Public Library.

3853. Phillips, Philip Lee. The Jeffersonian states. Rare caricatures of Bunker Hill. Some peculiar maps. Some old city directories. [N. Y.] 1918. [34]p.

Drawn from Library of Congress collections.

3854. Platt, Elizabeth T. "Books and national defense: a brief survey of some library resources of geographical pertinence." Geographical review, 31 (1941), 264-71.

A general survey of resources of many libraries and collections in this field.

3855. St. Louis Public Library. Maps in the St. Louis Public Library, by Mildred Boatman. [St. Louis] 1931. 16p. (Issued also as appendix to Library's Annual report, 1930-31)

3856. [Stevens, Henry, son and Stiles, firm, booksellers, London] "Lafreri's atlas. Rome, c1515. Folio. (Title) Geografia Tavole moderne di geografia de la maggior parte del mondo." [London, 1909] 6 l. Typed.

"Description of the copy now in the Division of maps and charts of the Library of Congress; and comparison with the copy owned by the Royal geographical society."

3857. U. S. Board of Surveys and Maps. Map collections in the District of Columbia. [Wash.] 1938. 50 numb. l.

Brief descriptions of collections.

3858. U. S. Library of Congress. "Annual reports on acquisitions: maps." Library of Congress quarterly journal of current acquisitions, 3 (Aug. 1946), 30-34; 4 (Aug. 1947), 55-61; 5 (Aug. 1948), 41-50; 6 (Aug. 1949), 63-74; 7 (Aug. 1950), 59-68.

3859. U. S. Library of Congress, Division of Maps. Check list of large scale maps published by foreign governments (Great Britain excepted) in the Library of Congress. Wash.: Govt. Print. Off., 1905. 58 numb. l.

3860. U. S. Library of Congress, Division of Maps. A list of atlases and maps applicable to the World War. Wash.: Govt. Print. Off., 1918. 202p.

Geographically arranged, world-wide in scope. Lists 784 maps. Detailed subject index.

3861. U. S. Library of Congress, Division of Maps. A list of geographical atlases in the Library of Congress, with bibliographical notes, comp. by P. L. Phillips. Wash.: Govt. Print. Off., 1909-20. 4v.

3862. U. S. Library of Congress, Division of Maps. A list of works relating to cartography, by P. Lee Phillips. Wash.: Govt. Print. Off., 1901. 90p. (Reprinted from A List of Maps of America, in the Library of Congress.)

3863. U. S. Library of Congress, Division of Maps. Noteworthy maps... no. [1]-3. Accessions... with acknowledgment of sources of gifts, exchanges, and transfers. 1925/26 - 1927/28. Wash.: Govt. Print. Off., 1927-1930. 3v.

"A continuation of the lists included in the annual reports of the librarian of Congress for the years 1899-1925."

3864. Virginia State Library. "Finding list of geography, anthropology, and hydrography," comp. by Earl G. Swem. Virginia State Library bulletin, 2 (1909), 191-228.

3865. Wagner, Henry Raup. "The manuscript atlases of Battista Agnese." Bibliographical Society of America papers, 25 (1931), 1-110.

Locates copies in American and foreign libraries of atlases by 16th century Genoese cartographer.

3866. Winsor, Justin. A bibliography of Ptolemy's geography. Cambridge, Mass.: University Press, J. Wilson and Son, 1884. 42p. (Harvard University Library, Bibliographical contributions, no. 18) (Reprinted from Harvard University bulletin, no. 24-29, 1883-84)

Locates copies in American libraries.

3867. Wright, John Kirtland and Platt, Elizabeth Towar. Aids to geographical research; bibliographies, periodicals, atlases, gazetteers and other reference works. 2d ed. N. Y.: Published for the American Geographical Society by Columbia University Press, 1947. 331p. (American Geographical Society research series, no. 22)

Based on collections in the Society's library and map department.

3868. Wroth, Lawrence C. "The early cartography of the Pacific." Bibliographical Society of America papers, 38 (1944), 87-268.

List appended of 194 principal maps mentioned, with location of copies consulted.

AMERICA (General)

3869. Brown, Horace. Maps pertaining to early America (collection of Horace Brown) the Fleming Museum, University of Vermont, October 5 to October 21, 1935. Burlington? 1935. 15p.

3870. Henry E. Huntington Library. America in maps, 1503-1600; notes on an exhibition, by Herbert C. Schulz. San Marino [1946]. 8p.

3871. LaGear, Clara Egli. "Sixteenth-century maps presented by Lessing J. Rosenwald." Library of Congress quarterly journal of current acquisitions, 6 (May 1949), 18-22.

Description of 5 maps of Americana interest received by the Library of Congress.

3872. Museum Book Store, London. A catalogue of maps of America from the sixteenth to the nineteenth centuries. London: Museum Book Store, 1924. 80p.

Collection now part of Henry E. Huntington Library.

3873. Museum Book Store, London. A catalogue of rare maps of America from the sixteenth to nineteenth centuries. London: Museum Book Store, 1927. 92p.

Acquired by Henry E. Huntington Library.

3874. New York Public Library. "The Western hemisphere, by Walter W. Ristow." New York Public Library bulletin, 46 (1942), 419-44. Reprinted. 27p.

Lists and describes maps shown in exhibition: "The Western Hemisphere in maps from 1492 to 1942."

3875. Newberry Library, Edward E. Ayer Collection. List of manuscript maps in the Edward E. Ayer collection, comp. by Clara A. Smith. Chicago: The Library, 1927. 101p. (Special publications, no. 24)

3876. Stevenson, Edward Luther. Early Spanish cartography of the new world, with special reference to the Wolfenbüttel-Spanish map and the work of Diego Ribero. Worcester, Mass.: Davis Press, 1909. 53p. (Reprinted from American Antiquarian Society Proceedings, n. s. 19 (April 1909), 369-419)

Occasionally locates a copy.

3877. U. S. Library of Congress, Division of Maps and Charts. List of Maps of America in the Library, preceded by a list of works relating to cartography, by P. Lee Phillips. Wash.: Govt. Print. Off., 1901. 1,137p.

3878. Winsor, Justin. The Kohl collection of maps relating to America. Cambridge: Harvard Univ. Library, 1886. 70p. (Harvard University Library, Bibliographical contributions, no. 19). Catalog reprinted, with index by P. L. Phillips, Wash., 1904. 189p.

Collection, containing 474 titles, transferred to Library of Congress in 1903.

NORTH AMERICA

3879. Brown, Lloyd A. "Manuscript maps in the William L. Clements Library." American Neptune, 1 (Apr. 1940), 141-48.

Description of selected items from Library's 550 manuscript maps of period from 1755 to 1800, relating chiefly to United States history.

3880. Brown, Ralph H. "Materials bearing upon the geography of the Atlantic seaboard, 1790-1810." Association of American Geographers annals, 28 (1938), 201-31.

Footnotes locate some books and manuscripts.

3881. Jenks, William L. "The Michael Shoemaker collection of maps." Michigan historical collections, 39 (1915), 297-300.

Collection of early maps of the Great Lakes region, held by Michigan Pioneer and Historical Society.

3882. Joerg, W. L. G. "Archival maps as illustrated by those in the National Archives." American archivist, 4 (1941), 188-93.

Notes on about 38,000 maps received from Department of State, Office of the Chief of Engineers in the War Department, Office of Indian Affairs, the Senate, etc.

3883. LeGear, Clara Egli. "The Hotchkiss maps collection." Library of Congress quarterly journal of current acquisitions, 6 (Nov. 1948), 16-20.

Description of printed and manuscript maps, in Library of Congress, of Major Jedidiah Hotchkiss, Confederate Army topograhical engineer.

3884. Martin, Lawrence. "John Mitchell's map." Library of Congress quarterly journal of current acquisitions, 1 (Apr.-June, 1944), 36-38.

Maps of British and French North America, published in London, 1755, and in Paris, 1756. Copies located in Library of Congress and other collections.

3885. Martin, Lawrence, "Mitchell's map." In: Miller, Hunter, ed. Treaties and other international acts of the United States of America. Wash.: Govt. Print. Off., 1933. v. 3, p. 328-56.

John Mitchell's map, issued 1755, was used to define boundaries of the United States in 1783 peace negotiations. Martin locates copies in the United States and England of various editions and impressions.

3886. Michigan, University, William L. Clements Library. British headquarters maps and sketches used by Sir Henry Clinton while in command of the British forces operating in North America during the war for independence, 1775-1782; a descriptive list of the original manuscripts and printed documents now preserved in the William L. Clements Library at the University of Michigan, by Randolph G. Adams. Ann Arbor: William L. Clements Library, 1928. 144p.

Describes portion of Library's 20,000-piece map holdings.

3887. Michigan, University, William L. Clements Library. British maps of the American revolution; a guide to an exhibit. Ann Arbor, 1936. 23p. (Bulletin, no. 24)

Describes maps made by or after surveys of British engineers.

3888. Michigan, University, William L. Clements Library. Early maps of the Mississippi valley, [by Louis C. Karpinski] Ann Arbor, 1925. 4p. (Bulletin, no. 7)

An exhibition.

3889. Michigan, University, William L. Clements Library. An exhibition of maps engraved within the present limits of the United States, mostly prior to 1800. Ann Arbor: The Library, 1933. 15p. (Bulletin, no. 20)

Description of 25 maps.

3890. Odgers, Charlotte H., comp. "Federal government maps relating to Pacific Northwest history." Pacific Northwest quarterly, 38 (1947), 261-72.

List of maps in National Archives, photostat copies in University of Washington and State College of Washington libraries.

3891. Phillips, Philip Lee. The rare map of the Northwest, 1785, by John Fitch; a bibliographical account, with facsimile reproduction including some account of Thomas Hutchins and William McMurray. Wash.: W. H. Lowdermilk & Co., 1916. 43p.

Pages 42-43 describe the collection of papers of John Fitch in Library of Congress.

3892. U. S. Library of Congress. The Lowery collection; a descriptive list of maps of the Spanish possessions within the present limits of the United States, 1502-1820, by Woodbury Lowery, ed. by Philip Lee Phillips. Wash.: Govt. Print. Off., 1912. 567p.

Describes 750 maps, all but 184 of which were in Library of Congress at time of publication.

3893. U. S. Library of Congress, Division of Maps. Alaska and the northwest part of North America, 1588-1898; maps in the Library of Congress, by P. Lee Phillips, Wash.: Govt. Print. Off., 1898. 119p.

Chronologically arranged.

3894. Wagner, Henry R. The cartography of the Northwest coast of America to the year 1800. Berkeley: Univ. of California Press, 1937. 2v.

Books and maps used in preparation of this work are now in Pomona College Library. Locates maps in 16 American libraries and many European collections.

3895. Webb, Willard. "The Hotchkiss papers; an additional note." Library of Congress quarterly journal of current acquisitions, 7 (Nov. 1949), 23-24.

Supplements article in Quarterly journal, 6 (Nov. 1948), 16-20.

UNITED STATES (Individual States and Cities)

Boston

3896. Boston, Engineering Department. List of maps of Boston published between 1600 and 1903, copies of which are to be found in the possession of the city of Boston or other collectors of the same. Boston: Municipal Printing Office, 1903. 248p. (Reprint of Appendix I, Annual report of the City Engineer. February 1, 1903) Supplement, 1904. 97p.

Locates maps in 40 public or private collections around Boston.

3897. Boston, Engineering Department. List of maps of Boston published between 1614 and 1822, copies of which are to be found in the possession of the city of Boston or other collectors of the same. Boston: Municipal Printing Office, 1902. 35p. (Reprint of Appendix J, Annual report of the city engineer. February 1, 1902.)

Locates maps in 40 public or private collections in or near Boston.

3998. U. S. Library of Congress, Division of Maps. "A descriptive list of maps and views of Boston in the Library of Congress, 1630-1865." Wash., 1922. 275p. Typed.

California

3899. California State Library, Sutro Branch. List of the maps showing the Californias in the Sutro Branch... list of maps and authors and list of all localities indicated in Lower and Upper California, comp. by Chas. B. Turrill. [San Francisco] 1917. 217 (i. e. 280) numb. l.

3900. California, University, Library. List of printed maps of California, comp. by J. C. Rowell. Berkeley: [State Print. Off.] 1887. 33p. (Library bulletin, no. 9)

3901. Henry E. Huntington Library. California in maps, 1541-1851; notes on an exhibition, by Willard O. Waters. San Marino, 1949. 8p.

3902. U. S. Library of Congress, Division of Maps. "A descriptive list of maps of California and San Francisco to 1865, inclusive, found in the Library of Congress." Wash., 1915. 173 l. Typed.

3903. Wheat, Carl I. The maps of the California gold region, 1848-1857; a bibliocartography of an important decade. San Francisco: Grabhorn Press, 1942. 153p.

Locates copies of 323 entries in 14 institutional and private libraries.

Detroit

3904. Detroit Public Library. "Old Detroit in maps, plans and views [to 1875]: an annotated list," comp. by Francis Waring Robinson. Detroit, 1942-43. 6p. Typed.

Based upon material in Library's Burton Historical Collection.

Florida

3905. Phillips, Philip Lee. Notes on the life and works of Bernard Romans. Deland: Florida State Historical Society, 1924. 128p.

Locates copies of Romans' 18th century maps of Florida.

Georgia

3906. Historical Records Survey - Georgia. Classified inventory of Georgia maps, 1941. East Point, Ga.: Ga. State Planning Board, 1941. 150p.

Kentucky

3907. Phillips, Philip Lee. The first map of Kentucky by John Filson; a bibliographical account... from the copy in the Library of Congress. Wash.: W. H. Lowdermilk, 1908. 22p.

Michigan

3908. Jenks, William L. "Some early maps of Michigan." Michigan Historical Society collections, 38 (1912), 627-37.

Locates copies of some maps.

3909. Karpinski, Louis Charles. Bibliography of the printed maps of Michigan, 1804-1880. Lansing: Michigan Historical Commission. 1931. 539p.

Locates over 1,000 Michigan maps in 29 libraries or collections; also includes descriptions and locations of 120 "fundamental maps of the Great Lakes area," issued before 1804.

New York

3910. Historical Records Survey - N. Y. (State) Inventory of maps (partial) located in various state, county, municipal and other public offices in New York State, (exclusive of New York City). Albany, 1942. 355p.

3911. New York Public Library. "Check list of maps and atlases relating to the City of New York in the New York Public Library." New York Public Library bulletin, 5 (1901), 60-73.

3912. New York Public Library. "Check list of maps in the New York Public Library relating to the City of Brooklyn and to Kings County." New York Public Library bulletin, 6 (1902), 84-88.

Chronologically arranged, 1750-1898.

3913. New York Public Library. "Manhattan maps-- a co-operative list," comp. by Daniel Carl Haskell. New York Public Library bulletin, 34 (1930), 241-56, 328-45, 541-56, 593-627, 653-75, 725-42. Reprinted. 128p.

Lists holdings of American Geographical Society, New-York Historical Society, New York Public Library, Library of Congress, etc.

North Carolina

3914. North Carolina State Department of Archives and History. The Eric Norden collection; an inventory of a group of survey plats drawn for the most part by the late Eric Norden and covering land areas located chiefly in southeastern North Carolina, comp. by Henry Howard Eddy and Frances Harmon. Raleigh: The Department, 1949. 40p.

Descriptive list of about 140 large-scale maps and plats.

Ohio

3915. Phillips, Philip Lee. The first map and description of Ohio, 1787, by Manasseh Cutler. A bibliographical account, with reprint of the "Explanation," Wash.: W. H. Lowdermilk & Co., 1918. 41p.

Description and bibliography based on material from Map Division of Library of Congress.

Philadelphia

3916. Phillips, Philip Lee. A descriptive list of maps and views of Philadelphia in the Library of Congress, 1683-1865. [Philadelphia: Geographical Society of Philadelphia] 1926. 91p.

Rhode Island

3917. Chapin, Howard M. "Chronological check list of maps of Rhode Island in the Rhode Island Historical Society library." Rhode Island Historical Society collections, 11 (1918), 47-55, 90-98, 124-32; 12 (1919), 26-32, 58-64, 89-95. Appeared also as Check list of maps of Rhode Island. Providence: Preston and Rounds, 1918. 48p. (Contributions to

Rhode Island bibliography, no. 5)

Lists 185 items, locating copies chiefly in Rhode Island Historical Society Library.

Vineland, N. J.

3918. [Ankenbrand, Frank, Jr.] "A bibliography of Vineland [N. J.] maps published, and originals in the possession of the Vineland Historical Society." Vineland historical magazine, 23 (1938), 134-40.

Covers period from 1851 to 1935.

Virginia

3919. Phillips, Philip L. "Some early maps of Virginia and the makers, including plates relating to the first settlement of Jamestown." Virginia magazine of history and biography, 15 (July, 1907), 71-81.

Describes Library of Congress collection of early Virginia maps, and locates a few rare maps elsewhere.

3920. Phillips, Philip L. Virginia cartography; a bibliographical description. Wash.: Smithsonian Institution, 1896. 85p. (Smithsonian miscellaneous collection, v. 37, art. 4)

Locates some Virginia maps in various collections, including Library of Congress.

3921. Roberts, Joseph Kent and Bloomer, Robert O. Catalogue of topographic and geologic maps of Virginia. Richmond: Dietz Press, 1939. 246p.

Locates copies of 970 maps in 14 libraries.

3922. Virginia State Library. "Maps relating to Virginia in the Virginia State Library and other departments of the Commonwealth, with the 17th and 18th century atlas-maps in the Library of Congress," by Earl G. Swem. Virginia State Library bulletin, 7 (1914), 37-263.

A chronological list, 1590-1914. In addition to maps in Library of Congress, maps of several other non-Virginia libraries are included.

Washington, D. C.

3923. U. S. Library of Congress, Division of Maps. "A descriptive list of maps and views of Washington and District of Columbia, including Mount Vernon." [1916?] 540p. Typed.

3924. U. S. Library of Congress, Division of Maps. List of maps and views of Washington and District of Columbia in the Library of Congress, by P. Lee Phillips. Wash.: Govt. Print. Off., 1900. 77p. (56th Cong., 1st sess. Senate. Doc. 154)

Chronologically arranged, 1782-1900.

West Virginia

3925. Historical Records Survey - West Va. Inventory of defense maps of West Virginia. Huntington, W. Va., 1942. 99p.

LATIN AMERICA

3926. American Geographical Society. A catalogue of maps of Hispanic America, including maps in scientific periodicals and books, and sheet and atlas maps, with articles on the cartography of the several countries, and maps showing the extent and character of existing surveys. N. Y., 1930-33. 4v. (American Geographical Society map of Hispanic America publication, no. 3)

Lists holdings of Library of Congress, New York Public Library, Pan American Union, American Geographical Society, Columbia, Harvard, and Yale Universities.

3927. Martin, Lawrence, and others. "Hispanic-American map exhibition at the Library of Congress at Washington; a selection of Hispanic-American maps representative of four centuries of historical, diplomatic and cartographic progress in the two Americas." Pan American Institute of Geography and History proceedings, (1937), 243-54.

3928. Martin, Lawrence. "South American cartographic treasures." Library of Congress quarterly journal of current acquisitions, 1 (Jan. - March 1944), 30-39.

Description of 22 early cartographic manuscripts and a printed map of South America acquired by the Library of Congress.

3929. Pan American Union, Columbus Memorial Library. Books and magazine articles on geography in the Columbus Memorial Library of the Pan American Union. Wash.: The Union, [1935] 72 numb. l. (Bibliographic series, no. 13)

3930. Pan American Union, Columbus

Memorial Library. Maps relating to Latin America in books and periodicals, comp. by A. Curtis Wilgus. Wash.: Pan American Union, 1933. 103p.

List of about 5,000 maps "taken generally from books and periodicals found in the Library of the Pan American Union and the Library of Congress."

3931. Phillips, Philip Lee. "Guiana and Venezuela cartography." American Historical Association annual report, (1897), 681-776.

Covers 16th through 18th centuries. Locates each map in either Library of Congress or one of 6 foreign sources.

3932. U. S. Library of Congress. "Maps relating to Cuba," comp. by P. Lee Phillips. In: Gonzalo de Quesada. Cuba. Wash.: Govt. Print. Off., 1905, p. 447-512.

3933. U. S. Library of Congress, Division of Maps. Catalogue of an exhibition in the Division of Maps, comprising some 200 Hispanic-American maps, atlases, geographies, globes, and portraits of historical, diplomatic and cartographic interest, ranging through four centuries. [Wash.] Govt. Print. Off., 1935. 20p.

3934. U. S. Library of Congress, Division of Maps. Disturnell's map, by Lawrence Martin. Wash.: Govt. Print. Off., 1937. p. [339]- 370.

"Study of an important American treaty map... made in the Library of Congress at the request of the Department of State. It is reprinted from the publication entitled: 'Treaties and other international acts of the United States of America,' v. 5, 1937, edited by Dr. Hunter Miller, historical adviser, Department of State."

Biography and Genealogy

GENERAL

3935. Fitch, Elizabeth H. Autobiographies, memoirs, letters and journals in Case Library. [Cleveland, 1910] 43p.
　Now part of Western Reserve University Library.

3936. Harvard University, Wm. Hayes Fogg Art Museum. Exhibition: Washington, Lafayette, Franklin; portraits, books, manuscripts, prints, memorabilia, for the most part from the collections of the University. [Cambridge] Fogg Museum of Art, Harvard University, 1944. 53p.

3937. O'Neill, Edward Hayes. Biography by Americans, 1658-1936; a subject bibliography. Philadelphia: Univ. of Penn. Press, 1939. 465p.
　Copies located in 8 libraries.

3938. U. S. Library of Congress, Division of Bibliography. Biographies of the presidents of the United States, a bibliographical list, comp. by Grace Hadley Fuller. n. p., 1937. 49p.

3939. U. S. Library of Congress, Division of Bibliography. List of references relating to notable American women, comp. by Florence S. Hellman. Wash., 1931. 144p. Supplementary lists, 1932, 1937; second supplement, 1941; comprehensive index, 1941.

3940. U. S. Library of Congress, General Reference and Bibliography Division. Biographical sources for foreign countries, comp. by Helen D. Jones. Wash., 1944-45. 4v.

3941. Virginia State Library. "Finding list of biography," comp. by Earl G. Swem. Virginia State Library bulletin, 1 (1908), 35-134.

INDIVIDUAL BIOGRAPHY

Adams, Abigail

3942. Eaton, Dorothy S. "Some letters of Abigail Adams." Library of Congress quarterly journal of current acquisitions, 4 (Aug. 1947), 3-6.
　Describes collection of 500 manuscripts received by Library of Congress.

Adams, John

3943. Boston Public Library. Catalogue of the John Adams library in the Public Library of the City of Boston. Boston: The Library, 1917. 271p.
　Records about 3,000 volumes. Especially strong on constitutional and political history of various countries, including Italian republics.

Adams, John Quincy

3944. Boston Athenaeum. A catalogue of the books of John Quincy Adams deposited in the Boston Athenaeum with notes on books, Adams seals and bookplates, by Henry Adams. Boston: The Athenaeum, 1938. 152p.

Baker, Ray Stannard

3945. Brand, Katharine E. "The personal papers of Ray Stannard Baker." Library of Congress quarterly journal of current acquisitions, 5 (Aug. 1948), 3-9.

Bell, Alexander Graham

3946. Historical Records Survey - D. of C. Calendar of Alexander Graham Bell correspondence in the Volta Bureau, Washington,

D. C. Wash.: Historical Records Survey, 1940. 41 numb. l.

Benjamin, Judah Philip

3947. U. S. Library of Congress, Division of Bibliography. "Judah Philip Benjamin: a bibliographical list." Wash., Dec. 18, 1931. 6p. Typed. General Reference and Bibliography Division. [Supplementary list] Nov. 19, 1946. 4p. Typed.

Benton, Thomas Hart

3948. U. S. Library of Congress, Division of Bibliography. "A list of references on Thomas Hart Benton (1782-1858)." Wash., Apr. 18, 1934. 16p. Typed.

Bolívar, Simón

3949. Pan American Union, Columbus Memorial Library. "Bibliographical list relative to Simón Bolívar, the Liberator." Hispanic American historical review, 10 (1930), 525-43.

Locates copies in Pan American Union and Library of Congress.

3950. Pan American Union, Columbus Memorial Library. Bibliography of the Liberator, Simón Bolívar, compiled in the Columbus Memorial Library of the Pan American Union. [Wash., 1933] 107p. (Bibliographic series, no. 1, rev. & enl.)

Includes holdings of Pan American Union, Library of Congress, and National Library at Caracas.

3951. Pan American Union, Columbus Memorial Library. Simón Bolívar; bibliography of the liberator Simón Bolívar. Wash.: Govt. Print. Off., 1931. 21p. (71st Cong., 3d sess. Senate, Doc. 231)

Bowditch, Nathaniel

3952. Peabody Museum of Salem [Mass.] A catalogue of a special exhibition of manuscripts, books, portraits, and personal relics of Nathaniel Bowditch (1773-1838), by Raymond C. Archibald. [Portland, Me.: Southworth-Anthoensen Press, 1937] 40p.

Drawn from institutional and private collections, with owners indicated.

Brackenridge, Hugh Henry

3953. Heartman, Charles F. A bibliography of the writings of Hugh Henry Brackenridge prior to 1825. N. Y., 1917. 37p.

Locates copies in 15 libraries.

Burr, Aaron

3954. Tompkins, Hamilton Bullock. Burr bibliography. A list of books relating to Aaron Burr. Brooklyn, N. Y.: Historical Printing Club, 1892. 89 numb. l.

Locates copies in 11 libraries.

Burton, Theodore Elijah

3955. U. S. Library of Congress, Division of Bibliography. "Theodore Elijah Burton, 1851-1929: a bibliographical list." Wash., Jan. 4, 1932. 21p. Typed.

Butler, Nicholas Murray

3956. Thomas, Milton Halsey. Bibliography of Nicholas Murray Butler, 1872-1932; a check list. N. Y.: Columbia Univ. Press, 1934. 438p.

Entire collection of Butler's writings, printed and manuscript, now in Columbia University Library.

Cabot, John

3957. Winship, George Parker. Cabot bibliography. N. Y.: Dodd, Mead & Co., 1900. 180p.

Locates copies of many of 579 titles relating to lives of John Cabot and Sebastian Cabot.

Clark, George Rogers

3958. Swem, Earl G. "Newly discovered George Rogers Clark material." Mississippi Valley historical review, 1 (1914), 95-97.

Description of an extensive collection of papers found in Virginia State Auditor's office.

Clinton, George

3959. New York (State) State Historian. Public papers of George Clinton, first governor of New York. Albany, 1911. v. 9-10 analytical index.

In New York State Library.

Cromwell, Oliver

3960. Lane, William Coolidge. The Carlyle collection. A catalogue of books on Oliver Cromwell and Frederick the Great, bequeathed by Thomas Carlyle to Harvard College Library. Cambridge: Harvard University Library, 1888. 22p. (Harvard University Library, Bibliographical contributions, no. 26)

Columbus, Christopher

3961. Boston Public Library. "Columbus. A list of writings... and works relating to him." Boston Public Library bulletin, 11 (1892), 221-33.

3962. Goff, Frederick R. "The letters of Christopher Columbus concerning the islands of India." Library of Congress quarterly journal of current acquisitions, 3 (May 1946), 3-7.

Description of Columbus Letter (Rome: Stephan Plannck, 1493) acquired by Library of Congress.

Coolidge, Calvin

3963. Coolidge papers offered to Library of Congress." Publishers weekly, 142 (1942), 1906-07.

About 9,000 items of White House correspondence given to Library of Congress in 1942, to remain sealed for 20 years.

Cooper, Peter

3964. New York Public Library. "Peter Cooper; a critical bibliography of his life and works," comp. by C. Sumner Spalding. New York Public Library bulletin, 45 (1941), 723-45. Reprinted. 25p.

Locates copies principally in New York Public Library, Cooper Union Library, and Library of Congress.

Crittenden, John Jordon

3965. U. S. Library of Congress, Division of Manuscripts. A calendar of the papers of John Jordon Crittenden; prepared from the original manuscripts in the Library of Congress, by Claudius Newman Feamster. Wash.: Govt. Print. Off., 1913. 335p.

Custer, George Armstrong

3966. U. S. Library of Congress, Division of Bibliography. "List of references on General George Armstrong Custer." Wash., June 11, 1921. 12p. Typed. "Additional titles." Wash., 1930. 2p. General Reference and Bibliography Division. [Supplementary list] Apr., 1945. 4p.

Daniels, Josephus

3967. Brand, Katharine E. "The Josephus Daniels papers." Library of Congress quarterly journal of current acquisitions, 7 (Aug. 1950), 3-10.

Collection of about 500,000 pieces presented to Library of Congress.

Davis, Jefferson

3968. Harwell, Richard Barksdale. "A brief calendar of the Jefferson Davis papers in the Keith M. Read Confederate collection of the Emory University Library." Journal of Mississippi history, 4 (1942), 20-30.

3969. Louisiana Historical Association. Calendar of the Jefferson Davis postwar manuscripts in the Louisiana Historical Association collection. [New Orleans]: The Association, 1943. 325p.

List of about 600 letters, 1863-91, preserved in Confederate Memorial Hall, New Orleans.

Edwards, Jonathan

3970. Johnson, Thomas Herbert. The printed writings of Jonathan Edwards, 1703-1758. A bibliography. Princeton: Princeton Univ. Press, 1940. [136]p.

Copies located in 76 libraries. Lists 346 titles.

3971. U. S. Library of Congress, Reading Room. "A list of printed materials on Jonathan Edwards, 1703-1758, to be found in the Library of Congress; including biographies, appreciations, criticisms, and fugitive references. With supplementary lists of material not in the library and with notes on his manuscripts and works." [Wash., 1934] 29 l. Typed.

Evans, Luther H.

3972. U. S. Library of Congress, General Reference and Bibliography Division. "Writings of Luther H. Evans: a partial list." Wash., May 16, 1945. 4p. Typed. "Additional references." Wash., Nov. 27, 1946. 2p. Typed.

Ford, Henry

3973. U. S. Library of Congress, Division of Bibliography. "Henry Ford: a bibliographical list," comp. by Florence S. Hellman. Wash., Nov. 12, 1942. 17p. Typed.

Franklin, Benjamin

3974. Boston Public Library. "Collection of Franklin portraits." Boston Public Library bulletin, 11 (Apr. 1892 - Jan. 1893), 139-50.

3975. Bridgwater, Dorothy W. "The Mason-Franklin collection." Yale University Library gazette, 15 (1940), 16-19.
General description of a collection of 11,000 books, 850 pamphlets, and 400 broadsides devoted to Benjamin Franklin and his period.

3976. Bridgwater, Dorothy W. "Notable additions to the Franklin collection." Yale University Library gazette, 20 (1945), 21-28.
124 groups of historical manuscripts relating to Benjamin Franklin, in Yale University Library.

3977. Crane, Verner W. "Certain writings of Benjamin Franklin on the British Empire and the American colonies." Bibliographical Society of America papers, 28 (1934), 1-27.
Locates several collections of Franklin manuscripts used in identifying authorship of printed material.

3978. Curtis Publishing Company. The collection of Franklin imprints in the museum of the Curtis Publishing Company; with a short-title check list of all the books, pamphlets, broadsides, etc., known to have been printed by Benjamin Franklin, comp. by W. J. Campbell. Philadelphia: Curtis Publishing Co., 1918. 333p.
Presented to University of Pennsylvania Library in 1920.

3979. Dwight, Theodore F. "Lost and found manuscripts of Benjamin Franklin." Magazine of American history, 9 (1883), 428-39.
Description and list of collection now in Library of Congress.

3980. Eddy, George Simpson. "A ramble through the Mason-Franklin collection." Yale University Library gazette, 10 (1936), 65-90.
Description of an extensive collection relating to Benjamin Franklin and his period, in the Yale University Library.

3981. Ford, Paul L. Franklin bibliography, a list of books written by or relating to Benjamin Franklin. Brooklyn, 1889. 467p.
Lists 1,002 titles, with locations in 15 libraries.

3982. Hays, I. Minis, ed. Calendar of the papers of Benjamin Franklin in the library of the American Philosophical Society. Philadelphia: The Society, 1908. 5v.

3983. Michigan, University, William L. Clements Library. An exhibition of books and papers relating to Dr. Benjamin Franklin, from the collections in this library and the library of William Smith Mason. Ann Arbor: Alumni Press, 1926. 11p. (Bulletin, no. 12)
Mentions other books in Library besides those collected for exhibit.

3984. Mugridge, Donald H. "Scientific manuscripts of Benjamin Franklin." Library of Congress quarterly journal of current acquisitions, 4 (Aug. 1947), 12-21.
Description of "some sixteen pieces and a few related fragments" acquired by Library of Congress.

3985. New York Public Library. "List of works in the New York Public Library by or relating to Benjamin Franklin." New York Public Library bulletin, 10 (1906), 29-83. Reprinted. 55p.
Includes manuscripts and portraits.

3986. Pennsylvania, University, Library. "Calendar of the papers of Benjamin Franklin in the Library." University of Pennsylvania publications, series in history, no. 3 (1908), 399-546.

3987. Rosengarten, Joseph G. "The Franklin papers in the American Philosophical Society."

American Philosophical Society proceedings, 42 (1903), 165-70.

3988. Stevens, Henry. Benjamin Franklin's life and writings; a bibliographical essay on the Stevens collection of books and manuscripts relating to Dr. Franklin. London, 1881. 40p.

Purchased by Congress in 1882 for State Department; now deposited in the Library of Congress.

3989. Swift, Lindsay. Catalogue of works relating to Benjamin Franklin in the Boston Public Library. Boston: The Library, 1883. 42p. (Bibliographies of special subjects 1.)

3990. U. S. Library of Congress, Division of Manuscripts. List of the Benjamin Franklin papers in the Library of Congress. Wash.: Govt. Print. Off., 1905. 322p.

Fulton, Robert

3991. New-York Historical Society. Official Robert Fulton exhibition of the Hudson-Fulton Commission. The New-York Historical Society in cooperation with the Colonial Dames of America. N. Y.: The Society, 1909. 66, [8]p.

Catalog of 354 Robert Fulton items, many owned by Society.

Gallatin, Albert

3992. Andrews, Wayne, "Gallatin revisited." New-York Historical Society quarterly, 34 (1950), 135-39.

First of a series of articles describing New-York Historical Society's collection of Albert Gallatin papers, totaling 16,000 items.

Garfield, James A.

3993. U. S. Library of Congress, Division of Bibliography. "List of references on James A. Garfield." Wash., Nov. 10, 1913. 29p. Typed.

Gibbon, Edward

3994. Norton, Jane E. A bibliography of the works of Edward Gibbon. Oxford: Oxford Univ. Press, 1940. 256p.

Copies located in American Antiquarian Society, Harvard University, and libraries abroad.

Grey, Lady Jane

3995. U. S. Library of Congress, Division of Bibliography. "Lady Jane Dudley, known as Lady Jane Grey, 1537-1554: a bibliographical list." Wash., July 24, 1936. 12p. Typed.

Hamilton, Alexander

3996. Ford, Paul Leicester. Bibliotheca Hamiltoniana, a list of books written by or relating to Alexander Hamilton. N. Y., 1886. 159p.

Copies of 270 items located in 11 libraries.

3997. Ford, Paul Leicester. A list of editions of "The Federalist." Brooklyn, 1886. 25p. Reprinted from author's Bibliotheca Hamiltoniana, 1886. p. 13-35.

Locates some copies.

3998. Ford, Paul Leicester, comp. A list of Treasury reports and circulars issued by Alexander Hamilton, 1789-1795. Brooklyn, 1886. 47 numb. l.

Locates copies in 11 libraries.

Hayes, Rutherford Birchard

3999. Hayes Memorial Library. An index and list of the letters and papers of Rutherford Birchard Hayes... with notes on other source material at the Hayes Memorial Library. Columbus: Ohio State Archaeological and Historical Society, 1933. 42p.

Also notes other source material of Reconstruction period in Library at Fremont, Ohio.

4000. Hayes Memorial Library. An index and list of the pamphlets and periodicals collected by Rutherford Birchard Hayes, nineteenth president of the United States. Columbus: Ohio State Archaeological and Historical Society, 1935. 45p.

Includes a listing of Ohio imprints.

Henderson, James Pinckney

4001. U. S. Library of Congress, General Reference and Bibliography Division. "A selected list of references relating to James Pinckney Henderson (March 31, 1808 - June 4, 1858)," comp. by Nelson R. Burr. Wash., Feb. 15, 1946. 6p. Typed.

Herrick, Myron T.

4002. Wilcox, Robert Calvin. "A bibliography of the speech manuscripts of Myron T. Herrick." Cleveland: Western Reserve University, 1950. 39 l. Unpublished M. A. thesis.

Lists Myron T. Herrick materials housed in Western Reserve Historical Society Library.

Hopkins, Gerard Manley

4003. U. S. Library of Congress, Division of Bibliography. "Gerard Manley Hopkins, 1844-1889: a bibliographical list." Wash., Sept. 5, 1940. 12p. Typed.

House, Edward Mandell

4004. Wanning, Andrews. "The Edward M. House collection." Yale University Library gazette, 7 (1932), 4-9.

Brief description of House collection of books in Yale University Library of particular value "to the student of the [1st world] war and of the peace settlement."

Houston, Samuel

4005. U. S. Library of Congress, Division of Bibliography. "General Samuel Houston: a bibliographical list." Wash., Mar. 25, 1930. 9p. Typed.

Hudson, William Henry

4006. Michigan, University, William L. Clements Library. The G. M. Adams - W. H. Hudson collection. An appreciation by Carlton F. Wells. Ann Arbor: Univ. of Michigan, 1943. 12p. (Bulletin, no. 39)

Describes Adams collection of about 100 items written by W. H. Hudson, and presented to Clements Library.

Hughes, Lewis

4007. Cole, George Watson. "Lewis Hughes, the militant minister of the Bermudas and his printed works." American Antiquarian Society proceedings, n. s. 37 (1927), 247-311. Reprinted. 1928. 67p.

Bibliography, p. 286-310, lists 14 works chronologically, 1615-41, with locations in 10 American and British collections.

Jackson, Andrew

4008. MacDonald, William. "The Jackson and Van Buren papers." American Antiquarian Society proceedings, n. s. 17 (1905), 231-38.

Papers in the Library of Congress.

4009. New York Public Library. Jackson, Andrew. "Calendar of the Jackson-Lewis letters, 1806-1864." New York Public Library bulletin, 4 (1900), 292-320. Selections from the correspondence, with title, "Letters and papers of Andrew Jackson," appeared in Bulletin, 4 (1900), 154-62, 188-98.

In New York Public Library's Ford collection.

Jefferson, Thomas

4010. Bullock, Helen Duprey. "The papers of Thomas Jefferson." American archivist, 4 (1941), 238-49.

Notes on principal depositories of Jefferson papers, with details of University of Virginia collection.

4011. Butterfield, Lyman H. "The Jefferson-Adams correspondence in the Adams Manuscript Trust." Library of Congress quarterly journal of current acquisitions, 5 (1948), 3-6.

A description of papers which the Adams Manuscript Trust of Boston has deposited at Library of Congress.

4012. Jefferson, Thomas. Thomas Jefferson and his unknown brother Randolph. Twenty-eight letters exchanged between Thomas and Randolph Jefferson... during the years 1807 to 1815. Charlottesville: Tracy W. McGregor Library, University of Virginia, 1942. 42p.

Source material in the McGregor Library, University of Virginia.

4013. Michigan, University, William L. Clements Library. Thomas Jefferson, 1743-1943; a guide to the rare books and manuscripts exhibited at the University of Michigan. Ann Arbor: William L. Clements Library, 1943. 32p. (Bulletin, no. 38)

Comments on books, manuscripts and maps by and about Jefferson.

4014. Tompkins, Hamilton Bullock. Bibliotheca Jeffersoniana: a list of books written by or relating to Thomas Jefferson. N. Y. and

London: G. P. Putnam's Sons, 1887. 187p.
Copies located in 9 libraries.

4015. U. S. Department of State. Calendar of the correspondence of Thomas Jefferson. Wash., 1894-1903. 3v. (U. S. Bureau of Rolls and Library bulletin, nos. 6, 8, 10)

Pt. 1, letters from Jefferson; pt. 2, letters to Jefferson; pt. 3, supplementary. Collection now in Library of Congress.

4016. U. S. Library of Congress. Catalogue of the library of Thomas Jefferson, 1815, a prospectus. Wash.: Govt. Print. Off., 1943. 17p.

4017. U. S. Library of Congress. The Thomas Jefferson Bicentennial, 1743-1943: a catalogue of the exhibitions at the Library of Congress opened on April 12th. Wash.: Govt. Print. Office, 1943. 170p.

Manuscripts, maps, music, books, prints, etc., drawn from Library of Congress collections and from other libraries and individuals.

4018. U. S. National Archives. The Thomas Jefferson bicentennial exhibit of historical documents. Wash., 1943. 9p.

4019. Virginia, University, Library. The Jefferson papers of the University of Virginia; a calendar. Charlottesville: The Library, 1950. 343p. (Univ. of Virginia bibliographical series, no. 8)

4020. Virginia, University, Library. Jefferson's ideas of a university library; letters from the founder of the University of Virginia to a Boston bookseller, ed. by Elizabeth Cometti. Charlottesville: Univ. of Virginia, Tracy W. McGregor Library, 1950. 44p.

Source materials in Library of Congress and University of Virginia Library.

Johnston, Joseph E.

4021. Swem, E. G. Joseph E. Johnston papers... (and) John Marshall papers in the Library of William and Mary College. Williamsburg, 1939. 19p. (College of William and Mary in Virginia bulletin, v. 33, no. 7, Nov. 1939)

Jones, John Paul

4022. U. S. Library of Congress, Division of Manuscripts. A calendar of John Paul Jones manuscripts in the Library of Congress, comp. by Charles Henry Lincoln. Wash.: Govt. Print. Off., 1903. 316p.

Includes 883 items, from the Peter Force collection purchased in 1867.

Lawrence, James

4023. Baker, Charles E. "The Eugene H. Pool collection of Captain James Lawrence." New-York Historical Society quarterly bulletin, 28 (1944), 81-95. Reprinted. 17p.

Collection of books, manuscripts, prints, paintings and memorabilia owned by the New-York Historical Society.

4024. Peabody Museum of Salem [Mass.] "Don't give up the ship;" a catalogue of the Eugene H. Pool collection of Captain James Lawrence. Salem: Peabody Museum, 1942. 82p.

Lists letters and manuscripts, prints and paintings, models, and personal memorabilia, now in possession of New-York Historical Society.

Lee, Robert E.

4025. Nicholson, John B. "General Robert E. Lee, 1807-1870, a preliminary bibliography." 1936. A thesis at Washington and Lee University, unpublished, containing data on manuscripts in Washington and Lee Library.

Lincoln, Abraham

4026. Angle, Paul M. "Famous Lincoln collections: the Illinois State Historical Library." Abraham Lincoln quarterly, 1 (1940), 58-63.

Describes Lincoln material available in collection of Illinois State Historical Library.

4027. Benjamin, Philip M. "Famous Lincoln collections: Tarbell collection, Allegheny College." Abraham Lincoln quarterly, 2 (1943), 226-34.

General description, listing rare items.

4028. Brown University Library. The McLellan Lincoln collection at Brown University, a sketch, by Esther Cowles Cushman. Providence: The Library, 1928. 21p. (Also in the McLellan Lincoln collection publication 2. "Reprinted with some changes from the

American collector for Sept. 1927.")
One of the 5 most notable collections of Lincolniana.

4029. Bullock, Helen D. "The Robert Todd Lincoln collection of the papers of Abraham Lincoln." Library of Congress quarterly journal of current acquisitions, 5 (Nov. 1947), 3-8.
Summary of contents of collection opened to public by Library of Congress in 1947.

4030. Byrd, Cecil K. "Famous Lincoln collections: the Indiana-Oakleaf collection." Abraham Lincoln quarterly, 2 (1942), 185-91.
A description of collection assembled by Joseph B. Oakleaf and acquired by Indiana University Library.

4031. Cincinnati Public Library. Abraham Lincoln, 1809-1865, by Margaret S. Thompson. Cincinnati: The Library, 1909. 21p. (Special reading list, no. 13)
All titles listed are in Cincinnati Public Library.

4032. Colby College Library. An exhibit of Lincolniana, February 12, 1944, with a checklist of the George F. Terry Lincoln collection, comp. by Mary D. Herrick. Waterville, Me.: Colby College Library, 1944. 8p.

4033. Columbia University Library. Lincolniana in the Columbia University Libraries. An exhibition. [N. Y.: Columbia Univ. Press] 1944. 4p.
General notes only.

4034. Dempster, Margaret. "Famous Lincoln collections: the Lincoln collection of the Western Reserve Historical Society." Abraham Lincoln quarterly, 2 (1942), 143-48.
General description, listing rare items.

4035. Dunlap, Leslie W. "Lincoln's 'Autobiography.'" Library of Congress quarterly journal of current acquisitions, 4 (May, 1947), 57-59.
Document presented to Library of Congress.

4036. Fish, Daniel. "Lincoln collections and Lincoln bibliography." Bibliographical Society of America proceedings and papers, 3 (1908), 49-64.
Describes 5 private collections and some printed catalogs of Lincolniana.

4037. Griffith, Albert H. "Lincoln literature, Lincoln collections, and Lincoln collectors." Wisconsin magazine of history, 15 (Dec. 1931), 148-67.
Describes 23 private and 7 public Lincoln collections.

4038. Harvard University Library. "The Lincoln room." Harvard Library notes, 2 (1925), 71-74.
Lincolniana, Harvard College Library.

4039. Illinois State Historical Library. The Lincoln collection of the Illinois State Historical Library, by Paul M. Angle. Springfield: The Library, 1940. 21p.

4040. Louisville, University, J. B. Speed Memorial Museum. Catalogue of Lincoln books, pamphlets, magazines. Louisville, 1942. 19p.
Lists 141 items of Lincolniana.

4041. McMurtry, Robert Gerald. "Famous Lincoln collections: Lincoln Memorial University." Abraham Lincoln quarterly, 1 (1941), 384-93.
General description, listing rare items.

4042. Mearns, David Chambers. "Famous Lincoln collections: the Library of Congress." Abraham Lincoln quarterly, 1 (1941), 442-53. Reprinted. 12p.

4043. Mearns, David Chambers. "The Lincoln papers." Abraham Lincoln quarterly, 4 (1947), 369-85.
General description of Robert Todd Lincoln collection bequeathed to Library of Congress.

4044. Mearns, David Chambers. The Lincoln papers; the story of the collection. Garden City: Doubleday, 1948. 2v.
Selections of over 500 letters and memoranda to Abraham Lincoln from Robert Todd Lincoln collection in Library of Congress. A history of collection appears in first volume.

4045. Meserve, Frederick Hill. The photographic portraits of Abraham Lincoln; a descriptive list of the portraits in the Meserve collection, copies of which were presented to Lincoln Memorial University by Carl W. Schaefer. [N. Y.: Charles J. Amm Co.] 1941. 21p.
Lists and describes 118 portraits.

4046. Monaghan, James. Lincoln bibliography, 1839-1939. Springfield: Illinois State Historical Library, 1943-45. 2v. (Illinois State Historical Library collections, v. 31-32)
Lists 3,958 items, with locations.

4047. Potter, David M. "The Jackson collection of Lincolniana." Yale University Library gazette, 19 (1944), 22-28.
Approximately 2,000 pieces, collection now in Yale University Library.

4048. Pratt, Harry E. "Famous Lincoln collections: the Henry Horner collection." Abraham Lincoln quarterly, 1 (1940), 106-11.
Description of a major Lincoln collection presented to Illinois State Historical Library.

4049. Randall, James G. "Manuscript collections." In his: Lincoln The President. N. Y., Dodd, Mead, 1945. v. 2, p. 349-53.
List of important manuscript sources, with locations, for Lincoln research.

4050. Raney, McKendree Llewellyn. "Famous Lincoln collections: the University of Chicago." Abraham Lincoln quarterly, 1 (1941), 273-80.
General description, listing some rare items.

4051. Raney, McKendree Llewellyn and others. If Lincoln had lived. Chicago: Univ. of Chicago Press, [1935] 62p.
Description of William E. Barton collection of Lincolniana at University of Chicago, p. 1-15.

4052. Starr, Thomas I. "Famous Lincoln collections: the Greenly collection." Abraham Lincoln quarterly, 2 (1942), 13-25.
An important Lincoln collection, now held by Clements Library, University of Michigan.

4053. Starr, Thomas I. The Greenly collection, a recent gift of Lincolniana. [Ann Arbor, Mich., 1941.] 318-27p. (Reprinted from Michigan alumnus quarterly review, July 26, 1941)
Description of a collection of Lincolniana in William L. Clements Library, University of Michigan.

4054. U. S. Library of Congress. Lincoln collections in the Library of Congress, by David C. Mearns. 2d ed. Wash., 1943. 12p.

4055. U. S. Library of Congress. A list of Lincolniana in the Library of Congress, by George Thomas Ritchie. Rev. ed. Wash.: Govt. Print. Off., 1906. 86p. First edition, Wash., 1903. 75p.

4056. Warren, Louis A. "Famous Lincoln collections: The Lincoln National Life Foundation." Abraham Lincoln quarterly, 1 (1940), 163-70.
Lincoln collection owned by Lincoln National Life Insurance Company, Fort Wayne, Indiana. Includes 3,000 pictures, 30,000 manuscripts, etc.

4057. Wessen, Ernest James. Campaign lives of Abraham Lincoln, 1860. [Springfield, Ill., 1938] 33p. (Reprinted from Illinois State Historical Society, Papers in Illinois history and transactions, 1937.)
Locates copies of various editions of 21 biographies of Abraham Lincoln issued in 1860.

4058. Western Michigan College of Education Library. The Waldo collection of Lincolniana in the ... Library. Kalamazoo, 1947. 25 numb. l.
Lists 184 items in Western Michigan College of Education Library; a second list refers by number to Monaghan's Lincoln bibliography, and locates copies also in Kalamazoo College Library and Kalamazoo Public Library.

4059. Worthington, Edna M. "Famous Lincoln collections: Brown University." Abraham Lincoln quarterly, 1 (1940), 210-15.

4060. Wright, Lyle H. "Famous Lincoln collections: the Huntington Library." Abraham Lincoln quarterly, 1 (1941), 323-30.

Lindbergh, Charles A.

4061. U. S. Library of Congress, Division of Bibliography. "A selected list of references on Charles A. Lindbergh," comp. by Grace H. Fuller. Wash., Feb. 17, 1942. 17p. Typed.

Lippmann, Walter

4062. Anthony, Robert O. "A Walter Lippmann collection." Yale University Library gazette, 22 (1947), 39-41.
Books, articles and manuscripts by and about Lippmann.

BIOGRAPHY AND GENEALOGY

Lovejoy, Elijah Parish

4063. Colby College Library. A check list of Colby's Elijah Parish Lovejoy collection. Waterville, Me.: Colby College Library, 1944. [11]p.

Luther, Martin

4064. Smith, Preserved. "Martin Luther." Harvard Library notes, 1 (1921), 77-78.
Harvard College Library's collection.

MacArthur, Douglas

4065. U. S. Library of Congress, Division of Bibliography. A list of references on General Douglas MacArthur, comp. by Florence S. Hellman. [Wash.] 1942. 30p.

McHenry, James

4066. Dunn, Caroline. "William Henry Smith memorial library of the Indiana Historical Society." Indiana magazine of history, 40 (1944), 280-82, 364-65.
Describes recent acquisition, to library, of James McHenry papers (documents and letters to McHenry as head of the U. S. War Department, 1796-1800).

Madison, James

4067. U. S. Department of State. Calendar of the correspondence of James Madison. Wash., 1894-1903. 2v. (Bureau of Rolls and Library of the Department of State bulletin, no. 4)
Now in Library of Congress.

Mahan, Alfred Thayer

4068. Duke University Library. Letters of Alfred Thayer Mahan to Samuel A'Court Ashe (1858-59), ed. by Rosa Pendleton Chiles. Durham, N. C., 1931. 121p. (Duke University Library bulletin, no. 4, July 1931)
An edition of part of a collection in Duke University Library.

Masaryk, Thomas Garrigue

4069. Chicago Public Library. Collection Masaryk, a catalog of the books by and about Thomas Garrigue Masaryk, presented by the Honorable John Toman to John Toman Branch of the Chicago Public Library. [Chicago], 1939. 18p.

4070. New York Public Library. "Tomáš Garrigue Masaryk," comp. by Avrahm Yarmolinsky. New York Public Library bulletin, 45 (1941), 989-96, 1029-44. Reprinted. 27p.
A list of works by and about Masaryk in New York Public Library.

Mather Family

4071. Cadbury, Henry Joel. "Harvard College Library and the libraries of the Mathers." American Antiquarian Society proceedings, n. s. 50 (1940), 20-48.
List of books owned by the Mathers, with their present locations in Harvard College Library, Andover Theological Seminary, Harvard Divinity School, and American Antiquarian Society.

4072. Holmes, Thomas James. Cotton Mather: a bibliography of his works. Cambridge: Harvard Univ. Press, 1940. 3v., 1,395p.
Contains a table showing comparative strength of most important Mather collections, and locates copies of 468 titles in about 90 libraries.

4073. Holmes, Thomas James. Increase Mather; a bibliography of his works. Cambridge: Harvard Univ. Press, 1931. 2v.
Locates all known copies of 175 titles, and lists comparative tables showing in 4 ways the relative strength of the largest Mather collections.

4074. Holmes, Thomas James. The minor Mathers; a list of their works. Cambridge: Harvard Univ. Press, 1940. 218p.
Lists for 12 members of the Mather family. Locations shown in numerous libraries.

4075. Potter, Alfred C. "The Mathers." Harvard Library notes, 3 (1935), 30-32.
Recent acquisitions, Harvard College Library.

4076. Tuttle, Julius Herbert. "The libraries of the Mathers." American Antiquarian Society proceedings, n. s. 20 (1910), 269-356.
Libraries belonging to various members of Mather family in New England traced to

present locations in Boston Public Library, Massachusetts Historical Library, American Antiquarian Society, etc.

Maury, Matthew Fontaine

4077. Brown, Ralph Minthorne. Bibliography of Commander Matthew Fontaine Maury. Blackburg, Va., 1930. 61p. (Virginia Polytechnic Institute bulletin, v. 24, no. 2). 2nd ed., 1944. 46p. (Bulletin, v. 37, no. 12).

Locates some of the titles in the Virginia Polytechnic Institute, Virginia State Library, Library of Congress, Naval Observatory, or the U. S. Copyright Office.

4078. Darter, L. J. "Federal archives relating to Matthew Fontaine Maury." American Neptune, 1 (April 1941), 149-58.

A general survey of collection in National Archives relating to Maury.

Mitchell, William

4079. U. S. Library of Congress, Division of Bibliography. A list of references on Brigadier General William Mitchell, 1879-1936, comp. by Ann Duncan Brown. [Wash.] 1942. 33p.

Monroe, James

4080. U. S. Dept. of State. Calendar of the correspondence of James Monroe. Wash.: Dept. of State, 1893. 371p. (Bureau of Rolls and Library bulletin, no. 2)

Now in Library of Congress.

4081. U. S. Library of Congress, Division of Manuscripts. Papers of James Monroe, listed in chronological order from the original manuscripts in the Library of Congress. Wash.: Govt. Print. Off., 1904. 117p.

"Intended to complement the alphabetical 'Calendar of the correspondence of James Monroe' issued as Bulletin of the Bureau of Rolls and Library of the Department of State, no. 2, November 1893."

Moore, Thomas

4082. U. S. Library of Congress, Division of Bibliography. "List of references in the Library of Congress relating to Thomas Moore, 1779-1852 (exclusive of music)." Wash., June 10, 1932. 23p.

Morgan, George

4083. Carnegie Library of Pittsburgh. "Calendar to Morgan letter books." Pittsburgh: The Library, 1938. 73p. Typewritten.

Calendar to three volumes of manuscript letters, 1775-1779, of Colonel George Morgan, Indian agent.

Napoleon Bonaparte

4084. Brown University Library. A catalogue of the Napoleon collection formed by William Henry Hoffman... given to Brown University... by Mira H. Hoffman. Providence: Brown University, 1922. 77p.

4085. De Paul University Library. A catalog of the Napoleon Library of the De Paul University, comp. by Virginia Boyd Goult. Chicago: De Paul University, 1941. 112p.

Lists 2,074 items, classified by subjects and types of material.

Nelson, Admiral Horatio

4086. Baxter, James P., 3d. "The Nelson manuscripts in the Harvard College Library." Harvard Library notes, 2 (1929), 213-20.

Description of a collection of letters, documents, portraits and printed material relating to Admiral Nelson.

Paine, Thomas

4087. Michigan, University, William L. Clements Library. "These are the times that try men's souls." Ann Arbor, 1942. 8p. (Bulletin, no. 36)

Lists early editions and manuscripts of Thomas Paine held by Clements Library.

Penn, William

4088. Drake, Thomas E. "Penn at Haverford." Haverford review, 3 (Summer 1944), 6-8.

Account of William Penn material in Haverford College Library.

Pierce, Franklin

4089. U. S. Library of Congress, Division of Manuscripts. Calendar of the papers of Franklin Pierce, prepared from the original manuscripts in the Library of Congress, by W. R. Leech. Wash.: Govt. Print. Off., 1917. 102p.

Prescott, William Hickling

4090. Hispanic Society of America. Prescott; unpublished letters to Gayangos in the library of the Hispanic Society of America, ed. by Clara Louisa Penney. N. Y., 1927. 215p. (Hispanic notes and monographs.)

Letters from William Hickling Prescott, 1847-59.

Raleigh, Walter

4091. Eames, Wilberforce. A bibliography of Sir Walter Raleigh. N. Y., 1886. 35p.

Reprinted from Sabin's Dictionary, v. 16. Locates copies.

Randolph, John

4092. U. S. Library of Congress, Division of Bibliography. "John Randolph of Roanoke, 1773-1833: a bibliographical list." Wash., Jan. 29, 1929. 10p. Typed.

Sheridan, Philip Henry

4093. U. S. Library of Congress, Division of Bibliography. "Philip Henry Sheridan, 1831-1888: a bibliographical list." Wash., Aug. 12, 1935. 11p. Typed.

Sherman, William T.

4094. U. S. Library of Congress, Division of Bibliography. "List of works in the Library of Congress relating to General William T. Sherman, including his writings," comp. by A. P. C. Griffin. In: Keim, DeB. R. Sherman. Wash.: Govt. Print. Off., 1904. p. 391-99. (58th Cong., 2d sess. Senate. Doc. no. 320)

Sill, Edward Rowland

4095. U. S. Library of Congress, Division of Bibliography. "Edward Rowland Sill (1841-1887): a bibliographical list." Wash., Mar. 1, 1933. 6p. Typed.

Smith, John

4096. Eames, Wilberforce. A bibliography of Captain John Smith. N. Y., 1927. 48p.

"Reprinted from Sabin's Dictionary of books relating to America," v. 17. Locates copies.

Stearns, Samuel

4097. Clark, John C. L. "The famous Doctor Stearns, a biographical sketch of Dr. Samuel Stearns with a bibliography." American Antiquarian Society proceedings, n. s. 45 (1935), 317-424.

Bibliography of Stearns's published writings, p. 388-424, lists 66 items, chronologically, locating copies in American Antiquarian Society and other collections.

Stephens, Alexander H.

4098. Young, James Harvey. "Alexander H. Stephens papers in the Emory University Library." Emory University quarterly, 2 (1946), 1, 30-37.

Straus, Oscar S.

4099. Brand, Katharine E. "The Oscar S. Straus papers." Library of Congress quarterly journal of current acquisitions, 7 (Feb. 1950), 3-6.

Papers of American diplomat, cabinet officer, and business man. Collection of 8,500 pieces, for period from 1856 to 1926.

Ticknor, George

4100. Hispanic Society of America. George Ticknor; letters to Pascual de Gayangos from originals in the collection of the Hispanic Society of America, ed. by Clara Louisa Penney. N. Y.: The Society, 1927. 578p. (Hispanic notes and monographs)

Van Buren, Martin

4101. U. S. Library of Congress, Division of Manuscripts. Calendar of the papers of Martin Van Buren, prepared from the original manuscripts in the Library of Congress, by Elizabeth Howard West. Wash.: Govt. Print. Off., 1910. 757p.

Vernon, Edward

4102. U. S. Library of Congress, Division of Manuscripts. List of the Vernon-Wager manuscripts in the Library of Congress. Wash.: Govt. Print. Off., 1904. 148p.

Correspondence of Sir Charles Wager and Edward Vernon, 18th century, relating to West Indies.

Vilas, William F.

4103. Nunns, Annie A. "The Vilas papers." Wisconsin magazine of history, 17 (1933), 228-31.

Description of papers of William F. Vilas, cabinet officer in Cleveland's administration, now in Wisconsin State Historical Society.

Vinci, Leonardo da

4104. Stevens Institute of Technology Library. Catalogue of the Lieb memorial collection of Vinciana, comp. by Maureen Cobb Mabbott. Hoboken, N. J.: Stevens Institute of Technology, 1936. 103p.

Lists 985 items by or about Leonardo da Vinci, now in Stevens Institute Library.

Washington, George

4105. Boston Athenaeum. A catalogue of the Washington collection in the Boston Athenaeum; compiled and annotated by Appleton P. C. Griffin... With an appendix. The inventory of Washington's books drawn up by the appraisers of his estate; with notes in regard to the full titles of the several books and the later history and present ownership of those not in the Athenaeum collection, by William Coolidge Lane. [Cambridge: University Press: J. Wilson and Son] The Boston Athenaeum, 1897. 566p. Index, by Franklin Osborne Poole, 1900. 85p.

4106. Boston Public Library. "Washington bicentennial exhibit." More books, 7 (1932), 79-97.

A description of most important of 300 items displayed.

4107. Boston Public Library. "Washington letters in this library." More books, 7 (1932), 43-55.

Describes the 16 letters in the Library.

4108. Connecticut Historical Society. Letters of George Washington in the library of the Connecticut Historical Society. Hartford: The Society, 1932. 53p.

4109. Edwards, Everett E. George Washington and agriculture; a classified list of annotated references. Washington, 1936. 77p. (U. S. Dept. of Agriculture Library, Bibliographic contributions, no. 22, ed. 2)

List compiled from catalogs of Library of Congress or the U. S. Department of Agriculture Library, or one of 8 bibliographical indexes.

4110. Henry E. Huntington Library. George Washington, 1732-1932; an exhibition at the Henry E. Huntington Library. [San Marino, Calif., 1932] 25p.

4111. Hough, Franklin B. Bibliographical list of books and pamphlets containing eulogies, orations, poems, or other papers, relating to the death of General Washington, or to the honors paid to his memory. Albany, 1865. 59p. From his: Washingtoniana, v. 2, p. 219-77.

Copies located in 12 libraries, institutional and private.

4112. New York Public Library. "Calendar of Washington's copy-press letters in the New York Public Library, with brief mention of those in the Department of State at Washington." New York Public Library bulletin, 2 (1898), 202-26.

4113. New York Public Library. "Checklist of eulogies and funeral orations on the death of George Washington, December, 1799 - February, 1800," comp. by Margaret Bingham Stillwell. New York Public Library bulletin, 20 (1916), 403-50. Reprinted, with some alterations, as Washington eulogies; a checklist. 68p.

Copies located in 11 libraries.

4114. New York Public Library. "The Washington bicentennial exhibition, 1732-1932; notes on some of the portraits displayed, and a brief account of the exhibition," by Charles Flowers McCombs. New York Public Library bulletin, 36 (1932), 207-17. Reprinted, with slight variation in title. 13p.

4115. New York Public Library. Washington's farewell address. Edited by Victor Hugh Paltsits. N. Y.: The Library, 1935. 102p.

Original manuscript in the Library.

4116. Toner, J. M. "Some account of George Washington's library and manuscript records, and their dispersion from Mount Vernon." American Historical Association report, (1892), 71-111.

Locates several collections of Washington's books and letters.

4117. U. S. Library of Congress, Division of Manuscripts. Calendar of the correspondence of George Washington, Commander in Chief of the Continental Army with the officers... prepared from the original manuscripts in the Library of Congress, by John C. Fitzpatrick. Wash.: Govt. Print. Off., 1915. 4v.

Covers period from June 17, 1775, to January 4, 1784. Fourth volume is index.

4118. U. S. Library of Congress, Division of Manuscripts. Calendar of the correspondence of George Washington... with the Continental Congress, prepared from the original manuscripts in the Library of Congress by John C. Fitzpatrick. Wash.: Govt. Print. Off., 1906. 741p.

For period from May 12, 1775, to April 14, 1789. Index.

4119. U. S. Library of Congress, Division of Manuscripts. A calendar of Washington manuscripts in the Library of Congress, comp. by H. Friedenwald. Wash.: Govt. Print. Off., 1901. 315p.

4120. U. S. Library of Congress Division of Manuscripts. List of the Washington manuscripts from the year 1592 to 1775, prepared from the original manuscripts in the Library of Congress, by John C. Fitzpatrick. Wash.: Govt. Print. Off., 1919. 137p.

Chronological list with index.

4121. U. S. Library of Congress, Legislative Reference Service. The United States Congress on George Washington, comp. by Myrtis Jarrell. 2d ed. Wash. [1932] 66p.

List of addresses on Washington, Acts of Congress, etc.

4122. Wisconsin State Historical Society Library. George Washington, 1732-1799; a list of manuscripts, books and portraits in the Library of the State Historical Society of Wisconsin, prep. by Ruth Pauline Hayward. [Madison]: The Society, 1932. 70p. (Bulletin of information, no. 98)

Webb, Samuel Blatchley

4123. Monaghan, Frank. "The Webb manuscripts." Yale University Library gazette, 11 (1936), 1-7.

Correspondence, diaries, and other personal records of General Samuel Blatchley Webb, General James Watson Webb, and General Alexander Stewart Webb.

Webster, Daniel

4124. Clapp, Clifford Blake. "The speeches of Daniel Webster." Bibliographical Society of America papers, 13 (1919), 3-63.

Locates copies of manuscript and printed speeches, when known.

Webster, Noah

4125. Skeel, Emily Ellsworth Ford. "Check list of the writings of Noah Webster." In her: Notes on the life of Noah Webster. N. Y., 1912. v. 2, p. 523-40.

Copies located in 22 libraries.

Weems, Mason Locke

4126. Skeel, Emily Ellsworth Ford, ed. Mason Locke Weems... a bibliography left unfinished by Paul Leicester Ford. N. Y., 1929. 418p.

Locates copies in 64 institutional and private collections.

4127. Skeel, Emily Ellsworth Ford, ed. Mason Locke Weems - his works and ways. N. Y., 1929. 3v.

Volume 1 contains a bibliography of Weems' works, with location of copies in 64 libraries or collections.

White, William Allen

4128. Burr, Nelson R. "The papers of William Allen White." Library of Congress quarterly journal of current acquisitions, 4 (Nov. 1946), 10-14.

Description of collection received by Library of Congress.

William II, Emperor of Germany

4129. New York Public Library. "Catalogue of a collection of books relating to Emperor William II of Germany, presented to the New York Public Library by Dr. John A. Mandel." New York Public Library bulletin, 17 (1913), 869-75. Reprinted. 9p.

Williams, Roger

4130. Chapin, Howard Miller. List of Roger Williams' writings. Providence: Preston and Rounds Co., 1918. 7p. (Contributions to Rhode Island bibliography, no. 4)

Locates copies of originals in public and private collections.

4131. Williams, Roger. Letters and papers of Roger Williams, 1629-1682. Boston: Mass. Hist. Soc., 1924. 294 l.

Photostatic reproductions of manuscripts of Roger Williams which are located in about 20 different libraries.

Wilson, Woodrow

4132. Bragdon, Henry W. "The Woodrow Wilson collection." Princeton University Library chronicle, 7 (1945), 7-18.

General survey of Wilson collection in Princeton University Library.

4133. Brand, Katharine E. "The Woodrow Wilson collection." Library of Congress quarterly journal of current acquisitions, 2 (Oct. - Dec. 1944), 3-10.

Description of Woodrow Wilson papers in the Library of Congress.

4134. Eaton, Vincent L. "Books and memorabilia of Woodrow Wilson." Library of Congress quarterly journal of current acquisitions, 4 (Nov. 1946), 2-6.

Description of Wilson's 9,000-volume library and other materials presented to the Library of Congress.

GENEALOGY

4135. Anderson, Russell H. "Genealogy: general resources of Western Reserve Historical Society Library." Indiana magazine of history, 44 (1948), 211-26.

Description of collection, including a list of recent accessions.

4136. Baker, Mary Ellen. "Bibliography of lists of New England soldiers." New England historical and genealogical register, 64 (1910), 61-72, 128-35, 228-37, 327-36; 65 (1911), 11-19, 151-60.

Printed books and pamphlets in catalog of New York State Library.

4137. Boston Public Library. A finding list of genealogies and town and local histories containing family records, in the Public Library of the City of Boston. Boston: Pub. by the Trustees, 1900. 80p.

4138. California State Library. "Catalogue of works on genealogy and American local history." California State Library quarterly bulletin, 1 (April-June 1900), 13-64.

4139. Colonial Dames of the State of New York. Catalogue of the Genealogical and Historical Library. N. Y.: The Society, 1912. 518p.

4140. Connecticut Historical Society. List of family genealogies in library of Connecticut Historical Society. Hartford: The Society, 1911. 42p.

4141. Connecticut State Library. "Connecticut cemetery records in Connecticut State Library; preliminary list Dec. 24, 1930." Connecticut State Library, Report of the State Librarian, (1930), 59-76.

4142. Connecticut State Library. "Probate files deposited" [in the Connecticut State Library] Connecticut State Library, Report of the State Librarian, (1914), 17-22.

4143. Daughters of the American Revolution Library. Catalogue of genealogical and historical works, library of the National Society, Daughters of the American Revolution. [Wash., 1940] 352p. Revised edition of 1920 bibliography.

4144. Delaware Public Archives Commission. Calendar of Kent County, Delaware, probate records, 1680-1800, comp. by Leon de Valinger, Jr. Dover: The Commission, 1944. 558, 133p.

4145. Dunn, Caroline. "Sources for Indiana genealogical research." Indiana magazine of history, 39 (1943), 413-19.

Describes records in the Archives Division of the State Library, and elsewhere in Indiana.

4146. Genealogical Society of Pennsylvania. "Collections of the Genealogical Society of Pennsylvania. List of manuscripts in the collections." Genealogical Society of Pennsylvania publications, 6 (1917), 309-18.

BIOGRAPHY AND GENEALOGY

Church and official records containing genealogical information.

4147. Genealogical Society of Utah. "Catalogue of family histories in the library of the... Society." Utah genealogical and historical magazine, 9 (1918), 83-96, 139-44, 184-92; 10 (1919), 41-48, 87-96, 136-44.

4148. Historical Records Survey - N. J. Guide to naturalization records in New Jersey. Newark: Historical Records Program, 1941. 185p.

4149. Historical Records Survey - West Va. Calendar of wills in West Virginia, no. 49. Upshur County. Charleston: W. Va. Historical Records Survey, 1941. 91p.

4150. Illinois State Historical Library. A list of the genealogical works in the Illinois State Historical Library, comp. by Georgia L. Osborne. [Springfield] 1914. 163p. (Publication, no. 18) Supplement. [Springfield] 1919. 182p. (Publication, no. 25)

4151. Indiana State Library. Genealogical sources available at the Indiana State Library for all Indiana counties, comp. by Margaret R. Waters. [Indianapolis?] 1946. 37 numb. l.

4152. Indiana State Library. Guide to genealogical material in Pennsylvania archives, series 1-6, published 1852-1914. [Indianapolis] 1937. 16 numb. l.

4153. Indiana State Library. Location of indexes of genealogical and historical publications in the Indiana State Library, comp. by Leona E. Tobey. [Indianapolis] 1936. 36p.

4154. Institute of American Genealogy Library. Library catalogue of the Institute of American Genealogy. Chicago: The Institute, [1939] 111p.
A list of books and manuscripts in Institute Library available to members for loan.

4155. Jacksonville Public Library. Genealogical material, local and state history in the Jacksonville Public Library, by Pattie Porter Frost. [Jacksonville, Fla.: Arnold Printing Co., 1929] 15p.

4156. Kenney, Mildred A. "Some genealogical collections in St. Louis and vicinity." Library journal, 53 (1928), 989-90.
Describes genealogical collections of Decatur (Ill.) Public Library, Illinois State Historical Library, Illinois State Library, Missouri Historical Society Library, Mercantile Library of St. Louis, and St. Louis Public Library.

4157. Long Island Historical Society Library. Catalogue of American genealogies in the Library. Brooklyn: The Society, 1935. 660p.
Lists 8,202 items, printed and manuscript.

4158. McIlwaine, Henry Read. "Material in the Virginia State Library of genealogical value." National Genealogical Society quarterly, 29 (1931), 25-33.

4159. Maine Genealogical Society. "List of family histories in the library of the Maine Genealogical Society." Maine Genealogical Society reports, (1911), 14-42.

4160. Michigan State Library. Genealogy and American local history in the Michigan State Library. 2d ed. rev. and enl. Lansing, Mich., 1915. 169p.

4161. Moody, Katharine Twining. "Genealogical material in the St. Louis Public Library." St. Louis Public Library monthly bulletin, n. s. 13 (1915), 223-54.

4162. National Society of the Colonial Dames of America Library. Catalogue of the genealogical and historical library of the Colonial Dames of the State of New York. N. Y.: The Society, 1912. 518p.

4163. New England Historic Genealogical Society Library. Catalogue of the A. D. Weld French heraldic collection in the New England Historic Genealogical Society's library, with extracts from the proceedings of the Society relating to the same, and a sketch of the life of Aaron Davis Weld French. Boston: The Society, 1897. 17p.

4164. New Jersey Historical Society Library. Genealogical-index to books, pamphlets, mss., etc. in the New Jersey Historical Society library. [Newark, N. J.? 1923] 45p. (Reprinted from the Society's Proceedings, n. s. 8 (1923), 83-123)

4165. New York Public Library. "American

genealogies." New York Public Library bulletin, 1 (1897), 247-56, 280-88, 316-22, 343-50.

List, alphabetically arranged by family names, of works in New York Public Library.

4166. New York Public Library. "Heraldry--a guide to reference books," comp. by Harold Lancour. New York Public Library bulletin, 42 (1938), 851-56. Reprinted. 7p.

4167. New York Public Library. "List of works in the New York Public Library relating to British genealogy and local history," comp. by Daniel C. Haskell. New York Public Library bulletin, 14 (1910), 355-99, 415-52, 467-508, 523-66, 578-635, 646-723, 735-800. Reprinted. 366p.

4168. New York Public Library. "Passenger lists of ships coming to North America, 1607-1825; a bibliography," comp. by A. Harold Lancour. New York Public Library bulletin, 41 (1937), 389-410. Reprinted. 24p.

4169. New York State Library. Supplementary list of marriage licenses. Albany: Univ. of the State of New York, 1898. 48p. (New York State Library bulletin, History, no. 3, April 1898)

4170. North Carolina State Library. "Genealogical material in the... Library." In: North Carolina State Library biennial report, 1926-28, p. 11-71.

Bibliography of general genealogy, state, county, and family histories, military rosters, newspaper clippings, and magazine articles.

4171. Owen, Thomas M. "How the National Archives can aid genealogists." Alabama historical quarterly, 8 (Spring 1946), 25-34.

Describes genealogical materials in National Archives.

4172. St. Louis Public Library. Genealogical material and local histories in the St. Louis Public Library, rev. ed. by Georgia Gambrill. [St. Louis] 1941. 219p.

4173. Schnitzer, Martha. "Genealogical collection of the Houston Public Library." Texas Library Association news notes, 21 (Apr. 1945), 1, 6.

Brief description of collection of over 2,000 volumes. "Consists principally of works of Southern ancestry."

4174. Smith, Elsdon C. "Personal names; an annotated bibliography." New York Public Library bulletin, 54 (1950), 315-32. To be continued.

Locates copies in 39 libraries.

4175. Syracuse Public Library. List of books on genealogy and heraldry in the Syracuse Public Library, including parish registers, visitations, history of names and allied subjects. Syracuse, N. Y.: The Library, 1910. 119p. Supplement, listing genealogies added since 1911, issued in 1926. 25p.

4176. U. S. Library of Congress. American and English genealogies in the Library of Congress. 2d ed., comp. by M. A. Gilkey. Wash.: Govt. Print. Off., 1919. 1,332p. Preliminary ed., 1910. 805p.

Lists about 7,000 titles.

4177. Virginia State Library. "Provisional list of works on genealogy." Virginia State Library bulletin, 1 (1908), 1-33.

DIRECTORIES

4178. California, University, Library. A union list of selected directories in the San Francisco Bay Region, comp. by Carolyn L. Hale and Mary H. Lathe. Berkeley: Univ. of California Press, 1942. 26p. (Library bulletin, no. 19)

Locates 186 directories in 14 libraries.

4179. New York Public Library. "Check list of Brooklyn directories in the New York Public Library." New York Public Library bulletin, 6 (1902), 89-92.

4180. New York Public Library. "Check list of directories of the City of New York in the New York Public Library." New York Public Library bulletin, 5 (1901), 190-95.

4181. New York Public Library. "Directory information material (printed) for New York City residents, 1626-1786, a bibliographic study," by John H. Moriarty. New York Public Library bulletin, 46 (1942), 807-64. Reprinted. 60p.

Records lists of residents in New York City, 1626-1786, a total of 356 titles.

4182. Smith, Philip M. "Directories in the

Library of Congress." American genealogist and New Haven genealogical magazine, 13 (1936), 46-53.

4183. Wegelin, Oscar. "Early American directories in the Library of the New York Historical Society." New York Historical Society quarterly, 30 (1946), 92-104.

Annotated list of 186 city directories, each earliest published for its city, and some unique, beginning 1785.

History

GENERAL

4184. Boston Public Library. Catalogue of books in the lower hall of the Boston Public Library, in the classes of history, biography, geography, and travel. 3d ed. Boston: Pub. by the Trustees, 1892. 362p.

4185. Conference of Historical Societies. Historical societies in the United States and Canada, a handbook. Indianapolis: The Conference of Historical Societies, 1936. 136p.

"An introductory source of information" about activities and resources of historical societies; excludes libraries and museums. Mentions special collections in societies' libraries.

4186. Fisher, Harold Henry. A tower to peace; the story of the Hoover Library on War, Revolution, and Peace. Stanford University: Stanford Univ. Press, 1941. 31p.

Describes history, contents and publications of Hoover Library.

4187. A guide to historical literature, ed. by George Matthew Dutcher, and others. N. Y.: Macmillan, 1937. 1,222p.

Many sections contain brief discussions of leading library collections.

4188. Léger, Aléxis Saint-Léger. A selection of works for an understanding of world affairs since 1914. Wash., 1943. 87p.

Based on Library of Congress collection.

4189. McLean, Philip T. "The Hoover Library on War, Revolution, and Peace." College and research libraries, 1 (1940), 154-58.

A general description.

4190. Powell, Lawrence Clark. "Resources of western libraries for research in history." Pacific historical review, 11 (1942), 263-80.

General survey of important historical collections in Western libraries.

4191. Stanford University, Hoover Library. Special collections in the Hoover Library on War, Revolution, and Peace, by Nina Almond and H. H. Fisher. Stanford University, California, 1940. 111p.

4192. U. S. Library of Congress. "Bibliographical activities of the Library of Congress." Library of Congress information bulletin, 9 (June 19, 1950), Appendix, p. 1-10.

Describes collections of Russian, Far Eastern, South Asiatic, Near Eastern, Hebraic, Latin American and European materials in Library of Congress.

4193. U. S. National Archives. Reference information circulars. Wash., 1942-49. 40 nos.

Nos. 1-40, materials in the National Archives relating to:

1. The Philippine Islands. Apr. 1942. 6p.
2. The Southern and Western Pacific areas. Apr. 1942. 6p.
3. Belgium, France and the Netherlands. Apr. 1942. 12p.
4. The Balkan states. Apr. 1942. 4p.
5. The Scandinavian countries. May 1942. 5p.
6. Alaska. May 1942. 10p.
7. The Caribbean region. June 1942. 10p.
8. Brazil. June 1942. 6p.
9. The west coast of South America. July 1942. 8p.

10. Labor and labor problems. Sept. 1942. 16p.
11. Latin America (in Records of emergency war areas, 1917-19). Oct. 1942. 17p.
12. The Netherland East Indies. Dec. 1942. 10p.
13. French possessions in Africa. Dec. 1942. 8p.
14. Spanish possessions in Africa. Dec. 1942. 5p.
15. Labor migration during the first world war and the post-war period. Jan. 1943. 5p.
16. Transportation. Mar. 1943. 17p. Superseded by no. 36.
17. Food production and distribution, 1917-40. Mar. 1943. 13p.
18. Portuguese possessions in Africa and the Atlantic. Apr. 1943. 4p.
19. Forest products. Apr. 1943. 7p.
20. Small business. Apr. 1943. 9p.
21. Dehydration of food. July 1943. 5p.
22. Personnel records in the National Archives. Rev. Mar. 1945. 26p. (No. 37)
23. The basic iron, steel and tin industries. Nov. 1943. 7p.
24. The termination or modification of contracts and the settlement of claims following the first world war. Jan. 1944. 15p.
25. Nutrition and food conservation by consumers, 1917-41. Jan. 1944. 11p.
26. Military government by the United States in the Caribbean area, 1898-1934. Feb. 1944. 14p.
27. The disposition of surplus property following the first world war. Feb. 1944. 13p.
28. The demobilization of the armed forces and to the relief, rehabilitation and employment of veterans following world war I. June 1944. 17p.
29. Rubber. June 1944. 15p.
30. The work of the Civilian Conservation Corps. Dec. 1944. 6p.
31. The liquidation of Federal agencies, 1917-44. Apr. 1945. 13p.
32. The termination of economic controls by government agencies following world war I. June 1945. 14p.
33. Materials in the National Archives containing statistical data on economic subjects, 1910-44. July 1945. 17p.
34. Cuba. 1948. 13p.
35. Dominican Republic. 1948. 12p.
36. Transportation. 1948. 40p. (Rev. and enl. ed. of no. 16)
37. Civilian personnel records in National Archives. 1948. 26p.
38. India. 1949. 12p.
39. World War II. 1949. 31p.
40. Haiti. 1949. 13p.

4194. Utah, University, Utah Humanities Research Foundation. A bibliography of the archives of the Utah Humanities Research Foundation, 1944-1947, comp. by Hector Lee. Salt Lake City [1947] 41p. (Utah University bulletin, v. 38. no. 9, December 1947)
Material in University of Utah Library.

4195. Virginia State Library. "Finding list of history (except American history)." Virginia State Library bulletin, 2 (1909), 3-190.

4196. Wilbur, Ray Lyman. The Hoover Library; a resource for world peace. Stanford University, Calif. [1940] 12p.

4197. Wilson, Louis Round and Downs, Robert B. "Special collections for the study of history and literature in the Southeast." Bibliographical Society of America papers, 28 (1934), 97-131. Reprinted.
Describes best collections in each of Southeastern states.

ANCIENT HISTORY

4198. Amundsen, Leiv. Greek ostraca in the University of Michigan collection. Ann Arbor: Univ. of Mich. Press, 1935. v. 1. (Univ. of Mich. studies. Humanistic series, v. 34)
Recovered in Egypt at Karanis; dated A. D. 270-330.

4199. Brooklyn Museum, Wilbour Library. Catalogue of the Egyptological library and other books from the collection of the late Charles Edwin Wilbour, comp. by William Burt Cook, Jr. Brooklyn: The Museum, 1924. 795p.
Descriptive catalog of important works on Egyptology given Brooklyn Museum.

4200. Columbia University Library. Catalogue of the Babylonian tablets in the libraries of Columbia University; a list of cuneiform documents from the Sumerian, old-Babylonian,

Kassita, and neo-Babylonian periods, with photographic reproductions of selected seals, and clay objects, by Isaac Mendelsohn. [N. Y.] 1943. 84p. (Catalogue series, no. I. Columbia University Libraries)

4201. Columbia University Library. "The Columbia collection of Greek papyri," by William Linn Westermann. Columbia University quarterly, 23 (1931), 276-85.

4202. Columbia University Library. "Near East collections at Columbia," by Isaac Mendelsohn. Columbia University quarterly, 32 (1940), 283-99.

Describes Columbia Library's holdings of cuneiform tablets, Hebrew books and manuscripts, and Arabic books and manuscripts.

4203. Committee of Ancient Near Eastern Seals. Corpus of ancient Near Eastern seals in North American collections, edited for the Committee of Ancient Near Eastern Seals, a project of the Iranian Institute, the Oriental Institute of the University of Chicago and the Yale Babylonian collection. [N. Y.]: Pantheon Books [1948] 187p.

Volume 1: "The collection of the Pierpont Morgan Library, catalogued and edited by Edith Porada in collaboration with Briggs Buchanan."

4204. Haverford College Library. Haverford library collection of cuneiform tablets or documents from the temple archives of Tellah, ed. by George Aaron Barton. Philadelphia: John C. Winston Co. [1905-14] 3v.

4205. Hussey, Mary I. "Tablets from Drehem in the Public Library, Cleveland, Ohio." American Oriental Society journal, 33 (1913), 167-79.

In White collection of folklore and orientalia, Cleveland Public Library.

4206. Michigan, University, Library. Latin papyri in the University of Michigan collection, by Henry Arthur Sanders. Ann Arbor: Univ. of Michigan Press, 1947. 126p. (Michigan papyri, v. 7, University of Michigan studies, humanistic series, v. 48)

4207. Michigan, University, Library. Papyri and ostraca from Karanis, ed. by Herbert Chayyim Youtie and Orasmus Merrill Pearl. Ann Arbor: Univ. of Michigan Press, 1944. 252p. (University of Michigan studies, humanistic series, v. 47)

Papyri, A.D. 364-428; ostraca, A.D. 700-971. Recovered in Egypt for Michigan University.

4208. Michigan, University, Library. Papyri from Tebtunis, by Arthur E. R. Boak. Ann Arbor: Univ. of Michigan Press, 1933-44. 2v. (University of Michigan studies, humanistic series, v. 28-29)

A collection of documents from record office of Tebtunis (Egypt), A.D. 7-56. Now in University of Michigan Library.

4209. Michigan, University, Library. Papyri in the University of Michigan collections; miscellaneous papyri. Ann Arbor: Univ. of Michigan Press, 1936. 390p. (University of Michigan studies, humanistic series, v. 40)

4210. Michigan, University, Library. Zenon papyri in the University of Michigan collection, by Campbell Cowan Edgar. Ann Arbor: Univ. of Michigan Press, 1931. 211p. (University of Michigan studies, humanistic series, v. 24)

A collection of letters and documents preserved by Zenon, who lived in Egypt in the 3d century A.D. Discovered on site of ancient Philadelphia (Egypt); now in University of Michigan Library.

4211. New York Public Library. "Ancient Egypt: a list of references to material in the New York Public Library," comp. by Ida Augusta Pratt. New York Public Library bulletin, 27 (1923), 723-66, 799-871, 899-944, 965-1010; 28 (1924), 11-86, 111-52, 179-207, 376-421. Reprinted, with additions and an index, 1925. 486p.

4212. New York Public Library. Ancient Egypt: 1925-1941; supplement to Ancient Egypt. A list of references to material in the New York Public Library, 1925, comp. by Ida A. Pratt. N. Y.: The Library, 1942. 340p. Reprinted from New York Public Library bulletin, 45 (1941), 791-820; 46 (1942), 3-102, 539-684.

4213. New York Public Library. "Armenia and the Armenians; a list of references in the New York Public Library," comp. by Ida Augusta Pratt. New York Public Library bulletin, 23 (1919), 123-43, 251-77, 303-35. Reprinted. 96p.

4214. New York Public Library. "Assyria and Babylonia; a list of references in the New York Public Library," comp. by Ida Augusta Pratt. New York Public Library bulletin, 21 (1917), 748-810, 841-90. Reprinted. 143p.

4215. New York Public Library. "The Hittites; a list of references in the New York Public Library," comp. by Benjamin Schwartz. New York Public Library bulletin, 42 (1938), 594-609, 711-32, 783-816. Reprinted, 1939. 94p.

4216. [Pierpont Morgan Library]. The Amherst papyri, being an account of the Egyptian papyri in the collection of the Right Hon. Lord Amherst of Hackney... at Didlington Hall, Norfolk, by Percy E. Newberry. With an appendix on a Coptic papyrus, by W. E. Crum, M. A. With twenty-four autotype plates. London: B. Quaritch, 1899. 61p., 24 facsims.
Papyri now in possession of Pierpont Morgan Library.

4217. Pierpont Morgan Library. Babylonian records in the library of J. Pierpont Morgan, ed. by Albert T. Clay. N. Y.: Priv. Print., 1912-23. 4v.

4218. Pierpont Morgan Library. Bybliothecae Pierpont Morgan codices coptici photographice expressi. Romae, 1922. 56v. in 63.

4219. Pierpont Morgan Library. A check list of Coptic manuscripts in the Pierpont Morgan Library. N. Y.: Priv. Print., 1919. 20p. 5 facsims.
Lists 53 items.

4220. [Pierpont Morgan Library]. Cuneiform inscriptions: Chaldean, Babylonian and Assyrian; collections contained in the library of J. Pierpont Morgan, cataloged by C. H. W. Johns. N. Y.: Robert Grier Cooke, Inc., 1908. 61p.

4221. [Pierpont Morgan Library]. Cylinders and other ancient oriental seals in the library of J. Pierpont Morgan, cat. by William Hayes Ward. N. Y.: Priv. Print., 1909. 129p. 39 plates.

4222. Pierpont Morgan Library. Manuscrits coptes de la bibliothèque du couvent de El-Hamouly (Egypte). Paris, 1911. 3 l., 24 plates.
Collection now in Pierpont Morgan Library.

4223. Pierpont Morgan Library. Mesopotamian art in cylinder seals of the Pierpont Morgan Library, by Edith Porada. N. Y.: [The Library], 1947. 81p.
Description and reproductions of 108 seals.

4224. Princeton University. Papyri in the Princeton University collections. Princeton: Princeton Univ. Press [1931]-42. 3v. (Princeton Univ. studies in papyrology)

4225. Princeton University Library. Catalogue of the Babylonian cuneiform tablets in the Princeton University Library, comp. by Edward Chiera. Princeton: The Library, 1921. 126p.

4226. Princeton University Library. Selected temple accounts from Telloh, Yokha and Drehem; cuneiform tablets in the library of Princeton University, ed. by Edward Chiera. Princeton: Princeton Univ. Press, 1922. 40, [59]p.

4227. Worrell, William Hoyt, ed. Coptic texts in the University of Michigan collection. Ann Arbor: Univ. of Michigan Press, 1942. 375p. (Univ. of Mich. studies, Humanistic series, v. 46)

EUROPEAN HISTORY

General

4228. American Historical Association. Committee on Bibliography. A union list of collections on European history in American libraries--- Trial ed., comp. by E. C. Richardson. Princeton, N. J., 1912. 114 numb. l. Supplement: Copies added 1912-15. Princeton, 1915. 114 numb. l. Alphabetical subject index, by A. H. Shearer. Princeton, 1915. 58 numb. l.
Union list covering 94 libraries.

4229. Augustana College, Denkmann Memorial Library. "Sources on revolutionary Europe, 1789-1828. A selected list from the Charles XV collection in the Augustana College Library." Augustana Historical Society publications, 5 (1935), 134-57.

4230. Betten, Francis S. [List of books dealing with the history of the middle ages] Milwaukee: Marquette University Library, 1935. 8 l. Typed.

Locates copies in 29 midwestern libraries.

4231. Cheyney, E. P. "The Henry C. Lea Library." University of Pennsylvania Library chronicle, 1 (March 1933), 4-5.

Collection relating to Inquisition and medieval history in University of Pennsylvania Library.

4232. Chicago, University, Library. "Catalog of the George G. Coulton collection." Chicago, 1947. 196 l. Typed.

Relates to medieval history and medieval church history.

4233. Cornell University Library. Catalogue of the historical library of Andrew Dickson White, first president of Cornell University. Ithaca: University Press, 1889-97. v. 1, 2, 4. v. 3 unpublished.

Collection, now owned by Cornell University, relating to Protestant Reformation and French Revolution.

4234. Howland, A. C. "Some manuscripts in the Lea Library." [University of Pennsylvania] Library chronicle, 14 (1947), 15-19.

Description of collection of source material for the Middle Ages in the Lea Library of the University of Pennsylvania.

4235. MacKinney, Loren C. "Manuscript photoreproductions in classical, medieval and renaissance research." Speculum, 21 (1946), 244-52.

Contains "a partial list of American collections of photoreproductions of mss.," stating only number of photoreproductions owned.

4236. Milhollen, Hirst. "Roger Fenton, photographer of the Crimean War." Library of Congress quarterly journal of current acquisitions, 3 (Aug. 1946), 10-12.

Describes collection of photographs received by Library of Congress.

4237. New York Library Association, Committee on Bibliographies and Surveys. A union list of printed collections of source materials on European history in New York state libraries. Prelim. ed. Lewis F. Stieg, ed. N. Y.: The Committee, 1944. 112 numb. l.

Copies located in 17 libraries.

4238. New York Public Library. "List of works in the New York Public Library relating to the Near Eastern question and the Balkan States, including European Turkey and modern Greece." New York Public Library bulletin, 14 (1910), 7-55, 199-226, 241-95, 307-41. Reprinted. 166p.

4239. Nussbaum, F. L. "A check-list of film copies of archival material in the University of Wyoming Library." University of Wyoming publications, 2 (1936), no. 11.

Films of manuscripts and documents - in British Public Record Office, India Office, British Museum, and Archives Nationales - on diplomatic and commercial events prior to French Revolution.

4240. Princeton University Library. "German Reformation pamphlets in Princeton University Library," by William Warner Bishop. Princeton University bulletin, 15 (1904), 183-99.

4241. "The private libraries of Philadelphia, seventh paper." Robinson's epitome of literature, 2 (1878), 137-39, 153-55, 169-72.

Description of Lea Library of Inquisition and medieval history in University of Pennsylvania.

4242. Siebert, Wilbur H. "Report on the collections of material in English and European history and subsidiary fields in the libraries of the United States." American Historical Association annual report, (1904), 651-96.

A report describing, by topics, collections to be found, and giving references to bulletins and special catalogs issued by various libraries.

4243. Thomson, Samuel H. "A cross-section of medieval and Renaissance holdings in American libraries." Progress of medieval and renaissance studies in the United States and Canada, bulletin 16 (1941), 50-57.

Locates 45 nonperiodical sets in 61 libraries.

4244. Thomson, Samuel H. "Monographic holdings of American libraries in the medieval and renaissance fields." Progress of medieval studies, no. 18 (June 1944), 28-52.

Tabulates monographs in 74 libraries and locates copies of about 30 titles.

4245. U. S. Library of Congress, Division of Bibliography. List of references on Europe and international politics in relation to the present issues. Wash.: Govt. Print. Off., 1914. 144p.

4246. U. S. Library of Congress, European Affairs Division. The United States and Europe; a bibliographical examination of thought expressed in American publications during 1949. Wash., 1949. 192p.

4247. U. S. Library of Congress, European Affairs Division. The United States and postwar Europe; a bibliographical examination of thought expressed in American publications during 1948. Wash., 1948. 123p.

Great Britain

4248. Alvord, Clarence Walworth. "The Shelburne manuscripts in America." Institute of Historical Research bulletin, 1 (1924), 77-80.

In William L. Clements Library, University of Michigan. Brief description of contemporary documents collected by Lord Shelburne during his public career in England.

4249. Boston Public Library. A list of books on modern Ireland in the Public Library of the City of Boston. Boston: The Library, 1921. 90p.

4250. Boston Public Library. "Tracts of the period of English history covered by the reign of Charles I, the Civil war, and the Commonwealth, 1625-1660." Boston Public Library bulletin, 13 (1894), 212-49.

4251. California State Library, Sutro Branch. Bibliography of books and pamphlets on the English poor laws (1639-1890). San Francisco: The Library, 1940. 53 numb. l. (Its: Occasional papers. Bibliographical series no. 2)

A list of the books on the English poor, the poor laws, and charities in the Sutro Branch.

4252. California State Library, Sutro Branch. New source material on Sir Joseph Banks and Iceland. San Francisco: The Library, 1941. 133 numb. l. (Its: Occasional papers. Manuscript series no. 3)

Documents and notes relating to Icelandic affairs, 1807-16, in Banks manuscript collection at Sutro Branch.

4253. California State Library, Sutro Branch. Pamphlets relating to the Jews in England during the 17th and 18th centuries. San Francisco: The Library, 1939. 141p. (Its: Occasional papers. English series no. 3)

A list of pamphlets on the Jews in England, in the Sutro Branch.

4254. Chicago, University, Library. Cromwelliana and English civil war books in library of George M. Eckels. August 1, 1912. [Chicago, 1912?] [215]p. Typed.

Acquired by University of Chicago Library.

4255. Cleveland Public Library. Works on seventeenth century British history, comp. by Arline Welch Colgrove. [Cleveland, 1941] 176 numb. l.

4256. Cleveland Public Library. Works on eighteenth century British history, comp. by Arline W. Colgrove. [Cleveland] 1936. 66 numb. l.

4257. Davenport, Frances Gardiner. A classified list of printed original materials for English manorial and agrarian history during the middle ages. Boston: Ginn & Co., 1894. 65p. (Radcliffe College monographs, no. 6)

Locates copies in Boston Public Library, Boston Athenaeum, and Harvard University.

4258. Edmands, John. "A Junius bibliography." Philadelphia Mercantile Library Co. bulletin, 2 (1890-92), 48-52, 64-68, [85]-88, 105-08, 121-24, 142-44.

Locates editions of Junius' letters and of publications about Junius in 7 American libraries.

4259. Evans, Luther Harris. The Beatific Bookman; or, Wales in the collections of the Library of Congress; an address before the Saint David's Society, New York, N. Y., March 1, 1949. [Wash., 1949] 29p.

4260. Great Britain Historical Manuscripts Commission. The manuscripts of the Duke of Leeds, the Bridgewater Trust, [etc.] London, 1888. 383p.

Bridgewater manuscripts listed (p. 126-67) now in the Henry E. Huntington Library.

Consist of the legal collections of Sir Thomas Egerton, 2 Earls of Bridgewater, and the Earls of Derby.

4261. Great Britain Historical Manuscripts Commission. Report on the manuscripts of the late Reginald Rawdon Hastings. London: H. M. Stat. Office, 1928-47. 4v.

Collection now in the Henry E. Huntington Library. Documents of the historic Hastings family.

4262. Harvard University Library. "The Crispe charters." Harvard Library notes, 2 (1925), 84.

About 800 English charters, 12th to 17th centuries, in Harvard College Library.

4263. Harvard University Library. The Gay collection of English Civil War tracts 1640-1661 in the Harvard College Library. Cambridge, 1916. 14p.

4264. [Henry E. Huntington Library] The Huntingdon papers (the archives of the noble family of Hastings). London: Maggs Bros., 1926. 6pts. in 1v.

Original documents dating from 1101 to 1776, now in Huntington Library.

4265. Henry E. Huntington Library. "The letters and accounts of James Brydges, 1705-1713," by Edward Léon Harvey. Huntington Library bulletin, 2 (1931), 123-47.

A survey of more than 5,300 copies of letters to and from James Brydges, first Duke of Chandos. "A valuable contribution to the sources available for the study of the War of the Spanish Succession."

4266. Henry E. Huntington Library. "Summary report on the Hastings manuscripts." Huntington Library bulletin, no. 5 (1934), 1-67.

Mainly British documents relating to Hastings family from 1101 to 1892. Collection contains 50,000 pieces.

4267. Michigan, University, William L. Clements Library. Eighteenth century documents relating to the royal forests, the sheriffs, and smuggling; selected from the Shelburne manuscripts. Arthur L. Cross, ed. Ann Arbor: Univ. of Michigan, 1928. 328p. (Univ. of Michigan publications. History and political science, v. 7)

Descriptions and texts of collection.

4268. Minnesota, University, Division of Library Instruction. A bibliography of English county histories in the University of Minnesota Library, by Myrtle J. Eklund. Minneapolis: The Division, 1934. 23p. (Bibliographical projects, no. 1)

4269. Minnesota, University, Library. Sources of English history of the seventeenth century, 1603-1689, in the University of Minnesota Library, with a selection of secondary material, comp. by James Thayer Gerould. Minneapolis: The University, 1921. 565p. (Bibliographical series, no. 1)

4270. New York Public Library. "List of works in the New York Public Library relating to Ireland, the Irish language and literature, etc." New York Public Library bulletin, 9 (1905), 90-104, 124-44, 159-84, 201-29, 249-80. Reprinted. 122p.

4271. New York Public Library. "List of works in the New Public Library relating to Scotland," comp. by George Fraser Black. New York Public Library bulletin, 18 (1914), 11-58, 109-48, 359-403, 441-517, 573-663, 723-80, 827-90, 939-1031, 1111-1242, 1295-1452, 1481-1636. Not printed in full in the Bulletin; final sections, with the index, appear only in the separate publication, 1916. 1,233p.

4272. New York Public Library. "List of works in the New York Public Library relating to the Isle of Man," comp. by George F. Black. New York Public Library bulletin, 15 (1911), 756-68. Reprinted. 15p.

4273. [Pennsylvania, University, Library] Catalogue of British parliamentary papers published prior to 1880, which are in the Library of the University of Pennsylvania. London: King, 1899. 32, 20p.

4274. Pierpont Morgan Library. The British tradition illustrated in historical documents, autograph and illuminated manuscripts, drawings and printed books, eleventh to nineteenth century; guide to an exhibition. [N. Y.: Pierpont Morgan Library, 1941] 46p.

Catalog of over 400 items illustrating British culture from medieval to modern times.

4275. Thorpe, Thomas. Descriptive catalogue of the... muniments of Battle Abbey. London,

1835. 221p.
Collection now in the Huntington Library.

4276. Union Theological Seminary Library (New York). Catalogue of the McAlpin collection of British history and theology, comp. and ed. by Charles Ripley Gillett. N. Y., 1927-30. 5v.
Covers period from 1501 to 1700.

4277. Union Theological Seminary (New York). "The McAlpin collection of British history and theology," by Charles R. Gillett. Union Theological Seminary bulletin, 7 (1924), no. 2, p. 1-21.
A general description.

4278. U. S. Library of Congress, General Reference and Bibliography Division. "The Stuart and Jacobite exiles, 1688-1807." Wash., Jan. 16, 1948. 13p. Typed.

France

4279. Dutcher, George. "French Revolutionary newspapers." Harvard Library notes, 1 (1922), 155-58.
In Harvard College Library.

4280. Harvard University Library. Books on the French Revolution and Napoleon. Collected by William L. Fish and presented to Harvard College by John A. Roebling. n. p., 1932. 36p.

4281. New York Public Library. "French Revolutionary pamphlets: a check list of the Talleyrand and other collections," comp. by Horace E. Hayden. New York Public Library bulletin, 43 (1939), 3-18, 359-64, 396-442, 513-22, 563-72, 687-97, 743-59, 859-67; 49 (1945), 73-88, 314-32, 701-28. Reprinted, 1945. 152p.

4282. New York Public Library. "Pamphlets relating to the French Revolution, in the New York Public Library." New York Public Library bulletin, 2 (1898), 256-64.

4283. Palmer, R. R. "The Beauharnais archives." Princeton University Library chronicle, 3 (1942), 45-[51]
30,000 documents, including some Napoleonana, from archives of Eugene Beauharnais, stepson of Napoleon.

4284. Stewart, John Hall. France, 1715-1815; a guide to materials in Cleveland. Cleveland: Western Reserve Univ. Press, 1942. 522p. (Flora Stone Mather College. Historical studies)
Includes holdings of Western Reserve University, Western Reserve Historical Society, and Cleveland Public Library. Lists 5,175 items.

4285. U. S. Library of Congress, Division of Bibliography. List of cartularies (principally French) recently added to the Library of Congress, with some earlier accessions. Wash.: Govt. Print. Off., 1905. 30p.

4286. U. S. Library of Congress, General Reference and Bibliography Division. France. A list of references on contemporary economic, social and political conditions, comp. by Helen F. Conover. Wash., 1944. 173p.

4287. Wesleyan University Library. "French revolution collection." Wesleyan University Library, About books, 10 (1940), 5-6.

4288. Western Reserve University. Flora Stone Mather College Library. A catalogue of the Henry Eldridge Bourne collection of books on Revolutionary France in Flora Stone Mather College. Richmond, Va.: Western Reserve University Alumnae Historical Association, 1942. 59p.

4289. Woodress, James L., Jr. "The 'cold war' of 1790-1791; documented by a collection of eighteenth-century pamphlets in the Duke University Library." Library notes, a bulletin issued for the Friends of Duke University Library, no. 20 (July 1948), 7-18.
Description of collection of 54 items, with attached list, 1789-92, relating to British reactions to French Revolution.

Spain and Portugal

4290. California, University, Library. Spain and Spanish America in the libraries of the University of California, a catalogue of books, comp. by Alice I. Lyser. Berkeley: [Univ. of California Press] 1928-30. 2v.
Lists 30,000 titles.

4291. Hardin, Floyd. The Spanish civil war and its political, social, economic and ideological backgrounds; a bibliography.

Denver, Colo., 1938. 57p. (Bibliographical Center for Research, Regional checklist, no. 2)

Locates copies of material listed in 13 libraries.

4292. Harvard University Library. A list of Portuguese books and books relating to Portugal and Brazil in Harvard College Library including accessions to date to the collection in memory of the Count of Santa Eulalia presented by John B. Stetson, Junior. [Cambridge?], 1923-24. Manifold copy. In 3 pts. (including 2 supplements).

4293. Jackson, William A. "The Lamont collection on the Spanish Armada." Harvard Library notes, 3 (1940), 303-07.

In Harvard College Library.

4294. Martin, Thomas P. "Spanish archive materials and related materials in other national archives copied for the Library of Congress... 1927-1929." Hispanic American historical review, 10 (1930), 95-98.

4295. New York Public Library. "Portugal... catalogue of an exhibition," comp. by Stanley R. Pillsbury. New York Public Library bulletin, 45 (1941), 124-36. Reprinted. 15p.

List with full descriptions of 15th to 17th century items exhibited.

4296. Solberg, Thorvald. Some notes on the Balearic Islands, with special reference to their bibliography. Chicago, Ill., 1929. p. 69-146. ("From the Papers of the Bibliographical society of America, volume twenty-two, 1928.")

Based upon Library of Congress holdings.

4297. Sylvia, Esther. "Chronicles of Spain." More books, 14 (1939), 135-50, 183-98.

A description of 100 volumes of Spanish chronicles in Boston Public Library.

Italy

4298. Huntington, Thomas Waterman, ed. The Italiana bibliography; an approach to a comprehensive selected record of books in the English language relating to Italy. N. Y.: Brentano's, 1928. 45p.

Classed, with author index. A record of books relating to Italian life and letters dealing only with modern Italy. Library of Congress card numbers included.

4299. Illinois, University, Library. Manuscripts and printed documents of the Archivio Cavagna Sangiuliani in the University of Illinois Library, comp. by Meta Maria Sexton. Urbana: The Library, 1950. 2v. in 1.

Lists contents of 138 bundles of unbound manuscripts formerly owned by Count Antonio Cavagna Sangiuliani; also some printed documents and manuscripts relating chiefly to Italian local history.

4300. Richards, Gertrude R. Florentine merchants in the age of the Medici; letters and documents from the Selfridge collection of Medici manuscripts. Cambridge: Harvard Univ. Press, 1932. 342p.

Describes business aspects of Florentine culture. Collection in Harvard University, Baker Library.

4301. Shay, Mary Lucille, comp. "Italy, 1922-1942; a bibliography of books, pamphlets, periodicals and newspapers in the University of Illinois Library." Urbana, 1942. 72 numb. l. Typed.

All items listed pertain to Fascism.

4302. U. S. Library of Congress, Division of Bibliography. Sicily and Sardinia: a bibliographical list, comp. by Florence S. Hellman. [Wash.] 1942. 38p.

4303. U. S. Library of Congress, General Reference and Bibliography Division. Italy, economics, politics and military affairs, 1940-1945, comp. by Helen F. Conover. Wash., 1945. 85p.

Scandinavia

4304. Augustana College, Denkmann Memorial Library. Guide to the material on Swedish history in the Augustana College Library, prep. by O. Fritiof Ander. Rock Island, Ill.: Augustana College Library and Augustana Historical Society, 1934. 75p.

4305. U. S. Library of Congress. Report on the Scandinavian collection, by Sigmund Skard. Wash.: Library of Congress, 1944. 96 l.

4306. U. S. Library of Congress, Division of Bibliography. "Denmark: a list of references in English, French and German." Wash., Sept. 4, 1931. 29p. Typed.

4307. U. S. Library of Congress, Division of Bibliography. "Sweden: a select list of recent references," comp. by Helen F. Conover. Wash., 1937. 30p. Typed.

4308. U. S. Library of Congress, General Reference and Bibliography Division. [List of books on Scandinavia] comp. by Sigmund Skard. Wash., [1946] 456p.

4309. U. S. Library of Congress, Photoduplication Service. "Norwegian culture, a list of books and periodicals," comp. by Sigmund Skard. Wash., [1946] 231 sheets. Photostatic copy.

Russia

4310. Cole, Toby. "A library on the Soviet Union." Library journal, 70 (1945), 476-79.

General description of facilities of library of American Russian Institute for Cultural Relations with the Soviet Union, New York City.

4311. Gsovski, Vladimir. "Early travels in Russia." Library of Congress quarterly journal of current acquisitions, 4 (Feb. 1947), 8-10.

Editions of works of Baron Sigismund Herberstain (1486-1566), and Adam Olearius (1603?-1671), owned by Library of Congress.

4312. Harvard University Library. "The Russian books." Harvard Library notes, 1 (1922), 203-08.

Account of over 3,000 items chiefly in history and art, added to Harvard College Library in 1922.

4313. Rodkey, F. S. "Unfreezing research materials in the United States: Russian historical sources as illustrative example." Journal of modern history, 20 (Sept. 1948), 226-30.

Survey of collections relating to Russian history in principal American libraries.

4314. U. S. Library of Congress. [Library of Nicholas II] [Wash.] 1931-1932. 7, 43, 4p. Typed.

Copy of order sheets for the first part of the Czar's Library.

4315. U. S. Library of Congress. Selected list of books on the Ukraine published in English, French, German and Italian, comp. by Sergius Yakobson and Francis J. Whitfield. Wash., 1941. 13 l.

4316. U. S. Library of Congress, Division of Bibliography. Soviet Russia: a selected list of recent references. Revised. Comp. by Helen F. Conover. Wash., 1944. 89p. 1943 ed. 85p.

4317. U. S. Library of Congress, Reference Department. Russia: a check list preliminary to a basic bibliography of materials in the Russian language. Wash., 1944-1946. 10 parts.

Balkan and Slavic countries

4318. Hornicek, John. "Czechoslovakiana." Harvard Library notes, 1 (1922), 208-10.

In Harvard College Library.

4319. Kerner, Robert Joseph. Slavic Europe; a selected bibliography in the western European languages, comprising history, languages and literatures. Cambridge: Harvard Univ. Press, 1918. 402p.

In Harvard University Library, unless otherwise indicated.

4320. Krassovsky, Dimitry M., comp. Slavica in the Hoover Library on War, Revolution and Peace. Stanford University, 1946-47. 80p.

4321. New York Public Library. "The Polish question since the war; a list of references in the New York Public Library," comp. by Lucien E. Kostrzewski. New York Public Library bulletin, 20 (1916), 585-609.

4322. U. S. Library of Congress. "Annual reports on acquisitions: Slavica." Library of Congress quarterly journal of current acquisitions, 4 (Feb. 1947), 44-54; 6 (Feb. 1949), 50-61; 7 (Feb. 1950), 43-57.

4323. U. S. Library of Congress, Division of Bibliography. The Balkans... a selected list of references, comp. by Helen F. Conover. Wash., 1943. 5v.

Contents: I. General; II. Albania; III. Bulgaria; IV. Rumania; V. Yugoslavia.

4324. U. S. Library of Congress, General

Reference and Bibliography Division. "The Balkan and Slavic countries--topography, history, government, psychology, economics and sociology; a suggested list of references in Russian to be used for textbooks and for supplementary reading," comp. by Elizabeth A. Gardner. Wash., 1949. 11p. Typed.

Other European countries

4325. U. S. Library of Congress, Division of Bibliography. Greece: a selected list of references, comp. by Ann Duncan Brown and Helen D. Jones. Wash., 1943. 101p.

4326. U. S. Library of Congress, Division of Bibliography. "A selected list of references on modern Switzerland, with special reference to economic, political, cultural, and social aspects." Wash., Feb. 4, 1936. 14p. Typed.

4327. U. S. Library of Congress, General Reference and Bibliography Division. Turkey: a selected list of references, comp. by Grace Hadley Fuller. Wash., 1944. 114p.

ASIATIC HISTORY

China

4328. Essex Institute Library. Catalog of books on China in the Essex Institute, comp. by Louise Marion Taylor. Salem, Mass.: The Institute, 1926. 392p.
Records about 4,000 volumes.

4329. Fairbank, John K. and Liu, Kwang-ching. Modern China; a bibliographical guide to Chinese works, 1898-1937. Cambridge: Harvard Univ. Press, 1950. 608p.
All works listed, with few exceptions, are in Chinese-Japanese Library of Harvard-Yenching Institute.

4330. Gardner, Charles S. A union list of selected western books on China in American libraries. 2d ed. Wash.: American Council of Learned Societies, 1938. 111p.
Lists 371 titles in 76 libraries.

4331. Hummel, Arthur W. "The journal of Harriet Low." Library of Congress quarterly journal of current acquisitions, 2 (June, 1945), 45-60.
Nine autograph volumes, acquired by Library of Congress, of journal kept by Harriet Low during her voyage to and sojourn in Macao and Canton, 1829-34.

4332. New York Public Library. "The Manchus, a list of references in the New York Public Library," comp. by John L. Mish. New York Public Library bulletin, 51 (1947), 635-39. Reprinted. 5p.

4333. New York Public Library. "Outer Mongolia, a selection of references," by Hugo Knoepfmacher. New York Public Library bulletin, 48 (1944), 791-801. Reprinted. 13p.
All are in New York Public Library.

4334. U. S. Library of Congress, General Reference and Bibliography Division. China; a selected list of references on contemporary economic and industrial development, with special emphasis on post-war reconstruction, comp. by Helen F. Conover. [Wash.] 1945. 102p. Rev. ed. Wash., 1946. 118p.

4335. U. S. Library of Congress, Orientalia Division. A catalog of Chinese local histories in the Library of Congress, by Chu Shih Chia. Wash.: Govt. Print. Off., 1942. 552, 21p.
Lists, in Chinese characters, about 3,000 histories of Chinese provinces, prefectures, and districts.

4336. U. S. Library of Congress, Orientalia Division. Official gazetteers of the provinces, prefectures, and districts of China in the Library of Congress, January 1934. 3d ed., prep. by B. A. Clayton. Wash., 1934. 61 l.

Japan

4337. New York Public Library. "List of works in the New York Public Library relating to Japan." New York Public Library bulletin, 10 (1906), 383-423, 439-77. Reprinted. 79p.
Stresses 16th and 17th century accounts of European intercourse with Japan.

4338. U. S. Library of Congress, Division of Bibliography. Japan -- economic development and foreign policy; a selected list of references, comp. by Helen F. Conover. Wash., 1940. 36p.

4339. U. S. Library of Congress, Division of Bibliography. The Japanese empire: industries and transportation, a selected list of references, comp. by Florence S. Hellman. Wash., 1943. 56p.

4340. U. S. Library of Congress, General Reference and Bibliography Division. "Background bibliography on Japan and the Far East," comp. by Helen F. Conover. Wash., Jan. 1946. 31p. Typed.

4341. Yale University Library. Catalogue of books, manuscripts and other articles of literary, artistic and historical interest, illustrative of the culture and civilization of old Japan, presented to Yale University, U.S.A. by Yale Association of Japan. [Tokyo: Taiheiyosha Press, 1934.] 4v.

Miscellany

4342. Boston Public Library. "Corea, Japan and China." Boston Public Library bulletin, 13 (1895), 283-325.

4343. Claremont College Library. Materials on the Pacific Area in selected libraries of the Los Angeles region; a second checklist. Claremont, Calif.: Claremont Colleges Library, 1943-44. 3v.

Pt. 1, books in western languages, 5,150 titles in 13 libraries; Pt. 2, periodicals and serials, 1,190 titles in 36 libraries; Pt. 3, books in Chinese and Japanese languages, 1,100 titles in 5 libraries. Pt. 2 includes holdings of all large libraries in California as reported in Union List of Serials. Preliminary check list, July 15, 1939. 141p., contained 2,840 titles.

4344. Claremont College Library. Materials on the Pacific area; in the Oriental library of Claremont Colleges Library and in the libraries of Pomona College and Scripps College, Claremont, California. [Claremont, 1939] 141 numb. l.

A preliminary check list of books, bound pamphlets, maps, periodicals and serials. Contains 2,840 titles, part not repeated in second check list.

4345. Gillis, I. V. and Pai Ping-ch'i, comps. Title index to the catalogue of the Gest Oriental Library. Peking, China: Kwei Li Press, 1941. 4v.

Catalog of collection, in Princeton University Library, not published.

4346. Glazer, Sidney. Bibliography of periodical literature on the Near and Middle East. [n. p.] 1947-48. 2v.

"[Vol. 1] reprinted from the Middle East journal, vol. 1, no. 1, January 1947." Quarterly list, continued through v. 2 (1948). Compiled in Near East Section, Library of Congress.

4347. Harvard University Library. Indochina: selected list of references, Widener Library, Harvard University. [Cambridge, 1944] 108 numb. l.

Comp. by Elizabeth Ford for U. S. Office of Strategic Services.

4348. Hobbs, Cecil Carlton. Current publications in southeast Asia. [n. p.] 1949. 296-318p. (Reprinted from the Far Eastern quarterly, v. 8, no. 3, May 1949.)

A description of books acquired by Library of Congress and arrangements made for exchanges of serial publications with Southeast Asia.

4349. New York Public Library. "Jewish life in Oriental countries." New York Public Library bulletin, 30 (1926), 868-80. Reprinted, 1927. 15p.

An exhibition of books and manuscripts by and about Jews, drawn from 10 public and private collections in New York and elsewhere.

4350. New York Public Library. "The Khazars; a bibliography." New York Public Library bulletin, 42 (1938), 695-710. Reprinted, 1939. 20p.

4351. New York Public Library. "List of works in the New York Public Library relating to Persia," comp. by Ida Augusta Pratt. New York Public Library bulletin, 19 (1915), 9-126. Reprinted. 151p.

Excludes works on Persian language, Mohammedanism, and numismatics, covered in other lists.

4352. Newberry Library. Catalogue of East Asiatic books on religion, history, literature and arts, collected by Dr. Berthold Laufer in 1908-1910, for the Newberry Library, Chicago, Ill. ... 1216 works in 21,403 volumes. 162p.

Manuscript in Newberry Library. Collection sold to University of Chicago.

4353. Poleman, Horace I. "Serial publications in India." Library of Congress quarterly journal of current acquisitions, 1 (July-Sept., 1943), 23-30.

Contains "selected, basic" list, all received currently by Library of Congress.

4354. Princeton, Institute for Advanced Study. Title index to the catalogue of the Gest Oriental Library, comp. by I. V. Gillis and Pai Ping-ch'i. Peking, China, 1941. 4v.

4355. Rockhill, William Woodville. "Catalogue of the Tibetan books in the Library of Congress, 1902." 97 unnumb. l. ms.

4356. U. S. Library of Congress, Division of Bibliography. "Bibliography of China, Japan and the Philippine Islands." American Academy of Political and Social Science annals, 122 (1925), 214-46. Supplementary list on China in the Annals, 152 (1930), 378-98.

4357. U. S. Library of Congress, Division of Bibliography. Select list of books (with references to periodicals) relating the the Far East. Wash.: Govt. Print. Off., 1904. 74p.

4358. U. S. Library of Congress, General Reference and Bibliography Division. British Malaya and British North Borneo: a bibliographical list, comp. by Florence S. Hellman. Wash., 1943. 103p.

4359. U. S. Library of Congress, Orientalia Division. "Burma: a selected check list of references," comp. in the Indic Section, rev. Nov. 1944, with "A selected list of microfilm materials on Burma in the Library of Congress," comp. by Cecil Hobbs, Apr. 30, 1945. Washington, 1944, 1945. 18, 6p. Typed.

4360. U. S. Library of Congress, Orientalia Division. Southeast Asia, 1935-45; a selected list of reference books, comp. by Cecil Hobbs. Wash., 1946. 86p.

4361. U. S. Library of Congress, Reading Room. "A list of recent references on the Sino-Japanese dispute, with special reference to the action of the League of nations." [Wash., D.C., 1933] Typed. 22 (i. e. 23) numb. l.

Library of Congress call numbers and card numbers are indicated when available.

4362. U. S. Office of Education Library. An annotated list of government publications of use to teachers: the Far East, by Ruth A. Gray. Wash.: U. S. Office of Education, 1943. 12p.

4363. U. S. Office of Education Library. An annotated list of inexpensive books and pamphlets on the Far East, by Ruth A. Gray and C. O. Arndt. Wash.: U. S. Office of Education. 1943. 10p.

4364. U. S. Office of Education Library. An annotated list of pamphlets on the Far East, by Ruth A. Gray and C. O. Arndt. Wash.: U. S. Office of Education, 1944. 13p.

4365. U. S. Office of Education Library. An annotated list of periodicals on the Far East for teachers and librarians, by Martha R. McCabe and C. O. Arndt. Wash.: U. S. Office of Education, 1943. 11p.

AFRICAN HISTORY

4366. Hamlin, Arthur T. "Aethiopica in the Harvard Library." Harvard Library bulletin, 38 (1935), 398-403.

4367. New York Public Library. "Ethiopia, and the Italo-Ethiopian conflict, 1928-1935; a selected list of references," comp. by Daniel Carl Haskell. New York Public Library bulletin, 40 (1936), 13-20. Reprinted, with additions. 13p.

4368. New York Public Library. "Ethiopica and Amharica; a list of works in the New York Public Library," comp. by George Fraser Black. New York Public Library bulletin, 32 (1928), 443-81, 528-62. Reprinted. 87p.

4369. New York Public Library. "List of works in the New York Public Library relating to Arabia and the Arabs, Arabic philosophy, science and literature." New York Public Library bulletin, 15 (1911), 7-40, 163-98. Reprinted. 70p.

4370. New York Public Library. "Modern Egypt; a list of references to material in the New York Public Library," comp. by Ida Augusta Pratt. New York Public Library bulletin, 32 (1928), 589-634, 660-92, 729-65, 825-49; 33 (1929), 17-58, 81-123, 162-91, 267-81. Reprinted, with index. 320p.

4371. New York Public Library. "Works

HISTORY

relating to South Africa in the New York Public Library." New York Public Library bulletin, 3 (1899), 429-61, 502-05. P. 502-05 called "Supplement."

4372. U. S. Engineer School Library. The South African war, 1899-1902; a bibliography of books and articles in periodicals, prep. by Henry E. Haferkorn. Fort Humphreys, Va., 1924. 72p.

Locates copies in Engineer School Library and Library of Congress.

4373. U. S. Library of Congress, Division of Bibliography. "The Belgian Congo: a list of selected references," comp. by Helen F. Conover. Wash., Sept. 21, 1942. 33p. Typed.

4374. U. S. Library of Congress, Division of Bibliography. "Bibliography; list of works in the Library of Congress on the Boer War." In: U. S. War Department, General Staff. Selected translations pertaining to the Boer War. Wash.: Govt. Print. Off., 1905. p. 205-31.

4375. U. S. Library of Congress, Division of Bibliography. British Empire in Africa: selected references, comp. by Helen F. Conover. [Wash.] 1942-43. 4v.

V. 1, General. 1942. 37p.; v. 2, British West Africa. 1942. 32p.; v. 3, British East and Central Africa. 1942. 52p.; v. 4, The Union of South Africa. 1943. 77p.

4376. U. S. Library of Congress, Division of Bibliography. French colonies in Africa; a list of references, comp. by Helen F. Conover. Wash.: Govt. Print. Off., 1942. 89p.

Call numbers noted for volumes in Library of Congress, and locations for titles not held by Library of Congress given in Yale, Harvard, John Crerar, New York Public Library, and several federal libraries.

4377. U. S. Library of Congress, Division of Bibliography. "Liberia: a selected list of references," comp. by Helen F. Conover. Wash., Oct. 7, 1942. 13p. Typed.

4378. U. S. Library of Congress, Division of Bibliography. "List of books relating to the West coast of Africa (excepting Liberia and Nigeria) in the Library of Congress." Wash., 1908. 25p. Typed.

4379. U. S. Library of Congress, Division of Bibliography. List of references on Ethiopia (Abyssinia) comp. by Helen F. Conover. Wash., July 23, 1935. 28p. General Reference and Bibliography Division. "Ethiopia: a selective list of recent works" [Supplementary list] Nov. 3, 1947. 42p. Typed.

4380. U. S. Library of Congress, Division of Bibliography. "A list of references on Ifni, Spanish Morocco," comp. by Florence S. Hellman. [Wash.] 1942. 6 numb. l. Typed.

4381. U. S. Library of Congress, Division of Bibliography. "A list of references on the Italian colonies in Africa (Libya, Eritrea, Italian Somaliland and Ethiopia)," comp. by Grace Hadley Fuller. [Wash.] 1942. 49p.

4382. U. S. Library of Congress, Division of Bibliography. A list of references on the Portuguese colonies in Africa (Angola, Cape Verde Islands, Mozambique, Portuguese Guinea, Sao Thomé, and Principe), comp. by Helen F. Conover. Wash., 1942. 29p.

4383. U. S. Library of Congress, Division of Bibliography. A list of references on the Spanish colonies in Africa, comp. by Florence S. Hellman. [Wash.] 1942. 20p.

4384. U. S. Library of Congress, Division of Bibliography. Madagascar: a selected list of references, comp. by Helen F. Conover. [Wash.] 1942. 22p.

4385. U. S. Library of Congress, Division of Bibliography. "Reunion & Island dependencies of Madagascar: a selected list of references," comp. by Helen F. Conover. Wash., Sept. 28, 1942. 6p. Typed.

4386. U. S. Library of Congress, Division of Bibliography. "A selected list of books on modern Palestine," comp. by Florence S. Hellman. American Academy of Political and Social Science annals, 164 (1932), 190-97.

4387. U. S. Office of Education Library. An annotated list of inexpensive publications on North Africa and the Middle and Near East, by Ruth A. Gray. Wash.: U. S. Office of Education, 1943. 9p.

CANADIAN HISTORY

4388. Doughty, Arthur George and Middleton, J. E. "Bibliography of the siege of Quebec, with a list of plans of Quebec by P. Lee Phillips of the Library of Congress, Washington." In: Doughty, A. G. The siege of Quebec. Quebec, 1901. v. 4, p. [149]-313.

Locates rare books and manuscripts in the United States and Europe.

4389. Harvard University Library. The Canadian collection at Harvard University, ed. by William Inglis Morse. Cambridge: Harvard Printing Office, 1944-49. 6v.

4390. Michigan, University, William L. Clements Library. Unique Canadiana; an exhibition of fifteen Canadian rarities in the Clements Library. Ann Arbor: The Library, 1949. 11p. (Bulletin, no. 56)

Manuscripts, etc., chiefly of 18th century.

4391. New York Public Library. "Canada; an exhibition commemorating the four-hundredth anniversary of the discovery of the Saint Lawrence by Jacques Cartier, 1534-1535; catalogue of the exhibition," comp. by Stanley Rolfe Pillsbury. New York Public Library bulletin, 39 (1935), 491-518, 605-34. Reprinted. 59p.

Drawn from New York Public Library's collections.

4392. Scott, S. Morley. "Material relating to Quebec in the Gage and Amherst papers." Canadian historical review, 19 (Dec. 1938), 378-86.

Describes manuscripts and printed materials on Quebec, 1763-1783, in Clements Library, University of Michigan.

4393. U. S. Library of Congress, Division of Bibliography. Selected list of recent books and pamphlets on Canada, comp. by Ann Duncan Brown. [Wash.] 1941. 145p.

4394. Wroth, Lawrence C. and Annan, Gertrude L. "Acts of French royal administration concerning Canada, Guiana, the West Indies and Louisiana prior to 1791." New York Public Library bulletin, 33 (1929), 789-800, 868-93; 34 (1930), 21-55, 87-126, 155-93. Reprinted. 151p.

Copies located in 12 American libraries.

UNITED STATES HISTORY

General

4395. Adams, Randolph G. The whys and wherefores of the William L. Clements Library, 3d ed. Ann Arbor: Univ. of Michigan Press, 1932. 31p.

4396. American Antiquarian Society. A guide to the resources of the American Antiquarian Society, by R. W. G. Vail. Worcester: The Society, 1937. 98p.

4397. American Association for State and Local History. Historical societies in the United States and Canada. A handbook comp. and ed. by Christopher Crittenden and Doris Godard. Wash.: The Association, 1944. 261p.

Lists 1,367 societies; gives general descriptions of 904 of them, including notes on libraries.

4398. American Philosophical Society Library. A catalogue of manuscript and printed documents chiefly Americana, selected from the... collections of the... Society. Philadelphia: The Society, 1937. 38p.

An exhibition catalog.

4399. Babb, James Tinkham. "The Yale University Library: its early American collections." William and Mary quarterly, 3d ser., 2 (1945), 397-401.

A brief history of resources in early American history and literature, from material in Yale University library.

4400. Boston Public Library. Historical manuscripts in the Public Library of the City of Boston. Boston: The Library, 1900-04. 5v.

4401. Brown University, John Carter Brown Library. The American tradition, an exhibition of books and manuscripts illustrating the development of the democratic principle. [Providence]: The Library, 1942. 75 l.

4402. Brown University, John Carter Brown Library. Bibliotheca Americana. Catalogue of the John Carter Brown Library in Brown University, Providence, Rhode Island. Providence: The Library, 1919-31. 3v. Supersedes 1865-71 catalog.

4403. Brown University, John Carter Brown

Library. In retrospect, 1923-1949; an exhibition commemorating twenty-six years of service to the John Carter Brown Library by Lawrence C. Wroth, librarian. Providence, 1949. 40p.

List with bibliographical descriptions of 113 notable items acquired by the Library during 26-year period, arranged by types, subjects and geographical areas.

4404. Bryant, Douglas W. "Geographical distribution of Sabin's 'Bibliotheca Americana.'" Library journal, 62 (1937), 559-61.

Locates 277 sets of Sabin in the United States, 10 in Canada, and 25 elsewhere.

4405. Cappon, Lester J. and Menk, Patricia H. "The evolution of materials for research in early American history in the University of Virginia Library." William and Mary quarterly, ser. 3, 3 (1946), 370-82.

4406. Clements, William L. Uncommon, scarce and rare books relating to American history... from the library of William L. Clements. Bay City, 1914. [41]p. Additions, Sept. 1, 1915. [Bay City, 1915] [4]p.

Now in Clements Library, University of Michigan.

4407. Connor, R. D. W. "The Franklin D. Roosevelt Library." American archivist, 3 (1940), 81-92.

History and general description of contents of the library at Hyde Park, N. Y.

4408. Duncan, Winthrop Hillyer. Josiah Priest, historian of the American frontier; a study and bibliography. Worcester: American Antiquarian Society, 1935. 60p. (Reprinted from American Antiquarian Society proceedings, n. s. 44 (1935), 45-102).

Bibliography of 65 items, 1825-44, locates copies in 38 public and private collections.

4409. Eliot, Margaret S., comp. "List of manuscript accessions in various depositories in the United States received during the year 1940." American Historical Association annual report, 1 (1941), 191-331.

1,278 items received in 1940 by a total of 67 collections, listed by states.

4410. Foglesong, Hortense. "The Charles G. Slack collection of manuscripts, Marietta College." Ohio Valley Historical Association report, 2 (1909), 20-25.

Manuscripts relating to American history.

4411. Ford, Worthington C. "Public records in our dependencies." American Historical Association annual report, (1904), 129-48.

Brief description of material available in the United States dependencies formerly under Spanish control.

4412. Friendland, Louis S. "Richard Hildreth's minor works." Bibliographical society of America papers, 40 (1946), 127-50.

Locates copies in Library of Congress.

4413. Griffin, Grace Gardner, comp. Writings on American history... a bibliography of books and articles on United States history published during the years 1906-1940. Wash.: Govt. Print. Off., 1908-49. 33v. (Imprint varies).

Prepared in the Library of Congress.

4414. [Harvard University Library] Bibliotheca Americo-Septentrionalis; being a choice collection of books in various languages, relating to the history, climate, geography, produce, population, agriculture, commerce, arts, sciences, etc. of North America, from its first discovery to its present existing government... with all the important official documents published... by the authority of Congress. Collection d'ouvrages, écrits en diverses langues, qui traitent... de l'Amérique Septentrionale...[Paris: Nouzou] 1820. 147p.

Received by Harvard University, 1823.

4415. Harvard University Library. Calendar of the Sparks manuscripts in the Harvard College Library, with an appendix showing other mss., by Justin Winsor. Cambridge: Harvard University Library, 1889. 88p. (Harvard University Library bibliographical contributions, no. 22)

4416. Historical Records Survey. Guide to depositories of manuscript collections in the United States; one hundred sample entries. Columbus, Ohio: Historical Records Survey, 1938. 134 numb. 1.

4417. Historical Records Survey. Inventory of federal archives in the states. Series II: The Federal courts. St. Louis, 1938-42. 43v.

Issued for all states except Idaho, New Jersey, South Carolina, West Virginia, and Wyoming.

4418. Historical Records Survey. Inventory of federal archives in the states. Series III.: The Department of the Treasury. Oklahoma City, 1938-42. 43v.

Issued for all states except Delaware, Idaho, Montana, Virginia, and Washington.

4419. Historical Records Survey. Inventory of federal archives in the states. Series IV: The Department of War. Oklahoma City, 1937-42. 44v.

Covers all states except Delaware, Idaho, Ohio, and Virginia.

4420. Historical Records Survey. Inventory of federal archives in the states. Series V: The Department of Justice. St. Louis, 1937-42. 46v.

Issued for all states except South Dakota and West Virginia.

4421. Historical Records Survey. Inventory of federal archives in the states. Series VII: The Department of the Navy. St. Paul, 1937-41. 42v.

Issued for all states except California, Delaware, Idaho, Montana, South Carolina, and Virginia.

4422. Historical Records Survey. Inventory of federal archives in the states. Series VIII: The Department of the Interior. St. Louis, 1938-42. 37v.

Issued for all states except Colorado, Delaware, Louisiana, Montana, New Mexico, Oklahoma, South Carolina, Vermont, Virginia, West Virginia, and Wyoming.

4423. Historical Records Survey. Inventory of federal archives in the states. Series IX: The Department of Agriculture. St. Paul, 1938-42. 42v.

Includes all states except New Mexico, Ohio, Oregon, South Carolina, South Dakota, and Washington.

4424. Historical Records Survey. Inventory of federal archives in the states. Series X: The Department of Commerce. Lincoln, Neb., 1938-42. 38v.

Issued for all states except Georgia, Nevada, New Mexico, North Dakota, South Carolina, South Dakota, Virginia, West Virginia and Wyoming.

4425. Historical Records Survey. Inventory of federal archives in the states. Series XI: The Department of Labor. St. Louis, 1938-42. 36v.

Issued for all states except Alabama, Georgia, Idaho, Montana, New Mexico, North Dakota, Ohio, South Carolina, South Dakota, Virginia, West Virginia, and Wisconsin.

4426. Historical Records Survey. Inventory of federal archives in the states. Series XII: The Veterans' Administration. St. Louis, 1937-41. 34v.

Issued for all states except California, Colorado, Delaware, Georgia, Idaho, Kansas, North Dakota, Ohio, South Carolina, South Dakota, Virginia, West Virginia, and Wyoming.

4427. Historical Records Survey. Inventory of federal archives in the states. Series XIII: The Civil Works Administration. St. Louis, 1938-41. 10v.

Issued for Arizona, Connecticut, Indiana, Mississippi, Missouri, New Mexico, North Carolina, Oregon, Washington, and Wisconsin.

4428. Historical Records Survey. Inventory of federal archives in the states. Series XIV. The Emergency Relief Administration. St. Louis, 1938-41. 9v.

Issued for Arizona, Indiana, Louisiana, Massachusetts, Mississippi, Missouri, Oklahoma, Oregon and Tennessee.

4429. Historical Records Survey. Inventory of federal archives in the states. Series XV: The Works Progress Administration. St. Louis, 1938-41. 12v.

Issued for Arizona, Arkansas, Louisiana, Mississippi, Missouri, New Hampshire, North Carolina, Oklahoma, Oregon, Tennessee, Washington, and Wisconsin.

4430. Historical Records Survey. Inventory of federal archives in the states. Series XVI: The Farm Credit Administration. Oklahoma City, 1938-41. 34v.

Issued for all states except California, Colorado, Connecticut, Idaho, New Mexico, New York, North Dakota, South Carolina, South Dakota, Vermont, Virginia, West Virginia, Wisconsin, and Wyoming.

4431. Historical Records Survey. Inventory of federal archives in the states. Series XVII: Miscellaneous agencies. St. Louis, 1938-42. 34v.

Issued for all states except California, Colorado, Delaware, Idaho, Montana, New Mexico, Ohio, Pennsylvania, South Carolina, Utah, Virginia, Washington, West Virginia, and Wyoming.

4432. Historical Records Survey. "List of manuscript accessions in various depositories in the United States received during the year 1940," comp. and ed. by Margaret S. Eliot. American Historical Association annual report, 1 (1941), 191-331.

Lists 1,278 recent accessions in many United States libraries.

4433. Historical Records Survey - Md. Calendar of the General Otho Holland Williams papers in the Maryland Historical Society. Baltimore, Md.: Historical Records Survey Project, 1940. 454p.

Records about 1,200 pieces from 1744 to 1839, dealing with colonial wars, setting up federal government, social life of period, etc.

4434. Illinois, University. Materials for historical research afforded by the University of Illinois, Department of History. Urbana: University of Illinois, 1922. 56p. (University of Illinois bulletin, v. 20, no. 1)

Survey of resources in University of Illinois Library, for research in various fields of history.

4435. Jackson, William A. "Matt B. Jones collection." Harvard University Library notes, 4 (1942), 95-96.

Americana collection, now in Harvard Library.

4436. McLaughlin, Andrew Cunningham. Writings on American history, 1903. Wash.: Carnegie Institution, 1905. 172p.

Prepared in the Library of Congress.

4437. Martin, Thomas P. "Transcripts, facsimiles, and manuscripts in the Spanish language in the Library of Congress, 1929." Hispanic American historical review, 9 (1929), 243-46.

Transcripts of documents in Spanish archives relating to American history.

4438. Massachusetts Historical Society Library. Catalogue of the library and collection of autograph letters, papers, and documents bequeathed to the Massachusetts Historical Society by the Rev. Robert Waterston, comp. by Julius H. Tuttle. Boston: The Society, 1906. 479p.

Collection includes papers of Washington, John Adams, Jefferson, Madison, Monroe, J. Q. Adams, Lincoln, and others.

4439. Maynard, Julia M. "The Sparks manuscripts." Harvard Library notes, 3 (1936), 126-29.

In Harvard College Library.

4440. Michigan, University, William L. Clements Library. About the Clements Library, 1923-48. Ann Arbor, 1948. 24p. (Bulletin, no. 53)

Brief survey of the Library and its collections.

4441. Michigan, University, William L. Clements Library. An exhibit of letters of British statesmen [who had an influence on American affairs from the time of George II to Victoria] Ann Arbor, 1933. 4p.

4442. Michigan, University, William L. Clements Library. Guide to the manuscript collections in the William L. Clements Library, by Howard H. Peckham. Ann Arbor: Univ. of Michigan, 1942. 403p.

4443. Michigan, University, William L. Clements Library. Netherlands and America. Ann Arbor: Univ. of Michigan Press, 1947. 64p. (Bulletin, no. 50)

Annotated bibliography of 70 rare books from 1607 to 1862.

4444. Michigan, University, William L. Clements Library. Report, 1923/24-1943. Ann Arbor, 1924-44.

Includes notes on selected titles of printed books, manuscripts and maps acquired by Library each year.

4445. Michigan, University, William L. Clements Library. The William L. Clements Library, a brief description and bibliographical record, 1923-1944. Ann Arbor: University of Michigan, 1944. 47p. (Bulletin, no. 43)

An outline of the three divisions of Library: printed books, manuscripts and maps. "Bibliographical record": p. 23-47.

4446. Michigan, University, William L. Clements Library. The William L. Clements

Library of Americana at the University of Michigan. Ann Arbor, 1923. 228p.

A description of source materials held by Library.

4447. Museum Book Store, London. A century of conflict in America; catalogue of a collection of tracts and manuscripts from Walker's expedition against Quebec in 1711 to the War of 1812. London: Museum Book Store, 1925. 79p.

Entire collection acquired by Henry E. Huntington Library.

4448. New-York Historical Society Library. "The Hawks-Niblo collection. Catalogue of books in the library of F. L. Hawks, presented to the New-York Historical Society by William Niblo." In: Duyckinck, Evert A. A memorial to Francis L. Hawks. N. Y., 1871. p. 47-166.

Mainly American and European history and literature.

4449. New-York Historical Society Library. Selected Americana exclusive of New York from the library of the New-York Historical Society. A short-title list of rare and important books, pamphlets and broadsides. N. Y.: The Society, 1945. 42p.

4450. New York Public Library. "American historical prints, early views of American cities, etc.," prep. by Daniel Carl Haskell. New York Public Library bulletin, 31 (1927), 991-1026. Reprinted. 44p. (For various editions of a more elaborate compilation, see Stokes and Haskell.)

4451. New York Public Library. "Early books, mostly relating to America, presented to the New York Public Library, by Alexander Maitland." New York Public Library bulletin, 3 (1899), 9-22.

4452. New York Public Library. "French travellers in the United States, 1765-1931; a bibliographical list," comp. by Frank Monaghan. New York Public Library bulletin, 36 (1932), 163-89, 250-61, 427-38, 503-20, 587-96, 637-45, 690-702. Reprinted, with additions and revisions, 1933. 114p.

Locates copies in 26 American and foreign libraries.

4453. New York Public Library. "Periodicals, collections and society publications relating to American history and genealogy, in the New York Public Library and Columbia University Library." New York Public Library bulletin, 2 (1898), 120-54. Reprinted. 35p.

4454. New York Public Library. "The Phelps Stokes Collection of American historical prints, early views of American cities, etc., including a group of important views, etc., from other collections belonging to the New York Public Library," by I. N. Phelps Stokes and D. C. Haskell. New York Public Library bulletin, 35 (1931), 511-88, 619-57, 789-818; 36 (1932), 21-66, 101-23. Reprinted with extensive additions and revisions, in two editions: 1932, 327p.; 1933, 235p.

4455. Parker, David W. Calendar of papers in Washington archives relating to the territories of the United States (to 1873). Wash.: Carnegie Institution, 1911. 476p. (Carnegie Institution publication, no. 148)

Locates papers in 9 government repositories.

4456. Penrose, Boies. "The Grenville Kane Americana." Princeton University Library chronicle, 11 (Autumn 1949), 4-25.

Purchased by Princeton University Library.

4457. Powers, Zara J. "American historical manuscripts in the Historical manuscript room." Yale University Library gazette, 14 (1939), 1-11.

A survey of holdings of Americana housed in Historical manuscript room of Yale University Library.

4458. Rhode Island Historical Society Library. Catalogue of books obtained by the Rhode Island Historical Society, from the sale of the library of the late Joseph J. Cooke, March-December, 1883. Providence: Kellogg Printing Co., 1884. 36p.

Principally Americana.

4459. Richardson, Ernest Cushing. Writings on American history, 1902. Princeton, N. J.: Library Book Store, 1904. 294p.

Library of Congress card numbers added.

4460. Robertson, James A. Lists of documents in Spanish archives relating to the history of the United States, which have been printed, or of which transcripts are preserved in American libraries. Wash.: Carnegie Institution, 1910. 368p.

Locates about 5,332 titles.

4461. Sabin, Joseph. Bibliotheca Americana. A dictionary of books relating to America, from its discovery to the present time. N. Y., 1868-1936. 29v. List of library location symbols, v. 29, p. 299-305.

Includes books, pamphlets and periodicals printed in America, and works about America printed elsewhere; in many cases, locates copies.

4462. Shaw, Charles Bunsen. The Swarthmore College British Americana collection. Philadelphia, 1947. 4p. (Special Libraries Council of Philadelphia and Vicinity bulletin, v. 13, no. 4, March 1947.)

Writings about United States by British visitors to this country..

4463. Sparks, Jared. Catalogue of the library of Jared Sparks; with a list of the historical manuscripts collected by him and now deposited in the library of Harvard University. Cambridge: Riverside Press, 1871. 230p.

Collection purchased by Cornell University, 1872. Strong in American history.

4464. U. S. Library of Congress. "Annual reports on acquisitons: Americana." Library of Congress quarterly journal of acquisitions, 3 (May 1946), 23-36; 4 (May 1947), 69-79; 6 (May 1949), 65-79.

4465. U. S. Library of Congress. Archives of government offices outside of the city of Washington. Wash.: Govt. Print. Off., 1913. 219p. (62d Cong. 3d sess. House. Doc. 1443)

4466. U. S. Library of Congress. Exhibition of prints relating to early American history; being a part of the prints contained in the Mabel Brady Garvan collection of American arts and crafts at Yale University. [Catalogue] Wash.: [Govt. Print. Off.] 1931. 28p.

Lists 322 items relating to various phases of American history from about 1650 to midnineteenth century.

4467. U S. Library of Congress. Writings reflecting American life and thought. [Wash., 1942] 299 l.

4468. U. S. Library of Congress, Division of Manuscripts. Check list of collections of personal papers in historical societies, university and public libraries and other learned institutions in the United States. Wash.: Govt. Print. Off., 1918. 87p.

4469. U. S. Library of Congress, Division of Manuscripts. A guide to manuscripts relating to American history in British depositories reproduced for the Division of Manuscripts of the Library of Congress, by Grace Gardner Griffin. Wash.: Govt. Print. Off., 1946. 313p.

Enumerates material in collection by archive or other depository, with description of contents of each volume.

4470. U. S. Library of Congress, Photoduplication Service. Pictorial Americana; a select list of photographic negatives in the Prints and Photographs Division of the Library of Congress, comp. by Milton Kaplan. Wash., 1945. 38 numb. 1.

4471. U. S. National Archives. A brief guide to the museum collections in the Franklin D. Roosevelt Library, Hyde Park, N. Y. Wash.: Govt. Print. Off., 1947. 6p.

4472. U. S. National Archives. Guide to the records in the National Archives. Wash.: Govt. Print. Off., 1948. 684p.

Arranged by departments, bureaus, and other agencies, with descriptions of collections. Supersedes Guide to the material in the National Archives, published in 1940.

4473. U. S. National Archives. Interior Department centennial, 1849-1949; an exhibit. [Wash., 1949] 23p.

Catalog of the exhibition.

4474. U. S. National Archives. List of file microcopies. Wash., 1947. 31p.

4475. U. S. National Archives. Preliminary checklist of the records of the Bureau of Refugees, Freedmen, and Abandoned Land, comp. by Elizabeth Bethel, Sara Dunlap, and Lucille Pendell. [Wash.] 1946. 64p.

4476. Utley, George Burwell. "Source material for the study of American history in the libraries of Chicago." Bibliographical Society of America papers, 16 (1922), 17-46. Reprinted.

Description of holdings of Newberry Library, Chicago Historical Society, University of Chicago, Chicago Public Library, and John Crerar Library.

4477. Van Tyne, Claude Halstead and Leland, Waldo Gifford. Guide to the archives of the government of the United States in Washington. 2d ed. Wash.: Carnegie Institution, 1907. 327p. (Carnegie Institute of Washington, Publication no. 92. Papers of the Dept. of Historical Research)

Locates important historical and administrative records in all branches of federal government.

4478. Virginia State Library. "Finding list of American history." Virginia State Library bulletin, 1 (1908), [137]-291.

Catalog of books on American history in State Library.

4479. Virginia, University, Library. Description of the Tracy W. McGregor Library, University of Virginia. Charlottesville: Univ. of Virginia, Tracy W. McGregor Library, 1949. 15p.

4480. Wegelin, Oscar. "Some rare Americana from eastern presses." New-York Historical Society quarterly bulletin, 27 (1943), 93-99.

Describes some rare books and pamphlets in collections of New-York Historical Society.

4481. Wemyss, Stanley. The general guide to rare Americana... with chronological and regional inventories of early printed books in the U. S. and key to American imprints, 1639-1889. Philadelphia: The Author, 1944. 2v.

Locates about 6,000 titles.

4482. Winsor, Justin. "Manuscript sources of American history - the conspicuous collections extant." American Historical Association papers, 3 (1887), 9-27.

Mentions some famous manuscript collections available for study of American history.

4483. Wisconsin State Historical Society. Descriptive list of manuscript collections of the Society, together with reports on other collections of manuscript material for American history in adjacent states, ed. by Reuben Gold Thwaites. Madison: The Society, 1906. 197p.

4484. Woodrow Wilson Foundation Library. Woodrow Wilson Memorial Library of the Woodrow Wilson Foundation, 8 W. 40th Street, New York. [1936]. 8p.

Describes scope of library and lists periodicals on file.

4485. Wroth, Lawrence C. The first century of the John Carter Brown Library; a history with a guide to the collections. Providence: Associates of the John Carter Brown Library, 1946. 88p.

American Indians

4486. Alden, John Richard. "The eighteenth century Cherokee archives." American archivist, 5 (1942), 240-44.

Description and list of documents originating with Cherokees, 1763-78, now in Manuscripts Division, Library of Congress.

4487. Anderson, Robert B., comp. "A preliminary check list of the laws of the Indian tribes." Law library journal, 34 (1941), 126-48.

Locates copies in 15 institutional and private collections.

4488. DePuy, Henry F. A bibliography of the English colonial treaties with the American Indians. N. Y.: Printed for the Lenox Club, 1917. 109p.

Includes census of copies of 50 treaties in 23 American libraries and the British Museum.

4489. Florida, University, Library. Bibliography on Seminole Indians. [Gainesville, 1940] 24 numb. l.

4490. Hargett, Lester. A bibliography of the constitutions and laws of the American Indians. Cambridge: Harvard Univ. Press, 1947. 123p.

Locates copies of 225 items in 51 institutional and private collections.

4491. McConnell, Winona. "California Indians (annotated list of material in the California State Library)." News notes of California libraries, 10 (1915), 485-523.

4492. Masterson, James R. "The records of the Washington Superintendency of Indian Affairs, 1853-1874." Pacific Northwest quarterly, 37 (Jan. 1946), 31-57.

Originals are in records of Office of

Indian Affairs in National Archives. Microcopies are at University of Washington and University of Oregon.

4493. Michigan, University, William L. Clements Library. Pontiac, chief of the Ottawas; a guide to an exhibition in the William L. Clements Library. Ann Arbor: Univ. of Michigan, 1939. 11p. (Bulletin no. 29)

A bibliography of 34 18th century printed books, manuscripts and maps.

4494. Newberry Library, Edward E. Ayer Collection. Narratives of captivity among the Indians of North America; a list of books and manuscripts on this subject in the Edward E. Ayer collection of the Newberry Library, comp. by Clara A. Smith. Chicago: The Library, 1912. 120p. (Publications of the Newberry Library, no. 3) Supplement I, by Clara A. Smith. Chicago: Newberry Library, 1928. 49p.

4495. U. S. Library of Congress, Division of Bibliography. A selected list of books on the Indians of North America, comp. by Helen F. Conover. Wash., Feb. 6, 1939. 25p.

4496. U. S. National Archives. List of documents concerning the negotiation of ratified Indian treaties, 1801-1869, comp. by John H. Martin. Wash., 1949. 175p. (Special list, no. 6)

Colonial period

4497. American Antiquarian Society Library. A calendar of the manuscripts of Col. John Bradstreet in the library of the Society, prep. by Charles Henry Lincoln. Worcester, Mass.: The Society, 1908. 55-133p. (Reprinted from American Antiquarian Society proceedings, n. s. 19 (1908), 103-82)

Autograph material for the study of British policy in America immediately preceding the American Revolution (1745-1774).

4498. American Antiquarian Society Library. "A calendar of the manuscripts of Sir William Johnson in the Library of the Society," prep. by Charles Henry Lincoln. American Antiquarian Society proceedings, n. s. 18 (1907), 367-410. Reprinted.

Includes 84 manuscripts, 1755-74, relating to Indian wars, events leading to American Revolution, etc.

4499. American Antiquarian Society Library. A list of additional manuscripts of the French and Indian War in the library of the Society, prep. by Charles Henry Lincoln. Worcester, Mass.: The Society, 1908. 49p. (Reprinted from the American Antiquarian Society proceedings, n. s. 19 (1909), 255-301)

Lists manuscripts in the Library relating to the period of the French and Indian War from 1754 to 1763 only.

4500. American Antiquarian Society Library. Manuscript records of the French and Indian War in the library of the Society, prep. by Charles Henry Lincoln. Worcester, Mass.: The Society, 1909. 267p. (Its: Transactions and collections, v. 11)

4501. Bartlett, John Russell. Bibliographical notes of rare and curious books relating to America... in John Carter Brown Library. Providence, R. I., 1882. 2v.

4502. Brown, Alexander. "An account of two manuscript volumes now in the Library of Congress, at Washington, D. C." Magazine of American history, 29 (1893), 371-80.

Description of the Virginia Company of London's "Records of the Courts," 1619-24.

4503. Butler, Ruth Lapham. "For the study of American colonial history: The Newberry Library." William and Mary quarterly, 3d ser., 2 (1945), 286-95.

General description of resources of the Ayer collection of the Newberry Library as a workshop for students of American colonial history. Mentions some important holdings.

4504. Carter, Clarence E. "Notes on the Lord Gage collection of manuscripts." Mississippi Valley historical review, 15 (1929), 511-25.

In William L. Clements Library, University of Michigan.

4505. Christie-Miller, Sydney Richardson. Catalogue of the magnificent series of early works relating to America from the renowned library at Britwell Court, Burnham, Bucks. [London]: Dryden Press [1916] 122p.

Collection acquired by Henry E. Huntington Library.

4506. Church, Elihu Dwight. A catalogue of books relating to the discovery and early history of North and South America forming a part of the library of E. D. Church, comp. by George Watson Cole. N. Y.: Dodd, Mead & Co. 1907. 5v.

Church collection now in Henry E. Huntington Library. Locations of works listed sometimes shown in other American libraries.

4507. Cole, George Watson. "Elizabethan Americana." In: Bibliographical essays; a tribute to Wilberforce Eames. [Cambridge: Harvard University Press] 1924, p. 161-78.

Describes 22 extremely rare books relating to America, printed between 1520 and 1641, now in Henry E. Huntington Library, and locates the few copies found in other American libraries.

4508. Columbus, Christopher. The letter of Columbus on the discovery of America. A facsimile of the pictorial edition. N. Y.: [DeVinne Press] 1892. 10 numb. 1. 61p.

Based upon original in New York Public Library. Includes reprint of 4 oldest editions in Latin, also found in Library.

4509. Greene, Evarts Boutell, and Morris, Richard B. A guide to the principal sources for early American history (1600-1800) in the City of New York. N. Y.: Columbia University Press, 1929. 357p.

Includes printed and manuscript sources, locating copies in 28 libraries.

4510. Harrisse, Henry. Bibliotheca Americana Vetustissima; a description of works relating to America, published between the years 1492 and 1551. N. Y.: G. P. Philes, 1866. 519p.

Records 304 titles with all known locations.

-----. Additions. Paris: Tross, 1872. 199p.
Records 186 titles, with locations where known.

4511. Henry E. Huntington Library. American manuscript collections in the Huntington Library for the history of the seventeenth and eighteenth centuries, comp. by Norma B. Cuthbert. San Marino: The Library, 1941. 93p. (Huntington Library lists, no. 5)

4512. Henry E. Huntington Library. "Loudoun papers. (a) Colonial, 1756-58. (b) French colonial, 1742-53," by Stanley M. Pargellis and Norma B. Cuthbert. Huntington Library bulletin, 3 (1933), 97-107.

Survey of papers in Huntington Library of Earl of Loudoun, commander in chief of British forces in North America, 1756-58.

4513. Historical Records Survey. Descriptive catalogue of the Du Simitière papers in the Library Company of Philadelphia. Philadelphia: The Survey, 1940. 196p.

The Du Simitière papers, purchased by Library Company in 1785, are a source of information on bibliography, natural history, Indian life, and colonial history.

4514. Lee, John Thomas. "A bibliography of [Jonathan] Carver's Travels." Wisconsin State Historical Society proceedings, 57 (1909), 143-83.

Lists, describes and locates 30 editions of Carver's Travels through the interior parts of North-America in the years 1766, 1767, and 1768.

4515. Long, John Cuthbert. The Plimpton collection of French and Indian War items presented to Amherst College and exhibited at the Lord Jeffery Inn, Amherst, Mass. Amherst, Mass.: Amherst College, 1934. 39p.

4516. Michigan, University, William L. Clements Library. A brief account of Raleigh's Roanoke colony of 1585, being a guide to an exhibition. Ann Arbor: [Ann Arbor Press], 1935. 18p. (Bulletin, no. 22)

Describes 35 books in Library about Roanoke colony.

4517. [Michigan, University, William L. Clements Library] Jesuit relations in the Library of William L. Clements. Bay City, Michigan, 1921. 6p.

Chronological list, 1632-88, of collection now in Clements Library, University of Michigan.

4518. Michigan, University, William L. Clements Library. Opportunities for investigation in colonial history. Ann Arbor, 1925. 4p. (Bulletin, no. 5)

Catalog of an exhibition of Richard Price, English pamphleteer, 1723-91, and Josiah Tucker, economist, 1712-99.

4519. New-York Historical Society. "Seventeenth century Americana in the library of the New-York Historical Society." New-York

Historical Society quarterly bulletin, 2 (1918), 4-8.
Includes partial check list.

4520. New York Public Library. Calendar of the Emmet Collection of manuscripts, etc., relating to American history. N. Y.: The Library, 1900. 563p.
Relates to colonial and Revolutionary periods.

4521. New York Public Library. "Columbus' letter on the discovery of America (1493-1497)," by Wilberforce Eames. New York Public Library bulletin, 28 (1924), 595-99.
Lists locations of original copies of "letter" in various languages.

4522. New York Public Library. "German works relating to America, 1493-1800; a list compiled from the collections of the New York Public Library," by Paul Ben Baginsky. New York Public Library bulletin, 42 (1938), 909-18; 43 (1939), 140-44, 349-58, 523-28, 575-80, 622-30, 671-86, 760-78, 921-46; 44 (1940), 39-56. Reprinted, with index, 1942. 217p.

4523. [Paine, Nathaniel] List of books received by the American Antiquarian Society from the sale of the first part of the Brinley library; to which is added a catalogue of the Mather publications previously in the Society's library. Worcester: C. Hamilton, 1879. 62p.
Strong in Mather and other early American imprints.

4524. Paltsits, Victor H. "A bibliography of the writings of Baron Lahontan." In: Lahontan's New voyages to North America, ed. by R. G. Thwaites. Chicago: McClurg, 1904. P. li-xciii. Reprinted. 1905.
Copies located in 13 American and Canadian libraries.

4525. Philadelphia Free Library. Three centuries of American history, 1493-1793; illustrated by contemporary books, manuscripts and maps from the collections of the Library Company of Philadelphia, the Free Library of Philadelphia and some of its trustees. Exhibiton held at the Free Library of Philadelphia, 1944. [Philadelphia, 1944] 62p.
Chronologically arranged with detailed annotations.

4526. Pierpont Morgan Library. Exhibition: the development of America, 1492-1792. [N. Y.: The Library, 1943] 8p.
Brief résumé of items shown in exhibition.

4527. Proctor, Robert George Collier. Jan van Doesborgh, printer at Antwerp; an essay in bibliography. London: Bibliographical Society, 1894. 101p.
Describes John Carter Brown Library's unique copy in Dutch of Vespuccius' letter to Lorenzo de' Medici narrating the story of his third voyage.

4528. Vail, Robert W. G. The voice of the old frontier. Philadelphia: Univ. of Pennsylvania Press, 1949. 492p.
Bibliography records 1,300 entries of American frontier literature, 1542-1800, with locations in 150 libraries.

4529. Virginia Company of London. The records of the Virginia Company of London, ed. by Susan Myra Kingsbury. Wash.: Govt. Print. Off., 1906-35. 4v.
Locates records, documents, manuscripts and other material pertaining to Company, 1600-1626, in 37 American and British depositories.

4530. Wainwright, Alexander D. "From Columbus to J. C. Adams; notable Americana in the McCormick collection." Princeton University Library chronicle, 10 (Nov. 1948), 41-50.
In Princeton University Library.

4531. Watertown Library Association. A selection of one hundred items from the Benjamin De Forest Curtiss collection of books in the Watertown Library. Watertown, Conn., 1937. 61p.
Chiefly Americana, 17th to 18th century.

4532. Wolf, Edwin. "Check list of the earliest English Americana." Bibliographical Society of America papers, 33 (1939), 49-54.
Locates copies of 32 titles in America and abroad.

Revolution and confederation

4533. Adams, Randolph G. "The cartography of the British attack on Fort Moultrie in 1776." In: Essays offered to Herbert Putnam. New Haven: Yale Univ. Press, 1929. p. 35-46.
Descriptions of maps, located in Clements

Library and Library of Congress, relating to Fort Moultrie in 1776.

4534. Adams, Randolph G. The headquarters papers of the British army in North America during the war of the American Revolution; a brief description of Sir Henry Clinton's papers in the William L. Clements Library. Ann Arbor: William L. Clements Library, 1926. 47p. (Bulletin, no. 14)

4535. Adams, Randolph G. "A new library of American revolutionary records." Current history, 33 (1930), 234-38.
Describes some documents on American Revolution in William L. Clements Library, University of Michigan.

4536. Adams, Randolph G. The papers of Lord George Germain; a brief description of the Stopford-Sackville papers now in the William L. Clements Library. Ann Arbor: William L. Clements Library, 1928. 46p. (Bulletin, no. 18)
Papers relating to American colonies, 1740 through Revolution.

4537. American Philosophical Society. "Calendar of the correspondence of Brigadier-General George Weedon, U. S. A., with celebrated characters of the American Revolution." American Philosophical Society transactions, 38 (1899), 81-114.
Calendar of collection owned by the Society.

4538. American Philosophical Society. Calendar of the correspondence relating to the American Revolution of Brigadier-General George Weedon, Hon. Richard Henry Lee, Hon. Arthur Lee, and Major-General Nathanael Greene, in the library of the American Philosophical Society. Philadelphia: The Society, 1900. 255p.
Chronologically arranged for each individual.

4539. Bowman, J. R. "A bibliography of the First book of the American chronicles of the times, 1774-1775." American literature, 1 (1929), 69-74.
Locates copies in about 10 libraries.

4540. Chicago Historical Society. "List of works on the Lewis and Clark expedition presented [to the Society]." Chicago Historical Society annual report, (1910), 342-50.
Lists 39 works recently acquired by Chicago Historical Society.

4541. Chinard, Gilbert. "The Berthier manuscripts; new records of the French army in the American Revolution." Princeton University Library chronicle, 1 (Nov. 1939), 3-[8].
Acquired by Princeton University Library. Maps and journals dealing with American operations of French army under Rochambeau, 1781-82.

4542. Conklin, Edwin G. "The American Philosophical Society and the founders of our government." Pennsylvania history, 4 (1937), 235-40.
Describes materials in the Society's archives relating to the colonial, revolutionary and confederation periods.

4543. Duke University Library. "The Purviance Courtenay collection in the Manuscript Department of Duke University Library," by N. L. Goodwin. Library notes, a bulletin issued for the Friends of Duke University Library, no. 16 (June 1946), 6-13.
Description of collection of 2,400 items relating to American Revolutionary era and after, written by Samuel Purviance, Baltimore patriot, and his relatives.

4544. Fay, Bernard. Bibliographie critique des ouvrages français relatifs aux États-Unis (1700-1800). Paris: Champion, 1925. 108p. (Bibliothèque de la Revue de littérature comparée, t. 7, 2. ptie.)
Locates copies in 8 American libraries.

4545. Ford, Paul Leicester. Some materials for a bibliography of the offical publications of the Continental Congress, 1774-89. Boston, 1890. 31p. (Boston Public Library, Bibliographies of special subjects, 6)
Lists 472 titles, arranged chronologically. Locations in 15 libraries.

4546. Ford, Worthington C., comp. Bibliographical notes on the issues of the Continental Congress, 1774-[1779]. Wash.,1904-[08]. 6 pts.
Locates copies.

4547. Goff, Frederick R. "A contemporary broadside printing of the Declaration of Independence." Library of Congress quarterly journal of current acquisitions, 5 (Nov. 1947), 12-16.
Acquired by Library of Congress.

4548. Goff, Frederick R. "Peter Force." Bibliographical Society of America papers, 44 (1950), 1-16.

Description of acquisition of Force collection of Americana by Library of Congress, with a general survey of this collection of "the sources of American history."

4549. Harvard University Library. Calendar of the Arthur Lee manuscripts in the library of Harvard University. Cambridge: University Press, 1882. 43p. (Harvard University Library bibliographical contributions, no. 8)

4550. Heartman, Charles Frederick. The cradle of the United States, 1765-1789; five hundred contemporary broadsides, pamphlets and a few books. Perth Amboy, N. J., 1922-23. 2v. (Vol. 2 published in Metuchen, N. J.)

Collection now in Yale University Library.

4551. [Henry E. Huntington Library] The Destouches papers relative to the American Revolution, comprising letters and documents. N. Y.: American Art Association [1926] [34]p.

Acquired en bloc by the Huntington Library.

4552. Heusser, Albert Henry. The forgotten general, Robert Erskine, (1735-1780). Paterson, N. J.: The Benjamin Franklin Press, [1928] 216p.

Pages 194-201 list Erskine-Dewitt collection of manuscript maps and surveys by Robert Erskine and others, 1778-81, in New-York Historical Society.

4553. Historical Records Survey - D. of C. Calendar of the letters and documents of Peter Force and his son William Q. Force on the Mecklenberg declaration of independence in the Loomis collection, Washington, D. C. Wash.: D. of C. Historical Records Survey, 1940. 35 numb. l.

4554. [Hunt, Gaillard] "Bibliographical notes," [on the issues of the Continental Congress, 1780-1781] In: U. S. Library of Congress, Journals of the Continental Congress. Wash.: Govt. Print. Off., 1910-1912. v. 18, p. 1233-37; v. 21, p. 1199-1203.

Locates some copies, chiefly in Library of Congress.

4555. James, James Alton, ed. George Rogers Clark papers, 1771-1784. Springfield: Illinois State Historical Library, 1912-26. 2v. (Illinois State Historical Library collections, v. 8, 19)

Original documents in Virginia State Library, U.S. State Department, Virginia State Historical Library, Library of Congress, Wisconsin State Historical Society, and foreign archives.

4556. Jenkins, Charles F. "The completed sets of the signers of the Declaration of Independence, 1925." Pennsylvania magazine of history and biography, 49 (1925), 231-49.

Gives history and description of 27 existing collections of autographs of signers of the Declaration, with present locations. See also Autograph collectors' journal, 3 (Jan. 1951), 15-19.

4557. McIlwaine, Henry R. "Revolutionary war material in the Virginia State Library." Magazine of history, 10 (1909), 143-50.

4558. Maggs Bros., booksellers. The American war for independence as related in the unpublished manuscript journals and plans of Alexander Berthier. London: Maggs Bros., Ltd., 1936. 36p.

Collection acquired by Princeton University Library.

4559. Marblehead Historical Society. "Revolutionary War manuscripts." Essex Institute historical collections, 75 (1939), 15-22.

Text of 4 manuscripts copied from originals in possession of Marblehead Historical Society.

4560. Michigan, University, William L. Clements Library. Beaumarchais and the American Revolution. Ann Arbor, 1925. 4p. (Bulletin, no. 8)

Catalog of an exhibition.

4561. Michigan, University, William L. Clements Library. Exhibition of some interesting papers from the archives of Sir Henry Clinton. Ann Arbor, 1926. 4p. (Bulletin, no. 13)

Brief description of collection of papers of commander in chief of British armies in North America, 1778-82, now in Clements Library.

4562. Michigan, University, William L. Clements Library. The headquarters papers of the British army in North America during the war of the American Revolution; a brief description of Sir Henry Clinton's papers. Ann Arbor, 1926. 47p. (Bulletin, no. 14)

4563. Michigan, University, William L. Clements Library. Lexington to Fallen Timbers; episodes from the earliest history of our military forces. Illustrated by original maps and papers in the Clements Library. Selected and described by Randolph G. Adams and Howard H. Peckham. Ann Arbor: Univ. of Mich. Press, 1942. 41p. (Bulletin, no. 37)

4564. Michigan University, William L. Clements Library. The one hundred and fiftieth anniversary of the Battle of Bunker's Hill, June 17, 1775. Ann Arbor, 1925. 4p. (Bulletin, no. 9)

Catalog of an exhibition.

4565. Michigan, University, William L. Clements Library. The one hundred and fiftieth anniversary of the meeting of the first Continental Congress, 1774-1924. Ann Arbor, 1924. 4p. (Bulletin, no. 2)

Description of an exhibition.

4566. Michigan, University, William L. Clements Library. Report on the Sir John Vaughan papers in the William L. Clements Library, by Edna Vosper. Ann Arbor: The Library, 1929. 37p. (Bulletin, no. 19)

"Outline of the contents of the Vaughan papers," p. 27-32.

4567. Michigan, University, William L. Clements Library. The surrender of Cornwallis. Ann Arbor, 1924. 4p. (Bulletin, no. 3)

Description of an exhibition.

4568. Museum Book Store, London. A catalogue of Americana, mainly dealing with the American Revolution; and English literature, from the libraries of a nobleman and a descendant of David Hartley, Franklin's friend. London: Museum Book Store, 1925. 92p.

Collection, numbering 768 items, acquired by Henry E. Huntington Library.

4569. New York Public Library. Collation of the various issues of the American diplomatic correspondence (1776-1783, 1783-1789) in the New York Public Library." New York Public Library bulletin, 9 (1905), 87-89.

4570. New York Public Library. "Documents of the First and Second Congresses of the United States in the New York Public Library." New York Public Library bulletin, 3 (1899), 462-69.

Lists original editions only.

4571. New York Public Library. "Exhibition commemorating the 150th anniversary of the adoption of the Declaration of Independence, 1776-1926," arr. by Charles F. McCombs and Ernest Leopold Hettich. New York Public Library bulletin, 31 (1927), 807-25, 904-39. Reprinted. 56p.

4572. New York State Library. "Preliminary checklist of printed Fourth of July orations." Albany, 1950. 141 numb. l. Typed.

4573. N. Y. (State) Secretary of State. Calendar of historical manuscripts relating to the war of the Revolution in the office of the Secretary of State. Albany, 1868. 2v.

Manuscripts were transferred in 1881 to New York State Library.

4574. Newberry Library. Check list of American Revolutionary War pamphlets in the Newberry Library, comp. by Ruth Lapham. Chicago: The Library, 1922. 115p. (Special publications, no. 19)

English and American political pamphlets, 1750-86.

4575. Pennsylvania Historical Society. The Constitution of the United States... an exhibit of books, pamphlets and documents from the collections of the Historical Society of Pennsylvania. Philadelphia: Historical Society of Pennsylvania, 1937. 35p.

4576. Philadelphia Library Company. Exhibition of books and manuscripts in commemoration of the one hundred and fiftieth anniversary of the signing of the Constitution of the United States of America, September 17th, 1787. [Philadelphia, 1937] 28p.

Drawn from Philadelphia Library Company's collection.

4577. "Philadelphia papers." Bibliographical Society of America papers, 14 (1920), 92-126.

Controversial news sheets of 1790's about refugees from San Domingo who lived in Philadelphia. Material located in John Carter Brown Library, or occasionally elsewhere as stated.

4578. Plumb, Milton M., Jr. "The Bill of Rights comes home." Library of Congress quarterly journal of current acquisitions, 2 (June, 1945), 30-44.
Original copy of American Bill of Rights presented to Library of Congress.

4579. Thomas, William S. "American Revolutionary diaries, also journals, narratives, autobiographies, reminiscences, and personal memoirs, cataloged and described." New-York Historical Society quarterly bulletin, 6 (1922), 32-35, 61-71, 101-07, 143-47; 7 (1923), 28-35, 63-71.
Lists more than 300 items, with few exceptions in New-York Historical Society.

4580. U. S. Library of Congress, Division of Bibliography. "Bibliography of Baron von Steuben," by H. H. B. Meyer. In: U. S. Congress, Joint Committee on Printing, Proceedings upon the unveiling of the statue of Baron von Steuben. [Wash.: Govt. Print. Off., 1913?] p. 215-26. (62d Cong., 3d sess. House. Doc. 1455)

4581. U. S. Library of Congress, Division of Bibliography. "Count Kazimierz (Casimir) Pulaski, 1748-1779: a bibliographical list." Wash., Aug. 16, 1929. 8p. Typed. General Reference and Bibliography Division. [Supplementary list] Feb. 27, 1948. 4p. Typed.

4582. U. S. Library of Congress, Division of Bibliography. List of works relating to the French alliance in the American Revolution, comp. by Appleton Prentiss Clark Griffin. Wash.: Govt. Print. Off., 1907. 40p.

4583. U. S. Library of Congress, Division of Bibliography. "The Saratoga campaign 1777: a bibliographical list," comp. by Florence S. Hellman. Wash., Feb. 2, 1939. 26p. Typed.

4584. U. S. Library of Congress, Division of Manuscripts. The Declaration of Independence, the Constitution of the United States, and other historic material in the Division of Manuscripts of the Library of Congress. [Wash., 1941] 14p, 2p.
Description of the documents.

4585. U. S. Library of Congress, Division of Manuscripts. Naval records of the American revolution, 1775-1788; prepared from the originals in the Library of Congress, by Charles Henry Lincoln. Wash.: Govt. Print. Off., 1906. 549p.

4586. U. S. Library of Congress, General Reference and Bibliography Division. "The loyalist exiles of the American Revolution." Wash., Jan. 5, 1948. 14p. Typed.

Early federal period to Civil War

4587. American Catholic Historical Society. "Americana in the library of the American Catholic Historical Society." American Catholic Historical Society records, 39 (1928), 263-70, 356-63.
Arranged chronologically, 1814-47.

4588. Haferkorn, Henry Ernest. The war with Mexico, 1846-1848; a select bibliography on the causes, conduct, and the political aspect of the war, together with a select list of books and other printed material on the resources, economic conditions, politics and government of the republic of Mexico and the characteristics of the Mexican people. With annotations and an index. Washington Barracks, D. C., 1914. 93p.
Locates copies in Library of Congress, Army War College, Engineer School, and War Department.

4589. Haight, Gordon S. "The John William De Forest collection." Yale University library gazette, 14 (1940), 41-46.
Brief description of "the family papers of John Hancock De Forest (1776-1839) and the literary manuscripts of his son, John William De Forest (1826-1906), the novelist," now in the Yale University Library. An intimate view of American life, 1820-40.

4590. Hoyt, William D., Jr. "The Warden papers." Maryland historical magazine, 36 (Sept. 1941), 302-14; 38 (Mar. 1943), 69-85.
Description of papers of David Baillie Warden, American consul to France, 1808-14, and resident of France to 1855.

4591. Louisville Free Public Library. Books and magazine articles on Battle of Tippecanoe, Battle of the River Raisin, Battle of the Thames. [Louisville] 1913. 11p.

4592. Louisville Free Public Library. Books and magazine articles on Oliver Hazard Perry and the battle of Lake Erie. [Louisville] 1913. 8p.

Items from the Library collected for the Perry centennial celebration at Louisville in 1913.

4593. New-York Historical Society. "Calendar of the American Fur Company's papers," ed. by Grace L. Nute. American Historical Association annual report, Part 1: 1831-1840, 2 (1944), 519-982; part 2: 1841-1849, 3 (1944), 983-1951.

Collection in possession of New-York Historical Society.

4594. New York Public Library. "The United States Exploring Expedition, 1838-1842, and its publications, 1844-1874; a bibliography," comp. by Daniel C. Haskell. New York Public Library bulletin, 45 (1941), 69-89, 507-32, 821-58; 46 (1942), 103-50. A preliminary introduction to this work appeared in Bulletin, 44 (1940), 93-112, the whole reprinted with additions and an index, 1942. 188p.

Locates copies in 88 libraries.

Civil War

4595. Boston Athenaeum. Confederate literature; a list of books and newspapers, maps, music and miscellaneous matter printed in the South during the Confederacy, now in the Boston Athenaeum, prep. by Charles N. Baxter and James M. Dearborn, with an introduction by James Ford Rhodes. [Boston]: Boston Athenaeum, 1917. 213p. (Robert Charles Billings Fund publication, no. 5)

Lists 733 volumes. New edition in process of compilation.

4596. Botkin, B. A. "The slave as his own interpreter." Library of Congress quarterly journal of current acquisitions, 2 (Nov. 1944), 37-63.

Collection of portraits and narratives of American ex-slaves, received by Library of Congress.

4597. Brigham, Clarence S. "Wall-paper newspapers of the Civil War." In: Bibliographical essays; a tribute to Wilberforce Eames. [Cambridge: Harvard Univ. Press] 1924. p. 203-09.

Locates copies in American Antiquarian Society, Boston Athenaeum, Boston Public Library, Library of Congress, Loyal Legion Library (Boston), Massachusetts Historical Society, and Yale University.

4598. Brooklyn Public Library. "The Halliday Civil War collection." Brooklyn Public Library bulletin, 4th ser., 11 (1932), 93.

4599. Columbia University Library. The Townsend Library of national, state, and individual civil war records at Columbia University, New York City. [N. Y., 1899] 15p.

4600. Columbia University Library. Townsend's library of national, state, and individual records, 1860-1870; including all attainable information up to the present time [1888] concerning individuals and events connected with that decade. N. Y., 1888. 12p.

4601. Confederate Memorial Literary Society. A calendar of Confederate papers, with a bibliography of some Confederate publications, prep. by Douglas Southall Freeman. Richmond, Va.: Confederate Museum, 1908. 620p.

Record of manuscripts in Confederate Museum Library.

4602. Emory University Library. "A short title list of books, pamphlets, newspapers and periodicals comprising the Keith M. Read Confederate collection of the Emory University Library." Atlanta, 1941. 154 numb. 1. Typed.

4603. Harwell, Richard Barksdale. "Atlanta publications of the Civil War." Atlanta historical bulletin, 6 (July 1941), 165-200.

A union list.

4604. Historical Records Survey. A calendar of the Ryder collection of Confederate archives at Tufts College. Boston, Mass., 1940. 168p.

A collection of archives of Confederate States of America, now in Tufts College Library.

4605. Historical Records Survey, District of Columbia. Calendar of the writings of Frederick Douglass in the Frederick Douglass Memorial Home, Anacostia, D. C. Wash.: D. of C. Historical Records Survey, 1940. 93 numb. 1.

4606. Historical Records Survey, Illinois. Calendar of the Robert Weidensall correspondence, 1861-1865, at George Williams College, Chicago, Illinois. Chicago: Illinois Historical Records Survey, 1940. 34 numb. 1.

4607. Historical Records Survey, Louisiana.

4608 HISTORY

Taber collection. University, La.: Department of Archives, Louisiana State University, 1938. 12p.

Calendar of letters from a Confederate soldier to his family, 1861-62.

4608. Illinois State Historical Library. The Civil War collection of the Illinois State Historical Library, by Donald J. Berthrong. Springfield: The Library, 1949. 23p.

Description of book collection, newspapers, manuscripts and archives held by Library.

4609. Joline, J. F. "Special collections at Princeton; VI. The Pierson Civil War collection." Princeton University Library chronicle, 2 (1941), 105-[10]

Comprehensive collection of 6,600 books and 2,000 pamphlets, assembled from 1869 to 1908.

4610. Milhollen, Hirst. "Mathew B. Brady collection." Library of Congress quarterly journal of current acquisitions, 1 (April-June 1944), 15-19.

Report on collection of 7,000 negatives, made by Mathew B. Brady, Civil War photographer, acquired by Library of Congress.

4611. Morrison, Hugh A. "A bibliography of the official publications of the Confederate States of America." Bibliographical Society of America proceedings and papers, 3 (1908), 92-132.

Copies located in Howard Memorial Library, New Orleans; Library of Congress; Virginia State Library; and State Historical Society of Wisconsin.

4612. Nicholson, John Page. Catalogue of library of Brevet Lieutenant-Colonel John Page Nicholson... relating to the war of the rebellion, 1861-1866. Philadelphia, 1914. 1,022p.

Collection acquired by Henry E. Huntington Library.

4613. Oberlin College Library. A classified catalogue of the collection of anti-slavery propaganda in the Oberlin College Library, comp. by Geraldine Hopkins Hubbard. Oberlin, Ohio: Oberlin College, 1932. 84p. (Library bulletin, v. 2, no. 3)

Records 1,590 items. A supplement, typewritten, comp. by Franklyn F. Bright, 1941, 63p., lists 239 items. Second supplement, 1941-45, typewritten, records 83 items.

4614. Princeton University Library. "Pierson Civil War collection." Princeton University Library classed list. Princeton, 1920. v. 6, p. 2985-3077.

4615. U. S. Library of Congress, General Reference and Bibliography Division. "The Dred Scott decision, 1857: a selected list of references," comp. by Donald H. Mugridge. Wash., June 23, 1948. 7p. Typed.

4616. U. S. War Dept. Library. Bibliography of state participation in the Civil War, 1861-1866. 3d ed. Wash.: Govt. Print. Off., 1913. 1,140p. (Subject catalogue, no. 6)

Catalog of material in War Department Library, with locations given for books not held by Library. Now in U. S. National War College Library.

4617. U. S. War Dept. Library. List of the photographs and photographic negatives relating to the war for the union, now in the War Department Library. Wash.: Govt. Print. Off., 1897. 219p. (Subject catalogue, no. 5)

Now in U. S. National War College Library.

4618. U. S. War Dept. Library. Military literature in the War Department Library relating chiefly to the participation of the individual states in the war for the union. 2d ed. Wash.: Govt. Print. Off., 1899. 266p. (Subject catalogue, no. 6)

Now in U. S. National War College Library.

4619. U. S. War Dept. Library. Military literature in the War Department Library relating to the campaign against Chattanooga, siege of Chattanooga, battle of Chickamauga, battle of Lookout Mountain, battle of Missionary Ridge, and the retreat of Bragg... August 1863, to December 1863. Wash.: Govt. Print. Off., 1898. 73p. (Subject catalogue, no. 7)

Now in U. S. National War College Library.

4620. Virginia State Library. "A list of the official publications of the Confederate States government in the Virginia State Library and the library of the Confederate Memorial Literary Society." Virginia State Library bulletin, 4 (1911), 1-72.

4621. Wait, Martha H. "American Civil War

pamphlets." Harvard Library notes, 1 (1922), 160-62.

In Harvard College Library.

4622. Wisconsin State Historical Society Library. Catalogue of books on the war of the rebellion, and slavery, in the library of the State Historical Society of Wisconsin. Madison: Democrat Printing Co., 1887. 61p.

Lists 1,617 titles.

4623. Wisconsin State Historical Society Library. The Keyes and the Civil War manuscript collections in the Wisconsin Historical Library. Madison, 1916. 20p. (Bulletin of information, no. 81)

UNITED STATES REGIONAL HISTORY

New England

4624. American Antiquarian Society Library. "A check list of New England election sermons," by R. W. G. Vail. American Antiquarian Society proceedings, n. s. 45 (1935), 233-66. Reprinted.

Locates copies in American Antiquarian Society and other libraries.

4625. Boston Public Library. Catalogue of a collection of early New England books made by the late John Allen Lewis and now in the possession of the Boston Public Library. Boston: The Library, 1892. 31p. (Reprinted from Boston Public Library bulletin, July 1892)

Includes about 200 items relating to Cotton and Increase Mather.

4626. Boston Public Library. Catalogue of the American portion of the library of the Rev. Thomas Prince. With a memoir, and list of his publications, by Wm. H. Whitmore. Boston: J. K. Wiggin & W. P. Lunt, 1868. 166p.

Rare books relating to the history of New England prior to 1758; about 1,899 vols.

4627. Boston Public Library. New England; a selected list of works in the Public Library of the City of Boston. Boston: The Library, 1920. 38p.

4628. Boston Public Library. The Prince Library; a catalogue of the collection of books and manuscripts which formerly belonged to the Rev. Thomas Prince... and is now deposited in the Public Library of the City of Boston. Boston: A. Mudge & Son, 1870. 160p.

Relates to history of New England before 1758.

4629. California State Library, Sutro Branch. An annotated bibliography of sermons and tracts delivered in New England between 1720 and 1810. San Francisco, 1939. 99 numb. l. (Its: Occasional papers. English series no. 1)

Lists 468 tracts in the Sutro Branch collection; tracts are mostly by New England ministers or political speakers.

4630. Forbes, Harriette M. New England diaries, 1602-1800; a descriptive catalogue of diaries, orderly books and sea journals. Topsfield, Mass.: Priv. print., 1923. 439p.

Locates each manuscript and indicates where a published extract or imprint may be found.

4631. [Gay, Frederick Lewis] A rough list of a collection of transcripts relating to the history of New England, 1630-1776, in possession of Frederick Lewis Gay. Brookline, Mass., 1913. 273p.

Collection now owned by Massachusetts Historical Society.

4632. Ham, Edward B. "The library of the Union St.-Jean-Baptiste d'Amérique." Franco-American review, 1 (1937), 271-75.

Brief description of resources, especially for New England history, of the library at Woonsocket, R.I.

4633. New York Public Library. "Books by and about the Rogerenes," by Ellen S. Brinton. New York Public Library bulletin, 49 (1945), 627-48. Reprinted. 24p.

Locates copies in 34 libraries. Works by and about John Rogers and his followers in New England, 1697-1842.

Middle Atlantic

4634. U. S. Library of Congress, Division of Bibliography. "A list of references on social life in New York, Philadelphia, and Washington 1789 to 1812." Wash., Mar. 12, 1935. 10p. Typed.

South

4635. Chapman, Lily May. "The Southern collection of books in the Birmingham Public Library." Southeastern Library Association papers, (1930), 44-52.
   Describes Tutwiler collection of Southern history and literature in Birmingham Public Library.

4636. Duke University Library. The centennial exhibit of the Duke University Library, consisting of material from the George Washington Flowers memorial collection of books and documents relating to the history and literature of the South. April 5 - June 5, 1939. Durham, N. C., 1939. 60p.

4637. Duke University Library. Guide to the manuscript collections in the Duke University Library, prep. by the Historical Records Survey, Works Progress Administration. Raleigh, N. C.: Historical Records Survey, 1939. 165 l.
   Brief descriptions of 1,097 collections; strong for Civil War and other Southern material.

4638. Duke University Library. Guide to the manuscript collections in the Duke University Library, by Nannie M. Tilley and Noma Lee Goodwin. Durham: Duke Univ. Press, 1947. 362p. (Historical papers of the Trinity College Historical Society, ser. 27-28)
   Describes 1,896 collections in the Library in 1942; strong for Civil War records and other Southern material. Based on and supersedes 1939 Guide.

4639. Hamilton, Joseph Grégoire de Roulhac. A national southern collection at the University of North Carolina. Chapel Hill: University of North Carolina, 1928. 14p.
   Description of the Southern historical collection, University of North Carolina Library.

4640. Maxwell, Sarah Alison. "Tutwiler collection of Southern history and literature." Special libraries, 33 (Dec. 1942), 367-69.
   Description of Birmingham Public Library collection containing 11,090 books, 8,739 pamphlets, and maps, mounted pictures, etc.

4641. New York Southern Society Library. Catalogue of the New York Southern Society. "Garden Library", of Southern Americana, comp. by John F. B. Lillard. N. Y.: The Society, 1891. 143p.

4642. North Carolina, University, Library. Guide to the manuscripts in the Southern Historical Collection of the University of North Carolina. Chapel Hill: Univ. of N. C. Press, 1941. 204p. (James Sprunt studies in history and political science, v. 24, no. 2)

4643. U. S. Library of Congress, Division of Bibliography. "A list of references on the Ozarks." Wash., Mar. 24, 1936. 16p. Typed.

4644. U. S. Library of Congress, Division of Bibliography. A selected list of recent books and pamphlets on the South, comp. by Ann Duncan Brown. [Wash.] 1940. 24p.

4645. U. S. Library of Congress, General Reference and Bibliography Division. "The south: economics and social conditions," comp. by Helen F. Conover. Wash., July 18, 1944. 34p. Typed. "Supplementary references, 1943-1947." June 30, 1947. 20p. Typed.

Midwest

4646. Benton, Elbert Jay. "The Western Reserve Historical Society and its library." College and research libraries, 6 (1944), 23-29.
   General description of collections of maps, manuscripts, newspapers, books, periodicals, genealogy, and special collections.

4647. Burton, Clarence M. "The Burton Historical Collection of the Public Library, Detroit." Bibliographical Society of America papers, 16, pt. 1 (1922), 10-16. Reprinted.

4648. Rusk, Ralph Leslie. The literature of the middle western frontier, 1700-1840. N. Y.: Columbia Univ. Press, 1925. 2v.
   Volume 2, p. 39-363, is entirely bibliographies of material in v. 1, and locates copies throughout.

4649. St. Louis Mercantile Library. Missouri and Illinois newspapers... manuscripts relating to Louisiana Territory and Missouri. St. Louis: The Library, 1898. 22p. (Reference lists, no. 1)
   Gives holdings of Missouri and Illinois newspapers in St. Louis Mercantile Library, and lists manuscripts in Library, with some description.

4650. "Source material of the Detroit Public Library as supplied by the acquisition of the Burton historical collection." Michigan history magazine, 6 (1922), 386-99.

4651. Streeter, Floyd Benjamin. "The Burton Historical Collection." American collector, 1 (Jan. 1926), 123-34.
In Detroit Public Library.

4652. U. S. Engineer School Library. The Mississippi River and Valley; bibliography, mostly non-technical, prep. by H. E. Haferkorn. Fort Humphreys, Va.: Engineer School, 1931. 116p.
Locations indicated, chiefly in Library of Congress.

4653. Western Reserve Historical Society. Partial list of manuscripts, field notes, and maps. [Cleveland] 1885. 16p.

Southwest

4654. Austin, Mary. "Spanish manuscripts in the Southwest." Southwest review, 19 (1934), 402-09.
Describes a collection of Spanish literature of Southwest in Santa Fe Laboratory Museum.

4655. Wagner, Henry Raup. The Spanish Southwest, 1542-1794; an annotated bibliography. Berkeley, Calif., 1924. 302p.
Locates copies in 18 public and private collections in the United States and in foreign libraries.

4656. Wagner, Henry Raup. The Spanish Southwest, 1542-1794; an annotated bibliography. Albuquerque: Quivira Society, 1937. 2v. (Quivira Society publications, v. 7, pt. 1-2)
Locates copies of editions of 177 author or title entries in 25 United States libraries or collections.

Northwest

4657. Appleton, John B. The Pacific Northwest: a selected bibliography. Portland, Ore.: Northwest Regional Council, 1939. 455p.
Locates copies of unpublished material.

4658. Bradley, Isaac S. "Available material for the study of the institutional history of the old Northwest." Wisconsin Historical Society proceedings, 44 (1896), 114-42. Also in American Historical Association annual report, 1 (1896), 296-319.
List of statutes, session laws, legislative journals and documents, journals of constitutional conventions, and newspaper files of the territory northwest of the Ohio River and the states of Ohio, Illinois, Michigan and Wisconsin, published prior to 1851, to be found in 22 libraries in those states.

4659. Eaton, Vincent L. "Legislative journals of the old Northwest Territory." Library of Congress quarterly journal of current acquisitions, 5 (Aug. 1948), 10-11.
Describes documents received by Library of Congress for period from 1799 to 1802.

4660. Gates, Charles M. "Some sources for Northwest history: Account books." Minnesota history, 16 (1935), 70-75.
Description of a collection, of interest for Northwest history, in Minnesota Historical Society.

4661. "Harmar papers of the Clements Library." Western Pennsylvania historical magazine, 19 (1936), 305-10.
Description of correspondence of Josiah Harmar, army officer, relating to Northwest Territory in decade following Revolution.

4662. Jackson, W. Turrentine. "Territorial papers in the Department of the Interior archives, 1873-1890: Washington, Idaho and Montana." Pacific Northwest quarterly, 35 (Oct. 1944), 323-41.
Papers are in National Archives collection.

4663. Knox College Library. An annotated catalogue of books belonging to the Finley collection on the history and romance of the Northwest, collected and presented to the library of Knox College, Galesburg, Illinois... Supplemented by a Bibliography of the discovery and exploration of the Mississippi Valley, by Appleton P. C. Griffin. Galesburg: Knox College, 1924. 67p.

4664. Knox College Library. A catalogue of books and maps belonging to the Finley collection on the history and romance of the Northwest. 2d ed. Galesburg, Ill.: Knox College, 1928. 61p.

4665. Knox College Library. Some recent additions to the Finley collection on the history and romance of the Northwest, collected and contributed by Edward Caldwell. [Galesburg? Ill., 1937?] 30p.

4666. "Pacific Northwest Americana." Washington historical quarterly, 13 (1922), 152-54, 239-40, 308-10; 14 (1923), 75-76, 156-58; 15 (1924), 76-78, 154-55, 234-36, 308-10; 16 (1925), 74-76, 158-59, 311-12; 17 (1926), 74-75, 154-56, 238-39, 310-11; 18 (1927), 77-78, 156-57, 238-39, 311-12.
Articles on acquisitions, collections and bibliographies of material.

4667. Pacific Northwest Library Association. A union list of manuscripts in libraries of the Pacific Northwest, comp. by Charles W. Smith. Seattle: Univ. of Washington Press, 1931. 57p.
Lists holding of 16 libraries in Pacific Northwest region.

4668. Smith, Charles W. "The Bagley collection of Pacific Northwest history." Washington historical quarterly, 10 (April 1919), 83-87.
Collection of newspapers, books and manuscripts in University of Washington Library.

4669. Smith, Charles W., comp. Checklist of books and pamphlets relating to the history of the Pacific Northwest. Olympia: Washington State Library, 1909. 191p.
Cooperative list, locating each title in one or more of 13 libraries of region. Second edition, N. Y.: Wilson, 1921. 329p.; third edition, Portland: Oregon Historical Society, 1950, in press.

4670. Smith, Charles W., comp. Manuscripts in libraries of the Pacific Northwest. Seattle: Univ. of Wash. Press, 1931. 57p.
Union list of logbooks, diaries, journals, and other manuscripts relating to Pacific Northwest history.

4671. Smith, Charles W. Pacific Northwest Americana; a checklist of books and pamphlets relating to the history of the Pacific Northwest. 2d ed. rev. and enl. N. Y.: H. W. Wilson, 1921. 329p.
Copies located in 18 libraries. Includes 4,501 items.

4672. Smith, Charles W., comp. Pacific Northwest Americana: a checklist of books and pamphlets relating to the history of the Pacific Northwest. Rev. by Isabel Mayhew. 3d ed. Portland: Oregon Historical Society, 1950. In press.
Lists holdings of 38 Pacific Northwest libraries.

4673. Stephenson, George M. "Some sources for Northwest history: Swedish immigration material." Minnesota history, 18 (1937), 69-75.
Describes various types of material in Minnesota Historical Society's collection.

4674. Swanson, Evadene B. "Some sources for Northwest history: the Dight papers." Minnesota history, 25 (March 1944), 62-64.
Describes a collection in Minnesota Historical Society.

West

4675. California, University, Library. "Report on the Bancroft Library," by Reuben G. Thwaites. University of California chronicle, 8 (1905-06), 126-43.
Estimate of value of Bancroft collection.

4676. Caughey, John Walton. Hubert Howe Bancroft, historian of the West. Berkeley: Univ. of California Press, 1946. 422p.
P. 391-407: "Epilogue: the Bancroft library." A general history and description of the collection.

4677. Dunne, Peter M. "Jesuit annual letters in the Bancroft Library." Mid-America, 20 (1938), 263-72.
Description of a collection of annual letters written by Jesuit missionaries in New Spain, now in the Bancroft Library of the University of California.

4678. Eberstadt, Edward. "The William Robertson Coe collection of Western Americana." Yale University Library gazette, 23 (1948), 37-130. Reprinted, with additions. 110p.
7,000 items embracing "the territory west of Missouri, north of Mexico, and south of the Arctic Circle" now in the Yale University Library.

4679. Hammond, George P. "Manuscript collections in the Bancroft Library." American archivist, 13 (1950), 15-26.
At University of California, Berkeley.

4680. Historical and Philosophical Society of Ohio Library. Catalogue of books relating to the state of Ohio, the West and Northwest. [Cincinnati, 190-?] 108p.

A catalogue of 783 books in Society's library.

4681. Illinois, University, Illinois Historical Survey. Guide to manuscript materials relating to western history in foreign depositories reproduced for the Illinois Historical Survey, by Marguerite Jenison Pease. Urbana, 1950. 85 numb. l.

Arranged by archives and libraries.

4682. Jackson, W. Turrentine. "Materials for western history in the Department of Interior archives." Mississippi Valley historical review, 35 (June 1948), 61-76.

Description of type of records and source material relating to history of West, in U. S. Department of the Interior archives.

4683. Powell, Benjamin E. "Western Americana in Columbia." M. L. A. quarterly, 3 (June 1942), 23-26.

Brief description of Western Americana (including Missouriana) in libraries of State Historical Society of Missouri and University of Missouri.

4684. Presbyterian Historical Society. Primary source materials on Western life in America at the Presbyterian Historical Society... Philadelphia, Pa. [Philadelphia, 1948] 4p. (Presbyterian key, 4, Dec. 1948, no. 1)

4685. Priestley, H. I. "Manuscript collections in the Bancroft Library." Archives and libraries, (1939), 64-70.

4686. Riverside Public Library. The Colorado River and its tributaries; a bibliography of books, magazine articles, and government documents in the Riverside Public Library, comp. by Bertha L. Walsworth. Riverside, Calif.: Riverside Public Library, 1922. 137 l.

4687. Shelley, Fred. "The papers of Moreton Frewen." Library of Congress quarterly journal of current acquisitions, 6 (Aug. 1949), 15-20.

General description of collection of about 30,000 documents, dated 1823-1934, relating to Western cattle trade, etc.

4688. Streeter, Thomas W. "The Rollins collection of Western Americana." Princeton University Library chronicle, 9 (1948), 191-210.

Collection of 2,300 books, now in Princeton University Library, relating to Western cattle ranches, the Oregon Trail, and general works issued in 19th century.

4689. U. S. Library of Congress, Division of Bibliography. List of references on the Colorado River and its tributaries (supplementing Bibliography compiled in 1922 by Bertha L. Walsworth, Riverside Public Library, Riverside, California), comp. by Florence S. Hellman, Wash., March 27, 1926. 28p. [Supplementary list] Nov. 19, 1927. 23p. [Supplementary list] with special reference to the Boulder Dam. Aug. 16, 1935. 47p.

4690. Wagner, Henry R. The plains and the Rockies; a bibliography of original narratives of travel and adventure, 1800-1865. San Francisco: John Howell, 1921. 193p.

Author's note: "In the case of the rarer books I have also noted where copies can be found."

EARLY AMERICAN ALMANACS

4691. American Antiquarian Society. Exhibition of American almanacs, October, 1925, in honor of the gift to the society from Samuel L. Munson of his notable collection of almanacs, comp. by Charles L. Nichols. [Worcester, 1925] 11p. (Reprinted from American Antiquarian Society proceedings, n. s. 35 (1925), 210-18)

4692. Bates, Albert Carlos. "Check list of Connecticut almanacs, 1709-1850." American Antiquarian Society proceedings, n. s. 24 (1914), 93-215.

Locates copies in 14 libraries. Additions and corrections in Arthur J. Riley's Catholicism in New England to 1788; p. 395-98 (Catholic University of America Studies in American church history, v. 24)

4693. Chapin, Howard Millar. "Check list of Rhode Island almanacs, 1643-1850." American Antiquarian Society proceedings, n. s. 25 (1915), 19-54. Reprinted.

Locates copies in 7 American libraries and in British Museum, with emphasis on holdings of Rhode Island Historical Society and American Antiquarian Society.

4694. Heartman, Charles F. Preliminary check list of almanacs printed in New Jersey prior to 1850. Metuchen, N. J., 1929. 39p.
Locates copies in public and private collections.

4695. Jerabek, Esther. "Almanacs as historical sources." Minnesota history, 15 (1934), 444-49.
Describes almanacs in Minnesota Historical Society, containing material relating to various nationality groups in the United States.

4696. Long Island Historical Society. "Early American almanacs in the library of the Long Island Historical Society," by Alberta Pantle. Long Island Historical Society quarterly, 2 (1940), 99-108.
Society has 1,265 almanacs, about 125 before 1800.

4697. McMurtrie, Douglas C. "A check-list of Kentucky almanacs, 1789-1830." Kentucky State Historical Society register, 30 (1932), 237-59.
Copies located in 11 public and 2 private collections.

4698. Morrison, Hugh Alexander. Preliminary check list of American almanacs, 1639-1800. Wash.: Govt. Print. Off., 1907. 160p.
Locates copies in 17 libraries.

4699. New York Public Library. "Check list of New York City almanacs in the New York Public Library." New York Public Library bulletin, 5 (1901), 186-89.

4700. New York Public Library. "List of almanacs, ephemerides, etc., and of works relating to the calendar, in the New York Public Library." New York Public Library bulletin, 7 (1903), 246-67, 281-302.

4701. New York Public Library. "A list of New York almanacs, 1694-1850," comp. by Alexander James Wall. New York Public Library bulletin, 24 (1920), 287-96, 335-55, 389-413, 443-60, 508-19, 543-59, 620-41. Reprinted, 1921. 122p.
Locates copies in 53 public and private collections in United States and in British Museum.

4702. Nichols, Charles L., comp. "Checklist of Maine, New Hampshire and Vermont almanacs." American Antiquarian Society proceedings, n. s. 38 (1928), 63-163. Reprinted. 1929. 103p.
Chronological lists by states: Maine, 1787-1850; New Hampshire, 1757-1850; Vermont, 1784-1850. Locations in 10 public and private collections.

4703. Nichols, Charles L. "Notes on the almanacs of Massachusetts." American Antiquarian Society proceedings, n. s. 22 (1912), 15-134. Reprinted. 1912. 122p.
"Chronological list of Massachusetts almanacs, 1639-1850," p. 41-134, locates copies in 10 libraries. Additions and corrections appeared in Arthur J. Riley's Catholicism in New England to 1788, p. 384-95 (Catholic University of America studies in American church history, v. 24)

4704. Page, Alfred B. "John Tulley's almanacs, 1687-1702." Colonial Society of Massachusetts transactions, 13 (1912), 207-23.
Locates copies in 8 libraries.

4705. Paltsits, Victor Hugo. "The almanacs of Roger Sherman, 1750-1761." American Antiquarian Society proceedings, n. s. 18 (1907), 213-58.
Includes chronologically arranged bibliography, with locations of copies in various libraries.

4706. U. S. Library of Congress. Preliminary check list of American almanacs, 1639-1800, by H. A. Morrison. Wash.: Govt. Print. Off., 1907. 160p.

4707. Webber, Mabel L. "South Carolina almanacs to 1800." South Carolina historical and genealogical magazine, 15 (1914), 73-81.
Locates all known copies of titles in libraries of Charleston, S. C.

UNITED STATES STATE AND LOCAL HISTORY

General

4708. Boston Public Library. Index of articles

upon American local history in historical collections in the Boston Public Library, by A. P. C. Griffin. Boston: The Library, 1889. 225p.

4709. Mereness, Newton D. "Historical material in Washington of value to the state." Mississippi Valley historical review, 10 (1923), 47-53.

Brief survey of material for history of states to be found in federal archives.

4710. New York Public Library. "Check list of American county and state histories in the New York Public Library." New York Public Library bulletin, 5 (1901), 434-40.

Arranged by states.

Alabama

4711. Alabama History Commission. "An account of manuscripts, papers and documents pertaining to Alabama in official repositories beyond the state... within the state... in private hands. War records of Alabama." In: Alabama History Commission, Report, 1900, ed. by Thomas M. Owen. Montgomery: Brown, 1901, p. 45-369.

Gives locations.

4712. Historical Records Survey - Ala. Inventory of the county archives of Alabama. Birmingham: Ala. Historical Records Survey, 1938-42. 14v.

Covers Clay, Colbert, Conecuh, Cullman, Greene, Hale, Lauderdale, Lowndes, Madison, Marengo, Sumter, Talladega, Wilcox, and Winston counties.

4713. Owen, Thomas M. "Alabama archives." American Historical Association annual report, (1904), 487-553.

Lists material in the Alabama Department of Archives and History, and in other state and local offices.

4714. Owen, Thomas M. "A bibliography of Alabama." American Historical Association annual report, (1897), 777-1248.

Locates books on Alabama in University of Alabama and 10 other libraries.

Arizona

4715. Arizona, University, Library. A bibliographical list of books, pamphlets and articles on Arizona in the University of Arizona Library, prepared by Estelle Lutrell. Tucson: Arizona Daily Star, 1913. 60p. (Univ. of Arizona record, ser. 6, no. 10)

4716. Historical Records Survey - Ariz. Inventory of the county archives of Arizona. Phoenix: Historical Records Survey, 1938-41. 3v.

Covers Maricopa, Pima and Santa Cruz counties.

4717. Munk, J. A. Features of an Arizona library. Los Angeles: Times-Mirror Print. and Bind. House, 1926. 55p.

Description of rarest titles in Munk library of Arizoniana in Southwest Museum, Los Angeles.

4718. Southwest Museum. Bibliography of Arizona: being the record of literature collected by Joseph Amasa Munk, M. D., and donated by him to the Southwest Museum of Los Angeles, by Hector Alliott. Los Angeles: The Southwest Museum, 1914. 431p.

The third catalog of Munk collection; the first issued in 1900, and the second in 1908.

Arkansas

4719. Arkansas History Commission. Catalogue, Arkansas State History Museum, by Dallas T. Herdnon. Ft. Smith: Calvert-McBride, [1923] 53p.

Lists manuscripts.

4720. Arkansas History Commission. "The Kie Oldham papers (1860-1875)." Its: Bulletin of information, no. 5, (March 1913), 107-73.

Manuscripts relating to Civil War and post-Civil War period in Arkansas. In the possession of Arkansas History Commission.

4721. Arkansas History Commission. "List of state papers in the collections of L. C. Gulley, Samuel W. Williams and John E. Knight in the custody of the Commission." Its: Bulletin of information, no. 2 (June 1912), 17-51.

Cover years from 1814 to 1892 in Arkansas history.

4722. Historical Records Survey - Ark. Inventory of the county archives of Arkansas. Little Rock: Arkansas Historical Records Survey, 1939-42. 17v.

Covers Baxter, Benton, Carroll, Cleburne, Cleveland, Cross, Faulkner, Hot Springs, Izard, Jackson, Madison, Monroe, Montgomery, Polk, Saline, Scott, and Searcy counties.

4723. Matthews, Jim P. and Jones, V. L., comps. Arkansas books. Fayetteville, 1931. 31p. (Univ. of Ark. bulletin, General extension service, v. 25, no. 8)

Lists 540 items, those with stars in University of Arkansas Library. Includes books written by Arkansans and about Arkansas.

4724. Reynolds, John Hugh. "An account of manuscripts, papers and documents concerning Arkansas in public repositories beyond the state." Arkansas Historical Association publications, 1 (1906), 43-94.

Describes and lists resources in federal offices and in libraries and societies.

4725. Reynolds, John Hugh. Papers and documents of eminent Arkansans: an account of books, manuscripts, documents, and papers in private hands." Arkansas Historical Association publications, 1 (1906), 230-52.

Locates papers in private collections.

4726. Reynolds, John Hugh. "Public archives of Arkansas." American Historical Association annual report, 2 (1906), 23-51.

An inventory of source materials for Arkansas history in public offices.

4727. Shinn, Josiah H. and Reynolds, John H. "An account of manuscripts in public repositories within the state." Arkansas Historical Association publications, 1 (1906), 95-185.

Describes types of manuscripts to be found in Arkansas state offices, county and municipal offices, educational institutions, churches, and benevolent societies.

California

4728. California Historical Survey Commission. Guide to the county archives of California, by Owen C. Coy. Sacramento: California State Printing Office, 1919. 622p.

General description and lists of records to be found in various counties of California.

4729. California Library Association, Committee on Local History. California local history; a centennial bibliography, ed. by Ethel Blumann and Mabel W. Thomas. Stanford: Stanford, Univ. Press, 1950. 576p.

Locates copies in 98 California libraries.

4730. California State Library. Bibliotheca Californiae; a descriptive catalogue of books in the State Library of California, by Ambrose P. Dietz. Sacramento: D. W. Gelwicks, State Printer, 1870-71. 2v.

A list of material relating to California. V. 1, Law Library.

4731. California, University, Library. A bibliography of the history of California, 1510-1930, by Robert Ernest Cowan and Robert Granniss Cowan. San Francisco: J. H. Nash, 1933. 3v.

Cowan's collection, including about 3,700 of 5,000 items listed, purchased by University of California Library, Los Angeles, in 1936.

4732. Cooley, Laura C. "Selected list of source material in the Los Angeles Public Library: California - from the discovery to the end of the Spanish period." Southern California Historical Society annual publications, 11 (1918), 91-101.

4733. Gieger, Bayard J. Calendar of documents in the Santa Barbara Mission archives. Wash., 1947. 291p. (Academy of American Franciscan History publications, bibliographical series, v. 1)

Records 3,939 items, 1521-1913, in Archives of the Santa Barbara Mission, relating to California church history.

4734. Head, Edwin L. "Report on the archives of the state of California." American Historical Association annual report, (1915), 277-309.

Report on "the archives and records of the elective offices of the State government which are located... at Sacramento."

4735. Henry E. Huntington Library. "California books and manuscripts in the Huntington Library," by John C. Parish. Huntington Library bulletin, no. 7 (1935), 1-58.

General survey of Library's resources for history of California. Especially strong for 1840's and 1850's.

4736. Henry E. Huntington Library. California from legendary island to statehood; an exhibition. [San Marino, Calif., 1933] 27p.

Books and manuscripts selected from Huntington Library's Californiana collection.

4737. [Henry E. Huntington Library] A list of books, Californiana and the Pacific, in the library of Augustine S. MacDonald. Oakland, Calif.: Enquirer Pub. Co., 1903. 76p.

Acquired en bloc by Huntington Library, 1916.

4738. Henry E. Huntington Library. Los Angeles: the transition decades, 1850-70; an exhibition, by Robert G. Cleland. San Marino, 1937. 25p.

Describes 40 items on Los Angeles history exhibited at Huntington Library in 1937.

4739. Historical Records Survey - Calif. Calendar of the Major Jacob Rink Snyder collection of the Society of California Pioneers. San Francisco: Northern California Historical Records Survey Project, 1940. 107 numb. l.

4740. Historical Records Survey - Calif. Guide to depositories of manuscript collections in the United States: California. Los Angeles: Southern California Historical Records Survey, 1941. 76 numb. l.

4741. Historical Records Survey - Calif. Inventory of the Bixby collection in the Palos Verdes Library and Art Gallery. Los Angeles: Southern California Historical Records Survey, 1940. 43p.

4742. Historical Records Survey - Calif. Inventory of the county archives of California. San Francisco: Historical Records Survey, 1937-42. 11v.

Covers Alameda, Fresno, Kern, Marin, Mono, Napa, San Benito, San Francisco, San Luis Obispo, San Mateo, and Santa Clara counties.

4743. Historical Records Survey - Calif. Inventory of the county archives of California. Los Angeles: Historical Records Survey, 1940-41. 5v.

Includes Los Angeles Tax Collector's Office, San Diego tax and financial offices, and title-line inventories of San Bernardino, Santa Barbara, and Ventura counties.

4744. Historical Records Survey - Calif. Inventory of the state archives of California. Department of Industrial Relations, Division of Immigration and Housing. San Francisco: Northern California Historical Records Survey, 1941. 47p.

4745. McMurtrie, Douglas C. A California broadside of 1849; the original... preserved in the archives of the Department of State at Washington. Chicago: Privately printed, 1935. 5p.

Consists of a facsimile of one broadside only.

4746. Maggs Bros., booksellers, London. Bibliotheca Americana, pt. II. Father Kino, "The Apostle of California." London, 1922. (Catalogue, no. 432)

Collection acquired by Henry E. Huntington Library. Autograph letters of Father Eusebio F. Kino of his discoveries and explorations in California as a missionary, 1680-87.

4747. U. S. Library of Congress. California; the centennial of the Gold Rush and the first state constitution. An exhibit in the Library of Congress, Washington, D. C., November 12, 1949 to February 12, 1950. Wash.: Govt. Print. Off., 1949. 97p.

4748. Vail, R. W. G. "Gold fever: a catalogue of the California Gold Rush Centennial Exhibition." New-York Historical Society quarterly, 33 (1949), 237-71. Reprinted. 40p.

Lists manuscripts, books, pamphlets, broadsides, newspapers, maps, paintings, prints, cartoons, and museum objects. Includes some loaned material.

4749. Wagner, Henry Raup. "The Templeton Crocker collection of Californiana." California history quarterly, 19 (March 1940), 79-81.

Collection of books and manuscripts in California Historical Society.

4750. Wheat, Carl I. "The Schweitzer collection of Californiana." California Historical Society quarterly, 11 (1932), 184-87.

Collection in California Historical Society, mainly concerned with Sonoma County history.

Colorado

4751. Historical Records Survey - Colo. Inventory of the county archives of Colorado. Denver: Colorado Historical Records Survey, 1938-42. 16v.

Covers Alamosa, Arapahoe, Bent, Conejos, Costilla, Fremont, Garfield, Hinsdale, Larimer, Logan, Morgan, Phillips, Prowers, San Miguel, Washington, and Yuma counties.

4752 HISTORY

4752. MacDowd, Kennie. Bibliography of Colorado authors from pioneer days to the present. Denver: Denver Public Library, 1935. 311p.

Locates copies in Denver Public Library.

4753. Paxson, Frederic L. "The public archives of the state of Colorado." American Historical Association annual report, 1 (1903), 415-37.

Describes "various instruments of administration in the state, and... an account of the public records created and preserved by them."

4754. U. S. Library of Congress, Division of Bibliography. "A list of the more important works in the Library of Congress relating to Colorado." Wash., 1906. 17p. Typed. "Additional references." Oct. 20, 1924. 2p. Typed.

4755. Willard, James F. "The public archives of Colorado." American Historical Association annual report, 1 (1911), 365-92.

Revises and supplements Paxson report, appearing in American Historical Association annual report, for 1903.

Connecticut

4756. Bates, Albert Carlos. "Report on the public archives of Connecticut." American Historical Association annual report, 2 (1900), 26-36.

Describes unprinted archives in office of the Secretary of State, State Library, and Comptroller's office; mentions a few collections in other public offices.

4757. Connecticut Examiner of Public Records. Connecticut town records, June 30, 1930. Hartford: Connecticut State Library, 1930. 53p. (Connecticut State Library bulletin no. 15)

Lists all land and vital records in offices of town clerks of Connecticut.

4758. Connecticut Historical Society. "Connecticut local histories in Connecticut Historical Society and Watkinson Library." Connecticut Historical Society papers and report, (1895), 22-38.

4759. Connecticut Historical Society. Manuscripts of Connecticut interest exhibited by the Connecticut Historical Society and the Watkinson Library. Hartford: [The Society] 1935. 23p.

4760. Connecticut Historical Society. "Some of the manuscript collections in the Connecticut Historical Society." Connecticut Historical Society papers and report, (1893), 26-30.

4761. Connecticut State Library. Select list of manuscripts in the Connecticut State Library. Hartford: The Library, 1920. 32p. (Bulletin, no. 9) (Reprinted from the Report of the state librarian to the governor for the two years ended Sept. 30, 1916.)

A subject list of some manuscripts in the Library.

4762. Farrand, Max. "The papers of the Johnson family of Connecticut." American Antiquarian Society proceedings, n. s. 23 (1913), 237-46.

Describes and lists manuscripts and letters deposited in Library of Congress, Columbia University or Connecticut Historical Society, with locations.

4763. Historical Records Survey - Conn. Inventory of the town and city archives of Connecticut. New Haven: Connecticut Historical Records Survey, 1938-40. 4v.

Covers towns in Fairfield, Hartford, and New Haven counties.

4764. Litchfield Historical Society. Catalogue of books, papers and manuscripts of the Litchfield Historical Society... Litchfield, Conn., August 1, 1906. [N. Y.: Brewer Press, 1906] 115p.

4765. Mead, Nelson P. "Public archives of Connecticut: county, probate, and local records." American Historical Association annual report, 2 (1906), 53-127.

Town and county records described, with individual holdings given.

Delaware

4766. Dawson, Edgar. "Public archives of Delaware." American Historical Association annual report, 2 (1906), 129-48.

Includes lists of records of the Federal courts in Delaware, the state archives, and the county records.

4767. Delaware Historical Society. Catalogue. Wilmington, 1871. 23p.
Lists manuscripts and printed material.

4768. Delaware Public Archives Commission. A calendar of Ridgely family letters, 1742-1899, in the Delaware state archives, ed. and comp. by Leon de Valinger, Jr. and Virginia E. Shaw. Dover, Del., 1948. v. 1, 349p. + 36p. Index.
The first of 3 projected volumes.

4769. Historical Records Survey - Del. Inventory of the county archives of Delaware. Dover: Public Archives Commission of Delaware, 1941. 325p.
New Castle County only.

4770. Michigan, University, William L. Clements Library. New Sweden, 1638-1938; a guide to an exhibition of rare books and maps in the William L. Clements Library arranged in commemoration of the tercentenary of the Swedish settlements on the Delaware. Ann Arbor: Univ. of Michigan, 1938. 12p. (Bulletin, no. 28)
Annotated bibliography of 34 rare printed books and maps.

4771. Pennsylvania Historical Society, Gilpin Library. New Sweden, 1638-1938; being a catalogue of rare books and manuscripts relating to the Swedish colonization of the Delaware River. Philadelphia: The Society, 1938. 51p.
List, with descriptions, of 95 items from Gilpin Library and private collections.

4772. U. S. Library of Congress. Books, maps and prints relating to New Sweden; tercentenary commemorating the first settlement of the Swedes and the Finns on the Delaware, 1638-1938. [Wash.: Govt. Print. Off., 1938] 51p.

District of Columbia

4773. Bethel, Elizabeth. "Material in the National Archives relating to the early history of the District of Columbia." Columbia Historical Society records, 42-43 (1942), 169-87.

4774. Historical Records Survey - D. of C. Inventory of the municipal archives of the District of Columbia. Wash.: District of Columbia Historical Records Survey, 1940. 31p.

4775. Phillips, Philip Lee. The beginnings of Washington, as described in books, maps and views. Wash.: For the author, 1917. 78p.
Based upon Library of Congress collection.

4776. U. S. Library of Congress, Division of Bibliography. "History and description of Washington, D. C.: a bibliographical list." Wash., Mar. 10, 1927. 8p. Typed [Supplementary list] Feb. 21, 1936. 17p. Typed.

4777. U. S. Library of Congress, Division of Bibliography. "Social life in Washington: a bibliographical list." Wash., Mar. 17, 1930. 17p. Typed.

4778. U. S. Library of Congress, Division of Bibliography. The White House: a bibliographical list, comp. by Ann Duncan Brown. [Wash.] 1939. 42p.

4779. U. S. Library of Congress, General Reference and Bibliography Division. The United States capitol: a selected list of references, comp. by Ann Duncan Brown. Wash., 1949. 34p.

Florida

4780. Connor, Jeanette T. Colonial records of Spanish Florida; letters and reports of governors and secular persons. DeLand: Florida State Historical Soc., 1925-30. 2v.
Locates copies in Florida State Historical Society and in 7 collections outside the state.

4781. Drewry, Elizabeth B. "United States National Archives. Materials relating to Florida, 1789-1870." Florida historical quarterly, 23 (Oct. 1944), 97-115.

4782. Florida Library Association. "Preliminary checklist of Floridiana, 1500-1865, in the libraries of Florida." Florida library bulletin, 2 (April 1930), 1-16.
Locates books, manuscripts, newspapers, periodicals, photostats, pictures, and maps in 21 libraries.

4783. Historical Records Survey - Fla. Guide to depositories of manuscript collections in the United States: Florida. Jacksonville: Florida Historical Records Survey, 1940. 27p.

4784. Historical Records Survey - Fla. Inventory of the county archives of Florida.

Jacksonville: Historical Records Survey, 1938-42. 12v.

Covers Charlotte, Clay, Collier, Duval, Flagler, Hardee, Hendry, Leon, Okaloosa, Pinellas, Sarasota, and Wakulla counties.

4785. Historical Records Survey - Fla. Spanish land grants in Florida. Tallahassee: State Library Board, 1940-41. 5v.

4786. Julien C. Yonge Library. Catalogue of Julien C. Yonge collection, Pensacola, Florida. Assembled by Historical Records Survey, 1936-37. Recataloged, 1938. [Miami, Fla., 1938] 283 numb. l.

Collection now in University of Florida Library, Gainesville.

4787. McMurtrie, Douglas C. Ordinances of the Provinces of the Floridas, but relating specifically to East Florida, proclaimed by Major General Andrew Jackson and printed in pamphlet form at St. Augustine in 1821... the only known copy of the original preserved in the Library of Congress. Chicago: John Calhoun Club, 1941. 9p. [30]p.

4788. McMurtrie, Douglas C. Ordinances of the Provinces of the Floridas, but relating specifically to West Florida, as proclaimed by Major General Andrew Jackson and printed in broadside form at Pensacola in 1821, reproduced in facsimile from the only known copies preserved in the National Archives, Washington, D. C. Chicago: John Calhoun Club, 1941. 6p., [6]p.

Facsimiles of 6 ordinances, originals of which are among State Department papers in National Archives.

4789. Manning, Mabel M. "The East Florida papers in the Library of Congress." Hispanic American historical review, 10 (1930), 392-97.

Covers period 1784-1821.

4790. Manucy, Albert C. "Florida history (1650-1750) in the Spanish records of North Carolina State Department of Archives and History." Florida historical quarterly, 25 (1947), 319-32; 26 (1947), 77-91.

Describes collection of about 10,000 items copied from archives of Spain.

4791. Mowat, Charles L. "Material relating to British East Florida in the Gage papers and other manuscript collections in the William L. Clements Library." Florida historical quarterly, 18 (1939), 46-60.

4792. Robertson, James A. "Archival distribution of Florida manuscripts." Florida historical quarterly, 10 (July 1931), 35-50.

Description of sources of early Florida history in foreign archives, Washington and elsewhere.

4793. Robertson, James A. "The Spanish manuscripts of the Florida State Historical Society." American Antiquarian Society proceedings, n. s. 39 (1929), 16-37.

General description of Society's collection.

4794. Thomas, David Y. "Report on the public archives of Florida." American Historical Association annual report, 2 (1906), 149-58.

Territorial and state archives found in offices of governor, secretary of state and surveyor-general.

4795. Thomas, David Y. "Report upon the historic buildings, monuments, and local archives of St. Augustine, Florida." American Historical Association annual report, 1 (1905), 339-52.

Describes public archives of St. Augustine.

4796. U. S. Library of Congress. Florida's centennial... with a catalog of the exhibition. Wash.: Govt. Print. Off., 1946. 36p.

Lists 212 rare books, manuscripts, maps, photographs and prints of Floridiana in Library of Congress collections.

4797. U. S. Library of Congress, Division of Bibliography. "List of books relating to Florida." Wash., Nov. 30, 1921. 7p. Typed. [Supplementary list] July 24, 1933. 19p. Typed.

4798. Wroth, Lawrence C. "Source materials of Florida history in the John Carter Brown Library." Florida historical quarterly, 20 (1941), 3-46. Reprinted. 46p.

Georgia

4799. Brooks, Robert Preston, comp. A preliminary bibliography of Georgia history. Athens, Ga.: McGregor Co., 1910. 46p. (University of Georgia bulletin, 10 (1910), no. 10A, serial no. 127)

List of 300 items, indicating those held by the University of Georgia.

4800. Cobb, Maud Barker. "Check list of the Georgia archival material in certain offices of the capitol." Georgia Historical Association proceedings, 1 (1917), 49-63.

Documents listed are from files of: Adjutant-General, Comptroller-General, Executive Department, Secretary of State, Western and Atlantic Railroad Commission.

4801. Flisch, Julia A. "Report on the local records of Georgia." American Historical Association annual report, 2 (1906), 159-64.

Covers public records of Richmond County, including newspapers and giving locations.

4802. Georgia State Library. Finding list of books and pamphlets relating to Georgia and Georgians. Atlanta: The Library, 1928. 129p.

Locates copies in 4 Georgia libraries and the Library of Congress.

4803. Historical Records Survey - Ga. Inventory of the county archives of Georgia. Atlanta: Georgia Historical Records Survey, 1938-42. 9v.

Covers Chatham, Clinch, Cook, Dougherty, Echols, Jefferson, Lee, Muscogee, and Richmond counties.

4804. Mackall, Leonard L. "The Wymberley Jones DeRenne Georgia Library." Georgia historical quarterly, 2 (June 1918), 63-86.

Describes collection now in University of Georgia Library.

4805. Phillips, Ulrich B. "Georgia local archives." American Historical Association annual report, (1904), 555-96.

Records of Oglethorpe, Habersham and Clarke counties and town of Athens, with locations.

4806. Phillips, Ulrich B. "Public archives of Georgia." American Historical Association annual report, 1 (1903), 439-74.

A list of state archives preserved in the capitol.

4807. Savannah Historical Research Association. "A guide to the unpublished papers in the files of the Savannah Historical Research Association." Georgia Historical quarterly, 28 (1944), 213-23.

Describes some unpublished papers of interest to students of Georgia history.

4808. U. S. Library of Congress. An exhibition commemorating the settlement of Georgia, 1733-1948. Wash.: Govt. Print. Off., 1948. 92p.

Catalog of 575 rare books, manuscripts, maps, prints, photographs, newspapers and music owned by Library of Congress, National Archives, National Gallery of Art, Georgia State Department of Archives and History, and other Georgia institutions and individuals.

4809. Wegelin, Oscar, comp. Books relating to the history of Georgia in the library of Wymberley Jones DeRenne. [Savannah: Morning News] 1911. 268p.

Collection now in University of Georgia Library.

4810. Wymberley Jones DeRenne Georgia Library. Catalogue. Wormsloe, Ga., 1931. 3v.

Especially rich in historical and literary material relating to Georgia as a colony and as a state. Now in University of Georgia Library.

4811. Yenawine, Wayne Stewart. "A checklist of source materials for the counties of Georgia." Georgia historical quarterly, 32 (1948), 179-229.

Locates copies in University of Georgia, Georgia Historical Society, Emory University, Georgia State Department of Archives and History, Georgia State Library, Atlanta Public Library, and Savannah Public Library.

Idaho

4812. Historical Records Survey - Idaho. Inventory of the county archives of Idaho. Boise: Historical Records Survey, 1937-42. 10v.

Covers Bingham, Boundary, Clark, Kootenai, Lemhi, Minidoka, Nez Perce, Power, and Teton counties.

4813. Marshall, Thomas M. "Report on the public archives of Idaho." American Historical Association report, (1917), 137-72.

A survey of "the archives in the old and new capitol buildings," listing contents of some of vaults.

4814. Vedelen, Harold C. "Historical materials at the Southern Branch of the University of Idaho." Pacific Northwest quarterly, 27 (1936), 174-75.

Records 5 collections of papers relating to Idaho history, acquired in 1935-36 by Historical Museum of University of Idaho, Southern Branch.

Illinois

4815. Alvord, Clarence Walworth and Pease, Theodore Calvin. "The archives of the state of Illinois." American Historical Association annual report, (1909), 379-463. Reprinted, 1911.

A history and description of public archives of Illinois, with lists and holdings of each office.

4816. Alvord, Clarence Walworth. "Eighteenth century French records in the archives of Illinois." American Historical Association annual report, 1 (1905), 353-66. Reprinted, 1906.

Locates documentary records of Kaskaskia and Cahokia, 2 French villages in Illinois.

4817. Buck, Solon Justus. Travel and description, 1765-1865, together with a list of county histories, atlases, and biographical collections and a list of territorial and state laws. Springfield: Illinois State Historical Library, 1914. 514p. (Illinois State Historical Library collections, v. 9, Bibliographical series, v. 2)

Locates copies in Illinois State Historical Library, Library of Congress, Wisconsin State Historical Society, New York Public Library, etc. A bibliography of accounts of travel in Illinois.

4818. Burr, Nelson R. "The charter of the Mormon city of Nauvoo." Library of Congress quarterly journal of current acquisitions, 6 (Feb. 1949), 3-5.

Description of copy in Library of Congress of 1840 charter, granted by Illinois Legislature.

4819. Historical Records Survey - Ill. Guide to depositories of manuscript collections in Illinois. Prelim. ed. Chicago: Illinois Historical Records Survey, 1940. 55 numb. l.

4820. Historical Records Survey - Ill. Inventory of the county archives of Illinois. Chicago: Historical Records Survey, 1937-42. 34v.

Covers Adams, Brown, Carroll, Champaign (printed), Clark, Cumberland, Dewitt, Douglas, Effingham, Fayette, Franklin, Jackson, Jo Daviess, Knox, Livingston, Logan, Macon, Macoupin, Menard, Montgomery, Morgan, Moultrie, Ogle, Peoria, Piatt, Pike, Rock Island, Saline, Sangamon, Scott, Shelby, St. Clair, Stephenson, and Vermilion counties.

4821. Historical Records Survey - Ill. Inventory of the state archives of Illinois. State Council of Defense of Illinois, 1917-1919. Chicago: Ill. Hist. Rec. Survey, 1942. 53p.

4822. Illinois State Historical Library. Alphabetic catalog of the books, manuscripts, maps, pictures and curios of the Illinois State Historical Library. Authors, titles and subjects. 1900, comp. by Jessie Palmer Weber. Springfield, Ill., 1900. 363p. (Publication, no. 5)

4823. Illinois State Historical Library. "Historical materials in the State Historical Library at Springfield," by George N. Black. Illinois State Historical Library publication, 4 (1900), 51-55.

4824. Illinois State Historical Library. "Important purchase of books by the Illinois State Historical Library." Illinois State Historical Society journal, 2 (1910), 49-70.

List of books on early history of Illinois and the West.

4825. Illinois State Library. "Illinois - a bibliography." Illinois libraries, 30 (1948), 386-408.

Locates copies in Illinois State Library and several other collections.

4826. Illinois State Library, Archives Division. The Archives Division of the Illinois State Library, by William J. Stratton. Springfield: [Journal Printing Co.] 1932. 32p.

"Records on deposit... Jan. 1, 1930."

4827. Norton, Margaret C. "The archives of Illinois," by Margaret C. Norton and others. Illinois libraries:

1. "The General Assembly and its records," 22 (Jan. 1940), 25-29; (April 1940), 17-22; (May 1940), 22-28; (June 1940), 23-28.
2. "The J. Nick Perrin collection," 22 (Oct. 1940), 22-24.

3. "Lincoln collection: Illinois State Archives," 25 (Feb. 1943), 114-25.
4. "Illinois & Michigan canal records," 25 (Oct. 1943), 340-41.
5. "Census records in the Archives Department of the Illinois State Library," 26 (May 1944), 178-84.
6. "Cahokia marriage records," 28 (May 1946), 260-72.
7. "Marriage records of St. Clair County, 1791-1807," 28 (June 1946), 321-34.
8. "St. Clair County marriage records, 1807-1810," 28 (Oct. 1946), 436-42.
9. "Letterheads, 1854-1900," (Feb. 1947), 106-16.
10. "Winning our freedom; an exhibit," 30 (Nov. 1948), 455-65.
11. "Significant documents in Illinois history," 31 (Feb. 1949), 126-30; 31 (March 1949), 159-64; 31 (April 1949), 187-96; 31 (May 1949), 223-27; 31 (June 1949), 263-68.

Descriptions and lists of materials in the Archives Department of the Illinois State Library.

4828. Pease, Theodore Calvin. The county archives of the state of Illinois. Springfield: Illinois State Historical Library, 1915. 730p. (Illinois State Historical Library collections, v. 3)

A survey and description of county records of Illinois, with specific holdings listed under each county.

Indiana

4829. Henley, Lillian E. "Bibliography of town and city histories in the Indiana State Library." Indiana magazine of history, 6 (1910), 91-95.

4830. Historical Records Survey - Ind. Inventory of the county archives of Indiana. Indianapolis: Indiana Historical Records Survey, 1936-42. 22v.

Covers Allen, Blackford, Boone, Clay, Delaware, Fulton, Greene, Howard, Jay, La Porte, Marion, Marshall, Monroe, Morgan, Posey, St. Joseph, Shelby, Tippecanoe, Tipton, Vanderburgh, Warrick, and Wells counties.

4831. Howe, Daniel Wait. A descriptive catalogue of the official publications of the territory and state of Indiana, from 1800 to 1890. Indianapolis: Bowen-Merrill Co., 1891. 91p. (Indiana Historical Society pamphlet, no. 5)

4832. Hurst, Roger A. "The New Harmony manuscript collection." Indiana magazine of history, 37 (March 1941), 45-49.

Description of collection of 14,000 manuscripts in the Workingmen's Institute Library, New Harmony, Ind. Manuscripts deal with the history of New Harmony, Ind., since 1814.

4833. Indiana State Library. "County histories." Indiana State Library bulletin, 11 (Sept. 1916), 17-25.

Bibliography of Indiana county histories in Indiana State Library.

4834. Indiana State Library. Reading list on Indiana in the Civil War. Indianapolis: W. B. Burford, 1902. 12p. (Indiana State Library bulletin, 3d ser. no. 9, May 1902)

4835. Indiana State Library. "A select bibliography of Indiana historical material in the Indiana State Library." Indiana State Library bulletin, 10 (Sept. 1915), 2-16.

4836. Lindley, Harlow. "Report on the archives of the state of Indiana." American Historical Association annual report, (1910), 315-30.

Brief survey of records available in the state offices, exclusive of printed records or papers.

4837. New Harmony Workingmen's Institute Library. List of books and pamphlets in a special collection in the library of the Workingmen's Institute, New Harmony, Ind., comp. by Rena Reese. [New Harmony] 1909. 21p.

"Collection relating to the early history of New Harmony and to Robert Owen and his disciples. Early New Harmony prints have also been listed."

4838. South Bend Public Library. Books about Indiana in the Public Library of South Bend, with a list of Indiana writers represented in the Public Library. [South Bend, Ind., 1920] 28p.

4839. Stoler, Mildred C. "Indiana Historical Society manuscript collections." Indiana magazine of history, 30 (1934), 267-69.

Brief description of collections.

4840. Stoler, Mildred C. "Manuscript accessions - Indiana State Library." Indiana magazine of history, 29 (1933), 44-47.

4841. Stoler, Mildred C. "Manuscripts in Indiana State Library." Indiana magazine of history, 27 (1931), 236-39.

4842. Wish, Harvey. "New Indiana archival documents." Indiana magazine of history, 32 (1936), 360-69; 33 (1937), 62-74.
 A list of 5,887 items relating to Indiana history, now in Indiana State Library.

Iowa

4843. Historical Records Survey - Iowa. Guide to depositories of manuscript collections in the United States: Iowa. Des Moines: Iowa Hist. Rec. Survey, 1940. 47 numb. 1.

4844. Historical Records Survey - Iowa. Guide to manuscript collections in Iowa. Des Moines: Iowa Historical Records Survey, 1940. V. 1. 57p.

4845. Historical Records Survey - Iowa. Inventory of the county archives of Iowa. Des Moines: Iowa Historical Records Survey, 1938-42. 11v.
 Covers Carroll, Cherokee, Dallas, Dubuque, Ida, Jasper, Montgomery, Polk, Sac, Taylor, and Woodbury counties.

4846. Mott, Frank Luther. Literature of pioneer life in Iowa, an address delivered before the Academy of Science and Letters at Sioux City in March 1923 with a partially annotated bibliography. Iowa City: State Historical Society of Iowa, 1923. 89p.
 Locates copies in 4 libraries.

4847. Shambaugh, Benjamin F. "Report on the public archives of Iowa." American Historical Association annual report, 2 (1900), 39-46.
 General description of archives in public offices of state.

4848. U. S. Library of Congress. Iowa centennial exhibition, December 28, 1946 - April 27, 1947. Wash.: Govt. Print. Off., 1947. 84p.
 Catalog of 561 rare books, manuscripts, maps, prints, photographs, newspapers, and music from Library of Congress, National Archives, National Gallery of Art, and certain Iowa institutions.

Kansas

4849. Becker, Carl. "Public archives of Kansas." American Historical Association annual report, (1904), 597-601.
 "A few of the most important of the printed archives are given here to indicate to what extent the archives have been published."

4850. Hill, Esther Clark. "The Pratt collection." Kansas historical quarterly, 1 (1932), 83-88.
 Papers relating to John G. Pratt, missionary printer and Indian agent in Kansas, 1837-70, now in Kansas State Historical Society.

4851. Historical Records Survey - Kan. Inventory of the county archives of Kansas. Topeka: Kansas Historical Records Survey, 1937-42. 14v.
 Covers Bourbon, Cherokee, Franklin, Gove, Graham, Gray, Greenwood, Johnson, Montgomery, Morris, Osage, Phillips, Seward, and Shawnee counties.

4852. Kansas State Historical Society Library. Catalog of the Kansas territorial and state documents in the library of the State Historical Society, 1854-1898, by Zu Adams. Topeka: State Printer, 1900. 93p. (Issued originally in Transactions of the Kansas State Historical Society, 6 (1897-1900), 383-475)

4853. Kansas State Historical Society Library. "Kansas books; a typical selection of books and pamphlets from the Kansas section of the library of the Kansas State Historical Society." In: Kansas State Historical Society, 14th biennial report, 1902-1904, p. 99-117.

Kentucky

4854. Coleman, J. Winston, Jr. A bibliography of Kentucky history. Lexington: Univ. of Kentucky Press, 1949. 516p.
 Locates copies in 113 public and private collections.

4855. Filson, John. Filson's Kentucke; a facsimile reproduction of the original Wilmington edition of 1784, with paged critique, sketch of Filson's life and bibliography, by Willard Rouse Jillson... Exact reprint of the first map of 1784. Louisville, Ky.: J. P. Morgan & Co., 1930. 198p.

Describes 11 known copies.

4856. Henry, Edward Atwood. "The Durrett collection now in the Library of the University of Chicago." Bibliographical Society of American papers, 8 (1914), 57-94. Reprinted. 38p.

Collection of Kentuckiana.

4857. Historical Records Survey - Ky. Inventory of the county archives of Kentucky. Louisville: Historical Records Survey, 1937-41. 9v.

Covers Anderson, Breckenridge, Carlisle, Fayette, Jessamine, Knox, Laurel, McCreary, and Meade counties.

4858. Jillson, Willard Rouse. "Early Kentucky history in manuscript - a brief account of the Draper and Shane collections." Kentucky State Historical Society register, 33 (1935), 137-50.

Draper and part of Shane collection are held by the Wisconsin State Historical Society. Remainder of Shane material, by Presbyterian Historical Society, Philadelphia.

4859. Jillson, Williard Rouse. The Kentuckie country; an historical exposition of land interest in Kentucky prior to 1790, coupled with facsimile reproductions of the London 1786 brochure of Alexander Fitzroy, and the "Whatman" edition of John Filson's map... with critical comment on Filson's map, by Lawrence Martin. Wash., D. C.: H. L. & J. B. McQueen, 1931. 63p.

Locates and describes rare copies of Filson's map in the United States and England.

4860. Jillson, Willard Rouse. "Kentucky acts and legislative journals 1792-1800; a preliminary locating index." Kentucky State Historical Society register, 35 (1937), 196-97.

Gives locations of 32 titles in Kentucky State Historical Society, State Library or the Court of Appeals, and/or one private collection.

4861. Jillson, Willard Rouse. Kentucky history; a check and finding list of the principal published and manuscript sources of the general, regional, and county history of the Commonwealth, 1729-1936. Louisville, 1936. 96p.

Copies located in 7 Kentucky libraries.

4862. Jillson, Willard Rouse. The Kentucky land grants; a systematic index to all of the land grants recorded in the State Land Office at Frankfort, Kentucky, 1782-1924. Louisville: Standard Print. Co., 1925. 1,844p. (Filson Club publications, no. 33)

Records are in the Kentucky Land Office.

4863. Jillson, Willard Rouse. Old Kentucky entries and deeds; a complete index to all of the earliest land entries, military warrants, deeds and wills. Louisville: Standard Printing Co., 1926. 571p. (Filson Club publications, no. 34)

An index to 2 groups of old manuscript documents: one in office of Clerk of the Court of Appeals; the other in Kentucky Land Office.

4864. Kentucky, Secretary of State. Catalogue records, documents, papers, etc. Kentucky governors, 1792-1926. Frankfort, 1926. 185p.

Archives now in Kentucky Historical Society.

4865. Kentucky State Historical Society. Catalogue no. 5 of Kentucky State Historical Society from 1914 to 1917 September, comp. by Sally Jackson. Frankfort: State Journal Co., 1917. 83p.

Lists books, pamphlets, periodicals, newspapers, paintings, and curios held by the Society.

4866. Lexington Public Library. Books relating to Kentucky history in the Lexington Public Library. Kentuckiana. [Lexington, Ky., 1913] [4]p.

4867. McMurtrie, Douglas C. "A bibliography of eighteenth century Kentucky broadsides." Filson Club history quarterly, 10 (1936), 23-30.

Describes 30 broadsides, located in 5 American libraries.

4868. Myers, Irene T. "Report on the archives of the state of Kentucky." American Historical Association annual report, (1910), 331-64.

Describes state archives to be found in state capitol at Frankfort. Lists important holdings of some departments.

4869. Staples, Charles R. "The Bryan family papers." Kentucky State Historical Society register, 34 (1936), 196-200.

A list of 108 papers of Bryan family, now

in Shane collections of Wisconsin State Historical Society or the Presbyterian Historical Society at Philadelphia. Relate to pioneer period of Kentucky history.

4870. Staples, Charles R. "New discoveries amongst old records." Kentucky State Historical Society register, 33 (1935), 307-25.

Describes materials for Kentucky history in governmental, legal, military, and county records, and in private collections.

4871. Tenney, S. M. "Materials on Kentucky history in the library of Historical Foundation of the Presbyterian and Reformed Churches, Montreat, North Carolina." Filson Club history quarterly, 5 (April 1931), 99-111.

Lists official records, books, periodicals, etc., on Kentucky.

4872. U. S. Library of Congress, Division of Bibliography. "List of books relating to Kentucky (supplementary to bibliography in Robert McNutt McElroy's Kentucky in the nation's history. N. Y.: Moffat, Yard and Co., 1909, p. 547-577)." Wash., Mar. 23, 1925. 26p. Typed.

4873. Wisconsin State Historical Society Library. Calendar of the Kentucky papers of the Draper collection of manuscripts. Madison: The Society, 1925. 624p. (Publications of the State Historical Society of Wisconsin, Calendar series II)

Louisiana

4874. Alabama, University, Library. A bibliography of Louisiana books and pamphlets in the T. P. Thompson collection of the University of Alabama Library, comp. by Donald E. Thompson. University: Univ. of Ala. Press, 1947. 210p.

Lists 3,339 items of books, pamphlets, collections of pictures, brochures, etc.

4875. Dart, Henry Plauche. "Cabildo archives." Louisiana historical quarterly, 3 (Jan. 1920), 71-99.

A selection of documents, with translations, from Louisiana Historical Society's archives at Cabildo or from the private collection of Gaspard Cusachs in New Orleans. Depicts life and history of early Louisiana, 1725-70.

4876. "Guide to depositories of manuscript collections in Louisiana." Louisiana historical quarterly, 24 (Apr. 1941), 305-53.

Lists and describes collections in Louisiana institutions.

4877. Historical Records Survey - La. Calendar of manuscript collections in Louisiana: Series I. The Department of Archives: No. 1. Taber collection. University, La.: Dept. of Archives, La. State Univ., 1938. 12p.

4878. Historical Records Survey - La. Guide to depositories of manuscript collections in Louisiana. 2d ed. University: Dept. of Archives, La. State Univ., 1941. 50 numb. l. First edition appeared in Louisiana historical quarterly, 24 (1941), 305-53.

4879. Historical Records Survey - La. Guide to the manuscript collections in Louisiana. The Department of Archives, Louisiana State University, ed. by William Ransom Hogan. University, La.: The Department of Archives, 1940. v. 1. 55 numb l.

"A guide to the important personal and business papers acquired... by the Dept. of Archives during its first four years."

4880. Historical Records Survey - La. Inventory of municipal and town archives: Louisiana. University: Dept. of Archives, La. State Univ., 1941-42. 2v.

For Franklinton and Thibodaux.

4881. Historical Records Survey - La. Inventory of the parish archives of Louisiana. University, La.: Dept. of Archives, La. State Univ., 1937-42. 21v.

Includes Allen, Assumption, Beauregard, Bossier, Calcasien, Grant, Jefferson, Lafayette, Lafourche, Morehouse, Natchitoches, Orleans, Ouachita, Plaquemines, Sabine, St. Bernard, St. Charles, Terrebone, Washington, and Webster parishes.

4882. Historical Records Survey - La. Inventory of the state archives of Louisiana. The judiciary. University, La.: Dept. of Archives, La. State Univ., 1941-42. 3v.

Covers the Superior Court of the Territory of Orleans, the Supreme Court of Louisiana, and the Courts of Appeal of Louisiana.

4883. Historical Records Survey - La. Inventory of state archives: Louisiana. The Lieutenant Governor. 1941. 11p.

4884. Illinois State Historical Library. "List of the editions of the works of Louis Hennepin in the Library." Illinois State Historical Society journal, 2, no. 4 (1910), 71-73.

Lists 11 editions of Hennepin's Description of Louisiana, The new discovery, and The new voyage.

4885. Kendall, John S. "Historical collections in New Orleans." North Carolina historical review, 7 (1930), 463-76.

Survey of manuscripts, newspapers, etc., relating to Louisiana history in New Orleans libraries.

4886. Louisiana Historical Society. A catalogue of the colonial exhibit of the Louisiana Historical Society and loan exhibit of members and friends, consisting of books, pamphlets, documents, maps, charts, views, pictures, plans, etc., New Orleans, December 20th, 1903, centennial transfer of Louisiana. [New Orleans, 1903] 32p.

Owners of 1,043 items listed.

4887. Louisiana State Museum. Handbook of information concerning its historic buildings and the treasures they contain, prep. by Robert Glenk. New Orleans, 1941. 400p.

Lists some items in Museum library, including source books on Louisiana history, p. 176-85.

4888. Porteus, Laura L. "Index to the Spanish judicial records of Louisiana." Louisiana Historical quarterly, 6 (1923)-29, no. 1 (1946). Continued in each quarterly issue from v. 6, no. 1, through v. 29, no. 1.

Locates copies in public offices in Louisiana.

4889. Scroggs, William O. "Report on the archives of the state of Louisiana." American Historical Association annual report, (1912), 275-93.

General description of archives in public offices in New Orleans and Baton Rouge.

4890. Swearingen, M. "The John McDonogh papers." Southwest review, 19 (1934), 348-50.

A collection of 5,000 manuscripts held by Tulane University library, relating chiefly to Louisiana economic and social conditions in first half of 19th century.

4891. Thompson, Thomas Payne. Index to a collection of Americana (relating principally to Louisiana), art and miscellanea, all included in the private library of T. P. Thompson. New Orleans: Perry and Buckley Co., 1912. 203p.

Now in University of Alabama Library.

Maine

4892. Hall, Drew Bert. "Reference list on Maine local history." New York State Library bulletin, 63 (1901), 775-917.

Resources of New York State Library and Bowdoin College Library in Maine local history.

4893. Historical Records Survey - Maine. Inventory of municipal and town archives: Maine. Portland: Hist. Records Survey, 1939-40. 7v.

Covers towns in Franklin, Hancock, and Piscataquis counties.

4894. Johnson, Allen. "Report on the archives of the state of Maine." American Historical Association annual report, 1 (1908), 257-318.

Survey of the state archives, county archives, proprietary records and local records.

4895. Maine. University, Dept. of History and Government. A reference list of manuscripts relating to the history of Maine, Parts I-III. Orono: Univ. of Maine Press, 1938-41. 3v. (University of Maine studies. Second series, no. 45) Index in Maine bulletin, 43 (Feb. 1941), no. 8.

Locates source materials on Maine in many local and out-of-state libraries. Excludes "archival material."

4896. Noyes, R. Webb. A guide to the study of Maine local history. [Ann Arbor, Mich.] 1936. 88p.

Locates copies in Bowdoin College, Bangor Public Library, Library of Congress, Maine State Library, University of Michigan, and compiler's own collection.

Maryland

4897. Catholic University of America Library. The Michael Jenkins collection of works on the history of Maryland. Wash.: The University, 1913. 28p.

Lists about 200 titles in Catholic University Library.

4898. Enoch Pratt Free Library. Catalog of the Cator collection of Baltimore views, 1933. [Baltimore, 1933] 47 numb. l.

4899. Historical Records Survey - Md. Inventory of the county archives of Maryland. Baltimore: Historical Records Survey, 1937-41. 8v.

Covers Allegany, Anne Arundel, Carroll, Jarrett, Howard, Montgomery, Washington, and Wicomico counties.

4900. Hoyt, William D., Jr. "The papers of the Maryland State Colonization Society." Maryland historical magazine, 32 (1937), 247-71.

Cover period from 1827 to 1875. Papers now held by Maryland Historical Society.

4901. Maryland Court of Appeals. Catalogue of manuscripts and printed matter in the possession of the Court of Appeals of Maryland, November 1926. [Baltimore: Daily Record Co., 1926] 29p.

Maryland manuscript and printed records dating from the 17th century.

4902. Maryland Hall of Records. Index holdings. [Annapolis, 1949?] 9p. (Bulletin, no. 8)

Lists unpublished indexes, in the Maryland Hall of Records, to probate, land, marriage, military service, and miscellaneous records.

4903. Maryland Hall of Records Commission. Calendar of Maryland state papers. No. 1: The black books. Annapolis, 1943. 297p. (Publications, no. 1)

Calendar of over 1,500 miscellaneous papers of the colonial period, 1630-1785.

4904. Maryland Hall of Records Commission. Calendar of Maryland state papers. No. 2, the bank stock papers, by Morris L. Radoff. Annapolis, 1947. 68p. (Publications, no. 5)

Papers in Maryland Hall of Records, 1780-1809, relating to Maryland diplomatic-financial affairs.

4905. Maryland Hall of Records Commission. Calendar of Maryland state papers. No. 3, the brown books, by Roger Thomas. Annapolis, 1946. 180p. (Publications, no. 6)

Largely official correspondence of Revolutionary period.

4906. Maryland Hall of Records Commission. Catalogue of archival material, Hall of Records, State of Maryland. Annapolis, 1942. 161p. (Publications, no. 2)

In addition to descriptions of archives, lists newspaper files, church records, and miscellaneous manuscript collections.

4907. Maryland Hall of Records Commission. Land Office and Prerogative Court records of colonial Maryland, by Elisabeth Hartsook and Gust Skordas. [Annapolis, 1946] 124p. (Publications, no. 4)

Collections in Maryland Hall of Records on colonial land and probate records.

4908. Maryland Historical Society. The Calvert papers. Number one... together with a calendar of the papers recovered, and selections from the papers. Baltimore, 1889. 334p. (Maryland Historical Society Fund publication, no. 28)

Calendar, p. 59-126, lists 17th and 18th century documents relating to Maryland, boundary disputes between colonies, and Calvert family.

4909. Maryland Historical Society. "Logs and papers of Baltimore privateers, 1812-15," by William D. Hoyt, Jr. Maryland historical magazine, 34 (1939), 165-74.

Describes Maryland Historical Society collection.

4910. Scisco, Louis Dow. "Baltimore county records of 1665-1667." Maryland historical magazine, 24 (1929), 342-48.

Records in courthouse archives.

4911. Scisco, Louis Dow. "Colonial records." Maryland Historical magazine: Charles County, 21 (1926), 261-70. Kent County, 21 (1926), 356-61. Anne Arundel County, 22 (1927), 62-67. Baltimore County, 22 (1927), 245-59. Somerset County, 22 (1927), 349-56. Talbot County, 22 (1927), 186-89. Cecil County, 23 (1928), 20-26. Dorchester County, 23 (1928), 243-46. Prince George's County, 24 (1929), 17-23. Queen Anne's County, 24 (1929), 224-28.

Digests of court records of various Maryland counties in the 17th and 18th centuries, in courthouse archives.

4912. Semmes, Raphael. "Vignettes of Maryland history from the Society's collection of broadsides." Maryland historical magazine, 39 (1944), 95-126; 40 (1945), 24-53.

Broadsides in Maryland Historical Society collection on agriculture, industry, dueling, transportation, politics and military affairs, 17th to 19th centuries.

4913. Society for the History of the Germans in Maryland Library. Catalog of the library of the Society for the History of the Germans in Maryland. 1907. [Baltimore, Press of Schneidereith & Sons, 1907] 47p.

4914. U. S. Library of Congress, Division of Bibliography. "A selected list of references on Maryland (with special reference to its government, finance, economic and social conditions)." Wash., Nov. 4, 1933. 18p. Typed.

Massachusetts

4915. Beebe Town Library. Histories of the Commonwealth of Massachusetts, its counties, cities and towns in the Lucius Beebe Memorial Library, Wakefield, Massachusetts. [Wakefield] 1930. n. p.

Arranged by localities.

4916. Bolton, Charles Knowles. "Some works relating to Brookline, Massachusetts, from its settlement to the year 1900." Brookline Historical Publication Society publications, nos. 19-20 (1900), 89-179.

Locates copies in 7 libraries.

4917. Boston Public Library. Boston and the Bay Colony; a tercentenary exhibit of rare books, broadsides and manuscripts. Boston: The Library, 1930. 31p.

Description of exhibit of over 250 items illustrating the history of Boston and the Bay Colony, especially during 17th century. Items are from Boston Public Library collection.

4918. Boston Public Library. The Pilgrims: a selected list of works in the Public Library of the City of Boston. A contribution to the tercentenary celebration, comp. by Mary Alice Tenney. Boston: The Library, 1920. 43p.

4919. Boston Public Library. Tercentenary celebration, 1630-1930. The Massachusetts Bay Colony and Boston; a selected list of works in the Public Library of the City of Boston. Boston: The Library, 1930. 165p.

A collection relating to Boston, England, and Boston, Mass.

4920. Cambridge Public Library. List of books in the Cambridge Public Library relating to the Pilgrim fathers and the settlement of Plymouth, Mass. in 1620. [Cambridge, Mass., 1920] 16p.

4921. Davis, Andrew McFarland. "Calendar of the papers and records relating to the Land Bank of 1740, in the Massachusetts archives and Suffolk court files." Colonial Society of Massachusetts publications, 4 (1910), 1-121.

I. Massachusetts archives; II. Suffolk court files.

4922. Davis, Andrew McFarland. "Report on the public archives of Massachusetts." American Historical Association annual report, 2 (1900), 47-59.

Primarily a study of archives kept in office of Secretary of the Commonwealth of Massachusetts.

4923. Edmonds, John H. "The Massachusetts archives." American Antiquarian Society proceedings, n. s. 31 (1921), 18-60.

History and description of contents of and facilities for archives in the State House, Boston, Mass.

4924. Flagg, Charles Allcott. A guide to Massachusetts local history; being a bibliographic index to the literature of the towns, cities and counties of the state, including books, pamphlets, articles in periodicals and collected works, books in preparation, historical manuscripts, newspaper clippings, etc. Salem, Mass.: Salem Press Company [1907] 256p.

Locates copies, mainly in Library of Congress or Library of New England Historic and Genealogical Society.

4925. Ford, Worthington Chauncey and Matthews, Albert. A bibliography of the laws of the Massachusetts Bay, 1641-1776. Cambridge, 1907. 186p. (Reprinted from Colonial Society of Massachusetts publications, 4 (1910), 291-480)

Copies located in 12 libraries.

4926. Ford, Worthington Chauncey. A bibliography of the Massachusetts House journals, 1715-1776. Cambridge: Priv. printed, 1905.

87p. (Reprinted from Colonial Society of Massachusetts publications, 4 (1910), 201-89)
Locates copies in 8 libraries.

4927. Historical Records Survey - Mass. A calendar of the General Henry Knox papers, Chamberlain collection, Boston Public Library. Boston: Historical Records Survey, 1939. 19p.
A part of Chamberlain collection of autographs in Boston Public Library.

4928. Historical Records Survey - Mass. Guide to depositories of manuscript collections in Massachusetts. Prelim. ed. Boston: Historical Records Survey, 1939. 160p.

4929. Historical Records Survey - Mass. Guide to the manuscript collections in the Worcester Historical Society. Boston: Historical Records Survey, 1941. 56p.

4930. Historical Records Survey - Mass. Inventory of municipal and town archives: Massachusetts. Boston: Historical Records Survey, 1939-42. 23v.
Covers towns and cities in Berkshire, Franklin, Hampden, Middlesex, Norfolk, Suffolk, and Worcester counties.

4931. Historical Records Survey - Mass. An inventory of the county archives of Massachusetts. Boston: Historical Records Survey, 1937. 370 numb. 1.
Essex County only.

4932. Historical Records Survey - Mass. Proclamations of Massachusetts issued by governors and other authorities, 1620-1936. Boston, 1937. 2v.
V. 1, 1620-1775; v. 2, 1776-1936.

4933. Illinois, University, Library. "The Pilgrims; a selected list of works in the University of Illinois Library," comp. by Alice S. Johnson and Fanny Dunlap. [Urbana]: University of Illinois, 1920. 26 l. Typed.

4934. Massachusetts Historical Society. Handbook of the Massachusetts Historical Society, 1791-1948. Boston, 1949. 182p.
List of collections of manuscripts owned by or deposited in Society, p. 118-41; files of early newspapers, p. 142-43; description of library, p. 143-44.

4935. Massachusetts Historical Society. Handbook of the publications and photostats, 1792-1935. Boston, 1937. 144p.
Lists refer to items in Society's collection.

4936. Massachusetts Historical Society Library. Catalogue of the library of the Massachusetts Historical Society. Boston: Printed for the Society, 1859-60. 2v.
The third catalog issued by Society. Others appeared in 1796, 1811.

4937. Morison, Samuel Eliot. "The custom-house records in Massachusetts, as a source of history." Massachusetts Historical Society proceedings, 54 (1922), 324-31.
Inventory of records important for history of commerce, fishing, shipping and shipbuilding since 1789.

4938. New York Public Library. "The Massachusetts Bay exhibition," comp. by Charles Flowers McCombs. New York Public Library bulletin, 35 (1931), 465-71. Reprinted with title, Massachusetts Bay: the founding and early years of the colony. 9p.
Catalog of an exhibition.

4939. Pilgrim Society Library. A catalogue of the collections of the Pilgrim Society in Pilgrim Hall, Plymouth, Massachusetts, comp. by Rose T. Briggs. Plymouth, Mass.: The Society, 1941. 79p.
Includes list of books of Pilgrims, maps, charts and prints.

4940. Shattuck, Frederick Cheever. "Cheever papers." Massachusetts Historical Society proceedings, 55 (1923), 286-89.
Describes collection of 18th century manuscripts.

4941. Swift, Lindsay. "The Massachusetts election sermons; an essay in descriptive bibliography." Colonial Society of Massachusetts publications, 1 (1897), 388-451. Reprinted, 68p.
Locates a few manuscripts and collections of election sermons in various libraries.

Michigan

4942. Conger, John L. "Report on the public archives of Michigan." American Historical Association annual report, 1 (1905), 369-76.

Manuscript records of interest to students of Michigan history, to be found in the public offices.

4943. Detroit Public Library. Antoine de la Mothe Cadillac and Detroit before the conspiracy of Pontiac; a bibliography. [Detroit]: The Library, 1912. 30p.
Material in Detroit Public Library.

4944. Detroit Public Library. "Descriptive list of the papers of Governor Austin Blair." Michigan history magazine, 1 (1917), 133-48.

4945. Detroit Public Library. "Father Gabriel Richard." Detroit Public Library, Burton Historical Collection leaflet, 1 (March 1923), 81-84.
Issues of his press.

4946. Doelle, J. A. "Historical materials owned by the Keweenaw Historical Society, Houghton, Michigan; bibliography." Michigan history magazine, 1 (1917), 129-55.
Books, documents, mining reports and maps relating primarily to Upper Michigan.

4947. Historical Records Survey - Mich. Guide to manuscript collections in Michigan. Detroit: Michigan Historical Records Survey Project, 1941-42. 2v.
V. 1, Michigan historical collections, University of Michigan; v. 2, University of Michigan collections (exclusive of those in Michigan historical collections). A guide to the 427 historical collections in the University of Michigan, and to the University of Michigan manuscript collection.

4948. Historical Records Survey - Mich. Guide to manuscript depositories in the United States: Michigan. Detroit: Michigan Historical Records Survey, 1940. 74 numb. 1.

4949. Historical Records Survey - Mich. Inventory of municipal and town archives: Michigan, Wayne County. Detroit: Michigan Historical Records Survey, 1940-42. 5v.
Covers City Treasurer, Arts Commission, Department of Recreation and Recorders Court in Detroit, and Office of Engineer in Hamtramck.

4950. Historical Records Survey - Mich. Inventory of the county archives of Michigan. Detroit: Historical Records Survey, 1937-42. 12v.
Covers Alger, Alpena, Baraga, Bay, Calhoun, Cheboygan, Genesee, Iosco, Iron, Jackson, Marquette, and Muskegon counties.

4951. Historical Records Survey - Mich. Inventory of the state archives of Michigan. State police. Detroit: Michigan Historical Records Survey, 1941. 46p.

4952. Marquette County Historical Society. Catalog of the... Society. Ishpeming, Mich.: Iron Ore Press, 1928. 45p.
Books, pamphlets, manuscripts, maps, periodicals and newspapers relating to Lake Superior region, and in particular to Marquette County, Mich., in Library of the Society.

4953. Michigan Department of State. "Report on the archives in the Department of State... Lansing." Michigan history magazine, 2 (1918), 437-54.
Lists archives in office of Secretary of State.

4954. Michigan Executive Department. "Report on the archives in the Executive Department... Lansing." Michigan history magazine, 2 (1918), 238-56.
Lists contents of vaults, boxes and storeroom in Governor's office in Lansing. Covers period 1812-1918.

4955. Michigan Historical Commission. Michigan bibliography. A partial catalogue of books, maps, manuscripts and miscellaneous materials relating to the resources, development and history of Michigan from earliest times to July 1, 1917; together with citation of libraries in which the materials may be consulted, and a complete analytic index by subject and author, prep. by Floyd Benjamin Streeter. Lansing: Michigan Historical Commission, 1921. 2v.
Locates copies in Michigan libraries, Library of Congress, and Wisconsin Historical Society.

4956. Michigan, University. "The Michigan historical collections," by Elizabeth S. Adams. University of Michigan official bulletin, 41 (July 29, 1939), 3-12.

4957. Michigan, University, Michigan Historical Collections. Bibliography of Michigan county histories; with a report on the holdings of 213 libraries in Michigan and neighboring states. Ann Arbor: Michigan Historical Collections [1948] 28 numb. l.

4958. Michigan, University, William L. Clements Library. Michigan through three centuries; a guide to an exhibition of books, maps and manuscripts in the William L. Clements library. Ann Arbor: Univ. of Michigan Press, 1937. 20p. (Bulletin, no. 27)
List of 50 items, 1636-1861.

4959. Person, Harlow S. "Report on the public archives of Michigan." American Historical Association annual report, 2 (1900), 60-63.
General statement of papers in Office of Governor, Secretary of State, and State Library.

Minnesota

4960. Historical Records Survey - Minn. Guide to depositories of manuscript collections in the United States: Minnesota. St. Paul: Minnesota Historical Records Survey, 1941. 84 numb. l.

4961. Historical Records Survey - Minn. Inventory of the county archives of Minnesota. St. Paul: Minnesota Historical Records Survey, 1937-42. 44v.
Covers Aitkin, Anoka, Beltrami, Benton, Big Stone, Blue Earth, Cass, Chippewa, Dakota, Dodge, Douglas, Fairibault, Fillmore, Freeborn, Goodhue, Grant, Houston, Hubbard, Jackson, Kanabec, Lincoln, Marshall, Martin, Meeker, Mille Lacs, Morrison, Murray, Nicollet, Nobles, Olmsted, Otter Tail, Pipestone, Redwood, Renville, Rice, Rock, Scott, Sherburne, Stearns, Traverse, Wabasha, Washington, Wright, and Yellow Medicine counties.

4962. Holbrook, Franklin F. "The Neill papers in the manuscript collection of the Minnesota Historical Society." Minnesota history bulletin, 1 (1916), 369-77.
Over 3,000 papers, 1836-93, relating to Minnesota history.

4963. Kellar, Herbert A. "A preliminary survey of the more important archives of the territory and state of Minnesota." American Historical Association annual report, 1 (1914), 385-476.

"Comprises a preliminary survey of the manuscript records of the more important offices."

4964. Loehr, Rodney C. "Some sources for Northwest history: Minnesota farmers' diaries." Minnesota history, 18 (1937), 284-97.
Collection of diaries for period preceding 1885 in Minnesota Historical Society.

4965. Minnesota Historical Society. Guide to the personal papers in the manuscript collections of the Minnesota Historical Society, comp. by Grace Lee Nute and Gertrude W. Ackermann. St. Paul, 1935. 146p.

4966. Minnesota Historical Society Library. Catalogue of the library of the Minnesota Historical Society. St. Paul: Pioneer Press Company, 1888. 2v.
A short-title author and subject catalog of about 28,000 works. Contains "almost every known work" on Minnesota, and a good collection of material relating to Northwest.

4967. Nute, Grace Lee. "The Mississippi Valley from Prairie du Chien to Lake Pepin; a survey of unpublished sources." Minnesota history, 7 (1926), 32-41.
Survey of some manuscripts in Minnesota Historical Society collection.

4968. Nute, Grace Lee. "Some sources for Northwest history; Minnesota county archives." Minnesota history, 15 (1934), 194-99.
A short survey of type of archives to be found in county records and historical societies.

4969. Thompson, Ruth. "The collection and preservation of local historical pictures in the Minneapolis Public Library." American archivist, 9 (1946), 219-25.
Description of collection of about 10,000 pictures relating to Minneapolis.

4970. U. S. Library of Congress. Centennial of the Territory of Minnesota exhibition, March 5, 1949 - June 15, 1949. Wash.: Govt. Print. Off., 1949. 74p.
Catalog of 351 rare books, manuscripts, maps, prints, newspapers, music, and photographs, from Library of Congress, National Archives, National Gallery of Art, Smithsonian Institution, and institutions in Minnesota.

4971. Virtue, Ethel B. "The Pond papers." Minnesota historical bulletin, 3 (1919), 82-86.

Collection of 200 letters, in Minnesota Historical Society, by missionaries to the Sioux in Minnesota, written 1833-50.

4972. Williams, J. F. "Bibliography of Minnesota." Minnesota Historical Society collections, 3 (1870), 13-75.

Lists numerous early Minnesota imprints. "A transcript of the[part of the]catalogue... of the Minnesota Historical Society which relates to this state."

Mississippi

4973. "An account of manuscripts, papers and documents in public repositories within the state of Mississippi." Mississippi Historical Society publications, 5 (1902), 119-227.

Describes and lists material in state offices, educational institutions, historical societies, etc.

4974. "An account of manuscripts, papers, and documents pertaining to Mississippi in public repositories beyond the state." Mississippi Historical Society publications, 5 (1902), 49-117.

Describes fully collections of Mississippi archives outside the state.

4975. Historical Records Survey - Miss. Inventory of the county archives of Mississippi. Jackson: Historical Records Survey, 1937-42. 9v.

Covers Amite, Forrest, Grenada, Humphreys, Lamar, Pearl River, Tippah, Tunica, and Walthall counties.

4976. Mississippi Department of Archives and History. Annual report, 1906-07. Nashville, Tenn.: Brandon Publishing Co., 1908. 59p.

Lists newspaper holdings, 1805-1905, and Mississippi pamphlets.

4977. Mississippi Department of Archives and History. "An official guide to the historical materials in the... Department." Mississippi Department of Archives and History, twelfth annual report, (1912-1913), 43-147.

A list of provincial, territorial and state archives, military records, and newspaper files of Department of Archives and History of Mississippi.

4978. Owen, Thomas McAdory. "A bibliography of Mississippi." American Historical Association annual report, 1 (1899), 633-828.

Copies located in 9 libraries.

4979. U. S. Library of Congress, Division of Bibliography. "A list of references relating to Mississippi." Wash., Oct. 29, 1935. 17p. Typed.

4980. Weathersby, William H. "Preservation of Mississippi history." North Carolina historical review, 5 (1928), 141-50.

Describes activities of Mississippi Historical Society in collecting Mississippi historical records, types of material in Society's library, and in other collections of archives.

4981. White, James M. and Riley, Franklin L. "Libraries and societies." Mississippi Historical Society publications, 5 (1902), 169-227.

Lists books, pamphlets, newspapers and materials relating to Mississippi history in various Mississippi libraries. Holdings of Mississippi Historical Society and University of Mississippi are given in detail.

Missouri

4982. Brown, Leighton B. "The Snyder collection in the University of Kansas City Library." The M. L. A. quarterly, 5 (Sept. 1944), 55-58, 61; 5 (Dec. 1944), 76-79.

Description of collection relating to travel in Missouri to 1900, poetry by Missouri authors to 1890, fiction by Missouri authors, or with Missouri setting, to 1900, Missouri River, Mormons, Osage Indians, early Missouri imprints, and Missouri outlaws.

4983. Historical Records Survey - Mo. County court records, St. Charles County. St. Louis: The Survey, 1941. 40p.

4984. Historical Records Survey - Mo. Early Missouri archives. St. Louis: Missouri Historical Records Survey, 1941-42. 3v.

4985. Historical Records Survey - Mo. Guide to depositories of manuscript collections in the United States: Missouri. Prelim. ed. St. Louis, 1940. 17 numb. l.

4986. Historical Records Survey - Mo. Inventory of the county archives of Missouri. St. Louis: Historical Records Survey,

1937-42. 15v.

Covers Cass, Cole, Dallas, Henry, Jasper, Johnson, Linn, McDonald, Macon, Marion, Pettis, Pike, Reynolds, Ripley, and Shelby counties.

4987. Sampson, Francis Asbury. "Bibliography of books of travel in Missouri." Missouri historical review, 6 (1912), 64-81.

"Only books found in the library of the State Historical Society of Missouri are included."

4988. Viles, Jonas. "The archives at Jefferson City." Missouri historical review, 2 (1908), 284-95.

4989. Viles, Jonas. "Report on the archives of the state of Missouri." American Historical Association annual report, 1 (1908), 319-64.

Description of most important holdings of state offices in Missouri.

Montana

4990. Historical Records Survey - Calif. Calendar of the Montana papers in the William Andrews Clark Memorial Library (University of California at Los Angeles). Los Angeles: Southern California Historical Records Survey, 1942. 103 numb. l.

4991. Historical Records Survey - Mont. Inventory of the county archives of Montana. Missoula: Historical Records Survey, 1938-42. 7v.

Covers Beaverhead, Carbon, Flathead, Gallatin, Lake, Lincoln, Madison, Mineral, Missoula, Park, Ravalli, Sanders, Silver Bow, Stillwater, Sweet Grass and Toole counties.

4992. Montana Historical Society Library. Catalogue of the library of the Historical Society of the state of Montana. Also a report of the librarian for the years 1891-92, being the first biennial report and catalogue ever published by the state or society. In two parts. Pt. 1: The publications of this state and of other states and general history. Pt. 2: Publications of the United States which have been received at this library to November 30, 1892, prep. by Wm. F. Wheeler. Helena, Mont.: C. K. Wells Co., 1892. 128p.

4993. Phillips, Paul C. "The archives of the state of Montana." American Historical Association annual report, (1912), 295-303.

Brief description of public archives in offices in state capitol at Helena.

Nebraska

4994. Historical Records Survey - Neb. Guide to depositories of manuscript collections in the United States: Nebraska. Prelim. ed. Lincoln: Nebraska Historical Records Survey, 1940. 43 numb. l.

4995. Historical Records Survey - Neb. Inventory of the county archives of Nebraska. Lincoln: Historical Records Survey, 1939-42. 7v.

Covers Gosper, Greeley, Howard, Loup, Merrick, Seward, and Webster counties.

4996. Omaha Public Library. Nebraska; material in the Omaha Public Library. [Omaha, 1931] 21 numb. l.

Arranged by subjects. Excludes books on Omaha.

4997. Sheldon, Addison E. "Report on the archives of the state of Nebraska." American Historical Association annual report, (1910), 365-420.

Gives holdings of important public offices in Nebraska. A subject list.

Nevada

4998. Historical Records Survey - Nev. Inventories of the county archives of Nevada. Reno: Nevada Historical Records Survey, 1937-41. 7v.

Covers Douglas, Elko, Eureka, Mineral, Nye, Ormsby, and Washoe counties.

4999. U. S. Library of Congress, Division of Bibliography. "A selected list of references on Nevada." Wash., Mar. 13, 1934. 33p. Typed.

New Hampshire

5000. Dover Public Library. A list of books and pamphlets in the Dover Public Library relating to New Hampshire. Dover: H. E. Hodgdon, 1903. 172p.

Includes a collection of 400 volumes of local (Dover) history.

5001. Historical Records Survey - N. H. Guide to depositories of manuscript collections in the United States: New Hampshire. Manchester: N. H. Historical Records Survey, 1940. 44 numb. l.

5002. Historical Records Survey - N. H. Inventory of municipal and town archives: New Hampshire. Manchester: New Hampshire Historical Records Survey, 1939-42. 10v.
   Covers towns in Belknap, Hillsboro, Merrimack and Rockingham counties.

5003. Historical Records Survey - N. H. Inventory of the county archives of New Hampshire. Manchester: Historical Records Survey, 1936-40. 6v.
   Covers Belknap, Carroll, Cheshire, Coos, Grafton, and Merrimack counties.

5004. New Hampshire State Library. A subject-author catalogue of history, biography, genealogy, geography and travel in the New Hampshire State Library. Manchester: A. E. Clarke, 1897. 146p.

New Jersey

5005. Andrews, Frank De Witte, comp. A bibliography of Vineland, its authors and writers. Vineland, N. J., 1916. 21p.
   Material listed in Vineland Historical and Antiquarian Society library.

5006. Historical Records Survey - N. J. Calendar of the New Jersey State Library manuscript collection... Trenton, New Jersey. Newark: Historical Records Survey, 1939. 168p.
   Material showing the development of New Jersey from early Colonial days.

5007. Historical Records Survey - N. J. Inventory of municipal and town archives: New Jersey. Wharton, 1939-42. 5v.
   Covers towns of Orange, East Newark, Belmar, Denville, and Wharton.

5008. Historical Records Survey - N. J. Inventory of the county archives of New Jersey. Newark: Historical Records Survey, 1937-40. 4v.
   Includes Bergen, Morris, Ocean, and Passaic counties.

5009. Kemmerer, Donald L. "Neglected source material on colonial New Jersey." New Jersey Historical Society proceedings, 57 (Jan. 1939), 29-34.
   Describes resources of 11 United States libraries outside New Jersey, which are rich in manuscript and printed source materials relative to New Jersey.

5010. Nelson, William. "Bibliography of the printed proceedings of the Provincial Assembly, 1707-1776 [and] of the printed acts of the Legislature of New Jersey, 1703-1800, and ordinances of the Governors." In: New Jersey, First report of the Public Record Commissioner, 1899. Somerville, N. J.: Unionist-Gazette Association, Public Printers, 1899, p. 31-48 (App. C.), p. 49-93 (App. D.).
   Locates copies if not in New Jersey State Library, chiefly in Lenox Library (New York Public Library).

5011. Nelson, William. "The public archives of New Jersey." American Historical Association annual report, 1 (1903), 479-541.
   Describes and locates archives and records in state, local and historical offices.

5012. New Jersey, Secretary of State. Calendar of records in the office of the Secretary of State, 1664-1703, ed. by William Nelson. Paterson: Press Print. and Pub. Co., 1899. 770p. (Documents relating to the colonial history of the state of New Jersey, v. 21)

5013. Newark Free Public Library. Newark-in-print; references to Newark in books, pamphlets, reports, newspapers and in records which tell the story of the growth of Newark from 1666 through 1930. Newark, N. J.: The Public Library, 1931. 24p.

5014. Nichols, Charles Lemuel. "Papers of William Livingston." Massachusetts Historical Society proceedings, 55 (1923), 225-28.
   Collection of letters and papers of governor of New Jersey, 1776-90, in Massachusetts Historical Society.

New Mexico

5015. Hammond, George P. "Manuscript collections in the Spanish archives in New Mexico." Archives and libraries, (1939), 80-87.
   A general description.

5016. Historical Records Survey - N. M. Inventory of the county archives of New Mexico. Albuquerque: Historical Records Survey, 1937-42. 15v.

Covers Bernalillo, Colfax, Dona Ana, Eddy, Grant, Hidalgo, Luna, Mora, Otero, Sandoval, San Miguel, Sierra, Torrance, Union, and Valencia counties.

5017. Lounsbury, R. G. "United States National Archives. Materials relating to history of New Mexico before 1848." New Mexico historical review, 21 (July 1946), 247-56.

5018. New Mexico Historical Society. Catalogue of books in English in the library of the Society relating to New Mexico and the Southwest. January 1910. Santa Fe: New Mexico Printing Co., 1910. 49p. (Historical Society of New Mexico publications, no. 15)

Includes books on Mexico and Central America.

5019. Saunders, Lyle, comp. A guide to materials bearing on cultural relations in New Mexico. Albuquerque: Univ. of New Mexico Press, 1944. 528p.

Lists references in history, geography, agriculture, etc. Locates many unpublished items.

5020. Twitchell, Ralph Emerson, comp. The Spanish archives of New Mexico. [Cedar Rapids, Iowa]: Torch Press, 1914. 2v.

Describes about 1,390 titles in Office of Surveyor-General, Santa Fe, and 3,100 titles in Library of Congress.

5021. Vaughan, John H. "A preliminary report on the archives of New Mexico." American Historical Association annual report, (1909), 465-90.

History and description of various state, county, church and historical society archives in New Mexico.

New York

5022. Buffalo Historical Society. "Rough list of manuscripts in the library of the... Society." Buffalo Historical Society publications, 14 (1910), 421-85. Reprinted, Buffalo, 1910. 65p.

5023. Chase, Franklin H. Where to find it; bibliography of Syracuse history. Published by the Onondaga Historical Association. Syracuse: Dehler Press, 1920. 219p.

Locates items in the Syracuse (N. Y.) Public Library or the Onondaga Historical Association.

5024. Cornell University, Collection of Regional History. Report of the Curator, 1942/45-1946/48. Ithaca, N. Y.: The University, [1945-48] 3v.

Each report lists acquisitions to collection of historical material on upstate New York.

5025. Day, Richard E. Calendar of the Sir William Johnson manuscripts in the New York State Library. Albany: University of the State of New York, 1909. 683p.

5026. "Dutch records in the City Clerk's Office, New York." Holland Society of New York year book, (1900), 110-82, 190-203; (1901), 121-76.

A digest of records of cases before Orphans Court, and a synopsis of items in books of the Notaries Public, etc. - cf. Pref. Preserved in the New York City Clerk's office.

5027. Flagg, Charles Allcott and Jennings, Judson T. "Bibliography of New York colonial history." New York State Library bulletin, 56 (1901), 289-558.

Locates copies in other libraries if not held by New York State Library.

5028. Gosnell, Charles F. and Jacobsen, Edna L. "History in the State Library." New York history, 27 (1946), 531-33; 28 (1947), 245-46.

Describes manuscript and archival material in the New York State Library.

5029. Gummere, Amelia M. "Manuscripts concerning the Otsego purchase of 1769." Friends Historical Association bulletin, 20 (1931), 21-24.

Description of a collection held by Haverford College.

5030. Hirsch, Felix E. "The Bard family." Columbia University quarterly, 33 (1941), 222-41.

Gives some locations for source material on the Bard family, associated with Hyde Park and Duchess County, N. Y., Columbia University, etc., 1706-1861.

5031. Historical Records Survey - N. Y.

Calendar of the Gerrit Smith papers in the Syracuse University Library. General correspondence. Albany, N. Y., 1941-42. 2v.

Covers period from 1819 to 1854. Letters, deeds, manuscripts, etc., given to Syracuse University.

5032. Historical Records Survey - N. Y. "Guide to ten major depositories of manuscript collections in New York State (exclusive of New York City)." Middle States Association of History and Social Science Teachers proceedings, 38 (1941), 1-78. Reprinted. 1941. 78p.

5033. Historical Records Survey - N. Y. (City). Guide to manuscript depositories in New York City. N. Y., 1941. 150p.

5034. Historical Records Survey - N. Y. (City). Inventory of municipal and town archives: New York City, Bronx Borough. N. Y., 1942. 302p.

5035. Historical Records Survey - N. Y. (City). Inventory of the county and borough archives of New York City. N. Y.: Historical Records Survey, 1939-42. 3v.

Covers Bronx, Kings, and Richmond counties.

5036. Historical Records Survey - N. Y. (State). Guide to depositories of manuscript collections in New York State (exclusive of New York City). Albany, 1941. V. 1, 424p.

5037. Historical Records Survey - N. Y. (State). Inventory of the county archives of New York State (exclusive of... New York City). Albany: Historical Records Survey, 1937-40. 6v.

Covers Albany, Broome, Cattaraugus, Chautauqua, Chemung, and Ulster counties.

5038. Hufeland, Otto. A check list of books, maps, pictures, and other printed matter relating to the counties of Westchester and Bronx. White Plains, N. Y.: Westchester County Historical Society, 1929. 320p. (Publication of the Westchester County Historical Society, v. 6)

Locates copies of unusual books in 6 libraries.

5039. Huntington, Edna and Downs, Robert B. "The Long Island Historical Society." New York history, 23 (1942), 522-26.

Brief description of history and scope of collections of Long Island Historical Society.

5040. Jacobsen, Edna L. "Manuscript treasures in the New York State Library." New York history, 20 (July 1939), 265-76.

5041. Long Island Historical Society. Catalogue of manuscripts, excerpts, prints and maps, available as material for a history of the Borough of Brooklyn. N. Y., 1909. 70p.

Collection now in office of Commissioner of Records, Hall of Records, Brooklyn, N. Y.

5042. Long Island Historical Society. Long Island Historical Society, 1863-1938; a record in commemoration of the seventy-fifth anniversary. Brooklyn, 1938. 76p.

A history, with information on library resources.

5043. McMurtrie, Douglas C. The first guides to Niagara Falls. Chicago, 1934. 12p. (Reprinted from American book collector, 4 (1933), 129-33. Bibliography, p. 8-12)

Locates copies of old guides in 13 libraries.

5044. Morris, Richard B. "The Federal archives of New York city; opportunities for historical research." American historical review, 42 (1937), 256-72.

A general description of survey in New York City, mentioning several important collections.

5045. New-York Historical Society. Collections. 1-5 (1809-30); 2nd series, 1-4 (1841-1859); 3rd series, 1-75 (1868-1943). N. Y., 1811-1944.

Contains in published form many original records held by Society.

5046. New-York Historical Society. The De Peyster Collection. Catalogue of books in the library of the New-York Historical Society, presented by John Watts De Peyster. Pt. 1, January, 1868. N. Y.: The Society, 1868. 24p.

Chiefly 17th to 19th century pamphlets.

5047. New-York Historical Society. "Old New York inventories of estates, 1717-1800." New-York Historical Society quarterly bulletin, 6 (1923), 130-37; 8 (1924), 43-46.

A list of several hundred official inventories in New-York Historical Society.

5048. New-York Historical Society. Survey of the manuscript collections in the New-York Historical Society. N. Y.: The Society, 1941. 96p.

5049. New-York Historical Society Library. Catalogue of books, manuscripts, maps, etc., added to the library of the New-York Historical Society, since January, 1839. N. Y.: Joseph W. Harrison, 1840. 32p.
A partial supplement to 1813 catalog.

5050. New-York Historical Society Library. Catalogue of printed books in the library of the New-York Historical Society. N. Y.: The Society, 1859. 653p. (New-York Historical Society, Collections, 2nd series, v. 4)

5051. New-York Historical Society Library. Catalogue of the books, tracts, newspapers, maps, charts, views, portraits and manuscripts in the Library of the New-York Historical Society. [N. Y., 1813] 139p. (New-York Historical Society collections, 1st ser., v. 2)

5052. New York Public Library. "Calendar of messages and proclamations of General George Clinton, first governor of the State of New York, with some legislative responses, August, 1777, to September, 1781," comp. by Mabel Clare Weaks. New York Public Library bulletin, 31 (1927), 539-67. Reprinted. 31p.

5053. New York Public Library. "Check list of engraved views of the City of New York in the New York Public Library." New York Public Library bulletin, 5 (1901), 222-26.

5054. New York Public Library. "Check list of works in the New York Public Library relating to the history of Brooklyn, and of other places on Long Island now included in the City of New York." New York Public Library bulletin, 6 (1902), 77-83.

5055. New York Public Library. "Check list of works relating to the history (general, political, etc.) of the City of New York in the New York Public Library." New York Public Library bulletin, 5 (1901), 97-127.

5056. New York Public Library. "Check list of works relating to the streets, markets, real-estate, public buildings, etc., of the City of New York." New York Public Library bulletin, 5 (1901), 151-59.

5057. New York Public Library. "Check list of works relating to the water front of the City of New York, its harbors, docks, ferries, etc.--and bridges--in the New York Public Library." New York Public Library bulletin, 5 (1901), 167-72.

5058. New York Public Library. "Daniel Denton's description of New York in 1670," by Victor Hugo Paltsits. New York Public Library bulletin, 28 (1924), 599-604.
Locates 20 known copies.

5059. New York Public Library. "The Eno Collection of New York City views," by Frank Weitenkampf. New York Public Library bulletin, 29 (1925), 327-54, 385-414. Reprinted, with additions. 82p.

5060. New York Public Library. "Greater New York's golden anniversary, with a selected list of books relating to New York City," by Cleveland Rodgers and Rebecca B. Rankin. New York Public Library bulletin, 52 (1948), 170-81. Reprinted. 14p.
Lists 150 books about New York, from collection of Municipal Reference Library, a branch of New York Public Library.

5061. New York Public Library. "List of works in the New York Public Library relating to Henry Hudson, the Hudson River, Robert Fulton, early steam navigation, etc." New York Public Library bulletin, 13 (1909), 585-613. Reprinted, with extensive additions, with slightly variant title, in two editions.

5062. New York Public Library. "New York State - boundaries; references to documents, reports, and other papers in the New York Public Library relating to the boundaries of the State of New York," by A. R. Hasse. New York Public Library bulletin, 4 (1900), 359-77.

5063. New York Public Library. "The New York tercentenary; an exhibition of the history of New Netherland," by Victor Hugo Paltsits. New York Public Library bulletin, 30 (1926), 655-84, 759-96. Reprinted. 63p.

5064. New York Public Library. "The North Eastern boundary. References to (selected) maps, documents, reports and other papers in the New York Public Library relating to the North Eastern boundary controversy," by A. R. Hasse. New York Public Library bulletin, 4 (1900), 391-411.

5065. New York Public Library. "Publications relating to New York affairs under Governor Cosby." New York Public Library bulletin, 2 (1898), 249-55.

Principally of interest for John Peter Zenger material. Includes manuscripts, prints, etc.

5066. New York Public Library. "Some materials for a bibliography of the official publications of the General Assembly of the Colony of New York, 1693-1775," comp. by Adelaide R. Hasse. New York Public Library bulletin, 7 (1903), 51-79, 95-116, 129-51. Reprinted. 73p.

Copies located in 7 American and 2 English libraries.

5067. New York Public Library. "Works relating to the State of New York in the New York Public Library." New York Public Library bulletin, 4 (1900), 163-78, 199-220, 359-78.

5068. New York State Historian. Historical account and inventory of records of the city of Kingston. Albany: Univ. of the State of New York, 1918. 48p.

5069. New York State Historian. Historical account and inventory of the records of Suffolk County. Albany: Univ. of the State of New York, 1921. 34p.

5070. New York State Historian. The records of Huntington, Suffolk County. Albany: Univ. of the State of New York, 1921. 17p.

Inventory of official archives.

5071. New York State Library. Annotated list of the principal manuscripts in the New York State Library. Albany: Univ. of the State of N. Y., 1899. p. 209-237. (New York State Library bulletin, History, no. 3, June 1899)

5072. New York State Library. Calendar of Council minutes, 1668-1783. Albany: Univ. of the State of New York, 1902. 720p. (New York State Library bulletin 58, History, no. 6, March 1902)

5073. New York State Library. 94th annual report, 1911. Albany: Univ. of the State of New York, 1913.

List of manuscripts salvaged from Capitol fire of 1911, p. 16-31.

5074. New York State Library, Manuscripts and History Section. Official document book, New York State freedom train. Albany: The Library, 1950. 72p.

Famous documents relating to New York state history, all except 10 in New York State Library.

5075. N. Y. (State) Secretary of State. Calendar of historical manuscripts in the office of Secretary of State, Albany, N. Y. Part I, Dutch manuscripts, 1630-1644. Part II, English manuscripts, 1664-1776, by E. B. O'Callaghan. Albany, 1865-66. 2v.

Transferred to New York State Library.

5076. N. Y. (State) Secretary of State. Calendar of New York colonial manuscripts, indorsed land papers; in the office of the Secretary of State of New York 1643-1803. Albany, 1864. 1,087p.

Manuscripts transferred to New York State Library.

5077. New York (State) Secretary of State. Catalogue of records of the office of Secretary of State. Albany, 1898. 142p.

Many series have been transferred to New York State Library.

5078. Oneida Historical Society. Catalogue of the library of the Oneida Historical Society of Utica. Utica, N. Y.: E. H. Roberts & Co., 1890. 127p.

Arranged by subjects and types of material.

5079. Osgood, Herbert L. "The public archives of New York." American Historical Association annual report, 2 (1900), 67-250.

Includes an annotated list of principal manuscripts in New York State Library, as well as a history and description of archives in public offices of New York state (including city and county offices).

5080. Osgood, Herbert L. "Public archives of the City of New York and of other jurisdictions lying wholly or partly within the same." American Historical Association, Public Archives Commission, First report. American

Historical Association annual report, 2 (1900), 163-235.

General survey of archives available in public offices of New York City; also gives some detailed holdings.

5081. Reynolds, James Bronson. Civic bibliography for Greater New York, ed. ... for the New York Research Council. N. Y.: Charities Publication Committee, 1911. 296p. (Russell Sage Foundation [Publications].)

Copies located in 10 New York libraries.

5082. Roach, G. W. "Guide to depositories of manuscript collections in New York State." New York history, 24 (1943), 265-70, 417-22, 560-64; 25 (1944), 64-68, 226-27.

Supplements Historical Records Survey Guide, issued 1941. Describes collections.

5083. Rowse, Edward F. "The archives of New York." American archivist, 4 (Oct. 1941), 267-74.

History and description of various depositories in New York state.

5084. Sealock, Richard Burl and Seeley, Pauline A. Long Island bibliography. Baltimore, 1940. 338p.

Copies located in more than 200 libraries, covering history of Long Island through 1939.

5085. Stokes, Isaac Newton Phelps. The iconography of Manhattan Island, 1498-1909, compiled from original sources and illustrated by photo-intaglio reproductions. N. Y.: R. R. Dodd, 1915-28. 6v.

Volume 6 covers archives. Locates material in New York and other libraries. Extends Osgood's work.

5086. Utica Public Library. Bibliography of Sullivan's expedition against the Six Nations in 1779. Utica, N. Y., 1929. 22p.

Material listed located in Utica Public Library.

5087. Utica Public Library. A bibliography of the history and life of Utica; a centennial contribution, compiled by Utica Public Library from its resources. Utica, N. Y.: Goodenow Print. Co., 1932. 237p.

5088. [Wall, Alexander J.] "De Peyster family papers." New-York Historical Society bulletin, 5 (1922), 105-06.

Describes collection of 1,754 miscellaneous family papers, 1682-1827.

5089. Winters, William H. Three hundredth anniversary of the settlement on Manhattan Island, 1614-1914. A literary and legal bibliography of the old Dutch Province of Nieuw Netherlandt (New Netherland) and the City of Nieuw Amsterdam (New Amsterdam). [N. Y., 1914]. 34p.

Locates some items in New York libraries.

North Carolina

5090. Bassett, John Spencer, and others. "North Carolina county archives." American Historical Association annual report, (1904), 603-27.

Brief listing of contents of some of county archives.

5091. Bassett, John Spencer. "Report on the public archives of North Carolina." American Historical Association annual report, 2 (1900), 251-66; 2 (1901), 345-52.

General description of public archives of the state.

5092. Cotten, Bruce, comp. Housed on the third floor; being a collection of North Caroliniana formed by Bruce Cotten; with some facsimile impressions of titles. Baltimore: [Horn-Shafer Co.] 1941. 65p.

Collection now owned by University of North Carolina Library.

5093. Fries, Adelaide L. Records of the Moravians in North Carolina. Raleigh: Edwards & Broughton, 1922-43. 6v. (Publications of the North Carolina Historical Commission).

Transcripts and translations of Moravian records, 1752-1808, now in possession of Wachovia Historical Society, Winston-Salem, N. C.

5094. Historical Records Survey - N. C. A calendar of the Bartlett Yancey papers in the Southern historical collection of the University of North Carolina. Raleigh: Historical Records Survey, 1940. 48p.

5095. Historical Records Survey - N. C. Guide to depositories of manuscript collections in North Carolina. Raleigh: North Carolina Historical Records Survey, 1940. 18p.

5096. Historical Records Survey - N. C. A guide to the manuscript collections in the archives of the North Carolina Historical Commission. Raleigh: North Carolina Historical Commission, 1942. 216p.

5097. Historical Records Survey - N. C. The historical records of North Carolina. Raleigh: North Carolina Historical Commission, 1938-39. 3v.
County records: v. 1, Alamance-Columbus; v. 2, Craven-Moore; v. 3, Nash-Yancey.

5098. Historical Records Survey - N. C. Inventory of the state archives of North Carolina. Raleigh: North Carolina Historical Records Survey, 1941. 32p.

5099. Historical Records Survey - N. C. Inventory of state archives: North Carolina. Miscellaneous agencies. Raleigh: Historical Records Survey, 1940-41. 4v.
Covers North Carolina Historical Commission, State Library, Library Commission, State Board of Elections, Board of Advisors of Veteran Loan Fund, and North Carolina Rural Electrification Authority.

5100. Historical Records Survey - N. C. Inventory of state archives: North Carolina. Regulatory agencies. Raleigh: Historical Records Survey, 1939-42. 4v.
Covers Utilities Commission, Insurance Department, State Board of Alcoholic Control, and Licensing Boards.

5101. Historical Records Survey - N. C. Inventory of state archives: North Carolina. Social service agencies. Raleigh: Historical Records Survey, 1941. 2v.
Covers North Carolina Board of Health and Stonewall Jackson Manual Training and Industrial School.

5102. Historical Records Survey - N. C. Inventory of the state archives of North Carolina. State Planning Board. Raleigh: Historical Records Survey, 1942. 7p.

5103. Lacy, Dan. "Records in the offices of registers of deeds in North Carolina." North Carolina historical review, 14 (1937), 213-29.
Brief descriptions, based largely on findings of Historical Records Survey.

5104. McConnell, Roland C. "Records in the National Archives pertaining to the history of North Carolina." North Carolina historical review, 25 (July 1948), 318-40.

5105. North Carolina Historical Commission. Calendars of manuscript collections; prepared from original manuscrpts in the collections of the... Commission, by D. L. Corbitt. Raleigh: Edwards and Broughton, 1926. v. 1, 351p. (No more issued)

5106. North Carolina Historical Commission. Handbook of county records deposited with the... Commission, by D. L. Corbitt. Raleigh: Edwards & Broughton, 1925. 45p.

5107. North Carolina State Library. "Bibliography of North Carolina." In: North Carolina State Library biennial repot, 1916-18, p. 23-80; 1918-20, p. 63.
Author list of books in State Library relating to North Carolina.

5108. Thornton, Mary Lindsay. "North Carolina collection at the University." North Carolina library bulletin, 6 (Dec. 1924), 11-14.
Account of extensive collection of Caroliniana at University of North Carolina.

5109. U. S. Library of Congress, General Reference and Bibliography Division. "Some references to Duplin County [N. C.]: its antecedents and historical background." Wash., June 1, 1949. 9p. Typed.

5110. Weeks, Stephen B. A bibliography of the historical literature of North Carolina. Cambridge: Harvard Univ. Press, 1895. 79p. (Harvard University Library bibliographical contributions, no. 48)
Compiled largely from material in University of North Carolina, North Carolina State Library, Trinity College (now Duke University), and Wake Forest College. Locations not given.

5111. Weeks, Stephen B. Weeks collection of Caroliniana. Raleigh: E. M. Uzzell, 1907. 31p.
Description of a collection now in University of North Carolina Library.

North Dakota

5112. Historical Records Survey - N. D. Inventory of the county archives of North Dakota.

Bismarck: Historical Records Survey, 1938-41. 3v.
Covers Golden Valley, Mercer, and Williams counties.

5113. Jackson, W. Turrentine. "Dakota territorial papers in the Department of the Interior archives." North Dakota historical quarterly, 11 (July 1944), 209-20.
Records now in National Archives.

Ohio

5114. Historical and Philosophical Society of Ohio Library. Catalogue of the Torrence papers. Cincinnati, 1887. 21p.
Chiefly private letters and papers relating to early history of Cincinnati.

5115. Historical and Philosophical Society of Ohio Library. A partial list of the books in its library relating to the state of Ohio. Cincinnati, 1893. 108p.

5116. Historical Records Survey - Ohio. Calendar of the Joshua Reed Giddings manuscripts in the library of the Ohio State Archaeological and Historical Society, Columbus, Ohio - twenty-five sample pages. Columbus, Ohio, 1939. 30 l.

5117. Historical Records Survey - Ohio. Inventory of municipal and town archives: Ohio, Cuyahoga County. Columbus: Ohio Historical Records Survey Project, 1938-41. 4v.
Covers Cleveland records, Cleveland Departments of Public Safety and Health and Welfare, and Cuyahoga County municipalities other than Cleveland.

5118. Historical Records Survey - Ohio. Inventory of the county archives of Ohio. Columbus: Historical Records Survey, 1936-42. 27v.
Covers Adams, Allen, Ashland, Athens, Brown, Columbiana, Cuyahoga, Fayette, Franklin, Geuga, Hamilton, Hancock, Jackson, Knox, Lake, Lorain, Lucas, Madison, Montgomery, Pike, Ross, Scioto, Seneca, Stark, Summit, Trumbull, and Washington counties.

5119. Historical Records Survey - Ohio. Inventory of the state archives of Ohio. Columbus: Ohio Historical Records Survey, 1940. 71p.

5120. Lindley, Harlow. "The Woodbridge-Gallaher collection." Ohio archaeological and historical quarterly, 44 (1935), 443-50.
Description of a collection, for period from 1754 to 1887, pertaining to Marietta, Indian affairs, etc. Held by Ohio State Archaeological and Historical Society Library.

5121. Ohio State Library. Martha Kinney Cooper Ohioana library; catalog of books, brochures, Sept. 1929 - July 1945. Columbus: The Library [1945] 76p.
A catalog of books by Ohioans, about Ohio or Ohioans, written while authors were residents of Ohio.

5122. Overman, William D. "Ohio archives." American archivist, 5 (1942), 36-39.
General description of collection in Ohio State Archaeological and Historical Society, official depository.

5123. Miami University Library. The Samuel F. Covington library of Ohio Valley history, with a sketch of Samuel Fulton Covington. Oxford, O.: Miami University, 1914. 75p. (Miami University bull. ser. 13. no. 2, 1914)
Catalog, arranged by subjects and types of material.

5124. Michigan, University, William L. Clements Library. The Maumee valley through fifty years, 1763-1813. Ann Arbor: Univ. of Mich., 1940. [20]p. (Bulletin, no. 33)
Indicates some of the original sources of the history of the region in Clements Library.

5125. Sioussat, St. George L. "The John Cleves Short collection of papers of the Short, Harrison, Symmes, and allied families." Library of Congress quarterly journal of current acquisitions, 2 (July - Sept. 1944), 76-85.
A collection of 13,000 personal papers, covering late 18th and first half of 19th centuries, centering principally in Ohio Valley.

5126. Stevenson, Richard Taylor. "A preliminary report on the Ohio archives." American Historical Association annual report, 2 (1906), 165-96.
Describes archives in public offices of state and counties, and a few other collections.

5127. Thomson, Peter G. A bibliography of the state of Ohio; being a catalogue of books and pamphlets relating to the history of the state. Cincinnati, 1880. 436p.

A collection bought by the Historical and Philosophical Society of Ohio in 1891.

5128. Weaver, Clarence Lahr. "County and local historical material in the Ohio State Archaeological and Historical Society library," comp. by Clarence L. Weaver and Helen M. Mills. Ohio State archaeological and historical quarterly, 54 (1945), 261-327.

5129. Weaver, Clarence L. and Mills, Helen, comps. "County historical material in the Ohio State Archaeological and Historical Society Library." Ohio archaeological and historical quarterly, 45 (1936), 95-150.

Oklahoma

5130. Foreman, Grant. "A survey of tribal records in the archives of the United States government in Oklahoma." Chronicles of Oklahoma, 11 (1933), 625-34.

History and general description of the survey.

5131. Historical Records Survey - Okla. Inventory of state archives: Oklahoma. A list of records of the state of Oklahoma. Oklahoma City: Historical Records Survey, 1938. 272 l.

5132. Historical Records Survey - Okla. Inventory of the county archives of Oklahoma. Oklahoma City: Historical Records Survey, 1937-41. 11v.

Covers Atoka, Beckham, Cherokee, Cimarron, Haskell, Lincoln, McIntosh, Mayes, Muskogee, Pittsburgh, and Pushmataha counties.

Oregon

5133. Historical Records Survey - Ore. Descriptions of county offices in Oregon and check list of their records. Portland, Ore.: Historical Records Survey, 1937. 36 numb. l.

5134. Historical Records Survey - Ore. Guide to depositories of manuscript collections in the United States: Oregon-Washington. Portland: Oregon Historical Records Survey, 1940. 42p.

5135. Historical Records Survey - Ore. Guide to the Angelus Studio collection of historic photographs. Portland: Oregon Historical Records Survey, 1940. 77p.

5136. Historical Records Survey - Ore. Guide to the manuscript collections of the Oregon Historical Society. Portland: Oregon Historical Records Survey, 1940. 133p.

"492 entries... arranged alphabetically by name of the author of the particular manuscript collection."

5137. Historical Records Survey - Ore. Inventory of the county archives of Oregon. Portland: Oregon Historical Records Survey, 1937-42. 14v.

Covers Benton, Clatsop, Coos, Hood River, Josephine, Klamath, Linn, Morrow, Multnomah, Tillamook, Umatilla, Wasco, and Washington counties.

5138. U. S. Library of Congress. Centennial of the Oregon Territory exhibition, September 11, 1948 - January 11, 1949. Wash.: Govt. Print. Off., 1948. 76p.

Catalog of 341 rare books, manuscripts, maps, prints, photographs, newspapers and music, drawn from Library of Congress, National Archives, and institutions in Oregon.

5139. Young, F. G. "Report on the archives of Oregon." American Historical Association annual report, 1 (1902), 337-55.

A list of "printed documents designated by the Secretary of State as the 'Archives' of the state."

Pennsylvania

5140. Ames, Herman V. and Kelker, Luther R. "Public archives of Pennsylvania." American Historical Association annual report, (1904), 629-49.

Supplements Ames and Shimmell report, appearing in American Historical Association annual report for 1900. A list of the contents of the "Pennsylvania Archives," 2d and 3d series.

5141. Ames, Herman V. and McKinly, Albert E. "Report on the public archives of the city and county of Philadelphia." American Historical Association annual report, 2 (1901), 231-344.

Locates copies in city and county offices "and in the 5 principal libraries of Philadelphia."

5142. Ames, Herman V. and Shimmell, Lewis S. "Report on the public archives of

Pennsylvania." American Historical Association annual report, 2 (1900), 267-93.

General description of state of collections, with some specific items located.

5143. Bausman, Lottie M. A bibliography of Lancaster County, Pennsylvania, 1745-1912. Philadelphia: Pennsylvania Federation of Historical Societies, [1916] 460p.

Locations given in Lancaster County Historical Society, Historical Society of Pennsylvania, and several private collections. Chronological arrangement.

5144. Connor, R. D. W. "The National Archives and Pennsylvania history." Pennsylvania history, 7 (April 1940), 63-78.

An address given on fifth anniversary of National Archives; gives a general survey of history, aims and contents.

5145. Historical Records Survey - Pa. Guide to depositories of manuscript collections in Pennsylvania. Harrisburg: Pennsylvania Dept. of Public Instruction, 1939. 126p.

5146. Historical Records Survey - Pa. Guide to manuscript collections of the Historical Society of Pennsylvania. 2d ed. Philadelphia: Historical Society of Pennsylvania, 1949. 350p.

Annotated list of manuscript collections in Historical Society of Pennsylvania.

5147. Historical Records Survey - Pa. Inventory of the county archives of Pennsylvania. Harrisburg: Historical Records Survey, 1938-42. 18v.

Covers Adams, Beaver, Berks, Blair, Bradford, Delaware, Erie, Fayette, Forest, Greene, Lancaster, Lawrence, Luzerne, Warren, Washington, Wayne, and Westmoreland counties.

5148. Kent, Donald H. "Sources for Pennsylvania history in the William L. Clements Library." Pennsylvania history, 14 (1947), 23-29.

Description based on "a complete survey for the Col. Bouquet period and a casual survey for earlier and later times," of sources for Pennsylvania history in the University of Michigan William L. Clements Library.

5149. Long, Amelia Reynolds. "Manuscript collections on early jurisprudence and legislation in Pennsylvania." Pennsylvania history, 2 (1935), 190-93.

Covers period from Revolution to Civil War. Description of 4 county historical society collections outside of Philadelphia.

5150. Pennsylvania Historical and Museum Commission. Inventory of the county archives of Pennsylvania. Gettysburg, Pa. [etc.]: Board of County Commissioners, 1941-46. 17v.

When completed, series will comprise 67 volumes, one for each county in Pennsylvania.

5151. Pennsylvania Historical Society. "Supplement to the 'Guide to the manuscript collections in the Historical Society of Pennsylvania.'" Pennsylvania magazine of history and biography, 65 (1941), 505-12; 67 (1943), 108-12; 68 (1944), 98-111; 70 (1946), 181-84; 71 (1947), 283-87; 72 (1948), 276-83; 73 (1949), 322-78.

Supplements to 1940 Guide.

5152. Pennsylvania State Library. "Bibliography of Pennsylvania history in the Pennsylvania State Library." In: Pennsylvania State Library report, 1901, p. 253-85.

Includes state, county, town and township histories.

5153. Pennsylvania State Library. "Checklist of Pennsylvania county, town and township histories." Harrisburg: E. K. Meyers, 1892. 24p. (From Pennsylvania State Library report, 1891, p. A3-A24)

5154. Pennsylvania State Library. "Check list of the laws, minutes, journals and documents of the state of Pennsylvania, 1682-1899." In: Pennsylvania State Library report for 1901, p. 325-421.

5155. Sewickley Public Library. An annotated catalog of the Alexander C. Robinson collection of western Pennsylvaniania, ed. by Lowell W. Nicols. [Sewickley]: Library Society of Sewickley, Penn., 1940, 229p.

5156. Shearer, Augustus H. "Bibliographical and descriptive notes on the issues of the journal of the Pennsylvania Assembly, 1776-1790." Pennsylvania magazine of history, 41 (1917), 359-64.

Locates only known copy in Historical Society of Pennsylvania.

5157. U. S. Library of Congress, General Reference and Bibliography Division. "Bedford County, Pennsylvania: a selected list of references," comp. by Charles Hancock Wentz. Wash., Aug. 1946. 23p. Typed.

5158. Western Pennsylvania Historical Survey. Inventory of the manuscript and miscellaneous collections of the Historical Society of Western Pennsylvania. Pittsburgh, 1933. 11 numb. l. (Bibliographical contributions, no. 1)

Chiefly collections of personal papers.

5159. Wood, Richard G. "Research materials in the National Archives pertaining to Pennsylvania." Pennsylvania magazine of history and biography, 69 (Apr. 1945), 89-102.

Rhode Island

5160. Bartlett, John Russell. Bibliography of Rhode Island. A catalogue of books and other publications relating to the state of Rhode Island, with notes, historical, biographical and critical. Printed by order of the General Assembly. Providence: A. Anthony, Printer to the State, 1864. 287p.

Locates books by classes rather than by specific titles.

5161. Brigham, Clarence S. "Report on the archives of Rhode Island." American Historical Association annual report, 1 (1903), 543-644.

"Attempts to list and describe all of the manuscript archives in possession of the State of Rhode Island, of the 5 county courts, and of each city and town in the State."

5162. Harvard University, Graduate School of Business Administration, Baker Library. "De Wolf family papers." Business Historical Society bulletin, 9 (1935), 41-44.

Collection of papers of James De Wolf (1764-1837), of Bristol, R. I. American privateer, in Baker Library, Harvard University.

5163. Historical Records Survey - R. I. Inventory of municipal and town archives: Rhode Island. Providence: Rhode Island Historical Records Survey, 1942. 2v.

For West Greenwich and North Providence.

South Carolina

5164. Charleston Library Society. Catalogue of the portraits, books, pamphlets, maps and manuscripts presented to the Charleston Library Society. Columbia, S. C., 1908. 148p.

Classified subject list of about 900 items relating to history of South Carolina and Charleston.

5165. Historical Records Survey - S. C. Inventory of the county archives of South Carolina. Columbia: Historical Records Survey, 1937-41. 14v.

Covers Abbeville, Aiken, Allendale, Anderson, Cherokee, Dillon, Florence, Jasper, Lee, McCormick, Oconee, Pickens, Richland, and Saluda counties.

5166. McCormack, Helen G. "A provisional guide to manuscripts in the South Carolina Historical Society." South Carolina historical and genealogical magazine, 45 (1944), 111-15, 172-76; 46 (1945), 49-53, 104-09, 171-75, 214-17; 47 (1946), 53-57, 171-78; 48 (1947), 48-52, 177-80.

Describes manuscripts owned by or deposited with the Society.

5167. Salley, A. S. "Preservation of South Carolina history." North Carolina historical review, 4 (1927), 145-57.

Describes activities of South Carolina Historical Commission in preserving various archival records of South Carolina.

5168. South Carolina Historical Commission. Documents relating to the history of South Carolina during the Revolutionary War, ed. by A. S. Salley, Jr. Columbia: The Commission, 1908. 118p.

5169. South Carolina Historical Commission. Report, Regular Session of 1906. Columbia: Gonzales and Bryan, 1905-1906. 21p.

Lists of legislative, executive and judicial documents held by Commission.

5170. South Carolina, University, Library. Author list of Caroliniana in the University of South Carolina Library, comp. by Elisabeth D. English. Columbia, 1923. 337p. (Bulletin of Univ. of South Carolina, no. 134)

5171. Uhlendorf, Bernhard Alexander, ed. & tr. The siege of Charleston, with an account of the province of South Carolina: diaries and letters of Hessian officers from the von Jungkenn papers in the William L. Clements

Library. Ann Arbor: Univ. of Mich. Press, 1938. 445p. (Univ. of Mich. publications. History and political science, v. 12)

German and English on opposite pages. A transcription and translation of some of letters and diaries from collection in William L. Clements Library, University of Michigan.

5172. Woody, R. H. "The public records of South Carolina." American archivist, 2 (1939), 244-63.

History and general description.

South Dakota

5173. Historical Records Survey - S. D. Inventory of the county archives of South Dakota. Rapid City: Historical Records Survey, 1937-42. 8v.

Covers Bennett, Buffalo, Clark, Faulk, Haakon, Jackson, Millette, Miner, and Washabaugh counties.

5174. South Dakota State Library. "Catalogue of books, pamphlets and newspapers in the South Dakota division of the South Dakota State Library." South Dakota historical collections, 4 (1908), 16-57.

Tennessee

5175. Historical Records Survey - Tenn. Guide to collections of manuscripts in Tennessee. Nashville: Tennessee Historical Records Survey, 1941. 38 numb. l.

5176. Historical Records Survey - Tenn. Guide to depositories of manuscript collections in Tennessee. Nashville: Tennessee Historical Records Survey, 1940. 27p.

5177. Historical Records Survey - Tenn. Inventory of the county archives of Tennessee. Nahsville: Tennessee Historical Records Survey, 1937-42. 13v.

Covers Anderson, Bedford, Blount, Bradley, Cheatham, Crockett, Hamilton, Haywood, Loudon, Rutherford, Sullivan, Tipton, and Wilson counties.

5178. Holt, Albert C. "Bibliography of works referred to..." In his: Economic and social beginnings of Tennessee. Nashville [1923?] p. 157-62.

Locates manuscripts, documentary material, newspapers, etc., when known.

5179. Lawson McGhee Library. Calvin Morgan McClung historical collection of books, pamphlets, manuscripts, pictures and maps relating to early western travel and the history and genealogy of Tennessee and other southern states. Knoxville, Tenn.: Knoxville Lithographing Co., 1921. 192p.

5180. Mellen, George F. "Calvin Morgan McClung and his library." Tennessee historical magazine, 7 (April 1921), 3-26.

A detailed analysis by states and subjects, of historical collection of McClung, presented to Lawson McGhee Library, Knoxville, Tenn.

5181. Sioussat, St. George L. "A preliminary report upon the archives of Tennessee." American Historical Association annual report, 2 (1906), 197-238.

Describes holdings in Office of the Secretary of State, Secretary of the Department of Archives, State Library, and other public offices.

5182. Tennessee State Library. "Catalogue-Tennesseeana." In: Tennessee State Library biennial report, 1911-12, p. 31-133.

Books listed are all in Tennessee State Library.

5183. U. S. Library of Congress. Tennessee's Sesquicentennial exhibition, held at the Library of Congress... June 1, 1946 - October 21, 1946. Wash.: Govt. Print. Off., 1946. 71p.

Catalog of 468 rare books, manuscripts, maps, photographs, prints, newspapers, and music from the Library's collections, and documents from National Archives.

5184. Wisconsin State Historical Society Library. Calendar of the Tennessee and King's Mountain papers of the Draper collection of manuscripts. Madison: The Society, 1929. 698p. (Publications of the State Historical Society of Wisconsin, Calendar series III)

Texas

5185. Barker, Eugene C. "Report on the public archives of Texas." American Historical Association annual report, 2 (1901), 353-58.

Locates public and private collections of Texas archives: Colonial (to 1836), Republican (1836-45), and State.

5186. Castañeda, Carlos Eduardo. A report

on the Spanish archives in San Antonio, Texas. San Antonio: Yanaguana Society, 1937. 167p. (Yanaguana Society publications, v. 1)

A calendar of over 2,000 manuscripts, 1736-1838, in the County Clerk's office of San Antonio.

5187. Evans, Luther H. "Texana in the Nation's capitol." Southwestern historical quarterly, 50 (1946), 220-35.

Describes Texas Centennial exhibition in Library of Congress, and materials in National Archives.

5188. Garrison, George P., ed. "Diplomatic correspondence of the republic of Texas." Pt. 1. American Historical Association annual report, 2 (1907), 1-646.

Materials found in archives of Texas; if location is not given, letters are in State Library.

5189. Gutsch, Milton R. "Texas and the preservation of war history materials." Mississippi Valley Historical Association proceedings, 10 (1918-19), 95-107.

Description of World War I collection in University of Texas.

5190. Harrison, Guy Bryan, Jr. The Texas collection of Baylor University. Waco: Baylor Univ. Press, 1940. 75p. (Baylor bulletin 44, no. 4, Dec. 1940; Baylor University historical publications, series 1)

General description of books on Texas in Baylor University. Lists some rare items.

5191. Historical Records Survey - Tex. An inventory of the colonial archives of Texas: municipality of Brazoria, 1832-37. San Antonio: Historical Records Survey, 1940. 120p.

5192. Historical Records Survey - Tex. Inventory of the county archives of Texas. San Antonio: Texas Historical Records Survey, 1937-41. 24v.

Covers Bandera, Bastrop, Brown, Caldwell, Calhoun, Denton, DeWitt, Fayette, Gillespie, Gregg, Guadalupe, Hays, Hood, Jackson, Marion, Milam, Mills, Orange, Robertson, Rockwall, Sabine, Somervell, Uvalde, and Wilson counties.

5193. Lounsbury, Ralph G. "Early Texas and the National Archives." Southwestern historical quarterly, 46 (1943), 203-13.

Survey of materials relating to Texas in National Archives.

5194. McLean, M. D. "The Bexar archives." Southwestern historical quarterly, 50 (1947), 493-96.

Describes collection of official Spanish documents accumulated in San Antonio de Béxar, then capital of Texas. Now located in University of Texas archives.

5195. Michigan, University, William L. Clements Library. Fifty Texas rarities, selected from the library of Mr. Everett D. Graff for an exhibition. Ann Arbor: The Library, 1946. 40p. (Bulletin, no. 46)

Locates copies in 57 libraries.

5196. Raines, C. W. A bibliography of Texas; being a descriptive list of books, pamphlets, and documents relating to Texas in print and manuscript since 1536. Austin: Gammel Book Co., 1896. 268p.

No locations, but author stated, "The materials noted... with comparatively few exceptions, may now be found within the limits of Texas. Many of them are owned by the Texas State Library."

5197. San Jacinto Museum of History Association. A checklist of Texana. Houston, Texas: San Jacinto Museum of History Association, 1949. 37p.

Calendar of 162 documents ranging in date from 1805 to 1891, a majority relating to the Mexican War.

5198. Smither, Harriet. "The archives of Texas." American archivist, 3 (1940), 187-200.

History and description of various depositories.

5199. Texas State Library. Calendar of the papers of Mirabeau Buonaparte Lamar, prepared from the original papers in the Texas State Library, by Elizabeth Howard West. Austin: Von Boeckmann-Jones Co., 1914. 355p.

5200. U. S. Library of Congress. Texas centennial exhibition, held at the Library of Congress... December 15, 1945 - April 15, 1946. Wash.: Govt. Print. Off., 1946. 54p.

Catalog of 371 rare books, manuscripts,

maps, photographs, and prints from the Library's collections.

5201. U. S. Library of Congress, Division of Bibliography. "Texas: a bibliographical list." Wash., Feb. 23, 1929. 25p. Typed.

5202. Whatley, W. A. "The historical manuscript collections of the University of Texas." Texas history teachers' bulletin, 9 (Nov. 1920), 19-25.

Utah

5203. Historical Records Survey - Utah. Introduction to inventory of state archives of Utah. The state of Deseret. Salt Lake City, 1940. 187p. Reprinted from Utah State Historical Society quarterly, 8 (1940), 65-251.

5204. Historical Records Survey - Utah. Inventory of the county archives of Utah. Ogden: Utah Historical Records Survey, 1937-41. 12v.
Covers Box Elder, Carbon, Daggett, Emery, Grand, Morgan, Sanpete, Tooele, Uintah, Utah, Wasatch, and Weber counties.

5205. U. S. Library of Congress. Centennial of the settlement of Utah exhibition, June 7, 1947 - August 31, 1947. Wash.: Govt. Print. Off., 1947. 72p.
Catalog of 414 rare books, manuscripts, maps, prints, photographs, newspapers and music from Library of Congress collections, National Archives, National Gallery of Art, U. S. Geological Survey, National Park Service, and Association of American Railroads.

Vermont

5206. Historical Records Survey - Vt. Inventory of municipal and town archives: Vermont. Montpelier: Vermont Historical Records Survey, 1939-41. 33v.
Covers towns in Addison, Chittenden, Franklin, Grand Isle, Lamoille, Oreans, Rutland, Windham, and Windsor counties.

5207. Historical Records Survey - Vt. Inventory of the county archives of Vermont. Montpelier: Historical Records Survey, 1936. 32p.
Lamoille County only.

5208. Shearer, Augustus Hunt. "Report on the archives of the state of Vermont." American Historical Association annual report, (1915), 311-55.
Describes collections held in state capitol and those public offices scattered around the state.

5209. U. S. Library of Congress, Division of Bibliography. "List of writings on the history of Vermont." Wash., [1908?] 13p. Typed.

5210. Vermont, University, Wilbur Library. Calendar of Ira Allen papers in the Wilbur Library, University of Vermont. Montpelier, Vt.: Historical Records Survey, 1939. 149p.

Virginia

5211. Cappon, Lester J. Bibliography of Virginia history since 1865. University, Va.: Institute for Research in the Social Sciences, 1930. 900p. (Institute monographs, no. 5)
Locates 6,242 items in 10 Virginia libraries, and in 18 libraries outside the state.

5212. Echenrode, H. J. "List of manuscripts exhibited by the Virginia State Library and the Virginia Historical Society at the Jamestown Exposition." Virginia State Library annual report, (1907), 66-101.
Composed of documents owned by the 2 libraries.

5213. Hariot, Thomas. A brief and true report of the new found land of Virginia. A facsimile reproduction. Ann Arbor: University of Michigan, William L. Clements Library, 1931. 46p. (Ann Arbor facsimile series, no. 1)
Includes a census of copies of 1588 quarto by Randolph G. Adams.

5214. Historical Records Survey - Va. Inventory of the county archives of Virginia. Richmond: Historical Records Survey, 1938-43. 9v.
Covers Amelia, Brunswick, Chesterfield, Dinwiddie, Isle of Wight, Middlesex, Powhatan, Prince George, and Southampton counties.

5215. Malone, Miles S. "Falmouth and the Shenandoah: trade before the Revolution." American historical review, 40 (1935), 693-703.
Description of the Allason manuscripts in the Virginia State Library. A picture of life in the Lower Shenandoah Valley up to 1775.

5216. Morison, Samuel Eliot. "Exhibition of Virginiana in the Widener Library treasure room." Harvard alumni bulletin, 37 (1934), 159-61, 196-99.

Description of rare books and manuscripts pertaining to early Virginia.

5217. New York Public Library. "List of works in the New York Public Library relating to Virginia." New York Public Library bulletin, 11 (1907), 64-83, 99-125, 143-68. Reprinted. 71p.

Includes state and local history.

5218. New York Public Library. "The Smyth of Nibley papers, 1613-1674." New York Public Library bulletin, 1 (1897), 186-90.

A calendar. Selections with title, "Virginia papers," appeared in the Bulletin, 3 (1899), 160-71, 208-23, 248-58, 276-95.

5219. Stanard, William G. "Virginia archives." American Historical Association annual report, 1 (1903), 645-64.

Describes records on file in Virginia State Library, Virginia Historical Society, Library of Congress, and elsewhere.

5220. Thompson, Edith E. B. "A Scottish merchant in Falmouth in the eighteenth century." Virginia magazine of history and biography, 39 (1931), 108-17, 230-38.

Description of William Allason papers in Virginia State Library, dealing with social and economic life of Virginia, relations with England, and Allason family.

5221. Tyler, Lyon G. "Preservation of Virginia history." North Carolina historical review, 3 (1926), 529-38.

Describes work of Virginia State Library in detail and other agencies more briefly.

5222. U. S. Library of Congress, Division of Bibliography. "References on the boundary controversies between Virginia (and West Virginia) and Maryland." Wash., Sept. 14, 1914. 9p. Typed.

5223. U. S. National Park Service, Historical Division. A bibliography of the Virginia campaign and siege of Yorktown, 1781. Yorktown, Va.: Colonial National Historical Park, 1941. 162p.

Classified list, with descriptions and locations of archival and manuscript materials.

5224. Virginia Historical Society. Catalogue of the manuscripts in the collection of the Virginia Historical Society, and also of some printed papers. Richmond: W. E. Jones, 1901. 120p.

A list of all manuscripts, including autograph letters and documents, in Society's collections.

5225. Virginia State Library. "A bibliography of Virginia. Part 1. Containing the titles of books in the Virginia State Library which relate to Virginia and Virginians, the titles of those books written by Virginians, and of those printed in Virginia but not including the titles of the official editions of the laws, of the journals of the legislative bodies, of the reports of administrative officers, and other published official documents," by Earl G. Swem. Virginia State Library bulletin, 8 (1915), 31-767.

5226. Virginia State Library. "A bibliography of Virginia. Part 2. Containing the titles of the printed official documents of the commonwealth, 1776-1916," by Earl G. Swem. Virginia State Library bulletin, 10 (1917), 1-1404.

5227. Virginia State Library. "A bibliography of Virginia. Part 3. The acts and the journals of the General Assembly of the colony, 1619-1776," by Earl G. Swem. Virginia State Library bulletin, 12 (1919), 1-71.

5228. Virginia State Library. "A bibliography of Virginia. Part 4. Three series of sessional documents of the House of Delegates: extra session, January 7 - April 4, 1861; called session, September 15 - October 6, 1862; and adjourned session, January 7 - March 31, 1863," by W. L. Hall. Virginia State Library bulletin, 18 (1932), 57-96.

5229. Virginia State Library. "List of manuscripts recently deposited in the Virginia State Library by the State Auditor," comp. by Earl G. Swem. Virginia State Library bulletin, 7 (1914), 1-32.

Lists some thousands of documents of Revolutionary and post-Revolutionary periods, important for economic and social history of state. Also included is a collection of George Rogers Clark papers.

5230. Virginia State Library. "A trial bibliography of colonial Virginia. Special report of the Department of Bibliography," by W. Clayton-Torrence. In: Virginia State Library annual report, 1908-10. 2v.

Lists publications issued from 1608 to 1776. Locates copies in Virginia State Library, Virginia Historical Society, and in libraries outside the South.

5231. Virginia State Library. Virginia and the Bill of Rights. Richmond, 1942. 14p.

Description of documents in Library pertaining to adoption of Bill of Rights.

5232. Virginia State Library, Archives Division. Calendar of transcripts in the Virginia State Library. Richmond: D. Bottom, Supt. Pub. Prtg., 1905. 658, 44p.

5233. Virginia, University, Library. Annual report on historical collections. Charlottesville, 1931-date.

Lists manuscript collections received by University of Virginia Library and occasionally mentions other accessions. For first 10 years entitled "Annual Report of the Archivist, University of Virginia Library."

5234. Virginia, University, Library. The Byrd library, a collection of Virginiana in the library of the University of Virginia, comp. by John S. Patton. Charlottesville: Univ. of Virginia Press, 1914. 45p.

5235. Virginia, University, Library. General index to first fifteen annual volumes on historical collections, University of Virginia Library, 1931-1945. [Charlottesville, 1947] 144p.

5236. Virginia War History Commission. "[Report] supplement," nos. 1-4. Virginia magazine of history and biography, 29 (1921), 65-96, 193-224, 305-36, 449-96.

No. 1, source material from Virginia counties; no. 2, source material from Virginia cities; no. 3, calendar of military histories, narratives and reports; no. 4, lists and calendars of source material. Material now in Virginia War Archives.

5237. Wisconsin State Historical Society Library. The Preston and Virginia papers of the Draper collection of manuscripts. Madison: The Society, 1915. 357p. (Publications of the State Historical Society of Wisconsin, Calendar series I)

Papers relate to frontier phase of American history in Virginia between 1651 and 1901.

5238. Wright, Louis B. "Materials for the study of the civilization of Virginia." Princeton University Library chronicle, 10 (1948), 3-15.

Describes books and manuscripts on Virginia held by Princeton University Library.

Washington

5239. Bowman, Jacob N. "Report on the archives of the state of Washington." American Historical Association annual report, 1 (1908), 365-98.

"A general view of the department archives and... a calendar of some of the records," with order of listings according to office vaults.

5240. Historical Records Survey - Wash. Inventory of the county archives of Washington. Pullman: Historical Records Survey, 1937-42. 15v.

Covers Adams, Asotin, Benton, Chelan, Cowlitz, Garfield, King, Lewis, Lincoln, Pend Oreille, Skagit, Snohomish, Spokane, Stevens, and Yakima counties.

5241. Murray, Keith. "The Wesley L. Jones papers." Pacific Northwest quarterly, 36 (Jan. 1945), 65-68.

Description of Senator Jones's papers, now in University of Washington.

5242. U. S. Library of Congress, Division of Bibliography. "List of works relating to the history of the state of Washington and of the Oregon country." Wash., 1908. 25p. Typed.

West Virginia

5243. Historical Records Survey - West Va. Calendar of the Arthur I. Boreman letters in the State Department of Archives and History. Charleston, W. Va., 1939. 91p.

5244. Historical Records Survey - West Va. Calendar of the Francis Harrison Pierpont letters and papers in West Virginia depositories. Charleston: West Virginia Historical Records Survey, 1940. 387p.

5245. Historical Records Survey - West Va. Calendar of the Henry Mason Matthews letters and papers in the State Department of Archives and History. [West Virginia] Charleston, W. Va., 1941. 327p.

5246. Historical Records Survey - West Va. Calendar of the J. J. Jacob letters in West Virginia depositories. Charleston: West Virginia Historical Records Survey, 1940. 251p.

5247. Historical Records Survey - West Va. Calendar of the William E. Stevenson letters in the State Department of Archives and History [West Virginia] Charleston, West Va., 1939. 105p.

5248. Historical Records Survey - West Va. Inventory of the county archives of West Virginia. Charleston: West Virginia Historical Records Survey, 1937-42. 13v.
  Covers Gilmer, Grant, Lincoln, Marion, Mineral, Monroe, Pendleton, Pocahontas, Putnam, Randolph, Ritchie, Roane, and Taylor counties.

5249. Lewis, Virgil A. "A bibliography of the journals and public documents of West Virginia which have been issued since the formation of the State." In: West Virginia Department of Archives and History, second biennial report, Charleston, 1908, p. 13-71.

5250. U. S. Library of Congress, Division of Bibliography. "A list of references on the Monongahela Valley, West Virginia (historical, industrial, agricultural and social development)." Wash., Apr. 11, 1934. 13p. Typed.

5251. U. S. Library of Congress, Division of Bibliography. "List of works on the formation of the state of West Virginia from the commonwealth of Virginia and their ensuing relations." Wash., Nov. 1, 1913. 13p. Typed.

5252. West Virginia Dept. of Archives and History. A bibliography of West Virginia, comp. by Innis Davis. Charleston, 1939. 143, 392p. (West Virginia Dept. of Archives and History, Biennial report, 1936-38)

5253. West Virginia Dept. of Archives and History. Third biennial report. Charleston: News-Mail Co., 1911. 279p.
  Contains a classified list of works relating to Virginia and West Virginia in the Department, edited by Virgil A. Lewis.

5254. West Virginia, University, Library, Division of Documents. First report... 1935-1936, with a descriptive list of manuscript collections. Morgantown: The University, 1936. 24p. (West Virginia University bulletin, ser. 37, no. 1-11, July 1936)

5255. West Virginia, University, Library, Division of Documents. Second report... 1936-1949, with a descriptive list of manuscript collections. Morgantown: The University, 1949. 28p. (West Virginia University bulletin, ser. 50, no. 2-1, August 1949)

5256. Wilson, Nancy. "The library of the Department of Archives and History." West Virginia history, 3 (Jan. 1942), 147-55.

Wisconsin

5257. Bradley, Isaac Samuel. A bibliography of Wisconsin's participation in the war between the states, based upon material contained in the Wisconsin Historical Library. Madison: Wisconsin History Commission, 1911. 42p. (Wisconsin History Commission: Original papers, no. 5)

5258. Fish, Carl Russell. "Report on the public archives of Wisconsin." American Historical Association annual report, 1 (1905), 377-419.
  Lists archives to be found in public offices.

5259. Historical Records Survey - Wis. Guide to manuscript depositories in Wisconsin. Madison: Wisconsin Historical Records Survey, 1941. 36 numb. l.

5260. Historical Records Survey - Wis. Inventory of municipal and town archives: Wisconsin. Madison: Wisconsin Historical Records Survey, 1941-42. 3v.
  Covers towns of Cudahy, Wauwatosa, and Greendale.

5261. Historical Records Survey - Wis. Inventory of the county archives of Wisconsin. Madison: Wisconsin Historical Records Survey, 1939-42. 18v.
  Covers Barron, Buffalo, Chippewa, Clark, Douglas, Dunn, Eau Claire, Grant, Jackson, La Crosse, Marathon, Monroe, Oneida, Pepin, Polk and Sheboygan counties.

5262. Historical Records Survey - Wis.

HISTORY

Inventory survey of the state archives of Wisconsin. Department of State. Madison: Wisconsin Historical Records Survey, 1942. 265 numb. 1.

5263. Kellogg, Louise Phelps. "The Fairchild papers." Wisconsin magazine of history, 10 (1927), 259-81.

Description and evaluation of Fairchild family papers, now in State Historical Society of Wisconsin. Especially rich in Wisconsin history, 1850-90.

5264. Kellogg, Louise Phelps. "The State Historical Society of Wisconsin." Bibliographical Society of America papers, 16 (1922), 47-52.

Description of the Society's source materials for the history of the West.

5265. Libby, Orin G. "Report on the public archives of Wisconson." American Historical Association annual report, 2 (1900), 294-97.

Locates some manuscript records in Executive Department, State Department and Land Office, of Wisconsin.

5266. Schlinkert, Leroy W. "The Charles McCarthy papers." Wisconsin magazine of history, 23 (1940), 308-12.

In Wisconsin State Historical Society. Papers relating to Wisconsin legislation from 1906-21.

5267. U. S. Library of Congress. Wisconsin centennial exhibition, May 29, 1948 - August 23, 1948. Wash.: Govt. Print. Off., 1948. 64p.

Catalog of 314 rare books, manuscripts, maps, prints, photographs, newspapers and music, from Library of Congress, National Archives, National Gallery of Art, and U. S. Forest Service.

5268. Wisconsin Legislative Reference Library. "Wisconsin's historical manuscripts," by Alice E. Smith. Wisconsin blue book, (1933), 1-17.

Describes manuscript collection of Wisconsin Historical Society.

5269. Wisconsin State Historical Society. Guide to the manuscripts of the Wisconsin Historical Society, ed. by Alice E. Smith. Madison: The Society, 1944. 290p.

Guide to a collection of 720,000 pieces and 2,500 volumes of manuscripts.

5270. Wisconsin State Historical Society Library. Catalogue of the library of the State Historical Society of Wisconsin, prep. by Daniel S. Durrie and Isabel Durrie. Madison: Pub. by order of the state, 1873-87. 7v.

5271. Wisconsin State Historical Society Library. Strong and Woodman manuscript collections in the Wisconsin State Historical Library. Madison: The Society, 1915. 22p. (Bulletin of information, no. 78)

Wyoming

5272. Historical Records Survey - Wy. Inventory of the county archives of Wyoming. Cheyenne: Historical Records Survey, 1938-42. 6v.

Covers Goshen, Laramie, Lincoln, Park, Platte, and Sweetwater counties.

5273. Jackson, W. Turrentine. "Territorial papers of Wyoming in the National Archives." Annals of Wyoming, 16 (Jan. 1944), 45-55.

5274. Mumey, Nolie. The Teton Mountains, their history and traditions. Denver: Artcraft Press, 1947. 462p.

Bibliography, p. 403-47, locates copies in some 60 libraries, chiefly in western United States.

5275. U. S. Library of Congress, Division of Bibliography. "Wyoming: a bibliographical list," comp. by Florence S. Hellman. Wash., Jan. 23, 1936. 98p. Typed.

5276. Willard, James F. "The public archives of Wyoming." American Historical Association annual report, 1 (1913), 275-317.

"Records, territorial and state, found in the capitol building or elsewhere in Cheyenne."

5277. Wyoming, University, Archives Department. University archives and western historical manuscripts collections, University of Wyoming. Laramie, 1949. 12p.

Briefly describes holdings of Department.

Territorial possessions

5278. Reid, Charles Frederick, ed. Bibliography of the Virgin Islands of the United States. N. Y.: H. W. Wilson, 1941. 225p.

"The major portion of the research work was done at the New York Public Library."

5279. U. S. Library of Congress, Division of Bibliography. Alaska: a selected list of recent references, comp. by Grace Hadley Fuller. Wash., 1943. 181p.

5280. U. S. Library of Congress, Division of Bibliography. Aleutian Islands: a list of references, comp. by Grace Hadley Fuller. Wash., 1943. 41p.

LATIN AMERICAN HISTORY

5281. Bealer, Lewis W. "Contribution to a bibliography on Artigas and the beginnings of Uruguay, 1810-1820." Hispanic American historical review, 11 (1931), 108-34.

No specific locations, but it is noted that most items are to be found in University of California (Berkeley), and greater part of balance in Stanford University Library.

5282. Bealer, Lewis W. "Some recent additions to the South American collection in the University of California libraries." Hispanic American historical review, 12 (1932), 103-06.

Mentions some notable acquisitions from 1927 to 1932.

5283. Boston College Library. Catalogue of books, manuscripts, etc. in the Carribbeana section (specializing in Jamaicana) of the Nicholas M. Williams memorial ethnological collection. Chestnut Hill, Mass.: Boston College Library, 1932. 133p.

By topics and places. 1,674 entries.

5284. Boston Public Library. "Manuscripts on the West Indies," by Margaret Munsterberg More books, 4 (1929), 313-21.

Description of a collection received by the Boston Public Library in 1877.

5285. Boston University, New England Institute of Inter-American Affairs. An informal list of books on Latin America for the general reader and a directory of Latin American collections in New England libraries. [Boston, 1943] 16p.

Describes collections of books on Latin America of 23 New England colleges.

5286. Brown University, Photographic Laboratory. Latin Americana. Providence, 1942-43. no. 1-2.

"Lists of Latin American titles filmed by Brown University for its library."

5287. Butler, Ruth Lapham. "Edward E. Ayer's quest for Hispano-Americana." Inter-American bibliographical review, 1 (1941), 81-90.

Ayer collection now in Newberry Library, Chicago. A description of the "Inter-American" books.

5288. Cardozo, Manuel S. "Guide to the manuscripts in the Lima Library, Catholic University of America." In: Handbook of Latin American studies. Cambridge, 1941. no. 6, (1940), 471-504.

5289. Castañeda, Carlos E. and Dabbs, J. Autrey. "The Manuel E. Gondra collection." Handbook of Latin American studies, 6 (1940), 505-17.

Describes collection of manuscripts and maps in Gondra collection of University of Texas. Sources for study of Paraguay, Argentina, Brazil, Uruguay, Chile, Bolivia and Peru.

5290. Catholic University of America Library. "The Portuguese manuscripts in the Ibero-American Library at the Catholic University of America," by Manoel de Oliveira Lima. Hispanic American historical review, 8 (1928), 261-80.

5291. Chicago, Library of International Relations. Titles chosen as representative of the collection on Central and South America. Chicago: The Library [1943] 36p.

5292. Chicago Public Library, Omnibus Project. Checklist of films and slides on Latin America, located in the Chicago area. Chicago, 1942. 33 l.

5293. Claremont College Library. American hemispheric solidarity; library resources. Claremont, 1943. 49 numb. l.

Lists books, pamphlets and magazine articles in Claremont College libraries.

5294. [Duke University Library] Catalogo de la Biblioteca Peruana, propiedad de Dn. Francisco Perez de Velasco. Lima: Libreria e Imprenta Gil, 1918. 195p.

Catalog of 3,000-volume Peruvian collection nearly all now in Duke University Library.

5295. Ford, Worthington C. The Isle of Pines, 1668; an essay in bibliography. Boston: Club of Odd Volumes, 1920. 116p.

Locates copies of 30 editions of this book.

5296. Hanke, Lewis. "The Luis Dobles Segreda collection." Library of Congress quarterly journal of current acquisitions, 1 (Jan.-March, 1944), 57-62.

Description of a 6,000-volume collection on Costa Rica acquired by the Library of Congress.

5297. Held, Ray E. "Hispanic American history and description in the University of Florida libraries: a bibliography." Gainesville: Univ. of Florida, 1946. 24 numb. l. Typed.

5298. [Henry E. Huntington Library] From Panama to Peru; the conquest of Peru by the Pizarros, the rebellion of Gonzalo Pizarro and the pacification by La Gasca. London: Maggs Bros., 1925. 620p.

Items described, consisting of 3,000 manuscript pages, 1537-80, now owned by Huntington Library.

5299. Henry E. Huntington Library. Mexico in the sixteenth century; an exhibition. San Marino, 1938. 18p.

Includes 38 of earliest histories and imprints of Mexico and several contemporary manuscripts.

5300. Hilton, Ronald, ed. Handbook of Hispanic source material and research organizations in the United States. Toronto, Canada: Univ. of Toronto Press, 1942. 441p.

Describes collections of Hispanic source materials in the United States.

5301. Historical Records Survey. List of the papeles procedentes de Cuba (Cuban papers) in the archives in the North Carolina Historical Commission. Raleigh: The Survey, 1942. 78p.

5302. Hussey, Roland D. "Manuscript Hispanic Americana in the Ayer collection of the Newberry Library, Chicago." Hispanic American historical review, 10 (1930), 113-18.

5303. Hussey, Roland Dennis. "Manuscript Hispanic Americana in the Harvard College Library." Hispanic American historical review, 17 (1937), 259-77.

5304. International Bureau of the American Republics. A list of books, magazine articles, and maps relating to Central America, including the republics of Costa Rica, Guatemala, Honduras, Nicaragua, and Salvador, 1800-1900, prep. by P. Lee Phillips. Comp. for the Bureau of the American Republics. Wash.: Govt. Print. Off., 1902. 109p.

Locates copies in Library of Congress, British Museum and the United States State Department.

5305. International Bureau of the American Republics. Mexico. A geographical sketch, with special reference to economic conditions and prospects of future development. Wash.: Govt. Print. Off., 1900. 385p.

Bibliography, p. 350-356; cartography, by P. L. Phillips, p. 356-74. Locates maps in Library of Congress, British Museum, or United States War Department.

5306. Jones, Cecil Knight. A bibliography of Latin American bibliographies. 2d ed. rev. & enl. Wash.: Govt. Print. Off., 1942. 311p. [U. S. Library of Congress. Latin American series, no. 2]

Gives Library of Congress card numbers for titles in Library of Congress.

5307. Jones, Cecil Knight. "Hispano-Americana in the Library of Congress." Hispanic American historical review, 2 (1919), 96-104.

5308. Keniston, Hayward. List of works for the study of Hispanic-American history. N. Y.: Hispanic Society of America, 1920. 451p. (Hispanic notes and monographs)

No locations given, but the larger part of the list is accessible in the Society's Library, and in four geographical centers in the United States.

5309. "Latin American collections in the United States." Library journal, 44 (1919), 223-28.

Describes collections in 9 libraries.

5310. Lima, Manoel de Oliveira. "The Portuguese manuscripts in the Ibero-American Library at the Catholic University of America." Hispanic American historical review,

8 (1928), 261-80.

Manuscripts chiefly diplomatic in character.

5311. Lord, Robert A. "Contribution toward a bibliography on the O'Higgins family in America." Hispanic American historical review, 12 (1932), 107-38.

Of particular interest for Peruvian and Chilean history. Lists 247 items with locations in Library of Congress, Pan American Union, and New York Public Library.

5312. NcNeil, Paul Alexander. Notes on the works of Ferdinand Denis, 1789-1890, Americanist, in the Oliveira Lima Collection, Catholic University of America. Washington, 1941. 8p.

5313. Manchester, Alan K. "Descriptive bibliography of the Brazilian section of the Duke University Library." Hispanic American historical review, 13 (1933), 238-66, 495-523. Reprinted. 69p.

"The various items are grouped, with convenient subdivisions, under three main heads: bibliographical aids; contemporary accounts, 1500-1822; and works written since 1822."

5314. Michigan, University, William L. Clements Library. The conquest of Mexico. Ann Arbor, 1924. 4p. (Bulletin, no. 1)

Description of an exhibition.

5315. Michigan, University, William L. Clements Library. The conquest of Peru, 1531-1546. Ann Arbor, 1925. 4p. (Bulletin, no. 10)

Catalog of an exhibition.

5316. Nachbin, Jac. "Descriptive calendar of South American manuscripts in the Northwestern University Library." Hispanic American historical review, 12 (1932), 242-59, 376-86, 503-21; 13 (1933), 124-42, 267-80, 402-19, 524-42.

Describes manuscripts dated 1574 to near end of 19th century.

5317. New-York Historical Society. "Latin Americana in the Society's collections," by Harold F. Nutzhorn and Susan E. Lyman. New-York Historical Society quarterly bulletin, 28 (1944), 11-20.

A selective list.

5318. New York Public Library. "List of works in the New York Public Library relating to Mexico." New York Public Library bulletin, 13 (1909), 622-62, 675-737, 748-829. Reprinted. 186p.

5319. New York Public Library. "List of works in the New York Public Library relating to the West Indies," comp. by Daniel Carl Haskell. New York Public Library bulletin, 16 (1912), 7-49, 231-78, 307-55, 367-440, 455-84, 503-46, 563-621. Reprinted. 392p.

5320. Notre Dame, University. "The library of South Americana of the University of Notre Dame." Hispanic American historical review, 2 (1919), 490-92.

Brief description of collection, taken from Bulletin of the University of Notre Dame, (July 1917), 9-11.

5321. [Pan American Union] A list of books, magazine articles, and maps relating to Central America, including the republics of Costa Rica, Guatemala, Honduras, Nicaragua, and Salvador, 1800-1900, prep. by Philip Lee Phillips. Wash.: Govt. Print. Off., 1902. 109p.

Copies located in Library of Congress and U. S. Department of State.

5322. Pan American Union, Columbus Memorial Library. Bibliographies pertaining to Latin America in the Columbus Memorial Library of the Pan American Union. Wash., 1928. 34 numb. l.

5323. Pan American Union, Columbus Memorial Library. Catalogue of books, pamphlets, periodicals and maps relating to the republic of Bolivia in the Columbus Memorial Library. Wash.: Govt. Print. Off., 1905. 23p.

5324. Pan American Union, Columbus Memorial Library. Fifty years of the library of the Pan American Union, 1890-1940, by Charles E. Babcock. Wash.: Pan American Union [1940] 9p. (Bibliographic series, no. 23)

General description of Library's resources.

5325. Pan American Union, Columbus Memorial Library. List of Latin American history and description in the Columbus Memorial Library. Wash., [1907] 98p. Supplement no. 1. 1909. 34p.; supplement no. 2. 1914. 136p.

5326. Pan American Union, Columbus Memorial Library. Selected list of books (in English) on Latin America. Wash.: The Union, 1945. 86 numb. 1. (Bibliographic series, no. 4. 7th ed. rev. & enl.)

5327. Pan American Union, Columbus Memorial Library. Source material and special collections dealing with Latin America in libraries of the United States, by A. C. Wilgus. Wash.: The Union, 1934. 23 numb. 1. (Pan American Union congress and conference series, no. 14)

General descriptions, arranged by libraries.

5328. Pan American Union, Columbus Memorial Library. Theses on Pan American topics, prepared by candidates for degrees in universities and colleges in the United States. Wash., 1941. 170 numb. 1. (Bibliographic series, no. 5. 3d ed. rev. & enl.)

5329. Peraza Sarausa, Fermín. Bibliografías cubanas. Wash.: [Govt. Print. Off.] 1945. 58p. ([U. S.] Library of Congress. [Latin American series, no. 7])

Lists only titles in Library of Congress.

5330. Phillips, Philip Lee. A list of books, magazine articles, and maps relating to Chile, comp. for the International Bureau of the American Republics. Wash.: Govt. Print. Off., 1903. 110p.

Locates copies in Library of Congress, U. S. State Department, etc.

5331. Pombo, Jorge. Biblioteca de Jorge Pombo. Catalogo de la sección historia y geografía de America. (Obras escogidas) 1906. Bogota: Impr. de "La Idea," [1906] 58p.

Most of collection now in John Crerar Library.

5332. Ragatz, Lowell Joseph. A guide for the study of British Caribbean history, 1763-1834, including the abolition and emancipation movements. Wash.: Govt. Print. Off., 1932. 725p. (American Historical Association annual report, 1930, v. 3)

Bibliography lists materials in 69 repositories in 7 countries.

5333. Rivera, Rodolfo O. "Peruvian collection of Duke University." Hispanic American historical review, 10 (1930), 255-56.

Brief description of a 3,000-volume collection.

5334. Robertson, James Alexander. "Recent acquisitions of German books in the Library of Congress referring to Hispanic America." Hispanic American historical review, 12 (1932), 522-29.

5335. Sánchez, Manuel Segundo. Bibliografía venezolanista; contribución al conocimiento de los libros extranjeros relativos a Venezuela y sus grandes hombres, pub. o reimpresos desde el siglo XIX. Caracas: Empresa el Cojo, 1914. 494p.

Collection purchased in 1913, and divided among John Crerar Library, Harvard University, and Northwestern University.

5336. Spell, Lota M. "Some of the Hispanic American resources of the University of Texas." Hispanic American historical review, 19 (1939), 100-01.

Brief summary of principal collections in field.

5337. Texas, University, Library. Guide to the Latin American manuscripts in the University of Texas Library, ed. by Carlos E. Castañeda and Jack A. Dabbs. Cambridge: Harvard Univ. Press, 1939. 217p. (Committee on Latin American Studies, American Council of Learned Societies, Miscellaneous publication, no. 1)

"A complete list... [with the exception of the Manuel Gondra papers] of the manuscript sources in the University of Texas for the study of the history and culture of Latin America and the former provinces of Spain within the present limits of the United States..." Introd.

5338. Tulane University, Department of Middle American Research. Its activities and its aims. New Orleans: Tulane University, 1932. 39p.

Includes a description of the library.

5339. Tulane University, Department of Middle American Research. Rare Americana. New Orleans: Tulane University, 1932. 26p.

5340. Tulane University, Department of Middle American Research Library. Manuscripts in the Department of Middle American

Research, described by Arthur E. Gropp. New Orleans: Department of Middle American Research, Tulane University of Louisiana, 1933. p. [217]-97. (Middle American pamphlets: no. 5 of Publication no. 5 in the "Middle American research series")

5341. Tulane University, Department of Middle American Research Library. An inventory of the collections of the Middle American Research Institute, Tulane University. 4v.

1. "Callander I. Fayssoux collection of William Walker papers." 1937. 28p. (Relates to Walker's filibustering expeditions against Nicaragua in the 1850's)
2. "Calendar of the Yucatecan letters." 1939. 240p.
3. "Maps in the Frederick L. Hoffman collection." 1939. 146p.
4. "Maps in the library of the Middle America Research Institute." 1941. 285p. 889 entries.

5342. U. S. Library of Congress. "Annual report on acquisitions: Hispanica." Library of Congress quarterly journal of acquisitions, 5 (Nov. 1947), 19-31; 7 (Nov. 1949), 27-33.

5343. U. S. Library of Congress. "Bermudiana collection." Wash., Jan. 16, 1929. 7p. Typed.
Copy of Library of Congress order sheets. 444 items.

5344. U. S. Library of Congress. "Books relating to Cuba," comp. by A. P. C. Griffin. In: Gonzalo de Quesada. Cuba. Wash.: Govt. Print. Off., 1905. p. 315-446.

5345. U. S. Library of Congress. A list of books, magazine articles and maps relating to Brazil, 1800-1900, comp. by P. L. Phillips. Wash.: Govt. Print. Off., 1901. 145p.

5346. U. S. Library of Congress. List of books relating to Cuba (including references to collected works and periodicals), by A. P. C. Griffin... with a bibliography of maps, by P. Lee Phillips. [2d ed. cor.] Wash.: Govt. Print. Off., 1898. 61p. (55th Congress, 2d sess., 1897-98. Senate document, no. 161)
Lists holdings of Library of Congress and U. S. State Department. Appendix, by Herbert Friedenwald; lists manuscripts in the Library of Congress relating to Cuba.

5347. U. S. Library of Congress, Division of Bibliography. "British Guiana: a bibliographical list," comp. by Florence S. Hellman. Wash., Oct. 20, 1937. 39p. Typed.

5348. U. S. Library of Congress, Division of Bibliography. "British Honduras: a bibliographical list." comp. by Florence S. Hellman. Wash., Mar. 15, 1940. 21p. Typed.

5349. U. S. Library of Congress, Division of Bibliography. British possessions in the Caribbean area: a selected list of references, comp. by Ann Duncan Brown. Wash., 1943. 192p.

5350. U. S. Library of Congress, Division of Bibliography. A list of books (with references to periodicals) on Porto Rico, by A. P. C. Griffin. Wash.: Govt. Print. Off., 1901. 55p.

5351. U. S. Library of Congress, Division of Bibliography. A list of books (with references to periodicals) on the Danish West Indies, by A. P. C. Griffin. Wash.: Govt. Print. Off., 1901. 18p.

5352. U. S. Library of Congress, Division of Bibliography. "A list of references on the Isle of Pines." Wash., July 16, 1936. 9p. Typed.

5353. U. S. Library of Congress, Division of Bibliography. List of references on the Panama Canal and the Panama Canal Zone. Wash.: Govt. Print. Off., 1919. 21p.

5354. U. S. Library of Congress, Division of Bibliography. "Lower California: a bibliographical list." Wash., Aug. 15, 1931. 11p. Typed. [Supplementary list] Dec. 23, 1938. 9p. Typed.

5355. U. S. Library of Congress, Division of Bibliography. The Panama Canal and the Panama Canal Zone; a selected list of references, comp. by Ann Duncan Brown. Wash., 1943. 57p. Supplement to 1919 edition.

5356. U. S. Library of Congress, Division of Bibliography. "Puerto Rico: a selected list of references." Wash., Oct. 5, 1939. 50p. Typed.

5357. U. S. Library of Congress, Division of Bibliography. Puerto Rico: a selected list of recent references, comp. by Ann Duncan Brown. Wash., 1943. 44p.

5358. U. S. Library of Congress, Division of Bibliography. A selected list of references on the Guianas, comp. by Florence S. Hellman. Wash., 1940. 17p.

5359. U. S. Library of Congress, Division of Manuscripts. The Harkness collection in the Library of Congress; calendar of Spanish manuscripts concerning Peru, 1531-1651, prep. by Stella R. Clemence. Wash.: Govt. Print. Off., 1932. 336p.

Chronologically arranged, 1531-1740. Collection comprises 1,405 folios.

5360. U. S. Library of Congress, Division of Manuscripts. The Harkness collection in the Library of Congress; documents from early Peru, the Pizarros and the Almagros, 1531-1578. Wash.: Govt. Print. Off., 1936. 253p.

5361. U. S. Library of Congress, General Reference and Bibliography Division. "The Falkland Islands and its dependencies: a list of recent references," comp. by Helen F. Conover. Wash., Dec. 1, 1944. 8p. Typed.

5362. U. S. Library of Congress, Reference Dept. Martinique: a selected list of references, comp. by Linn R. Blanchard and supplementing a list prepared by the Division of Bibliography in 1923. Wash., 1942. 57p.

5363. U. S. National Archives. List of records of the Bureau of Insular Affairs relating to the Dominican customs receivership, 1905-1940, comp. by Kenneth Munden. Wash., 1943. 29p. (Special lists, no. 5)

5364. U. S. National Archives. Preliminary checklist of the records of the Military Government of Cuba, 1899-1903, comp. by Margareth Jorgenson. [Wash.] 1946. 52p.

5365. U. S. National Archives. Preliminary checklist of the records of the Military Government of Santo Domingo, 1916-1924, comp. by Lyman Hinckley. [Wash., 1945] 10p. (Preliminary checklist, no. 27)

5366. U. S. National Archives. Records of the Bureau of Insular Affairs relating to Puerto Rico, 1898-1934, a list of selected files, comp. by Kenneth Munden and Milton Greenbaum. Wash., 1943. 47p. (Special lists, no. 4)

5367. U. S. National Archives. Records of the Bureau of Insular Affairs relating to the United States military government of Cuba, 1898-1902, and the United States provisional government of Cuba, 1906-1909, a list of selected files, comp. by Kenneth Munden. Wash., 1943. 43p. (Special lists, no. 3)

5368. U. S. Office of Education Library. An annotated list of periodicals useful in the study of Latin American countries, by Martha R. McCabe. Wash.: U. S. Office of Education, 1943. 11p.

5369. U. S. War Dept. Library. Index of publications, articles and maps relating to Mexico, in the War Department Library. Govt. Print. Off., 1896. 120p. (Subject catalogue, no. 3)

Now in U. S. National War College Library.

5370. Wilgus, Alva Curtis, comp. Source materials and special collections dealing with Latin America in libraries of the United States. Wash.: Pan American Union, 1934. 22p. (Pan American Union congress and conference series, no. 14)

OCEANIAN AND POLAR REGIONS HISTORY

Australia and New Zealand

5371. Stanford University Library. Australiana in the Leland Stanford Junior University. [Stanford University, 1901?] 172p. Supplement, 1903; revised, 1906. [Stanford University, California, 1906] 22p. Supplement: Checklist (books recently received) 1906. [Stanford University, 1906]

5372. U. S. Library of Congress, Division of Bibliography. New Zealand: a selected list of references, comp. by Helen F. Conover. [Wash.] 1942. 68p.

5373. U. S. Library of Congress, Division of Bibliography. A selected list of references on Australia, comp. by Grace Hadley Fuller. [Wash.] 1942. 101p.

Philippine Islands

5374. Blair, Emma H. and Robertson, James A. The Philippine Islands, 1493-1898. Bibliography. Cleveland, O.: Arthur H. Clark Co., 1908. 433p.

Forms volume 53 of their "The Philippine Islands, 1493-1898." Lists and describes printed books and manuscripts relating to Philippine Islands, with locations for many items, and descriptions of large collections.

5375. New York Public Library. "Works relating to the Philippine Islands in the New York Public Library." New York Public Library bulletin, 4 (1900), 19-29.

5376. U. S. Library of Congress. A list of books (with references to periodicals) on the Philippine Islands in the Library of Congress, comp. by A. P. C. Griffin... With chronological list of maps in the Library of Congress, by P. Lee Phillips... Wash.: Govt. Print. Off., 1903. 397p. (57th Cong., 2d sess. Senate. Doc. no. 74).

5377. U. S. Library of Congress, Division of Bibliography. List of works relating to the American occupation of the Philippine Islands, 1898-1903; by Appleton P. C. Griffin. Wash.: Govt. Print. Off., 1905. 100p. (Reprinted from the List of books (with references to periodicals) on the Philippine Islands, 1903, with some additions to 1905.)

5378. U. S. Library of Congress, Division of Bibliography. Philippine Islands, with special reference to the question of independence: a bibliographical list of recent writings, comp. by Anne L. Baden. [Wash., 1931] 25p.

5379. U. S. National Archives. Records of the Bureau of Insular Affairs relating to the Philippine Islands, 1898-1935, a list of selected files, comp. by Kenneth Munden, Wash., 1942. 91p. (Special lists, no. 2)

Polar Regions

5380. Brooklyn Public Library. The Polar regions; a list of books in the Brooklyn Public Library, September, 1909. Brooklyn: The Library, 1909. 28p.

5381. John Crerar Library. Union catalogue of literature on Greenland. Chicago: The Library, 1940. 45 numb. l. (Reference list, no. 45)

Includes holdings of Chicago Public Library, John Crerar Library, Newberry Library, and University of Chicago.

Miscellany

5382. Delaware, University, Memorial Library. Calendar of the George Handy Bates Samoan papers at the University of Delaware, prep. by William Ditto Lewis. Wilmington: W. N. Cann, 1942. 41p.

5383. U. S. Library of Congress. Islands of the Pacific; a selected list of references, comp. by Helen F. Conover. Wash., 1943. 154p. Supplement. 1945. 68p.

5384. U. S. Library of Congress. List of books relating to Hawaii (including references to collected works and periodicals), by A. P. C. Griffin. Wash.: Govt. Print. Off., 1898. 26p.

5385. U. S. Library of Congress, Division of Bibliography. A list of books (with references to periodicals) on Samoa and Guam. Wash.: Govt. Print. Off., 1901. 54p.

5386. U. S. Library of Congress, General Reference and Bibliography Division. Netherlands East Indies; a bibliography of books published after 1930, and periodical articles after 1932 available in U. S. libraries. Wash., 1945. 208p.

MILITARY AND NAVAL HISTORY AND SCIENCE

Military history and science

5387. Bethel, Elizabeth. "Early records of the War Department General Staff in National Archives." American archivist, 9 (1945), 241-47.

Description of records for period from 1903 to 1919.

5388. Carnegie Endowment for International Peace Library. Conscientious objectors and war resisters. [Washington, 1939] 8p.

Collection now a part of George Washington University Library.

5389. Carnegie Endowment for International

5390 HISTORY

Peace Library. Conscription of men, material resources and wealth in time of war; with select references on war profiteering, comp. by Mary Alice Matthews. [Wash.] 1940. 15p.

Collection now a part of George Washington University Library.

5390. Haferkorn, Henry Ernest. Poisonous gas in warfare. Wash.: Engineer School, 1917. 27p. (Reprinted from U. S. Corps of Engineers professional memoirs, 9 (1917), no. 48)

Locates titles in Library of Congress and 4 other government libraries.

5391. Hellman, Florence Selma. "Military training for national defense." The booklist, 37 (1941), 337-48.

A bibliography, compiled in Library of Congress.

5392. Huber, Elbert L. "War Department records in the National Archives." Military affairs, 6 (1942), 247-54.

5393. Michigan, University, Library. Early military books in the University of Michigan libraries, by Thomas M. Spaulding and Louis C. Karpinski. Ann Arbor: Univ. of Michigan Press, 1941. 45p.

Lists 372 items, 1493-1800, with locations in 31 American libraries.

5394. Oakland Public Library. Training for national defense, a selected list of technical books in the Oakland Public Library on trades related to the National defense program (exclusive of aviation). 2d ed., rev. [Oakland, Calif.]: The Library, 1941. 51 numb. 1.

5395. Pan American Union, Columbus Memorial Library. Selected list of books and magazine articles on hemisphere defense. Wash.: The Union, 1941. 14p. (Bibliographic series, no. 24)

All material listed held by Pan American Union Library except a few items marked with asterisk.

5396. Peckham, Howard H. "Military papers in the Clements Library." Journal of the American Military History Foundation (Military Affairs), 2 (1938), 126-30.

Describes 23 collections of military papers, 1745-85, in Clements Library, University of Michigan.

5397. Princeton University Library. The art of war, an exhibition of books, maps, prints and manuscripts pertaining to military strategy, the Princeton University Library, December 1943. [Princeton, 1943] 11p.

5398. San Antonio Public Library. A list of books that treat of service and life in the regular army of the United States of America, by Charles G. Sturtevant. San Antonio: The Library, 1942. 12p.

5399. Shriver, Harry Clair. A bibliography of military law, militia law, and the law of the home guard. Wash.: Law Library, Library of Congress, 1941. 56 numb. 1. Photostat reproduction (positive)

5400. U. S. Army War College Library. List of authors and titles and catalogue of maps from August 15, 1903 to September 1, 1904. Wash.: Govt. Print. Off., 1904. 179p. First catalog of library. Supplement. 1905. 65p.

5401. U. S. Army War College Library. Monthly list of military information carded from books, periodicals, and other sources. [Wash.: Govt. Print. Off., 1915-21] 67 nos. in 5 v.

References are available in War College Library.

5402. U. S. Army War College Library. Selected reading list... psychology of leadership. [Wash.] 1944. 9p.

5403. U. S. Coast Artillery School Library. Analytical catalogue of the professional library of the United States Artillery School at Fort Monroe, Va., comp. by Capt. James Chester... and 1st Lieut. Albert Todd... 1881 and 1885. Wash.: Govt. Print. Off., 1886. 341p.

5404. U. S. Command and General Staff School, Fort Leavenworth, Library. Library catalog 1927. The General Service Schools, Fort Leavenworth, Kansas. 55,650 books, pamphlets, and documents, and 1,160 maps and atlases classified by subjects and countries, with alphabetic subject index. Fort Leavenworth: General Service Schools Press, 1927. 754p. Supplement. Fort Leavenworth, 1930. 315p.

5405. U. S. Engineer School Library. Arctic

warfare; a bibliography. Fort Belvoir, Va.: The Library, 1946. 28p.

5406. U. S. Engineer School Library. Engineer troops. Wash.: Engineer School, 1911. 15p. (Engineer School, U. S. Army, Occasional papers 47)

5407. U. S. Library of Congress, Division of Bibliography. Bibliography of tanks and other military tracklaying vehicles, comp. by Douglas W. Bryant. Wash., 1941. 22p. (Cooperative bibliographies, no. 1)

5408. U. S. Library of Congress, Division of Bibliography. Compulsory military training; a selected list of references, comp. by Ann Duncan Brown. [Wash., 1940] 25p. A supplementary list of references. [Wash. 1941] 38p.

5409. U. S. Library of Congress, Division of Bibliography. "Compulsory military training and service in foreign countries," comp. by Ann D. Brown. Wash., Jan. 7, 1942. 13p. Typed.

5410. U. S. Library of Congress, Division of Bibliography. Industrial mobilization; a selected list of references, comp. by Anne L. Baden. [Wash.] 1941. 22p.

5411. U. S. Library of Congress, Division of Bibliography. A list of bibliographies on questions relating to national defense, comp. by Grace Hadley Fuller. [Wash.] 1941. 21p. Supplementary list, 1942. 59p.

5412. U. S. Library of Congress, Division of Bibliography. A list of references on camouflage, comp. by Grace Hadley Fuller. [Wash.] 1942. 16p. Supplementary to mimeographed list of November 1940.

5413. U. S. Library of Congress, Division of Bibliography. A list of references on flags, insignia, medals, decorations, and uniforms of the United States and certain foreign countries. Wash., 1942. 13p.

5414. U. S. Library of Congress, Division of Bibliography. A list of references on priorities. Wash., 1940. 16p.

5415. U. S. Library of Congress, Division of Bibliography. A list of references on western hemisphere defense, comp. by Helen F. Conover. Rev. ed. [Wash.] 1942. 39p.

5416. U. S. Library of Congress, Division of Bibliography. Powdered metals. A bibliography, prep. by Norma B. McDonald. Wash., 1943. 108p.

5417. U. S. Library of Congress, Division of Bibliography. "Selected list of recent references on American national defense." Wash., June 16, 1936. 18p. Typed.

5418. U. S. Library of Congress, Division of Bibliography. Selected list of recent references on American national defense (supplementary to typewritten list of June, 1936), comp. by Grace Hadley Fuller. [Wash.] 1939. 42p.

5419. U. S. Library of Congress, General Reference and Bibliography Division. Firearms, ammunition, explosives and fireworks; a selected list of books and pamphlets, comp. by Anne L. Baden. Wash., 1943. 44p.

5420. U. S. Library of Congress, General Reference and Bibliography Division. "Military administration: a partial bibliography with special reference to the unification of the armed services," comp. by Donald H. Mugridge. Wash., 1946. 2pts. Typed.
  Contents: Pt. I, United States, 60p.; pt. II, foreign countries, p. 61-75.

5421. U. S. Library of Congress, General Reference and Bibliography Division. "Negroes in the armed services of the United States from the earliest times to the present: a selected list of references," comp. by Blanche Prichard McCrum. Wash., 1949. 22p. Typed.

5422. U. S. Library of Congress, General Reference and Bibliography Division. Universal military training; a selected and annotated list of references, comp. by Frances Cheney. Wash., 1945. 138p. Supplement, comp. by Janice B. Harrington. Wash., 1945. 118p.

5423. U. S. Library of Congress, Legislative Reference Service. Raw materials (April 1941 - March 1942); selected and annotated bibliography on raw materials in a wartime economy. Wash., 1942. 69p.

5424. U. S. Library of Congress, Reference Department. Chemical warfare; a check list, March 1, 1943, and Supplement no. 1, June 1, 1944, prep. by Charles H. Wentz. Wash., 1944. 17, 38p.

5425. U. S. Military Academy. The centennial of the United States Military Academy at West Point, New York. 1802-1902. Wash.: Govt. Print. Off., 1904. 2v. (58th Cong., 2d sess. House, Doc. no. 789)
    Bibliography (v. 2, p. 1-396) of works on West Point, the Academy, and by graduates of the Academy, locates copies in Academy Library.

5426. U. S. Military Academy Library. Catalogue of the Library, U. S. Military Academy, West Point, N. Y., 1873. Newburgh, N. Y., 1876. 723p. Supplement. Poughkeepsie: A. V. Haight, 1882. p. 725-1027.

5427. U. S. Military Academy Library. Library manual. Reference books, prep. by E. S. Holden. West Point: U. S. Military Academy, 1905. 20p.
    Description of Library's resources.

5428. U. S. Military Academy Library. Library manual II. Manuscripts, rare books, memorabilia, and the like in the Library, prep. by E. S. Holden. West Point: U. S. Military Academy, 1908. 93p. (U. S. Military Academy, West Point. Bulletin, no. 2)

5429. U. S. National Archives. Preliminary checklist of the records of the Headquarters of the Army, 1825-1903, comp. by Jerome Thomases. [Wash.] 1946. 12p.

5430. U. S. National Archives. Preliminary checklist of the records of the National Guard Bureau and its predecessors, 1822-1941, comp. by Lucy E. Weidman. [Wash., 1946] 3p. (Preliminary checklist, no. 33)

5431. U. S. National Archives. Preliminary checklist of the records of the Office of the Commissary General of Subsistence, 1818-1912, comp. by Roland C. McConnell. [Wash., 1946] 14p. (Preliminary checklist, no. 34)

5432. U. S. National Archives. Preliminary checklist of the records of the Office of the Inspector General, 1814-1939, comp. by Richard Giroux. [Wash.] 1946. 5p.

5433. U. S. National Archives. Preliminary checklist of the records of the Office of the Secretary of War, 1800-1942, comp. by Lucille H. Pendell. [Wash., 1945] 34p. (Preliminary checklist, no. 25)

5434. U. S. National Archives. Preliminary inventory of the records of the Adjutant General's Office, comp. by Lucille H. Pendell and Elizabeth Bethel. Wash., 1949. 149p. (Preliminary inventory, no. 17)

5435. U. S. National Archives. Preliminary inventory of the records of the Office of the Paymaster General, comp. by Roland C. McConnell. Wash., 1948. 16p. (Preliminary inventory, no. 9)

5436. U. S. Ordnance Dept. Library. Catalogue of the Ordnance Office Library. 1875. Wash.: Govt. Print. Off., 1875. 78p.

5437. U. S. Strategic Bombing Survey. Index to records of the United States Strategic Bombing Survey. Wash., 1947. 317p.
    Statistical and documentary materials indexed are in National Archives.

5438. U. S. War Dept. Library. Alphabetical catalogue of the War Department Library (including Law Library). Authors and subjects. Wash.: Govt. Print. Off., 1882. 325p.
    Now in U. S. National War College Library.

5439. U. S. War Dept. Library. Alphabetical list of additions made to the War Department Library. Wash.: Govt. Print. Off., 1884-94. 3v.
    Now in U. S. National War College Library.

5440. U. S. War Dept. Library. Author and title list of the most important accessions to the War Department Library, with subject entries in biography, military history, and military science, and index of periodicals received during the calendar year 1904. Wash.: Govt. Print. Off., 1905. 95p.

5441. U. S. War Dept. Library. Check list of serial publications in the War Department Library. Wash.: Govt. Print. Off., 1903. 42p.
    Indicates holdings.

5442. U. S. War Dept. Library. Finding list of military biographies and other personal literature in the War Department Library.

2d ed. Wash.: Govt. Print. Off., 1899. 145p. (Subject catalogue, no. 4)

Now in U. S. National War College Library.

5443. U. S. War Dept. Library. Finding list of the principal reference works in the War Department Library, October 1, 1903. Wash.: Govt. Print. Off., 1903. 34p.

5444. U. S. War Dept. Library. Index of periodicals, annuals, and serials in the War Department Library. Rev. ed. Wash.: Govt. Print. Off., 1895. 37p. (Subject catalogue, no. 2)

5445. U. S. War Dept. Library. Late additions made to the War Department Library. Wash.: Govt. Print. Off., 1894. 30p. (Subject catalogue, no. 1)

Now in U. S. National War College Library.

5446. U. S. War Dept. Library. National planning and strategy; a working bibliography for the educational system of officers of the Army. Wash., 1946. 376p.

Most of titles listed in U. S. Army Library, Washington, D. C.

Naval history and science

5447. Browne, Margaret F. "The rare collection of the Naval History Society with its wealth of priceless information regarding the wars of the United States." Naval History Society annual, 13th year (1922), 47-54.

Collection now in the New-York Historical Society.

5448. Glenn, Bess. "Navy Department records in the National Archives." Military affairs, 7 (1943), 247-60.

5449. Harbeck, Charles Thomas. A contribution to the bibliography of the history of the United States Navy. Cambridge: Riverside Press, 1906. 247p.

About 700 volumes on naval history purchased by Henry E. Huntington Library from Harbeck.

5450. Kerr, Willis. "Source materials on Pacific coast marine history." Special libraries, 36 (1945), 365-66.

Records of 12 Pacific coast steamship companies, 1866-1935, in Claremont College Library.

5451. Lincoln, Charles Henry. "Material in the Library of Congress for a study of U. S. naval history." Bibliographical Society of America proceedings and papers, 1 (1904-05), 84-95.

5452. Naval History Society. Catalogue of the books, manuscripts, and prints and other memorabilia in the John S. Barnes Memorial Library of the Naval History Society. N. Y.: Naval History Society, 1915. 377p.

Collection now in New-York Historical Society.

5453. New York Public Library. "List of works in the New York Public Library relating to nautical and naval art and science, navigation, and seamanship, shipbuilding, etc." New York Public Library bulletin, 11 (1907), 239-87, 299-345, 359-98, 420-36. Reprinted. 151p.

5454. New York Public Library. "Naval architecture and shipbuilding; a list of references in the New York Public Library," comp. by Rollin Alger Sawyer. New York Public Library bulletin, 23 (1919), 13-50, 73-94. Reprinted. 59p.

5455. New York Public Library. "A selected list of works in the New York Public Library relating to naval history, naval administration, etc." New York Public Library bulletin, 8 (1904), 261-95, 323-51, 369-93, 423-63, 570-75.

5456. New York Public Library. "Submarines; a list of references in the New York Public Library," comp. by Mary Ethel Jameson. New York Public Library bulletin, 22 (1918), 18-69, 91-132. Reprinted. 97p.

5457. New York Public Library. "Torpedoes; a list of references to material in the New York Public Library," comp. by William A. Ellis. New York Public Library bulletin, 21 (1917), 657-726. Reprinted. 85p.

5458. U. S. Bureau of Navigation. Catalogue of works by American naval authors, comp. by Lucien Young. Wash.: Govt. Print. Off., 1888. 149p.

5459. U. S. Library of Congress, Division of Bibliography. London Naval Conference, 1930: a bibliographical list, comp. by Florence S. Hellman. [Wash., 1930] 19p.

5460. U. S. Library of Congress, Division of Bibliography. Selected list of references on safety at sea, comp. by Grace Hadley Fuller. [Wash.] 1940. 39p.

5461. U. S. Library of Congress, Division of Bibliography. A selected list of references on the expansion of the U. S. Navy, 1933-1939, comp. by Grace Hadley Fuller. [Wash.] 1940. 34p.

5462. U. S. National Archives. List of logs of United States Coast Guard vessels in the National Archives, 1790-1941, by Thornton W. Mitchell and Arthur Dyer. Wash., 1944. 32p.

5463. U. S. National Archives. Preliminary checklist of the general records of the Department of the Navy, 1804-1944, comp. by James R. Masterson. [Wash., 1945] 103p. (Preliminary checklist, no. 31)

5464. U. S. National Archives. Preliminary checklist of the naval records collection of the Office of Naval Records and Library, 1775-1910, comp. by James R. Masterson. [Wash., 1945] 149p. (Preliminary checklist, no. 30)

5465. U. S. National Archives. Preliminary checklist of the records of the Boston Navy Yard, 1811-1942, comp. by Richard G. Wood. [Wash., 1946] 17p. (Preliminary checklist, no. 40)

5466. U. S. National Archives. Preliminary checklist of the records of the Bureau of Supplies and Accounts (Navy) 1885-1942, comp. by James R. Masterson and Fred G. Halley. [Wash., 1946] 6p. (Preliminary checklist, no. 41)

5467. U. S. National Archives. Preliminary checklist of the records of the Office of the Judge Advocate General (Navy) 1799-1943, comp. by James R. Masterson. [Wash., 1945] 49p. (Preliminary checklist, no. 32)

5468. U. S. National Archives. Preliminary checklist of the records of the United States Marine Corps, 1798-1944, comp. by Fred G. Halley. [Wash.] 1946. 21p.

5469. U. S. National Archives. Preliminary inventory of the records of the Bureau of Yards and Docks, comp. by Richard G. Wood. Wash., 1948. 28p. (Preliminary inventory, no. 10)

5470. U. S. National Archives. The sesquicentennial of the Department of the Navy, 1798-1848; an exhibit, by Elizabeth E. Hamer. Wash., 1948. 13p.

5471. U. S. Naval Academy. Catalogue of historic objects at the United States Naval Academy, comp. by Herman F. Krafft. [Baltimore: Industrial Printing Co., 1925] 250p.

5472. U. S. Naval Academy Library. Bibliography of naval literature in the United States Naval Academy Library, comp. by Louis H. Bolander. [Annapolis, 1929] 3v. in 1.

5473. U. S. Naval Academy Library. Catalogue of the library of the U.S. Naval Academy, Annapolis, Maryland, June 30, 1860. Annapolis: R. F. Bonsall, 1860. [252]p.

5474. U. S. Navy Dept. Library. Alphabetical catalogue. Wash.: Govt. Print. Off., 1891. 601p. Author catalog. Supplement. 1892. 90p.; second Supplement. 1896. 105p.

5475. U. S. Navy Dept. Library, Naval War Records Office. List of log-books of U. S. vessels, 1861-1865, on file in the Navy Department. Wash.: Govt. Print. Off., 1898. 49p. (Office memoranda, no. 5)

Civilian defense

5476. "Bibliography of selected references on civil defense, 1939-49. Selected from a compilation by Deborah S. Peck and Janie E. Mason, Legislative Reference Service, Library of Congress." In: U. S. Congress. Joint Committee on Atomic Energy. Civil defense against atomic attack: preliminary data, February 1950. Wash.: Govt. Print. Off., 1950. p. 63-70.

5477. John Crerar Library. Blackouts, a bibliography, comp. by Constance A. Strandel. Chicago, 1942. 15p. (Reference list 51)

5478. Los Angeles Public Library, Municipal Reference Library. Air raid shelters. 1941. 8 numb. 1. (Defense bibliographies, no. 1) Supplemented by Air raid protection. 1941. 10 numb. 1. (Defense bibliographies, no. 9)
   Locates titles in 4 Los Angeles libraries.

5479. Los Angeles Public Library, Municipal Reference Library. Defense housing. 1941.

11 numb. l. (Defense bibliographies, no. 8)
Locates titles in 4 Los Angeles libraries.

5480. Los Angeles Public Library, Municipal Reference Library. Defense planning for local governments. 1941. 3 numb. l. (Defense bibliographies, no. 2)
Locates titles in Los Angeles Public Library, University of California at Los Angeles, or University of Southern California, Los Angeles.

5481. Los Angeles Public Library, Municipal Reference Library. Fire service during wartime. 1942. 9 numb. l. (Defense bibliographies, no. 10)
Locates titles in 4 Los Angeles libraries.

5482. Los Angeles Public Library, Municipal Reference Library. Health in a national defense program. 1941. 20 numb. l. (Defense bibliographies, no. 4)
Locates titles in 4 Los Angeles libraries.

5483. Los Angeles Public Library, Municipal Reference Library. Police service during wartime. 1942. 9 numb. l. (Defense bibliographies, no. 11)
Locates titles in 4 Los Angeles libraries.

5484. Los Angeles Public Library, Municipal Reference Library. The preparation of electric and water utilities during wartime. 1941. 4 numb. l. (Defense bibliographies, no. 5) Supplemented by Problems of public utilities in wartime. 1942. 10 numb. l. (Defense bibliographies, no. 12)
Locates titles in 4 Los Angeles libraries.

5485. Los Angeles Public Library, Municipal Reference Library. Protection of civilians in wartime. [1943] 7 numb. l. (Defense bibliographies, no. 13)
Locates titles in 4 Los Angeles libraries.

5486. Los Angeles Public Library, Municipal Reference Library. Public protection in defense plants. 1941. 4 numb. l. (Defense bibliographies, no. 3)
Locates titles in 4 Los Angeles libraries.

5487. Los Angeles Public Library, Municipal Reference Library. Recreation and national defense. 1941. 3 numb. l. (Defense bibliographies, no. 6)
Locates titles in 4 Los Angeles libraries.

5488. Los Angeles Railway Corporation Library. Mass transportation in relation to national defense; a selected bibliography. Los Angeles: The Library, 1941. 20 numb. l. (Los Angeles Public Library, Municipal Reference Library, Defense series, no. 7)
Locates copies in several Los Angeles libraries.

5489. Northwestern University Library. Selected current references to official publications on civilian defense. [Evanston, Ill., 1942] 18p. Supplement I-II. March 5, 1942 - May 5, 1942. Evanston, 1942. 2v.

5490. Oakland Public Library. Civil defense; subject list of information on civil defense in the library of the Oakland Defense Council and the Reference Dept. of the Oakland Public Library. Oakland, Calif.: The Library, 1941. 2pts.

5491. U. S. Library of Congress, Division of Bibliography. Civilian defense; a selected list of recent references, comp. by Helen F. Conover. [Wash.] 1941. 43p.

5492. U. S. Library of Congress, Division of Bibliography. Civilian defense; a selection of available guide books and pamphlets, comp. by Helen F. Conover. rev. ed. [Wash.] 1942. 24p.

5493. U. S. Library of Congress, Legislative Reference Service. Civilian defense (April 1941 - March 1942); selected and annotated bibliography on the organization and administration of air raid protection. Wash., 1942. 38p.

5494. U. S. Library of Congress, Reference Dept. A check list, Civilian defense collection, section D, sub-section 5. Chemical warfare, decontamination, prep. by Charles H. Wentz. Wash.: Library of Congress, 1943. 17 numb. l.
Locates titles in Library of Congress by call number.

5495. U. S. National Archives. Inventory of the records of Office of Civilian Defense, 1941-1945, comp. by Raymond P. Flynn. Wash.: Records Retirement Unit, Office of Civilian Defense, 1945. 2v.
V. 1, National Office; v. 2, regional offices.

WORLD WAR I

5496. Allen, Lafon. "Lafon Allen collection of posters of the World War." Yale University Library gazette, 12 (1937), 1-16.
Describes poster collection of World War I in Library.

5497. Carnegie Library of Pittsburgh. Imbrie memorial collection presented by Mr. B. V. Imbrie. Pittsburgh: The Library, 1939. 42p.
Collection of World War I material.

5498. Clark University Library. The war collection at Clark University Library, by Louis N. Wilson. Worcester: Clark Univ. Press, 1918. 53p. (Clark University Library publications, VI, no. 1)

5499. Coles, Harry L., Jr. "The Federal food administration of Tennessee and its records in the National Archives, 1917-1919." Tennessee historical quarterly, 4 (1945), 23-57.
A general statement of how records in National Archives can contribute to the economic and social history of a state, and the type of records collected in Tennessee Federal Food Administration.

5500. Currier, Thomas F. "Germany in war and revolution." Harvard Library notes, 1 (1922), 171-76.
World War I collection, Harvard College Library.

5501. Curtis, Lewis P. "The Gibson collection." Yale University Library gazette, 20 (1946), 57-64.
Describes a collection of some 2,500 volumes on naval history of World War I.

5502. Duniway, David C. "The California Food Administration and its records in the National Archives." Pacific historical review, 7 (1938), 228-40.
Records for World War I.

5503. Emerson, Guy. "Harvard collection of war posters." Harvard alumni bulletin, 21 (1919), 279-83.

5504. Historical Records Survey - La. Inventory of the records of world war emergency activities in Louisiana, 1916-1920. University: Dept. of Archives, Louisiana State University, 1942. 61p.

5505. Historical Records Survey - Minn. Inventory of records of World War (I) emergency activities, Minnesota. St. Paul: Minnesota Historical Records Survey, 1941. 85 numb. 1.

5506. Leland, Waldo Gifford and Mereness, Newton D. Introduction to the American official sources for the economic and social history of the world war. New Haven: Yale Univ. Press, 1926. 532, 18p. (Carnegie Endowment for International Peace. Div. of Econ. and Hist. Economic and social hist. of the world war. American series.)
Records and official publications of the federal government are located in some governmental libraries.

5507. Lokke, Carl L. "The Food Administration papers for the state of Virginia in the National Archives." Virginia magazine of history and biography, 50 (July 1942), 220-26.

5508. McCain, William D. "The papers of the Food Administration for Louisiana, 1917-1919, in the National Archives." Louisiana historical quarterly, 21 (1938), 869-74.

5509. McCain, William D. "The papers of the Food Administration for Missouri, 1917-1919, in the National Archives." Missouri historical review, 32 (1937), 56-61.

5510. McCain, William D. "The papers of the Food Administration for North Carolina, 1917-19, in the National Archives." North Carolina historical review, 15 (1938), 34-40.

5511. Meany, Edmond S., Jr. "Food Administration papers for Washington, Oregon and Idaho, deposited in the National Archives." Pacific Northwest quarterly, 18 (1937), 373-82.

5512. New York Public Library. "Diplomatic history of the European War; a list of references in the New York Public Library," comp. by Rollin Alger Sawyer. New York Public Library bulletin, 21 (1917), 413-31. Reprinted. 21p.

5513. Perry, Ruth Mary (Robinson). "Clandestine publications issued in Belgium during the German occupation, 1914-1918, with a checklist of clandestine serials in the Hoover Library on War, Revolution, and Peace." [Berkeley? Calif.] 1939. 67 numb. 1. (M. A. thesis, University of California, unpublished)

5514. Princeton University Library. European war collection; alphabetical author list. [Princeton] The Library, 1918. 92p.

5515. Princeton University Library. European war collection; classed list. [Princeton]: The Library, 1918. 97p.

5516. Princeton University Library. A finding list of books on the war. [Princeton: The Library, 1918] 2v.

A union list of books on World War I in Princeton University Library, New York Public Library, Library of Congress, etc.

5517. Princeton University Library. Princeton University Library war poster collections. [Princeton]: The Library, 1919. 134, 18, 29p.
List of about 2,500 posters.

5518. Stanford University Library, Hoover Library on War, Revolution and Peace. A catalogue of Paris Peace Conference delegation propaganda in the Hoover War Library. Stanford University: Stanford Univ. Press, 1926. 96p. (Stanford University publications. Hoover War Library, Bibliographical series I)

5519. Stanford University Library, Hoover Library on War, Revolution and Peace. An introduction to a bibliography of the Paris Peace Conference collection of sources, archive publications and source books, by Nina Almond and Ralph Haswell Lutz. Stanford University: Stanford Univ. Press, 1935. 32p. (Hoover War Library, Bibliographical series II)

5520. U. S. Library of Congress, Division of Bibliography. A check list of the literature and other material in the Library of Congress on the European war. Wash.: Govt. Print. Off., 1918. 293p.

5521. U. S. Library of Congress, Division of Bibliography. List of bibliographies of the European war, June 18, 1919. [Wash., 1919] 31 l.

5522. U. S. Library of Congress, Division of Bibliography. List of recent references on the reparations problem. Wash., 1932. 41p.

5523. U. S. Library of Congress, Division of Bibliography. List of references on casualties in the European war and strength of the armies in the field. [Wash., 1918] 22 l.

5524. U. S. Library of Congress, Division of Bibliography. List of references on the work of the American Red Cross in the European war. [Wash., Press of Gibson Bros., 1917] 7p. ([Red Cross. U. S. American National Red Cross] A. R. C. [Circular] 156. April 2, 1917)

5525. U. S. Library of Congress, Division of Bibliography. "A list of the histories of regiments and other units of the U. S. Army in the European war." Wash., Sept. 29, 1921. 19p. Typed.

5526. U. S. Library of Congress, Division of Bibliography. The United States at war, organizations and literature. Wash.: Govt. Print. Off., 1917. 115p.

5527. U. S. Library of Congress, Division of Bibliography. The world war; a list of the more important books published before 1934, selected by Dr. Henry Eldridge Bourne. [Wash.] 1934. 20p. [Supplementary list] June 28, 1936. 17p. Typed.

5528. U. S. Library of Congress, Division of Documents. "Tentative check list of state publications relating to the European war, 1917-1919." Wash.: Govt. Print. Off., 1920. Monthly list of state publications, 10 (December, 1919) [579]-648.

"Includes state war publications issued during 1917-1919 which were received by the Library of Congress."

5529. U. S. Library of Congress, Reading Room. A list of references on reparations of the European war, 1914-1918, prep. by Donald G. Patterson and James T. Rubey. [Wash.] 1932. 136 numb. l.
Lists 2,201 titles.

5530. U. S. National Archives. Handbook of federal world war agencies and their records, 1917-1921. Wash.: Govt. Print. Off., 1943. 666p. (Publication, no. 24)

5531. U. S. National Archives. Preliminary checklist of the records of the Headquarters, American Expeditionary Forces 1917-1921, comp. by Elizabeth Bethel. [Wash., 1946] 47p. (Preliminary checklist, no. 35)

5532. U. S. National Archives. Preliminary checklist of the records of the Selective Service System 1917-1919, comp. by Lucy E. Weidman. [Wash., 1945] 13p. (Preliminary checklist, no. 26)

5533. U. S. National Archives. Preliminary checklist of the records of the War Department Claims Board, 1918-1922, comp. by Stuart Portner and Victor Gondos, Jr. Division of War Department Archives. [Wash., 1943] 105p.

5534. U. S. National Archives. Preliminary inventory of the Council of National Defense records, 1916-1921. Wash., 1942. 75p. (Preliminary inventory, no. 2)

5535. U. S. National Archives. Preliminary inventory of the records of the United States Food Administration. Pt. 1, The headquarters organization, 1917-1920. Wash., 1943. 335p. (Preliminary inventories, no. 3)

5536. Van Schreeven, William J. "Indiana Food Administration papers." Indiana magazine of history, 33(1937), 422-27.

Records now in National Archives.

5537. Whitney, Edward A. "The World War collection." Harvard Library notes, 1 (1922), 158-59.

In Harvard College Library.

5538. Wood, Marjorie P. "The war collection." Harvard Library notes, 1 (1922), 162-70.

In Harvard College Library.

5539. Wright, Almon R. "Sources for Ohio world war history in the papers of the Food Administration in the National Archives." Ohio archaeological and historical quarterly, 47 (Oct. 1938), 355-62.

Source material for study of Ohio history during World War I, in National Archives.

WORLD WAR II

5540. Lovett, Robert W. "A university cares for its war contract records." American archivist, 10 (1947), 41-46.

Description of Harvard University collection.

5541. McCloy, Elizabeth J. "Japanese-American relocation collection." California Library Association bulletin, 8 (1946), 22, 29.

Brief description of collection in Occidental College Library.

5542. McFarland, Marvin W. "The General Spaatz collection." Library of Congress quarterly journal of current acquisitions, 6 (May 1949), 23-55. Reprinted. 33p.

Description of papers of General Carl Spaatz, former Chief of Staff of the U. S. Air Force, presented to Library of Congress.

5543. New York Public Library. "The trojan-horse bibliography; the European 'fifth column' and American morale-resistance, 1939-1940." New York Public Library bulletin, 44 (1940), 741-44.

Limited principally to periodical references.

5544. Novossiltzeff, George A. "Soviet Union war posters." Library of Congress quarterly journal of current acquisitions, 2 (Feb. 1945), 68-79.

Description of Library of Congress collection.

5545. Stanford University, Hoover Library on War, Revolution and Peace. List of the Polish underground collection, 1939-1945. Stanford University, 1948. 18p.

5546. U. S. Library of Congress. "The underground press in France, Belgium, Norway, Denmark and the Netherlands." Library of Congress quarterly journal of current acquisitions, 2 (Jan. - June, 1945), 3-29.

Discussion and listing of Library of Congress collection.

5547. U. S. Library of Congress, Division of Bibliography. Children and war, a selected list of references, comp. by Helen F. Conover. Rev. ed. [Wash.] 1943. 56p.

5548. U. S. Library of Congress, Division of Bibliography. Foreign relief and rehabilitation, a selected list of references, comp. by Grace Hadley Fuller. [Wash.] 1943. 32p.

5549. U. S. Library of Congress, Division of Bibliography. "German militarism: a selected list of recent writings," comp. by Grace H. Fuller. Wash., Aug. 2, 1940. 27p. Typed.

5550. U. S. Library of Congress, Division of Bibliography. "The Malayan campaign: a list of references," comp. by Florence S. Hellman. Wash., June 11, 1943. 11p. Typed.

5551. U. S. Library of Congress, Division of Bibliography. Women's part in World War II, a list of references, comp. by Florence S. Hellman. [Wash.] 1942. 84p.

5552. U. S. Library of Congress, European Affairs Division. The displaced persons analytical bibliography [prepared under the supervision of Harry J. Krould, by Helen F. Conover assisted by Hildegarde Lobel] Report (supplemental) of a special subcommittee of the Committee on the Judiciary, House of Representatives, pursuant to H. Res. 238, a resolution to authorize the Committee on the Judiciary to undertake a study of immigration and nationality problems. Wash.: Govt. Print. Off., 1950. 82p. (81st Cong., 2d sess. House. Rept. 1687)
   Bibliography based on Library of Congress collection.

5553. U. S. Library of Congress, General Reference and Bibliography Division. "The defence of Leningrad, 1941-1944: writings published in America," comp. by Helen F. Conover. Wash., Dec. 5, 1946. 26p. Typed.

5554. U. S. Library of Congress, General Reference and Bibliography Division. Demobilization: a selected list of references, comp. by Grace Hadley Fuller. Wash., 1945. 193p.

5555. U. S. Library of Congress, General Reference and Bibliography Division. Nazi fifth column activities: a list of references, comp. by Florence S. Hellman. Wash., 1943. 42p.

5556. U. S. Library of Congress, General Reference and Bibliography Division. The Nazi state, war crimes and war criminals, comp. by Helen F. Conover. Wash., 1945. 132p.

5557. U. S. Library of Congress, Legislative Reference Service. Bibliographies of the world at war; no. 1-10. Wash.: The Library, 1942-43.
   Contents: 1. Political developments and the war; 2. Agriculture in a war economy; 3. Raw materials; 4. Industry in wartime; 5. Labor in wartime; 6. Economics of war; 7. Civilian defense; 8. Social and cultural problems in wartime; 9. Conduct of the war; 10. Postwar planning and reconstruction.

5558. U. S. Library of Congress, Legislative Reference Service. Bibliography on the major phases of the war and civilian participation. Wash., 1943. 18p. (War service bulletin F-133)

5559. U. S. Library of Congress, Legislative Reference Service. Conduct of the war (April 1941 - March 1942); selected and annotated bibliography on the operations of the armed forces in the war. Wash., 1942. 95p.

5560. U. S. Library of Congress, Legislative Reference Service. Economics of war (April 1941 - March 1942); selected and annotated bibliography on economic problems and policies in wartime. Wash., 1942. 120p.

5561. U. S. Library of Congress, Legislative Reference Service. Industry in wartime (April 1941 - March 1942); selected and annotated bibliography on industrial problems and policies in a wartime economy. Wash., 1942. 103p.

5562. U. S. Library of Congress, Legislative Reference Service. List of references on various aspects of wartime conditions; selected mainly from German sources. Restricted list no. 1-6. [Wash., 1942?-43] 6v. in 1.

5563. U. S. Library of Congress, Legislative Reference Service. Manpower problems; a selected and annotated list of references, prepared for the Office for Emergency Management, by John P. Umbach. Wash., 1943. 22p. (War service bulletin H-5)

5564. U. S. Library of Congress, Legislative Reference Service. Political developments and the war (April 1, 1941 - March 31, 1942); selected and annotated bibliography on world politics under the impact of war. Wash., 1942. 238p.

5565. U. S. Library of Congress, Legislative Reference Service. Postwar planning and reconstruction (April 1941 - March 1942); selected and annotated bibliography on postwar plans and problems. Wash., 1942. 181p.

5566. U. S. Library of Congress, Legislative Reference Service. Social and cultural problems in wartime (April 1941 - March 1942); selected and annotated bibliography. Wash., 1942. 80p.

5567. U. S. National Archives. Preliminary checklist of the records of the Industrial Incentive Division and the Navy Board for Production Awards, 1941 - 1945, comp. by Vivian D. Wiser. [Wash., 1946] 4p. (Preliminary checklist, no. 36)

5568. U. S. National Archives. Preliminary inventory of records of the Chemical Warfare Service, comp. by Raymond P. Flynn. Wash., 1948. 5p. (Preliminary inventory, no. 8)

5569. U. S. National Archives. Preliminary inventory of records of the War Production Board, comp. by Fred G. Halley and Josef C. James. Wash., 1948. 59p. (Preliminary inventory, no. 15)

5570. U. S. National Archives. Preliminary inventory of the records of naval establishments created overseas during World War II, comp. by Richard G. Wood. Wash., 1948. 8p. (Preliminary inventory, no. 13)

5571. U. S. National Archives. Preliminary inventory of the records of the Board of Investigation and Research-Transportation, comp. by Leo Pascal. Wash., 1949. 12p. (Preliminary inventory, no. 19)

5572. U. S. National Archives. Preliminary inventory of the records of the United States Counsel for the Prosecution of Axis Criminality, comp. by Fred G. Halley. Wash., 1949. 182p. (Preliminary inventory, no. 21)

5573. U. S. National Archives. Preliminary inventory of the War Industries Board records. Wash., 1941. 134p. (Preliminary inventory, no. 1)

5574. U. S. National Archives. Selective list of records in the files of the War Industries Board, relating to the supply, production, and control of certain commodities in wartime: steel, copper, nickel, tin, zinc, lumber, wool, machine tools, comp. in the Division of War Department Archives by Edward G. Campbell and Marie C. Stark. [Wash., 1941] 66p.

5575. U. S. National Security Resources Board, Mobilization Procedures and Organization Office. Selected list of documents in the mobilization planning file of War Production Board records pertaining to problems and methods of production control administration during World War II. [Wash.] 1949. 373p.
Documents listed are in National Archives.

5576. U. S. Office of Education. Women's contributions in wartime: a list of references to recent material, by Helen Ellis Wheeler. Wash.: Federal Security Agency, 1942. 7p. (U. S. Office of Education, Vocational Division. Miscellany, no. 2951)

5577. U. S. Price Administration Office. OPA bibliography, 1940-1947; publications of the Office of Price Administration and its predecessor agencies, by W. J. Wilson and others. [Wash., 1948] 441p.
Collection described is deposited in National Archives.

5578. Wabeke, B. H. "Dutch underground publications." Library of Congress quarterly journal of current acquisitions, 4 (Feb. 1947), 3-7.
Description of a collection of 1,000 pieces acquired by the Library of Congress. An earlier article, "The underground press of France, Belgium, Norway, Denmark, and the Netherlands," appeared in the Quarterly, 2 (June 1945), 3-29.

Index

(Numbers refer to individual items)

Abbot, Ezra, 983
Abbott, Jacob, 3273
Aborigines, Australia, 2310
Absenteeism in industry, 1581
Abstract services, 8
Academy of Motion Picture Arts and Sciences, 3086
Accidents, industrial, 2344, 2355, 2359
Accounting, 2765-72; government, 1863; railroad, 2768-69
Ackermann, Gertrude W., 1051-52, 4965
Adams, Abigail, 3942
Adams, George C. S., 3162
Adams, George M., 3303
Adams, Henry, 258, 3944
Adams, James, 727
Adams, John, 3943, 4438
Adams, John Q., 3944, 4438
Adams, Joseph Q., 3524
Adams, Léonie, 3325
Adams, Marion, 2993
Adams, Randolph G., 684, 3886, 4395, 4533-36, 4563, 5213
Adams, Zu, 4852
Adamson Law, 1628
Addison, Agnes, 2946
Adler, Cyrus, 1232
Adler, Elkan N., 1215
Advertising, 301, 2773-80
Aerial photography, 2569
Aerodynamics, 2575
Aeronautics, 2545-81; periodicals, 2573, 2576
Aeropolitics, 2126
Aesop, 3723, 3730
Africa, 4193 (13-14, 18); history, 4366-87
Agnese, Battista, 3841, 3865
Agricultural credits, 2602 (7, 23)
Agricultural economics, 2620-39
Agricultural engineering, 2594

Agricultural experiment stations, 2598 (4), 2613-14
Agricultural extension, 2599 (18)
Agricultural marketing, 2599 (7), 2602 (37, 43), 2623-24
Agricultural museums, 2599 (29)
Agricultural periodicals, 2602 (18), 2610-14
Agricultural relief, 2626 (41-42, 45, 50, 52-53, 76, 84, 92)
Agriculture, 2183, 2591-2673; Alabama, 2626 (15); California, 2626 (31); English, 2599 (24), 4257; Greece, 2626 (39); Oklahoma, 2626 (21); Rumania, 2626 (49); Switzerland, 2626 (35); U. S. history, 2599 (26, 32-33, 35), 3615-19; Virginia, 2593
Aguilera, Francisco, 3710
Aiken, Walter H., 2204
Air brakes, 2513
Air conditioning, 2528
Air freight, 2560, 2578
Air raid protection, 5478, 5493
Airplane manufacture, 2568
Airports, 2567
Akron University, Bierce Library, 3390
Alabama, authors, 3255; history, 4711-14
Alabama Dept. of Archives and History, 283, 3255, 4713
Alabama History Commission, 4711
Alabama Polytechnic Institute Library, 178
Alabama Supreme Court Library, 1669
Alabama, University, Library, 179, 4714, 4874, 4891
Alaska, 4193 (6), 5279
Albania, 4323
Albany, N. Y., authors, 3250
Albany Institute and Historical and Art Society Library, 3250
Albee, Louise B., 3139
Albers, C. C., 2432
Albertus Magnus, 623

INDEX

Albrecht, Otto E., 3000
Alchemy, manuscripts, 2276
Alden, John E., 549, 865
Alden, John R., 4486
Aldine editions, 234, 604
Aldrich, Thomas B., 3274
Aleut language, 3187
Aleutian Islands, 5280
Algebra, 2220
Algonquian languages, 3177
Allason, William, 5215, 5220
Allegheny College Library, 180, 4027
Allegheny County Law Library, 1670
Allen, Albert H., 709, 720-21, 745-46, 751-53, 845
Allen, Don C., 664
Allen, Francis P., 2329
Allen, Francis W., 3688
Allen, George, 3120
Allen, Ira, 5210
Allen, Jay, 3015
Allen, Lafon, 5496
Alliott, Hector, 4718
Allison, William H., 1199
Almanacs, 4691-4707; Connecticut, 4692; Kentucky, 4697; Maine, 4702; Massachusetts, 4703; New Hampshire, 4702; New Jersey, 4694; New York City, 4699, 4701; Rhode Island, 4693; South Carolina, 4707; Vermont, 4702
Almond, Nina, 5519
Almonds, 2628 (23)
Altsheler, Brent, 2297
Alvord, Clarence W., 4248, 4816
American Antiquarian Society Library, 181, 388, 406, 451, 497, 685-86, 700, 765, 881, 961, 1014, 2742, 2947, 2950, 3221, 3231, 3801, 3994, 4071, 4076, 4097, 4396, 4497-4500, 4523, 4597, 4624, 4691, 4693
American Assoc. for State and Local History, 4397
American Assoc. of Law Libraries, 1761
American Assoc. of Museums, 2157
American Assoc. of Port Authorities, 2118
American Baptist Historical Society Library, 1056
American Bible Society Library, 1015
American book-prices current, 2
American Catholic Historical Society Library, 1155, 1175, 4587
American Chemical Society, 2251; Cincinnati Section, 2195; Library, 2264
American Colonization Society, 1397
American Council on Education, 68
American drama, 3232-38
American Entomological Society, 2330

American fiction, 3239-49
American Foundation for the Blind, 1917
American Fur Company, 4593
American Geographical Society Library, 2272, 3172, 3822-24, 3828, 3867, 3913, 3926
American Historical Assoc., 4228
American Home Missionary Society, 1051-52
American Imprints Inventory, 708, 710-11, 717, 730-32, 742, 744, 748, 751-53, 755, 774, 785, 787, 793, 796-97, 803, 806, 809, 817-18, 827, 847, 873-75, 887, 889, 891, 894
American Indian, 154, 2599 (23), 4486-96, 4498-4500
American Institute of Accountants, 2765-66; Library, 2772
American Institute of Electrical Engineers, 2481-82
American Institute of Mining Engineers, 2495
American Library Assoc.: Art Reference Round Table, 2830; Comm. on Foreign Documents, 49; Comm. on Library Coop. with Latin America, 452; Junior Members Round Table, 1
American library directory, 69
American literature, 3219-3347
American Mathematical Society, 2209
American Merchant Marine, 2130
American Missionary Association, 1053
American Numismatic Society Library, 2903
American Oriental Society Library, 3795
American Patent Law Association Library, 1671
American Philatelic Society, 2045
American Philosophical Society Library, 182, 3982, 3987, 4398, 4538, 4542
American poetry, 3219-31, 3356, 3359
American Red Cross, 1919, 5524
American Russian Institute Library, 4310
American Scientific Congress, 3825
American Society of Civil Engineers, 2454, 2505-06
American Society of Mechanical Engineers, 2473
American Telephone and Telegraph Co., 2767
American Type Founders Co., 928, 932
Ames, Herman V., 5140-42
Ames Foundation, 1762
Amhara history, 4368
Amherst College Library, 2022, 3576, 4515
Ammunition, 5419
Amory, Harcourt, 2232, 3446
Amphibians, 2338
Amundsen, Leiv, 4198
Amusements, 3086-3145
Amylases, 2800

Ander, O. Fritiof, 367, 4304
Anderson, Gregg, 773
Anderson, Hans C., 3632
Anderson, Henry J., 2158
Anderson, Robert B., 1763-64, 4487
Anderson, Russell H., 4135
Anderson, Sherwood, 3275
Andover Theological Seminary Library, 984, 4071
Andrews, Clement W., 318
Andrews, Frank De W., 5005
Andrews, Wayne, 3992
Andrews, William L., 614
Anesthesia, 2375, 2416
Angell, Joseph W., 3605
Angelus Studio, 5135
Angle, Paul M., 4026, 4039
Animal culture, 2635-39
Ankenbrand, Frank, 3918
Annan, Gertrude L., 4394
Annmary Brown Memorial, 615-16
Anonyms, 15
Anthony, Robert O., 4062
Anthracite coal, 2293
Anthropology, 134, 2307-14, 2626 (89), 2847, 3864
Antrim, Edward, 1714
Apel, Willi, 3001
Apiculture, 2599 (21), 2639
Apple industry, 2626 (19)
Appleseed, Johnny, 3268
Appleton, John B., 4657
Arabia, history, 4369
Arabian nights, 3771
Arabic languages, 3170
Arabic literature, 3767-68, 3770-71, 4202, 4369
Arbitration: industrial, 1641, 1654; international, 1821
Archibald, Raymond C., 3952
Architecture, 2874-2902; American, 2886; colonial, 2874; English, 2885, 2928; Greek, 2884; Pennsylvania, 2845
Archives, U. S., 4416-31, 4465, 4472, 4477
Arctic warfare, 5405
Arents, George, 2640-42
Argentine history, 5289
Aristotle, 3722
Arithmetics, 2213, 2216, 2221, 2223, 2226
Arizona, history, 4715-18
Arizona State Library, 183
Arizona Statewide Archival and Records Project, 1272
Arizona Territorial Library, 183
Arizona, University, Library, 284, 3694, 4715

Arkansas Geological Survey, State Map Library, 3826
Arkansas: government publications, 23; history, 4719-27
Arkansas History Commission, 4719-21
Arkansas State History Museum, 4719
Arkansas, University, Library, 23, 4723
Armajani, Yahya, 545
Armenia, 4213
Armenian Apostolic Church, 1081
Armstrong, A. Joseph, 3430, 3432
Armstrong, Eva V., 2252-55, 2268
Armstrong, Nellie C., 1794
Arndt, C. O., 4363-65
Art, 2830-2993; auctions, 2842; Indian, 2831; Latin American, 2841, 2848, 2852-54; Negro, 2832-33; Pennsylvania, 2845; periodicals, 2830
Arthurian romances, 2151-52
Artigas, José Gervasio, 5281
Asakawa, Kanichi, 3777
Asbestos, 2465
Asch, Sholem, 1237
Asia, history, 4328-65
Assemblies of God, 1197
Associated Knit Underwear Manufacturers of America, 2807
Association books, 3204
Association of American Railroads, 5205
Association of Casualty and Surety Executives, 1946
Association of Research Libraries, 368
Association of the Bar of the City of New York Library, 1672, 1765-66
Assyria, 4214
Astor Library, 231-32, 3796
Astronomy, 2229-44
Athapascan languages, 3178
Athletics, 3129-38
Atkinson, Fred W., 3232
Atkinson, Geoffroy, 3827
Atlanta Public Library, 4811
Atlanta University Library, 1385
Atlantic neptune, 2124
Atomic bomb, 2502
Atomic energy, 2179, 2181-82
Atwood, Alice C., 2315
Auction catalogs, 9
Audio-visual aids, 2602 (28)
Augustana College Library, 184, 367, 4229, 4304
Auslander, Joseph, 3189
Austin, Mary, 4654
Australia, history, 5371, 5373
Autographs, 483, 488, 503, 509, 511, 552, 569, 578, 612

INDEX

Automobile industry, 1635, 2544
Automobile parking, 2135
Automobile tires, 2542
Avery, Ellen Walters, 555
Avery, Mary, 1200
Avianus, 3733
Ayer, Joseph C., 1003
Ayer, Mary F., 369
Ayres, Frank C., 2698

Babb, James T., 4399
Babbitt, Charles J., 1854
Babcock, Charles E., 5324
Babine, Alexis V., 3745
Babson Institute Library, 2184
Babylonian history, 4200, 4214, 4217
Backus, Edythe N., 3011
Backus, Richard C., 1736
Bacon, Francis, 3421-22
Baden, Anne L., 971, 1355, 1486-87, 1505,
    1510, 1526, 1537, 1558-59, 1563, 1867-69,
    1888, 1947, 2130, 2358-59, 2494, 2544,
    2696, 2777, 2826, 3117, 5378, 5410, 5419
Baer, Carlyle S., 54
Baer, Elizabeth, 762
Baginsky, Paul B., 4522
Baha'i Assemblies, 1196
Baig, Samuel, 2172
Bailey, Philip J., 3423-24
Bailey, Thomas P., 969
Bakelite, 2814
Baker, C. H. C., 2948
Baker, Charles E., 4023
Baker, Eugene C., 5185
Baker, Frank S., 3431
Baker, George H., 3191
Baker, Mary E., 285, 4136
Baker, Ray S., 3945
Baker University Library, 1016
Balch, Ruth, 955
Balderston, Katharine C., 3472
Baldwin, Loammi, 2713
Baldwin, Muriel F., 2931
Balearic Islands, 4296
Balkans, 4193 (4), 4238, 4323-24
Ballads, 769, 783, 2147, 3221, 3227, 3355
Ballard, James F., 2417
Ballet, 3023
Baltimore and Ohio Railroad, 2059
Baltimore, history, 4898, 4910
Banana industry, 2628 (19)
Bancroft, Hubert H., 4676
Bangor Public Library, 4896
Bangorian controversy, 1006
Bank for International Settlements, 1478
Bank of the U. S., 1476, 1495

Banker, Howard J., 2201
Banking, 1476-1503
Bankruptcy, 1492, 1498
Banks, Joseph, 4252
Baptist Church, 1056-72, 1207
Baptist Mission Press, 746
Barberini family, 2714, 2717
Barck, Dorothy C., 2699
Bard family, 5030
Barlow, Joel, 3276
Barnard, Henry, 1961
Barnason, Gudrun, 3606
Barnes, John S., 5452
Barnett, Claribel R., 2601 (16)
Barnett, George E., 1645-46
Barnett, John, 3094
Barnhart, J. H., 2300
Barrett, Lawrence, 3095
Barter commerce, 2626 (40)
Barthold, Allen J., 370
Bartlett, Hazel, 3035
Bartlett, Henrietta C., 3419, 3514-16, 3530,
    3541
Bartlett, John R., 4501, 5160
Bartlett, Kenneth F., 2239, 2382
Barton, George A., 4204
Barton, William E., 4051
Basanoff, V., 1080
Baseball, 3134
Baskerville, John, 682-83
Bassett, John S., 5090-91
Batchelder, John D., 511, 610-11
Bates, Albert C., 723, 1767, 3802, 4692, 4756
Bates, George H., 5382
Bates, W. N., 3722
Battle Abbey, 4275
Bauer, Harry C., 116
Baughman, Roland, 593, 716
Baum, P. F., 3506
Baumgardt, David, 958, 1514
Baumgartner, Leona, 3660
Bausman, Lottie M., 5143
Baxter, Charles N., 4595
Baxter, James P., 4086
Bay, J. Christian, 132, 1156, 2159
Bay psalm book, 768, 783
Baylor University Library, 306, 3430, 3432-33,
    5190
Beach, Helen, 1932
Beaches, 2288
Beal, Edwin G., Jr., 3778
Beale, Joseph H., 1762, 1764, 1768
Bealer, Lewis W., 5281-82
Beall, Rachel H., 2932
Beane, L. E., 2827
Beardsley, Arthur S., 1769

Beardsley, Aubrey, 2909
Beauharnais, Eugene, 4283
Beaumarchais, Pierre, 3650, 4560
Beaumont, Francis, 3372
Beaumont, William, 2412
Becker, Carl, 4849
Bedford County, Penn., history, 5157
Bedinger, Margery, 2793
Beebe Town Library, 4915
Beer, William, 286
Beerbohm, Max, 3425
Beethoven, Ludwig van, 3043-44
Beggars, 1921
Behrens, William B., 2248
Belgian Congo, 4373
Belgium, 4193 (3)
Bell, Alexander G., 3946
Bell, Martha S., 2138
Bellamann, Henry, 3678
Bemis, Samuel F., 1404
Bender, Albert M., 598
Bender, Harold S., 1091
Bender, John E., 1476
Benedict, Russell, 1770
Benedictis, Jack de, 453
Benjamin, Judah P., 3947
Benjamin, Mary A., 1157
Benjamin, Philip M., 4027
Bennett, Richard, 580, 605
Benson, Adolph B., 3625-26
Benson, Nettie L., 1405
Bentley, William, 180
Benton, Elbert J., 4646
Benton, Joel, 813
Benton, Josiah H., 1118
Benton, Thomas H., 3948
Bergson, Henri, 950
Berkeley, Francis L., Jr., 2743
Berkeley, George, 995
Berkeley Public Library, 2873
Bermuda, history, 5343
Berry, W. J. C., 1765
Berryman, Clifford K., 2921
Berryman, John R., 1729
Berthier, Alexander, 4558
Berthold, Arthur B., 70
Berthrong, Donald J., 4608
Bestor, Arthur E., Jr., 1512
Bethel, Elizabeth, 4475, 4773, 5387, 5434, 5531
Betten, Francis S., 4230
Beveridge, William, 491
Bible, 234, 572, 1014-46, 1227; American,
    1037-38, 1042, 1044-45; Catholic, 1038;
    drama, 3368; English, 1018-19, 1035-37,
    1046; Greek, 1019, 1021-22; Hungarian,
    1027; in literature, 3368; Latin, 1025;
    New Testament, 1017, 1020-23, 1026, 1030;
    Old Testament, 1029, 1031
Bibliographical Center for Research, Rocky
    Mountain Region, 287
Bibliographical Planning Comm. of Philadel-
    phia, 71, 117
Bibliographie géographique internationale,
    3828
Bibliography: American, 13; English, 13;
    French, 20; general, 1-22; German, 20,
    468; international, 59; Italian, 20; national,
    4; Russian, 21; Slavonic, 11; subject, 6
Bigelow, Frank B., 371
Bigelow, Kennard and Co., 2715
Bill of rights, 1841, 1848, 4578, 5231
Bimetallism, 1480
Biography, 1997, 3935-4134
Biology, 2297-2314; periodicals, 2300-02,
    2306, 2390, 2610
Birdsong, Robert E., 1934
Birkbeck, Morris, 1374
Birmingham Public Library, 3255, 4635, 4640
Bishop, Crawford M., 1737
Bishop, William W., 665, 4240
Bitting, Katherine L., 2582
Bitzer, David R., 1017
Black, George F., 963-67, 2310, 3401, 4271-72,
    4368
Black, George N., 4823
Black, J. William, 1571
Black, Robert K., 3375
Blackouts, 5477
Blackstone, William, 1732
Blair, Austin, 4944
Blair, Emma H., 5374
Blake, William, 2949, 2980, 3426
Blanchard, Linn R., 5362
Blanck, Jacob N., 3803-04
Blast cleaning, 2474
Blast furnaces, 2475
Blind, 1917
Blondheim, David S., 3163
Bloomer, Robert O., 3921
Blumann, Ethel, 4729
B'Nai B'rith, 1987
Boak, A. E. R., 4208
Boardman, Samuel L., 759
Boatman, Mildred, 3855
Bobbitt, Mary R., 2154
Bodde, Dirk, 3779
Bolander, Louis H., 5472
Bolívar, Simón, 3949-51
Bolivia, history, 5289, 5323
Bolton, Charles K., 4916
Bolton, Henry C., 2196
Bonaparte, Louis-Lucien, 3154

INDEX

Bond, Richmond P., 454, 3376
Bontemps, Arna, 1386
Bonus pay, 1624
Book design, 927-48
Book illustration, 673, 914-17, 2912-14, 2953, 2957, 2960; Icelandic, 3612; oriental, 3781
Book of Common Prayer, 985, 1118, 1137
Book reviews, technical, 2435
Bookbinding, 524, 527, 568-69, 572, 604, 611, 918-26; English, 922
Bookmaking, 539
Bookplates, 54-55, 57, 60
Books, deterioration, 61
Books of Hours, 519, 985
Booktrade, 65
Book-worms, 63
Booth, Ada P., 3235
Booth, Bradford A., 3561
Borchard, Edwin M., 1734, 1756, 1759
Boreman, Arthur I., 5243
Born, Lester K., 3164
Borneo, 4358
Borrenstein, David A., 806
Bossuet, Jacques B., 3651
Boston: history, 4917, 4919; maps, 3896-98
Boston Athenaeum, 185, 582, 927, 3543, 3944, 4105, 4257, 4595, 4597
Boston College Library, 3559, 5285
Boston Elevated Railway Co. Library, 2132
Boston, Engineering Dept., 3896-97
Boston Medical Library, 2417
Boston Museum of Fine Arts, 2831, 3652
Boston Navy Yard, 5465
Boston Philatelic Society, 2044
Boston Public Latin School, 1995
Boston Public Library, 166, 186-87, 288, 483-84, 581-82, 617, 630, 687, 700, 927, 985, 1018, 1118, 1216, 1254, 2044, 2139, 2231, 2266, 2312, 2856, 2875-76, 2936, 2955, 3002, 3044, 3063, 3087, 3104, 3165, 3193, 3201, 3286, 3349, 3423, 3429, 3431, 3466, 3516-19, 3543, 3551, 3581, 3583, 3592, 3635, 3661, 3674, 3681, 3690-91, 3695, 3726, 3738, 3805, 3809, 3943, 3961, 3974, 3989, 4076, 4106-07, 4137, 4184, 4294-50, 4257, 4297, 4342, 4400, 4597, 4625-28, 4708, 4917-19, 4927, 5284
Boston Social Law Library, 1673
Boston Society of Natural History Library, 2298
Boston University: New England Institute of Inter-American Affairs, 5285; School of Medicine Library, 2361
Boswell, James, 3427-28
Botany, 2315-28, 2601 (42); medical, 2323; periodicals, 2317, 2321

Botkin, B. A., 4596
Bourland, Benjamin P., 3683
Bourland, Caroline B., 3690
Bourne, Henry E., 4288, 5527
Bowditch, Nathaniel, 3952
Bowdoin, W. G., 60
Bowdoin College Library, 188, 3158, 4892, 4897
Bowerman, Elizabeth G., 2450
Bowers, Fredson, 3362, 3511
Bowker, Howard F., 2904
Bowman, J. R., 4539
Bowman, Jacob N., 5239
Boxing, 3131
Boycotting, labor, 1658
Boys, R. C., 3350
Brachenridge, Henry H., 3953
Bradford, John, 749
Bradley, Isaac S., 4658, 5257
Bradley, R. H., 1711
Bradstreet, John, 4497
Brady, Mathew B., 4610
Bragdon, Henry W., 4132
Bragg, Clara W., 3318
Brahms, Johannes, 3047, 3049
Braille books, 17
Brand, Denis, 756
Brand, Katharine E., 3945, 3967, 4099, 4133
Brantley, Rabun L., 373
Brasch, Frederick E., 2229-30, 2245
Brazil, 4193 (8); history, 4292, 5286, 5313, 5345
Bray, Ruth K., 1618, 1840
Brayer, Herbert O., 372, 2054
Bread making, 2626 (2)
Breckenridge, James M., 792
Breckenridge, William C., 792
Breton literature, 3743
Brewing, 2795
Brick, 2783
Bridgeport Public Library, 1158
Bridges, 2516
Bridgwater, Dorothy W., 3975-76
Briggs, Rose T., 4939
Briggs, Walter B., 3310
Brigham, Clarence S., 374-75, 4597, 5161
Bright, Franklyn F., 4613
Brincklé, Gertrude, 2914
Brinton, Ellen S., 972, 978, 4633
Brinton, Margaret, 2384
Briscoe, Ruth L., 2402
British Central Africa, 4375
British East Africa, 4375
British Guiana, 5347
Britton, Roswell S., 3780
Brockett, Paul, 2545

INDEX

Brockton Public Library, 3202
Brody, Fannie M., 289
Brome, Richard, 3429
Bronson, Leisa, 1567
Brontë, Charlotte, 3386
Bronx County, N. Y., history, 5038
Brook Farm, 1512
Brookline, Mass., history, 4916
Brooklyn, N. Y., history, 1462, 5041, 5054
Brooklyn Botanic Garden Library, 2316-17
Brooklyn Museum Library, 518-19, 4199
Brooklyn Public Library, 189, 2278, 2937, 3121, 3377, 4598, 5380
Brooks, Aurelia E., 3433
Brooks, Jerome E., 2642
Brooks, Robert P., 4799
Broughton, Leslie N., 3572-73
Browder, Philip P., 1540
Brower, Philip P., 2828
Brown, Alexander, 4502
Brown, Allen A., 3002, 3087
Brown, Ann D., 1267, 1532, 1556, 1851, 1864-65, 1891, 1894, 1904-05, 2115, 2146, 2526, 2670, 2899, 2998, 3316, 4079, 4325, 4393, 4644, 4778-79, 5349, 5355, 5357, 5408-09
Brown, Carleton F., 3351
Brown, Gertrude L., 3009
Brown, Guy A., 225
Brown, Herbert R., 3239
Brown, Horace, 3869
Brown, Ira V., 882
Brown, Karl, 139, 281, 2149, 2448, 2689, 3133
Brown, Leighton B., 4982
Brown, Lloyd A., 3879
Brown, Ralph H., 3880
Brown, Ralph M., 4077
Brown, Robert B., 3721
Brown, W. N., 3772
Brown, Walter V., 2688
Brown, Warren, 376
Brown University, 2021; John Carter Brown Library, 479, 618, 868, 896-98, 902, 2243, 2728, 2993, 4401-03, 4485, 4501, 4527, 4577, 4798; Photographic Laboratory, 5286; University Library, 190, 618, 3051, 3219-20, 3222, 3231, 4028, 4059, 4084
Browne, Margaret F., 5447
Browning, Elizabeth B., 3431
Browning, Robert, 3430-33
Bruce, David W., 628
Brumbaugh, A. J., 68
Bruner, Helen M., 118
Bryant, Douglas W., 4404, 5407
Bryant, William C., 3277
Brydges, James, 4265

Bryn Mawr College Library, 320
Buck, Solon J., 4817
Bucks County Historical Society Library, 290
Buddhism, 1214
Budgets, government, 1530, 1534, 1863
Buffalo Historical Society Library, 342, 5022
Buffalo Museum of Science, 2185
Buffalo Public Library, 342, 3584
Buffalo, University: Lockwood Memorial Library, 3251, 3288; Medical School Library, 2386
Buffum, Imbrie, 3654
Bühler, Curt F., 619-20, 646
Building and loan associations, 1500
Bulgaria, 4323
Bullen, Henry L., 928
Bullock, Charles J., 1456
Bullock, Helen D., 2857, 4010, 4029
Bulwer-Lytton, Edward, 3405
Bunker Hill, 3853, 4564
Bunnell, Ada, 2388
Bunyan, John, 233-34, 3434-35
Bureau of Railway Economics Library, 1601, 1627-29, 1634, 1651, 2055-95, 2110-11, 2483, 2507-12, 2745, 2768-69
Burke, William J., 3149
Burlington Railroad, 2103
Burma, 4359
Burmese literature, 3787
Burney, Fanny, 3436
Burnham, John M., 191
Burr, Aaron, 3954
Burr, Nelson R., 4001, 4128, 4818
Burton, Clarence M., 4647
Burton, Theodore E., 3955
Busby, William, 2163
Buschke, Albrecht, 3122
Business, 2674-2780; cycles, 2031; history, 2698-2744; services, 64, 2685, 2692
Business Historical Society, 2698, 2700, 2706
Business men, photographs, 2680
Butler, Nicholas M., 3956
Butler, Pierce, 643, 929
Butler, Ruth L., 455, 485, 3174-75, 4503, 5287
Butler, Samuel, 3437-39
Butter oil, 2598 (5)
Butterfield, Lyman H., 4011
Byrd, Cecil K., 4030
Byron, George Gordon, 3440-43

Cabeen, David C., 3656
Cabon, Adolphe, 456
Cabot, John, 3957
Cabot, Sebastian, 3957
Cadbury, Henry J., 1142, 4071
Cadillac, Antoine de la Mothe, 4943

381

INDEX

Caldwell, Edward, 4665
California: fiction, 3240-41; government publications, 24-25; history, 572, 4728-50; maps, 3899-3903
California Academy of Sciences, 2160
California, Dept. of Industrial Relations, 4744
California Historical Society, 4749-50
California Historical Survey Commission, 4728
California Library Association, 291-92, 377; Comm. on Local History, 4729; Southern District, 24
California State Library, 25, 192-93, 3240-41, 3829, 4138, 4730; Law Dept., 1674; Sutro Branch, 118, 666, 986, 1159, 3696, 3716, 3899, 4251-53, 4629
California State Mining Bureau Library, 2496
California Supreme Court, 1771
California, University (Berkeley): Bancroft Library, 3718-19, 4675-77, 4679, 5685; Dept. of Music, 3052; History of Science Club, 2186; Library, 138, 194, 293, 453, 918, 949, 969, 987, 995, 1949, 2873, 3157, 3160, 3592, 3641, 3900, 4178, 4290, 5281-82
California, University (Los Angeles): Library, 119, 163, 3003, 3392-94, 3590, 4731, 5480; William Andrews Clark Memorial Library, 119, 494, 667, 713, 3014, 3287, 3458, 3568-69, 4990
California, University (Mt. Hamilton), Lick Observatory Library, 2233
Calligraphy, 2916-17
Cam, Gilbert A., 1604, 1901, 2867
Cambridge (Mass.) Press, 765, 781
Cambridge Public Library, 3675, 4920
Camden and Amboy Railroad, 2061
Cameron, K. W., 1119
Camouflage, 5412
Campbell, Edward G., 5574
Campbell, Frank C., 3045
Campbell, Jean, 511, 550, 610
Campbell, Ruth B., 3243
Campbell, W. J., 3978
Canada, history, 1375; 4388-94
Canada Bureau of Statistics, 1269
Canadian Pacific Railway Co., 2062
Canal boats, 2105
Canals, 2112-14, 2726
Cancer Research Laboratories, 320
Cannon, Carl L., 72, 481
Cannon, Lucius H., 1927
Canny, James R., 3321
Capital punishment, 1850, 1852
Cappon, Lester J., 378, 882, 1072, 1140, 4405, 5211
Carberry, Hilda M., 294

Cardozo, Manuel S., 5288
Careers, 1987-91
Caribbean, 4193 (7, 26), 5283, 5332, 5349
Carlson, William H., 73, 3627
Carlyle, Thomas, 3960
Carmack, Elizabeth M., 1468
Carman, Bliss, 3348
Carnegie Endowment for International Peace Library, 973-76, 1350, 1803, 5388-89
Carnegie Institution of Washington, 3
Carnegie Library of Pittsburgh, 249, 853, 1552, 2045, 2161-62, 2197, 2246, 2256-58, 2279-80, 2331, 2343-45, 2435-36, 2455, 2474-77, 2497, 2513-15, 2520-21, 2528-32, 2540, 2583, 2651, 2666, 2773, 2781-92, 2808-12, 3004, 3806-07, 4083, 5497
Carroll, Lewis, 3445-48
Carruthers, Ralph H., 63
Carson, Hampton L., 1719
Cartels, 1564, 1567
Carter, Clarence E., 4504
Carter, Constance, 930, 3662
Cartier, Jacques, 4391
Cartography, 3837, 3877
Cartoons, 2921, 2959
Cartularies, 4285
Carver, Jonathan, 4514
Cary, Austin, 2652
Case, Arthur E., 3352
Case Institute of Technology Library, 357
Cassady, Theodore J., 1446
Castañeda, Carlos E., 988, 5186, 5289, 5337
Casting, 2460
Castlemon, Harry, 3803
Cataloging, 59
Catechisms, 990
Catholic Historical Society (St. Louis), 1174
Catholic Library Association, 1160
Catholic University Library, 295, 3697, 4897, 5288, 5290, 5310, 5312
Cattle trade, 2636, 4687-88
Caudill, Watson G., 1447
Caughey, John W., 4676
Cavagna Sangiuliani, Antonio, 4299
Cavanaugh, Cortes W., 3462
Cavender, Curtis H., 1094
Cawley, F. Stanton, 3607
Caxton, William, 650, 655
Cellophane, 2815
Cellulose, 2602 (24, 44)
Celtic literature, 3742-44
Cement, 2829
Central America: government publications, 46; history, 5304, 5321
Centralization of government, 1903
Century Association Library, 195, 551

INDEX

Century of Progress Exposition, 2443
Ceramics, 2799
Cervantes, Miguel de, 595, 3709-15
Chamberlain, Jacob C., 3304
Chamberlin, Ellen F., 1819, 2035, 2107, 2136-37
Chamberlin, Waldo, 1467, 1639
Chambers of commerce, 2039
Chapbooks, 836, 2147-48, 2150
Chapin, Howard M., 688, 2638, 3917, 4130, 4693
Chapin, Peter, 2638
Chaplin, W. E., 379
Chapman, John, 3268
Chapman, Lily M., 4635
Charities and corrections, 1917-24
Charles I of England, 4250
Charleston, S. C., history, 5171
Charleston Library Society, 5164
Charlton, Henry B., 3520
Charters, English, 4262
Chase, Franklin H., 5023
Chase, Gilbert, 3073, 3076
Chaucer, Geoffrey, 3379, 3404
Chausson, Ernest, 3047
Chekhov, Anton P., 3751, 3753
Chemical abstracts, 2251
Chemical technology, 2781-2806
Chemical warfare, 5390, 5424, 5494
Chemistry, 2251-76; periodicals, 2251, 2259, 2261-64, 2271-73, 2275, 2610
Chemists' Club Library, 2264
Chenery, Winthrop H., 363
Cheney, Frances, 1271, 1564, 3230, 5422
Cherokee Indians, 4486
Chess, 3120-26
Chester, James, 5403
Chesterfield, Philip D. S., 3413
Cheyney, E. P., 4231
Chicago and North Western Railway Co., 2063
Chicago Art Institute, Ryerson Library, 3781
Chicago Historical Society, 396, 737, 2738, 4476, 4540
Chicago Joint Reference Library, 1856
Chicago Law Institute Library, 1676-77
Chicago Library Club, 74, 296
Chicago, Library of International Relations, 5291
Chicago Municipal Reference Library, 1872-73, 2133
Chicago Public Library, 196, 297, 1161, 1255, 1874-75, 2005, 3194, 3203, 3378, 3628-29, 3746-47, 4069, 4476, 5381; Omnibus Project, 689, 2832, 5292
Chicago Scottish Rite Library, 1935

Chicago Theological Seminary Library, 1051-52
Chicago, University: Dept. of New Testament, 1020; Library, 120, 380, 486, 621, 1019, 1659, 1833, 1875, 1918, 2311, 2412, 3232, 3365, 3582, 3595, 3782, 3791, 3830, 3832, 4050-51, 4232, 4254, 4352, 4476, 4856, 5381; School of Commerce Library, 1460
Chiera, Edward, 4225-26
Child, Sargent B., 5
Child labor, 1664-68
Child psychology, 959
Childs, James B., 43-47, 50-51, 1804
Chile, history, 5289, 5311, 5330
Chiles, Rose P., 4068
China, history, 4328-36, 4342, 4356
Chinard, Gilbert, 4541
Chinchona, 2598 (9)
Chinese Americans, 1381
Chinese literature, 3779-83, 3785-86, 3788-94
Chinookan languages, 3179
Chisholm, William W., 1717
Ch'iu, A. K., 3783
Christian art, 2844
Christian Science Church, 1073-74
Christie-Miller, Sydney R., 4505
Christmas, 526, 528, 2156
Chromium, 2808
Church, Elihu D., 3391, 4506
Church and state, 1006
Churchill, William, 3172
Cincinnati history, 5114
Cincinnati Public Library, 197, 4031
Cincinnati, University, Library, 191
Cincinnati Young Men's Mercantile Library Association, 198
Circus, 3112, 3115
Citrus fruits, 2646
City planning, 2856-73, 2875
Civil service, 1857, 1861-62, 1864-66
Civil war, English, 4250, 4254, 4263
Civilian defense, 5476-95
Clagett, Helen L., 1735, 1738-44
Clandestine publications, 5513, 5545-46, 5578
Clapp, Clifford B., 4124
Claremont College Library, 2533, 4343-44, 5293, 5450
Clark, Ethel B., 552
Clark, Frederick C., 2813
Clark, George R., 3958, 4555, 5229
Clark, John C. L., 4097
Clark, Jonas G., 553
Clark, Josephine A., 2601 (20)
Clark, Kenneth W., 1021-22
Clark, T. D., 405
Clark, William A., 667, 3392-94, 3458, 3568

383

INDEX

Clark University Library, 298, 553, 5498
Clarke, J. F., 905
Classification: agricultural, 2602 (30); library, 66
Clay, Albert T., 4217
Clayton, B. A., 4336
Clayton-Torrence W., 5230
Cleland, Robert G., 4738
Clemence, Stella R., 5359
Clementi, Muzio, 3046
Clements, William L., 4406
Clemons, Harry, 75
Clemson College Library, 199
Cleveland, history, 5117
Cleveland Institute of Art Library, 357
Cleveland Medical Library, 357, 2420
Cleveland Museum of Art Library, 357
Cleveland Museum of Natural History Library, 357
Cleveland Public Library, 1162, 1988, 2153, 3053, 3088, 3125-26, 3355, 3585, 3748, 3797, 4205, 4255-56, 4284
Cliff dwellings, 2309
Clifford, William, 2170
Climatology, 2238, 2662
Clinton, George, 3959, 5022
Clinton, Henry, 3886, 4534, 4561-62
Coal industry, 1552, 1565
Coal mines, nationalization, 1504
Coats, Nellie M., 2203
Cobb, Maud B., 4800
Cobb, Ruth, 2198
Cochran, Alexander D., 537
Coe, William R., 4678
Cogswell, Joseph G., 231
Cohen, Boaz, 1217
Coking, 2784
Colby, Elbridge, 3481
Colby College Library, 167, 584-85, 668, 3006, 3204, 3273, 3278, 3281, 3298, 3301, 3326, 3438, 3475-79, 3485, 3501, 4032, 4063
Cold storage, 2599 (10), 2602 (11)
Cole, Arthur H., 1457, 2674-75, 2701-05
Cole, Betty Joy, 2273
Cole, Eva A., 1997
Cole, George W., 3391, 3398, 4007, 4506-07
Cole, Toby, 3749, 4310
Coleman, Edward D., 3368-69
Coleman, J. Winston, 4854
Coleridge, Samuel T., 3360, 3449
Coles, Harry L., 5499
Colgate University Library, 1057, 1071
Colgrove, Arline W., 4255-56
Collective bargaining, 1589
College of the City of New York Library, 200
Collier, Thomas, 776

Collins, Varnum L., 802
Collins, Victor, 3154
Collins, Wilkie, 3387
Collmann, Herbert L., 3353
Colombia, government publications, 44
Colonial Dames of the State of New York, 4139
Colonization, 1370-84
Colorado: authors, 3253; government publications, 26; history, 4751-55
Colorado Historical Society, 722
Colorado River, 4686, 4689
Colorado State Board of Library Commissioners, 26
Colorado State College of Agriculture Library, 299, 2259
Colorado State Library, 201
Colorado Supreme Court Library, 1678
Colorado, University, Library, 300
Columbia Broadcasting System Reference Library, 2484
Columbia University: Avery Architectural Library, 2884, 2893-95, 2901; College of Pharmacy, 2369; Library, 121, 202-03, 535, 554-55, 586, 928, 931-32, 950, 1452, 1458, 1466, 1512, 1806, 1925, 1950, 1985, 1998, 2158, 2209, 2212-13, 2219, 2221-26, 2686, 2740, 2770-71, 2877-78, 2956, 2994, 3109, 3151, 3191, 3205, 3279, 3318, 3445, 3493, 3531, 3560, 3592, 3656, 3751, 3784, 3798, 3926, 3956, 4033, 4200-02, 4290, 4453, 4599-4600, 4762; Plimpton collection, 496, 570; School of Mines Library, 2498; Teachers College Library, 555, 2403, 2932
Columbus, Christopher, 3961-62, 4508, 4521, 4530
Commission government, 1893
Committee of Ancient Near Eastern Seals, 4203
Common law, 1693, 1719
Communal settlements, 1512-13
Communism, 1514
Communities, 2602 (46)
Community centers, 2898
Compulsory military training, 5408-09, 5422
Conat, Mabel L., 1879
Concrete, 2461
Confederate literature, 3227, 3257, 4595, 4601-04
Confederate Memorial Hall, New Orleans, 3969
Confederate Memorial Literary Society, 4601, 4620
Confederate Museum, 440, 4601
Confederate States of America, 2046; publications, 4611, 4620
Conference of Eastern College Librarians, 301

INDEX

Conference of Historical Societies, 4185
Conferences, international, 311
Conger, John L., 4942
Congregational Church, 1075-78
Congresses, international, 311; medical, 2377
Conklin, Dorothy G., 2456
Conklin, Edwin G., 4542
Connecticut: authors, 3252; history, 4756-65
Connecticut College for Women, Palmer Library, 3570
Connecticut Examiner of Public Records, 4757
Connecticut Historical Society, 723-24, 3252, 4108, 4758-60
Connecticut State Library, 122, 587, 1201, 1642, 1679, 2879, 2889, 4141-42, 4756, 4761-62
Connelly, D., Boiler Co., 2730
Connolly, James B., 3278
Connolly, Terence L., 3559
Connor, Jeanette T., 4780
Connor, R. D. W., 4407, 5144
Conover, Helen F., 982, 1270, 1356, 1362-64, 1383, 1413, 1415, 1472, 1499, 1522, 1621, 1820, 1916, 1930, 1986, 2031, 2504, 2778, 2806, 2935, 3762, 4286, 4303, 4307, 4316, 4323, 4334, 4338, 4340, 4373, 4376-77, 4379, 4384-85, 4495, 4645, 5361, 5372, 5383, 5415, 5491-92, 5547, 5552-53, 5556
Conrad, Joseph, 3379, 3450-51
Conscientious objectors, 5888
Constitution, U. S., 1401-02, 1834-36, 1839, 1844-45, 1847-48; Virginia, 1849
Constitutional conventions, 1835, 1837-38, 1849, 1854
Constitutional law, 1833-49
Constitutions, 1260
Consular service, 1826
Consumers' cooperatives, 1509
Container cars, 2509
Containers, 2777
Convict labor, 1580, 1593
Conway, William E., 3569
Cook, Dorothy E., 2942
Cook, Elizabeth, 3429
Cook, Elizabeth C., 381
Cook, Eugene B., 3122, 3124
Cook, Olan V., 645
Cook, William B., Jr., 4199
Cookery, 2583-85, 2587-89
Cooley, Elizabeth F., 879
Cooley, Laura C., 4732
Coolidge, Bertha, 3495
Coolidge, Calvin, 3963
Coomaraswamy, Amanda K., 2831
Cooper, James F., 3279
Cooper, Martha K., 5121

Cooper, Peter, 3964
Cooper Union Library, 2457, 3964
Cooperation, 1509-11, 2602 (41)
Copernicus, Nikolaus, 2230
Copinger, Harold B., 906
Copinger, Walter A., 989
Copper, 2806
Coptic manuscripts, 4216, 4218-19, 4222, 4227
Copybooks, 2024
Copyright records, 19, 589, 703, 735
Corbitt, D. L., 5106
Cork oak, 2598 (7)
Corn, 2626 (87)
Corn laws, 1543
Cornell University: Collection of Regional History, 5024; Library, 1023, 2210, 2880, 3166, 3571-73, 3608-09, 3611-23, 3676, 3685, 3750, 4233, 4463
Corning, Howard, 2706-07
Cornwallis, Charles, 4567
Corporations, 2675, 2677
Corrosion, metal, 2256
Cost of government, 1523
Cost of living, 1561
Costa Rica, 5296, 5304, 5321
Costume, 2936-45
Cotten, Bruce, 5092
Cotton, John, 1007
Cotton, 2626 (44, 61, 63, 91), 2628 (8-9, 18, 22), 2648
Cotton textile industry, 2626 (57), 2628 (3, 7), 2825
Coues, Elliott, 2332
Coulton, George G., 4232
Council on Foreign Relations Library, 1805, 1810
County government, 1875, 1886, 1888-90
Courtenay, Purviance, 4543
Courtesy, 970
Coverdale Bible, 1035
Covington, Samuel F., 5123
Cowan, Robert E., 714, 4731
Cowan, Robert G., 4731
Cowles, Katharine C., 778
Cowley, John D., 1772
Cox, Carolyn, 1581
Coy, Owen C., 4728
Craftsmanship, 2725
Craig, Mary E., 457
Crane, Ronald S., 458
Crane, Stephen, 3280
Crane, Verner W., 3977
Crawford, J. P. W., 3698-3700
Cremation, 2347
Cremation Association of America, 2347
Criminal law, 1850-52, 1933

385

INDEX

Criminology, 1698, 1926-33
Crittenden, Charles C., 382, 4397
Crittenden, John J., 3965
Crocker, Templeton, 4749
Cromwell, Oliver, 3960, 4250, 4254
Cross, Arthur L., 4267
Cross, Wilbur L., 3470-71
Crowne, John, 3452
Cruikshank, George, 673, 2910-11, 2920, 3458
Cruikshank, Isaac, 2910
Cruikshank, Robert, 2910
Crusades, 254
Cryptogamic botany, 2320
Cuba, 4193 (34); history, 5301, 5344, 5346, 5364, 5367; maps, 3932
Cundall, Frank, 899
Cuneiform inscriptions, 503, 4200, 4202, 4204-05, 4220, 4225-26
Cunninghame Graham, R. B., 3453
Currie, Florence B., 123
Currier, Margaret, 683, 2307-08
Currier, Thomas F., 1951, 1982, 3344, 3653, 5500
Currier and Ives, 2968
Curti, Merle E., 2023
Curtis, Carolyn, 2103
Curtis, Florence R., 58
Curtis, Lewis P., 5501
Curtis, Nathaniel C., 2881
Curtis Publishing Co., 3978
Curtiss, Benjamin De F., 4531
Cushing, Harvey, 2364, 2384, 2404
Cushman, Esther C., 4028
Cusick, Margaret R., 2720
Custer, George A., 3966
Cuthbert, Norma B., 4511-12
Cutler, Manasseh, 3915
Cutts, Elmer, 3773
Czechoslovakia, 4318

Dabbs, Autrey J., 5289
Dabbs, Jack A., 5337
Dairying, 2599 (6), 2626 (71, 97)
Daley, Charles M., 622-23
Dallas Public Library, 306, 315
Damon, Samuel F., 3220
Dams, 2524
Dana, Maria T., 1999
Dancing, 3104
Daniels, Josephus, 3967
Dante, Alighieri, 3674-84
Dante Society, 3677
Dart, Henry P., 4875
Darter, L. J., 4078
Dartmouth College: Library, 674, 766, 798, 800, 1344, 3280, 3285, 3303, 3333, 3453; Tuck School, 2676
Darwin, Charles R., 2190
Date palm, 2650
Daughters of the American Revolution Library, 4143
Daumier, Honoré, 2959
Davenport, Frances G., 4257
David, Hans T., 3069
Davies, David, 1835
Davis, Andrew M., 2000, 2004, 4921-22
Davis, Caroline H., 3109
Davis, Emily G., 2354
Davis, Harry, 3089
Davis, Herbert F., 3552
Davis, Innis, 5252
Davis, Jefferson, 3968-69
Davis, Richard B., 3511
Dawson, Edgar, 4766
Day, Cyrus L., 2007
Day, George E., 1055
Day, Joseph P., 2747
Day, Richard E., 5025
Dayton Public Library, 204
Dean, Hazel, 2390
Dean, Helen E., 77
Dearborn, James M., 4595
Debating, 3218
DeBow, James D. B., 322
Debt, public, 1527-28
Decalcomania, 2926
Decatur Public Library, 4156
Declaration of Independence, 4547, 4556, 4571, 4584
Decoration and design, 2875, 2890, 2923-35
Deering, F. P., 1720
Defense financing, 1521
Defoe, Daniel, 3454-57
DeForest, John H., 4589
DeForest, John W., 4589
Dehydrated foods, 2586, 2598 (6), 4193 (21)
DeLand, Fred, 1924
Deland, Margaret, 3281
Delaware, history, 4766-72
Delaware and Hudson Co., 2070
Delaware Historical Society Library, 446, 4767
Delaware Public Archives Comm., 4144, 4768
Delaware State Library, 205, 1680
Delaware, University, Library, 446, 2006, 3840, 5382
Delivery of goods, 2080, 2094
Delta County, Colo., 2628 (21)
Demobilization, military, 4193 (28), 5554
Democracy, 1357
Demography, 1272-1343
Demorest, Rose, 853

INDEX

Dempster, Margaret, 4034
Denis, Ferdinand, 5312
Denmark, history, 4306
Dentistry, 2353, 2387, 2393, 2400; periodicals, 2387, 2393, 2400
Denver Art Museum, 2833, 2847
Denver Public Library, 536, 2211, 2309, 2437, 2555, 2793, 2833, 3008, 3054, 3253, 4752
Denver, University, Library, 302
DePaul University Library, 4085
Depew, Ganson G., 3415
DePeyster, John W., 5046, 5088
Depressions, economic, 1483
DePuy, Henry F., 4488
DeRenne, Wymberly J., 4804, 4809-10
Detroit: history, 4943; maps, 3904
Detroit Public Library, 206, 1509, 1635, 1876, 2030, 2032, 2301, 2438-39, 2541, 2858, 2882, 2923, 2938, 3339, 3586, 3642, 3904, 4647, 4650-51, 4943-45
Deutsch, Herman J., 1202
DeWolf, James, 5162
Dexter, Franklin B., 2001
Dexter, Gordon, 2120
Dexter, Henry M., 1075
Dextrins, 2800
Dialects: American, 3152; European, 3154; French, 3162; German, 3158
Diamond drilling, 2480
Diaries, 4630
Dickens, Charles, 3405, 3458-64
Dickinson, Emily, 3282
Dickson, Frederick, 3470
Dictionaries, 7, 550, 3147, 3155-56, 3162, 3165, 3169; scientific, 2172; Spanish, 2172; technical, 2172
Dietz, Ambrose P., 4730
Dillard, Henry B., 3482
Dime novels, 3244
Dinitrophenol, 2348
Diorama, 2887
Directories, 7, 4178-83; commercial, 2039, 2816; N. Y., 4179-81
Disarmament, 1817, 1827
Disaster relief, 2066
Disciples (Christian) Church, 1079
Disease prevention, 2355
Displaced persons, 5552
Dissertations, 1967, 2015
District of Columbia, history, 4773-79
District of Columbia Bar Assoc. Library, 1681
District of Columbia Grand Lodge Library, 1936
District of Columbia Public Library, 1163-64
Disturnell, John, 3934
Divorce, 980-82

Dixon, Maxey R., 1501
Dobell, Bertram, 588
Dock, George, 2362
Docke, 2323
Dockweiler, J. F., 1773
Doctrina Christiana, 907
Doe, Janet, 2405
Doelle, J. A., 4946
Doesborgh, Jan van, 4527
Dogs, 2638
Doheny, Estelle, 572
Doll, Eugene E., 854
Domestic allotment plans, 2626 (41)
Dominican Republic, 4193 (35), 5363, 5365
Donne, John, 3465
Donovan, Frank P., 3206
Dorosh, John T., 21, 3168
Doty, Marion F., 2267
Doughty, Arthur G., 4388
Douglass, Frederick, 4605
Dover Public Library, 5000
Doves Press, 667
Dowell, E. Foster, 1895
Downing, Margaret B., 1165
Downs, Robert B., 78-83, 4197, 5039
Dowse, Thomas, 221
Drake, Thomas E., 4088
Drama, 3191-92
Drama recordings, 3213
Dramatic music, 3037
Drawing, 2909-22
Dreiser, Theodore, 549
Drepperd, Carl W., 2915
Drewry, Elizabeth B., 4781
Dropsie College Library, 1219
Drug control, 2357
Druids, 966
Drury, Francis K. W., 316, 2199
Dryden, John, 3466-67
Dubester, Henry J., 1333, 1335, 1339, 1341
Dudley, Laura H., 2957
Duff, Edward G., 624
Duke University Library, 124, 383, 433, 706, 1022, 1400, 2200, 3020, 3254, 3283, 3340-41, 3506, 3678, 4068, 4289, 4543, 4636-38, 5110, 5294, 5313, 5333
Dumbarton Oaks Library, 552
Duncan, Winthrop H., 4408
Duniway, David C., 5502
Dunklin, Gilbert T., 3574
Dunlap, Fanny, 4933
Dunlap, Leslie W., 4035
Dunlap, Mollie E., 1387
Dunlap, Sara, 4475
Dunn, Caroline, 4066, 4145
Dunn, George, 1796

INDEX

Dunne, Peter M., 4677
Duplin County, N. C., history, 5109
DuPont de Nemours & Co. Technical Library, 303
Dure, Charlotte A., 1705
Durkin, Joseph T., 3663
Durrie, Daniel S., 5270
Durrie, Isabel, 5270
Duryea, Samuel B., 597
Dust explosions, 2534
Dutcher, George M., 4187, 4279
Dwight, Theodore F., 3937
Dyeing, 2804
Dyer, Arthur, 5462
Dysentery, 2346

Eames, Wilberforce, 690, 767-68, 834, 990, 3831, 4091, 4096, 4521
Earthquakes, 2278
Earths, 2282
Eastern Orthodox Church, 1080-81
Eaton, Charles C., 2677
Eaton, Dorothy S., 3942
Eaton, Vincent L., 3292, 4134, 4659
Echenrode, H. J., 5212
Eckel, John C., 3459
Eckels, George M., 4254
Eckler, Albert R., 2708
Economic entomology, 2598 (8)
Economic planning, 1562, 1569
Economics, 1420-32, 1452-1570, 2599 (27, 31); French, 1459; Latin American, 1454, 1465; Russian, 1472; U. S., 1470-71
Economics of war, 5560
Eddas, 3613
Eddy, George S., 3980
Eddy, Harry L., 2091
Eddy, Henry H., 3914
Eddy, Isaac, 881
Eder, Phanor J., 1736
Edes, Peter, 759
Edgar, Campbell C., 4210
Edgeworth, Maria, 3468
Edmands, John, 4258
Edmonds, Albert S., 883
Edmonds, Cecil K., 669
Edmonds, John H., 4923
Edmunds, Albert J., 1143
Edmunds, Charles C., 1026
Education, 1949-2029; elementary, 2026; higher, 1997-2022; secondary, 1995-96, 2026
Edwards, Everett E., 2615, 4109
Edwards, Jonathan, 3970-71
Edwards County, Ill., 1374
Eells, Richard, 2546-47

Egbert, Donald D., 522
Egbert, Victor, 2979
Egerton, Thomas, 4260
Eggs, 2628 (4)
Egypt, history, 4199, 4211-12, 4370
Eichhorn, Hermene, 3055
Einstein, Albert, 2245, 3041
Eklund, Myrtle J., 4268
Elections, 1365-69
Electoral college, 1367
Eliot, George, 3386
Eliot, Jared, 2618
Eliot, John, 767
Eliot, Margaret S., 4409, 4432
Elkins, Kimball C., 1144, 1351, 3610
Eller, Catherine S., 1732
Eller, Mabel H., 2360
Ellesmere, Francis E., 3521
Elliott, Agnes M., 1942
Elliott, Mary B., 3811
Ellis, John T., 1166
Ellis, William A., 5457
Ellison, Rhoda C., 707
Elzevir press, 906
Embargoes, 1853
Emeneau, Murray B., 3774
Emerich, J. Oscar, 1670
Emerson, Guy, 5503
Emerson, Ralph W., 3251, 3264, 3283
Emig, Wilmer J., 385
Emory University Library, 125-26, 556, 2046, 3968, 4098, 4602, 4811
Employers' liability, 1642-44
Employment, 1566, 1586
Enamel, 2790
Encyclopedias, 7
Engineering, 2448-49, 2454-2581; automotive, 2540-44; ethics, 2455; history, 2457; 2468; hydraulic, 2520-27; marine, 2503-04; mechanical, 2473-80; mining, 2495-2501; periodicals, 2458, 2462, 2473, 2481-82; sanitary, 2528-39
Engineering index, 2458
Engineering Societies Library, 2440, 2454, 2458-62, 2473, 2478, 2480-82, 2495, 2505, 2678
Engineers, 2161
English, Elisabeth D., 5170
English, Thomas H., 556
English drama, 3362-74
English fiction, 3198, 3375-89
English poetry, 3225, 3349-61
Engraving, 2954-93
Engstfeld, Caroline P., 3255
Enoch Pratt Free Library, 3319, 3330, 4898
Entomology, 2321, 2599 (20), 2601 (55)

INDEX

Ephrata Cloisters, 854
Epictetus, 3734
Equitable Life Assurance Society, 1682
Eritrea, 4381
Erosion, 2667 (1), 2669 (1)
Erskine, Robert, 4552
Eskimo language, 3180
Essex County (Mass.), Law Library, 1684
Essex County (N. J.), Bar Assoc. Library, 1683
Essex Institute Library, 2707, 2729, 2905, 3345, 4328
Esthetics, 949
Ethics, 969-71
Ethiopia, 4366-68, 4379, 4381
Ethiopic languages, 3171
Ethnology, American, 2311
Etiquette, 2154
Europe, history, 4228-4327
Evangelical Church, 1082-84
Evans, Charles, 691
Evans, Clara T., 54
Evans, Louise, 340
Evans, Luther H., 1830, 3972, 4259, 5187
Evanston Public Library, 1989, 3009
Evelyn, John, 3469
Exhibits, 2602 (45), 2628 (17)
Explosives, 5419
Expositions, 2452
Ezekiel, Jacob, 1218

Faber du Faur, Curt von, 3587
Fables, 3727, 3730, 3733
Fairbank, John K., 4329
Fairchild family, 5263
Fairs, 2452
Falkland Islands, 5361
Fall River Law Library, 1685
Falmouth, Va., 5215, 5220
Faris, Nabih Amin, 531-32
Farmhouses, 2602 (19)
Farm labor, 2602 (4), 2626 (26, 64, 72, 95)
Farm migration, 2602 (38)
Farm mortgages, 2626 (47)
Farm production, 2602 (49)
Farm taxes, 2626 (94)
Farm tenancy, 2602 (2), 2626 (70, 85)
Farrand, Max, 1833, 4762
Fascism, 4301
Fassett, Frederick G., 386
Faxon, Frederick W., 3207
Fay, Bernard, 4544
Faye, Christopher U., 625, 1024
Fayer, Margaret L., 3256
Fayssoux, Callander I., 5341
Feamster, Claudius N., 3965

Fearing, Daniel B., 55, 3140-43
Federal Reserve Banking System, 1479
Federalist Party, 1448
Fellman, Jerome D., 3832
Felton, Samuel M., 2098
Fenton, Roger, 4236
Fernandez de Lizardi, J. J., 3716-19
Ferrand, Gabriel, 3797
Fertilizers, 2602 (27)
Fiction, 3193-3200
Field, Alston G., 2709
Field, William B. O., 3491-92
Field Museum Library, 2311, 2333
Fielding, Henry, 3470-71
Fifth columns, 5543, 5555
Filar, Leo, 2475
Filing, 2678
Filson, John, 3907, 4855, 4859
Finance, 36
Finch, Jeremiah S., 3488-89
Fine, Ruth, 2356
Fink, Albert, 2058
Finney, Charles G., 1211
Finotti, J. M., 1167
Firdausī, 3798
Fire departments, 1884
Fire prevention, 2410
Fire protection, 5480
Firearms, 5419
Fireworks, 5419
Fisch, Max H., 2420
Fish, Carl R., 5258
Fish, Daniel, 4036
Fish, fisheries and fishing, 55, 2334, 2338-39, 2637, 3139-45
Fisher, Harold H., 4186
Fisher, Jennie D., 227
Fisher, Samuel H., 776
Fisk University Library, 1053, 1389, 3056, 3079
Fiske, Pliny, 2054
Fiske, Willard, 3165, 3676, 3685
Fitch, Elizabeth H., 3935
Fitch, John, 3891
Fitz, Reginald, 2363, 2406
Fitzpatrick, John C., 4117-18, 4120
Fitzroy, Alexander, 4859
Flagg, Charles A., 4924, 5027
Flags, 1347, 5413
Flanders, Bertram H., 304
Flanders, Louis W., 692
Flanders, Ralph B., 305
Fleisher, Edwin A., 3016, 3030
Fletcher, Harris F., 3496-97
Flint, F. C., 2781
Flisch, Julia A., 4801

INDEX

Floods, 2520-21, 2525, 2628 (13)
Floras, 2321
Florence, history, 4300
Florida: government publications, 27; history, 4780-98; maps, 3905
Florida Library Assoc., 4782
Florida State Historical Society, 4780, 4793
Florida, University: Library, 27, 2652, 4489, 4786, 5297; Yonge Library, 406
Flour milling, 2626 (2)
Flower, George, 1374
Flowers, George W., 4636
Flute, 3021
Flynn, Raymond P., 5495, 5568
Foglesong, Hortense, 4410
Folger Shakespeare Library, 671, 3374, 3419, 3520, 3522-24, 3540
Folk, Edgar E., 207
Folk dances, 3088
Folk music, 3024, 3028, 3052-54, 3067, 3073-75, 3077
Folklore, 2147-56; Brazilian, 2149
Food: preservation, 2599 (4); production and distribution, 4193 (17); supply, 2599 (9), 2626 (82)
Foote, Henry W., 1047
Foote, Lucy B., 755
Forbes, Charles H., 3736
Forbes, Harriette M., 4630
Force, Peter, 4022, 4548, 4553
Force, William Q., 4553
Ford, Elizabeth, 4347
Ford, Henry, 3973
Ford, Paul L., 195, 693, 814, 1834, 3981, 3996-98, 4126, 4545
Ford, Worthington C., 387, 769, 3221, 4411, 4546, 4925-26, 5295
Fore-edge paintings, 2953
Foreign relations, U. S., 1375, 1404-18
Foreign trade, 2038, 2040-42
Foreman, Carolyn T., 851
Foreman, Edward R., 815
Foreman, Grant, 5130
Forest, A. N., 3633
Forest fires, 2602 (34), 2655
Forest products industry, 2653, 4193 (19)
Forestry, 2601 (24, 76), 2602 (36), 2651-65, 2856; periodicals, 2663
Fort Worth Public Library, 315
Fossils, 2296
Foster, John, 687, 771
Foster, Stephen C., 3083
Fourth of July, 4572
Fowler, Mary, 3676, 3685
Fox, Louis H., 388
Fox Film Corporation, 3090

Foxwell, Herbert S., 2727
Francastoro, Girolamo, 3660
France, 4193 (3); government publications, 49; history, 123, 4279-89
Frank, John C., 2112, 3224
Franklin, Benjamin, 684, 690, 3936, 3974-90
Franklin, E. M., 3395
Franklin Institute Library, 2441, 2492
Frazier, E. Franklin, 1388
Frederick the Great, 3960
Free speech, 1359-60
Freedley, George, 3091
Freedom of press, 1360-61
Freedom of seas, 1818, 1820
Freeman, Douglas S., 4601
Freeman, Edmund A., 2059
Freemasons, 559, 1935-42; Supreme Council Library, 2163
Freight rates, 2631
Freimann, Aron, 599
French, A. D. W., 4163
French, Robert D., 3507
French Africa, 4376
French and Indian War, 4499-4500, 4515
French bibliography, 20
French drama, 3633-34
French fiction, 3198, 3264, 3635-40
French Institute Library, 3648
French language, 3162
French literature, 123, 3633-59
French Revolution, 578, 4233, 4279-82, 4287-89
Freneau, Philip, 3284
Frewen, Moreton, 4687
Frey, Ellen F., 3340
Frick, Bertha M., 884, 2212-13
Friedenwald, Herbert, 4119, 5346
Friedmann, Robert, 1092
Friedrich, Gerhard, 1370
Friedus, A. S., 3769
Friend, William L., 1800
Friendland, Louis S., 4412
Fries, Adelaide L., 5093
Frisian literature, 3161
Frost, Pattie P., 4155
Frost, Robert, 3285
Frozen food industry, 2628 (2)
Fry, William H., 3080
Fuller, Grace H., 1348, 1451, 1488, 1492, 1498, 1511, 1533-34, 1592, 1624, 1828, 1841, 1847-48, 1870, 1923, 2117, 2294, 2898, 3155-56, 4061, 4327, 4381, 5279-80, 5373, 5411-12, 5418, 5460-61, 5548-49, 5554
Fulton, John F., 2260, 2270, 2364, 2416, 3660
Fulton, Robert, 3991, 5051

INDEX

Funk, Anneliese M., 854
Fur trade, 1555
Furniture, 2890, 2923-25, 2928, 2930
Furuseth, Andrew, 1592
Fyfe, Arthur W., Jr., 2798

Gabler, Anthony J., 460
Gadd, L. H., 1703
Gaeddert, G. Raymond, 389
Gages, 2479
Gaine, Hugh, 814
Galbreath, C. B., 333
Gallatin, Albert, 3992
Gallatin, Albert E., 2909, 3425
Gallup, Donald, 3331
Gambet, Adrien, 3123
Gamble, William B., 2465, 2558, 2797, 2820, 2822, 2997, 3108
Gambrill, Georgia, 4172
Game animals, 2341
Gardening, 2602 (15), 2643
Gardner, Charles S., 3785, 4330
Gardner, Elizabeth A., 1565, 2042, 2650, 3820, 4324
Garfield, James A., 3993
Garner, W. W., 2644
Garrett, Robert, 487, 544-46
Garrett Biblical Institute, 1095
Garrison, Curtis W., 514, 2710
Garrison, Fielding H., 2385, 2421
Garrison, George P., 5188
Garvan, Mabel B., 4466
Gary, Elbert H., 1749, 1795
Gas, natural, 2281
Gaskell, Elizabeth C., 3386
Gaskill, Nelson B., 694
Gassett, Henry, 1940
Gastronomy, 2582
Gates, Alice J., 2440
Gates, Charles M., 4660
Gates, Elizabeth, 2261
Gaul, John J., 2519, 2995
Gay, Ernest L., 127, 3653
Gay, Frederick L., 127, 4631
Gay, George H., 127
Gay, Henry N., 3663-64, 3668, 3673
Gazetteers, Chinese, 4336
Geiser, Samuel W., 306
Genealogical Society of Pennsylvania, 4146
Genealogical Society of Utah, 4147
Genealogy, 141, 4135-77; Tennessee, 5179
General Society of Mechanics and Tradesmen Library, 2883
General Theological Library (Boston), 991
General Theological Seminary Library (N. Y.), 999, 1025-26, 1134

Genetics, plant, 2328
Geography, 2283, 3822-3934; American, 3869-3934; periodicals, 3832, 3851
Geology, 2086, 2277-95; Mississippi Valley, 2287; Virginia, 2285
Geopolitics, 1453
George, Henry, 1519
George IV, King of England, 2928
George Washington University Library, 973-75, 1350, 1803, 5388-89
George Williams College, 4606
Georgetown University: Library, 56, 1038, 1157, 1182, 1187; School of Foreign Service, 1453
Georgia: history, 4799-4814; maps, 3906
Georgia Historical Society, 4811
Georgia State Dept. of Archives and History, 4808, 4811
Georgia State Law Library, 1686
Georgia State Library, 4802, 4811
Georgia, University, Library, 208, 4799, 4811
Germain, George, 4536
German Americans, 1370-71, 1380
German bibliography, 20, 468
German drama, 3580
German fiction, 3581-82
German literature, 3580-3605
Germanic languages, 3157-61, 3624
Germany: government, 53; government publications, 53
Gerould, James T., 4269
Gershwin, George, 3056, 3084
Gesamtkatalog der wiegendrucke, 626
Gessiness, Gernard, 2195
Gibbon, Edward, 3994
Giddings, Joshua R., 5116
Gieger, Bayard J., 4733
Gilbert, A. H., 3678
Gilbert, John, 3113
Gilbert, W. H., 1500
Gilder, Rosamond, 3091
Gilkey, M. A., 4176
Gillett, Charles R., 4276-77
Gillis, I. V., 4345, 4354
Gilmer, Gertrude C., 307-08
Gilmore, Barbara, 770
Gipsies, 2155
Giroux, Richard, 5432
Glass, 2781, 2796, 2799
Glazer, Sidney, 4346
Gleason, Frances E., 1158
Glenk, Robert, 4887
Glenn, Bess, 5448
Glidden, Sophia H., 2711
Gliders, 2580
Glossaries, scientific, 2165

INDEX

Goan, Fava E., 309
Godard, Doris, 4397
Goethe, Johann W. von, 3595-99
Goff, Frederick R., 557-58, 577, 589, 627, 908, 3010, 3962, 4547-48
Gohdes, Clarence, 3283
Gold standard, 1480
Goldsmith, Alfred F., 3342
Goldsmith, Oliver, 3472-73
Gondos, Victor, Jr., 5533
Gondra, Manuel E., 5289
Góngora y Argote, Luis de, 3720
Goodnight, Scott H., 3588
Goodrich, F. L. D., 779
Goodrich, Nathaniel L., 3195
Goodspeed, Edgar J., 486
Goodwin, Noma L., 4543, 4638
Goold, Clarissa L., 3208
Gordan, John D., 3322, 3400, 3556
Gordon, Reginald B., 2192, 2282, 2479, 2486
Gorham, Rex, 2149
Göring, Hermann, 2991
Gorky, Maxim, 3761
Goshen College, Mennonite Historical Library, 1092
Gosnell, Charles F., 5028
Goss, W. F. M., 2468
Goudy, Frederic W., 939, 946
Goult, Virginia B., 4085
Gourley, James E., 2585, 2587
Government: Great Britain, 1915; U. S., 1896, 1899, 1901-03, 1905-15
Government publications, 23-53, 223; Chicago, 1875; Great Britain, 1434; Louisiana, 755; N. Y., 1882-83; U. S., 1722; U. S. local, 30; U. S. state, 31, 34, 36, 40
Grabhorn Press, 716
Grade crossings, 2508
Grady, Catharine C., 105
Graf, Dorothy W., 2594
Graff, Everett D., 5195
Graham, James L., 195
Graham, John W., 962
Graham, Mary E., 310
Graham, Walter J., 310
Grammars, 3147, 3165
Grand Lodge of Iowa Library, 1937
Grand Rapids Public Library, 2924
Granier, James A., 3706
Granniss, Ruth S., 935, 938
Grants in aid, 1840, 1842, 1923
Grape industry, 2626 (36)
Gratwick Laboratory Library, 2386
Graves, F. P., 1952
Graves, William B., 1895-96

Gray, Asa, 2190
Gray, Francis C., 2984
Gray, John C., 1774
Gray, Roland, 1774
Gray, Ruth A., 1967, 4362-63, 4387
Gray, Thomas, 3474
Great Britain, history, 490, 4242, 4248-78
Great Britain, Historical Manuscripts Comm., 4260-61
Great Britain, Ministry of Reconstruction, 1473
Great Britain, Parliament, 4273
Great Lakes, maps, 3881, 3909
Greece, 4238, 4325
Greek and Latin literature, 237, 3722-41
Greek ostraca, 4198, 4207
Greely, Adolphus W., 28-29
Green, Harriet E., 1448
Green, O. H., 3700
Green, Samuel A., 695, 771-72
Green, Thomas, 723
Greenaway, Kate, 572
Greenbaum, Milton, 5366
Greene, Belle Da Costa, 565
Greene, Evarts B., 4509
Greene, Jane, 1541
Greene, Nathanael, 4538
Greenland, 5381
Greenly, Albert H., 3312
Greenwood, Jane L., 1775
Greenwood, John, 2971
Greer, Sarah, 1857-58, 1860, 1877
Greg, Walter W., 3364
Gregory, Julia, 3034
Gregory, Winifred, 52, 311, 362, 366
Grey, Lady Jane, 3995
Grieder, Elmer M., 1859
Griffin, A. P. C., 1419, 1545, 2050, 4094, 4105, 4582, 4663, 4708, 5344, 5346, 5350-51, 5376-77, 5384
Griffin, Grace G., 1404, 4413, 4469
Griffin, Max L., 312
Griffith, Albert H., 4037
Griffith, H. W., 269
Griffith, Reginald H., 3442, 3502
Grinstead, S. E., 1389
Griswold, Ada T., 448
Griswold, Rufus W., 3286
Griswold, Stephen B., 1709
Grolier Club, 590, 628-29, 919, 933-38, 2958, 3665
Gropp, Arthur E., 5340
Grossman, Moses H., 1789
Grosvenor Library, 559, 1188, 1191, 2262, 2386, 3057, 3354

Grotius, Hugo, 1806-07
Gsovski, Vladimir, 4311
Guam, 5385
Guatemala, 5304, 5321
Guayule, 2602 (10), 2667 (4)
Gudger, Eugene W., 2334
Guerber, Louise, 2309
Guianas, 3931, 4394, 5358
Guild, Edward C., 3158
Gulley, L. S., 4721
Gummere, Amelia M., 5029
Gutenberg, John, 581
Gutenberg Bible, 569, 637, 661
Guthrie, Chester L., 1553
Gutsch, Milton R., 5189
Gyroscope, 2540

Haferkorn, Henry E., 390, 2287-88, 2569, 4588, 4652
Hagedorn, Ralph, 1246, 2164
Haight, Gordon S., 4589
Haines, Donal H., 2746
Haiti, 4193 (40)
Hale, Carolyn L., 4178
Haley, Emilie L., 1162
Hall, Drew B., 4892
Hall, Edward B., 3092-94
Hall, Lillian A., 3095-99, 3101
Hall, W. S., 2906
Hall, Wilmer L., 1542, 5228
Halley, Fred G., 5466, 5468-69, 5572
Hallidie, Andrew S., 987
Halliwell-Phillips, James O., 3543
Halper, Benzion, 1219
Ham, Edward B., 4632
Hamer, Elizabeth E., 5470
Hamilton, Alexander, 3996-98
Hamilton, Joseph G. de R., 4639
Hamilton, Milton W., 1941
Hamilton, Sinclair, 914
Hamlin, Arthur T., 3291, 4366
Hamlin, Talbot F., 2878, 2884
Hammond, George P., 4679, 5015
Hammond, James, 236
Hampton Institute, 1390
Handicapped, 1578
Handicrafts, 2935
Handwriting, 3214
Hanke, Lewis, 5296
Hanson, J. C. M., 621
Haquinius, Eric, 2292
Haraszti, Zoltan, 617, 630, 2231
Harbeck, Charles T., 5449
Harbors, 2118, 2125, 2523
Hardin, Floyd, 959, 4291
Harding, George L., 715

Harding, Jane D., 2151
Hardwicke, Robert E., 2281
Hardy, Thomas, 3006, 3405, 3475-80
Hargett, Lester, 4490
Hariot, Thomas, 5213
Harmar, Josiah, 4661
Harmon, Frances, 3914
Harper, George M., 3574
Harrington, Janice B., 5422
Harrington, Thomas F., 2407
Harris, Caleb F., 3222
Harris, Chauncy D., 3832
Harris, Joel Chandler, 556
Harrison, Guy B., 5190
Harrison, Thomas P., Jr., 2432
Harrisse, Henry, 4510
Harrsen, Meta P., 1027
Hart, Richard H., 3319
Harte, Francis Bret, 3287
Hartford Seminary Foundation, 3771
Hartford Theological Seminary Library, 1001
Hartsook, Elizabeth, 4907
Hartwell, Edith, 2002
Harvard, John, 250
Harvard College, 2000, 2004-05, 2008, 2020
Harvard Law School Assoc., 1776
Harvard University, 2003, 2009, 2012-14;
    Arnold Arboretum Library, 657, 2318,
    2322; Baker Library, 1455, 1477, 1636,
    2097-98, 2122-23, 2564, 2616, 2674-75,
    2678-83, 2698, 2700-06, 2708, 2711-27,
    2733-34, 2737, 2747, 2774, 2817, 3400,
    4300, 5162; Bureau of Economic Research
    in Latin America, 1454; Engineering
    Library, 2456, 2467; Farlow Herbarium
    and Library, 2320, 2327; Fogg Museum
    Library, 2840, 2996, 3936; Gray Herbar-
    ium Library, 2325; Houghton Library,
    560-61; Isham Memorial Library, 3001;
    Kress Library, 2704-05, 2719, 2727;
    Institute of Geographical Exploration, 3833;
    Law School Library, 1687, 1763-64, 1768,
    1774, 1776-79, 1782-84, 1790-93, 1796,
    1809; Library, 55, 57, 67, 127, 151, 168,
    209-11, 259, 274, 459, 488-89, 508, 579,
    582, 631, 905, 911, 927, 930, 951, 985, 989,
    992, 1142, 1144, 1242, 1248, 1349, 1351,
    1457, 1808, 1859, 1951, 1953, 1960, 1982,
    1995, 2000, 2003-05, 2147, 2187, 2194,
    2232, 2342, 2645, 2834, 2837, 2910, 2957,
    2974, 2984, 2992, 3092-3101, 3103-04,
    3113, 3119, 3123, 3139-43, 3161, 3167,
    3188, 3213, 3238, 3274, 3299-3300, 3305,
    3310, 3314, 3346, 3348, 3352, 3356, 3358,
    3360, 3372, 3374, 3376, 3381, 3396-97,
    3423, 3425, 3431, 3446, 3449, 3452, 3460,

INDEX

3465, 3485, 3487, 3492, 3498, 3503, 3526, 3541, 3543, 3549, 3551, 3564, 3566, 3577, 3592, 3596, 3600, 3603-04, 3606-07, 3610, 3624, 3643-44, 3651, 3653, 3655, 3657, 3662-64, 3666, 3668, 3673, 3677, 3681, 3690, 3702, 3713, 3717-18, 3723-24, 3728, 3740, 3743-44, 3754, 3783, 3786, 3808, 3842, 3926, 3960, 3994, 4038, 4064, 4071, 4075, 4086, 4257, 4262-63, 4280, 4292-93, 4312, 4318-19, 4347, 4366, 4376, 4389, 4414-15, 4435, 4439, 4549, 4621, 5216, 5303, 5335, 5500, 5503, 5537-38, 5540; Medical School Library, 2363, 2365-66, 2406-07, 2409; Museum of Comparative Zoology, 2335; Peabody Museum Library, 2307-08; School of Landscape Architecture Library, 2860; Semitic Museum, 3767

Harvard-Yenching Institute, 3783, 3786, 4329
Harvey, Edward L., 4265
Harvey, Perry W., 682
Harvey, William, 2411
Harwell, Richard B., 2046, 3257, 3968, 4603
Harzberg, Hiler, 2939
Haselden, R. B., 490
Haskell, Daniel C., 281, 329, 424, 675, 1240, 1926, 2689, 2907, 3192, 3236, 3647, 3913, 4367, 4450, 4454, 4594, 5319
Hassall, Albert, 2374, 2380
Hasse, Adelaide R., 1420-32, 5062, 5064, 5066
Hastings, Reginald R., 4261, 4264, 4266
Haswell, Anthony, 782
Hatch, W. H. P., 1026
Hatfield, Henry R., 2772
Hatheway, Nicholas, 1685
Haverford College Library, 320, 533, 1145, 1148, 1154, 3313, 4088, 4204, 5029
Hawaiian Islands, 485, 2121, 5384
Hawaiian language, 3174
Hawkins, Dorothy L., 726-27
Hawkins, R. R., 3347
Hawkins, Richmond L., 3643, 3657
Hawks, Emma B., 2601 (18)
Hawley, Edith J. R., 3834
Hawley, Emma A., 3271
Hawthorne, Nathaniel, 3251, 3288-89
Hayden, Horace E., 3646, 4281
Hayes, Rutherford B., 3999-4000
Hayes Memorial Library, 3999-4000
Haykin, David J., 939
Hayne, Paul H., 3254
Hays, I. Minis, 3982
Hayward, Ruth P., 4122
Hazen, Allen T., 3486, 3565
Hazen, Margaret P., 2796
Head, Edwin L., 4734
Hearn, Lafcadio, 3290

Heartman, Charles F., 696-97, 3320-21, 3338, 3953, 4550, 4694
Hebrew Education Society, 1232
Hebrew literature, 4202
Hebrew periodicals, 289
Hebrew Union College, 1218, 1245, 3042
Hedges, James B., 2728
Hedrick, Ellen A., 2601 (41)
Heers, William H., 1902
Hegel, G. W. F., 954
Heifitz, Anna, 3751, 3753-54
Heindel, Richard H., 2188
Heine, Heinrich, 3600-02
Helbig, Richard E., 1371
Held, Ray E., 5297
Hellman, Florence S., 1347, 1489, 1493, 1525, 1562, 1863, 1889, 1905, 1909-11, 2040, 2293, 2451-52, 2485, 2664, 2871, 3306, 3761, 3973, 4065, 4339, 4358, 4380, 4383, 4386, 4583, 4689, 5275, 5347-48, 5358, 5391, 5459, 5550-51, 5555
Heltzel, Virgil B., 970
Hemphill, William E., 1141, 2019
Henderson, James P., 4001
Henderson, Robert W., 3129
Henderson, Rose, 1391
Hendrickson, G. L., 3725
Henley, Lillian E., 4829
Hennepin, Louis, 4884
Hennepin County, Minn., Medical Library, 2302
Henry, Edward A., 4856
Henry E. Huntington Library, 128-30, 390, 460, 490-91, 591-93, 633, 654-55, 669-70, 673, 698-700, 716, 737, 773, 900, 1345, 1688, 1780-81, 1835, 2023, 2189, 2408, 2422, 2548, 2556-57, 2835, 2885, 2948-49, 2960, 3011, 3130, 3352-53, 3365-66, 3373-74, 3379, 3391, 3398-99, 3418-19, 3440, 3461, 3465, 3469, 3512, 3521, 3870, 3872-73, 4060, 4110, 4260-61, 4264-66, 4275, 4447, 4505-07, 4511-12, 4551, 4568, 4612, 4736-38, 4746, 5298-99, 5449
Hepburn, William M., 739, 2468, 3309
Heraldry, 4163, 4166, 4175
Herbals, 2323, 2424, 2532
Herberstain, Sigismund, 4311
Herbert, George, 3358
Hering, Hollis W., 1054
Hermannsson, Halldór, 3608-09, 3611-23
Herdnon, Dallas T., 4719
Herrick, Mary D., 4032
Herrick, Myron T., 4002
Hertzberg, Harry, 3112
Hess, Henry E., 1944
Hettich, Ernest L., 4571

394

Heuser, Frederick W. J., 3589
Heusser, Albert H., 4552
Hewett, Anna B., 1145
Heyer, Anna H., 3012
Hiatt, Caroline W., 1597
Hibernation, 2336
Hidy, Muriel E., 2729
Higginson, Thomas W., 2139
Highway engineering, 2505
Hildeburn, C. S. R., 855
Hildreth, Richard, 4412
Hiler, Hilaire, 2940
Hiler, Meyer, 2940
Hill, David S., 84
Hill, Edwin C., 1458
Hill, Esther C., 4850
Hill, Frank P., 802, 3233
Hill, Richard S., 3013
Hill, William H., 816
Hilton, Ronald, 5300
Hinckley, Lyman, 5365
Hintz, Carl W., 85
Hirsch, Felix E., 5030
Hispanic Society of America Library, 212, 492-93, 594-95, 634, 2836, 2960, 3293, 3687, 3690, 3711-12, 3715, 3719-20, 3835-36, 4090, 4100, 5308
Historical and Philosophical Society of Ohio Library, 4680, 5114-15
Historical Foundation of the Presbyterian and Reformed Churches Library, 1103-04, 4871
Historical Records Survey, 5, 2730, 2748-63, 3014, 4416-32, 4513, 4604, 5301; Ala., 708, 1120, 1273-74, 4712; Ariz., 711, 4716; Ark., 394, 710, 1073, 1275, 4722; Calif., 717, 1276-77, 3287, 4739-44; Col., 1220, 1278, 4751; Conn., 1086, 1121, 1279, 4763; Del., 1087, 4769; D. of C., 1122, 3058, 3946, 4553, 4605, 4774; Fla., 1058, 1280-81, 2652, 4783-85; Ga., 1059, 1282, 3906, 4803; Idaho, 730-31, 1283, 4812; Ill., 732, 894, 1095, 1105, 1284-85, 4606, 4819-21; Ind., 1286, 4830; Iowa, 742, 1287, 4843-45; Kan., 744, 1288, 4851; Ky., 748, 1289, 4857; La., 397, 1221, 1290, 4607, 4877-83, 5504; Maine, 4893; Md., 1123, 4433, 4899; Mass., 774, 1124, 1193, 1291, 2190, 4927-32; Mich., 785, 1060, 1082-83, 1096, 1106, 1125, 1168, 1194-95, 1203-04, 1222, 1292-93, 4947-51; Minn., 787, 1294-95, 4960-61, 5505; Miss., 392, 1126, 1223, 1296, 4975; Mo., 793, 1061-62, 1297-98, 4983-86; Mont., 1299-1300, 4990-91; Neb., 796, 1301, 4994-95; Nev., 797, 1127, 1131, 1169, 1302, 4998; N. H., 1170, 1303, 5001-03; N. J., 803, 1064, 1076, 1084, 1107-08, 1128, 1192, 1196, 1205, 1304, 4148, 5006-08; N. M., 809, 1305, 5016; N. Y., 817-18, 1130, 1306-08, 3910, 5031-37; N. Y. (City), 1081, 1088, 1097, 1109-10, 1129, 1146; N. C., 1063, 1099, 1309, 5094-5102; N. D., 1310-11, 5112; Ohio, 847, 1172, 5116-19; Okla., 1206, 1312, 5131-32; Ore., 1313, 5133-37; Pa., 5145-47; Philadelphia, 395; R. I., 1065, 1147, 1314-15, 5163; S. C., 5165; S. D., 1316, 5173; Southern Calif., 494; Tenn., 873-75, 1066, 1224, 1317-18, 5175-77; Texas, 393, 1319, 5191-92; Utah, 313, 1320, 5203-04; Vt., 5206-07; Va., 1067-69, 5214; Wash., 887, 1208, 1321-22, 5240; W. Va., 889, 1111, 1132, 1209, 1323-24, 3925, 4149, 5243-48; Wis., 391, 891, 1079, 1100, 1133, 1173, 1197-98, 1225, 1325-26, 1897-98, 5259-62; Wyo., 1327-28, 5272
Historical societies, 4185, 4397
Historical Society of Western Pennsylvania, 398
History, 4184-5578; ancient, 4198-4227
Hitchcock, Henry R., 2886
Hitchcock, Jeannette M., 2764
Hitti, Philip K., 3768
Hittites, 4215
Hoaxes, 3211
Hobbs, Cecil C., 3787, 4348, 4359
Hodgson, James G., 30, 2259, 2263
Hoernlé, Reinhold F. A., 951
Hofer, Philip, 520, 921, 2837
Hoffman, William H., 4084
Hofmannsthal, Hugo von, 3603
Hogan, Charles B., 3508
Hogan, William R., 4879
Hogarth, William, 2992
Holbrook, Franklin F., 4962
Holcroft, Thomas, 3481
Holden, Edward S., 2233, 2241, 5427-28
Holden, William, 239
Holgate, Josephine, 1508
Holland Society of New York Library, 1112-13, 1806
Hollins College Library, 596
Holmes, Dorothy P., 5
Holmes, Pauline, 1995
Holmes, Ruth E. V., 3697
Holmes, Thomas J., 920, 3355, 4072-74
Holt, Albert C., 5178
Holt, Anna C., 2366, 2409
Holt, Roland, 3089
Holverstott, Lyle J., 1501, 1871
Holweck, F. G., 1174
Home economics, 2582-90, 2599 (18)
Homer, Thomas J., 288

INDEX

Homer, Winslow, 2912
Homsher, Lola M., 2635
Honduras, 5304, 5321; British, 5348
Hoole, William S., 314-15
Hoover Library. See Stanford University, Hoover Library
Hopkins, Gerard M., 4003
Hopkinson, Francis, 549
Hopp, Ralph, 2474
Hoppe, A. J., 3437
Hopper, Elizabeth G., 2612
Horace, 3726, 3729, 3737, 3739
Hornberger, Theodore, 2189
Hornbooks, 1983, 1985
Horner, Henry, 4048
Hornicek, John, 4318
Horology, 549
Horsch, John, 1093
Horticultural Society of N. Y. Library, 2604
Hospital service, railroad, 2092
Hotchkiss, Jedidiah, 3883, 3895
Houdini, Harry, 3114
Hough, Franklin B., 4111
Houghten, Mattie L., 2794
Hours of work, 1627-33
House, Edward M., 4004
House plans, 2878-79, 2889, 2896
Housing, 5479
Housman, Alfred E., 3482-83
Houston, Samuel, 4005
Houston Public Library, 4173
Howard Memorial Library, 755, 4611
Howard University Library, 1392, 1398
Howe, Daniel W., 4831
Howe, W. T. H., 3288
Howell, James, 3484
Howells, William D., 3291
Howland, A. C., 4234
Hoyt, William D., Jr., 4590, 4900, 4909
Hubbard, Gardiner G., 2988
Hubbard, Geraldine H., 4613
Hubbard, James M., 3518
Hubbard, Lucius L., 3551
Hubbard, Theodora, 2859-60
Huber, Elbert L., 5392
Hudson, Henry, 5051
Hudson, William H., 4006
Hudson River, 5051
Hufeland, Otto, 5038
Hufford, Harold E., 1446-47
Hughes, Lewis, 4007
Hughes, Thomas, 3385
Huguenot Society of America Library, 1085
Hulbert, Archer B., 1101
Hull, Callie, 2275
Hulsius, Levinus, 233

Hummel, Arthur W., 1746, 3788-89, 4331
Humphrey, Constance M., 804
Hunnewell, James, 2121, 3281, 3438
Hunt, Gaillard, 4554
Hunter College Library, 3380
Huntington, Edna, 5039
Huntington, Thomas W., 4298
Hurst, Roger A., 4832
Hussey, Mary I., 4205
Hussey, Miriam, 2731, 2736
Hussey, Roland D., 5302-03
Hutchings, C. E., 2324
Hutchins, Henry C., 3454-56
Hutchins, Margaret, 2549
Hutchinson, Edward P., 1329-30
Hutchinson, Susan A., 518-19
Hydrography, 3864
Hydroponics, 2591
Hymnology, 1047-50

Iben, Icko, 86-87
Ice cream, 2599 (17)
Iceland, 4252
Icelandic literature, 3606-24
Idaho, history, 4812-14
Idaho, University, Southern Branch, 4814
Ide, Simeon, 692
Ifni, 4380
Illinois, history, 4815-28
Illinois and Michigan Canal, 2113
Illinois Central Railway System, 2068, 2096, 2102
Illinois Dept. of Agriculture Library, 2605
Illinois Railroad and Warehouse Comm. Library, 2099
Illinois State Council of Defense, 4821
Illinois State Historical Library, 4026, 4039, 4048, 4150, 4156, 4608, 4817, 4822-24, 4884
Illinois State Library, 213, 4825; Archives Div., 4826-27
Illinois State Museum of Natural History, 2299
Illinois Supreme Court, Law Library, 1689
Illinois, University: Library, 58, 316, 430, 495, 625, 755, 1024, 1226, 1572, 1878-79, 1887, 2214, 2549, 2673, 3496, 4299, 4301, 4434, 4681, 4933; Music Library, 3015; Ricker Library, 2881; Visual Aids Service, 3102
Illumination, 2488, 2538
Imbrie, B. V., 5497
Imitatio Christi, 1011
Immigration, 1370-84
Impeachment, 1846
Imperial County, Cal., 2628 (25)
Income statistics, 2626 (73)
Income tax, 1522, 1524, 1531

INDEX

Incunabula, 56, 146, 572, 578, 594, 596, 607, 613, 615-63, 915, 956, 1041; Dominican, 622; English, 619, 624, 650, 655; Hebrew, 632, 640, 649; medical, 2417-34; miniature, 638
Indexes, 1, 8, 10, 16
India, 4193 (38)
Indian languages, 3175-86
Indian primers, 696
Indiana: authors, 3258; history, 4829-42
Indiana Academy of Science, 2201-03
Indiana Historical Society Library, 4066, 4839
Indiana State Law Library, 1690
Indiana State Library, 214, 400, 2925, 3059, 4145, 4151-53, 4829, 4833-35, 4840-42
Indiana Supreme Court, Law Library, 1691
Indiana University Library, 131, 400, 1959
Indianapolis Bar Assoc., 1692
Indianapolis Public Library, 400, 3258
Indic literature, 3772-76
Indochina, 4347
Induction heating, 2490
Industrial accidents, 2344, 2355, 2359
Industrial diseases, 1577
Industrial education, 1992
Industrial mobilization, 5410
Industrial relations, 1467, 1634-41
Industrial surveys, 2442
Inflation, economic, 1488-90
Information services, 2042
Inglis, Margaret I., 136
Ingpen and Stonebill, 3381
Inheritance, land, 2602 (22)
Inheritance taxation, 1523, 1531-32
Initiative, referendum and recall, 1354
Injunctions, labor, 1655-56, 1658
Inks, 2797
Inland Empire Council of Teachers of English, 88
Inquisition, 4231, 4241
Insignia, 5413
Installment plan, 2696
Institute of Aeronautical Science, 2550-51
Institute of American Genealogy Library, 4154
Institute of Public Administration Library, 1857-58, 1860, 1877
Insulating oil, 2798
Insulation, electrical, 2486
Insurance, 1944-48
Insurance: farm, 2602 (47), 2626 (67), 2628 (24); government control, 1947-48; group, 1620; health, 1621; life, 1622; unemployment, 1617, 1623
Insurance Co. of North America, 2410
Insurance Library Association of Boston, 1944
Insurance Society of N. Y., 1945

Interior decoration, 2923-25, 2928, 2930, 2932
International Bureau of the American Republics, 5304-05
International law, 1756, 1795, 1803-32
Internationalism, 1355
Interstate commerce, 2033-34
Inventors, 2161
Iowa, history, 4843-48
Iowa Historical, Memorial and Art Dept., 420
Iowa State College Library, 1990
Iowa State Library, 215
Iowa State University Library, 1693
Ioway and Sac Mission Press, 745
Ireland, William, 3538
Ireland, history, 4249, 4270
Irish literature, 3742, 4270
Iron, 2497, 2787-89, 2805, 4193 (23)
Iroquoian languages, 3181
Irrigation, 2601 (41)
Irving, Washington, 3292-97
Irwin, Theodore, 2961
Isaacs, Lewis M., 3327
Isham, Ralph H., 3427
Isidore of Seville, 3721
Isle of Man, 4272
Isle of Pines, 5295, 5352
Italian bibliography, 20
Italian literature, 549, 3360-86, 3999
Italian Somaliland, 4381
Italy, history, 4297-4303
Ives, S. A., 496
Ivins, W. M., 941

Jackson, A. V. W., 537
Jackson, Andrew, 4008-09, 4787-88
Jackson, Elisabeth C., 2103
Jackson, Joseph, 3302
Jackson, Margaret H., 3672
Jackson, Sally, 4865
Jackson, W. Turrentine, 4662, 4682, 5113, 5273
Jackson, William A., 560-61, 3713, 4293, 4435
Jacksonville Public Library, 4155
Jacob, J. J., 5246
Jacobsen, Edna L., 5028, 5040
Jacoby, Karl, 3603
Jaggard, William, 3527
Jahr, Torstein K. T., 59
Jamaica, 5283
James, A. E., 3209
James, Edmund J., 401
James, Eldon R., 1782-83
James, Henry, 3299
James, James A., 4555
James, Josef C., 5569
James, Margaret A., 3457

INDEX

James, William, 3298-99
Jameson, Mary E., 5456
Jamestown, Va., maps, 3919
Jantz, Harold S., 3223
Japan, history, 4337-43, 4356
Japanese-American relocation program, 5541
Japanese in America, 1382, 2598 (3)
Japanese literature, 3777-78, 3781, 3783-84, 3786, 3789-92
Japanese prints, 2963, 2967, 2974, 2987
Jarrell, Myrtis, 4121
Jefferson, Thomas, 266, 2602(8), 4010-20, 4438
Jefferson National Expansion Memorial. 2891
Jenkins, Charles F., 4556
Jenkins, Michael, 4897
Jenkins, William S., 1433
Jenkinson, Richard C., 602
Jenks, William L., 3881, 3908
Jennings, Judson T., 5027
Jerabek, Esther, 32, 4695
Jesuit relations, 4517
Jet propulsion, 2559
Jewett, James R., 3767
Jewett, Sarah O., 3300-01
Jewish music, 3042
Jewish Theological Seminary Library, 649, 1028, 1215, 1217, 1227-29, 1233
Jews: in drama, 3769; in England, 4253; in literature, 3368-69; in Orient, 4349
Jillson, Willard R., 749-50, 4855, 4858-63.
Jiu-jitsu, 3137
Joerg, W. L. G., 3882
Johansen, Dorothy O., 2732
John Crerar Library, 6-8, 132, 216, 317-18, 635-36, 1269, 1434, 1459-60, 1645-46, 1874-75, 1899-1900, 1954, 2039, 2140, 2165-67, 2192-93, 2234, 2247, 2282, 2336-37, 2346-52, 2442-45, 2463, 2479, 2486-87, 2499, 2534-35, 2552-53, 2591, 2684, 2795, 2814-16, 2887, 2926, 3790, 4376, 4476, 5331, 5335, 5381, 5477
John of Garland, 3164
Johns, C. H. W., 4220
Johns Hopkins University Library, 1230, 1645-47, 3580; Tudor and Stuart Club, 3548
Johnson, Alice S., 4933
Johnson, Allen, 4894
Johnson, Duncan S., 2300
Johnson, E. D. H., 2838
Johnson, Edgar A. J., 2733
Johnson, Francis R., 3548
Johnson, H. Earle, 3060
Johnson, James G., 3242
Johnson, Samuel, 3485-86
Johnson, Samuel (president, King's College), 2011

Johnson, Thomas H., 3970
Johnson, Thomas M., 952
Johnson, Wanda M., 1475
Johnson, Sir William, 4498, 5025
Johnston, Joseph E., 4021
Johnston, William D., 89-90
Joint Comm. on Library Research Facilities for National Emergency, 72
Joline, J. F., 4609
Jones, Cecil K., 5306-07
Jones, Harold W., 2367, 2423
Jones, Helen D., 1382, 1513, 1831, 2178, 2180, 2452, 2778, 3137, 4325
Jones, John P., 4022
Jones, Matt B., 775, 993, 4435
Jones, Perrie, 2586
Jones, Samuel A., 3444
Jones, Silas P., 3636
Jones, Theodore F., 2010
Jones, V. L., 4723
Jones, Wesley L., 5241
Jones Library, Amherst, Mass., 3282
Jordan, Alice M., 3809
Jordan, Philip D., 409, 3061, 3811
Jorgensen, Inge B., 2535
Jorgenson, Margareth, 5364
Josephson, A. G. S., 282, 636, 2191, 2445
Journalism, 480-82
Judaism, 1215-51
Judo, 3137
Julien C. Yonge Library, 4786
Juniata College Library, 1370
Junius, 4258
Juvenal, 3725
Juvenile literature, 836, 3801-21

Kahn, Herman, 2636
Kahrl, George M., 3356
Kaiser, John B., 1436
Kalamazoo College Library, 1060, 4058
Kalamazoo Public Library, 4058
Kane, Grenville, 620, 4456
Kansas, history, 4849-53
Kansas City, University, Library, 4982
Kansas Court of Industrial Relations, 1585
Kansas State Historical Society Library, 389, 402-03, 4852-53
Kansas State Library, 217, 1694
Kapitsa, Petr L., 2249
Kaplan, Milton, 4470
Kaplan, Mitchell M., 1231
Karow, Otto, 3778
Karpinski, Louis C., 2215-16, 2235, 3837, 3844, 3888, 3909, 5393
Kastor, Robert, 2168
Kaye, F. B., 458

INDEX

Keating, George T., 3450
Keats, John, 3487
Kebler, Leonard, 3292
Keefer, Pearl M., 351
Keep, Austin B., 141
Keeweenaw Historical Society, 4946
Kehl, Mary M., 2685
Keidel, George C., 404
Kelker, Luther R., 5140
Kellar, Herbert A., 4963
Kelling, Lucile, 3544
Kellogg, Louise P., 5263-64
Kelly, Howard A., 2319
Kelmscott Press, 572, 667-68, 673, 676
Kemmerer, Donald L., 5009
Kendall, John S., 4885
Keniston, Hayward, 3701, 5308
Kennedy, Edward G., 937
Kennedy, Frances B., 3290
Kenney, Mildred A., 4156
Kent, Donald H., 5148
Kent, Henry W., 934
Kent County, Del., probate records, 4144
Kentucky, history, 4854-73; maps, 3907
Kentucky Court of Appeals, 4860, 4863
Kentucky gazette, 749
Kentucky Library Association, 405
Kentucky, Secretary of State, 4864
Kentucky State Historical Society, 4860, 4864-65
Kentucky State Land Office, 4862-63
Kentucky State Library, 218
Keogh, Andrew, 637, 3545
Kepler, Johann, 2229
Ker, Annita M., 48
Kerner, Robert J., 4319
Kerr, Ruth A., 164
Kerr, Willis, 5450
Keyes, Virginia, 2342
Keynes, Geoffrey, 2411, 3426, 3465, 3469
Khazars, 4350
Kilgour, Frederick G., 2194
Killeffer, D. H., 2264
Killingworth, Charles T., 1647
Kilmer, Kenton, 3189
Kilroe, Edwin P., 1925
Kimball, Fiske, 2888
Kimball, LeRoy E., 3838
King, Charles G., 2945
King, Solomon, 836
King's College (Columbia), 1998
King's Mountain, 5184
Kingsley, Charles, 3385, 3405
Kingston, N. Y., history, 5068
Kinhead, Ludie, 405
Kino, Eusebio F., 4746
Kipling, Rudyard, 3415

Kites, 2549
Klebs, A. C., 2424
Kletsch, Ernest, 3739
Klinge, Norma, 1399
Knapp, William I., 3165
Knauss, James O., 406-07
Knight, John E., 4721
Knitting industry, 2807
Knoepfmacher, 4333
Knowles, Edwin B., Jr., 3710
Knox, Henry, 4927
Knox College Library, 4663-65
Koch, Theodore W., 3676, 3679-80
Kolchin, Morris, 1520
Konstanzer, Marcia B., 2542
Koran, 1252
Korea, 4342
Kornhauser, Henrietta, 352
Kostrzewski, Lucien E., 4321
Krafft, Herman F., 5471
Krassovsky, Dimitry M., 4320
Krebs, Emil, 3146
Krieger, L. C. C., 2319
Krueger, Paul, 1754
Kuhlman, A. F., 31, 1928
Kulsrud, Carl J., 2620
Küp, Karl, 2943
Kuroda, Andrew Y., 3778
Kyle, Eleanor R., 848

Labor, 4193 (10, 15), 1571-1668; disputes, 1651-58; newspapers, 1583-84; periodicals, 1583-84, 1638; unions, 1645-50
Laciar, S. L., 3016
Lacy, Dan, 5103
Ladd, Mary B., 1651
Lafayette, Marquis de, 3936
LaFontaine, Jean de, 3652
Lafreri, Antoine, 3856
Lagarde, Paul de, 237
LaGrange, Marie J., 2925
Lahontan, Baron, 4524
Lake Superior, 4952
Lallou, William L., 1175
Lamar, Mirabeau B., 5199
Lamb, Charles, 3488-90
Lamberton, John P., 319
Lammers, Sophia J., 3259
Lampblack, 2345
Lancaster County Historical Society, 5143
Lancaster County, Penn., history, 5143
Lancour, A. H., 2842, 4166, 4168
Land Bank of 1740, 4921
Land: drainage, 2601 (41); settlement, 2602 (9), 2621; titles, 2602 (21); utilization, 2622
Landa, Louis A., 3552

INDEX

Landau, Baron Horace de, 3013
Landauer, Bella C., 2775
Landevennec Gospels, 521
Landrey, Kathleen B., 3805
Landscape: architecture, 2856-73; gardening, 2602 (35)
Lane, William C., 992, 2005, 3677, 3681, 3960, 4105
Lange, Otto, 1755
Langfeld, William R., 3296
Lansing, John G., 994
Lapham, Ruth, 4574
Larkey, Sanford V., 2408
Larpent, John, 3365
Larsen, Henrietta M., 2734
Larson, Cedric, 3752
Laskey, Julia H., 1164
Lathe, Mary H., 4178
Latin America, 4193 (9, 11); government publications, 43-48; history, 4290, 5281-5370; maps, 3926-34
Latin and Greek literature, 237, 3722-41
Latrobe, Benjamin H., 2888
Latvian literature, 3746
Laufer, Berthold, 3790-91
Laurvik, J. Nilsen, 2922
Law, Robert A., 133
Law, 183, 205, 220, 260, 273, 609, 1436, 1669-1855; American Indians, 4487, 4490; Argentina, 1734; Bolivia, 1735; Brazil, 1738; Chile, 1734; China, 1752; Colombia, 1736; Connecticut, 1767; Cuba, 1737; District of Columbia, 1775; Dominican Republic, 1737; Ecuador, 1738; England, 1762, 1764, 1768, 1772, 1780, 1789, 1796, 1800; European, 123, 1749, 1756; France, 1758; Germany, 1759; Haiti, 1737; Indiana, 1794; Kentucky, 1785; Korea, 1746; Latin America, 1732-45; libraries, 1761; library catalogs, 1669-1732; Mexico, 1739, 1742; Mohammedan, 1748, 1750; New York, 1770; Paraguay, 1740; Peru, 1741; Roman, 1754-55; Russia, 1751; Spain, 1757, 1760; Uruguay, 1743; U. S. Civil War, 1693; U. S. colonial, 1675, 1688, 1716, 1770, 1783; Venezuela, 1744; Virginia, 1786
Law Library Association of St. Louis, 1696
Lawrence, James, 4023-24
Lawrence Law Library, 1697
Laws, A. C., 3682
Lawson McGhee Library, 5179-80
Lea, Henry C., 4231, 4234, 4241
Leach, Howard S., 3367
League of Nations, 1819, 1829, 4361
Leake, Chauncey D., 2375
Leake County, Miss., 2628 (27)

Lear, Edward, 3491
Leatherman, Marian, 1879
Lee, Arthur, 4538, 4549
Lee, Guy A., 1913, 2672
Lee, Hector, 4194
Lee, John T., 4514
Lee, Richard H., 4538
Lee, Robert E., 4025
Lee, Sidney, 3536-37
Leech, John, 3492
Leech, W. R., 4089
Leeser, Isaac, 1232
Lefferts, Marshall C., 3503
Legal biography, 1698
Legal fiction, 1698
Legal medicine, 2365
Le Gear, Clara E., 3839, 3871, 3883
Léger, Aléxis S., 4188
Legislation, 1419-47, 1854-55
Lehigh University Library, 3538
Lehmann-Haupt, Hellmut, 909, 931
Leikind, Morris C., 2168, 2179, 2249, 2360
Leisy, Ernest, 3260
Leland, Charles G., 3302
Leland, Waldo G., 4477, 5506
Leningrad, battle, 5553
Lenox Library, 233-34
Lermontov, Mikhail Y., 3754, 3762
Leslau, Wolf, 3170-71
Lessing, Gotthold, 3604
Letter-writing, 3263
Letters, 503
Lewinson, Paul, 1393
Lewis, John Allen, 687
Lewis, John F., 523, 541
Lewis, Virgil A., 5249, 5253
Lewis, William D., 2006, 3840, 5382
Lewis, Wilmarth S., 134
Lewis and Clark expedition, 4540
Lexington Public Library, 4866
Libby, Orin G., 5265
Liberia, 1397, 4377
Liberty, 1363
Liberty of conscience, 1004
Libraries: Arizona, 73, 96; Boston, 103; California, 92; Chicago, 74; Colorado, 73; District of Columbia, 84, 98, 107, 109; Idaho, 73, 111; Illinois, 66; Indiana, 106; Los Angeles, 97; Missouri, 77; Montana, 73, 111; Nevada, 73; New Jersey, 93; New Mexico, 73; New Orleans, 94; New York City, 62, 82, 89, 104; Northwest, 88; Oklahoma, 87, 145; Oregon, 111; Pacific Northwest, 95, 111; Philadelphia, 71, 105; scientific, 2176; southern states, 83; Texas, 108; United States, 78-81, 85, 99, 101-02,

INDEX

110, 114-15; university, 76; Utah, 73; Virginia, 75, 112; Washington, D. C., 84, 98, 107, 109; Washington (state), 111; Wyoming, 73
Library architecture, 2876
Library catalogs, 177-280
Library Company of the Baltimore Bar, 1698
Library science, 54-67
Library surveys, 68-115
Libya, 4381
Lice, 2598 (1)
Lieber, Francis, 1345
Lillard, John F. B., 4641
Lilly Research Laboratories, 2446
Lima, Manoel de O., 5310
Limouze, A. S., 461
Lincoln, Abraham, 4026-60, 4438, 4827 (3)
Lincoln, Charles H., 497, 4022, 4497, 4499-4500, 4585, 5451
Lincoln, Jonathan T., 2817
Lincoln, Robert T., 4029, 4043-44
Lincoln, Waldo, 451, 2584, 2950
Lincoln Memorial University Library, 4041, 4045
Lincoln National Life Foundation, 3056
Linda Hall Library, 2169
Lindbergh, Charles A., 4061
Linder, David H., 2320
Lindley, Harlow, 4836, 5120
Lindsey, Vachel, 3303
Lingel, Robert, 2124
Linguistics, 237, 485, 3146-88
Linnaeus, Charles, 2326
Lippmann, Walter, 4062
Liquor, 2718; laws, 1869
Liszt, Franz, 3050
Litchfield, Dorothy H., 320
Litchfield Historical Society, 776, 4764
Literary Anniversary Club, 3550
Literary annuals, 3207-09, 3212, 3266
Literary criticism, 3191
Literary forgeries, 3210, 3214, 3399, 3401, 3406, 3411, 3538
Literary geography, 3834
Literature, 3189-3821
Lithographs, 2959, 2968, 2986
Little, Eleanor N., 1784
Little, Homer P., 2283
Little, Thomas, 3346
Little magazines, 331
Little Red Riding Hood, 3821
Littlefield, George E., 777
Littleton, A. C., 2772
Littmann, Enno, 547
Liu, Kwang-ching, 4329
Liveright, Frank I., 2908

Livestock industry, 2626 (62)
Livingston, Dorothy F., 3421
Livingston, Flora V., 3446
Livingston, Luther S., 3304, 3528
Livingston, Mary W., 1599
Livingston, William, 5014
Lloyd Library, 2174-75, 2204, 2321, 2371-72
Loacker, E. M., 3590
Lobel, Hildegarde, 5552
Local government, 1872-94
Local transit, 2132-37
Locke, Edwin, 1256
Locke, Robinson, 3110
Loeffler, Charles M., 3085
Loehr, Rodney C., 2735, 4964
Lokke, Carl L., 5507
London Naval Conference, 5459
Long, Amelia R., 5149
Long, John C., 4515
Long Island, N. Y., history, 5084
Long Island Historical Society Library, 60, 384, 597, 4157, 4696, 5039, 5041-42
Longfellow, Henry W., 3251
Longhead, Flora H. A., 92
Longyear, E. J., Co., 2480
Lope de Vega, 3698
Lord, Robert A., 5311
Los Angeles, history, 4738
Los Angeles Public Library, 135, 1358, 1573, 2963, 3017, 3028, 4732; Municipal Reference Library, 1880, 2861, 5478-87
Los Angeles Railway Corporation Library, 5488
Lotteries, 971, 1503, 1526
Louis XVI of France, 574
Louis XVII of France, 3648
Louisiana: fiction, 3243; history, 4394
Louisiana Historical Assoc., 3969
Louisiana Historical Society, 4875, 4886
Louisiana State Bar Assoc. Library, 1700
Louisiana State Library, 219; Law Dept., 1701
Louisiana State Museum, 4887
Louisiana State University Library, 408, 755, 2205, 3163, 4607, 4877, 4879
Louisiana Supreme Court, 4882
Louisville Free Public Library, 1176, 1394, 2839, 3018, 4591-92
Louisville, University, Speed Museum, 4040
Lounsberg, Ralph G., 5017, 5193
Lovejoy, Elijah P., 4063
Loveless, Milo J., 401
Lovett, Robert W., 1636, 5540
Low, Harriet, 4331
Lowe, John A., 2007
Lowell, James R., 3251, 3304-05
Lowell City Library, 3637

INDEX

Lower California, 5354
Lowery, Woodbury, 3892
Loyal Legion Library, 4597
Lucas, E. Louise, 2834, 2840
Luckhardt, A. B., 2412
Lumber industry, 2664
Luquiens, Frederick B., 3708
Luther, Martin, 4064
Lutheran church, 184, 1086-90
Lutheran Historical Society Library, 1089-90
Lutheran Theological Seminary, 1089-90
Lutrell, Estelle, 321, 3694, 4715
Lutz, Ralph H., 5519
Lycanthropy, 967
Lydenberg, Harry M., 140
Lyman, Susan E., 5317
Lynch, Mary M., 352
Lynch law, 1851
Lyser, Alice I., 4290

Mabbott, Maureen C., 2843, 3686, 4104
Mabbott, Thomas O., 409
McAdam, Edward L., Jr., 3486
McAneny, Marguerite L., 3315
Macao, 4331
MacArthur, Douglas, 4065
McBride, Roberta, 1635
McCabe, Martha R., 1966, 4365, 5368
McCain, William D., 5508-10
McCarthy, Charles, 5266
McClelland, E. H., 1552, 2529, 2782, 2786, 2790
McCloy, Elizabeth J., 5541
McClung, Calvin M., 5179-80
McColvin, Lionel R., 3019
McCombs, Charles F., 601, 3434, 4114, 4571, 4938
McCombs, Lois F., 2497
McConnell, Roland C., 5104, 5431, 5435
McConnell, Winona, 4491
McCormack, Helen G., 5166
McCormick Historical Association, 2617
McCosker, M. J., 2410
McCrum, Blanche P., 5421
McCulloch, Champe C., 2425
McCusker, Honor, 3063, 3286
MacDonald, Augustine S., 4737
Macdonald, Duncan B., 540
MacDonald, Grace E., 38
McDonald, Norma B., 5416
MacDonald, Pirie, 2951
MacDonald, William, 4008
McDonogh, John, 4890
MacDowd, Kennie, 4752
MacDowell, Edward, 3081-82
MacDowell, Lillian I., 1958

McFarland, Marvin, 2554, 5542
McGregor, Tracy W., 4479
McGuire, James C., 1983
McHenry, James, 4066
Machinery foundations, 2478
Machinery in industry, 1594
McIlwaine, Henry R., 4158, 4557
Mackall, Leonard L., 4804
McKay, George L., 9
McKeen, Newton F., 778
McKelvey, Susan D., 2322
McKenzie, Kenneth, 3727
McKinly, Albert E., 5141
MacKinney, Loren C., 4235
McLaughlin, Andrew C., 4436
MacLean, John P., 1189
McLean, M. D., 5194
McLean, Philip T., 4189
MacLeish, Archibald, 3306-08
McLeod, Malcolm, 3103
McManaway, James G., 671, 3374
MacMillan, Dougald, 3365
McMillen, James A., 322
McMurtrie, Douglas C., 323, 410-12, 638, 712, 720-22, 728-29, 733-37, 740, 745-47, 751-54, 756-58, 760, 786, 788-90, 794-95, 799, 805, 810-11, 819-33, 841-43, 846, 849, 852, 856, 866, 869-70, 876, 878, 888, 890, 892-93, 895, 901-02, 910-11, 940, 1785, 2426, 4697, 4745, 4787-88, 4867, 5043
McMurtry, Robert G., 4041
McNay, Ralph R., 2536
McNeil, Paul A., 5312
McNutt, John C., 1690
Macon, Ga., Public Library, 305
Macpherson, Harriet D., 3650
Macpherson, James, 3401
McVoy, Lizzie C., 3243
Madagascar, 4384-85
Madan, Falconer, 672, 3448
Maddox, J. Eric, 1501
Madison, James, 4067, 4438
Maggot therapy, 2349
Maggs Bros., London, booksellers, 2555-56, 4558, 4746
Magicians, 3114
Magnetic recording, 2487
Magoun, Francis P., 3498
Magriel, Paul D., 3104, 3131
Magurn, Ruth S., 2996
Mahan, Alfred T., 4068
Mahoney, Frances, 2135
Maine, history, 4892-96
Maine Genealogical Society, 4159
Maine State Library, 1702

402

INDEX

Maine, University, Dept. of History and Government, 4895
Maitland, Alexander, 4451
Major, Charles, 3309
Malaya, 4358, 5550
Malikoff, G. E., 362
Malloch, Archibald, 2430
Malone, Miles S., 5215
Mampoteng, Charles, 1134
Manchester, Alan K., 5313
Manchus, 4332
Mandates, 1352, 1383
Manganese, 2786
Mango, 2602 (29)
Mangosteen, 2602 (32)
Mann, Thomas, 3605
Manning, Mabel M., 4789
Manpower, 5563
Manucy, Albert C., 4790
Manufactures, 2807-28
Manuscripts, 483-548; Arabic, 531-32, 535-38, 540, 546-47; British, 512; Greek, 546, 570; illuminated, 498, 502-04, 518-30, 566, 568-69, 572, 580, 3135, 4274; Indic, 543, 545-46, 548; medical, 2417, 2431, 2433; medieval, 484, 496, 498, 502, 506; Oriental, 531-48; Persian, 534-35, 537, 544-46; Renaissance, 496, 506; Spanish, 492; Turkish, 535, 537, 540, 544-45
Manwaring, Elizabeth W., 2862
Maps, 210, 2836, 3822-3934
Marblehead Historical Society, 4559
Marchant, Anyda, 1737
Marietta, Ohio, history, 5120
Marietta College Library, 4410
Marine paintings, 2410
Marquette County Historical Society, 4952
Marriage, 980, 982
Marriner, Ernest C., 3278
Marsh, George P., 3216
Marshall, John, 4021
Marshall, Thomas M., 4813
Marston, Thomas E., 639
Martin, F. R., 534
Martin, John H., 4496
Martin, Lawrence, 3825, 3841, 3884-85, 3927-28, 4859
Martin, Mamie R., 787
Martin, Thomas P., 1395, 4294, 4437
Martin, William H., 1786
Martineau, Harriet, 3494
Martinique, 5362
Martinovitch, Nicholas N., 535, 544
Marx, Alexander, 640, 1228-29, 1233
Maryland, history, 4897-4914
Maryland Court of Appeals, 4901

Maryland Hall of Records, 4902-07
Maryland Historical Society, 308, 404, 4433, 4900, 4908-09, 4912
Maryland State Colonization Society, 4900
Maryland State Library, 220, 1703
Maryland, University, Medical Library, 2402, 2413
Masaryk, Thomas G., 4069-70
Mascaro, Stephen A., 1700
Mason, Janie E., 2182, 5476
Masonic Library Association (Pa.), 1942
Massachusetts, history, 4915-41
Massachusetts Historical Society Library, 221, 387, 695, 772, 1448, 4076, 4438, 4597, 4631, 4934-35, 5012
Massachusetts Horticultural Society Library, 2606-07
Massachusetts Institute of Technology Library, 2536, 2796, 2964
Massachusetts State Board of Agriculture Library, 2608
Massachusetts State Library, 222, 1515, 1747, 1854
Masterson, James R., 2239, 4492, 5463-64, 5466-67
Maté, 2628 (16)
Mathematics, 495, 2158, 2209-28, 2235-36; periodicals, 2206, 2227
Mather, Cotton, 4072, 4625
Mather, Frank J., 914, 2911-12
Mather, Increase, 4073, 4625
Mather family, 4071-76, 4523
Mathis, Treva, 3055
Mattfeld, Julius, 3067-68
Matthews, Albert, 324, 2008
Matthews, Brander, 3205
Matthews, Charles D., 536, 994
Matthews, Henry M., 5245
Matthews, Jim P., 4723
Matthews, Mary A., 973, 975, 5389
Maumee Valley, 5124
Maurer, Konrad von, 3624
Maury, Matthew F., 4077-78
Maxwell, Sarah A., 4640
Mayer, Claudius F., 2414, 2427
Mayhew, Dorothy F., 3842
Mayhew, Isabel, 4672
Maynard, George S., 2543
Maynard, Julia M., 4439
Mayo Clinic Library, 2302
Mazarinades, 3646
Mead, Herman R., 633, 995, 2422
Mead, Nelson P., 4765
Meany, Edmund S., 412, 5511
Mearns, David C., 4042-44, 4054
Meat industry, 2633

INDEX

Mecklenberg Declaration of Independence, 4553
Mecom, Benjamin, 690
Medals, 5413
Medical Library Association, 2387
Medical prints, 2434
Medical Society of County of Kings Library, 2428-29
Medici family, 2721, 2724
Medicine, 196, 306, 609, 2343-2434; Arabic, 2414; eclectic, 2371-72; Latin American, 2423; military, 2351; periodicals, 2385-2401; socialization, 2356, 2358
Medieval history, 2402-16, 4230-32, 4234-35, 4241, 4243-44, 4257
Meehan, Thomas F., 1177
Meeker, Jotham, 746
Meinecke, Bruno, 2368
Meixell, Granville, 2686
Mekeel, Arthur J., 1148
Mellen, George F., 5180
Melville, Herman, 3310-11
Mendelsohn, Isaac, 4200, 4202
Mendenhall, J. C., 3382
Mendenhall, Thomas C., 3843
Menk, Patricia H., 4405
Mennonite Church, 1091-93
Mennonite Historical Library, 1093
Mercantile Library Assoc. of the City of New York, 3196, 3383, 3638
Mercantile Library of St. Louis, 4156
Mercantile marine subsidies, 1545
Meredith, George, 3495
Mereness, Newton D., 4709, 5506
Merrill, Harold, 1902
Merrill, William S., 1178
Merritt, Percival, 700
Merrymount Press, 773
Merz, Karl, 3004
Meserve, Frederick H., 4045
Metals, 2793; powdered, 5416
Metcalf, Frank J., 1048-49
Metcalf, Jessie L., 2301
Metcalf, Keyes D., 1234
Meteorology, 2294-95
Methodist Church, 556, 1094-98
Metropolitan Museum of Art Library, 534, 537, 941, 2170, 2841, 2913, 2965, 3652
Mettee, Andrew H., 1699
Metzdorf, Robert F., 509
Metzgar, Judson D., 2963
Metzger, Ethel M., 857
Mexican literature, 3694, 3696, 3703, 3716-19
Mexican War, 4588, 5197
Mexicans, U. S., 1372

Mexico: government publications, 48; history, 5299, 5314, 5318, 5369
Meyer, Herman H. B., 1497, 2687, 2818, 2824, 3529, 4580
Meyer-Baer, Kathi, 3020
Meyers, Charles L., 2941
Mezzotints, 2958, 2971
Miami University Library, 5123
Mica, 2279
Michelmore, G. W., 2557
Michigan: history, 4942-59; maps, 3908-09
Michigan Dept. of State, 4953
Michigan Executive Dept., 4954
Michigan Historical Commission, 4955
Michigan Pioneer and Historical Society, 3881
Michigan State Library, 223, 1881, 4160, 4959; Law Dept., 1704
Michigan, University: Audio-Visual Education Center, 3105, 3210-11; Library, 136, 641-42, 903, 911, 1029-31, 1574, 2235, 2319, 2329, 2464, 3444, 3551, 3683, 3688, 4198, 4206-10, 4896, 4947, 4956-57, 5393; Medical Library, 2368; Transportation Library, 2746; William L. Clements Library, 583, 684, 701-02, 779, 1077, 1114, 1807, 2217, 2338, 3234-35, 3844, 3879, 3886-89, 3983, 4006, 4013, 4052-53, 4087, 4248, 4267, 4390, 4392, 4395, 4406, 4440-46, 4493, 4504, 4516-18, 4533, 4560-67, 4661, 4770, 4791, 4958, 5124, 5148, 5171, 5195, 5213, 5314-15, 5396
Microfilms, 12
Middlebury College Library, 3256, 3261-62
Middleton, J. E., 4388
Middleton, Thomas C., 1179
Midwest history, 4646-53
Milam, Carl H., 1970
Milhollen, Hirst, 1919, 4236, 4610
Military administration, 5420
Military conscription, 5389
Military government, 1828
Military history and science, 2183, 2448, 2470, 5387-5495
Military law, 5399
Military pensions, 1867
Military training, 5391
Milkweeds, 2598 (2)
Millard, Alice, 591
Millard, George, 591
Miller, C. William, 680
Miller, Charles C., 2639
Miller, Daniel, 413-14
Miller, Dayton C., 3021
Miller, Dorothy P., 1406
Miller, George J., 806
Miller, Joaquin, 113

404

INDEX

Millington, Yale O., 415
Mills, Helen M., 5128-29
Mills College Library, 598
Milton, John, 233-34, 3496-99
Milwaukee Municipal Reference Library, 325
Miner, Dorothy E., 498
Mineral resources, 2499
Mineral wool, 2463
Mineralogy, New Jersey, 2284
Miniature books, 590, 638
Minimum wage, 1603, 1609, 1615
Mining directories, 2499
Mink, Arthur D., 427
Minneapolis, history, 4969
Minneapolis Public Library, 3631, 4969
Minnesota: government publications, 32-33; history, 4960-72
Minnesota Historical Society: Forest Products History Foundation, 2653; Library, 32-33, 1052, 2735, 3061, 4660, 4673-74, 4695, 4962, 4964-67, 4971-72
Minnesota State Library, 1705
Minnesota, University, Library, 326, 416-17, 1257, 2302, 4268-69
Minstrels, 3097
Missionary Research Library, 1054
Missions, 1051-55
Mississippi, history, 4973-81
Mississippi delta, 2602 (40)
Mississippi Dept. of Archives and History, 4976-77
Mississippi Historical Society, 4980-81
Mississippi River, 4652
Mississippi State Library, 224
Mississippi, University, Library, 4981
Mississippi Valley, 3888, 4652, 4663, 4967
Missouri, history, 4683, 4982-89
Missouri Baptist Historical Society, 1061
Missouri Botanical Garden Library, 363, 2323-24
Missouri Historical Society Library, 4156
Missouri Library Association, 327
Missouri State Historical Society Library, 418, 792, 4683, 4987
Missouri State Library, Law Dept., 1706
Missouri, University, Library, 123, 137, 952, 4683
Mitchell, Eleanor M., 1588
Mitchell, John, 3884-85
Mitchell, Thornton W., 5462
Mitchell, William, 4079
Mix, David E. E., 3845
Mizener, Arthur, 3308
Mock, James R., 1396
Modern Language Association of America, 499-500

Moffit, Alexander, 743
Moghadam, Mohamad E., 545
Mohammedanism, 1252-53
Molière, Jean B., 3653, 3655
Monaghan, Frank, 4123, 4452
Monaghan, James, 4046
Money, 1476-1503
Mongan, Elizabeth, 2980
Mongolia, 4333
Mongolian literature, 3791
Monmouth County Historical Association, 419
Monongahela Valley, West Va., 5250
Monrad, Anna M., 1046, 1078
Monroe, James, 4080-81, 4438
Monroe doctrine, 1407, 1414
Montaigne, Michel E. de, 3654-55
Montana, history, 4990-93
Montana Historical Society Library, 4992
Montana State Library, Law Dept., 1707
Montesquieu, Charles de S., 3656
Montessori, Maria, 2027
Montignani, John B., 2841
Mood, Fulmer, 138
Moody, Katharine T., 4161
Moore, John, 3119
Moore, Julia A., 3312
Moore, Thomas, 4082
Morand, Julia P. M., 1085
Moravian Church, 1099-1101, 5093
More, Hannah, 997
More, Thomas, 3500
Morey, Charles R., 521
Morgan, Bayard O., 3591-92
Morgan, George, 4083
Morgan, J. Pierpont, 2922
Morgan, James D., 1165
Morgan, Katherine L., 466, 2206
Morgan, Morris H., 3728
Morgan, S. Rowland, 962
Moriarty, John H., 4181
Morison, Samuel E., 2009, 4937, 5216
Morison, Stanley, 2917
Morize, André, 462, 3644
Morley, Christopher, 3313
Mormon Church, 1102, 1212
Morris, Richard B., 4509, 5044
Morris, William, 572, 605, 676
Morrison, Hugh A., 445, 2114, 3190, 4611, 4698, 4706
Morrogh, Charles A., 673
Morsch, Lucile M., 803, 807
Morse, Willard S., 113, 2914, 3336
Morse, William I., 3348, 4389
Mose, H. Einar, 2166, 2347
Moseley and Motley, 2734
Mosher, Frederic J., 15

INDEX

Mothers' clubs, 1976
Mothers' pensions, 1922
Motor fuels, 2598 (10)
Motor transport, 2035, 2136-37
Mott, David C., 420
Mott, Frank L., 480, 4846
Mott, Margaret M., 3064
Mountaineers, 1342, 2599 (28)
Moving pictures, 1978, 2722, 3086, 2090, 3102, 3105, 3117-18
Mowat, Charles L., 4791
Mudd, Seeley W., Foundation, 956
Mudge, Isadore G., 90
Mugridge, Donald H., 1836, 3984, 4615, 5420
Muller, Joseph, 3065
Mumey, Nolie, 5274
Munden, Kenneth, 5363, 5366-67, 5379
Munk, Joseph A., 4717-18
Munro, Isabel S., 2942
Munsterberg, Margaret, 3583, 3729, 5284
Murra, Kathrine O., 2016, 2025, 2178
Murray, C. Fairfax, 2918
Murray, Keith, 5241
Murrie, Eleanore B., 3007
Muscle Shoals, 2485, 2493
Museum Book Store, London, 3872-73, 4447, 4568
Museums, 2157, 2170
Mushabac, Ruth L., 2996
Mushrooms, 2601 (20)
Music, 203, 234, 549, 552, 3000-85; American, 3051-85; California, 3052, 3066; education, 3008; libraries, 3019; Moravian, 3069; Oriental, 3035, 3040; Portuguese, 3025; religious, 1047-50; therapeutics, 2352
Music Library Assoc., Southern California Chapter, 3066
Muskhogean languages, 3182
Muss-Arnolt, William, 1118
Myers, Denys P., 1808
Myers, Irene T., 4868

Nachbin, Jac, 5316
Names, personal, 4174
Napoleon Bonaparte, 4084-85, 4280, 4283
Nash, Ray, 674, 800, 2024, 3285
Nashville, Chattanooga and St. Louis Railway, 2060
National Academy of Design, 2927
National Association of State Libraries, 34
National banks, 1501
National bibliography, 4
National Broadcasting Co., 3106
National Bureau of Casualty and Surety Underwriters Library, 1946
National Carbon Co., 2447

National defense, 72, 2087, 5391, 5394, 5411, 5417-18
National Gallery of Art, 3652, 4808, 4848, 4970, 5205, 5267
National parks, 2870
National planning, 5446
National Research Council, 960, 2171, 2236, 2265, 2283, 2303
National Socialist Party, German, 53
National Society of the Colonial Dames of America-Connecticut, 2889
Nationalism, 1353
Natural resources, 1504-08, 1537, 1570
Nauvoo, Illinois, 4818
Naval architecture, 2503, 5454
Naval history and science, 2183, 2448, 5447-75, 5501
Naval History Society, 5447, 5452
Navigation, 2242-44
Nazarene, Church, 1194
Nebraska: authors, 3259; history, 4994-97
Nebraska State Library, 225
Nebraska, University, Library, 3259
Needlework, 2929
Negro authors, 3265
Negroes, 1385-1403; in armed services, 5421
Nelen, Eleanor W., 3730
Nelson, Charles A., 1950, 1998
Nelson, Horatio, 4086
Nelson, William, 421, 5010-12
Nemoy, Leon, 538, 1235-37, 1249-50
Nerboso, Salvatore D., 1597
Netherland East Indies, 4193 (12), 5386
Netherlands, 4193 (3), 4443
Neuburger, Otto, 53
Neurology, 2394
Neutrality, 1820
Nevada, history, 4998-99
Nevada State Library, 226-27
New Bedford Free Public Library, 228, 942, 2592
New England, history, 4624-33
New England Assoc. of Chemistry Teachers Library, 2266
New England courant, 387
New England Historic Genealogical Society Library, 4163, 4924
New England History Teachers' Assoc., 3846
New England primer, 693, 697
New Hampshire: government publications, 35; history, 5000-04
New Hampshire State Library, 35, 229, 5004
New Harmony, Ind., 4832, 4837
New Harmony Workingmen's Institute Library, 4837
New Haven Free Public Library, 3810

New Jersey, history, 5005-14
New Jersey Historical Society Library, 802, 4164
New Jersey Library Association, 93
New Jersey, Secretary of State, 5012
New Jersey State Library, 5006, 5010
New Mexico, history, 5015-21
New Mexico Historical Society, 5018
New Mexico, University, Library, 328, 422
New Orleans Library Club, 94
New Orleans Public Library, 3197
New Sweden, 4770-72
New York: government publications, 37; history, 4634, 5022-89; maps, 3910-13
New York Academy of Medicine Library, 2353, 2373, 2430-31
New York City, history, 1463, 5053-60, 5080-81, 5085, 5089
New York College of the City of New York Library, 1238
New York College of Pharmacy, 2369
New-York Historical Society Library, 384, 388, 406, 442, 723, 1135, 1503, 2699, 2775, 2951, 3913, 3991-92, 4023-24, 4183, 4448-49, 4480, 4519, 4552, 4579, 4593, 5045-51, 5317, 5447, 5452
New York Law Institute, 1708, 1787
New York Library Association, 10, 4237
New York Mercantile Library Association, 230
New York, New Haven and Hartford Railroad, 2095
New York Public Library, 11, 36, 61-63, 139-40, 169, 231-34, 281, 289, 329-31, 384, 388, 423-24, 463-64, 479, 481, 501-02, 508, 520-22, 539, 562, 599-601, 675, 700, 737, 816, 834-36, 911-12, 915-17, 921-22, 943, 953, 961, 963-67, 977, 980, 990, 996-999, 1034, 1037, 1102, 1190, 1214, 1239-40, 1252-53, 1258-61, 1371, 1391, 1397, 1406, 1420-32, 1449, 1461-64, 1478-83, 1504, 1516-20, 1543, 1554, 1602-05, 1652, 1748, 1833, 1882-86, 1901, 1920-21, 1926, 1955-56, 1983, 2100-2101, 2112, 2119, 2124, 2134, 2141-42, 2148-50, 2154-55, 2172, 2218, 2248, 2267, 2284, 2310, 2339, 2354, 2370, 2448-49, 2465-66, 2488-89, 2516, 2522, 2537, 2542-43, 2558, 2586-88, 2637, 2640-43, 2688-89, 2776, 2797-2800, 2820-23, 2842-46, 2863-68, 2907, 2915, 2928-32, 2943, 2966-73, 2997, 3022-26, 3067-68, 3104, 3107-10, 3131-34, 3145, 3147-49, 3170-71, 3187, 3192, 3212, 3224-25, 3236, 3244, 3263, 3289, 3294-96, 3322, 3327, 3347, 3368-69, 3400-01, 3423, 3434, 3462, 3481, 3493-94, 3530, 3541, 3547, 3556, 3575, 3592, 3645-47, 3650, 3652, 3656, 3667, 3690, 3714, 3731, 3751, 3753-57, 3769-70, 3796, 3799, 3811-13, 3834, 3847-52, 3874, 3911-13, 3926, 3964, 3985, 4009, 4070, 4112-15, 4129, 4165-68, 4179-81, 4211-15, 4238, 4270-72, 4281-82, 4295, 4321, 4332-33, 4337, 4349-51, 4367-71, 4376, 4391, 4450-54, 4508, 4520-22, 4569-71, 4594, 4633, 4699-4701, 4710, 4817, 4938, 5010, 5052-67, 5217-18, 5278, 5311, 5318-19, 5375, 5453-57, 5512, 5516, 5543
New York Society Library, 141-42, 235-36, 371, 384
New York Southern Society Library, 4641
New York State Historian, 3959, 5068-70
New York State Library, 37, 816, 1210, 3195 3845, 3959, 4136, 4169, 4572-73, 4892, 5025, 5027-28, 5040, 5071-74, 5076-77, 5079; Law Library, 1709, 1788; Medical Dept., 2388
New York (State) Secretary of State, 4573, 5075-77
New York Supreme Court Library, 1710
New York Times, 425
New York University Library, 237, 358, 954, 1241, 1789, 1961, 2010, 3264
New Zealand, history, 5372
Newark, N. J., history, 5013
Newark Free Public Library, 64, 602, 802, 2690-91, 2932, 5013
Newark Museum, 2908
Newberry Library, 143, 170, 455, 540, 563, 603, 638, 643-44, 676-78, 955, 970, 1004, 1035, 1837-38, 1874, 2024, 2096, 2102-03, 2151-52, 2311, 2916-17, 3134, 3175, 3245, 3275, 3357, 3435, 3592, 3684, 3732, 3791, 4352, 4476, 4503, 4574, 5381; Ayer collection, 3875, 4493, 5287, 5302; Wing Foundation, 929
Newman, John Henry, 1186
Newspapers, 283, 297, 305, 310, 313, 321, 335, 341, 355-56, 359, 366-479, 942; Alaska, 445; Arizona, 321, 712; Arkansas, 394; Bermuda, 451; Boston, 369; California, 442; Cincinnati, 434; Cleveland, 356; Colorado, 432, 721; Delaware, 446; District of Columbia, 415; English, 454, 458, 460; European, 469, 475-76; Florida, 385, 406; foreign, 297, 451-79; French, 459, 478; French-American, 370; Georgia, 305, 373; German, 1371; German-American, 407, 413-14; Haiti, 456; Illinois, 341, 401, 409, 4649; indexes, 372; Indiana, 400, 435; Iowa, 420; Irish, 460; Jamaica, 899; Kansas, 389, 402-03; Kentucky, 405, 435; Louisiana, 323, 359, 397; Maine, 386; Maryland, 404, 764;

INDEX

Masonic, 1941; Michigan, 399; Midwest, 429; Milwaukee, 892; Mississippi, 392, 4976-77; Missouri, 435, 4649; Monmouth County, N. J., 419; Montana, 442; Negro, 376; Nevada, 410; New Mexico, 422; New York, 384, 388; Newport, R. I., 447; North Carolina, 382, 426; Ohio, 333, 427, 435, 444; Oklahoma, 431; Oregon, 442; Pennsylvania, 413-14, 435; Philadelphia, 395, 428; Russian, 453; Scottish, 460; Swedish-American, 366; Texas, 393; Turkish, 469; Utah, 313, 442; Virginia, 378, 439; wallpaper, 4597; Washington (state), 411-12, 442; West Indies, 451; Winchester, Va., 374; Wisconsin, 391; Wyoming, 379
Newton, Isaac, 2184
Niagara Falls, history, 5043
Nicaragua, 5304, 5321, 5341
Nicholas II of Russia, 4314
Nichols, Charles L., 780, 4691, 4702-03, 5014
Nichols, Nelson, 3547
Nicholson, John B., 4025
Nicholson, John P., 4612
Nicholson, Natalie N., 2467
Nickerson, Mildred E., 3717
Nickles, John M., 2289
Nicols, Lowell W., 5155
Nitze, William A., 2152
Noble, Frank H., 1693
Noise, 2247
Nolan, James B., 858
Nolen, Eleanor W., 3814
Nordbeck, Theodore M., 2974
Norden, Eric, 3914
Norfolk and Western Railway, 2071
Norlie, Olaf M., 1036
North Africa, 4387
North Carolina: history, 5090-5111; maps, 3914
North Carolina College Library, 1400
North Carolina fiction, 3248
North Carolina Historical Commission, 382, 5096, 5099, 5105-06, 5301
North Carolina State Dept. of Archives and History, 3914, 4790
North Carolina State Library, 238, 426, 844, 4170, 5099, 5107, 5110
North Carolina Supreme Court Library, 1711-12
North Carolina, University: Dramatic Museum, 3089; Hanes collection, 645; Library, 144, 382, 844, 1400, 3544, 4639, 4642, 5092, 5094, 5108, 5110-11; Woman's College Library, 2143, 3055
North Dakota, history, 5112-13
North Dakota State Law Library, 1713

North Texas State Teachers College, 315
Northup, Clark S., 3474
Northwest, history, 4657-74
Northwestern University: Gary Library of Law, 1749, 1795, 1933; Library, 2144, 5316, 5335, 5489; Technological Institute Library, 2490-91, 2502, 2559
Norton, Charles E., 3314
Norton, Jane E., 3994
Norton, Margaret C., 4827
Norway, history, 4309
Norwegian American Historical Association, 1373
Notre Dame, University, Library, 5320
Novossiltzeff, George A., 3169, 5544
Noyes, Crosley S., 2987
Noyes, R. Webb, 760-61, 4896
Numismatics, 2903-08; Oriental, 2904-05
Nunns, Annie A., 4103
Nuremberg chronicle, 653
Nursing, 2403
Nussbaum, F. L., 4239
Nute, Grace L., 4593, 4965, 4967-68
Nutrition, 4193 (25)
Nutzhorn, Harold F., 5317

Oakland Public Library, 2873, 3027, 5394, 5490
Oakleaf, Joseph B., 4030
Oberlin College Library, 1211, 1571, 3689, 4613
O'Callaghan, Edmund B., 1037, 5075
Occidental College Library, 5541
Occult sciences, 962-68
Occupational therapy, 2354
Ocean transport, 2118-22, 2124-25, 2127-31
Ochs, Robert D., 2113
O'Connor, Thomas F., 1180
Odd Fellows Library, 1943
Odgers, Charlotte H., 3890
Official gazettes, 51
Offset printing, 947
O'Higgins family, 5311
Ohio, history, 4680, 5114-29; maps, 3915
Ohio Historical and Philosophical Society, 5127
Ohio Library Association, 332
Ohio State Archaeological and Historical Society, 427, 5116, 5120, 5122, 5128-29
Ohio State Library, 239, 333, 5121
Ohio Supreme Court Law Library, 1714
Oil shale industry, 2794
Okfuskee County (Okla.), 2628 (28)
Oklahoma, history, 5130-32
Oklahoma A. and M. College Library, 1929
Oklahoma Historical Society, 431

INDEX

Oklahoma Library Commission, 145
Oklahoma, University, Library, 146
Oldfather, William A., 3733-34
Oldham, Kie, 4720
Olearius, Adam, 4311
Olivart, Ramón de D., 1809
Oliveira Lima, Manoel de, 5290
Oliver, Peter, 3567
Olmsted, Frederick L., 2857
Olympics, 3133
Omaha Public Library, 4996
Oneida Historical Society, 5078
O'Neill, Edward H., 3937
O'Neill, Eugene, 3315-16
Oneirocritica, 961
Onondaga Historical Association, 5023
Opera music, 3023, 3036-37, 3068
Ophthalmia neonatorum, 2343
Optics, 2250
Orchestral music, 3016, 3022, 3039
Oregon, history, 5133-39
Oregon Historical Society, 5136
Oregon State College Library, 334
Oregon State Library, 240, 2869
Oregon Supreme Court Library, 1715
Oregon Trail, 4688
Oregon, University, Library, 4492
Oriental literature, 237, 3767-3800
Ornament, 2931
Ornithology, 2331-33, 2337, 2340-42
Osborn, James M., 3467
Osborne, Georgia L., 4150
Osborne, Harriet, 1016
Osborne, Lucy E., 613
Osgood, Herbert L., 5079-80
Ossian, 3401
Ostrom, John W., 3323
Overman, William D., 5122
Owen, Robert, 4837
Owen, Thomas M., 4171, 4711, 4713-14, 4978
Ozarks, 4643

Pacific Coast Gas Assoc. Library, 2801
Pacific islands, 5383
Pacific Northwest: history, 4666; maps, 3890
Pacific Northwest Library Association, 95, 4667
Pacific Ocean, 4193 (2)
Packaging, 2602 (42)
Packard, Frederick C., 3213
Paganini, Nicolò, 3048
Page, Alfred B., 4704
Pageants, 3109, 3116
Paine, Nathaniel, 685-86, 765, 4523
Paine, Thomas, 4087
Painter, William T., 1959

Painting, 2946-53
Pajanovitch, Cecile, 2823
Paleography, 191
Paleontology, 2284, 2296
Palestine, 4386
Palha, M. Fernando, 37.02
Pallets, 2459
Palmer, George H., 951, 3358, 3361
Palmer, R. R., 4283
Palmer, T. S., 2340
Palmer, Thomas W., Jr., 1760
Palmieri, Aurelio, 3758
Palos Verdes, Calif., Library, 4741
Paltsits, Victor H., 1033, 3284, 3289, 4115, 4524, 4705, 5058, 5063
Pan American Railway, 2079
Pan American Sanitary Bureau Library, 2389
Pan American Union, 5321; Columbus Memorial Library, 65-66, 335-36, 465-66, 1372, 1407-09, 1465, 1575, 1733, 2206, 2277, 2644, 3692, 3815, 3926, 3929-30, 3949-51, 5311, 5322-28, 5395
Panama Canal, 2114, 5353, 5355
Pantle, Alberta, 4696
Papal documents, 1157
Paper industry, 2813, 2818
Papyri, 503, 546, 568, 4201, 4206-10, 4216, 4224
Paraguay, history, 5289
Parcels post, 2051
Paré, Ambroise, 2405
Parent-teacher associations, 1976
Pargellis, Stanley, 3150, 4512
Paris Peace Conference, 5518-19
Parish, John C., 4735
Parish, William A., 2885, 2959
Parker, Alice L., 2975
Parker, David W., 4455
Parks, William, 886
Parma, V. Valta, 564
Parrish, Morris L., 923, 3384-87, 3447, 3463, 3557, 3562
Parsons, Arthur J., 2976, 2988
Parsons, Wilfrid, 56, 1038, 1181-82
Parsons, William B., 2448, 2956
Partch, Clarence E., 1984
Parvin, T. S., 1937
Parvin, Thomas, 749
Pascal, Leo, 1599, 5571
Patents, 1567, 1671, 1724, 2453, 2776, 2780
Patristics, 191
Pattee, Fred L., 3269
Patterson, Donald G., 5529
Patterson, Eugenia, 331
Patterson, Robert W., 3737
Patton, Cornelius H., 3576

INDEX

Patton, John S., 5234
Patton, Mollie M., 3421
Pauli, A. F., 3735
Paxson, Frederic L., 4753
Paylore, Patricia P., 96
Peabody, Francis G., 1351
Peabody, George, 2729
Peabody Institute Library, Baltimore, 241-43, 2890
Peabody Institute Library, Peabody, Mass., 244
Peabody Museum of Salem, 3952, 4024
Peace and war, 972-79
Peanut industry, 2626 (80)
Pearce, Betty J., 2269
Pearl, Orasmus M., 4207
Pearlove, Shirley, 161
Pears, Thomas C., Jr., 1116
Pearson, Constance, 3028
Pease, Marguerite J., 4681
Pease, Theodore C., 4828
Peat, 2599 (12)
Peck, Deborah S., 5476
Peckham, Howard H., 4442, 4563, 5396
Peckham, Morse, 3423-24
Pendell, Lucille, 4475, 5433-34
Penn, William, 4088
Pennell, Elizabeth R., 2589, 2977, 2979, 2989
Pennell, Joseph, 2977, 2979, 2986, 2989
Penney, Clara L., 594-95, 3293, 4090
Penney, Freeland F., 2672
Penniman, James H., 1975
Penniman, Maria Hosmer, 1952, 1957
Pennsylvania, history, 5140-59
Pennsylvania Historical and Museum Comm., 5150
Pennsylvania Historical Society Library, 861, 1410, 1716, 2709, 2731, 2978, 3302, 4575, 4771, 5143, 5146, 5151
Pennsylvania Historical Survey, 428, 1149, 1410
Pennsylvania Horticultural Society Library, 2609
Pennsylvania Museum and School of Industrial Art Library, 2933, 3176
Pennsylvania State College Library, 3269, 3408
Pennsylvania State Library, 1717-18, 2710, 5152-54
Pennsylvania Turnpike, 2514
Pennsylvania, University: Library, 117, 155, 171, 245, 320, 548-49, 574, 1039, 1219, 1476, 1952, 1957, 2002, 2252-55, 2268, 2946, 3159, 3302, 3370, 3382, 3423, 3534-35, 3633, 3682, 3698-3700, 3722, 3759, 3772, 3779, 3978, 3986, 4231, 4234, 4241, 4273; Wharton School, 2736
Penrose, Boies, 2978, 4456
Pensions, 1601, 1604-05, 1607, 1610, 1612-14, 1616, 1619, 1626, 1866-67
Peoria Public Library, 737, 3029, 3195, 3593
Peraza Sarausa, Fermín, 5329
Periodicals, 281-365; African, 473, 477; Alaskan, 445; Arizona, 321; Asiatic, 471, 473, 477; Australian, 473, 477; Baltic, 464; Buffalo, N. Y., 342; California, 291; Charleston, S. C., 314; Cleveland, 356; economic, 2038; English, 454, 458, 460-61, 666, 3409; European, 471, 473, 475-77; foreign, 451-79; French, 462; Georgia, 304-05, 307; German, 468, 474-76, 1371; Illinois, 341; indexes, 329, 358, 2436; Indiana, 309; Irish, 460; Jewish, 289, 330; Latin American, 335-36, 452, 455, 463, 465-67, 470, 479, 2602 (5), 3701, 3703-04; Louisiana, 323, 359; Maryland, 308; New England, 324; New Orleans, 312; Ogden, Utah, 313; Russian, 453, 464; scientific, 471; Scottish, 457, 460; technical, 2435-36, 2440, 2446-47, 2450; women's, 2145
Perkins, Frances, 1582
Perkins, Henrietta T., 2384
Perkins, Norton, 3360
Permanent Court of International Justice, 1822, 1824
Perry, Josepha M., 2737
Perry, Oliver H., 4592
Perry, Ralph B., 3299
Perry, Ruth M., 5513
Persia, 4351
Persius, 3728
Person, Harlow S., 4959
Personnel administration, 1857, 1861-62, 1864, 2602 (33), 2667 (2), 4193 (22, 37)
Peru, history, 5289, 5294, 5298, 5311, 5315, 5333, 5359-60
Peters, Charlotte H., 2260
Peters, Harry T., 2968
Peterson, Clarence S., 1411
Petrarch, Francesco, 3685
Petroleum, 1559, 2281, 2500-01, 2803
Pettengill, George E., 1652
Pettit, Henry, 3579
Pforzheimer, Carl, 3402
Pharmacy, 2321
Philadelphia: history, 4634; maps, 3916
Philadelphia Academy of Natural Sciences, 2188
Philadelphia Bibliographical Center, 12
Philadelphia Board of Public Education Library, 1958

Philadelphia College of Physicians Library, 2411, 2418-19
Philadelphia Free Library, 337, 523, 541, 1719, 1987, 1991, 2979, 3016, 3030, 3079-80, 3199, 3302, 3423, 3464, 3473, 3532, 3816, 4525
Philadelphia Friends' Library, 1150
Philadelphia International Electrical Exhibition, 2492
Philadelphia Library Association of Friends, 1151
Philadelphia Library Company, 246-47, 3080, 3120, 4513, 4525, 4576
Philadelphia Mercantile Library Company, 248
Philadelphia Museum of Art, 2980
Philately, 2044-48
Philippine Islands, 485, 4193 (1), 4356, 5374-79
Philippine languages, 3173
Phillips, Albertine F., 1701
Phillips, John C., 2341
Phillips, Paul G., 4993
Phillips, Philip L., 3853, 3861, 3877-78, 3891-93, 3905, 3907, 3915-16, 3919-20, 3924, 3931, 4388, 4775, 5304-05, 5330, 5345-46, 5376
Phillips, Ulrich B., 4805-06
Phillips, Wendell, 3317
Phillips Academy Library, 3736
Philosophy, 196, 306, 949-58; periodicals, 958
Phobias, 2350
Photo-facsimiles, 18
Photography, 2990-91, 2994-99
Photo-mapping, 2292
Physics, 2236, 2245-50
Pickering, Timothy, 1448
Pierce, Franklin, 4089
Pierpont, Francis H., 5244
Pierpont Morgan Library, 147-50, 503-04, 524-30, 565-69, 604-05, 638, 646-47, 924, 941, 1040, 1136-37, 2918-20, 2958, 2961, 2981-82, 3135, 3371, 3403, 3434, 3632, 3658, 4203, 4216-23, 4274, 4526
Pike, Charles B., 2738
Pilgrim Holiness Church, 1195
Pilgrim Society Library, 4939
Pilgrims, 4918, 4920, 4933, 4939
Pilling, James, 3177-86
Pillsbury, Stanley R., 4295, 4391
Pinger, W. R. R., 3157
Pinkett, Harold T., 1484, 2654, 2665, 2671
Pinthus, Jurt, 3111
Piranesi, Giovanni B., 2919
Pittsburgh Etching Club, 2983

Planning, government, 1902
Plant culture, 2640-50
Plant pathology, 2599 (1-2, 8, 16)
Platonism, 955
Platt, Elizabeth T., 3854, 3867
Play and playgrounds, 1979
Playing cards, 3127-28
Plenn, Abel, 452
Plimpton, Frances T. P., 3672
Plimpton, George A., 570, 1951, 1985, 2219, 2221, 2223, 2226, 3151, 3404, 3531
Plumb, Milton M., 4578
Plunkett, Mattie, 224
Pluto (planet), 2234
Poe, Edgar Allan, 3264, 3318-23
Poetry, Negro, 3226
Poetry recordings, 3213, 3229
Poinsett, Joel R., 1410
Pol, Nicolaus, 2420
Poland, history, 4321
Polansky, Victor S., 2246, 2514, 2786-89, 2791-92, 2808, 2810-11
Polar regions, 3833, 5380-81
Poleman, Horace I., 542-43, 3775, 4353
Police, 1877, 5483
Polish literature, 3748, 3756, 3760
Polish Roman Catholic Union, 3760
Political associations, 1925
Political parties, U. S., 1448-51
Political science, 1344-1451, 3943
Pollard, Alfred W., 616, 679, 3514
Polynesian languages, 3172
Pombo, Jorge, 5331
Pomona College Library, 3894, 4344
Pomrenze, Seymour J., 1913
Pontiac, Indian chief, 4493
Pool, Eugene H., 4023-24
Poole, Franklin O., 4105
Poor laws, England, 4251
Poor Publishing Co., 2701
Pope, Alexander, 3501-04
Population, 1272-1343; British Africa, 1339; Europe, 1335, 1340; France, 1336; Germany, 1337; Italy, 1338; Sweden, 1329; U. S., 1272-1328, 1341-43
Population index, 1331
Porada, Edith, 4203
Porter, Dorothy B., 1398, 3226, 3265
Porter, E. F., 1713
Porter, William A., 1476
Porteus, Laura L., 4888
Portland Cement Assoc. Library, 2829
Portland Public Library, 3388
Portner, Stuart, 5533
Portolan charts, 3835-36
Portraits, 2946-47, 2950-52

INDEX

Ports, 2118, 2125
Portugal, history, 5310
Portuguese Africa, 4382
Portuguese literature, 3695, 3702, 3705
Postal money order service, 2049
Postal savings banks, 1491
Postal service, 2044-52
Potter, Alfred C., 151, 250, 2645, 3305, 3372, 4075
Potter, David M., 4047
Potter, Harriet S., 3261
Potter, Margie, 2380
Pottery, 2851
Pottle, Frederick A., 3427-28, 3501
Poultry, 2601 (18), 2602 (12), 2626 (24)
Powell, Benjamin E., 4683
Powell, C. Percy, 515
Powell, John H., 3464
Powell, Lawrence C., 119, 4190
Power, Ralph L., 97
Powers, Zara J., 4457
Pratt, Harry E., 4048
Pratt, Ida A., 1214, 1748, 4211-14, 4351, 4370
Pratt, John G., 4850
Pratt, Willis W., 3443
Pratt Institute Library, 2932
Prayer books, 985, 1118, 1137
Presbyterian Church, 1103-17, 1212
Presbyterian Historical Society Library, 1115-17, 4684, 4858, 4869
Prescott, William H., 4090
President, U. S., 1907, 1909, 1912, 3938
Press, freedom, 942
Price, Francis W., 3794
Price, Richard, 4518
Prices, 1468, 1554, 1558, 1561, 2599 (5), 2626 (18, 48, 58, 79, 86), 2629
Prichard, Louise G., 347
Priest, Joseph, 4408
Priestley, H. I., 4685
Priestley, Joseph, 2260, 2270
Primary elections, 1366
Prime, George W., 1041
Primers, 696
Prince, Huberta, 98
Prince, Thomas, 4626, 4628
Princeton, Institute for Advanced Study, 4354
Princeton Theological Seminary Library, 1000-01
Princeton University: Industrial Relations Section Library, 1637; Library, 172, 251-52, 487, 531-32, 544-47, 620, 648, 914, 923, 2047, 2054, 2156, 2538, 2906, 2909, 2911-12, 3122, 3124, 3144, 3315, 3334, 3384-87, 3405, 3412, 3423-24, 3447, 3463, 3488-89, 3510, 3541, 3557, 3561-63, 3574, 3654, 3727, 3737, 3768, 3780, 4132, 4224-26, 4240, 4283, 4345, 4456, 4530, 4541, 4558, 4609, 4614, 4688, 5238, 5397, 5514-17; Marquand Art Library, 2849
Printing: Abingdon, Va., 885; Alabama, 706-08; Albany, N. Y., 826; Alexandria, Va., 694; Amherst, Mass., 778; Antigua, 690, 901; Arizona, 711-12; Arkansas, 709-10; Auburn, N. Y., 821, 832; Batavia, N. Y., 818, 837; Belgian, 908; Boston, 687; Brooklyn, N. Y., 828; Buffalo, N. Y., 819, 829, 839; Bulgarian, 905; California, 713-19; Canandaigua, N. Y., 824; Carlisle, Pa., 864; Charleston, S. C., 869, 872; Chicago, 733, 736; Colorado, 720-22; Confederate States, 699; Connecticut, 723-25; Dayton, Ohio, 849; Delaware, 726-27; District of Columbia, 728; Dresden, N. H., 800; English, 664-83; Fredericksburg, Va., 885; French, 912; French-American, 688; Geneva, N. Y., 820-822, 830; Georgia, 729; Greenland, 913; Hartford, Conn., 723; Hebrew, 599; history, 559, 580-948; Idaho, 730-31; Illinois, 732-38; Indiana, 739-41; inks, 2797; Iowa, 742-46; Italian, 648; Ithaca, N. Y., 823, 833; Jamaica, 899; Kansas, 744-47; Kentucky, 748-54; Latin American, 896-904; Lima, Peru, 896-97; Los Angeles, 719; Louisiana, 755-58; Maine, 759-61; Malta, 910-11; Maryland, 762-64; Massachusetts, 765-84; Mexican, 900, 903-04; Michigan, 785-86; Milwaukee, Wis., 892; Minnesota, 787; Mississippi, 788-91; Missouri, 792-94; Montana, 795; Morristown, N. J., 805, 808; Nebraska, 796; Nevada, 797; New England, 687; New Hampshire, 692, 798-801; New Jersey, 694, 802-08; New Market, Va., 882-83; New Mexico, 809-12; New Orleans, 756-57; New York, 813-40; Newark, N. J., 802; North Carolina, 841-44; North Dakota, 845-46; Northampton, Mass., 770; Northampton County, Pa., 862; Ohio, 847-50; Oklahoma, 851; Oregon, 852; Oxford, England, 672; Pennsylvania, 853-64; Peoria, Ill., 734, 737; Petersburg, Va., 885; Philadelphia, 694; Philippines, 907; Pittsburgh, Pa., 853; Reading, Pa., 858; Rhode Island, 865-68; Rochester, N. Y., 831; Russian, 909; Sag Harbor, N. Y., 827; Salem, Mass., 784; Schenectady, N. Y., 825; South Carolina, 869-72; South Dakota, 845; Tennessee, 873-76; Texas, 877; United States, 684-895; Utah, 878; Utica, N. Y., 817, 840; Vermont, 692, 879-81; Virginia, 882-86; Washington (state), 887-88; West Virginia, 889-90;

INDEX

Wisconsin, 891-93; Wyoming, 894-95; York, Pa., 856
Prints, 2836, 2838-39, 2954-93; historical, 4450, 4454, 4466; railroad, 2956
Priorities, 5414
Prison labor, 1580, 1593
Private presses, 588
Probasco, Henry, 563
Proctor, Robert G. C., 4527
Profit sharing, 1606, 1611, 1624
Proportional representation, 1365
Prosody, 3153
Protestant Episcopal Church, 1118-41
Protestant Episcopal Church Divinity School, 1003
Protestant Reformation, 986, 4233, 4240
Provençal language, 3162
Provençal literature, 3645, 3647
Providence Athenaeum, 253
Pseudonyms, 15
Psychiatry, 2394
Psychological index, 960
Psychology, 959-61, 2394; periodicals, 960; rural, 2626 (78)
Ptolemaeus, Claudius, 3831, 3852, 3866
Public administration, 1856-1916
Public Affairs Information Service, 1261
Public finance, 1515-42
Public health, 2356, 2358, 2389, 5481
Public relations, 2778
Public utilities, 2030, 2036-37
Public works, 1591
Puerto Rico, 5350, 5356-57, 5366
Pulaski, Count Kazimierz, 4581
Pulling, Arthur C., 1790-93
Purcell, George W., 429
Purdue University Library, 739, 2269, 2468, 2610, 3309
Purdy, Richard L., 3480
Purviance, Samuel, 4543
Pushkin, Aleksandr S., 3755, 3763
Pyle, Howard, 2914

Quakers (Friends), 1142-54
Qualey, Carlton C., 1373
Qualls, LeRoy L., 430
Quaritch, firm, booksellers, 3125
Quayle, William A., 1016
Quebec, history, 4388, 4392
Queens Borough Public Library, 2939
Quenzel, Carrol H., 2739
Quesnel, Louise, 3330
Quinn, Arthur H., 3319
Quintana, Ricardo, 3440

Race relations, 1358, 1362, 1364, 1400

Racquet and Tennis Club, 3136
Radar, 2491
Raddin, George G., 3246
Radiant heating, 2535
Radin, Max, 649
Radin, Paul, 3718
Radio, 1868, 2484, 2494
Radioactive substances, 2360
Radoff, Morris L., 4904
Raff and Gammon, 2722
Ragatz, Lowell J., 5332
Railroad literature, 3206
Railroad prints, 2956
Railroads, 2054-2109, 2726; bibliography, 2082; cars, 2509, 2511-12; consolidations, 2072, 2083; conventions, 2084; economics, 2054, 2057-58, 2067, 2069, 2072, 2074, 2076, 2080-81, 2085, 2109; electrification, 2483; European, 2097, 2108; gages, 2510; government ownership, 2055-56, 2077, 2101, 2106; Great Britain, 2064; Iowa, 2091; N. Y. City, 2089-90; periodicals, 2507; Scandinavian, 2093; transport, 2065; U. S., 2098, 2100, 2107
Railway motor cars, 2511
Raines, C. W., 5196
Raleigh, Walter, 4091
Ramage, Allene, 383
Ramsey County, Minn., Medical Library, 2302
Randall, James G., 4049
Randers-Pehrson, N. H., 2572
Randolph, John, 4092
Randolph-Macon Woman's College Library, 2138
Raney, M. Llewellyn, 120, 4050-51
Ranger, Edmund, 920
Rankin, Rebecca B., 5060
Rare books, 549-79
Rastell Press, 674
Ratchford, Fannie E., 3406, 3411, 3504, 3553, 3555
Ratcliff, John, 920
Rationing, 2602 (3)
Rau, Albert G., 3069
Rauch, John G., 1794
Raw materials, 1570, 5423
Ray, Grace E., 431
Read, Keith M., 4602
Reade, Charles, 3387
Real estate prices, 2626 (60)
Rebec, Estelle, 2043
Reciprocal trade, 1546, 1550
Reclamation, 2519
Recreation, 5487
Redfield, Robert, 2311
Redgrave, G. R., 679

INDEX

Reed, Simeon G., 2732
Reed College Library, 2732
Reese, Rena, 4837
Reeves, Harold, 3019
Reference books, 14
Reformed Church, 1103-04, 1107, 1110, 1112-13
Refrigeration, 2599 (10)
Reichmann, Felix, 859
Reid, Charles F., 5278
Reid, Winnifred, 2270
Religion, 196, 237, 983-1253; periodicals, 999, 1001
Religious drama, 3368
Religious education, 1012
Rembrandt, 2922, 2982-83
Remick, A. E., 2271
Renaissance, 608, 4243-44
Renstrom, Arthur G., 2126, 2554, 2560-62, 2572, 2574, 2576, 2579
Reparations, 5522, 5529
Reptiles, 2338
Research, 2178, 2180, 2451, 2626 (90)
Rex, Frederick, 1873, 2133
Rex, Wallace H., 432
Reynolds, James B., 5081
Reynolds, John H., 4724-27
Reynolds, Lloyd G., 1647
Rhode Island: government publications, 38; history, 5160-63; maps, 3917
Rhode Island Historical Society, 867-68, 2728, 3917, 4458, 4693
Rhode Island School of Design Library, 2934
Rhode Island State Library, 38
Riant, Paul E. D., 254
Ribero, Diego, 3876
Riccardi, Saro J., 2845, 2928
Ricci, Seymour de, 13, 502, 506, 650
Rice, Carlton C., 2038
Rice, 2602 (31)
Richard, Father Gabriel, 4945
Richards, Gertrude R., 4300
Richardson, Ernest C., 99, 507-08, 1001, 4228, 4459
Richardson, Helen R., 2063, 2068, 2077
Richardson, Mary H., 2921
Richardson, Wilson G., 179
Richart, Genevieve, 1074
Richmond, University, Library, 1072
Rider, Fremont, 165, 651-52
Rieck, Waldemar, 3023
Riggs, J. M., 1669
Riley, Franklin L., 4981
Rimington-Wilson, J. W., 3126
Ringer, Gladys W., 1692
Ripley, William Z., 2312

Risorgimento, 3663-64
Ristow, Walter W., 3850, 3874
Ritchie, George T., 4055
Rivera, Rodolfo O., 5333
Riverside Public Library, 4686
Rivlin, Joseph B., 3494
Roach, George W., 837, 5082
Road dust, 2515
Roads, 2517-18
Roanoke Colony, 4516
Roback, Abraham A., 1242
Robbins, Rossell H., 3351
Robbins, Roy M., 338
Roberts, Elizabeth M., 3324
Roberts, Ethel D., 3509
Roberts, Joseph K., 2285, 3921
Roberts, Martin A., 157, 703
Robertson, James A., 4460, 4792-93, 5334, 5374
Robertson, Thomas W., 3505
Robinson, Alexander C., 5155
Robinson, Benjamin L., 2325
Robinson, Edwin A., 3325-27
Robinson, Francis W., 3904
Robinson, Fred N., 3744
Robinson, John, 2905
Robson, Charles B., 1345
Rochambeau, Count Jean, 4541
Roche, Alphonse V., 3645
Rochester Public Library, 339
Rochester, University, Library, 152, 509
Rockets, 2559
Rockhill, William W., 4355
Rockwell, William W., 1002
Roden, Robert F., 781
Rodger, Grace, 3359
Rodgers, Cleveland, 5060
Rodkey, F. S., 4313
Rogerenes, 4633
Rogers, Bruce, 739, 944
Rogers, Francis M., 3167
Rogers, John, 4633
Rogers, Paul P., 3689
Rogers, Robert W., 533
Rolfe, Franklin P., 3461
Roman Catholic Church, 1155-87, 1212; newspapers, 1166; periodicals, 1160, 1177, 1179
Roman de la Rose, 3643
Romance languages, 3162-67, 3216
Romans, Bernard, 3905
Romansch language, 3166
Roosevelt, Franklin D., 1418, 4407, 4471; Library, 1418
Roosevelt, Robert B., 1806
Rose, Grace D., 808

Rosenbach, A. S. W., 209, 1243, 2910, 3460, 3549, 3532, 3812, 3816
Rosenberg, Henry, 153
Rosenberg Library, 133, 153
Rosengarten, Joseph G., 3987
Rosenthal, Solomon, 1241
Rosenwald, Lessing J., 571, 3871
Rosicrucians, 1934
Ross, T. Edward, 1039
Rossetti, Dante G., 3506
Roth, William M., 3578
Rousseau, Jean J., 3657-58
Rowell, J. C., 3900
Rowlandson, Thomas, 2838
Rowse, Edward F., 5083
Rowson, Susanna H., 3328
Royal primers, 696, 700
Rubber, 2827-28, 4193 (29)
Rubey, James T., 1902, 5529
Rudolph, E. L., 3227
Rugg, Harold G., 880-81, 3407
Rumania, 4323
Rumball-Petre, Edwin A. R., 1042
Rural life, 2603
Rush, Charles E., 144
Rusk, Ralph L., 4648
Ruskin, John, 3507-10
Russell Sage Foundation Library, 1262, 3109
Russia, history, 4310-17
Russian bibliography, 21
Russian language, 3169
Russian literature, 3745, 3747, 3749-55, 3757-59, 3761-66
Rutgers University Library, 173, 1984, 2741, 3209
Rutherford, Livingston, 838

Sabin, Joseph, Bibliotheca Americana, 4404, 4461
Safety, 2344, 2355, 2359, 2602 (14); at sea, 5460
Sagas, Icelandic, 3614-16, 3623
St. Aubin, Ernst, 1625
St. Augustine, Fla., history, 4795
St. Charles' Seminary, 1183
St. Clement's Church, 1003
St. John, Wallace, 1004
St. John's Seminary Library, 572
St. John's University Library, 2772
St. Lawrence seaway, 2111, 2115, 2526, 2599 (30)
St. Louis Mercantile Library, 401, 4649
St. Louis Public Library, 1399, 1555, 1927, 2563, 2870, 2891-92, 3031, 3152, 3359, 3533, 3855, 4156, 4161, 4172
Saint Olaf College, 1036

Sakanishi, Shio, 3040
Salem Athenaeum, 255
Sales tax, 1529, 1539
Salishan languages, 3183
Salley, Alexander S., Jr., 871, 5167-68
Salmagundi Club Library, 2944, 3648
Salmon, Lucy M., 482
Salmonsen, Ella M., 2346, 2348-50, 2352, 2534, 2552
Salvador, 5304, 5321
Salvation Army, 1204-05
Salvemini, Gaetono, 3668
Samoa, 5382, 5385
Sampley, Arthur M., 340
Sampson, Francis A., 4987
San Antonio, Texas, history, 5194
San Antonio Public Library, 3112, 5398
San Bernardino Free Public Library, 2646
San Francisco, maps, 3902
San Francisco Art Assoc., 2922
San Francisco Law Library, 1720
San Francisco Public Library, 256, 2173, 3032, 3389, 3817
San Jacinto Museum of History Assoc., 5197
Sanborn, Ruth A., 2564
Sánchez, José, 2172
Sanchez, M., 2208
Sánchez, Manuel S., 5335
Sand, 2280, 2288
Sandburg, Carl, 3329
Sanders, Henry A., 1029, 4206
Sandys, George, 3511
Sanskrit literature, 3772, 3776
Santa Barbara Mission, 4733
Santa Fe Laboratory Museum, 4654
Sardinia, 4302
Sargent, Ralph M., 3313
Saunders, Lyle, 5019
Savage, Grace O., 2240
Savage, J. B., Co., 2730
Savage, J. E., 2413
Savannah Historical Research Assoc., 4807
Savannah Public Library, 4811
Saville, Marshall H., 2313
Savord, Ruth, 351, 1810
Sawyer, Ellen M., 1747
Sawyer, Rollin A., 1478-79, 1482, 1504, 1519, 1886, 5454, 5512
Sayer, William L., 942
Scandinavian countries, 4193 (5); history, 4304-09
Scandinavian literature, 254, 3216, 3606-32
Schad, Robert, 593
Schapiro, Israel, 1244
Schecter, Abraham I., 1246
Schelling, F. E., 3534-35

INDEX

Schilling, Hugo K., 3160
Schinz, Albert, 3658
Schlinkert, Leroy W., 5266
Schlundt, Esther M., 2610
Schmidt, Carl, 1029
Schmidt, John J., 3747
Schneider, Henrich, 3596
Schneider, Herbert, 2011
Schnitzer, Martha, 4173
Schoneman, Ruth E., 2830
School lunches, 2602 (26)
Schools: Brooklyn, N. Y., 1955; N. Y. City, 1956
Schreiber, Carl F., 3597
Schreiber, L. W., 2981
Schrero, Morris, 2258, 2497, 2666, 2781
Schroeder, Theodore, 1359
Schubert, Franz, 3045
Schullian, Dorothy M., 2433
Schulz, Herbert C., 3870
Schwab, Marguerite J., 302
Schwartz, Benjamin, 4215
Schwegmann, George A., Jr., 368
Schwerin, Kurt, 1795
Sciarra-Colonna family, 2717
Science, 2157-2342; history, 2184-94; periodicals, 2195-2208, 2385
Scientific management, 2687-88
Scientists, 2161, 2168
Scisco, Louis D., 4910-11
Scotland, history, 4271
Scott, Dred, 4615
Scott, Franklin W., 341
Scott, Lorene L., 3253
Scott, Mary A., 3669
Scott, S. Morley, 4392
Scott, Temple, 3473
Scott, Walter, 3512-13
Scott, Will, 2201
Scrip, 2629 (40)
Scripps College Library, 4344
Scroggs, William O., 4889
Scudder, Samuel H., 2296
Sealock, Richard B., 860, 5084
Seals: Massachusetts Bay Colony, 775; Near East, 4203, 4221, 4223
Sealts, Morton M., 3311
Seattle Public Library, 364, 2523, 2565, 2647
Seaver, William N., 1464
Secret societies, 1934-43
Seeley, Pauline A., 5084
Seely, Caroline E., 2227
Seidensticker, Oswald, 861
Selenium, 2267
Seligman, E. R. A., 1452, 1458, 1466
Seminole Indians, 4489

Semitic languages, 3170-71
Semitic literature, 3767-71
Semmes, Raphael, 4912
Seneca, 3738
Seniority, 2693-94
Serís, Homero, 3715
Sermons, 4624, 4629; New England, 1010, 4941
Sesame, 2602 (20)
Seton, Grace T., 2144
Severance, Frank H., 342
Severance, Henry O., 137
Severance taxes, 1537
Sewage disposal, 2530-31, 2537
Sewickley Public Library, 5155
Sexton, Meta M., 4299
Shaffer, Ellen K., 653, 3336
Shakers, 1188-91
Shakespeare, William, 233-34, 3390-91, 3514-43
Shambaugh, Benjamin F., 4847
Shapiro, Karl J., 3153, 3330
Shattuck, Frederick C., 4940
Shaver, Mary M., 612
Shaw, Charles B., 4462
Shaw, George B., 3544-45
Shaw, Gertrude M., 3651
Shaw, Nathaniel, 2744
Shaw, Ralph R., 2466
Shaw, Robert G., 3113
Shaw, Thomas, 2744
Shaw, Thomas S., 2900, 3329
Shaw, Virginia E., 4768
Shay, Mary L., 4301
Shearer, Augustus H., 1837-38, 4228, 5156, 5208
Shearer, James F., 872
Sheets, Marian L., 2847
Shelby, Charmion, 467
Sheldon, Addison E., 4997
Sheldon, Charles, 2341
Shelley, Fred, 4687
Shelley, Percy B., 3546
Shelley, Philip A., 3408
Shelterbelts, 2659
Shenandoah Valley, 5215
Sheridan, Philip H., 4093
Sherman, Roger, 4705
Sherman, William T., 4094
Shields, Nancy C., 3670
Shimmell, Lewis S., 5142
Shinn, Josiah H., 4727
Shipbuilding, 2128, 2503-04, 5453-54
Shipping, 2628 (6), 2749-63
Shipton, Clifford K., 2012-13
Shirley, William W., 1483
Shoe industry, 2823

Shoemaker, Alfred L., 862
Shoemaker, Michael, 3881
Shooting, 3132
Short, John C., 5125
Shorthand, 2689
Shriver, Harry C., 5399
Shumaker, Elizabeth M., 1437
Shuster, E. A., Jr., 2292
Sibley, John L., 2014
Sicily, 4302
Siebert, Wilbur H., 4242
Signor, Nelle, 1887
Silas Bronson Library, 257
Sill, Edward R., 4095
Silliman, Benjamin, 1999
Sills, R. Malcolm, 725
Silver standard, 1480
Simkhovitch, V. G., 554
Simmons College Library, 3846
Simon, H., 3046
Simons, Corinne M., 2174-75, 2371-72
Simons, Lao G., 2220
Simple Simon, 3813
Simpson, Bernice, 2165
Simsar, Muhammed A., 541
Sinclair Refining Co., 2802
Single tax, 1519
Siouan languages, 2184
Sioussat, St. George L., 5125, 5181
Sit-down strikes, 1652
Skaggs, Alma S., 343
Skard, Sigmund, 4305, 4308-09
Skarstedt, Marcus, 184
Skeel, Emily E. F., 4125-27
Skordas, Gust, 4907
Slack, Charles G., 4410
Slade, Bertha C., 3468
Slade, William A., 159, 1497
Slang, 3149
Slavery, 3267, 4613, 4622
Slavic languages, 3168-69
Slavic literature, 3745-66
Slavonic bibliography, 11
Slum clearance, 2867, 2899
Small, Norman J., 1895
Smith, Adam, 1455-56
Smith, Alice E., 5268-69
Smith, Charles L., 207
Smith, Charles W., 95, 1374, 4667-72
Smith, Clara A., 3875, 4494
Smith, David E., 2212, 2221-27, 3798
Smith, Dorothy, 344
Smith, Edgar F., 2252-55, 2268, 2274
Smith, Edward R., 2893-95
Smith, Elsdon C., 4174
Smith, George D., booksellers, 654

Smith, Gerrit, 5031
Smith, Glenn C., 441
Smith, Henry L., 1959
Smith, J. William, 607
Smith, Joel S., 3766
Smith, John, 4096
Smith, John D., 2315
Smith, Lester W., 1474
Smith, Philip M., 4182
Smith, Preserved, 4064
Smith, Robert C., 2848, 2854
Smith, Robert M., 3538
Smither, Harriet, 5198
Smithsonian Institution, 345, 2315, 2545, 4970; Freer collection, 1029-31; Library, 2566
Smoke and smoke prevention, 2529, 2532
Smyth, Herbert W., 3724, 3740
Snider, Helen G., 3582
Snow, Samuel, 2737
Snyder, Jacob R., 4739
Social credit, 1482
Social reform, 1254, 1263
Social Science Research Council, 1928
Social sciences, 1254-2156
Social Security Act, 1604, 1626
Social work, 1262
Socialism, 1512-14, 1600
Societies, scientific, 2171
Society for the History of the Germans in Maryland Library, 4913
Society of California Pioneers, 4739
Society of Friends, 1142-54
Society of the New York Hospital, 2373
Sociology, 1254-68, 1344
Sodium nitrate, 2257
Soil conservation, 2665-73
Soils, 2599 (13, 14)
Solberg, Thorvald, 4296
Sommer, Francis E., 2433
Soncino, printers, 649
Sondley Reference Library, 154, 704
Songs, 3007, 3051-54, 3057, 3064; English, 3355; Negro, 3220
Sonneck, O. G. T., 3036-37, 3043, 3070, 3072, 3081-83
Sotheby, Wilkinson and Hodge, 655, 1796, 3373
Sotheran, H. & Co., 3154
South Africa, history, 4371-72, 4374-75
South Bend Public Library, 4838
South Carolina, history, 5164-72
South Carolina Historical Commission, 5167-69
South Carolina Historical Society, 5166
South Carolina, University, Library, 5170
South Dakota, history, 5173-74
South Dakota State Library, 5174

INDEX

South Sea Bubble, 1477
Southeast, history, 154
Southern California, University: Hoose Library, 956; Library, 3028, 5480
Southern fiction, 3242
Southern history, 4635-45
Southern Methodist University Library, 306, 315
Southey, Robert, 3547
Southwest, history, 4654-56, 5018
Southwest Museum, 4717-18
Southwestern Baptist Theological Seminary, 315
Sower, Christopher, 859
Soybeans, 2626 (74), 2647
Spaatz, Carl, 5542
Spain, history, 4290-91, 4293-94, 4297
Spalding, C. Sumner, 3964
Spanish Africa, 4380, 4383
Spanish American printing, 594
Spanish Armada, 4293
Spanish drama, 3687-89
Spanish fiction, 3690-93
Spanish language, 3165
Spanish literature, 3687-3708
Spanish Morocco, 4380
Spanish printing, 594-95
Spanton, Albert I., 3390
Spargo, John W., 14, 782
Sparks, Jared, 4415, 4439, 4463
Spaulding, Stephen, 641
Spaulding, Thomas M., 5393
Special collections, 76-78, 86, 89-91, 93, 95-96, 99, 101-02, 125-26
Special Libraries Association, 101-04, 2390; Biological Sciences Group, 2304; Boston, 346; Chemistry Section, 2272-73; Cincinnati, 347; Illinois, 348-49, 2692; Michigan, 350; Minnesota, 2207; New York, 351; Pittsburgh, 352; San Francisco, 353; Science-Technology Group, 2450; Social Sciences Group, 1648; Southern California, 354
Special Libraries Council of Philadelphia, 105
Speck, William A., 3597-99
Spell, Jefferson R., 3704, 3719
Spell, Lota M., 5336
Spence, Thomas H., 1104, 1212
Spenser, Edmund, 3548
Sper, Felix, 3409
Spiller, Robert E., 91
Spinning, 2819
Spivacke, Harold, 3047-48
Spivey, Herman E., 3277
Sports, 3129-38
Spratt, Hereward P., 2176

Sprong, Olive T., 3066
Stanard, William G., 5219
Standardization, 2695
Standards of living, 2625
Stanford University: Hoover Library, 453, 1467, 1639, 4186, 4191, 4196, 4320, 5513, 5518-19, 5545; Hopkins Transportation Library, 2104, 2764; Industrial Relations Division Library, 1638; Krabbe Library, 913; Library, 355, 606, 1467, 3592, 5281, 5371
Stanton, Madeline E., 2416
Staples, Charles R., 4869-70
Star spangled banner, 3065, 3070
Starch, Taylor, 3161
Starch, 2800
Stark, Lewis M., 2588, 3225
Stark, Marie C., 5574
Starr, Edward C., 1057, 1070-71
Starr, Thomas I., 4052-53
State government, 1895, 1897-98, 1900, 1904
State rights, 1903
State trade barriers, 2628 (1)
Statistics, 1269-1343; commercial, 2041
Steam railways, 2074
Steam turbines, 2476
Stearns, Bertha M., 1263
Stearns, Mae I., 677
Stearns, Samuel, 4097
Steel, 2497, 2782, 2786-89, 2805, 2810, 2826, 4193 (23)
Steele, Helen M., 1576, 1578
Steeves, H. Alan, 943
Steffan, T. G., 3441
Stein, Gertrude, 3331-32
Stephens, Alexander A., 2046, 4098
Stephenson, Douglas R., 2061, 2512, 2745
Stephenson, George M., 4673
Stern, William B., 1750
Stern-Taeubler, Selma, 1245
Steuben, Baron von, 4580
Stevens, Harry R., 433
Stevens, Henry, 3856, 3988
Stevens Institute of Technology Library, 2748, 4104
Stevenson, Edward L., 3836, 3852, 3876
Stevenson, Richard T., 5126
Stevenson, Robert L., 3549-50
Stevenson, William E., 5247
Stewart, John H., 4284
Stewart, Roland C., 1574
Stieg, Lewis F., 4237
Stiles, Charles W., 2374
Stillwell, Margaret B., 615, 656, 4113
Stinnecke Maryland Episcopal Library, 1139
Stock raising, 2599 (19)

INDEX

Stockbridge, John C., 3219
Stohlman, W. Frederick, 2849
Stokes, I. N. P., 384, 4454, 5085
Stoler, Mildred C., 4839-41
Stone, Edna L., 1580-81, 1609, 1613-14, 1650
Stone, Wilbur M., 3812, 3818-19
Storage batteries, 2543
Storkan, Charles J., 356
Strandel, Constance A., 2684, 5477
Stratton, W. C., 192
Stratton, William J., 4826
Straus, Oscar S., 4099
Strawberry, 2626 (28)
Street railways, 2132, 2134, 2137
Streeter, Floyd B., 4651, 4955
Streeter, Mary E., 258, 357
Streeter, Thomas W., 4688
Stricker, Thomas Perry, 713
Strikes, 1651-53, 1657
Strohm, Adam J., 59
Strong, Katherine B., 347
Strout, Elizabeth, 3795
Strunk, W. O., 3071
Student self-government, 1980
Stumberg, George W., 1758
Stump, Vernon C., 434
Stuntz, Stephen C., 2611
Sturtevant, Charles G., 5398
Sturtevant, E. Lewis, 2323-24
Submarines, 5456
Subsidies, maritime, 2127, 2130
Subways, 2133, 2137
Suez Canal, 2114, 2123
Suffolk County, N. Y., history, 5069-70
Suffrage, 1365-69
Sugar, 1560
Sugar beet, 2601 (16)
Sullivan, Frank, 3500
Sullivan, Henry B., 2277
Sullivan, Majie P., 3500
Sumner, Charles, 259
Sunday laws, 1009
Sunflowers, 2628 (20)
Surveying, 2726
Surveys, industrial, 2442
Swan, Bradford F., 783
Swan, Marshall W., 3738
Swanson, Evadene B., 4674
Swanton, Walter I., 107
Swarthmore College Library, 320, 962, 972, 978-79, 1152-53, 4462
Swearingen, M., 4890
Sweden, history, 4304, 4307
Swedish literature, 3626, 3628-30
Sweet, William M., 1213

Swem, Earl G., 478, 948, 1849, 2183, 2593, 2619, 2855, 2952, 3200, 3217-18, 3539, 3864, 3941, 3958, 4021, 5225-27, 5229
Swift, Jonathan, 3551-54
Swift, Lindsay, 3989, 4941
Swingle, Walter T., 2326
Switzerland, 4326
Sydnor, Charles S., 791
Sylvia, Esther, 4297
Symbolism, religious, 530
Syracuse Public Library, 607, 4175, 5023
Syracuse University Library, 5031

Taggard, Genevieve, 3333
Taggart, W. T., 2274
Tammany, 1925
Tanks, 5407
Tannenbaum, Samuel A., 3493
Tansill, William R., 1445
Tapley, Harriet S., 784
Taracanzio, Timothy A., 1751
Tariff, 1536, 1543-51
Tarkington, Booth, 3334
Tashjian, Nouvart, 358
Tate, Allen, 3228, 3230, 3324
Tate, Vernon D., 2796
Tax exemption, 1493, 1525; homestead, 2628 (15)
Taxation, 2626 (25); war, 1520
Taylor, Archer, 15, 608
Taylor, Edith S., 863
Taylor, Henry C., 3843
Taylor, Irwin, 1710
Taylor, John, 3819
Taylor, Kanardy L., 2591
Taylor, Louise M., 1960, 4328
Taylor, Oliver A., 984
Taylor, Ruby L., 1434
Taylor, Thomas, 955
Teachers and teaching methods, 1976-81
Teachers pensions, 1981
Technology, 2435-2829; periodicals, 2195-2208
Teggart, Frederick J., 2104
Telephone, 2053
Television, 2484
Temple, Phillips, 56
Tennessee, history, 5175-84
Tennessee, Dept. of Archives, 5181
Tennessee, Secretary of State, 5181
Tennessee State Library, 260, 1435, 5181-82
Tennessee Valley Project, 2871
Tenney, Mary A., 4918
Tenney, S. M., 4871
Tennyson, Alfred, 3555
Teton Mountains, 5274
Texas, authors, 3270; history, 5185-5202

INDEX

Texas Christian University, 315
Texas Engineers Library, 2469
Texas Library Association, 108
Texas State College for Women, 315
Texas State Library, 877, 1436, 3270, 5188, 5196, 5199
Texas, University: Library, 16, 174, 573, 877, 988, 1246, 1405, 2432, 3395, 3410-11, 3441-43, 3490, 3502, 3504, 3546, 3553-55, 3704, 3718-19, 5189, 5194, 5202, 5289, 5336-37; Medical Library, 2375; Wrenn Library, 133
Textbooks, 1982-86
Textile industry, 2817, 2824-25
Thackeray, William, 3415, 3556-58
Thaxten, Roland, 2327
Thayer, Evelyn, 2342
Thayer, Gordon W., 2153, 3188, 3355
Theatre, 3086-3119
Thévenot, Melchisédech, 233
Thies, Louis, 2984
Thom, Emma M., 2290
Thomas à Kempis, 989
Thomas, Allen C., 1154
Thomas, David Y., 4794-95
Thomas, Elizabeth, 1929
Thomas, Isaiah, 180, 705, 766, 779-80, 3221
Thomas, Mabel W., 4729
Thomas, Milton H., 3956
Thomas, Roger, 4905
Thomas, Sister Ursula, 1184
Thomas, William S., 4579
Thomases, Jerome, 5429
Thompson, Alma M., 1400
Thompson, C. Seymour, 155, 574
Thompson, David W., 864
Thompson, Donald E., 4874
Thompson, Edgar T., 1400
Thompson, Edith E. B., 5220
Thompson, Francis, 3559
Thompson, Laura A., 1469, 1579, 1585, 1589, 1608, 1632, 1656, 1660, 1664-66, 2693
Thompson, Margaret S., 4031
Thompson, R. T., 2741
Thompson, Ralph, 3266
Thompson, Ruth, 4969
Thompson, Thomas P., 4874, 4891
Thompson Products, Inc., 1636
Thomson, James, 3560
Thomson, Peter G., 5127
Thomson, Samuel H., 4243-44
Thomson, Thomas R., 2100
Thordarson, Chester H., library, 2159, 2164
Thoreau, Henry D., 3251, 3256, 3335
Thorndike, Israel, 2711
Thornton, Mary L., 5108

Thorp, Willard, 3510
Thorpe, James, 3412
Thorpe, Thomas, 4275
Thurber, Charles H., 1951
Thursfield, Richard E., 1961
Thurston, Ada, 646
Thwaites, Reuben G., 435, 4483, 4675
Tibetan literature, 3791, 4355
Tickhill Psalter, 522
Ticknor, George, 3695, 4100
Tilley, Nannie M., 4638
Tillinghast, William H., 2147
Time and motion study, 2684
Tin, 2791, 4193 (23)
Tinker, Edward L., 359
Tippecanoe, Battle of, 4591
Tobacco, 2626 (75), 2640-42
Tobey, Leona E., 4153
Tobin, James E., 3552
Tod, George-Anna, 1399
Toda, Kenji, 3781
Todd, Albert, 5403
Todd, William B., 3413
Toedteberg, Emma, 60
Tolstoy, Leo N., 3757
Tomato industry, 2628 (10)
Tomlinson, S. Arthur, 1704
Tompkins, Hamilton B., 3954, 4014
Toner, J. M., 4116
Toovey, James, 604
Torpedoes, 5457
Totten, Ellsworth, 261
Tower, Charlemagne, 1716, 3759
Tower, Joseph T., Jr., 3833, 3842
Tower, William H., 2047
Townsend, John W., 748
Townsend, Rebecca D., 683
Townsend Plan, 1605, 1616
Tractors, agriculture, 2628 (26)
Trade cards, 2775
Trade catalogs, 2686
Trade marks, 2773, 2776
Trade unions, 1645-50
Traffic Club of Chicago, 2105
Transportation, 2035, 2105, 2448, 2732, 2745-64, 4193 (36), 5488; of crops, 2626 (81)
Transylvania College Library, 575, 609, 3414
Trappists (monastic order), 1156
Treaties, 1808, 1814, 1825; Indian, 4488; Latin American, 1804
Tregaskis, James, bookseller, 3560
Trenton Public Library, 1185
Trinity College Library, 360, 1005-06, 1098, 2305, 2539
Trollope, Anthony, 3405, 3561-63

Tropical medicine, 2395
Trotter, Massey, 2967
Troxell, Gilbert M., 3415-16
True, Rodney H., 2618
Trusts, 1557, 1564
Tsunoda, Ryusaku, 3784
Tubes, 2811
Tucker, Dorothy F., 3457
Tucker, Ethelyn M., 657, 2318
Tucker, Josiah, 4518
Tucker, Mildred M., 3566
Tucker, Sara J., 2314
Tufts College Library, 881, 4604
Tulane University, Dept. of Middle American Research, 5338-41
Tulane University Library, 4890
Tulley, John, 4704
Tulsa Public Library, 2803
Turkey, 4238, 4327
Turner, Joseph B., 1117
Turner, Lorenzo D., 3267
Turrill, Charles B., 3899
Tuttle, Julius H., 1007, 4076, 4438
Twain, Mark, 113, 3336-37
Twitchell, Ralph E., 5020
Tyler, Lyon G., 5221
Typewriters, 2822
Typography, 927-48
Typothetae of the City of New York Library, 945

Uhlendorf, Bernhard A., 5171
Ukraine, 4315
Ukranian literature, 3747
Ulrich, Carolyn F., 331
Ultra-violet rays, 2248
Umbach, John P., 5563
Unemployment, 1659-63
Uniforms, 5413
Union catalogs, 70
Union County, Miss., 2628 (27)
Union League Club, 261
Union lists, 281-83
Union Pacific Railroad, 2075
Union Saint-Jean-Baptiste d'Amèrique Bibliothèque, 1375, 4632
Union Theological Seminary Library, N. Y., 999, 1001, 4276-77
Union Theological Seminary Library, Richmond, 1008, 1017
Unitarian Church, 1192
United Brethren in Christ Church, 1198
United Nations, 1811
United Nations Educational, Scientific and Cultural Organization, 1830-31
U. S. government publications, 28-29; history, 2729, 4395-5280; colonial period, 4497-4532; Revolution, 4533-86, 5168
U. S. Adjutant General, 5434
U. S. Agricultural Adjustment Program, 2620
U. S. Agricultural Marketing Service, 2628 (5)
U. S. Army, 5398; Library, 5446
U. S. Army Medical Library, 2376-79, 2381, 2391-2400, 2411, 2414-15, 2421, 2423, 2425, 2433-34
U. S. Army War College Library, 2277, 4588, 5400-02
U. S. Attorney General's Advisory Committee on Crime, 1932
U. S. Board of Investigation and Research-Transportation, 5571
U. S. Board of Surveys and Maps, 3857
U. S. Bureau of Agricultural Economics Library, 2615
U. S. Bureau of Agricultural Engineering, 2594
U. S. Bureau of American Ethnology Library, 3186
U. S. Bureau of Animal Industry, 2374, 2380
U. S. Bureau of Foreign and Domestic Commerce, 1752
U. S. Bureau of Insular Affairs, 5363, 5366-67, 5379
U. S. Bureau of Labor Statistics Library, 2355
U. S. Bureau of Medicine and Surgery, 2382
U. S. Bureau of Mines, 2500
U. S. Bureau of Navigation, 5458
U. S. Bureau of Plant Industry, 2599 (3)
U. S. Bureau of Refugees, Freedmen and Abandoned Land, 4475
U. S. Bureau of Yards and Docks, 5469
U. S. Chemical Warfare Service, 5568
U. S. Circuit Court of Appeals Library, 1721
U. S. Civil Aeronautics Administration Library, 2567-68
U. S. Civil Service Commission Library, 1861-62
U. S. Civil War, 4595-4623
U. S. Civil Works Administration, 4427
U. S. Civilian Conservation Corps, 1484, 2670-71, 2673, 4193 (30)
U. S. Coast and Geodetic Survey, 2286
U. S. Coast Artillery School Library, 5403
U. S. Coast Guard, 5462
U. S. Command and General Staff School, Fort Leavenworth, Library, 5404
U. S. Commissary General, 5431
U. S. Congress, 1440-41, 1444-45; House Library, 1437; Senate, 1419, 1443, 1446-47; Senate Library, 1438-39
U. S. Constitution, 4575-76, 4584
U. S. Constitution Sesquicentennial Comm., 1839

INDEX

U. S. Continental Congress, 4545-46, 4554, 4565
U. S. Council of National Defense, 5534
U. S. Counsel for Prosecution of Axis Criminality, 5572
U. S. Dept. of Agriculture, 4423; Library, 465, 1653, 2328, 2595-2602, 2611-12, 2614-15, 2621-33, 2648-49, 2655-58, 2667-69, 4109
U. S. Dept. of Commerce, 4424; Library, 1340, 1468
U. S. Dept. of Interior Library, 262-63, 4422, 4473, 4662, 4682, 5113
U. S. Dept. of Justice, 4420; Library, 1722, 1753
U. S. Dept. of Labor, 4425; Library, 1264-65, 1469, 1576-90, 1606-17, 1630-32, 1640, 1645-46, 1649-51, 1654-56, 1660, 1664-66, 1922, 2356, 2693-94
U. S. Dept. of Navy, 4421, 5448, 5463, 5470
U. S. Dept. of State, 3882, 4015, 4067, 4080, 4555; Library, 1812-16, 4112, 4745, 5304, 5321, 5330, 5346
U. S. Dept. of Treasury, 4418; Library, 1475, 1914
U. S. Dept. of War, 4066, 4419, 5387, 5392, 5533; Library, 4588, 4616-19, 5305, 5369, 5438-46
U. S. Direct Tax Commission, 1541
U. S. Emergency Relief Administration, 4428
U. S. Engineer Dept. Library, 2470-71
U. S. Engineer School Library, 2287-88, 2501, 2524, 2569, 4372, 4588, 4652, 5390, 5405-06
U. S. Exploring Expedition, 4594
U. S. Farm Credit Administration, 1485, 4430
U. S. Farm Security Administration, 1256, 2990
U. S. federal courts, 4417
U. S. Federal Housing Administration Library, 2896
U. S. Federal Security Agency Library, 1618-19, 1840
U. S. Federal Trade Commission, 2043
U. S. Federal Works Agency: Law Library, 1591; Library, 2135
U. S. Food Administration, 5499, 5502, 5507-11, 5535-36, 5539
U. S. Forest Service, 2654, 2659, 2665, 5267; Library, 2660-63
U. S. General Land Office, 1540
U. S. Geological Survey, 2289-92, 2296, 5205; Library, 1902, 2277
U. S. Grain Corporation, 1553
U. S. Hydrographic Office Library, 2237
U. S. Hygienic Laboratory Library, 2374
U. S. Industrial Incentive Division, 5567
U. S. Inspector General, 5432

U. S. Judge Advocate General (Navy), 5467
U. S. Library of Congress, 47-48, 156-62, 175, 264-68, 333, 345, 388, 400, 406, 415, 439, 445, 467-68, 499-500, 508, 511, 543, 548, 564, 575, 588-89, 610-11, 623, 627, 658-61, 663, 719, 722-23, 750, 901, 903, 907, 910, 939, 944, 946-47, 957, 961, 1027, 1043, 1074, 1165, 1189, 1244, 1247, 1256, 1330-31, 1346, 1388, 1401, 1411, 1645-46, 1651, 1723, 1752, 1754-55, 1797-98, 1804, 1833, 1890, 1919, 2025, 2048, 2114, 2177, 2208, 2229, 2245, 2277, 2281, 2287-88, 2332, 2340, 2381, 2554, 2570-71, 2589, 2611, 2615, 2687, 2794, 2818, 2848, 2850, 2872, 2888, 2897, 2921, 2941, 2954, 2962, 2975-77, 2983, 2985-87, 2991, 3033, 3104, 3109, 3111, 3114, 3118, 3131, 3146, 3153, 3164, 3189-90, 3206, 3228, 3292, 3312, 3324-25, 3335, 3342, 3417, 3423, 3482, 3529, 3592, 3594, 3634, 3639-40, 3649, 3652, 3671, 3687, 3705, 3709-10, 3730, 3745, 3751-52, 3754, 3758, 3773, 3778, 3787-89, 3800, 3804, 3812, 3814-15, 3825, 3834, 3853, 3858, 3871, 3878, 3883-84, 3891-92, 3895, 3907, 3913, 3916, 3919-20, 3922, 3926-28, 3930-32, 3942, 3945, 3949-50, 3962-67, 3979, 3984, 3988, 4008, 4011, 4015-17, 4020, 4029, 4035, 4042-44, 4054-55, 4067, 4077, 4080, 4109, 4128, 4133-34, 4176, 4182, 4188, 4192, 4236, 4259, 4294, 4296, 4298, 4305, 4311, 4314-15, 4322, 4331, 4346, 4348, 4355, 4413, 4436-37, 4459, 4464-67, 4502, 4533-36, 4547-48, 4554-55, 4579, 4588, 4596-97, 4610-11, 4652, 4659, 4687, 4747, 4762, 4772, 4787, 4789, 4796, 4802, 4808, 4817-18, 4848, 4896, 4924, 4955, 4970, 5020, 5125, 5138, 5183, 5187, 5200, 5205, 5219, 5267, 5296, 5304-07, 5311, 5321, 5329-30, 5334, 5342-46, 5376, 5383-84, 5390-91, 5451, 5516, 5542, 5544, 5546, 5578; Acquisitions Dept., 20; Catalog Div., 2015; Census Library Project, 1332-41; Copyright Office, 19, 3237; Div. of Aeronautics, 2126, 2545-47, 2560-62, 2566, 2572-79, 2581; Division of Bibliography, 971, 981-82, 1009, 1186, 1266-67, 1270, 1347-48, 1352-55, 1360, 1365-69, 1376-81, 1402-03, 1412-16, 1440-44, 1450-51, 1470-73, 1486-98, 1505-07, 1510-11, 1521-37, 1544-49, 1556-63, 1592-95, 1620-24, 1633, 1641, 1643-44, 1657-58, 1662-63, 1667-68, 1817-28, 1841-48, 1850-53, 1863-69, 1888-94, 1903-11, 1915, 1923, 1930-31, 1947-48, 1992, 2031-36, 2040-41, 2049-53, 2106-09, 2115-17,

INDEX

2127-31, 2136-37, 2178, 2293, 2357-59, 2451-52, 2493-94, 2503-04, 2517, 2525-26, 2544, 2580, 2664, 2670, 2695-96, 2777-79, 2804-07, 2824-26, 2871, 2898-99, 2935, 2998, 3115-17, 3137, 3155-56, 3214-15, 3268, 3276, 3306, 3316-17, 3329, 3337, 3422, 3436, 3505, 3513, 3761-63, 3938-39, 3947-48, 3955, 3966, 3973, 3993, 3995, 4003, 4005, 4061, 4065, 4079, 4082, 4092-95, 4245, 4285, 4302, 4306-07, 4316, 4323, 4325-26, 4338-39, 4356-57, 4373-87, 4393, 4495, 4580-83, 4634, 4643-44, 4689, 4706, 4754, 4776-78, 4797, 4872, 4914, 4979, 4999, 5201, 5209, 5222, 5242, 5250-51, 5275, 5279-80, 5348-58, 5372-73, 5377-78, 5385, 5407-18, 5459-61, 5491-92, 5520-27, 5547-51; Div. of Documents, 53, 5528; Div. of Fine Arts, 2874; Div. of Manuscripts, 512-17, 1395, 3965, 3990, 4022, 4081, 4089, 4101-02, 4117-20, 4468-69, 4486, 4584-85, 5360; Div. of Maps, 3839, 3856, 3858-63, 3877, 3893, 3898, 3902, 3915, 3923-24, 3933-34; Div. of Music, 3013, 3021, 3033-39, 3045-50, 3064-65, 3070, 3072-77, 3082-85, 3229; European Affairs Div., 469, 1361, 1986, 4246-47, 5552; General Reference and Bibliography Division, 21, 39, 958, 1271, 1362-64, 1382-83, 1513-14, 1564-65, 1811, 1830-31, 1870, 1912, 1916, 2016, 2042, 2179-81, 2249, 2294, 2453, 2650, 2900, 3168, 3230, 3307, 3764, 3820, 3972, 4001, 4278, 4286, 4303, 4308, 4324, 4327, 4334, 4340, 4358, 4586, 4615, 4645, 4779, 5109, 5157, 5361, 5386, 5419-22, 5553-56; Hispanic Foundation, 470, 2852-53, 3706; John Boyd Thacher collection, 578; Legislative Reference Service, 109, 1445, 1453, 1500, 1538, 1566-68, 1596, 1734-45, 1756-60, 1773, 1775, 1797-1801, 1832, 1855, 1895-96, 2182, 2694, 2827, 4121, 5399, 5423, 5476, 5493, 5557-66; Orientalia Div., 3040, 3792-93, 4335-36, 4359-60; Periodical Div., 436-37, 472-77; Photoduplication Service, 4309, 4470; Photograph Section, 2999; Prints and Photographs Div., 2854, 2976, 2988-90; Processing Dept., 40, 3765; Reading Rooms, 1357, 1384, 1569, 2582, 3010, 3169, 3247, 3803, 3971, 4361, 5529; Reference Dept., 4317, 5362, 5424, 5494; Rosenwald collection, 550, 557-58, 571, 577, 627, 907-08; Science and Technology Project, 2360; Serials Div., 438; Union Catalog Div., 471, 3739; Vollbehr collection, 658-61, 663
U. S. Light-house Board Library, 2527

U. S. Marine Corps, 5468
U. S. Maritime Labor Board, 1597
U. S. Military Academy Library, 5425-28
U. S. National Archives, 1393, 1396, 1411, 1418, 1446-47, 1474, 1484, 1501, 1540-41, 1553, 1597-99, 1625, 1871, 1913, 1932, 2043, 2238-39, 2314, 2382-83, 2620, 2636, 2654, 2665, 2671-72, 2828, 3882, 3890, 4018, 4078, 4171, 4193, 4471-75, 4492, 4496, 4662, 4773, 4780, 4788, 4808, 4848, 4970, 5017, 5104, 5138, 5144, 5159, 5183, 5187, 5193, 5205, 5267, 5273, 5363-67, 5379, 5387, 5392, 5429-35, 5437, 5448, 5462-70, 5495, 5499, 5507-11, 5530-36, 5539, 5567-75, 5577
U. S. National Guard Bureau, 5430
U. S. National Park Service, 5205, 5223
U. S. National Recovery Administration, 1460
U. S. National Resources Comm., 2872
U. S. National Resources Planning Board, 1474
U. S. National Security Resources Board, 5575
U. S. National War College Library, 4616-19, 5369, 5438-39, 5442, 5445
U. S. National War Labor Board, 1598
U. S. National Youth Administration, 1267
U. S. Naval Academy, 5471; Library, 5472-75
U. S. Naval Observatory, 2239-41; Library, 4077
U. S. Navy, history, 4585
U. S. Navy Board for Production Awards, 5567
U. S. Office for Emergency Management, 2827
U. S. Office of Civilian Defense, 5495
U. S. Office of Education Library, 177, 1962-74, 1976-81, 1993-94, 1996-97, 2017-18, 2026-29, 2590, 2603, 4362-65, 5368, 5576
U. S. Office of Experiment Stations, 2613-14
U. S. Office of Indian Affairs, 3882, 4492
U. S. Ordnance Dept. Library, 5436
U. S. Patent Office, 1724, 2780
U. S. Paymaster General, 5435
U. S. Petroleum Administration, 1902
U. S. Price Administration Office, 5577
U. S. Public Roads Administration, 2135
U. S. Public Works Housing Div., 1902
U. S. Rubber Survey Committee, 2828
U. S. Secret Service, 1871
U. S. Secretary of War, 5433
U. S. Securities and Exchange Commission Library, 1502, 2037
U. S. Selective Service System, 5532
U. S. Social Security Board Library, 1626
U. S. Soil Conservation Service, 2672
U. S. Soil Erosion Service, 1902
U. S. Solicitor of the Treasury Library, 1725
U. S. Strategic Bombing Survey, 5437

INDEX

U. S. Supreme Court, 1906, 1911
U. S. Tariff Commission, 2038; Library, 1550-51, 1570
U. S. territorial possessions, 4411, 4455, 5278-80
U. S. Veterans' Administration, 4426
U. S. War Industries Board, 5573-74
U. S. War Labor Policies Board, 1599
U. S. War Production Board, 5569, 5575
U. S. Weather Bureau Library, 2295
U. S. Works Progress Administration, 4429
Universal languages, 3148
Universalist Church, 1193
Universities and colleges, 1997-2022
Updike, Daniel B., 773
Upton, William T., 3072, 3078, 3080
Uruguay, history, 5281, 5289
Ustick, Stephen C., 694
Utah, history, 5203-05
Utah State Library, 269
Utah, University, Utah Humanities Research Foundation, 4194
Utamaro, Kitagawa, 2967
Utica Public Library, 5086-87
Utley, George B., 4476
Utopias, 1351

Vail, Robert W. G., 1010, 2742, 3295, 3328, 4396, 4528, 4624, 4748
Valentine Museum, 440
Valinger, Leon de, 4768
Value, theory, 1461
Van Buren, Martin, 4008, 4101
Vance, John T., 1739
Vanderbilt, Paul, 2991
Vanderbilt University Library, 270
VanDerpool, James G., 2901
Van Duzer, Henry S., 3558
Vanilla, 2602 (13)
VanMale, John, 110-11
Vann, William H., 3484
VanName, Addison, 614
Van Patten, Nathan, 913
Van Schreeven, William J., 5536
Van Sinderen, Adrian, 3343
Van Tyne, Claude H., 4477
Varney, Edith, 1555
Vassar College Library, 482, 612
Vaughan, John, 4566, 5021
Vedelen, Harold C., 4814
Venezuela: history, 5335; maps, 3931
Vermont, history, 5206-10
Vermont State Library, 723
Vermont, University: Fleming Museum, 3869; Library, 271, 3216, 5210
Vernon, Edward, 4102

Vesalius, Andreas, 2404
Veterinary medicine, 2374, 2380
Viaducts, 2516
Vilas, William F., 4103
Viles, Jonas, 4988-89
Vinci, Leonardo da, 2843, 3686, 4104
Vineland, N. J., maps, 3918
Vineland Historical and Antiquarian Society Library, 3918, 5005
Virgil, 3731-32, 3736
Virgin Islands, 5278
Virginia: government publications, 41; history, 5211-38; maps, 3919-22
Virginia Baptist Historical Society, 1067, 1072
Virginia Company of London, 4502, 4529
Virginia Historical Society Library, 439, 4555, 5212, 5219, 5224
Virginia Polytechnic Institute Library, 4077
Virginia State Library, 41, 439-40, 478, 885, 948, 1141, 1268, 1542, 1849, 2183, 2593, 2619, 2855, 3200, 3217-18, 3539, 3864, 3922, 3941, 4077, 4158, 4177, 4195, 4478, 4555, 4557, 4611, 4620, 5212, 5215, 5219-21, 5226-32
Virginia, University, Library, 272, 441, 680, 1140-41, 2019, 2250, 2743, 3375, 4010, 4012, 4019-20, 4405, 4479, 5233-35
Virginia War History Comm., 5236
Virtue, Ethel B., 4971
Vocational education and guidance, 1987-94
Vogel, Emil, 3041
Vogt, George M., 3360
Volcanoes, 2278
Volta Bureau Library, 1924, 3946
Vormelker, Rose, 102
Vosper, Edna, 4566
Vosper, Robert, 163
Voyages, 3843, 3847

Wabeke, B. H., 5578
Wachovia Historical Society, 5093
Wade, Joseph S., 3335
Wager, Charles, 4102
Wages, 1602-03, 1608-09, 1615, 1625
Wagner, B. M., 56
Wagner, Henry R., 113, 718, 812, 900, 904, 3865, 3894, 4655-56, 4690, 4749
Wainwright, Alexander D., 4530
Wainwright, J. C. J., 3123
Wait, Martha H., 4621
Wakashan languages, 3185
Wake Forest College Library, 207, 5110
Waldbott, Sigmund, 2204
Wales, history, 4259
Walker, Ella K., 2873
Walker, John W., 3418

Walker, Mary A., 741
Walker, William, 5341
Wall, Alexander J., 442, 1503, 2902, 4701, 5088
Wallis, Talbot H., 1674
Walls, Howard L., 3118
Walpole, Horace, 3564-66
Walsh-Healey Act, 1588
Walsworth, Bertha L., 4686
Walter, Raleigh, 4516
Walter, Yvonne, 3359
Walters, Henry, 662
Walters Art Gallery, 498, 662
Walton, Clarence E., 67, 2020, 3300
Walton, Izaak, 233, 3567
Walton, Robert P., 61, 2800
Wanning, Andrews, 4004
War: contracts, 1870; economic aspects, 1453, 1464, 1556, 1568, 1596, 1639; industry, 5561; posters, 5496, 5503, 5517, 5544; production, 1568; profiteering, 5389; referendum, 1350
War of 1812, 4447
War Services Program, Louisiana, 1343
Ward, Christopher, 3840
Ward, William H., 4221
Warden, David B., 4590
Warrell, William H., 4227
Warren, Katherine, 3119, 3238
Warren, Louis A., 4056
Warrington, James, 1050
Washington, Booker T., 1388
Washington, George, 2599 (22), 3936, 4105-22, 4438
Washington, D. C.: history, 4634, 4773-79; maps, 3923-24
Washington (state), history, 5239-42
Washington State College Library, 664, 3890
Washington State Library, 42, 273, 1508, 1726, 2518
Washington University Library (St. Louis), 363
Washington, University (Seattle), Law Library, 1769; Library, 116, 364, 3890, 4492, 4668, 5241
Water, 2667 (3); power, 1563; rights, 1506; softening, 2477; supply, 2533
Water-glass, 2258
Waters, Edward N., 3049-50, 3084-85
Waters, Margaret R., 4151
Waters, Willard O., 698-99, 719, 1688, 3901
Waterston, Robert, 4438
Watertown Library Assoc., 4531
Waterways, 2110-17
Watkins, V. G., 2200
Watkinson Library of Reference, 164, 365, 723-24, 3252, 3707, 4758

Wayne University Library, 2301
Wead, Eunice, 925-26
Wead, Mary E., 3444
Weaks, Mabel C., 5052
Weather, 2294, 2595
Weaver, Clarence L., 5128-29
Weaver, William D., 2482
Weaving, 2819
Webb, Alexander S., 4123
Webb, James W., 4123
Webb, Samuel B., 4123
Webb, Willard, 3639, 3895
Webber, Mabel L., 4707
Weber, Albrecht F., 3776
Weber, Carl J., 2953, 3273, 3301, 3477-78, 3483
Weber, Clara C., 3301
Weber, Hilmar H., 1349, 3604
Weber, Jessie P., 4822
Webster, Daniel, 4124
Webster, Noah, 4125
Webster, William, 3330
Weedon, George, 4537-38
Weeks, Stephen B., 844, 5110-11
Weems, Mason L., 4126-27
Wegelin, Oscar, 839, 3231, 4183, 4480, 4809
Weidensall, Robert, 4606
Weidman, Lucy E., 5430, 5532
Weigand, Hermann J., 3601-02
Weights and measures, 2740
Weinberger, Bernhard W., 2353
Weis, Frederick L., 2947
Weiss, Harry B., 63, 836, 961, 998, 2148, 2150, 3263, 3812-13, 3821
Weitenkampf, Frank, 916, 2844, 2868, 2971-72, 2992, 5059
Welch, Doris, 3173
Welding, 2820-21
Welfare work, 1917-24
Wellesley College Library, 3361, 3431, 3509, 3665, 3672
Wells, Carolyn, 3342
Welsh, Charles, 2147
Welsh Americans, 1384
Wemyss, Stanley, 4481
Wentz, A. R., 1090
Wentz, Charles H., 5157, 5424, 5494
Werewolves, 967
Werner, Eric, 3042
Werner, William L., 3269
Wesleyan University Library, 165, 3735, 4287
Wesson, Ernest J., 4057
West, Clarence F., 2275
West, Elizabeth H., 4101, 5199
West, Herbert F., 3280, 3303, 3453
West African languages, 3188

INDEX

West Indies, 4102, 4394, 5284, 5319; Danish, 5351
West Point, 5425-28
West Virginia, history, 5243-56; maps, 3925
West Virginia State Dept. of Archives and History, 5243, 5245, 5247, 5252-53, 5256
West Virginia State Library, 1727
West Virginia University Library, 1728, 2739, 5254-55
Westchester County, N. Y., history, 5038
Westcott, Mary, 383
Western history, 4675-90
Western Michigan College of Education Library, 4058
Western Pennsylvania Historical Society, 5158
Western Pennsylvania Historical Survey, 443, 5158
Western Reserve Historical Society Library, 357, 444, 2945, 4002, 4034, 4135, 4284, 4653, 4646
Western Reserve University Library, 258, 357, 3355, 3935, 4284, 4288
Westwood, Thomas, 3145
Wetherill, Samuel, 2736
Wetmore, Hester A., 2272
Whaling, 2592, 2964
Whatley, W. A., 5202
Wheat, Carl I., 3903, 4750
Wheat, 2626 (33)
Wheatley, Phillis, 3338
Wheeler, Helen E., 5576
Wheeler, Joseph T., 763
Whicher, George F., 3282, 3540
Whistler, James A., 2975, 2977, 2989
White, Andrew D., 4233
White, James M., 4981
White, Viola C., 3262
White, William A., 3419, 3541, 4128
Whitfield, Francis J., 4315
Whitman, Walt, 3251, 3264, 3339-43
Whitmore, William H., 4626
Whitney, Edward A., 5537
Whitney, James L., 2876, 3695
Whittemore, Caroline, 801
Whittier, John G., 3344-45
Whittingham, W. R., 1138-39
Whittlesey, Walter R., 3083
Wickersham, James, 445
Widener, Harry E., 209, 274, 2910, 3460, 3549
Wiener, Minnie, 1591
Wigglesworth, Michael, 993
Wigmore, John H., 1933
Wilbour, Charles E., 4199
Wilbur, Ray Lyman, 4196
Wilcox, Fannie M., 3270
Wilcox, Jerome K., 1460, 1899-1900, 1954, 2039, 2167, 2234, 2442-43, 2463, 2499, 2553, 2795, 2814-16, 2887, 2926
Wilcox, Robert C., 4002
Wilde, Oscar, 3568-69
Wilder, Elizabeth, 2848
Wilgus, A. Curtis, 3692, 3930, 5237, 5370
Wilkie, Florence, 850
Wilkin, R. H., 1689
Wilkinson, W. W. J., 56
Willard, James F., 4755, 5276
Willey, Robert H., 1485
William II, Emperor of Germany, 4129
William and Mary College Library, 2638, 2952, 4021
Williams, Edwin E., 114
Williams, Frederick W., 3794
Williams, J. F., 4972
Williams, John C., 840
Williams, Nicholas M., 5283
Williams, Otho H., 4433
Williams, Ralph C., 3640
Williams, Roger, 4130-31
Williams, Samuel W., 4721
Williams, Sidney H., 3448
Williams, Stanley T., 3297, 3343
Williams, William, 840
Williams College, 2007; Chapin Library, 613, 3439; Library, 275
Williamson, Charles C., 932, 1603
Williamson, Roland, 1801
Willson, Robert W., 2232
Wilmington Institute Free Library, 276, 446, 2914
Wilson, Carmen, 2487
Wilson, Carroll A., 3283, 3536
Wilson, James, 3838
Wilson, Louis N., 5498
Wilson, Louis R., 3248, 4197
Wilson, Nancy, 5256
Wilson, William J., 506, 2276, 5577
Wilson, Woodrow, 3251, 4132-34, 4484
Winchell, Constance M., 115
Wine, 2795
Wing, Donald G., 681
Winkler, Ernest W., 877
Winship, George P., 447, 479, 579, 663, 1011, 2021, 3274, 3314, 3452, 3577, 3957
Winsor, Justin, 968, 3542-43, 3866, 3878, 4415, 4482
Winter, E. C., 1191
Winters, William H., 5089
Winthrop, James, 180
Winthrop, John, 235
Wire, 2812
Wirick, Harriet P., 738
Wisconsin: authors, 3271; history, 5257-71

INDEX

Wisconsin, Land Office, 5265
Wisconsin Legislative Reference Library, 5268
Wisconsin, State Dept., 5265
Wisconsin State Historical Society Library, 333, 448-49, 892-93, 1600, 3271, 3588, 4103, 4122, 4483, 4555, 4611, 4622-23, 4817, 4858, 4869, 4873, 4955, 5184, 5237, 5257, 5263-64, 5266, 5269-71
Wisconsin State Library, 1729
Wisconsin, University: Agriculture Library, 2639; Library, 2159, 2164, 3592
Wisdom, William B., 3346
Wise, Murray M., 470
Wise, Thomas J., 3399, 3406, 3410-11
Wiser, Vivian D., 5567
Wish, Harvey, 4842
Wistar Institute, 320, 2306
Wit and humor, 3215
Witchcraft, 963-65, 968
Witherspoon, A. M., 3499
Withington, Mary C., 1975, 2744
Witmark, Isadore, 203
Wolanin, Alphonse S., 3760
Wolf, Edwin II, 523, 3652, 4532
Wolfe, Thomas, 3346
Wolfson, Harry A., 1248
Women, 2138-46, 3939; as physicians, 2146; education, 2023; in Congress, 1444
Wood, Marjorie P., 3673, 3740, 5538
Wood, Richard G., 5159, 5465, 5469, 5570
Wood, Samuel and Sons, 3812
Wood engraving, 2954, 2957, 2960, 2962, 2965, 2993
Woodard, Clement M., 3162
Woodberry, George E., 3347
Woodress, James L., 4289
Woodrow Wilson Foundation Library, 4484
Woodward, Gertrude L., 678, 3374
Woody, R. H., 5172
Woody, Thomas, 1957
Worcester County Law Library, 1730
Worcester Historical Society, 4929
Wordsworth, William, 3360, 3570-77
Workers' leisure, 1590
Workingmen's Institute Library, 4832, 4837
Workingmen's insurance, 1595
Workmen's compensation, 1642-44
World government, 1355-56
World War I, 4004, 5189, 5496-5539; poetry, 3190
World War II, 4193 (39), 5540-70
Worthington, Edna M., 4059
Wrenn, John H., 3406, 3410
Wright, Almon R., 5539
Wright, Charles H. C., 3655

Wright, Edith A., 2026
Wright, Frank V., 1684
Wright, John, 1044-45
Wright, John C., 3823
Wright, John K., 3867
Wright, Louis B., 5238
Wright, Lyle H., 128, 2548, 3130, 3249, 4060
Wright, Orville, 2554
Wright, Wilbur, 2554
Writing, history, 539
Writing manuals, 2024
Wroth, Lawrence C., 647, 764, 886, 2242-43, 2993, 3272, 3868, 4394, 4403, 4485, 4798
Wu, K. T., 3040
Wyckoff, Lola A., 1578
Wymberley Jones DeRenne Georgia Library, 4810
Wynne, Marjorie G., 3138
Wyoming, history, 5272-80
Wyoming Historical Society, 379
Wyoming State Library, 1731
Wyoming Stock Growers' Association, 2635
Wyoming, University, Archives Dept., 5277; Library, 2635, 4239

X-ray, 2246
Xylographica, 605, 625, 646

Yakobson, Sergius, 4315
Yale College, 2001
Yale Theological Seminary, 1001
Yale University: Brothers in Unity Library, 277; Calliopean Society Library, 278; Divinity School, Day Missions Library, 1055; Law Library, 1732, 1802; Library, 134, 176, 279, 450, 538, 614, 639, 672, 682-83, 723, 725, 1012, 1045, 1075, 1078, 1235-37, 1249-50, 1975, 1999, 2001, 2244, 2341, 2401, 2472, 2618, 2744, 2862, 3138, 3297, 3308, 3331-32, 3336, 3343, 3352, 3374, 3415-16, 3420-21, 3423, 3427, 3450-51, 3454, 3456, 3470-71, 3480, 3486, 3495, 3499, 3507, 3545, 3551, 3578, 3587, 3597-99, 3601-02, 3605, 3625-26, 3643, 3708, 3718, 3725, 3741, 3766, 3777, 3794-95, 3843, 3926, 3975-76, 3980, 4004, 4047, 4062, 4123, 4341, 4376, 4399, 4457, 4466, 4550, 4589, 4597, 4678, 5496, 5501; Linonian and Brothers Library, 280; Medical Library, 2364, 2384, 2416, 2420; Sheffield Scientific School Library, 2228
Yancey, Bartlett, 5094
Yarmolinsky, Avrahm, 3187, 3755, 4070
Yassukovitch, Antonina, 3757
Yates, Garard F., 1187
Yeats, William B., 3578

INDEX

Yenawine, Wayne S., 2673, 4811
Yiddish literature, 1242
Yohannan, Abraham, 537
Yorktown, Va., history, 5223
Yoshipe, Harry B., 1540
Young, Edward, 3579
Young, F. G., 5139
Young, James H., 4098
Young, Lucien, 5458
Young, Malcolm O., 2022
Young, Perry, 2118
Youth, 2626 (17, 65)

Youth movement, 1267
Youtie, Herbert C., 4207
Yugoslavia, 4323

Zahm, Albert F., 2581
Zellars, W. C., 3693
Zenger, John Peter, 838, 5065
Zimmer, John T., 2333
Zinc, 2792
Zion Research Library, 1013
Zionist Archives and Library, 1251
Zoology, 2329-42, 2374, 2380; periodicals, 2329